AF361337

PERILOUS PASSIONS

Ethics and Emotion
in Early Modern Spain

Perilous Passions

*Ethics and Emotion in
Early Modern Spain*

HILAIRE KALLENDORF

UNIVERSITY OF TORONTO PRESS
Toronto Buffalo London

© University of Toronto Press 2024
Toronto Buffalo London
utorontopress.com
Printed in the USA

ISBN 978-1-4875-2703-7 (cloth)
ISBN 978-1-4875-2705-1 (EPUB)
ISBN 978-1-4875-2704-4 (PDF)

Library and Archives Canada Cataloguing in Publication

Title: Perilous passions : ethics and emotion in early modern Spain /
Hilaire Kallendorf.
Names: Kallendorf, Hilaire, 1974– author. Series: Toronto Iberic ; 87.
Description: Series statement: Toronto Iberic ; 87 | Includes
bibliographical references and index.
Identifiers: Canadiana (print) 20230573193 | Canadiana (ebook) 20230573258 |
ISBN 9781487527037 (cloth) | ISBN 9781487527044 (PDF) |
ISBN 9781487527051 (EPUB)
Subjects: LCSH: Spanish drama – Classical period, 1500–1700 – History and criticism. |
LCSH: Emotions in literature. | LCSH: Ethics in literature. | LCSH: Theater – Spain –
History – 16th century. | LCSH: Theater – Spain – History – 17th century.
Classification: LCC PQ6105 .K35 2024 | DDC 862/.309–dc23

Cover design: Heng Wee Tan
Cover image: Guido Reni, *Cupid*. Artefact/Alamy Stock Photo

We wish to acknowledge the land on which the University of Toronto Press operates. This
land is the traditional territory of the Wendat, the Anishnaabeg, the Haudenosaunee, the
Métis, and the Mississaugas of the Credit First Nation.

University of Toronto Press acknowledges the financial support of the Government of
Canada, the Canada Council for the Arts, and the Ontario Arts Council, an agency of the
Government of Ontario, for its publishing activities.

For my sister Sarah,
the most emotionally intelligent person I know

Contents

List of Figures

Acknowledgments

This research was supported by grants from the Academy for the Visual and Performing Arts, the Vice President for Research, the Dean of Faculties, the Melbern G. Glasscock Center for Humanities Research, and the Department of Hispanic Studies at Texas A&M University. A very special thanks to my student research assistants: Carolyn Biery, Judit Urrea, Elizabeth Sigala, Ana Chaires, Darcey Rydl, and Julia Bordonaro. Without their help – christened so cleverly by Carolyn as "emotional support" – this work would have taken me much, much longer. For writing the reference letters for my research sabbatical, and for countless other recommendation letters they have written for me through the years, I wish to thank my two scholarly "godfathers," Fred de Armas and Ed Friedman. Thanks to UTP senior acquisitions editor Suzanne Rancourt for believing in me and this project and to associate managing editor Barb Porter for bringing it to fruition. I want to express heartfelt gratitude to Carolina de Leon in Interlibrary Loan services at the Texas A&M University Libraries. I could not possibly wish for higher-quality librarians to aid me with my research. Finally, a big word of thanks to Juliana Cuyler for many yoga sessions at the blueberry patch – the perfect fix for my poor, muddled brain after a long day of writing. Thank you for always asking how my book was coming along, and for helping me soothe my seething passions through the practice of mindfulness. This kind of work can be hazardous to one's health!

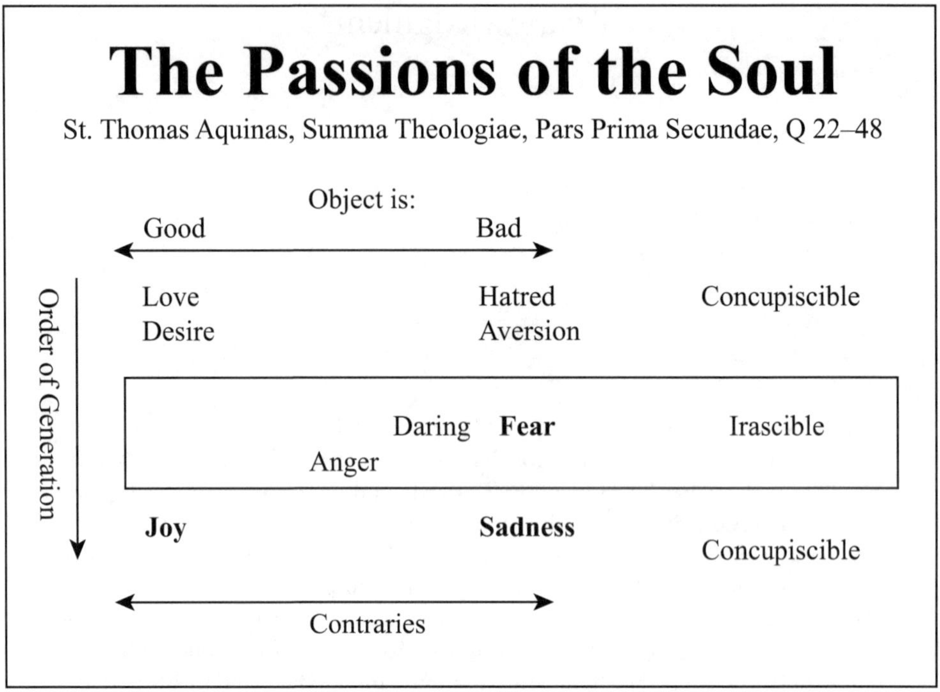

The Passions of the Soul

St. Thomas Aquinas, Summa Theologiae, Pars Prima Secundae, Q 22–48

1. The passions according to Saint Thomas Aquinas. Public Domain, https://en.wikipedia.org/w/index.php?curid=12283043.

2. Diego Velázquez, *The Fable of Arachne* (*Las Hilanderas*) (1657). Canvas, 220 × 289 cm. Museo del Prado (Madrid), Cat. 1173. Photo credit: Erich Lessing / Art Resource, NY.

3. Guido Reni, *Cupid* (1637–38). Oil on canvas, 101 × 88 cm. Museo del Prado (Madrid), NP 150. Photo credit: Album / Art Resource, NY.

4. *The Sun, the Moon and a Basilisk*, drawing (ca. 1512) on a page of a manuscript English translation of Horapollo's *Hieroglyphica* done by Willibald Pirkheimer, humanist and friend of Albrecht Dürer. British Museum (London), PD 1932-7-9-2. Photo credit: Erich Lessing / Art Resource, NY.

5. Andrea Domenico Remps, *Cabinet of Curiosities* (ca. 1690). Oil on canvas, 99 × 137 cm. Opificio delle Pietre Dure (Florence, Italy). Photo Credit: Scala / Art Resource, NY.

6. *Wheel of Fortune* from illuminated manuscript of Dante, *The Divine Comedy*.
Biblioteca Apostolica Vaticana / Vatican Museums.
Photo Credit: Album / Art Resource, NY.

7. Chimera of Arezzo with three heads (serpent, goat, and lion) (Etruscan bronze sculpture, 400–350 BC). Museo Archeologico Nazionale (Florence, Italy). Photo credit: Scala / Art Resource, NY.

8. Caravaggio, *The Cardsharps* (ca. 1597). Oil on canvas, 94.2 × l30.9 cm. Kimbell Art Museum (Fort Worth, Texas), AP 1987.06. Photo credit: Kimbell Art Museum, Fort Worth, Texas / Art Resource, NY.

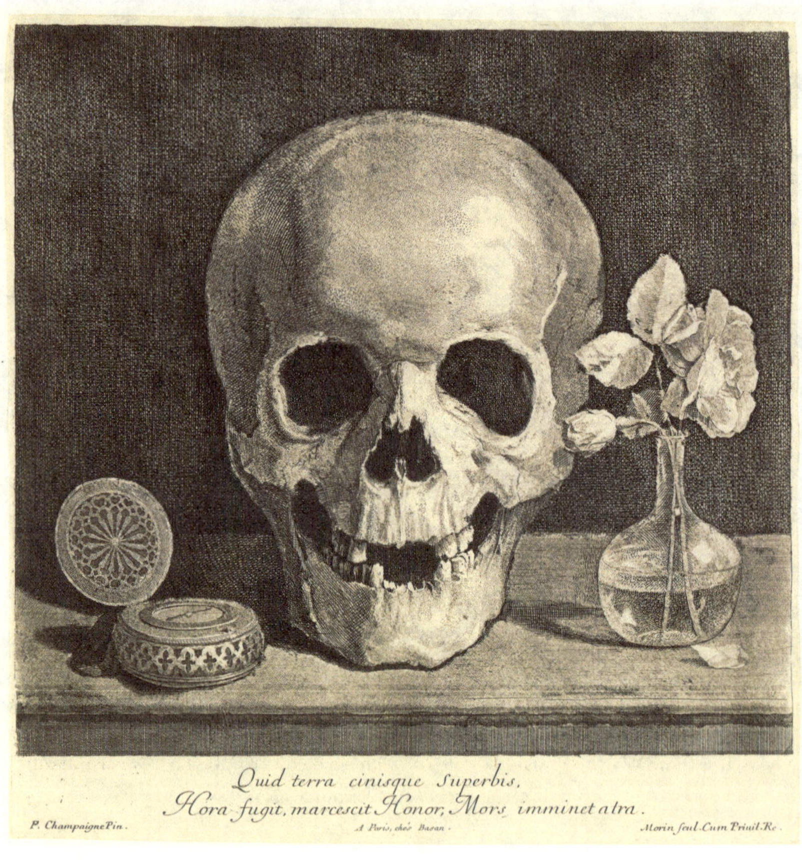

9. Jean Morin (ca. 1605–1650). After Philippe de Champaigne (1602–1674), *Still Life with Skull, Pocket Watch, and Roses (Memento Mori)*, 1640–1650. Etching and engraving. Image: 12 11/16 × 12 1/2 in. (32.2 × 31.8 cm) (cropped). Museum purchase, Achenbach Foundation for Graphic Arts Endowment Fund, 1994.13. Photography by Joseph McDonald, © courtesy Fine Arts Museums of San Francisco.

10. Hieronymus Bosch, *The Temptation of Saint Anthony* (ca. 1501), oil on oak panel, 73 × 52.5 cm. Museo del Prado (Madrid), P002049. Photo credit: Erich Lessing / Art Resource, NY.

11. Juan van der Hamen, seventeenth-century portrait of Francisco de Quevedo wearing the symbol of a red cross in the shape of a sword, representing his knighthood in the Order of Santiago. Instituto Valencia de Don Juan (Madrid).
Photo credit: Album / Art Resource, NY.

12. Raimundi Vicent, *Santiago Matamoros combatiendo*. Miniature in manuscript antiphonal belonging to Holy Roman Emperor Carlos V, fol. 20v. Biblioteca Nacional (Madrid). Photo credit: Album / Art Resource, NY.

13. *The Hanging of Judas* (Mozarabic Spain, Navarra, second half of the tenth century). Carved bone plaque, 7.7 × 6.8 cm. Musée National du Moyen Age - Thermes de Cluny (Paris), CL17050vv. Photo by Michel Urtado.
Photo credit: © RMN-Grand Palais / Art Resource, NY.

14. Manuscript drawing showing temptation to despair. *Ars moriendi*, editio princeps, Photographisches Facsimile des Unicum im Besitze von T.O. Weigel (Leipzig: 1869). Photo courtesy of the British Library.

15. Wolfgang Amadeus Mozart (1756–1791), *Don Giovanni*, Royal Opera House, Covent Garden, London. Dress rehearsal, for opening night on 12 September 2003. The Commendatore (Robert Lloyd) and Don Giovanni (Gerald Finley). End of act II. Conductor: Antonio Pappano. Photo credit © Laurie Lewis / Bridgeman Images.

16. Dante and Virgil walking through the Wood of the Suicides, from Dante Alighieri, *The Divine Comedy: Hell* (Circle VII, Ring II, Canto XIII), with commentary by Guiniforte delli Bargigi. Illuminated manuscript (Italy, fifteenth century), folio 14v. Biblioteca Comunale, Imola (Italy). Photo credit: Alfredo Dagli Orti / Art Resource, NY.

17. Philippe de Champaigne (1602–1674), *Vanitas* with wilting flower. Musée de Tessé (Le Mans, France). Photo credit: Erich Lessing / Art Resource, NY.

18. Columns of Hercules on title page of Francis Bacon, *Instauratio Magna* (London, 1620). Photo credit: HIP / Art Resource, NY.

19. The goddess *Spes* holding a flower representing Hope on a silver *denarius* (Roman imperial coin of Antoninus Pius, 431 AD). American Numismatic Society (New York), 1911.23.278 (reverse). Photo courtesy of the American Numismatic Society.

20. Tirso de Molina, *Don Gil de las calzas verdes*, advertising poster for performance, Teatre Nacional de Catalunya (Barcelona, Spain).

21. Diego Velázquez, portrait of Gaspar de Guzmán, Conde-Duque de Olivares, wearing the green Cross of Alcántara on his cape because he was a Comendador Mayor of that Order (1623). Colección Várez-Fisa (Madrid). Photo credit: Erich Lessing / Art Resource, NY.

SUMARIO DE LAS GRACIAS

E INDULGENCIAS PERPETUAS QUE GOZAN

LOS HERMANOS DE LA COFRADIA

DE LA PRECIOSA SANGRE DE CHRISTO

Y Nuestra Señora de los Dolores,

AGREGADA A LA ILUSTRE COFRADIA

DEL SEÑOR SAN HOMOBONO,

Fundada en nuestra Iglesia de la Santísima Trinidad por el Alcalde, Vedor, Guardianes de la Ilustre Archicofradia y demas Maestros del Arte de la Sastrería de la muy Noble é Imperial Ciudad de México, agregada á dicha Ilustre Archicofradia, y aprobada por nuestro Santísimo Padre el Señor Inocencio Duodecimo, quien se dignó concederlas por su Apostólico Breve, dado en Santa Maria la Mayor, debaxo del Anillo del Pescador el dia veinte y quatro de Enero de mil seiscientos noventa y ocho, al séptimo de su Pontificado.

22. Bull of indulgence (Mexico, 1807). Cushing Memorial Library and Archives, Texas A&M University (College Station, Texas).

PERILOUS PASSIONS

1
Introduction: Can Feelings Be Wrong?

Can feelings be wrong? This is the research question from which I began this project. It is also a quandary about which my husband and I have argued fiercely for nothing short of twenty-five years, with him telling me my feelings were wrong, and me telling him that couldn't be the case if emotions were not fully within my power to change. The tables have been turned only recently, when he was diagnosed with brain cancer. Now I am absolutely certain – and this was confirmed to me by his brain surgeon – that in a very real sense, some of his emotions are "wrong."

It turns out, there was some truth to both of our perspectives. Scientists now agree that emotions contain both a cognitive and a physiological component. The cognitive part can be modified, while the physiological response is involuntary. But what are the implications of this odd yoking for morality? Can people be held responsible for their feelings, or only for their actions?

In religious terms, the answer is clear. Part of what was so new about the New Testament was its legislation of heart motives: love your enemies, lust is equivalent to adultery, hate is the same thing as murder, etc. We aren't even supposed to be able to change these feelings on our own. Believers are helpless without the empowering work of the Holy Spirit.

But have emotions always been understood this way, i.e., as central to ethics? One would never know this had been the case, looking at popular culture today. The self-help industry, campaigning against co-dependency, trumpets that *Love Is a Choice*[1] while simultaneously hawking the latest anger management strategies, with no hint that love is an imperative or that anger might be sinful. In the fields of literary criticism and cultural studies, likewise, Hélène Cixous and Georges Bataille lead us (indiscriminately?) down pathways of desire,[2] while Julia Kristeva explores our (selfish) aversion to the abject.[3] What is missing here is an account of emotions that incorporates their ethical elements. This is by definition highly variable and thus only possible to execute for one specific place at one specific time – in this case, Renaissance Spain.[4]

This project participates in the so-called affective turn, which has been hailed recently in the humanities and social sciences as a much-needed corrective to the false dichotomies propagated by Cartesian dualism, that is, the supposed split between mind and body. Because they are both cognitive and physiological, emotions cannot be situated properly either exclusively in the mind or exclusively in the body. Victims of PTSD who experience sudden surges of adrenaline in response to sounds as mundane as the crackling of a potato chip bag can attest to the viscerality of the body's involuntary emotional response. But most psychotherapists would be wasting their time if some aspect of emotions were not amenable to change via cognition; this is the principle underlying the practice of cognitive-behavioural therapy. A "third term" or some combination of the two approaches is needed.

There is a growing recognition of this gap in our knowledge within the fields of literature and cultural studies, as evidenced by recent books such as Paul Johnson's *Affective Geographies* (2021).[5] But that book focuses only on Cervantes's prose. To my knowledge there exists no book-length treatment (either comprehensive or even representative) of emotions in Spanish Golden Age theatre. This is truly uncharted territory.

In recent years scholars have started to speak of a "Renaissance of emotion" in Renaissance studies[6] arising in response to the affective turn taken by humanities and social science fields more generally:

> The passions have occupied a central space in recent innovations in early modern studies. This has taken place both in the field of intellectual history and of literary studies, prompting some to speak of an "affective turn." Whereas the emotions were once thought of as a distinctively modern philosophical concern, it is now apparent … that "the passions were at the heart of early modern philosophy." However, to state this is to acknowledge a sea-change in intellectual sympathy. Since ancient times, the passions have been the disowned children of moral philosophy.[7]

The editors of *Passions and Subjectivity in Early Modern Culture* strive to justify this affective turn further: "In the last two decades, intellectual history has worked voraciously to end the neglect of the passions in the understanding of early modern thought and assumptions. In part this can be seen as reclaiming the legacy of Aristotle against that of Plato."[8]

Jon Elster[9] dates the scientific study of emotions from the publication of Darwin's *Expression of the Emotions in Man and Animals* (1872) and William James's paper "What Is an Emotion?" (1884). Since then the University of Amsterdam has come to house the Institute for the Study of Motivation and Emotion; the Australian Research Council hosts a Centre of Excellence for the History of Emotions; Florida State University boasts an Institute for the Study of Emotion; there is a "Languages of Emotion" Research Center at Berlin's Freie Universität; we find the Queen Mary Centre for the History of Emotions at the University of London; there is now a section called "Emotional Culture and Identity" at the Institute for Culture and Society in the University of Navarra (Spain); and the list goes on and on. The Center for the History of Emotions at the Max Planck Institute for Human Development (Berlin) is what Jan Plamper calls a "feel tank."[10] (There is an actual Feel Tank in Chicago to which emotions scholar Deborah Gould belonged.)[11] Oxford University Press publishes an Emotions in History book series. This is a truly vibrant scholarly field.

During the 1980s Peter and Carol Stearns coined the term "emotionology"[12] to describe cultural norms, expectations, and prescriptive standards concerning emotions. Medievalist Barbara Rosenwein pioneered the concept of "emotional communities,"[13] while historian William Reddy adapted John Austin's notion of "performatives" to study "emotives" that create or alter emotional environments.[14] The American Sociological Association established the Section for the Sociology of Emotion in 1986. An Emotions Network sprang up from within the European Sociological Association in 2004 (the British Sociological Association had a section on emotions as early as 1990). Some of the many recent art exhibitions on emotions include Antwerp's Museum of Modern Art show *Emotion Pictures* (April 2005) and the Berlin Kunstwerke's *Real Emotions* (Spring 2014). Further important developments include the foundation in 2009 of the scholarly journal *Emotion Review* by Lisa Feldman Barrett and James Russell. There is now a popular magazine called *Emotion* as well as an organization called Emotions Anonymous (modelled after Alcoholics Anonymous) that currently boasts more than one thousand branches in Europe and the United States. In *Generation Emotion*, Christian Ankowitsch proclaimed ostentatiously, "The 'Generation E' (E for Emotion) has realized that emotions are a world power."[15] Having thus established the timeliness and relevance of this research for multiple humanities-based and scientific fields, let us now turn to questions of terminology in order to delineate more clearly our object of study.

The word *feelings* is obviously not specific enough, given that we "feel" sorry but at the same time "feel" an insect stinging our arm. During the early modern period, "apart from its religious context, the word 'feeling' was not understood in its modern sense and was used mostly to refer to 'touch.'"[16] The most important current thinker to give any credence to this term is the neuroscientist Antonio Damasio. Basically, he calls *emotion* the physical response to a stimulus, and *feeling* the perception of an emotion.[17] But overwhelmingly, most other scholars consider emotion to be more than a physical response. Recently acolytes of Gilles Deleuze and Félix Guattari tried to use these terms together in a confusing combination: "Feelings are complex strings of ideas traversing emotions as they remap them."[18] But clearly feelings are more than just strings of ideas.

The word *emotion* comes the closest, among the words in current usage, to denoting what we mean to study. But actually, that doesn't narrow it down much:

"[e]ven in such a limited field as English-language experimental psychology, ninety-two different definitions of emotion have been counted between 1872 and 1980."[19] Here are some sample definitions:

– "Emotion is a contamination of empirical space by affect."[20]
– "[E]motion is the articulation of affect and ideology. Emotion is the ideological attempt to make sense of some affective productions."[21]
– Emotion is "a cognitive-physical sensation which is object-directed and, as such, structured within a belief system to which the emotional subject is responding."[22]
– "An emotion is a range of loosely connected thought material, formulated in varying codes, that has goal-relevant valence and intensity … that may constitute a 'schema' (or a set of loosely connected schemas or fragments of schemas); this range of thoughts tends to be activated together … but, when activated, exceeds attention's capacity to translate it into action or into talk in a short time horizon."[23]

Huhhhh??? These waters could not possibly be murkier.

Let's start with etymology: "The … root of the word *emotion* is *motere*, the Latin verb 'to move,' plus the prefix 'e-' to connote 'move away,' suggesting that a tendency to act is implicit in every emotion."[24] Richard Meek and Erin Sullivan claim that the word *emotion* emerged in late sixteenth-century England but did not enter common usage until the nineteenth century:[25]

> The term "emotion" early referred not to feelings but to physical movement or migration (it originally came from the Latin *emoveo*, to move out or move away). Thus Knolles's *History of the Turks* (1621) refers to "The divers emotions of that people." It continued to be used to mean a moving, stirring agitation in a physical sense until the early nineteenth century … [T]he word "emotion" was used figuratively to refer to an agitation or disturbance of the mind, that is passion, from the late sixteenth century, but was not in common use in this sense until the nineteenth century.[26]

Jonathan Ree confirms that the word *emotion* originally referred to civil unrest.[27] One of the earliest recorded uses of the term in a Romance language is by the French philosopher René Descartes:

> [I]n *Les Passions de l'Ame* (1649), Descartes made use of the term "émotions" in two ways, first as a synonym for "*passions*" in the broadest sense, and secondly in the phrase "*émotions intérieures*" to refer to a restricted class of intellectual feelings … Descartes' use of "*émotions*" as a broad umbrella term for movements of the soul was quite possibly the source of the term "emotions" in the writings of Scottish philosophers from Hume onwards.[28]

In his seminal work *From Passions to Emotions: The Creation of a Secular Psychological Category*, Thomas Dixon engages in some scholarly detective work to uncover the first official use of the new (psychological) definition of the word *emotion* in English in the writings of such luminaries as Thomas Brown and Charles Bell.[29] Dixon calls Thomas Brown (1778–1820), Doctor of Medicine and Professor of Moral Philosophy (notice the combination of fields!) at the University of Edinburgh, who wrote *Lectures on the Philosophy of the Human Mind* (published in 1820), the "inventor of the emotions":[30] "Brown was the first major mental philosopher systematically to replace 'passions' and 'affections' with 'emotions' in his lectures."[31] Dixon comments upon the secularizing tendency implicit in this move:

> The fact that the psychological category "emotions" gained widespread currency in the way that it did during the nineteenth century was indicative of the fact that the most popular and influential psychological works of the time were those produced within the positivist and secular tradition ... as opposed to Christian and moralist theories of "passions and affections" and "moral sentiments."[32]

It is just such a secularizing tendency that my study seeks to resist.

The early modern word most commonly used in reference to what we might call emotion is *passion* (sometimes equated to *affect*, which will be discussed momentarily).[33] Etymologically "*[p]assion* (derived from the deponent verb *patior*) suggested inactivity and suffering."[34] *Patior* means to suffer or endure. Thus even in modern dictionaries *passion* is defined as "to be subject to, to suffer intense and violent emotions."[35] But as my colleague Tim Mitchell points out in his book *Passional Culture: Emotion, Religion, and Society in Southern Spain*, this too is a slippery term: "Passion can refer to fervor and enthusiasm; it can refer to libidinal drives; it can imply the preponderance of external forces over personal freedom; it is synonymous with strong emotion of all kinds."[36] So which of these things are we talking about?

In a medieval and early modern context, Elena Carrera refers to the "Aristotelian definition of the passions as movements of the embodied soul causing alterations in the body in response to a perceived good or evil" and summarizes this same "understanding of the passions as cognitive-physiological events, located in the mind and the body simultaneously" as Aristotle was interpreted by Aquinas.[37] We shall return to these two thinkers shortly. Thomas Dixon clarifies: "Aquinas' passions (*passiones animae*) were conceived ... simply as special cases of the fundamental state of being acted upon (*passio*)."[38] This passive sense of being acted upon has proven to be important historically, for example in legal trial documents from Spain's early modern empire:

> This alleged passivity of emotions is particularly evident in criminal records of colonial Mexico. Facing a judge, defendants ... often explained their actions by claiming

to have been "seized by anger," "consumed by jealousy," or "paralyzed by fear." By invoking the idea of passivity, the defendants tried to excuse their behavior and mitigate their sentences.[39]

This sounds an awful lot like my students claiming the dog ate their homework, or early modern instances where demons were conveniently blamed as scapegoats for crimes up to and including murder.[40]

The so-called passivity of passion was not limited to negative emotions, however. It could also operate within the parameters of something so positively regarded as love. Agneta Fischer remarks, "the western conception of romantic love is a passion in *optima forma*: people see love as something that happens to them, it pops up out of nowhere."[41] Jan Plamper reminds us that there is a long and venerable history to this way of viewing emotion: "'Homer's literary figures saw themselves as more or less helpless in the face of the power of feelings', and the pre-Socratic philosophers also defined emotions as something that was external ... not something produced within men themselves."[42] This may have something to do with the fact that emotions were viewed as deities in the context of ancient religion and were the recipients of votive offerings and sacrifices at their respective shrines.[43] As Craig Kallendorf and I argued in a different context, if we take this fact into account, then Aristotle's much-debated poetic notion of dramatic catharsis should technically be viewed as a form of exorcism.[44] The result would be an emptying-out of emotional content epitomized by the Stoic idea of apathy.[45] Alternatively, within the cultural constructs of ancient Greece, *metriopatheia* was a term used to denote good emotionality[46] as opposed to lack of emotion, or *apatheia*. Muller mentions this term but then asks the obvious question: "[W]ho sets the standards for good emotionality, and what defines the norm against which its excesses and defects may be measured?"[47] This perceptive query cuts to the very heart of my research project.

Before we proceed further, however, I should like to offer a word or two about some additional terms one is likely to encounter in the course of doing early modern emotions research. The word *afecto*, or affect, seems to be synonymous with *passion* for Spanish Golden Age lexicographer Sebastián de Covarrubias: "*afecto ...* es pasión del ánima, que redundando en la voz, la altera y causa en el cuerpo un particular movimiento, con que movemos a compasión y misericordia, a ira y a vengança, a tristeza y alegría; cosa importante y necessaria en el orador."[48] The context here is specifically rhetorical. Etymologically *affection* (from the Latin *affectus*) suggests yearning or desire;[49] and for Saint Thomas Aquinas, "*[A]ffectus*, or 'affect' ... was a voluntary act 'without passion.'"[50] Thomist scholars of the early modern period held that "affections" of the will were like passions except that they did not induce a movement of the soul.[51] Renaissance Spanish Christian humanist Juan Luis Vives wrote: "The acts of those faculties which nature gave to the soul to follow what is good and avoid what is evil are called 'affects' or 'affections'; through them we are led to the good and move away from or against evil."[52] Thomas Dixon likewise refers to the "distinction between voluntary movements or affections … and unruly passions."[53]

The term *affect* does have its recent advocates, who note the "multiplicity, fluidity, and openness that the term *affect* provokes cultural theory to think with."[54] But the term also carries much baggage. As Lucía Díaz Marroquín explains for the early modern Spanish context, in reference to Saint Ignatius Loyola:

> En los *Ejercicios espirituales* el término *afecto* y sus derivados traen consigo matices tan peyorativos como los que en la tradición aristotélica venían siendo asimilados al término *pasión* y los suyos … [D]esestimando el fin de "mover los afectos para en todo amar y servir a Dios nuestro Señor" que mantenían San Jerónimo, San Agustín o San Gregorio, el fin último de los ejercicios es, de hecho, el de "quitar de sí todas las affecciones desordenadas."[55]

Díaz Marroquín comments further on the negative connotations of the word "passion" during this period: "las *pasiones* … [son] relativas a la expresión de aquellos sentimientos que exceden los límites de la ética o el decoro"[56] (hence the term *perilous* in my book's title).

As Juan Goytisolo famously quipped, there is no such thing as innocent syntax.[57] But on balance, the term *affect* seems to create more problems than it solves, given its close kinship with the English word *affection*, which typically bears positive connotations. What we need is a more flexible term to talk about both positive and negative emotions.

Let us briefly run through a few more relevant words, if only for the purpose of considering and then discarding them for our purposes. One of these is *apetito*, or appetite. The poet / playwright Lope de Vega uses this word almost at the outset in the first poem of his *Rimas sacras*:

> Al apetito sensitivo encuentro,
> de quien la voluntad mal respetada
> se queja al cielo, y de su fuerza armada
> conduce el alma al verdadero centro.[58]

This appetite would seem to be a very bad thing if free will complains to heaven about it. Sure enough, Thomas Dixon confirms that such is indeed the case:

> [A]ppetites, which were movements of the lower animal soul, were distinguished from the affections, which were acts of the higher rational soul. The appetites were hunger, thirst and sexual desire. The disobedience of the lower soul to the higher, and of the body to the soul, experienced in sexual appetite and in the passions was a sign of, and punishment for, the original sin of Adam and Eve. Often, passions were unruly

and disturbed the body; they included love, hate, hope, fear and anger. The higher affections of love, sympathy and joy were signs of relatedness to God … The will was divided by Aquinas into two "appetites": the higher intellectual appetite (the will proper), whose movements were the affections; and the lower, non-rational sense appetite, whose movements were the appetites and passions … It was in the world to come that a unified, ordered self, experiencing no passions but only the pure affections of love and joy, could be hoped for.[59]

This beatific vision of the "unified, ordered self" sounds indeed like one we might aspire toward. But it is certainly *not* the self we currently have – nor was that ever the case for emotional subjects in early modern Spain.

To list out quickly some other terms of possible relevance (some classical, some Renaissance, some modern), we might start with *perturbation* (from *perturbare*, to disturb), which obviously suggested disturbance.[60] Sometimes the enhancing or augmentative prefix was omitted, as in Saint Teresa's "nada te turbe, nada te espante."[61] This term as negative exemplum became a byword for Neostoic idealizations of *ataraxia*.[62] A somewhat later development was the discourse of the passions in contrast to *interests*, which in the eighteenth century took on a technical meaning:

> [T]he eighteenth-century discourse of the passions was political … [I]n this period an important distinction emerged between troubling "passions" and more cool and calculated "interests," such as the interest in acquiring wealth, which could override the wilder human passions and provide more innocuous motivations for action.[63]

This term has been studied in recent years by my former teacher Victoria Kahn, among others.[64]

Hurtling forward through the centuries, the current boom in emotions research has produced a few ridiculous neologisms like "cogmotive" (= cognitive + emotional),[65] along with some overly complicated words like "cathexis" (= investment of affect).[66] But the only additional word I'd like to comment on here is a simple one, *mood*, for which there is a surprisingly succinct definition: "Mood is sustained emotion."[67] So presumably whatever conclusions we reach about early modern passions / present-day emotions will be true of mood as well, simply by extending the duration or time frame under consideration.

A couple of these additional terms – while I've discarded them for the purpose of this research – do point to thorny problems that, conceptually, still need to be resolved. For example, the volitional aspect of *afecto* begs the exact question with which I began work on this topic in the first place: can feelings be wrong? It turns out that the Stoics, in particular, recognized this aspect of discourse on the passions and came up with a solution: the idea of *propassio*, or pre-passion. Simo Knuuttila explains:

At the beginning of the second book of his treatise *On Anger*, Seneca says that certain appearances can induce an affective thought which is accompanied by bodily changes. This first motion of the soul is involuntary. Seneca calls it a preparation for emotion … This Stoic theory of the first motions (pre-passions) proved to be very influential.[68]

Raphaële Garrod traces this discourse from the Stoics to Saint Thomas Aquinas:

> In the Stoic tradition – taken up by Aquinas in his explanation of the sadness of Christ on the Cross – a *propassio* was the drive of the sensitive appetite prior to any intervention of the will. A Stoic *propassio* was a mere "pre-emotion": it only became a perfect or fully fledged emotion once the will had assented to it and allowed it to become a motive for action.[69]

What might be some examples of these *propassiones*, or pre-passions? They could include things like involuntary blushing when one is embarrassed, shivering after drinking cold ice water too quickly, feeling vertiginous or dizzy when perched on the edge of a cliff, sensing the hair on the back of your neck rise at an uncanny coincidence, or even – for men – experiencing an erection in the presence of a scantily clad woman. So now the question becomes, are "first movements" or pre-passions sinful? Philippa Maddern offers some insight on this question:

> For Anselm of Laon and his contemporaries, a sin or passion did not consist simply in the original pleasurable response to a carnal stimulus; this constituted … a *propassio* (pre-passion). Only cognitively willed consent to such pleasure, leading ultimately to consent to action, produced fully blown sins (or passions) such as lust or anger. *Propassio* thus became an accepted medieval term for "the initial state of an unpremeditated desire or emotional response."[70]

Anselm lived from 1050 to 1117. Skipping ahead about one century, though, Saint Thomas Aquinas began to have doubts about this received wisdom. As Pierre Payer explains,

> [T]he common view up to Aquinas was that the first movements of sensuality were very minor venial sins … The individualized existentiality of the manifestations of sensuality is sufficient ground for Aquinas to claim that sensuality is subject to rational, voluntary control … [but] Aquinas was never able to resolve this conundrum.[71]

As the notion of *propassio* became lost in the maelstrom of Saint Thomas Aquinas's doubts, a very important piece of this puzzle was lost to future generations. (Had you ever heard of a *propassio* before reading this book? I certainly hadn't.) We now no longer possess the vocabulary required to talk about the ethics of emotion.

This is bad news for us. The good news is, though, that the ensuing centuries of confusion provide ample material for this study.

The first three figures in our story all have names that start with the letter "A": Aristotle, Avicenna, and Aquinas. In Aristotle's *Nicomachean Ethics*, "Emotions such as fear, anger, envy, and hatred are listed (1105b21–b23) under the heading of *pathē*, i.e., short-term states of the *appetitive* soul (1102b30–1103a3)."[72] As we might have guessed from this adjectival qualifier, "The human soul is divided into three parts, the reasoning (*logistikon*), the spirited (*thumoeides*, Lat. *irascibilis*) and the appetitive (*epistumêtikon*, Lat. *concupiscibilis*), of which the spirited and the appetitive give rise to emotional reactions and guide judgements accordingly."[73] This "divided soul" was something Aristotle had inherited from Plato. We should comment on two other important words in this tripartite scheme, namely *irascibilis* and *concupiscibilis*, which have given rise to our English words *irascible* and *concupiscible*.[74] The simplest definition I have found is that "the concupiscible power commands motion towards things, while the irascible power commands motion away from things."[75]

As is well known, the transmission of Aristotle's Greek texts in Spain (and indeed the rest of Europe) was largely accomplished by means of commentaries written by the Muslim philosopher Avicenna (980–1037 AD). Avicenna elaborated upon Aristotle's basic scheme, offering concrete examples of irascibility and concupiscence:

> Avicenna's examples of the concupiscible acts involve desires for food, wealth, and sexual intercourse, which are forms of seeking pleasure for oneself … The irascible power is directed toward victory and repelling antagonistic things. Avicenna's examples of its acts are pain, sadness, fear, and anger (*De anima*, 4.4, 58.26–32).[76]

Lest we doubt the extent of this philosopher's influence, Simo Knuuttila affirms that "Avicenna's *De anima* was the main source for medieval philosophical psychology until the middle of the thirteenth century and influenced its terminology even later."[77]

Middle of the thirteenth century: enter Saint Thomas Aquinas (1225–1274). Aquinas's *Summa theologiae* contained twenty-seven *quaestiones* (each comprising several *articuli*) on the *passiones animae*.[78] Elena Carrera narrates how "Aquinas drew on Christian revisions of Aristotle to explain the 'passions of the soul' (*animales passiones*) as involving the soul's functions related to embodied life."[79] Nicholas Lombardo adds that "Aquinas's account of the passions also represents an original synthesis of every major thinker available to him, particularly Aristotle, Augustine, Nemesius of Emesa, John Damascene, and his teacher, Albert the Great."[80] The Thomist canon of eleven passions or basic emotions includes six that are labelled concupiscible (aversion, desire, hatred, love, sorrow, and joy) plus five labelled irascible: fear, courage, despair, hope, and anger. Courage and anger – which appear in boldface in the list below – will not be treated in this book because I have already covered them under different auspices elsewhere.[81]

Saint Thomas arranged his schema for the passions into pairs of opposites (see figure 1):

1) AVERSION / DESIRE
2) HATRED / LOVE
3) SORROW / JOY
4) FEAR / **COURAGE**
5) DESPAIR / HOPE
6) **ANGER**

The concupiscible passions form three pairs of binaries, while the irascible ones form two pairs plus the dangling passion of anger, which stands alone. This was the chart or tree diagram that would have been sketched out in the notebook of every late medieval and Renaissance young pupil: "Aquinas's philosophy, as renovated by the Jesuits in the sixteenth century, was official doctrine in the Catholic world, and constituted the fundamental intellectual equipment imparted even to schoolboys."[82] This was the case particularly in Spain. As Alejandro Cañeque asserts, "Aquinas's ideas became mainstream thought in the Spanish world, and we find his influence in every political treatise written in this period."[83]

But Aquinas's influence was felt not only within the realm of politics. Indeed, one of the Spanish Golden Age's foremost literary theorists, Alonso López Pinciano, repeats Aquinas's scheme for the passions almost verbatim:

> El apetito se divide en dos escuadras: a la una dicen irascible y a la otra, concupiscible. Irascible se dice aquella potencia que tiene por objeto lo arduo y dificultoso y por fin, el gozo. Concupiscible, la que tiene por objeto lo deleitoso y por fin, también el gozo. De la una y de la otra el fin es uno; y aun el objecto también realmente, que es lo bueno. Distínguense en que la concupiscible sólo atiende a lo bueno como bueno, y la irascible lo mira como dificultoso y arduo. Quiérome declarar con un ejemplo: el amor, considerado simplemente como un deseo de gozar la cosa amada, toca a la parte concupiscible; pero, si se considera en cuanto está acompañado con la esperanza o desesperación, compete a la irascible. Esto se entenderá mejor, si digo los soldados con que cada una de las potencias o escuadras milita, los cuales son dichos afectos y passiones, como antes fue dicho; de los cuales digo así, según el orden de su generación: son los primeros amor y odio, y luego, deseo, huida, esperanza y desesperación, temor y osadía y ira; y más, el gozo y la tristeza, las cuales acompañan a las demás passiones todas. Las primeras cuatro (que son amor y odio, deseo y fuga) son soldados de la concupiscible y las otras cinco (esperanza, desesperación, temor y osadía y la ira) pertenecen a la irascible; y el gozo y la tristeza, a la una y a la otra. Todas tienen sus contrarios, salvo la ira.[84]

Given the extensive influence and prevalence of this model within the culture of early modern Spain, it is the basic one I shall follow in organizing this book's chapters.

Aquinas's taxonomy was further enlarged and elaborated by Renaissance Spanish humanist Juan Luis Vives. Vives studied at Montaigu College in Paris, the alma mater also of his compatriot Saint Ignatius Loyola. There he was immersed in Scholastic thought, including Thomist texts and methods. His *De Anima et Vita* was published in Bruges in 1538, two years before Vives's death. Eduardo Ruiz Jaren calls him the "fundador de la psicología moderna."[85] His modern translator Carlos Noreña notes that Vives's classificatory scheme for the passions "is very close to that of Saint Thomas, except for … the analysis of shame, which Saint Thomas reduces to a kind of fear (1aIIae. 41,4)."[86] In the treatment that follows – with all due deference to Vives – I have decided to stick with Aquinas's original schema instead of writing a separate chapter on shame.

The greatest rival system for understanding the passions, in competition with Aquinas's rewriting of Aristotle, was the corporeal model of the human body's four humours (blood, phlegm, yellow bile, and black bile). As Thomas Wright wrote in *Passions of the Minde in Generall* (1604), "there is no Passion very vehement, but that it alters extreamely some of the foure humors of the bodie."[87] The problem with this model, for our purposes, is that it reduces the passions to merely their physiological component, ignoring their cognitive component altogether. Thus, while many bodily symptoms for various emotions will be discussed in the following pages, the humoral system proves inadequate for explaining the passions' ethical dimension. As Muller notes, quoting Roger Smith: "'to ignore the theological dimension [of this discussion] … is badly ahistorical.' The marriage of faith and reason stands at the heart of early modern psychology."[88]

In the course of writing my previous monographs *Conscience on Stage: The* Comedia *as Casuistry in Early Modern Spain* (2007), *Sins of the Fathers: Moral Economies in Early Modern Spain* (2013), and *Ambiguous Antidotes: Virtue as Vaccine for Vice in Early Modern Spain* (2017) – all published by the University of Toronto Press – I have developed a trademark methodology for which I am known as a pioneer in the field of early modern Hispanic casuistry studies.[89] My method consists of training a team of undergraduate research assistants to comb through a database of 800 digitalized plays; this database is called Teatro Español del Siglo de Oro (TESO), distributed by ProQuest. These research assistants perform word searches for emotion words wherever they occur in the texts of these plays. They then cut and paste from the database, compiling Word files of "hits," which I then divide into relevant or irrelevant, depending on whether those lines spoken by dramatic characters can tell us anything new about the emotion in question. Finally, I go back to the play texts themselves and carve out longer excerpts for the most relevant passages, reading and studying entire plays selected empirically as having the most to say about emotion. The chapters vary in length according to how many "hits" each emotion word does (or does not) generate. (Incidentally, this in itself already tells us something about which emotions the *comedia* as a genre tends to emphasize: the love chapter is predictably long, as we might expect, while the despair chapter is the shortest – which we would also anticipate, given that despair is more germane to tragedy.)

I must emphasize that this method is not quantitative, nor is it meant to be. Each new metaphor I find to describe a discrete emotion is like one data point in a pointillist painting, a composite portrait or phenomenology that draws upon representative qualitative descriptions. Many of these plays are largely unknown to scholars because relatively few of the 800 theatrical works in this database have been published in modern editions.

This research participates in a larger trend for which Franco Moretti coined the term "distant reading." His phrase designates a new kind of digital humanities work that starts with a large corpus of texts and tries to look at the total to find consistent patterns. It is explicitly designed to serve as an antidote to New-Critical-style "close reading." As Moretti explains this paradigm shift,

> The trouble with close reading … is that it necessarily depends on an extremely small canon … [I]f you want to look beyond the canon … close reading will not do it. It's not designed to do it, it's designed to do the opposite. At bottom, it's a theological exercise – very solemn treatment of very few texts taken very seriously – whereas what we really need is a little pact with the devil: we know how to read texts, now let's learn how *not* to read them. Distant reading: where distance … *is a condition of knowledge*: it allows you to focus on units that are much smaller or much larger than the texts: devices, themes, tropes – or genres and systems … If we want to understand the system in its entirety, we must accept losing something. We always pay a price for theoretical knowledge.[90]

He emphasizes that for this new type of research, the criteria for evaluating the quality of this scholarship must undoubtedly shift as well: "The ambition is now directly proportional *to the distance from the text*: the more ambitious the project, the greater must the distance be."[91]

My guess is that even Moretti would say a corpus of 800 texts is suitably ambitious. But his underlying message is salutary: this kind of work is new, and the old criteria we typically used in past generations to evaluate it simply won't work for something this far outside the box. My hope is that open-minded readers will appreciate this work on its own terms – especially for the germs of future studies it holds – instead of trying to cram a square peg into a round hole. This might, in the end, turn out to be wishful thinking on my part. But then again, as you are about to find out in the last chapter on hope: hope springs eternal.

2

The Impure: Disgust

The criterion of disgust is the impure.[1]

No society can do without intolerance, indignation, and disgust; they are the forces behind the moral law.[2]

Disgust, in the Thomistic conception, involves movement away from its object; etymologically *aversion* comes from the Latin root for turning or looking away. Colin McGinn hazards the generalization, "To be disgusted by something is, crucially, to want to avoid contact with it – either by sight or touch or smell or taste."[3] Metaphorically disgust is a bad taste, as in "Disgusto del Gusto mío, / causa de mis desazones."[4] A disgusting kiss, for example, tastes like dirt in one's mouth.[5] If the bad taste is not so extreme, it might be compared to watered-down wine, like the kind served in taverns of ill repute in Madrid.[6] Disgust produces a queasy stomach, as in the case of overly rich food that makes the stomach upset: "La comida me ha dado algún disgusto, / de dulces que me dan fastidio llena."[7] Scientists confirm that "[d]isgust helps us avoid noxious foods and odors"[8] and "[d]isgust is, first of all, a gustatory response, an aversion to food that may contain contaminants."[9] Spoiled food can act like poison, stopping just short of killing a person but still making him sick.[10] Daniel Goleman observes, "The facial expression of disgust … suggests a primordial attempt … to close the nostrils against a noxious odor or to spit out a poisonous food."[11] The result is nausea or feeling sick to one's stomach: "pudiera ser que me hicieran / algún disgusto en la panza."[12] Aversion is described by analogy as what fire feels with regard to water[13] or what poisonous animals do when confronted with certain aromatic herbs: "como muchos animales ponzoñosos de algunas plantas Aromáticas, así la calumnia huye de los hombres sabios."[14]

How is disgust expressed? Aversion shows on a person's face as well as in the tone or inflection of his or her voice, like when Hipólita says to Don Álvaro: "Algún disgusto muestra / tu semblante."[15] It is indicated by facial expression or change of colour in one's complexion, like for example losing colour or becoming pale.[16]

Alternatively a disgusted person might blush, as with embarrassment.[17] Jennifer Biddle describes the facial expressions most often associated with disgust:

> [A]s disgust … causes annoyance, it is generally accompanied by a frown, and often by gestures as if to push away or to guard oneself against the offensive object … With respect to the face, moderate disgust is exhibited in various ways; by the mouth being widely opened, as if to let an offensive morsel drop out; by spitting; by blowing out of the protruded lips; or by a sound as of clearing the throat … Extreme disgust is expressed by movements round the mouth identical with those preparatory to the act of vomiting.[18]

Disgust might also be expressed vocally in complaints[19] or by not speaking at all.[20] As disgust or aversion escalates, it can be communicated by the act of leaving or turning away. Dixon affirms,

> [W]e now, when feeling a range of emotions, including disdain, contempt and disgust, carry out movements that would have been connected in the past with the rejection or avoidance of a noxious object. These actions include half-closing our eyes, turning away, or even retching or vomiting.[21]

Thus Saint Teresa laments to God, feeling He has turned away from her: "De vuestro disgusto / me avisa vuestro retiro."[22]

To what specifically did early modern Spaniards feel averse? The inventory of repulsive objects is extensive, starting with simple preferences according to personality. The *comedias* include instances of aversion to food or eating, as on the part of the melancholy Amón, who complains that nothing tastes good to him: "En nada / hallo sazón, y por eso, / o porque es conservación / de la vida, la aborrezco."[23] Characters might abhor certain colours due to their emotional resonance; for instance, Don Pedro dislikes black and white,[24] while Perejil dislikes yellow (the reason being, in this instance, that this colour represents fear or cowardice).[25] Others express an aversion to singing,[26] or to poetry and music.[27] This holds true especially for unwanted nocturnal serenades outside one's window,[28] or to poetry written by a "foolish" woman, as in Lope de Vega's *La dama boba*.[29] What we might call life-cycle aversion includes disgust at growing old ("El disgusto / de la edad, que acaba al hombre")[30] or simply the repugnance of boredom, which might indicate a youthful preference for variety.[31] People with a certain vocation might express aversion to engaging in activities typical of a different occupation. For example, Enrique describes himself and his twin brother, one devoted to arms and the other to letters:

> Solo que en los dos tuvo
> un algo de repugnancia,
> fueron los genios, dado él
> a las letras, yo a las armas.[32]

A soldier does not want to be a scholar, nor vice versa.

Of similar importance to vocation was location in terms of geographical or physical space. Our soldier from the last example will object to staying home in time of war, as he would prefer to be where the action is: "Da el ocio disgusto / si Marte la furia amansa."[33] Another frequently expressed preference is aversion to the royal court because of intrigue. For instance, Laura says to Roberto:

> Sé yo que vas engañado,
> que piensas que hay en la Corte,
> que de unas cartas en porte
> ya esperas un grande Estado.
> La esperanza, y ambición
> te meterán por su puerta,
> luego a la privanza abierta
> aumento, y estimación.
> Entregaránte al servicio
> lisonja, y solicitud,
> y éstos luego a la inquietud
> del favor, y del oficio.
> La envidia, y murmuración
> te harán luego compañía,
> tu esperanza cada día
> sentirá diminución.
> Las cautelas, los engaños,
> el corto premio, el disgusto,
> más a prisa que era justo
> irán segando tus años.
> Verás a la ingratitud
> entregarte a la vejez,
> que es el último juez,
> ya sin fuerza, y sin salud.
> No verás más la esperanza,
> sino al arrepentimiento
> que te muestra el sufrimiento
> junto a la desconfianza.
> Quejoso, pues, de esta suerte
> verás con triste partida,
> que en la Corte cualquier vida
> va por la posta a la muerte.[34]

This trope will be familiar to readers of Antonio de Guevara's Horatian *beatus ille* and *locus amoenus* motifs in *Menosprecio de corte y alabanza de aldea*. Aside from this critique of the court, however, *comedia* characters often express a simple preference for rural life, as when the Duke attributes to Rogerio an aversion to the royal courtly scene:

> ¿Rogerio, pues qué es esto?
> ¿Tú, triste, ahora, cuando manifesto
> secretos que ha tenido
> el tiempo, en las entrañas del olvido?
> ¿Cuando sólo creías
> heredar las groseras alquerías
> que viste el sayal pardo,
> hijo de un Duque ya, no de Pinardo,
> en posesión segura
> del estado Bretón, donde te jura
> por señor la nobleza,
> melancólico tú? ¿Tú con tristeza?
> Pudiera hacerte agravio,
> creyendo que echas menos
> montes de riscos, y de encinas llenos,
> rústico por costumbre,
> y que te da la Corte pesadumbre
> el palacio tristeza,
> y bárbaro disgusto esta belleza;
> que aunque ilustre has nacido,
> podrás, como entre montes has vivido,
> de la costumbre hacer naturaleza.[35]

An even more extreme example of space- or place-related aversion occurs with exile. Thus Adam with Eve after expulsion from the Garden of Eden wants to "templar el disgusto / de nuestro destierro impío."[36]

In addition to disgust with location, disgust could be experienced as a reaction to social customs. Aversion to social customs might object to duelling to solve disagreements, as between the rival clans depicted in Antonio Zamora's *Mazariegos y Monsalves*.[37] Likewise, devout members of monastic orders such as Franciscan friars or Clarisan nuns who had taken a vow of poverty might object to the social custom of sumptuous adornment.[38] This is not actually very far from simply the aversion of austere Castilians to extravagant displays of fashion that wasted money unnecessarily.[39] Another waste of money was addiction to gambling, to which devout (or simply prudent) laypeople might object.[40] Part of this aversion was undoubtedly tied to burgeoning notions of good taste and class consciousness, such as we see in these lines about aversion to improper lineage:

> Que el ser la buena mujer
> don de Dios habrás leído,

mas no por eso sabido
que a tiento se ha de escoger.
Porque si eso fuera así,
cualquiera se disculpara,
cuando muy mal se casara
sin poner la culpa en sí.
Que si comprando un melón
se ha de escoger en doscientos,
yo pienso que casamientos
de más importancia son.
Tiente, huela, tome a peso,
pesia tal el que se casa,
pero que no lleve a casa
algo que le quite el seso.
No melón como pepino,
ni de maduro badea,
pero que disgusto sea,
y para estimarle digno.
Llaman partes del melón
Los mequetrefes de España,
buen olor, buena calaña,
y estas dos las mismas son
que hacen buena a la mujer.
Buen olor es buena fama,
buena calaña es la rama
de quien ha de proceder,
que nunca de madre ruin,
vimos hija virtuosa.[41]

We should notice that here "good odour" is equated to "good reputation." The discourse of disgust often plays up such visceral equivalencies: "The poor smelled bad, as part of their feckless, uncivilized habits more generally."[42] Peter Stallybrass and Allon White confirm that disgust is central to preserving social hierarchies: "Differentiation … is dependent upon disgust. The division of the social into high and low, the polite and the vulgar, simultaneously maps out divisions between the civilized and the grotesque body, between author and hack, between social purity and social hybridization."[43]

Not surprisingly, the lines of theatrical dialogue quoted above occur in Lope de Vega's *La mal casada*. Almost as bad as lacking good lineage oneself was association with people who lacked adequately good ancestry. Thus Enrico expresses to Celia an aversion to letting unsavoury characters into the house:

¿No te he dicho, que no gusto
que entren estos marquesotes

todos guedejas, bigotes,
a donde me dan disgusto?
¿Qué provecho tienes de ellos?
¿Qué te ofrecen, qué te dan,
estos que continuo están
rizándose los cabellos?
De peña, de roble, o risco,
es el dar su condición,
su bolsa hizo profesión,
en la orden de San Francisco.
¿Pues para qué los admites?
¿Para qué los das entrada?
¿No te tengo yo avisada?
Tú harás algo que me incites
a cólera.[44]

This kind of aversion rapidly boils down to economic or social class considerations. As Martha Nussbaum explains,

[C]ertain disgust properties – sliminess, bad smell, stickiness, decay, foulness – have repeatedly and monotonously been associated with, indeed projected onto, groups by reference to whom privileged groups seek to define their superior human status. Jews, women, homosexuals, untouchables, lower-class people – all of these are imagined as tainted by the dirt of the body.[45]

In like manner, Pompeyo communicates to Lisardo his aversion to selling the last piece of family property.[46] Many *comedia* characters express an aversion to showing outward signs of poverty, like the squire in *Lazarillo de Tormes*, who ostentatiously uses a toothpick to make it seem to all observing him like he has just eaten a good meal. A theatrical parallel to this picaresque situation may be found in Lope de Vega's *Los peligros de la ausencia* when Don Pedro declares to Blanca:

No está ahora nuestra hacienda
para vivir como es justo
en la Corte; este disgusto
no será bien que os ofenda.
Alma de mi propia vida,
que es echarnos a perder
vivir no pudiendo ser
con la ostentación debida.[47]

Comedia characters voice similar concerns about infringements of the social code, which were considered to be discourtesy or just plain bad manners. An example might be the faux pas of making long social calls on a day set aside for writing letters or taking care of other necessary business ("No hay disgusto / como en día de cartas, dilatada / visita").[48] Upper-class characters express an aversion to servants who do not fulfil promptly their masters' wishes, as we see in this hilarious caricature by a servant of a bossy master:

> Da acá, muestra, desvía,
> la limpiadera, el espejo.
> Los guantes, limpia, desata,
> descalza, tira de aquí,
> vuelve, torna, ¿fuiste allí?
> ¿Qué dijo Doña Alpargata?
> Lleva este papel, ¿no acaba
> el sastre la cuera? Bestia,
> necio, tonto, qué molestia,
> qué disgusto, cosa brava.
> No hay sufrimiento, yo solo
> sufriera este criado:
> majadero, porfiado,
> si le hay de polo a polo.[49]

This satire arguably pushes the boundaries of socially acceptable class resistance, perhaps hiding behind a veil of humour to make the critique more palatable to a heterogeneous audience.

Social classes remained rigidly stratified in Golden Age Spanish society, and relations between them were often tense. Thus we hear an upper-class woman rebuke a male labourer who does not even necessarily work for her, objecting that he has failed to show proper deference:

> Pensad, señor labrador,
> quien quiera que vos seáis,
> cuánto más sujeto estáis
> a mi disgusto y rigor.
> De aquel castillo soy dueño,
> y con una voz que, de
> gente a caballo, y a pie
> os sabrán quitar el sueño.
> Hacedme la cortesía
> que se debe a una mujer,
> porque estáis en mi poder,
> y toda esa hacienda es mía.[50]

We hear in this instance the inflection of gender as well – i.e., how a man is supposed to treat a woman – but the main problem she finds with his behaviour is a lack of deference toward her as a landowner. Lines like these have long prompted critics to conclude that the *comedias'* ideological function in Golden Age Spanish culture was to maintain a rigidly stratified social hierarchy. Martha Nussbaum confirms, "disgust … has the function of protecting and reinforcing hierarchical boundary lines."[51]

One of the chief mechanisms by which Spanish culture held its hierarchy firmly in place was the much-contested notion of honour.[52] Characters on stage routinely express an aversion to offending honour, as when Luis retorts to Doña María:

> ¿Aconsejara
> cosa yo, que indigna fuera
> a tu honor? Con una amiga
> de su calidad, y prendas,
> debiera hacerlo hoy el gusto
> cuando el disgusto no fuera.[53]

Interpersonal relationships could be solidified further by emotion rules, such as Lisardo's avowed aversion to speaking ill of a friend: "Se me hace gran repugnancia / el decir mal de un amigo."[54] An even greater taboo was set firmly in place against betraying one's beloved; thus Ascanio feels aversion to Serafina even though she is beautiful because he has already given his heart to Lucrecia:

> Yo no tengo voluntad
> a Serafina, si bien
> conozco de su beldad
> que cuantos sus ojos ven
> la rinden su libertad.
> Lucrecia es de mis desuelos
> ocupación peregrina,
> ¿qué importa que forme celos?
> Y sé los de Serafina
> a Alfonso, cuando los cielos
> niegan la correspondencia,
> que por oculta aversión
> la apartan de su presencia.
> Donde no hay inclinación
> no puede haber competencia.
> No inclinándome a su dama,
> mal con él competir puedo.[55]

Characters further express aversion to being cast aside as a casualty of someone else's political aspirations, as when Laura laments being ignored by her husband:

> Mi esposo me va olvidando
> cuando le estoy adorando,

> pues con su privanza entiendo,
> que al paso que él va subiendo
> voy en su afición bajando.
> Su privanza, o su locura
> son causa de mi disgusto.[56]

On the other side of this equation, we find an aversion to losing one's friends in order to obtain political power.[57] We likewise see an aversion to not keeping one's promise or honouring one's vow, as when Enrico laments that he has not kept his promise to make a pilgrimage to Jerusalem:

> Yo hice voto al cielo en un peligro
> de ir a Jerusalén con mis soldados.
> No lo he cumplido, y vivo con disgusto.[58]

It was believed that this failure to make a pilgrimage as promised could lead to misfortune occasioned by supernatural wrath.

Interpersonal relationships within families could become particularly tense and thereby evoke disgust. In a familiar grievance, some characters complain about what we might recognize as "too much togetherness." Thus the King says to Florisandro about Leonora:

> Acompañarla fue justo
> hasta Londres, y mostrar
> de mi casamiento gusto,
> pero tanto acompañar
> ¿a quién no causa disgusto?[59]

Other, similar complaints by *comedia* characters often have a familiar ring to them, as with young Lucinda's aversion to receiving advice on matters of love from her mother:

> Qué infernal pena, y disgusto.
> Madre, ¿para qué te cansas?
> Que no me conoces bien.[60]

Another common feminine complaint within the family was aversion to caring for another woman's children (here we might think about the evil stepmother in *Cinderella*); this aversion is implied in the following curse spoken upon a character named Elisa:

> Siempre vivas con disgusto,
> con mala opinión y fama,

ni en la mesa, ni en la cama
tengas una hora de gusto.
Todo se os pase en reñir,
no te dé jamás placer,
ni regalos a comer,
ni galas para vestir.
Deshónrese de su suegro,
y siempre tenga cuestiones;
cubra vuestros corazones
llanto triste y luto negro.
Los hijos de otra mujer
traiga a tu casa a criar,
y te los haga limpiar,
mecer, cantar y envolver.[61]

The reverse side of this equation in the realm of family relationships is the aversion of a son as heir to his new stepmother, whom he perceives to be an interloper. Thus Federico declares to Batín:

Mi disgusto
no me permite, como fuera justo,
más prisa, y más cuidado.
Antes la gente dejo, y fatigado
de varios pensamientos,
y al dosel de estos árboles, que atentos
a las dormidas ondas de este río
mirando están sus copas,
después que los vistió de verdes ropas.
De mí mismo quisiera retirarme,
que me cansa el hablarme
del casamiento de mi padre, cuando
pensé heredarle, que si voy mostrando
a nuestra gente gusto, como es justo
el alma llena de mortal disgusto
camino a Mantua de sentido ajeno,
que voy por mi veneno,
en ir por mi madrastra, aunque es forzoso.[62]

His woes are compounded by the fact that he has been sent to fetch his new stepmother.

A similarly awkward family situation arises when a man feels aversion to his own wife once he has started having an affair with another woman. Thus Doña

Clara speaks to the "other woman," Celia, describing her husband's diminished desire for her:

> Comienza a mostrar disgusto,
> y el gusto en desdén resuelve,
> que cuando la espalda vuelve,
> cobrar de batalla el gusto;
> mas viendo que no era justo
> dejarme tan obligado,
> de tal manera a mi lado
> las noches amanecía,
> que amor vergüenza tenía
> de verse a su lado helado.
> Con esto quise saber
> la causa, que claro estaba,
> que hombre a quien mujer helaba
> abrasaba otra mujer;
> no fue difícil de ver,
> pues yo propia entrar le vi
> en vuestra casa.[63]

Here she attempts to get to the root of the problems in her marriage by confronting the other woman, her rival.

This stereotypically "feminine" jealousy regarding her wayward husband is one of many aversions attributable characteristically to one traditionally defined gender or the other. For example, the alleged aversion of women to intellectual life is depicted in a humorous exchange among Leonor, Elvira, and Mondragón (a boy who is dressed up like a student peddling books for sale):

> MONDRAGÓN: Traigo de todo el Derecho
>   libros ...
>   Hay Odofredos y Dinos,
>   Olrados, Bartulos, Baldos,
>   Paulos Castrenses, Ubaldos,
>   Albericos y Aretinos.
>   Decios, Jasones, Rosatos,
>   Curzios, Decios, Amodeos,
>   Fulgosios, Ripas, Budeos,
>   Tiraquelos, Purpuratos
>   y otros mil.
> LEONOR: ¡Qué lindo necio!

MONDRAGÓN: Si los quisiere comprar
   yo le volveré a buscar,
   y darélos en buen precio.
ELVIRA: Para mí son bernardinas,
   todos esos Doctores
   que nuestras leyes mejores
   son perdices, y gallinas.
   Buenas joyas, buenas galas,
   paz en casa, hijos y gusto.
LEONOR: Los libros me dan disgusto.
ELVIRA: Quítannos las buenas salas
   y ocúpannos los maridos,
   que en entrándose a estudiar
   no hay hacerlos acostar,
   ni volverles los sentidos.
   Si esta lista dijera
   cambrayes, tocas, holandas,
   cortes, mantos, ricas bandas,
   raso de oro, primavera,
   damascos, telas, tables,
   joyas, cadenas, diamantes,
   medias, zapatillas, guantes,
   y papeles carmesíes,
   aun fueran libros, Leonor,
   para nuestra librería.[64]

Scenes such as this one, which show women feeling "disgusted" by books, only served to reinforce unfortunate and potentially damaging misogynistic stereotypes. Patrick Hogan confirms:

> Among objects of disgust, it appears that those related to sex are the most intensively regulated and those that give rise to the most intense moral revulsion. In keeping with the intensity of disgust-based moral revulsion relating to sex … [we see] the importance of disgust to homophobia and misogyny.[65]

A similar cultural attitude conveyed on stage with reference to disgust was men's aversion to freedom for women. Sancho expresses extreme aversion to anything that might hint of liberty on the part of his wife, Inés:

¿Tú quieres que no riñamos?
Pues la vida que te aguarda

conmigo quiero decirte,
dame la oreja tan larga.
Lo primero, aunque seas buena,
has de parecerme mala,
porque es muy necio el marido
que con su mujer se casa.
A cuanto yo te dijere
no has de replicarme nada,
que te has de ir muy en hora buena,
si te envío en hora mala.
Tú no has de afeitarte el rostro,
no ha de haber muda que valga
si le tienes en tizona,
no has de ponerle en colada.
Que por si acaso algún día
(Dios me libre de esta plaga)
tuviera bubas, no quiero
que tú me gastes la pasta.
Moño, ni por qué se dijo,
si ponértele pensabas,
bien se te puede quitar
de la cabeza esa alhaja.
Las razones serán buenas,
llamaréte mentecata,
puerca, sucia, que no pienso
tratarte mal de palabra.
He de dejarte con llave
siempre que fuera me vaya,
porque si viene algún diablo
se vuelva a puerta cerrada.
Jamás has de entrar en coche,
que pudiendo andar a pata
no he de tratar yo en tinteros,
para que tú trates en cajas.
Nunca saldrás sino a Misa,
y no has de salir tapada,
que no has de darme un disgusto
por un ojo de la cara.
No irás al río en Verano,
que allá suelen muchas damas

en lugar de agua del río
bañarse en agua rosada.
A la comedia, hosse puto,
eso no, que arregostada,
querrás si hoy comes cazuela
irte a pasear mañana.
Aunque tengas un cuarto,
no has de dar una migaja
de tu honra, que más quiero
verte pobre que alcanzada.
Que siendo tan convenible
no hayas miedo, Inés amada,
que te dé más que ocho vueltas
de palos cada semana.[66]

Martha Nussbaum theorizes the dynamic at work here as misogyny directed toward the female body:

Misogynistic disgust has some empirical starting points that help to explain why this form of projection turns up with such monotonous regularity in more or less all societies. Women give birth, and are thus closely linked to the continuity of animal life and the mortality of the body. Women also receive semen: thus, if (as research suggests) semen disgusts males only after it leaves the male body, males will very likely come to view women as contaminated by this (to them) disgusting substance, while the male will view himself as uncontaminated, except insofar as he is in contact with her. In connection with these facts, women have often been imagined as soft, sticky, fluid, smelly, their bodies as filthy zones of pollution.[67]

But thankfully, misogyny does not always get to have the last word, either in life or on the stage. In the scene above, Inés replies tartly to her husband's chauvinistic tirade with what we can imagine to be a smirk on her face:

O quién tuviera testigos
que esta relación bastaba
para pedir yo divorcio.[68]

Unfortunately, in her society, divorce was much frowned upon as an option.[69] With regard to such problem-fraught relations between the sexes, the play's title in the form of an axiom or proverb says it all: *Con amor no hay amistad*.

Inés is not the only woman to invoke the concept of disgust while expressing aversion to her husband's manner and behaviour. Witness this exchange between Quiteria and Estela:

> QUITERIA: Soy casada.
> ESTELA: ¿Y ése es tanto mal?
> QUITERIA: Si es a disgusto,
>   ¿parécete que hay mal como él, hermana?
> ESTELA: Ése no es mal, que es muerte cotidiana,
>   y dime, ¿en qué te enfada tu marido?
> QUITERIA: En todo:
>   en la cara, en el talle, y en el modo,
>   que no hay cosa en el mundo mala, o buena,
>   que no le enfade, y de que no se pudra,
>   y fuera de esto toma sin embargo
>   todas las pesadumbres a su cargo:
>   de suerte, que en eterno movimiento
>   se quita la salud, y a mí el contento.[70]

These unhappily married women, like the titular character in Lope de Vega's *La mal casada*, show signs of this aversion to their husbands in their face, hair, and manner. Thus Ordóñez, a servant, declares concerning the lady of the house:

> No hemos visto levantar
> a mi señora con risa.
> Siempre sale desgraciada,
> siempre el cabello tranzado;
> ya da voces al criado,
> ya riñe con la criada.
> Y cuando por la mañana
> sale una mujer compuesta,
> y a todas riñe, y molesta,
> y come de mala gana,
> anda el rostro deslucido,
> y el sobrecejo en los pies,
> creedme que todo es
> disgusto de su marido.[71]

Not surprisingly, women show particular aversion to their husbands' infidelity. For example, we hear Fabia say to Celio:

Celio, aunque te escucho hablar
en esta nueva quimera,
no entiendas que es porque gusto
de tan locos disparates;
mas sólo porque me trates
de su engaño, y mi disgusto;
que a no haberme prevenido,
de que es mi esposo traidor,
ni yo escuchara tu amor,
ni tú fueras atrevido.
Deja, por Dios, si no quieres,
que te mande matar luego,
de ser tan loco, y tan ciego,
y dime cuáles mujeres,
o bajas, o principales,
Laureano quiere bien.[72]

Here she attempts to investigate the extent of her husband Laureano's philandering.

Laureano and his cronies might well defend themselves against these charges of misbehaviour with their own set of aversions. The *comedias* contain numerous lines expressing the aversion of men to "irritating" women, as when Julio exclaims, "¡O qué enfadosa mujer! / Siempre me ha de dar disgusto."[73] As Robert Wilson observes, "[r]acism, sexism and homophobia, or any other form of identity chauvinism, all may invoke the sense of foulness and filth that leads to disgust and contamination."[74]

But within family relationships, far and away the most common context for disgust within characters' discourse is to express an aversion to arranged marriage, an accepted practice by which couples were forced to marry against their own wishes. Thus in Francisco de Rojas Zorrilla's *Casarse por vengarse* (note the play's title), Blanca says to Enrique, King of Sicily:

Casarse a disgusto,
vienen a ser dos ahogos:
uno no poder jamás
desechar el amor propio,
que es natural el primero:
y es el otro tener odio
por los impulsos de amante
a los afectos de esposo.[75]

Aversion to arranged marriage could be so extreme that in certain cases it even led
to suicide. Thus the Muslim Jarifa warns the "tyrannical" Abindarráez:

> Vete, pues, tirano injusto,
> con tu gusto, y mi deshonra,
> que es mejor quedar sin honra,
> que casada con disgusto.
> Y yo me sabré matar.[76]

This ominous last line predicts her future suicide.

But not all *comedia* characters object merely to arranged marriage – some object
to all marriage in general. Don Juan is averse to marrying anyone (he just wants
to seduce women):

> [¿]Pues creíste …
> que me entregue
> yo a una prisión voluntaria?
> No, Camacho, que mi genio
> no es para andar de reata
> con mujer a todas horas.[77]

Don Juan is a rather extreme example, however; more typically, the objection to
marriage comes from the women on stage. Carlos describes Diana's condition of
mujer esquiva as encompassing an aversion to all men:

> Nunca pude sacar
> de su condición esquiva
> más, que más causa a la queja,
> y más culpa a la malicia.
> De esto nació el inquirir,
> si ella conmigo tenía
> alguna aversión, o queja
> mal fundada, o presumida:
> y averigüé, que Diana
> del discurso las primicias,
> con las luces de su ingenio
> le dio a la Filosofía.
> De este estudio, y la lección
> de las Fábulas antiguas,
> resultó un común desprecio
> de los hombres, unas iras
> contra el orden natural

del amor, con quien fabrica
el mundo a su duración
alcázares en que viva:
tan estable en su opinión
que da con sentencia fija
el querer bien por pasión,
de las mujeres indigna.
Tanto, que siendo heredera
de esta corona, y precisa
la obligación de casarse,
la renuncia, y desestima,
por no ver que haya quien triünfe
de su condición altiva.[78]

As Melveena McKendrick has shown us, the stereotypical *mujer esquiva* was a readily recognizable figure on the *comedia* stage.[79]

Not fitting exactly within the *mujer esquiva* model – but nonetheless objecting to any marriage with any man – was the saintly woman who refused betrothal because she wanted to follow a religious vocation instead. Witness the following exchange between Saint Rose of Peru and her suitor, Don Juan:

ROSA: Yo me hallo en estado ahora
    de no poderos querer,
    ni esperado, ni hallo forma
    de imaginarlo; mirad
    si me queréis por esposa.
DON JUAN: Para poder responderos
    me dad licencia, señora,
    de preguntaros la causa
    de aversión tan rigurosa.[80]

She goes on to explain that she plans to "marry" God instead by becoming a nun. Patrick Hogan explains this kind of sexual renunciation: "chastity in both deed and thought is a prime case of moral 'cleanliness' … [A]n ethics of disgust commonly entails an ethics of negation focused particularly on bodily pleasure, primarily sexual pleasure."[81]

A man like Don Juan, when confronted with this situation, should probably not take too great offence – after all, who was he to compete with God as bridegroom? However, in many other situations female characters make it clear they *are* objecting to specific characteristics of their suitors which they find repulsive or disgusting. These might include corpulence (referred to euphemistically as the quality of being "robust")[82] or lack of physical appeal. Susan Miller explains objections of this sort: "the concepts of physical ugliness, disease, and inferior race … are steeped in the brew of revulsion. To this trio, we can add inferior gender."[83] The inevitable counterpart to this kind of sexual disgust on the part of women was the aversion of men to inordinately tall females or those they perceived to show "defects" of physical appearance, personality, or other qualities. A wonderful speech from one *comedia* makes the point that beauty is in the eye of the beholder:

> Una dama, que es hermosa,
> para los ojos de muchos,
> a otros les parece fea,
> porque tiene el rostro oscuro.
> Si es pequeña, que es juguete,
> y si es alta, causa disgusto;
> si es discreta, no es hermosa,
> si es hermosa, es hielo puro.
> Si es trigüeña, que es muy negra,
> si blanca, no tiene gusto;
> que ya no hay nadie que pueda
> contentar a varios gustos.[84]

As this stage character wisely concludes, no human being alive can please everyone.

Women's aversion to men, within certain contexts, might be considered laudable because it denotes chastity ("La dama que al galán muestra disgusto, / funda en la honestidad el descontento"),[85] but emotion rules dictate that women are not supposed to show aversion to powerful men. One woman shows that she understands this dictum with regard to two of the powerful males in her life: "deja de pensar que puedo tener a mi padre miedo, ni al Conde mostrar desdén. Yo nací para servir."[86] She was born to serve – like most other women of all epochs, throughout history.

The topic of power relations between genders quickly leads to a discussion of power relations in general, where characters often express aversion to someone or something that looks different or unusual. Such is the case with the titular figure in *Hijo de los leones*, the appropriately named character Leonido, described by the hunters as "el monstruo."[87] In this scene Lisardo tells Perseo that he considers it his obligation to kill the lion-man. Perseo convinces him instead to take him prisoner, but subjects him to being bound like a beast. Carolyn Korsmeyer confirms with regard to "disgusting" animals: "animals that are aversive but not fearsome are merely odious and more likely to arouse disgust than sublimity."[88]

Other less obviously animalistic characters nevertheless provoke disgust due to their "monstrous" habits such as polygamy. Here Blanca declares to her renegade husband Leandro:

Que deseas pagar mal
la fe, y lealtad, que me debes,
y que por deleites breves
pierdes un bien inmortal.
Que te ha pegado la ropa
del Asia la pestilencia
y que se te ve el ausencia
de las costumbres de Europa.
Que desde que renunciaste
el hábito generoso
de tu fe, y el victorioso
principio degeneraste,
con bárbaros pensamientos
tu fama infamas, y aspiras
a los regalos que miras,
y a sus dulces movimientos.
Ya me tendrás con disgusto,
no me espanto; porque es llano,
que ya de Turca, y Cristiano,
tendrás Genízaro el gusto.
Eres absoluto Rey
de Asia, y querrás vivir
por su estilo, y no acudir
a las deudas de tu ley.
Ea, ten cuatro mujeres,
y ten quinientas amigas,
pues a bárbaro te obligas,
por gusto de sus placeres.
Mas no he de ser una yo.
Envíame a Italia luego;
vista tengo, si estás ciego;
perderte quieres, yo no.
Que dentro de un pensamiento
me quitaré este traje,
con que infamé mi linaje,
sólo por darte contento.
Y quedarás descansado

> sin mí, bien claro se entiende,
> que a quien nuevo amor pretende,
> mucho le enoja el pasado.[89]

Here she renounces her own renegade status with a symbolic change of clothing back to Christian-style garments and voices her intention to leave him, asking to be sent to Italy.

The association of Turkish culture with polygamy is no accident; instead, it taps into a wellspring of ethnic stereotypes exploited on the *comedia* stage to define Spanish culture in contrast to a cultural Other. As Martha Nussbaum affirms,

> Disgust operates by representing the other as a base animal, utterly unlike the (allegedly) pure and transcendant self. Disgust often, in effect, denies the reality of the (dominant group's) body, projecting bodily vulnerability onto the subordinate group … and then using that projection as an excuse for further subordination.[90]

Accordingly, we hear aversion to Islamic customs on the part of another so-called Turk by profession (i.e., renegade) named Pinelo:

> Heme aquí trocado en Moro.
> ¿Hay mayor bellaquería,
> que hacer Moro, y Luterano
> por fuerza un pobre Cristiano,
> y natural de Bugia?
> Aquí le han dado a entender
> al Rey que habemos nacido,
> y que yo también he sido
> pariente de Lucifer,
> y sobrino de Mahoma,
> siendo Cristiano perfecto,
> por el Bautismo sujeto
> al Pontífice de Roma.
> Y como tienen creído
> que aquí el origen tenemos,
> no piden que reneguemos,
> sino de sólo el vestido.
> ¡O maldito sea el patrón
> que tal industria le dijo!
> Todo es alcuzcuz, y mijo,

aceite, arroz, y cabrón,
comer en el suelo yermo
higos, datiles, y pasas,
pobre Pinelo que pasas
Dieta, sin estar enfermo.
ADAXA: ¡A, Cristiano!
PINELO: Que no soy
    quien soy; llamadme mi nombre.
ADAXA: Hasta este es gentilhombre;
    de él aficionada estoy.
    ¿Y qué nombre, Artemidoro,
    te han dado con el vestido?
PINELO: El que cuando fui nacido
    me dieron para ser Moro.
ADAXA: ¿Cómo?
PINELO: Cuchuchubali.
ADAXA: Extraño nombre te han dado.
PINELO: Dios sabe lo que ha costado
    de estudiar …
ADAXA: ¿Era mejor tierra Francia?
    ¿Hallábaste allá mejor?
PINELO: Cuánta es del cielo mayor
    la pérdida, o la ganancia.
    Y fuera de que esto es cierto,
    es tierra de bendición,
    donde se come a sazón
    vaca, y carnero bien muerto,
    no mirando al Sol, ni haciendo
    desatinos excusados,
    ni estos malos guisados,
    que ni los como, ni entiendo.
    Bébese vino del Rin,
    de Candia, Griego, y Falerno,
    ricas ollas, y pan tierno,
    y sobre la mesa en fin.
    No me entiendo con alfombras,
    ni con estas opalandas.
ADAXA: ¿Que en fin a disgusto andas,
    Moro por fuerza te nombras?
PINELO: Soylo si verdad te digo.[91]

These so-called *cristianos de Alá* pretended to be Muslim converts in order to obtain favourable treatment while in captivity.[92] Susan Miller describes perfectly the alleged "disgust" Spaniards felt toward Muslims:

> Across the centuries, those anxious about having their societies invaded or over-taken have at times been especially expressive in their use of disgust and contempt imagery to describe the gross nature of outsiders from other religions, classes, or races who may flood through the gate and pollute one's own group. Racist speech regularly uses the language and imagery of disgust to separate *us* from *them*.[93]

Although anti-Muslim propaganda was perhaps the norm in the century or two following the end of the Reconquest, Muslims were not the only ethnic group to provoke Spanish disgust. As Patrick Hogan explains, "Disgust … is readily extended to disgust at other people, entering into bias against out-group members, including racial bigotry."[94] Thus we see aversion by noble Spaniards to the "uppitiness" of an African slave named Amete (who, as it turns out, was himself a nobleman within Africa before being sold into slavery):

DOÑA LEONOR: ¡Jesús, y qué disgusto!

AMETE: ¡Ay, cielo airado!

GASPAR: Perro, bellaco, bárbaro insolente.

DOÑA LEONOR: Dejadle, buena cena me habéis dado.

GASPAR: En sufriendo a un esclavo impertinente,
    por momentos será desvergonzado.
    Yo os haré que sepáis que las criadas
    han de ser en mi casa respetadas.
    ¿Vos tomalles la cena de la mesa?

DOÑA LEONOR: Basta, señor, entráos, por vida mía.

GASPAR: La desvergüenza del perrazo.

AMETE: Hoy cesa
    la vida, la esperanza, y la porfía.
    Hoy me levanto a la mayor empresa,
    ya que la rabia del furor me guía,
    que ha cabido en esclavo eternamente,
    pues he sufrido que Gaspar me afrente.
    ¿Palos a mí, que general he sido?
    ¿Palos a mi galán de Meliona?
    ¿Palos a mí, que tantos he vencido
    en los campos de Orán por mi persona?

> ¿Al bárbaro más noble, y bien nacido
> de cuantos hoy el África corona?
> ¿Palos con una caña, y en España,
> donde es mayor la infamia con la caña?
> ¿Qué guardo yo la vida, si en Toledo,
> tan lejos de mi patria, pobre esclavo,
> la tengo de acabar? Afuera miedo,
> pues la desdicha con la vida acabo,
> con un cuchillo remediarlo puedo.
> Vitupero el vivir, la muerte alabo,
> blasfemo de Mahoma: ¿a mí dé palos?
> Los buenos con agravios se hacen malos.[95]

It is sobering to note that here he threatens suicide as a remedy for the misery of his servitude.

But Spaniards did not need to look outside their own country in order to find objects for their disgust; within Spain's own borders, regions like Galicia were despised as backward by Castile's more sophisticated city dwellers. Susan Miller describes this intercultural dynamic:

> Disgust responds to an encounter with something experienced as outside the self. That "Other" is felt to be noxious and ready to transfer noxiousness to the self. Therefore, one wants distance from the bad "Other." Disgust thus involves jeopardy to the self, which responds to that danger by devaluing – even despising – something outside, and determining to keep free of it.[96]

According to one ethnic stereotype perpetuated by the *comedias'* discourse, Galicians were thought to be dirty because of their alleged aversion to taking a bath. Thus a Galician woman is said to find "holy cleanliness" repugnant:

> Sábanas echaba ahora
> una entre Gallega, y galga
> que con la santa limpieza
> tiene inmortal repugnancia.[97]

Offensive stereotypes such as this one go a long way toward explaining modern-day Castilians' attitudes toward marginalized Galicians and vice versa.[98]

Ethnic aversion rapidly becomes political. Political disgust runs rampant through the *comedia* corpus. For example, we might categorize as political the aversion of people to the absence of their king, whom they expect to reside among them (such was the expectation imposed by Spaniards upon Holy Roman Emperor Carlos V, who had grown up in northern Europe among the Austrian Hapsburgs and when he arrived in Spain, spoke not a word of Spanish). Thus the Prior converses with the King in Tirso de Molina's *Averígüelo Vargas*:

> REY: ¿Cómo llegó mi señora
>   la Reina?
> PRIOR: Con mucho gusto
>   de Castilla, que la adora,
>   aunque lleva con disgusto,
>   señor, vuestra ausencia ahora.[99]

Here both the Queen and her people lament the King's absence. In addition to feeling aversion to a monarch who is missing in action, early modern Spaniards in general did not wish to see their ruler or that ruler's family imprisoned. Thus Prince Otón refers to the love his subjects bear him:

> OTÓN: La prisión mía,
>   que debe de tomar con el disgusto
>   que el amor de su Príncipe les mueve.
> EUFRASIA: Pues ¿cómo dicen, armas, guerra, guerra?
> OTÓN: Venme preso, y libertarme esperan.[100]

Here he predicts that his subjects' loyalty to him will compel them to seek his release.

But loyalty to a ruler was conditional upon that ruler's being worthy of esteem. *Comedia* discourse expresses aversion to swearing loyalty to a ruler considered to be unworthy to reign. Here a character describes a realm swarming with sedition and class conflict and predicts that there might be a problem erupting during the ritual of swearing the oath of allegiance:

> Y como siempre este Reino
> lleno está de sediciones,
> y suele haber controversia
> entre plebeyos, y nobles,
> cuando por Príncipe todos
> le juren, si en los rumores
> accidentalmente hubiera
> repugnancia que lo estorbe.[101]

The attitude of those who might potentially prove unwilling to swear allegiance to this objectionable Prince is here described as "repugnance."

A similar disgust or aversion might be felt by one ruler concerning another, as for example with rival maritime empires such as Spain's and Portugal's. Here Don Juan de Sosa discusses with the King of Portugal his aversion to efforts at diplomacy surrounding the Treaty of Tordesillas, in which Spain and Portugal brokered a compromise with regard to how the newly encountered territories would be divided between them:

> DON JUAN: Dícenme que os dio disgusto
>   la embajada en que tratáis
>   cómo se han de repartir
>   los mares que abrió Colón.
> KING: Yo perdí buena ocasión,
>   pues pudiéndome servir
>   de Colón en esta empresa,
>   perdimos por no admitirla
>   un mundo que dio a Castilla
>   de que ya tarde nos pesa.
> DON JUAN: Otro mayor os darán
>   presto vuestros Capitanes.[102]

Here Don Juan attempts to assure the King that his own mariners will soon present him with conquests equal to those of Columbus.

Imperialism provided further contexts for disgust by Spaniards when they encountered resistance to conquest on the part of Indigenous peoples they sought to subdue. In one dialogue, stage characters who are supposed to represent Natives of the Canary Islands discuss the need to be prepared to face the Spaniards' wrath. Specifically, King Bencomo speaks to his daughter Dacil regarding the danger of her desire to bathe in a specific lake where the Spaniards are likely to attack.[103]

But imperialistic aversion cuts both ways; other lines address explicitly the aversion of Native peoples to being conquered: "Viene un Reino a sujeción / y a veces dueño a disgusto."[104] Some of the more philosophical plays express the sentiment that free will always feels an aversion to subjugation, as in the allegorical figure Man's comment, "siempre sujeto / con repugnancia."[105]

Some of the most vocal defenders of free will in the *comedias* are actually women. For instance, the King of Albania frets about who will succeed him to the throne and laments his daughter Fénix's refusal to marry because of her fierce aversion to being controlled by a man. He describes

> [e]l rebelde dictamen
> de Fénix, en la crueldad

> de su condición tirana,
> su violento natural.
> Dígalo aquel que supiere,
> que fiera con su beldad,
> haciendo injuria al aplauso
> de su todo celestial,
> vive negada al comercio,
> tanto, que de racional,
> mal regida su razón
> confusos avisos da,
> que abonan su entendimiento,
> y culpan su voluntad,
> pues el pretexto terrible
> de su retiro, no es más
> que una aversión mal fundada,
> que una pasión pertinaz
> contra el dominio del hombre,
> con tanta severidad
> regida de su altivez,
> que sin ser posible hallar
> razón para divertirla
> de esta antipatía, da
> pretextos a mi desgracia
> la suma dificultad
> de vencer su horror, supuesto
> que lo haya intentado ya
> con diferentes cautelas,
> que no me sirven de más
> que de irritar su obstinado
> parecer, dando lugar
> con el ruego a que acredite
> su rebelde natural.[106]

Her "natural rebellion" inspires a fierce aversion to any form of masculine control.

In this as in so many other areas, the pride[107] of early modern combatants dictated that they remain averse to all peace treaties, preferring an honourable death to defeat. Thus we hear in the following dialogue that a certain French warrior feels "repugnance" toward diplomacy, wishing to die in battle rather than concede victory to the enemy:

> ENRICO V (KING OF ENGLAND): ¿Qué traes de nuevo de Orleans?
>   ¿Porfía Alenquer soberbio

en no rendir a partidos
la Plaza?
DUKE OF ZELEBERIA: Aunque siempre ha hecho
    repugnancia a los Tratados,
    queriendo morir primero,
    que entregarla, hoy, Gran Señor,
    si no me engaña el deseo,
    la habrá de rendir por fuerza.[108]

Apparently this captain will be forced to yield to his opponent, despite his natural aversion to doing so.

Political conflicts such as this one were often couched in the rhetoric of good vs. evil, which readily brings the discourse of disgust into the moral or ethical realm. Colin McGinn explains this translation: "there is a vague analogy between core cases of disgust and moral disgust: namely, in the notion of mental hygiene or orderliness or being governed by rules."[109] Patrick Hogan asserts that "moral disgust is continuous with 'core' disgust (the disgust response to food) and takes as its object a limited number of moral faults. These include racism and betrayal."[110] William Miller extends the discourse of moral disgust to other specific ethical realms: "Disgust deals with harms that sicken us in the telling, things for which there could be no plausible claim of right: rape, child abuse, torture, genocide, predatory murder and maiming."[111]

The discourse of aversion of virtue to vice is at least as old as Prudentius's *Psychomachia*, in manuscripts of which warlike virtues (usually pictured as female) are shown in the act of savagely slaughtering their corresponding vices.[112] The *autos sacramentales* paint this scenario with words in ekphrastic passages such as this one, where love tramples lust: "[¡]con qué ansia, resistencia, / y repugnancia el cariño, / pisa la concupiscencia!"[113] These gory scenes become less allegorical and more literally visceral in the *comedias*, as when Don Juan reports:

Un gran disgusto dos calles
de aquí he tenido, sospecho
que queda un hombre (no sé
lo que digo) herido, o muerto,
de la Justicia seguido
(mortal estoy) venía huyendo.[114]

Of course, the gorier, the better, for sensationalistic popular theatre where blood and guts (like in a Quentin Tarantino film) could at least be reported on stage, if not actually shown. Martha Nussbaum defines disgust as "a negative response toward substances with marked bodily characteristics: ooziness, bad smell, stickiness, sliminess, decay."[115] Colin McGinn confirms, "the soupy processes that make life possible excite our disgust quite dependably – the soft and soggy tissues of the body, the numerous trickles and spurts of our bodily fluids."[116] To illustrate this viscerality, witness the following exchange:

> ZARAOJA: No estaba el baño a mi gusto,
>   y víneme con disgusto
>   de este caso funesto.
> HAZÁN: Pues ¿qué caso?
> ZARAOJA: A Yusuf mató
>   Hazén, y el Cadí al momento
>   a empalarle sentenció.[117]

Here a punishment by impalement is reported as happening offstage. It is worth noting that this form of gruesome "justice" is attributed to Muslims, thereby participating in Spain's self-fashioning in contrast to an ethnic and religious Other. Martha Nussbaum describes the psychology of this process:

> The parts of the self that are disgust's focus are found disgusting after they leave the body, and the wish of disgust is to remove them to expel them from the sphere of the self. This wish typically issues ... in magical projections of the disgust properties onto people or groups who from then on become a device by which people create more secure boundaries between themselves and aspects of their own animality and mortality.[118]

Even "New" World Natives – for example, in Brazil – are portrayed as abhorring human sacrifice, in accord with "natural" law, as when this Indigenous person relates:

> Aunque pudiera valerme
> de la repugnancia que hace
> a toda ley natural,
> que un dios beba humana sangre,
> y dentro de una ley misma,
> el fiel muera, y el fiel mate;
> no lo he de hacer, que no quiero
> (aunque en mí esta razón cabe)
> escandalizar.[119]

The only reason given here for not objecting to human sacrifice openly is the desire to avoid scandal, presumably among other Native peoples who see no problem with this practice. Muslims are also portrayed as practising a variety of human sacrifice, in particular by Islamic warriors considered to be especially cruel, such as the notorious Almanzor.[120] In this speech, his theatrical avatar reports that he has built to Allah and Mohammed 100 altars upon which he is planning to decapitate 100 male victims, whose blood will then be sprinkled on the altars and whose bodies will be burned in ritual sacrifice:

> En cien altares que en honor y nombre
> del profeta Mahoma, y Alá santo
> tengo del bajo suelo levantados,
> la Mola ofreceré que estima en tanto,
> decabezando en cada uno un hombre;
> todos serán de sangre rociados,
> y al puro fuego dados
> de la feliz Arabia los olores,
> sin repugnancia alguna
> al Alcorán y Zuna.
> Haré una caja tal, que en sus labores
> y en esmaltes sea una
> en todo el mundo, y no se iguale a ella
> la de Meca, en riqueza ni en ser bella.[121]

Here he announces his plan to build a memorial afterward to rival the rich adornment of the Kaaba at Mecca, the destination all Muslim pilgrims must theoretically visit at least once in their lifetime even to this day.

As we can see from the above passages, extreme violence is often justified by religion, and indeed it is within the context of religion that we see some of the most intense rhetoric of repugnance. Jews showed an aversion to accepting Jesus as the Messiah, as when this Jewish man defies Christ: "Yo rebelde a tu precepto, / llegaré con repugnancia / de no conocerte Dueño."[122] Logically, Jews also showed an extreme aversion to the Eucharist, which Catholics believed to be transformed through the miracle of transubstantiation into the body of Christ through the ceremony of the mass. The *autos sacramentales* – a popular theatrical genre designed to make this theology accessible even to the illiterate – thus contain lines such as a Jewish person's question: "La duda es, / en que confuso encuentro / más repugnancia: ¿qué es / Comunión?"[123]

The edicts of faith[124] announced by the Inquisition provoked aversion in Judaizing *conversos*, depicted onstage as feeling repugnance toward the true Catholic faith. Thus Immanuel rebukes the allegorical figure of Synagogue concerning "la esquivez de tu pecho, / la repugnancia que ha hecho / el Edicto de la Fe."[125] Crypto-Jews were not the only targets of Inquisitorial persecution; any "heretics" or free thinkers would also naturally have felt aversion to Inquisitorial censorship. Robert Wilson opines, "disgust is a culture-specific affect that does precise work in entrenching taboos, limiting pollution, defending the sacred and generally contributing to a culture's cohesiveness."[126] Thus in one sacramental play Human Nature (conveniently aligned with ecclesiastical authority) reads a papal pronouncement on the dogma of the Immaculate Conception aloud on stage and then declares that any books not conforming to this dogma are to be expurgated and their heretical opinions silenced:

> Mandando, como mandamos,
> que de la opinión opuesta
> los Libros, que en cuanto al punto
> de que haya sido, y que sea
> la intención dar al Instante
> el culto, y la reverencia
> se opusieran, se corrijan,
> que quede esta materia
> tan en perpetuo silencio,
> que ser castigado pueda
> el que a nuestro Edicto haga
> repugnancia, o resistencia,
> por Tribunales de Fe,
> como reo.[127]

Any "heretic" opposed to the dogma of the Immaculate Conception is thus to be treated like a criminal by the Tribunal of Faith.

Susan Miller explains the function of disgust in maintaining sharp religious divisions:

> The more dangerously punitive God's condemnations are conceived as being, the more likely the believer will find comfort dividing mankind sharply into those who are good and those who are evil, with the evil group becoming the target of the believer's condemnation and presumably drawing God's disgust and rage, deflecting it from the struggling believer. What we have then is a belief system in which the believer's attitudes toward his fellow man precisely parallel his God's polarizing posture toward mankind. We might argue as easily that the believer's prior attitudes toward himself and his fellow man have cast their shadow across his conception of God, so that God's radical condemnations and grace reflect the

believer's inner world, as does God's finely tuned nose for the vulgar, abominable, and revolting.[128]

The Catholic Church was so averse to heresy that hagiographical *autos sacramentales* frequently depict saints expressing aversion to it, for example St. Augustine confronted with Manicheism:

> APOSTASÍA: Si dijiste,
>   que no sólo represento
>   un Apóstata, mas toda
>   la Apostasía, mal puedo
>   no conocer a Agustino,
>   más que por su Entendimiento,
>   por Discípulo de Manes,
>   que fue el que dio al Maniqueo
>   Nombre, en cuya Escuela, y cuya
>   Doctrina estudia, diciendo.
> AGUSTINO: Gran repugnancia me hace
>   esta Opinión.[129]

A similarly orthodox repugnance is expressed by Christians on stage in response to certain aspects of ancient Greek and Roman pagan mythology. Witness the following dialogue between the magician Cipriano and a demon appearing in bodily form (i.e., an actor wearing a demon's costume):

> DEMONIO: ¿Qué repugnancia
>   halláis en esto?
> CIPRIANO: No hallar
>   el Dios de quien Plinio trata;
>   que si ha de ser bondad suma,
>   aun a Jupiter le falta
>   suma bondad, pues le vemos
>   que es pecaminoso en tantas
>   ocasiones, Danae hable
>   rendida, Europa robada:
>   pues ¿cómo en suma bondad,
>   cuyas acciones sagradas
>   habían de ser divinas,
>   caben pasiones humanas?[130]

Here Cipriano questions the morality of ancient pagan mythology, pointing out the abundant sinfulness of the god Jupiter in episodes like the rape of Europa.

Conversely, heresy shows an aversion to orthodoxy, as when the allegorical figure of Apostasy expresses repugnance toward the mysteries of Catholic sacraments: "Yo fuera, Misericordia, / contigo, si no me hicieran / repugnancia los Misterios, / que de sus Manjares cuentan."[131]

This same repugnance might be felt in response to dubious spiritual experiences such as the ecstasy of Saint Teresa, which was much scrutinized for possibly heretical content. Thus Fray Juan de la Cruz Racimo describes a combination of attraction and repulsion in response to seeing Saint Teresa remain in ecstasy for fourteen hours:

> Aunque alguna repugnancia
> muy dentro de mi sentido,
> hallo también grande impulso,
> que me mueve a su designio;
> y así pues la reverencia,
> no se aja estando conmigo,
> acerquémonos a donde
> pueda verla, sin ser visto.[132]

Here he invites another ecclesiastical spectator to witness her supernatural trance from a safe distance in a place where their voyeuristic presence could go undetected.

The spiritual experiences of mystical nuns, accounts of which circulated widely thanks to the printing press[133] (and thus would have been familiar to playgoers), provided sensationalistic material for playwrights to explore in hagiographical dramas. Thus Juan Bautista Diamante in *Santa Maria Magdalena de Pazzi* depicts this saintly figure feeling aversion to the Eucharist when the devil afflicts her with spiritual malaise, *acedia*[134] or sloth:

> Con qué pereza que voy
> a lo que antes deseaba
> tanto; sin duda, Dios mío,
> que no debo de ir en gracia
> a recibiros; mi culpa
> es, Señor, mi repugnancia,
> ¡ay de mí, infeliz! ¡Si acaso
> a la mesa soberana
> pretendo llegar sin todas
> las precisas circunstancias
> que requiere acto tan grande!
> Sí, porque si yo llegara
> como antes, aquel consuelo
> que Dios me comunicaba

en la Comunión, ¡es cierto,
que ahora no me faltara![135]

Here she blames her sinful nature – and perhaps some covert, unconfessed sin she has committed – for preventing her from receiving communion in the state of spiritual consolation she had enjoyed previously. A hermit similarly laments his corporeal aversion to monastic discipline:

El alma, que a Dios imita
en vida, y eternidad,
adora la soledad
de esta preciosa Hermita.
Algún disgusto padece
el cuerpo donde se encierra,
que como es todo de tierra,
cosas de tierra apetece.[136]

Spiritual aversion was not always so subtle as monastic wavering or a lack of desire to receive the Eucharist, however; in a demoniac, it could manifest itself through wailing and gnashing of teeth. Here Judaism describes the whole demonically possessed Human Race:

Ni oye, ni ve,
ni habla: sin duda el disgusto
le hace del pasado susto,
que tan fuera de sí esté.
Pues sin hablar, sin oír;
ni ver, con mortal despecho,
despedazándose el pecho,
prorrumpe sólo en gemir.[137]

This howling demoniac is portrayed as lacking the ability to see, or speak, or hear. This poor person's experience of living hell is confirmed time and again in *comedia* lines about the sensations suffered by those condemned to eternal torment: "¿Puede haber en el infierno / pena de mayor disgusto?"[138]

This association of hell with disgust goes back at least as far as Dante:

Hell is all about disgust. The tradition in which Dante is working represents the punishment of sinners in Hell, and the sinners themselves as objects of a violent and visceral disgust that serves to cordon off good Christians from sin, reinforcing their determination not to be contaminated by the foulness of the sin they inspect. Such, presumably, is the motivation for portraying Hell as stinking, sulfurous, sticky, a stagnant swamp.[139]

This Christian place of suffering became conflated in the popular imagination with Hades, or the underworld of Greek and Roman mythology. Thus a theatrical Eurídice exclaims to Orfeo: "¡Con qué disgusto me quedo!"[140]

This conflation of pagan mythology with Church doctrine so typical of Christian humanism can be seen likewise in the explanations offered on stage for why people feel certain aversions. One explanation proffered openly was that attractions and aversions could be traced to the stars' influence. Thus Doña Inés says to Don Diego in rejecting his offer of marriage, which her father had tried to arrange:

> La aversión, o simpatía,
> con que se apartan, o acercan
> las almas, pende en el Cielo
> de influjo de sus Estrellas.
> Ésta es más, o menos grave,
> según es más la violencia
> de los Astros que la influyen,
> o la sangre en que se engendra,
> de donde la inclinación
> no puede ser acción nuestra,
> pues sin albedrío un alma,
> o se inclina, o se desdeña.
> Siendo así, cuando yo os diga
> que mi inclinación no es vuestra,
> no os ofendo en la razón,
> aunque en el gusto os ofenda.
> Esto supuesto, señor,
> no sólo eso el alma os niega,
> mas a mi pecho, y mis ojos
> hace horror vuestra presencia.
> Desde el instante que os vi
> discurrió un hielo mis venas,
> a que no halla el alma amparo,
> mas que el que de vos intenta.
> Y advertid, que ya os declaro
> mi aversión con tal llaneza,
> porque antes he prevenido
> que la inclinación no es nuestra.[141]

Here she describes in minute detail the "horror" she feels at his mere presence, a visceral reaction she characterizes as a sensation like ice in her veins. She vehemently disavows any responsibility for – or control over – this reaction, blaming the influence of the stars for "inclining" her to contempt or scorn. In a similar scene, Margarita describes in conversation with Mauricio her aversion to Ricardo as suitor:

> Ha dado en galantearme,
> sin que mis desprecios puedan,
> ni vencerle, ni templarme;
> y mi padre que le anima
> en lugar de refrenarle,
> cruel tercero le busca
> lugar para que me hable:
> yo le aborrezco, y de forma
> me ofende oírle, y hablarle,
> que de sus ojos lo atento,
> y de su voz lo agradable,
> a violencias me conquista,
> y a desvíos me persuade.
> Ésta es aversión.[142]

Later on in the same play, she continues: "Éste es un odio natural, / que de las estrellas nace, / y que mal podré vencerle, / cuando aun no puedo explicarle."[143] This woman, too, disavows the aversion she feels, declaring that she has no control over her hatred; this emotion is so intense that it offends her to speak to (or even to look at) him.

When stage characters are not busy blaming the stars, sometimes they instead excuse their aversions on the grounds of reason of state. One typical king expresses aversion to dividing up his kingdom, to which Duke Leopold of Clèves responds in solidarity: "Que es extraña, / y a toda razón de estado hace grande repugnancia."[144] Reason of state is said to introduce antipathy where neither faith, religion, zeal, law, or parentage could drive a wedge between parties:

> Aunque no se opongan nunca
> en Fe, Religión, ni Celo,
> la razón de Estado puede
> Guerra introducir entre ellos:
> y la mayor, sin que toque
> en la Ley, ni el Parentesco,
> es la de la antipatía.[145]

Reason of state can even conquer aversion to marriage,[146] which might otherwise be hard to trump with any other card, as we have seen above.

How do stage characters tend to talk about disgust? Interestingly, characters go to great lengths to explain away their aversion to each another, in an early modern version of "it's not you; it's me." Thus a King says to his Queen:

Señora, mi sentimiento
al veros, no es aversión
que os tengo, sino pesar
de ver mi delito yo,
debiéndoos tantas finezas,
como reconozco en vos.
El verme ingrato me obliga
a que os mire con horror;
ni el serlo, ni el enmendarlo
está en mi mano, pues son
acciones de un albedrío,
sin quien padeciendo estoy.[147]

In this passage we hear once again the familiar plea by a character for another person to forgive a feeling he can neither control nor change.

This mention of "amending" an emotion begs the question: can disgust be transformed into something else? If so, into what? Colin McGinn thinks it is a visceral response beyond our control:

Will power can help suppress the behavioral symptoms of disgust, and may even reduce strong initial disgust; but that is not to say that it can *nullify* disgust, that is, simply erase it from the psyche. The dedicated nurse can negotiate her feelings of disgust, not revealing them, bracketing them; but I doubt that she can simply eliminate them from her mind, or replace them with something positive. No amount of self-admonition to the effect that one *ought* not to feel disgust will simply make it disappear. The case is somewhat like the sensation of vertigo: it wells up involuntarily and no amount of firm conviction of one's physical safety can make it go away … Disgust … bypasses the rational faculties: it is reflexive, not deliberative. We do not *decide* to be disgusted, nor can we decide not to be.[148]

Early modern Spanish stage plays offer their own answers to these questions. A few intriguing lines relate the possibility that aversion can change to esteem, as when Luisa declares: "Tú sabes cuánto a Don Diego / estimo, desde que grata / rendí a su ruego la activa, / generosa repugnancia / de mi desdén."[149] These lines describe a process by which active repugnance gives way to esteem. It is even possible for aversion to serve as a precursor for attraction or desire, because at least a response of disgust means that the other person has caught one's attention: "disgust may actually kindle desire by putting certain things off limits, thus inflaming the human instinct to breach barriers, desiring what we cannot or ought not have."[150] Beatriz refers to this possibility when she observes, "Puede ser que sea, / como dices, tercero / el disgusto del gusto."[151]

A few lines seem to hold out the possibility that aversion might be resisted, or at least hidden or disguised. Don Íñigo says in an aside:

> Corazón, disimulemos
> el disgusto que me ha dado
> haber hallado aquí dentro
> a Don Antonio, pues son
> las joyas disculpa de ello,
> que no lo han de llevar todo
> hasta el fin mis sentimientos.[152]

Note that here he actively fights off the notion that he should let feelings rule him completely. But a visceral disgust is one of the more difficult passions to mitigate, a fact recognized by Ana when she says to her sister Leonor about Don Lope, their cousin: "En su desdén y retiro / se conoce su disgusto, / por más que quiera encubrirlo."[153] Instead, we are given the impression that aversion always tells the truth, which is what trauma theorists confirm regarding psychosomatic symptoms in general.[154] Laura goes so far as to contrast the apparent truthfulness of disgust with "lying" attraction: "Ha de pensar que siempre el gusto miente, / y que el disgusto siempre verdad diga."[155]

If disgust cannot be avoided – and if it always, albeit surreptitiously, tells the truth – then it may prove strong enough to topple prudence and lead to rash actions. A different character, also named Laura, confirms: "Fue tan grande mi disgusto, / que derribó la prudencia."[156] We see disgusted characters fleeing from themselves in a violent, instinctive, inadvertent reaction:

> A mí me tuvo violento
> un gran disgusto que tuve,
> y esperar no puede a nadie
> el que de sí mismo huye.[157]

And so (aside from the few caveats mentioned above), disgust would seem to be one of the more difficult passions to control.

Perhaps this is because – and this forms a convenient segue to our next chapter – disgust is so intricately bound up with desire. In the words of Jonathan Dollimore,

> One of the most significant conflicts is that between desire and disgust. We experience a profound attraction to the natural world (life as excess, expenditure, dissolution), yet alongside (or rather inside) that attraction is a revulsion, steeped in "lasting

repulsions and insurmountable disgust." Freud had found in the individual a similar conflict between desire and disgust which replicates the larger conflict between
instinct and civilization. And one reason why this conflict threatens to wreck the
human subject is because it entails the hostile, unstable, radical intimacy of each term
with the other: at one moment desire finds, in what was once disgusting, a pleasure
whose intensity it could never have known without the history of disgust; at another
moment desire gives way to a civilizing revulsion the more intense because its history
is grounded in the very desire it displaces.[158]

Let us turn now to the companion passion for disgust which is described here:
desire.

3

Question Your Desires

Our desires erupt like a swarm, endlessly and out of any proportion.[1]

Desire attain'd is not desire, but is the cinders of the fire.[2]

To have no desire is to be dead.[3]

Question your desires.[4]

At the outset, a clarification: desire is not the same thing as love. We know this from lines such as "en el querer, es preciso que haya deseo, y amores,"[5] which imply they are two different things. Other lines state outright that the two concepts are "very distinct": "es afecto muy distinto el quererse con deseo, o el amarse con cariño."[6] We glean more information about the relationship between them from the axiom "amor es hijo del deseo."[7] But this ideational parentage for love does not necessarily always ensue: as one womanizer says, "de todas me mata igual deseo, todas las quiero bien, mas poco dura."[8] In other words, desire is fleeting; love is lasting; and desire does not always morph into love.

The *comedias* offer remarkably exact definitions of the passions, as in the following exchange:

ARIADNA: ¿Qué es deseo y esperanza?
DIANA: El deseo es de algún bien, y la esperanza por quien vive mientras no se alcanza.[9]

In its most basic conceptualization,[10] desire is movement toward some good thing,[11] and hope is the emotion experienced until that good thing is attained. The relationship between these two passions is reflected in their colour schemes; both desire and hope are symbolized by the colour green: "mis deseos vienen ricos de verdes esmeraldas, que las acota amor para guirnaldas."[12] Here the colour green is mentioned in the context of both emerald gemstones and garlands of flowers. Further symbols of desire include roses,[13] veils,[14] and oars.[15]

Roses, being the gifts of a lover, are desire's weapons; veils hide the beloved's beauty and therefore incite further desire;[16] the beloved's desires are oars rowing on the sea of love.

Where is desire located in the body? Desire is often portrayed as profound, coming from deep inside one's entrails (e.g., "un deseo entrañable de verme en su compañía").[17] Desire resides in the homeland of the soul, as in "Tuya es el alma, patria del deseo."[18] Desire weighs down the soul or makes it heavy: "de un cabello me tienes pendiente el alma, pesada con un deseo."[19]

How does desire feel? The dramas are unanimous in declaring that desire burns hot; as one lover says to another, "ha de abrasarme el deseo de mirarme en tus brazos."[20] In fact, it is hot enough to melt ice.[21] Desire is a skillet[22] that heats up when one is cooking. It afflicts[23] like a fever.[24] In the end, desire burns hot as hell.[25]

Desire appears as an allegorical figure in multiple *autos sacramentales*.[26] In some of these, Desire's costume is richly adorned,[27] while in others Desire's physical appearance is scruffy.[28] Appearances can be deceiving, however, for Desire is judged rich even when surrounded by poverty: "el Deseo aun entre pobres es rico."[29]

A close reading of one of these plays will give us an idea of how this passion is typically acted on stage. In Calderón's *A tu prójimo como a ti* the stage directions read: "un Peñasco, y en él el Hombre dormido, y el deseo, como que le habla al Oído."[30] Desire is described as speaking to the soul when Lascivia says "Al Alma le habla su mismo deseo." Desire persuades Man to act, saying to him: "Pues ya que de tu deseo hoy te miras persuadido, salgamos de aquestos Montes." Man responds: "Otra, y mil veces me afirmo, en que dices bien, deseo." Man imagines a false protection which is not there: "imagino, que quien va tras su deseo, no dé en algún precipicio." Desire leads Man astray, in the estimation of another character who affirms: "persuadido de su deseo salió de su centro." Desire is dressed as a Villager, so Culpa asks him: "Pues ¿cómo vienes vestido de villano? ¿Si el deseo, aun entre Pobres, es rico?" Desire characterizes his own inclinations as always choosing that which is most agreeable: "como deseo, elijo siempre lo más agradable." In the course of the dialogue it becomes clear that Man's role in the matter is to acquiesce, or "consentir," to his Desire.[31] This choice results in Desire's dragging Man along after him into perdition.[32] Mundo ends up diverting the attention of / providing entertainment for Desire.[33] In the course of the *auto* the verdict is pronounced that whoever has lost the Desire for salvation, even if he hears the voice of Grace, will scorn its aid.[34] It seems that Man will lack nothing if only he attains his Desire.[35] This Desire includes indulging in pleasure and public festivities[36] and enjoying all the delicious things the World has to offer.[37] Conversely, nothing gives him pleasure while his Desire remains unsatisfied.[38] In fact, his unfulfilled Desire is described as "agony."[39] Man is taught didactically in the play: "tu Enemigo más cruel es tu deseo." Desire deceives the heart; as Lascivia explains, "un deseo te engañó el corazón." In fact, if left unchecked, Desire will ultimately murder Man: Deseo asks rhetorically, "¿Pues cuándo el deseo no es homicida de su Dueño?"

But a dialogue between Man and Desire makes it clear that the role of Desire is to persuade, not force:

HOMBRE: ¿Adónde me traes, deseo?
DESEO: Donde tú venir quisiste; que yo persuado, y no fuerzo.

This sentiment is repeated in another play by the same author when a character states, "Obligarte, y persuadirte, siempre mi deseo fue, más amante con finezas, que tirano con poder."[40] The good news, moreover, is that even after the wrong Desire has been followed, repentance can still change one's Desire.[41]

In the more secular plays, we find similar adjectives describing desire. Desire is impatient,[42] awaiting its fulfilment fretfully[43] in irritated anticipation,[44] while it seems that its object is moving in slow motion.[45] We find desirous characters asking each other what took them so long: "¿Cómo tardaste tanto? Pies de plomo te puso mi deseo."[46] It seems to be a truism that the hours of desire come clad with shoes made out of heavy lead.[47] Desire is ambitious[48] in aspiration[49] – e.g., to rule[50] – often relentlessly so, knowing neither restraint nor governing law.[51] Desire can be foolish,[52] audacious, and imprudent,[53] so rash as to literally jump out the window.[54] Desire is germane to immature youth[55] and impetuosity, while old age can temper its heat.[56] Desire is deceitful[57] enough to enchant[58] or cast a spell; specifically, it deceives modesty.[59] Desire can be jealous,[60] tenacious,[61] and insatiably[62] greedy.[63] Desire is so gigantic[64] that it knows no boundaries: "¡Quién creerá que cabe un mundo, donde no cabe un deseo!"[65] In *Desire and Its Discontents*, Eugene Goodheart confirms this characterization of desire: "the word [desire] ... does not require a predicate. Desire moves, floats, negates, shatters, aspires, it is itself a subject. Its freedom ... consists in its refusal to be constrained by the satisfactions that would extinguish it."[66] Desire can wound or injure[67] and cause sorrow.[68] In fact, Stephen Levine reports a proverb that states, "desire is the mother of the 10,000 sorrows."[69] When it becomes desperate,[70] desire can turn violent.[71]

The metaphors and similes for desire to be found in these plays are revealing. Desire is an astrologer[72] who can predict the future; it guides[73] a person like the North Star ("Norte ha sido mi deseo").[74] Desire is drawn to beauty[75] like a magnet,[76] especially if the woman in question is mysterious and unknown.[77] Desire's force is best exerted through physical appearance – if not in person, then via miniature portrait[78] (a common "token" exchanged by lovers to console each other in times of absence) – because it enters through the eyes.[79] In fact, desire is many-eyed[80] like Argos[81] because it is so vigilant;[82] alternatively, desire is sharp-eyed as the lynx.[83] Desire is like the lynx in other ways too, namely by being clever[84] and crafty.[85] Desire is fomented by the imagination[86] but polished and adorned by art. Desire paints[87] the image of its object in the will[88] and engraves its shape upon the heart.[89] If this sounds like idolatry, it is, for desire is called specifically heretical or "apostate."[90] It eats away at one's insides like a moth eating wool fabric.[91] Desire is a poisonous cup from which we choose to drink;[92] or alternatively, we are the liquid it pours or empties out ("una esquivez me cuaja, un deseo me derrite").[93] Desire is thirsty[94] and assiduous; it finds no rest.[95] As sociologist of religion Émile Durkheim wrote in the context of suicide, "Unlimited desires … cannot be quenched. Inextinguishable thirst is constantly renewed torture."[96] Desire never sleeps,[97] for the desiring person still experiences desire even in dreams: "el deseo en sus inquietudes, dormido te aflija, y despierto te asuste."[98] Jean-Michel Oughourlian confirms this characteristic of desire: "Desire … knows neither satisfaction nor rest; pierced by the other's desire, it never stops but pursues its object tirelessly."[99] Desire is a ravenous monster who feeds on impossibilities.[100]

In pursuing impossible things, however, desire draws upon an arsenal of weapons. It facilitates pleasure[101] even if it must go begging[102] in order to do so. Desire gallops forward at full speed, dancing faster and faster like the *tarantella* dance.[103] Desire is always in a hurry.[104] Desire runs away from us[105] and delays[106] our instant gratification. It leaves us hanging in suspense.[107] Eugene Goodheart reminds of the ramifications of this aspect of desire for literature: "Desire is the source of narrative. It generates the obstacles it must overcome or circumvent through ruses, deceptions, and displacements. It creates the devious shapes of narrative by aiming for satisfaction as well as agony in deferral."[108] Desire is fully capable of hurling us off a cliff[109] unless instead it carries us away on its wings.[110] But like Icarus, desire has a tendency to fly too close to the sun; in the words of Ulises to Circe:

> Un deseo, ¡ay de mí! tan remontado,
> que osó con harto vuelo
> calarse entre las nubes de algún cielo,
> donde al fuego vecino
> con ligereza suma,
> abrasada la pluma
> subió deseo, y mariposa vino.[111]

Like the moth flying too close to the fire, desire's wings sometimes get burned.

More frequently, however, we are the ones who get burned by it: desire incites and moves us,[112] making empty promises[113] and playing tricks ("mi deseo debió de burlarme").[114] Desire hunts reasons[115] to justify itself[116] with subtle rhetorical arguments.[117] Desire can lie ("mintió mi deseo")[118] or simply give bad advice ("Creo que le aconseja mal algún deseo").[119] Catherine Belsey theorizes, "it is not possible to tell the truth of desire, or about desire. Between the lovers truth merely distances, and the desire for truth is 'perverse' … [T]he truth of desire can neither be seen nor shown."[120]

Desire causes one to sigh[121] and simultaneously makes the tongue slip.[122] Desire rules the soul[123] as well as the memory.[124] Desire is all-consuming enough to flood the mind with rapid thoughts,[125] but ironically it can also restrain the steps and bring us up short ("tiéneme los pasos el deseo").[126] Desire squeezes us tightly[127] in a suffocating embrace until we feel locked inside its confusing prison: "esta ignorada prisión, donde mi confusión tiene atado mi deseo."[128]

We might well ask at this point: desire for what? Early modern Spanish stage plays enumerate multiple objects of desire. These range from basic needs and wants like survival[129] or escaping grave injury to pretty much anything the playwrights' creativity could dream up. Dramatists relished rehearsing corporeal desires for food and drink,[130] as we saw in my *Sins of the Fathers* book in the chapter on gluttony.[131] Specific delicacies mentioned in the context of desire include generically dessert,[132] empanadas,[133] and even heavenly manna from the sky.[134] Desire for money[135] is frequently mentioned, as is the wish to increase one's estate.[136] Desire for conquest[137] characterized Spain's conquistadores, especially the military variety (as opposed to explorer types).[138] Desire for empire ("el deseo del Imperio")[139] would be requited with victory's laurels ("de cada deseo fabrica un laurel"),[140] even if theoretically the glory should be given to God.[141] Patriotism was scripted to take pride of place,[142] ranking first before all other desires. Nothing compared with promoting the greatness of Spain: "tengo yo deseo de la grandeza de España."[143]

Desire for one's homeland was quickly transmuted into desire for one's actual home: "¡quisiera que sus paisanos lograran la victoria, y yo el deseo de poder irme a mi casa!"[144] The long-term stability of a "place to call home" for a family could be assured through laws and institutions such as the *mayorazgo*,[145] essentially a system of primogeniture. Spanish country estates provided an ideal seclusion for sad misanthropes[146] or simply those who were more introverted.[147] These getaways were especially suited to avid readers like Don Quijote or those whose foremost desire was a thirst for knowledge ("es natural propiedad el deseo de saber").[148] Not just any knowledge, but specifically puzzles, mysteries, or enigmas[149] – as Roger Shattuck explains in *Forbidden Knowledge*,[150] human nature typically desires that which is forbidden, prohibited,[151] or taboo.[152] As Foucault wrote in his *Lectures on Sade*: "desire and truth are endlessly multiplied in the unfolding, the scintillation, the infinite continuation of desire."[153]

We might go so far as to say that desire is fundamentally characterized by curiosity.[154] One need not even invoke the example of Faust to extend this desire to academic knowledge, as in

el deseo, la afición,
el gusto, y la inclinación,
con que a las letras se ha dado.[155]

In the wake of the Jewish diaspora occasioned by the tragic Edict of Expulsion in 1492, the memory of erudite Hebrew scholars was not too dim to recall their desire for study.[156] In the Renaissance the pursuit of knowledge was directly tied to the ability and opportunity to learn different languages, especially the ones (such as Latin, Greek, and Hebrew) associated with classical erudition.[157] However, still in this chauvinistic society the desire for knowledge was viewed differently in women.[158]

Women, in fact, were thought to be much more prone to desire;[159] however, in the pursuit of their desires they were believed to be fickle[160] and inconstant ("es inconstante el deseo en condición de mujer").[161] More acceptable female desires could be found in the area of religion, such as those expressed on stage by the character of Saint Teresa:

> [N]o puede consentir
> mi deseo fervoroso,
> el camino licencioso
> de este modo de vivir.
> Lutero infiel, contra vos
> tremola sus estandartes,
> hagamos, pues, baluartes
> en que se defienda Dios.[162]

This fervent religious zeal extends in countless hagiographical plays to a desire for martyrdom.[163] A similarly generous (and Christ-like) impulse is the desire to give one's life for another[164] – such as a relative being held in capitivity[165] – or else to die with someone[166] who is beloved rather than continue living without that person. These noble motives in some sense transcend gender but are also seen as acceptable "feminine" desires.

Traditionally "masculine" desires might include a desire for revenge[167] or else a desire to die a noble death,[168] for example in order to avoid being sold into slavery. Revenge provides the primary motive for countless stage plays (some influenced by Seneca)[169] and thus we hear lines such as "ya deseo verme de Carlos a morir vengado."[170] The preference to die and thereby avoid enslavement is expressed in the line spoken by Federico to his friend Fineo: "más deseo que me mate el enemigo, que no que me venda."[171]

Lust is of course another stereotypically masculine desire which is allegorized in many of the *autos sacramentales*; for instance, "a otro lleva su deseo al Cuarto de las Mujeres."[172] Men's lascivious desire is criticized, especially by women, as libidinous[173] and certainly not to be confused with love.[174] This ugly or base desire is aided by the cover of night.[175] Men tended to boast of their prowess at romantic conquests[176] using the same language they might employ to describe dexterity at swordfighting ("siempre mi deseo tuvo aceros de galán").[177] The "trophy" to which they aspired was convincing a woman to surrender the prize of her virginity[178] – a "favour" considered "licit" if there was a promise of matrimony.[179] Depending on her (primarily economic) circumstances, a woman who was being so pressured dared not refuse, for powerful men were used to having their way: "al poder nunca le agradan estorbos de su deseo."[180] Though it might seem offensive or even incredible to us today, this trophy was often described using the language of bullfighting: "gozaré el trofeo a que aspira mi deseo hoy en la postrera suerte."[181]

What is the teleology of desire?[182] Are desires ever obtained? New desires can strike one suddenly, as when a character exclaims, "Cielos, ¿qué nuevo deseo es aqueste con que lucho?"[183] Note that here desire is perceived as an external force to be fought against. As Catherine Belsey writes regarding Harlequin-style popular romance novels,

> Disasters mark the limits of human mastery. This is also the character of sexual desire in popular romance. The texts depict sex as an irrational, arbitrary otherness which seems to come from elsewhere, overwhelming the subject from outside, to the extent that it is not under conscious rational control.[184]

In similar fashion, a male character describes love at first sight[185] as "violent": "yo la he visto, obró el deseo, yo la adoré, fue violencia."[186]

Consistently in the *comedias*, desire is a glimmering mirage on the horizon,[187] promising the seeker that if only it is attained, then everything else will fall into place.[188] Counsellor Stephen Levine describes this never-ending illusion:

> We want something and try again and again to get hold of it, and then just when it at last comes within our grasp, in that moment of acquiring as burning desire momentarily disappears, we experience a moment of satisfaction. One of the great ironies of the fulfillment of desire is that the experience of satisfaction only arises in the momentary abeyance of desire. The fleeting experience of satisfaction is a glimpse of the source of satisfaction, revealed when desire momentarily abates in its instant of fulfillment. Satisfaction is a glimpse of the luminosity exposed when the clouds of desire briefly part.[189]

As a consequence, one will do anything to fulfil his desire – up to and including pawning one's freedom[190] – as when Gómez Arias asks rhetorically: "¿Qué no haré por ti, deseo?"[191] Desire that is not reciprocated will only intensify,[192] as will desire that is faced with competition.[193] In general, the harder a thing is to achieve, the more earnestly it is wished for ("Los peligros en el gusto / despiertan siempre el deseo"),[194] although waiting for something for too long can come with a high cost:

> [U]n bien esperado, es menos
> todo aquello que le quita
> de estimación el deseo,

> que aunque la dicha es gran joya,
> esperarla es mucho precio.[195]

Desire is fickle, abating at the slightest changing wind ("a cualquier soplo se abate, como cifra del deseo").[196] Different desires can sometimes be at odds with one another ("en un pecho pelea un deseo contra mil")[197] to the point where they start fighting among themselves within a person's breast.[198]

It is quite possible to desire something in vain;[199] in fact, the cynical view is that desire will always be disappointed: "nunca encuentra la mano, lo que prometió el deseo."[200] As Jean-Michel Oughourlian (disciple of René Girard) theorizes,

> [I]f the subject succeeds in attaining the coveted object, the satisfaction he gets from it will be short-lived and is virtually guaranteed to be disappointing. Once the object is possessed, it will lose its glittering splendor. It will obviously fail to bring the increase in fullness of being, of enjoyment and power, that seemed to shine like a nimbus around the mediator. Still less will it bring the radical transformation that it seemed to promise – perhaps it will even bring the opposite of what it seemed to offer.[201]

If not expressed openly, desire can remain buried in one's chest in silence.[202] Even expressed desires can be thwarted[203] or watered down,[204] or the object of desire replaced by an unsatisfactory substitute, as when Fauno in Calderón's *El castillo de Lindabridis* confesses:

> Muerto de Amor de una Beldad me veo,
> y he de curar con otra mi deseo,
> aunque aplicarle una al que otro ama,
> será matarle el humo, no la llama.[205]

He laments than any effort to cure one lovesickness with a different woman will only put out the smoke, not the fire.

Even without overt attempts to snuff it out, desire may die[206] or cease,[207] resulting in a period of mourning[208] equivalent to that following a death.[209] The inevitable result is despair, which is treated separately in a different chapter of this study:

> Turbó el imán del deseo,
> y ya de todo perdido
> el norte de la esperanza,
> dio por escollo en el risco
> de la desesperación.[210]

However, paradoxically, despair only increases desire: "crece al paso el deseo de la desesperación."[211] Eventually, one may become fed up and disillusioned enough with desire to cast it away altogether:

> [E]s como quien tiene un vidrio,
> del gusto de su deseo,
> que es por hechura y fineza
> tan singular en extremo,
> que como él no ha de hallar otro,
> y acaso con él bebiendo
> le da un golpe, y asustado,
> por de fuera, y por de dentro
> le mira, y viéndole roto,
> lo que buscó con desvelo
> le da tal pesar al lado,
> que le arroja con despecho.[212]

Here desire is likened to a fragile glass goblet tossed scornfully down to the floor once the cracks in it are noticed.

Not achieving one's desires can be frustrating;[213] but occasionally desires can be attained.[214] Indeed, desire must combine with occasion[215] in order to be fulfilled.[216] In fact, the language of casuistry[217] is specifically employed within the discourse of these plays to enumerate the conditions for sin about which confessors routinely interrogated their penitents: for example, "Ha sido un deseo que ha tenido tiempo, ocasión y lugar."[218] As I noted in *Conscience on Stage*, the circumstances of sin as elaborated in García López de Alvarado's *Breve compendio de confesión* (1552) are "which, when, why, in what place, in what time, with what instruments, how many times," etc.[219]

Some desires are described as so intense that they break down all barriers, as in "rompiendo las entrañas de la tierra, por conseguir su deseo, a pesar de las murallas que se le ponían en medio."[220] This fierce kind of desire is either consummated or else consumes itself (as Emanuel says, "Consumóse mi deseo").[221] However, just because a desire is satisfied does not necessarily mean that it is satisfied in the right way. Indeed, one character predicts scornfully that "saldrá de empresa tan vil el deseo mal logrado."[222] Such "triumphs" are perceived as ill-gotten gains.

When desire is finally satisfied, the pleasurable experience is often described as picking fruit[223] – or, alternatively, flowers, as in Ausonius's "Collige, virgo, rosas"[224] – or else as finding a safe harbour from the waves.[225] Once the thing desired is attained, however, the object of desire almost immediately loses its lustre: "es la esperanza, y deseo mejor que la posesión."[226] What is more, desires that are quickly obtained are esteemed less highly after the fact.[227] Thus the Count in Alarcón's *Examen de maridos* cites Ovid's *Ars amatoria* on the nature of desire:

> Ovidio dice que amor
> se yela y muda, si aquello
> lo halla en la posesión,
> que le prometió el deseo;

> pues hombre perfecto en todo
> no es posible hallarse: luego
> aunque Inés amase ahora
> al que tiene por perfecto,
> lo aborreciera, después
> que con el trato y el tiempo
> sus defectos descubriera.[228]

He predicts that Inés's love will turn to hate once she discovers her beloved's defects. Only in rare cases of good fortune is happiness measured out according to one's desires: "mucha fortuna es medirse las dichas a mi deseo."[229]

What are the moral valences of desire? Are they mostly negative?[230] Not at all – in fact, the *comedias* emphasize that desire in itself can be benign, as in "su deseo tan benigno."[231] This view is echoed in the work of current psychologists: "desires are often benign, functional, and evolutionary adaptive for the individual."[232] We frequently find a positive valuation of desire in the *comedias*, such as the belief that some desires are natural,[233] licit,[234] decent,[235] good,[236] or just.[237] Some are pious,[238] loyal,[239] praiseworthy[240] – even meritorious.[241] Some desires are defined as high and noble, as when a character says of the Sphinx: "Yo llevado del noble, alto deseo de ver qué en sí tanto prodigio encierra."[242] Surprisingly enough, within the xenophobia of orthodox Catholicism, even Muslims could have noble desires.[243] Desire, after all, can equate to aspiration,[244] such as a wish to see the world.[245] Desire promises great good to those who follow it.[246] Desire is the arbiter deciding what will please the most.[247] Desire heals like a physician[248] and, in selfless magnanimity, would give anything for the beloved. As Federico spells it out for Rosamira:

> El querer bien, Rosamira,
> nace de un deseo forzado,
> de dar al sujeto amado
> a cuya belleza aspira,
> cuanto el amante posee.[249]

Here the lover pledges "all he has" to the woman to whose beauty he aspires.

If this audacity seems rather bold – it is. Desires can both be bold[250] in themselves and make the person bold[251] who experiences them. Desire animates and inspires courage ("cuánto aquí el deseo me anima").[252] In its most extreme version, desire can make a person fearless. As one desiring character boasts, "temo el rigor, mas es tanta la pasión de mi deseo, que en ningún temor repara."[253]

When directed toward honest ends,[254] desire can be Christian[255] or even saintly;[256] an example would be the desire for martyrdom. We see these desires portrayed most frequently on stage in the *comedias de santos*, or hagiographical dramas. Less dramatic – but still pious – would be the desire for conversion[257] or perhaps a religious vocation.[258] Such godly desires could not possibly offend.[259] In fact, they are specifically believed to be honoured by God, as when a princely character declares: "Dios honra mi buen deseo, y acá otro Reino me ha dado."[260] As Jean Leclercq describes this form of desire,

> [O]ne can obtain from God the gift of real anticipation which is the desire itself. To desire Heaven is to want God and to love Him with a love the monks sometimes call impatient. The greater desire becomes, the more the soul rests in God. Possession increases to the same proportion as desire.[261]

A corollary to this belief is that one's true desires can be known only by God.[262]

Even if one's desires do not exactly qualify as saintly, often in these humanizing plays they are presented as at least not unworthy or undignified.[263] In the best casuistical tradition, an otherwise questionable desire can be excused or cleared of blame[264] under the right circumstances, as in "ya que disculpado … merece mi deseo esta ocasión."[265] If not, then even an evil desire can later be atoned for. The *comedias* make provision for this eventuality in lines such as "pudieras (ya que erraste en un deseo) acogerte en una enmienda."[266]

This mention of "erroneous" or wrong desire brings us to a discussion of desire's negative moral aspects, which – on balance – do outweigh its positive qualities in the majority of these plays. In the view of Saint Augustine, "desire is bad and slavish because it entails dependence on what is, in principle, unattainable."[267] In the *comedias*, desire is capricious[268] to the point of being dangerous,[269] especially for a person who surrenders his senses to its allure.[270] Leading its followers to risk honour,[271] desire is synonymous with worry and care.[272] Desire can be treacherous,[273] brutish,[274] and barbaric.[275] It can make us all look like fools.[276] In one of the biblically inspired dramas, it is said of Sara, Abraham's wife, that she named her son Isaac (a name which means "laughter") "temiendo que su deseo la burle"[277] – in other words, worried that her great desire for a son would play tricks on her by making her believe she was pregnant when she really wasn't; thereby her desire would have the last laugh. An alternative standard explanation is that Sara laughed when it was prophesied that she would bear a son at her advanced age (well past menopause) because the idea seemed so preposterous, barring divine intervention.

But most of the time, desire is no laughing matter. Quite the opposite: desire (and its inevitably tangled outcomes) can form the stuff of tragic rigour, as in "el trágico rigor de su deseo."[278] Desire can be inhuman[279] to the point of becoming murderous,[280] even toward a formerly beloved person like a spouse[281] or – in the case of the crazy Roman Emperor Nero – toward an entire capital city full of Roman citizens.[282] On the sensationalistic *comedia* stage, murderous desires come dripping with poison[283] and swimming in blood.[284] Ultimately desire becomes a martyrdom, in one particularly picturesque turn of phrase, as imagined glories metamorphose into the executioners of one's memories.[285]

For the real problem with desire is that it is fundamentally anti-rational,[286] crazy,[287] or insane.[288] As one character exclaims, "¡bravo amor, terrible furia, loco deseo, y poder sin resistencia ninguna!"[289] The ancient Greek poet Pindar had preceded Lope in this assessment: "too sharp is the madness of unattainable desire."[290] Another figure asks on stage whether desire causes delirium.[291] In an unanticipated twist, Rosamira uses her desire to prove she is *not* crazy: "No estoy loca, mi deseo me provoca."[292] Presumably, the two conditions of madness and desire are so similar in their symptoms that an observer could easily confuse them with each other.

Even when they do not seem crazy, desires are not always convenient, as in "vi en el primer deseo el primer inconveniente."[293] A basic rule is that desire wants more than one already has. German philosopher Arthur Schopenhauer long ago noted that the will's "desires are unlimited, its claims inexhaustible, and every satisfied desire gives birth to a new one. No possible satisfaction in the world could suffice to still its craving, set a final goal to its demands, and fill the bottomless pit of its heart."[294] William Irvine offers the following commentary on this point:

> [T]he psychological phenomenon known as adaptation … [means that] we tend to get used to what we have and therefore we like it less with the passage of time. We grow indifferent to the spouse, home, or car that once was our pride and joy, and because we are no longer satisfied with what we have, we form new desires in the belief that satisfying them … will lead to lasting happiness. These two psychological phenomena, miswanting and adaptation, lie at the heart of human insatiability …[295]

Desire breeds phantoms,[296] chimeras,[297] and illusions,[298] sometimes literalized on a *comedia* stage addicted to the use of special effects. With the use of newly available theatrical machinery, desire could literally "go up in smoke."[299] Catherine Belsey employs the discourses of painting and psychoanalysis to theorize about the nature of desire:

> *Trompe-l'oeil* invokes the *objet a*, the cause of desire. Like the duck-rabbit or the reversing cube, the *trompe-l'oeil* is first one thing, then another, now an object, now a picture of an object. It works only if it persuades as an illusion, deludes; and it works only if we can see that it is an illusion, that we are deluded. The gap between the two moments, Lacan proposes, is the location of desire.[300]

Desire brings heartache[301] until its host begins to exclaim, "this thing is killing me."[302]

Morally speaking, desire can be bad[303] or flat-out wrong:[304] low,[305] unworthy,[306] and discourteous[307] or vile,[308] ugly,[309] and malicious.[310] Thus Carlos describes his unsuccessful courtship of Diana, a *mujer esquiva*, and why he still desires her after being consistently rebuffed:

> Que aunque sea la codicia
> de más precio, lo que alcanza,

que lo que se le retira
sólo por la privación,
de más valor lo imagina,
y da el precio a lo difícil,
que su mismo ser le quita.[311]

Wrong desires are shameful,[312] such as wanting to gossip invidiously[313] or commit adultery.[314] Inventing perceived insults or offences,[315] evil desires prove indicative of treachery.[316] Desire is tyrannical,[317] leading not to freedom but instead to feeling trapped[318] and vanquished.[319] It wears us out, causing fatigue.[320] It exhausts us like a siege[321] or an enemy assault.[322] A series of rhetorical questions likens desire to a military campaign: "¿qué más guerra, que un cuidado? ¿más asalto, que un deseo? ¿más campaña, que un amor?"[323]

Unjust desires are called "crimes"[324] because they incline one towards evil.[325] But the *comedias* hasten to emphasize that desire itself is not a crime: "tan limpio afecto, que está el deseo tan lejos de ser delito."[326] Desire alone, without the power to accomplish one's goals, is impotent: "más se enojan, cuando miran a un hombre alfeñique, todo deseo sin manos."[327] *Alfeñique* was a word borrowed from Arabic to describe a person of weak or delicate physical constitution. The fact that this figure is pictured here "without hands" only adds to the xenophobic portrait which participates in the stereotype of Muslims as effeminate.[328]

But if many – if not most – desires bear a pejorative moral valence, then the question arises: can we control our desires?[329] Some plays answer with an emphatic "yes," as in "fue un voluntario deseo, y no fue un forzoso mal."[330] This is similar to the approach taken by the Buddha, albeit with a different rationale or motivation: "'The pull of desire is to be resisted and eventually abandoned,' and the reason we should overcome our desires is not because they are morally evil but because we will suffer until we overcome them."[331] Jean-Michel Oughourlian emphatically agrees:

I can also choose to resist being swept along by my desire, to let it flow through me without my submitting myself to its motion. If one of my desires begins to conflict with my convictions, I always retain the ability to reject it – not simply to follow it, but to choose another model.[332]

We might recall here that the purpose of *symposia* in ancient Greek culture was not merely to satisfy desires, but also to learn how to regulate them.[333]

But some of these plays imply "no" in answer to the question of whether desires can be controlled, as when Alonso laments to Fabia: "Un deseo es dueño de mi albedrío."[334] This is the perspective of philosophical psychologist Joel Marks, who states: "Desire is also evidently responsive to nonintentional influences such as biological homeostasis, heredity, conditioning, surgery, drugs, warm baths, and cold showers."[335] More graphically, Anna Clark asks: "Did a man have a rational and coherent self if he could not control his own desires? Did he have free will if he had an erection when he did not want to?"[336]

The one thing these plays can agree on is that desire is difficult to resist, like when Flor predicts: "Mal podré resistirme a mi deseo cuando estoy queriendo bien."[337] Attempts at resistance can be counterproductive:

> [S]ucédele a tu deseo
> lo que a los barcos que reman
> contra corriente de río,
> que los vuelve con más fuerza,
> el ímpetu de las ondas,
> no viendo la resistencia
> con las esferas del agua,
> pues cuando piensan que llegan
> a las riberas, están
> más lejos de las riberas.[338]

Here the attempt to resist desire is compared to a boat rowing against the river's current.

Some of these passages bear a fatalistic tinge, such as "a los hados forzosos resiste en vano el deseo."[339] In this line, playgoers are cautioned not to try to resist the Fates, those ghostly arbiters of the human race pictured in Diego Velázquez's *Las hilanderas* (see figure 2). Indeed, it is predicted that no force will be powerful enough to resist desire: "no hay fuerza para impedir un deseo, que lleva, con más violencia, al mayor riesgo."[340]

If desire cannot be resisted successfully, can it at least be influenced by our efforts? Some plays suggest that it can.[341] Positive desires can be permitted,[342] encouraged,[343] stimulated,[344] incited,[345] or otherwise set in motion.[346] On the flip side, some negative desires can be repressed,[347] particularly through the use of reason: "la razón pudiera a cualquier deseo cerrarle las puertas."[348] William Irvine recognizes a problem with this strategy, however, when the desires themselves are irrational:

> Reason tends to be the servant rather than the master of desire … [M]any of our most profound, life-affecting desires are not rational, in the sense that we don't use rational thought processes to form them. Indeed, we don't form them; they form themselves within us. They simply pop into our heads, uninvited and unannounced. While they reside there, they take control of our lives. A single rogue desire can trample the plans we had for our lives and thereby alter our destinies.[349]

He goes on to explain the neurological basis for this oddity:

> [D]ifferent desire-generating systems (or "functional modules") operate within the brain. Some of these systems work in conjunction with and are under the control

of the brain's dominant verbal system and thereby give rise to conscious, "rational" desires. Other desire-generating systems operate without the knowledge of the brain's verbal system and are therefore outside its control. We become aware of the existence of these systems only when they give rise to desires that we – that is, the "we" represented by our dominant verbal system – find to be objectionable.[350]

What about those desires that are neither all good nor all bad, but rather somewhere in between? Such desires can be adjusted,[351] corrected,[352] reduced,[353] or even "lost" on purpose, as with the command, "Pierde, sobrino, ese mal deseo."[354] But this is problematic, as most desires cannot be quieted or pacified ("ninguno me quieta mi deseo").[355] Instead, they can be subjected to other goods, such as love; we glimpse this capability in the line spoken by Segismundo: "Dichoso tú, que al amor no sujetas el deseo."[356] William Irvine advocates this more moderate approach:

> Perfect mastery of our desires is probably impossible. Even Buddha did not succeed in extinguishing desire: after his enlightenment, he retained a number of desires – to breathe, to eat, and most notably, to share with others the source of his enlightenment. What we should therefore seek is relative mastery: we should learn to sort through our desires, working to fulfill some of them, while working to suppress others.[357]

A desire experienced by one of the senses can be compensated or substituted for[358] by a different one of the body's *cinco sentidos*, as in "el deseo de los ojos se suple con el oído."[359] If the lady one adores cannot be seen, at least her voice can be heard. Desire can be alternately hunted with diligence[360] or reined in[361] by honour.[362] But the difficulty of curbing it[363] is reflected in the fact that under duress, often the leather straps of the reins will break.[364]

Perhaps predictably, some characters choose honour over desire: "allá quedarás, deseo, que a mí me basta el honor."[365] Others struggle to maintain desire within the bounds of courteous propriety.[366] Desire can be tempered[367] or moderated, or at least measured out with good judgment ("ir midiendo con el juicio las pisadas del deseo").[368] In an effort to tame it, it can be flattened[369] or ironed out – like in a convent[370] full of nuns – or even exorcized,[371] to borrow an image from the language of demonic possession. William Irvine urges us to explore these areas of potential control over our desires:

> We … would do well to develop some backbone and become a gatekeeper with respect to our desires, admitting and acting on some of them but rejecting many of them. Then we could, to the extent that it is possible to do so, live the life of our choosing, rather than the life our evolutionary past is attempting to foist upon us.[372]

The bottom line is: we can give way to our desires or not. One character asserts forcefully, "no doy lugar al deseo."[373] It is possible to indulge or give way to desire,[374] or even to deliver one's soul into its hands. We see this possibility in the question, "¿vos entregáis toda el alma a deseo tan injusto?"[375] Characters can choose to act on their desires or not, as when the *gracioso* Tritón observes, "Mas que pongo el deseo en ejercicio."[376] Or instead, one can act in a manner contrary to one's desire, an option we see reflected in the line, "hoy darle la pena, creo, mas contraria a su deseo, por hacer más importuno su dolor."[377]

Throughout the *comedias* and the *autos sacramentales*, characters are constantly evaluating their own desires and each other's. For example, Doña Leonor recognizes, "Ya conozco cuán injusto es mi deseo, o mi error."[378] Don Alonso expostulates with Enrique:

> Enrique, ya veo
> que culparéis mi deseo
> intentando corregirle
> con razones, pero bien
> sabéis la fuerza de amor.[379]

We find characters at war with their own desires, as in the lament "en mi contra mi deseo,"[380] or else feeling the conflict of desire on the one hand with prudent caution on the other.[381] Jonathan Dollimore posits that this conflict is a product of the war between a person's conscious thought and his or her Freudian unconscious: "unconscious desire, permanently at odds with the demands of civilization, is what will always wreck the ego's attempt to forge a coherent sense of self."[382] William Irvine describes the dilemma of conflicting desires from a more biological, evolutionary perspective:

> When our desires conflict, we are in effect at war with ourselves, and this makes it harder for us to cope with the world around us. One side of us will try to undo what the other side accomplishes. Our evolutionary ancestors who were at war with themselves were unlikely to survive. For this reason, evolution has given us an incentive to avoid internal discord: we experience the feeling of distress psychologists call cognitive dissonance. The only way to eliminate this feeling is to declare a winner of the internal debate and proceed with life.[383]

Free will is presumably the referee in this contest. Free will gives licence to desire;[384] but paradoxically, desire demands that free will be surrendered to its jurisdiction.[385] Desire is free and cannot be given away: "¿Es joya la inclinación? ¿Es la voluntad alhaja? ¿Es el deseo presea, ni menaje la esperanza, para hacer dádiva de ellas?"[386] Desire finds the means to accomplish what the will proposes ("a cuánto la Voluntad la propone el deseo es quien dispone los medios").[387]

There are, in these plays, some references to desire forcing someone to do something;[388] but there are clearly limits to how much desire itself can be forced.[389]

There seems to be virtually universal agreement that desire incites[390] insistently.[391] Desire inclines[392] a person toward a certain action or even dictates that action to him. However, even in this last scenario, Man admits that he follows Desire voluntarily: "Estos me dicta el deseo, a quien voluntario sigo."[393] The dramas seem frankly conflicted about the interface of desire with free will.[394]

In their interactions with each other, how do characters manipulate or even weaponize this emotion? Some characters curse desire,[395] while others try to inflame desire in each other by dressing up seductively[396] or else by engaging in overt rhetorical flourish.[397] To look favourably on someone else's desire is equated to giving it shelter like a pilgrim: "Ya Timoteo dio albergue a nuestro deseo."[398] Desire is frequently mentioned in connection to other passions; for example, desires are said to be love's children ("Los deseos son los hijos del amor").[399] Desire might be hampered or held back by fear,[400] but it is also guided by hope.[401] Desire fulfils hopes,[402] but the prudent person does not desire more than he or she can reasonably expect to obtain.[403] Desire still stays alive past the point where hope has died.[404] Life without desire is impossible, but ideally desires should be kept at a modest level. The *Oxford English Dictionary* defines the adjective "content" as "[h]aving one's desires bounded by what one has (though that may be less than one could have wished); not disturbed by the desire of anything more, or of anything different."[405] This *desideratum* (literally, "thing desired") of temperance[406] brings us back to the four Cardinal Virtues, which we have discussed elsewhere.[407]

Now let us turn to the next pair of passions in Aquinas's scheme after the disgust / desire dichotomy, namely hatred vs. love.

4

The Problem of Hate

Hatred ... is inveterate anger.[1]

Hate traps us by binding us too tightly to our adversary.[2]

The real root of humanity's difficulties lies in ... the problem of hate.[3]

The most extreme of Saint Thomas Aquinas's concupiscible passions is hatred, described in the *comedias* as fierce, cruel, and deep.[4] Hatred is stubborn, translated alternately into Spanish as "obstinate," "pertinacious," or "rigid."[5] Hatred is perpetual, as in the wording of the curse, "esté en odio perpetuo de mi tierra,"[6] or eternal, especially where honour is involved.[7] Daniel Smail explains in his essay "Hatred as a Social Institution in Late-Medieval Society" that

> [i]n a world with a limited commodity culture, in which architectural and sartorial fashions, public offices, and education were only just beginning to be sources of cultural capital routinely available to a wide spectrum of the population, social hatred was a relatively egalitarian and inexpensive source of honor.[8]

In an honour-obsessed culture such as early modern Spain, this assessment proved itself to be perpetually valid.

Hatred is self-assured, as when the allegorical figure of Odio refers to "mis conjeturas, que salirme tal vez suelen seguras";[9] but paradoxically, it is also sad.[10] Hatred is all-consuming, as when a character admits, "ya en mí todo es odio,"[11] and can be mortal – i.e., fatally wounding in its vehemence. Daniel Smail comments upon the concept of mortal hatred:

> The language of capital enmity ... can be found in legal documents throughout medieval Europe ... [T]he expression "mortal enmity" is found in the *Corpus iuris civilis* and surfaces in thirteenth-century Roman-canon procedural law. Legal tracts written by the

thirteenth-century Bolognese jurists Thomas de Piperata and Albertus Gandinus discussed the implications and relevance of mortal hatred. The expression "capital enemy" also surfaces in records from the north of France and in the English common law.[12]

Some early modern Spanish *comedias* repeat this "mortal" adjective.[13]

Some of the metaphors for hatred are similar to the ones used for love. As happens with love, hatred burns like fire: "el fuego al odio apagase, y amor le encendiese."[14] It can be rekindled, as in the scenario described by the lines "difunta brasa, que abriga el pecho, ceniza, después que el odio empezó, temo que se ha de encender."[15] Hatred blows cold, dry wind, as when the allegorical figure of Odio refers to "Respirando en mí el Cierzo de mortal rencor"[16] (the *Cierzo* was a cold, dry wind specific to the region of Aragon which blew from the northeast through the valley of the Ebro River). Hatred is a fatal poison for harmonious relations, as described by the related allegorical figure of Discord:

> Mi definición (según
> Divinos, y humanos Textos)
> es íntimo odio del Alma,
> que para mortal veneno
> de concordes voluntades,
> pasando a aborrecimiento
> el que primero era amor,
> en el Corazón me engendro.[17]

Once Discord or a grievance engenders itself in the heart, it becomes so permanent as to be figuratively carved in stone: "el agravio en piedra está eternamente esculpido; el odio que su marido tuvo a todos durará."[18] Here, in Tirso de Molina's *La mejor espigadera*, written about the Old Testament figure of Ruth, the specific hatred described is that of a husband toward "everyone."

What are the symptoms of hatred? How does a person know if he or she has become ensnared in hatred's grip? One indicator is that hearing the speech of a hated person causes distress. The Duchess of Amalfi describes this experience thus:

> Se te ofrecen dos que intentan
> hasta el fin acompañarte,
> y cada cual por su parte
> a tu lado se presentan.
> Al uno de estos dos tienes
> natural inclinación,
> en cuya conversación
> te regalas, y entretienes.
> Al otro aborrecimiento

> con tal fuerza de pesar,
> que solo el oírle hablar
> te causa desabrimiento.[19]

Even mentioning the name of a hated person causes offence, as when Casandra says of a man she does not know, but who loves her and has sent her his portrait:

> La fama, las noticias que me han dado
> de su estilo, y su traje,
> su soberbia, y lenguaje,
> indigno de quien es, me han obligado
> a un aborrecimiento,
> con que aun su nombre ofende el pensamiento.[20]

This gentleman is not likely to get very far with his courtship.

How is hatred expressed? Apparently it cannot be communicated only with hand gestures,[21] but instead requires words; however, facial expressions can get the job done as well.[22] Hatred can also be expressed by weeping, but there is some potential for ambiguity here, since crying can alternatively express fright.[23] Emotion rules for early modern Spanish society dictate that kings are permitted to show hatred on their faces: "En el rostro de los Reyes se vel el odio, o el temor."[24] Hatred is "printed" on the soul, even when it is not expressed by the mouth: "Calló entonces la fiera Miquilene el odio que entre el alma impreso tiene."[25]

Is there a characteristic manner in which hatred is portrayed on the stage? It turns out that the allegorical figure of Hatred does wear a particular costume: in one *auto sacramental*, Odio appears dressed as a demon on a black horse.[26] Even in non-sacramental plays such as hagiographical dramas (which still contain overtly religious content), demons frequently appear onstage, and one of their hallmark characteristics is hatred. Thus the Demon in Juan Bautista Diamante's *Santa Juliana* refers to "el odio con que a todos los mortales aborrezco."[27] Hatred is a characteristic often attributed to the devil by other characters, as when one speaks of the devil by saying, "Este rebelde a su Dios, desde entonces odio tiene a los hombres, y procura ser Dios engañosamente."[28] Here mortal hatred is held to be a permanent feature of the dynamics among deities, human beings, and fallen angels.

What actions does hatred inspire? Hatred holds characters in fierce subjection, as in the curse "muera en un destierro miserable … sujeto a su odio fiero."[29] Hatred calls for revenge.[30] In the intensity of its furore, hatred breaks every law,[31] to the point where hateful activities are said to find law repugnant: "ejercicio tan odioso en odio de la ley vive."[32] Hatred produces sin, which theologians of the time often referred to as "error": "en cualquier persona me cansa, enoja y fastidia ver el odio que en vosotros es causa de tantos yerros."[33]

Where does hatred come from? In early modern Spain hatred not only produced sin; it also was derived from it, as we see in the following exchange between "Edad 3" (the Third Age [of man], i.e. old age) and Hatred:

> EDAD 3: ¿Tan aprisa pasa del Amor al Odio el miserable que peca?
> ODIO: Sí.[34]

Hatred also stems from crime, particularly when wrongdoing does not remain hidden.[35] Hatred is born of evil actions ("de las malas acciones / nace el aborrecimiento"),[36] specifically deceit. The widow Clara complains explicitly about this problem: "el que engaña ofende, y causa / la ofensa aborrecimiento."[37] Daniel Smail confirms, "certain scripted behavioral patterns – assaults, insults, threats, and especially the calculated refusal to converse politely – formed a widely understood idiom or language of hatred that served to publicize and activate a hatred."[38] He goes on to specify an explicit form of deceit known as *barratry*, which he sees as widespread in the medieval period throughout Europe. The litigious form of barratry was "routinely assimilated to hatred":

> This response manifested itself linguistically in the increasing use of the insult *baratier*, cognate of the English "barrator," meaning one who defrauds another, accepts bribes, or falsely accuses another in court … Barratry, however, could also mean nasty litigiousness … Contemporaries elided all distinctions between these meanings – any misuse of legal apparatus was liable to be called barratry … [T]he insult came into common usage at some point between 1331 and 1406 … Dante devoted two cantos of the *Inferno* to barratry. The term itself was not invented in the fourteenth century; but to judge by the evidence, this century saw the origins of the systematic practice of barratry throughout Europe.[39]

However, other – less egregious – actions can also cause hatred, even if they do not reach the level of "sins," "crimes," or "offences." They can be merely transgressions, slight deviations from the social norm, or what Petronila refers to as Don Guillén's "crazy" behaviour:

> las travesuras,
> por no llamarlas locuras,
> que en don Guillén han causado
> común aborrecimiento.[40]

Hatred can be provoked by arrogance, as when another character sends the message to King Alfonso: "a ti, Alfonso, Rey de España, no salud, mas odio, y saña envío, por tu arrogancia."[41] This is the early modern Spanish equivalent of today's "nastygram."

But really, hatred does not even require a provocation. Ruy admits that his hateful "rancour" weighs more heavily than the worst actual grievance: "el odio, / y el rencor que os tengo, pesa / más que el agravio mayor."[42] As the saying goes, familiarity breeds contempt, as we see in these chilling lines spoken by King David's son Amón to his sister Tamar (whom he has raped, thus committing incest):

> Que yo te quise, ¿es posible?
> ¿que yo te tuve afición?
> Fruta de Sodoma horrible
> en la médula carbón,
> si en la corteza apacible.
> Sal fuera, que eres horror
> de mi vida, y su escarmiento,
> vete, que me das temor:
> más es mi aborrecimiento
> que fue mi primero amor.[43]

Here Amón declares that his hatred of Tamar is more powerful than his love for her ever was. This about-face is observed by other characters in the same play, as when Ionadab comments to Eliazar in the second act: "¡Extraño caso, Eliazar! ¡Tal odio tras tanto amar!"[44]

In the progression from love to hatred, one step on the pathway is disdain. Disdain or scorn felt by Clemencia is said by Enrique to be "almost hatred": "Clemencia, cuyo desdén / ya es casi aborrecimiento."[45] Hatred works in conjunction with envy, which amplifies it, as when one character confesses to having lied about a Cardinal because he was envious of him.[46] For this lie, the offender is punished publicly. This particular moral equation seems to function also in reverse: hatred kindles the fire of envy in the same way that envy enhances hatred. Thus we hear lines such as "a la llama de la envidia aviva el odio el incendio."[47] Hatred often results from perceived injuries or wrongs, as in "Daños, en cuya ofensa en odio ardo."[48] Hatred can stem from anger, but it does not have to – "el odio arguye ira"[49] – but we also find commands such as "no hagas odio de la ira."[50] This imperative would seem to indicate the potential for moral choice.

However, any space for human agency concerning hatred must also intersect with the power exerted by supernatural forces; for ultimately, hatred is believed to come from hell. Hell is described in one of these plays as "Patria horrible, y cruel del odio infame, del rencor infiel."[51] Perhaps more than any other passion, except maybe despair – and we might draw a connection here also to one of the Seven Deadly Sins, namely Pride – hatred was believed to be demonic in origin. It is in this context that one of Tirso de Molina's characters alludes quite literally to "el espíritu grande que ha vivido en mí, espíritu de odio, y de ira ha sido, de rencor, y discordia."[52] The "spirit" he is referring to is most definitely a demon. We see this diabolical parentage for hatred especially when villains show hatred for holy things like the cross. For instance, Mohammed describes the Christian battle flag adorned with the cross of Christ in lines dripping with hatred for the Catholic religion:

> Una Cruz trae por bandera.
> Heraclio osado, y severo,
> si él es en vencer primero,
> ésta es la insignia primera
> que suspende mi furor,
> y que mi aliento acobarda,
> mas cobarde en que se tarda
> mi osadía, y mi valor.
> Soldados a acometer,
> que cuando esta insignia veo,
> tanto me hiela el deseo
> que mi estatua vengo a ser.
> Pero ya el discurso ofrece
> porque la aborrezco así,
> rígeme el demonio a mí,
> y él a la Cruz aborrece.
> Y así entre la injuria fiera
> con que mis impulsos hiere,
> la aborrezco porque él quiere,
> y no porque yo quisiera.[53]

Here he speaks the language of demonic possession to describe the devil acting within him against his own wishes. It is a testament to the supernatural power of the Cross as symbol that the mere sight of it causes him to freeze in his tracks.

Such supernatural explanations for the negative passions were most likely to gain traction in early modern Spain due to the prevalence of Catholicism as the state-sanctioned religion; but hatred flourished even in plays where the Christian framework was absent. It is intriguing to look at the various explanations characters give for their passions, especially the ones perceived to pose some ethical or moral problem. In some of the more "secular" plays, hatred could be influenced by the stars; belief in astrology was still prevalent at this time within popular culture and even sanctioned, to some degree, by ecclesiastical authority. In this vein Margarita says to the Count: "Este es odio natural, que de las estrellas nace, y que mal podré vencerle."[54] She describes her hatred as "natural" and therefore something she cannot overcome. In what we might see now as almost a genetic or – at least – psychological interpretation, hatred is said to be inherited (and thus not the hater's fault). This is the phenomenon described in paediatrician G.H. Katzman's article "Neurobiological and Psychological Mechanisms Explaining How Hatred Is Programmed into the Minds of Children."[55] Sentiments expressed along these lines in the *comedias* range from "mal se podrá olvidar el odio heredado, y viejo"[56] to "daba lo ilustre de nuestra sangre dejar el odio en herencia."[57] In an interesting twist or variation on this theme, one man declares that he has "inherited" the hatred borne by another character named Otón toward his now-deceased brother: "hermano del difunto, os parece que sea yo heredero del odio que le habéis, Otón, tenido; podrá ser que lo sea."[58] These pernicious "bequests" might not have been listed in a dying person's last will and testament, but they were still very much a part of his legacy.

In fact, "inherited" hatreds were so strong as to leave a large footprint on the *comedia* corpus. These enmities are described explicitly as being passed down to one's descendants.[59] Familial hatreds were most powerful among noblemen, regardless of whether the current generation found anything to fight about or not.[60] Younger members of a family were expected to carry on their ancestors' quarrels: "el odio mantenemos de las familias."[61] One consequence of this reflexive loathing was that no thought would be given to marrying a member of a rival clan. Thus Admento says of Anfión: "nunca quiso con el aborrecimiento de nuestro heredado odio dar plática al casamiento."[62] Stoking the flame of this burning hatred was described as an "obligation" not to be abdicated.[63] Even when the older generation passed on, the memories of their fierce enmity (defined by David Konstan as "the state of affairs that obtains when people regard each other with mutual hatred")[64] remained vivid in the minds of youths who had heard their parents rehearse old grievances. We hear echoes of these tirades in the line, "El vuestro [enemigo] mi padre fue, y tengo siempre delante el odio, y enemistad que a este linaje tenía."[65]

Aside from a person's "lineage" being perceived to pose a problem, some synonyms often used to describe hereditary targets of hatred were "blood" and "house." For example, "tu sangre, y tu casa en odio tiene, y con sus armas viene a hacerte guerra."[66] A negative example – or absence of hatred – occurs in the line, "no ha tenido odio jamás a esta casa."[67]

Blood feuds tended to become notorious, extending well beyond the confines of a single house or village (here we might think of the early modern gang warfare fought between the Italian Capulet and Montague families, immortalized in Shakespeare's *Romeo and Juliet*). Daniel Smail recalls in the context of medieval Italy that

[a]s Albertanus of Brescia observed in the thirteenth century, vendettas were costly, and maintaining them for any length of time required considerable investments of time, money, and other resources ... Social hatreds were useful for testing and displaying one's ability to recruit kin, friends, and dependents. Full-blown feuds,

vendettas, or raids throughout medieval Europe demanded such extensive resources that only warrior aristocrats, wealthy patricians, or the free farmer-stockbreeders of Iceland could afford to practice them routinely.[68]

To this list he might well have added certain noble families in Spain. In the *comedias* we find lines such as "Sancho, y García, sin duda los dos Moncadas, que el odio, como la sangre les hace en Aragón tan notorios,"[69] which indicates that the Moncada family was known for pugnacity throughout the region of Aragon.

Which hatreds were thought to be worst or most extreme? Most *comedia* texts concur with the argument that hatred is worst when it occurs between brothers. In "The Dread of Sameness," Karl Figlio describes the hatred between siblings thus:

> In the narcissism of the child's love, its sibling depletes its narcissism, and thereby becomes a threat to its existence. A sibling … is a preserve of narcissism lost to the ego in its finite existence in the world … [T]he sameness between siblings constitutes an essential ambivalence, in which a threat to existence shadows sibling love … Uncannily, a sibling is both a comforting reassurance and at the same moment the thief of one's being.[70]

One *comedia* character asks this as a rhetorical question: "Di, ¿qué delito mayor que envidia, y odio entre hermanos? Mira en Caín, y en Abel este ejemplo."[71] Another Old Testament example appearing in the *autos sacramentales* is that of the Hebrew patriarch Joseph being sold into slavery by his brothers. The stage character Joseph says of this experience: "es el aborrecimiento / infeliz Mayorazgo, / con Herederos forzosos."[72]

Hatreds occurring in the microcosms of families were liable to mushroom and expand into the sphere of the macrocosm until they encompassed entire nations. We see this tendency in the line "la antigua guerra de aquel heredado odio, que hay entre Rusia, y Suebia."[73] This "ancient war" between Russia and the German region of Swabia was mirrored by a similar rivalry between countries in even closer geographical proximity – namely, Spain and Portugal. Thus a Spanish character, Doña Mayor, in Lope de Vega's *El más galán portugués Duque de Braganza* speaks frankly about "el odio de mi nación."[74]

The hatred was even more intense between countries that did not share a common religion; such was the case with Turkey and its relationships with various European nations. This hatred produced specific consequences such as an unwillingness to ransom captives taken by pirates or as prisoners of war: "por odio antiguo el Turco ningún Alemán rescata."[75] The hatreds of nations towards one another became most apparent during wartime, as with the Eighty Years' War, or Dutch Revolt, chronicled in Lope de Vega's historical drama *Los españoles en Flandes*. In this play, a character arrives to report onstage the arrival of French noblemen brought by "hatred" to participate in the conflict:

> Vienen otros titulados
> que odio, y envidia han traído
> muchos Monsiures, que han sido
> de Henao, Lila y Duay llamados.[76]

As Howard Thurman reminds us in the context of racial justice, "During times of war hatred becomes quite respectable, even though it has to masquerade often under the guise of patriotism."[77]

Even stronger than nationalistic hatreds were racial and ethnic ones. In "The Affective Turn: Political Economy, Biomedia, and Bodies," Patricia Clough writes, "the mutual hatred among races, or the projection of hate and fear onto a population that makes it into a mythical adversary, may come to function as a support of evaluations of populations, marking some for death and others for life."[78] Here many cultural stereotypes are brought into play, such as "el odio que siempre con los Gitanos tenéis los Hebreos."[79] Whether Jewish people harboured a particular hatred toward Gypsies or not, the important point here is that enough Spaniards believed they did for a line such as this one to resonate with playgoing audiences.

A perennially intense generator of hatred between people groups was the vexed issue of religion. Lope de Vega's *Roma abrasada* describes a "barbarian" who kills Christians: "bárbaro vestido de soberbia, arrogancia, crueldad e ira, venganza, enemistad, odio y mentira." Calisto asks in response to this description, "¿Tantos Cristianos mata?"[80] As Karl Figlio asserts,

> Religious differences … are treated as … external, solid, evident targets of hatred … The sacrilegious pole, which includes the otherwise surmounted suspicion that one's beliefs are illusory, can be projected on to the other culture and eradicated. It is similarity that evokes the uncanny, which can turn into psychotic terror, and it is one's shaky belief that is projected into another religious group and attacked.[81]

A similarly violent hatred could be expressed not between races or ethnic groups, but instead between the two traditionally defined genders. However, the language used to describe these enmities is (more often than not) mind-blowingly gender-bending. For example, the wide-eyed Galindo declares, when speaking about the *serrana de la vera*: "si destroza, si desmiembra hombres, por odio que a los hombres tiene, buscar otro remedio nos conviene."[82] Apparently this virile mountain girl hates all men enough to dismember them. Ironically, some *comedia* characters defend such hatreds by protesting that in hating all men (or women) equally, they are at least not giving some of them preference over others: "Las iras detén, pues no es odio desigual, si a todas las quiero mal."[83] Here a man asserts that his hatred is egalitarian, since it extends to all women. We might call this equal-opportunity hatred.

Not all hatred between the two traditionally defined genders results from such blanket assertions, however. Often the hatreds ascribed to men against women and vice versa are presented as excruciatingly specific. Such is the case with the hatred of one spouse towards the other in an arranged marriage. Thus Erifila announces that she has never loved anyone, but that this general hatred was originally caused by being forced to marry against her wishes:

> A nadie en mi vida amé.
> Antes fue aborrecimiento
> de casarme a mi disgusto,
> porque donde falta el gusto,
> no sobra el entendimiento.[84]

Just as Erfila did not set out to hate all men at the beginning, so too other hatreds frequently do not stem from hate, but instead from some other, hidden cause that has yet to come to light. We glimpse this possibility in the dialogue,

> DON ROQUE: ¿Aborreces de odio?
> DOÑA MATEA: No.[85]

Presumably his hatred does not stem from hatred, but rather from some other source.

If some hatred does not start out as hatred, then how does it begin? Love scorned might turn into hatred, as in "el amor despreciado / se vuelve aborrecimiento."[86] So, too, does love that lies forgotten: "como está sin calor, se trueca en odio el amor luego que el olvido empieza."[87] This "cold" or lifeless love morphs into hatred once it starts to be ignored. Similarly, the pity or compassion felt by a nobleman towards poor people might turn to hatred as irritation builds at their importunity: "de apiadarse de ellas la persona de su pobreza, las tiene odio según sus importunidades y sus ahíncos."[88] As the Renaissance Spanish humanist Juan Luis Vives wrote in his treatise on the passions, "The first emotion against evil is irritation, the opposite of liking. When confirmed, it becomes hatred."[89] Here what started as a "good" or "positive" emotion such as pity winds up being transformed by irritation into the ultimate aversion.

This last example begins to show us an inkling of the class struggle[90] that underlies some of the *comedias*, the most frequently cited example being Lope de Vega's *Fuenteovejuna*. Specific lines from these plays acknowledge the cold, harsh reality that leaders everywhere will be hated, no matter if they are paradigms of virtue: "el gusto del Rey lo contrario sienta … [O]dio engendra el mandar y llaman malo al más bueno."[91] Some of these dramatic works go even further in placing within the mouths of certain characters a well-developed hatred of civil authority. Thus

Leonor describes the queasy feeling in her stomach produced by the appearance
of an officer who arrives to make an arrest:

> No hay cosa que venga a ser
> para todo entendimiento
> de más aborrecimiento,
> que aquel que viene a prender:
> que puesto que viene a hacer
> no más de la ejecución,
> como el miedo y confusión
> solo en la vista repara,
> no sé qué tiene la vara,
> que causa poca afición.[92]

Here she admits that the officer is only doing his job. But her impression
is that the mere sight of him provokes "fear and confusion," such that the
reflexive response is hatred. The visual symbol of his authority – the *vara* or
rod signifying his office – is enough to inspire in its viewers "little affection"
("poca afición").

This "natural" aversion to authority[93] is of course only made worse when that
authority is abused. Tyranny always breeds hatred in a ruler's subjects. This situation is described by Demetrio in the context of Russia: "Moscovia / con tanto
aborrecimiento / hablaba de su tirano."[94] It has often been observed that such
potentially subversive political sentiments are more safely expressed onstage in
settings depicted as "long ago and far away."

What does hatred do? What are some of its ramifications? Hatred overcomes
respect, as with Cupid's rhetorical question, "¿Cuándo no supo el odio vencer
respetos?"[95] Hatred leads to scorn.[96] Hatred outshouts the praises of love – "que
el odio tiranice aplausos del amor"[97] – and even conquers paternal affection.[98]
Hatred destroys peace ("la cosa que más la paz destierra, el odio antiguo")[99] and
abolishes contentment.[100] Mari Matsuda describes the psychosomatic effects of
hatred on its targets or victims:

> The negative effects of hate messages are real and immediate for the victims.
> Victims of hate propaganda experience physiological symptoms and emotion
> [*sic*] distress ranging from fear in the gut to rapid pulse rate and difficulty in
> breathing, nightmare, post-traumatic stress disorder, hypertension, psychosis and
> suicide.[101]

Obviously, hatred causes unhappiness to its object;[102] but for the hating subject,
hatred actually gains more credit than love.[103] It is difficult to love after hating,[104]
or even to become friends: "del odio a la amistad, es difícil el camino."[105] Hatred

causes damage, as in "ha de ser el odio de los dos causa de un daño."[106] It produces ill treatment, as in the case of a captor towards his captives:

> Con este aborrecimiento
> tan mal trató sus cautivos
> que se mueren ciento a ciento,
> y aun esos que quedan vivos
> lo tienen por más tormento.[107]

In this play, hatred reportedly fostered such poor treatment of these captives that they died by the hundreds, with the survivors wishing they had also succumbed.

Hatred makes one bloodthirsty, as with one *comedia* character who "[a] los dos aborreció con tal temor, con tal odio, que estaban de nuestra sangre hidrópicos sus enojos."[108] This vivid image of annoyances becoming thirsty for the blood of hated enemies combines fear with hatred in recognition that sometimes we hate most that which we also fear.[109] As Spanish humanist Juan Luis Vives wrote, "Hatred is a deeply rooted irritation by which we wish to hurt seriously those we think have offended us … From hatred proceeds slander, and when it becomes more intense, violence and cruelty."[110] In the ultimate instance, hatred leads to murder, as in the accusation that "Fratricidio es; la muerte a su Hermano dio en venganza, odio, y rencor."[111] Here hatred is mentioned in conjunction with rancour and revenge as the motivating factors behind the assassination of a character by his own brother.

If this kind of murderous hatred toward one's own sibling seems to go against the laws of nature, well – it does. One child recounts the opposite responses his own birth engendered in his parents: "amor, que engendré en mi madre, y de odio en el padre mío, contra la naturaleza."[112] It might contravene the laws of nature for a father to hate his own progeny, but it still happens. Anfión, King of Cyprus, likewise says of the goddess Diana:

> Deidad, que en sus estatutos,
> contra naturales leyes,
> manda al aborrecimiento,
> que a pesar del amor reina.[113]

This hatred attributed to Diana was particularly appropriate because in addition to being the goddess of chastity, she was also patron goddess of hunting.

Hatred breaks "natural" laws governing human relations, especially if the person doing the hating obtains a special exemption from these rules by virtue of the fact that he or she is a monarch. We witness an accusation of "unreasonable" hatred being made against a King in the line, "Supe, Rey, que sin razón darle la muerte querías por odio que le tenías."[114] Here the King's hatred extends so far as to condemn its object to death.

One of the problems with hatred is that it accumulates: "que un odio sobre otro caiga."[115] It becomes a vicious cycle.[116] Public health experts Izzeldin Abuelaish and Neil Arya confirm: "Hatred self-perpetuates, usually through cycles of hatred and counter-hatred, violence and counter-violence (sometimes as revenge)."[117] Hatred which has been set aside momentarily can always be returned to, as in "Bien está, al odio volvamos antiguo; ¿tú no me ofendes?"[118] Here one character decides to perceive offence from another character, evidently as an excuse to return to a previous enmity.

Some hatreds are described as lasting since childhood, vividly stamped upon the soul from hearing unloving words that marred a young girl's innocence: "Yo aunque niña la escuchaba, y aquel odio, y desamor, dentro del alma estampaba."[119] These hatreds, although hidden ("tendrá el odio encubierto")[120] and disguised well by the shrewd politico, nonetheless remain visible to the eyes of God: "Dios sabe lo que siente, y el odio fiero que en su pecho esconde."[121]

If hatred is apparently so inescapable, then what are the desired responses to it? How is it to be dealt with? We hear some stage characters advise their confidants to keep hatred hidden or in the dark: "Pues a nadie digas tu oculto aborreci-miento."[122] Others counsel dissimulation as the best strategy.[123] Some claim hatred should be forgotten,[124] while others think hatred can be voluntarily stopped or left behind. We find numerous exhortations to this effect, all expressed in the impera-tive mood: "parad, el odio, y saña dejad, y el coraje despedid";[125] "Deja aparte ese odio ciego, y esa voluntad se tuerza";[126] and "que cese en vuestro disgusto el odio heredado vuestro."[127] It is noteworthy that in this last instance specifically "inher-ited" hatred is targeted for extermination. Aurel Kolnai validates this hypothetical possibility with his pronouncement that "[t]he central and unifying act of hatred seems ... to be a ... *commitment* to hostility. Hatred connotes a tinge of free will more than do fear (fright, dread) or disgust."[128]

Alternative scenarios are also presented in the *comedias*, however – namely, to illustrate the hypothesis that hatred cannot in fact be controlled by reason. We hear this exact argument being made in the line, "¡Qué rigor! Sin que oprimir pueda al odio la razón, se me inquieta el corazón."[129] Here the character professes to feel a "disquieted heart" due to reason's failure to "oppress" (perhaps a better English translation for sentiment would be "suppress") the hatred felt. This failure of reason in the battle against hatred is therefore experienced as "rigor," i.e. harsh cruelty.

If rationality is theoretically useless against hatred, what other weapons might be used against it instead? One option might be to flee ("es pequeño discurrir en esta materia quien desea huir del odio"),[130] or even to exile hatred: "Martín, el odio destierra si a Laura no quieres mal."[131] Apparently hatred can be placated,[132] especially with a friend's help. One King boasts of wielding this powerful an influ-ence over his comrade: "Su amigo soy, yo haré que el odio pierda."[133] In this way hatred can be tempered or moderated, although sometimes this reform comes too late.[134] The effort to do so is pictured like putting out a fire, the embers of which are still smouldering.[135] Daniel Smail describes a judicial case from the archives of fourteenth-century Marseilles in France:

> A ... striking legal device was to treat hatred as a *ius* that could be ceded. At some point early in the year 1354, for example, a fight broke out between the cobbler Uguo Blanc and the laborer Peire Gontard, during the course of which Uguo gave Peire a serious wound. Because of this wounding, "rancor, anger, and hatred were born and echoed between the two men (*rancor ira et odium inter partes predictas orta erant et etiam resultabant*)." Uguo was thrown in prison, and a peacemaker named Peire Ferrier came to the wounded man's house, begging him to make peace with his enemy. According to the narrative of the event provided in the peace act, "Peire Gontard, without any haste, freely, and from his own free will, having listened to and understood the words spoken and offered by Peire Ferrier without insistence, out of reverence for God ... remitted, ceded, and renounced any injury, wrath, rancor, and hatred that he has and could have by reason of the wound (*remisit cessit et dezamparavit omnem iniuriam iram rancorem et odium quas et quos habet et habere potest ratione vulnerationis predicte*)."[136]

Another way to extinguish the sparks of hatred was to offer a reminder of racial or religious solidarity, as with the injunction: "Muera el odio, sed amigos, tiemblen los Turcos de ver que amigos vuelven."[137] Here the soldiers so exhorted are encouraged to cooperate with each other in making common cause against the Turks.

The classic method for burying the hatchet in the *comedias*, as one might anticipate, was to end the play with a wedding; this generic expectation has struck more than one viewer or critic as uncomfortably "forced." This potential objection to the tidy convenience of the conventional ending seems to be anticipated by the line, "parará la guerra en bodas, si a parentesco acomodas un odio tan pertinaz."[138] Notice here the notion of hatred being adjusted or "accommodated" to the new paradigm of kinship.

Often within the *comedias*, however, no happy ending seems possible, in what is perhaps a tacit recognition of the genre's inherent limitations. The King of Albania lashes out against the

vulgo incapaz
de razón, y de consejo,
bárbaro, infiel, desleal
contra su Rey, pues aleve,
con pretexto de templar
el odio de mi razón,
se ha atrevido a articular,
que ... están

> los rencores decididos,
> y obviada la enemistad,
> como si fuera posible,
> que este fuego, que tenaz
> guarda el corazón, sujeto
> pueda a menos fuerza estar,
> que al incendio que le atiza,
> en cuya llama voraz,
> Fénix consumirse deja
> sólo por resucitar.[139]

He excoriates the "disloyal" *vulgo* for attempting to placate his wrath. In these cases, hatred can only be extinguished by death, as when one character recognizes the possibility that "con mi vida, o con la suya acabe el odio de tantas."[140] One or the other of them will need to die before their hatred can abate.

With such apparent inevitability for this passion, we might well ask: is there such a thing as "good" hatred? If it cannot be avoided, then how is it ethically wrong? Indeed, the *comedia* corpus seems to point toward specific instances where some kinds of hatred are thought to be wise, such as hatred of corruption at the royal court. Juan speaks of

> el provechoso olvido
> del Palacio, y de la Corte,
> de quien mil veces nos dijo
> tanto mal, tantos engaños,
> ceremonias, artificios,
> dobleces, contradicciones,
> envidias, falsos amigos,
> que connaturalizó
> en nosotros desde niños
> su sabio aborrecimiento.[141]

Here he adduces the lies, envy, artifice, and false friends of the courtly environment as ample reasons why a "wise" hatred for the court was cultivated in him from earliest infancy. Some hatred such as this kind can be justified if its object is ugly enough: "también puede una fealdad hacer un odio razón."[142] Such hatred is licit and just ("ya el amor se ha convertido en lícito rigor, en odio justo"),[143] particularly if supported by sufficient cause.[144] Still another kind of hatred is even considered "natural,"[145] especially between rival nations (this same idea appears in the English phrase *natural enemies*).[146]

And in early modern Spain, so often the fault lines were drawn simultaneously based upon both difference of nationality and difference of religion. Hatred of heretics by Catholics was considered to be a good thing, as when the Visigothic Ildefonso bids farewell to the dead Hermenegildo:

A Dios Príncipe de España
Hermenegildo, que el Reino
por el del cielo trocastes,
mucho os amo, mucho os quiero,
porque al hereje tuvistes
tan grande aborrecimiento.[147]

Here he explains his deep love for the Spanish prince as rooted in the hatred he had borne toward heretics. "Heresy" in this context could mean either other religious faiths, or else unorthodox sects within the larger umbrella of Christian faith: "medieval sources described the Moslems with the same spectrum of negative emotions that were used to reproach different groups within Christendom itself – the heretical sects provide a clear example of this approach."[148]

If it does not end in death, then what is the end of hatred? What happens when hatred runs its course? A few instances can be found of hatred subsiding, as when one character predicts of an erstwhile hating woman: "El odio perderá, y será benigna."[149] Apparently it is possible to lose one's hatred to the point of one's attitude becoming benign. But more often, as we have indicated, hatred only ends in the death of either the hating person or the hated one, as when Fineo exclaims, "un largo aborrecimiento / halla en la muerte descanso."[150] A hatred nurtured for a long time can find rest only in death.

If that moment ever comes, then the end of hatred finally means peace; but of course *comedia* characters question whether such a resolution is ever possible: "¿Si será en paz su odio reducido, / en amistad, su enemistad volviendo?"[151] If it works, the cessation of hatred will mean pleasure and great rejoicing. Thus one *comedia* character counsels another one, "Vuelve el odio riguroso en placer, y regocijos, toma esposo, y habrás hijos."[152] But of course this all-too-convenient happy ending risks the trite banality we described earlier as one of the perennial hazards of this art form.

Can hatred be successfully transformed into anything else? If so, into what? Sometimes love's first attraction masquerades as hatred, as when Juana declares confidently, "De grande aborrecimiento / suele nacer grande amor."[153] The logic behind this transformation seems to be that the same person who caught one's attention in a negative way at first at least did catch the attention, as opposed to never having been noticed at all. In the ultimate transformative scenario, hate can be conquered or vanquished and turned into love, as when Teodora boasts of her prowess:

Mal sabes mi pensamiento,
porque tu aborrecimiento
voy conquistando también.[154]

In "Kleinian Psychodynamics and Religious Aspects of Hatred as a Defense Mechanism," Paul Vitz and Philip Mango affirm that "in psychotherapy itself, the patient is confronted with a choice. He or she must decide to start, or not to start, the process of letting go of hatred and moving toward forgiveness."[155] This sort of love-hate relationship sometimes ends well, but other times it ends badly. To understand the complicated phenomenon we might today call "frenemies," let us turn now to the other half of this equation: love.

Writers and intellectuals through the centuries have long suspected that hate and love might be opposite sides of the same coin. Catullus famously quipped, "Odi et amo."[156] In his novel *The Scarlet Letter* (1850), set in colonial New England, Nathaniel Hawthorne wrote:

> It is a curious subject of observation and inquiry, whether hatred and love be not the same thing at bottom. Each, in its utmost development, supposes a high degree of intimacy and heart-knowledge; each renders one individual dependent for the food of his affections and spiritual life upon another; each leaves the passionate lover, or the no less passionate hater, forlorn and desolate by the withdrawal of his object. Philosophically considered, therefore, the two passions seem essentially the same, except that one happens to be seen in a celestial radiance, and the other in a dusky and lurid glow.[157]

Sara Ahmed explains well the interconnectedness – indeed, inseparability – of love and hate:

> Hate … cannot be opposed to love. Certainly, within psychological theories of prejudice, hate is seen as tied up with love. Or, to put it more precisely, love is understood as the pre-condition of hate … Such arguments allow us to consider the *ambivalence* of hate. If the demand for love is the demand for presence, and frustration is the consequence of the necessary failure of that demand, then hate and love are intimately tied together, in the intensity of the negotiation between desire and loss, presence and absence. To some extent, hate is an affect/effect of the impossibility of love; the impossibility that the subject can be satisfied.[158]

C. Fred Alford goes even further in claiming, "Hatred is not the opposite of love, love's eternal enemy. Hatred is the imitation of love, creating and preserving imitations of those love relationships on which psychic structure depends."[159] H. Guntrip declares succinctly, "hatred is love grown angry because of rejection."[160] We shall now study hatred's companion emotion – love – as the reverse side of this same coin.

5

Loneliness for Two (a.k.a. Love)

Love sees what is invisible.[1]

Love and the gentle heart are one same thing.[2]

Love can consummate an unholy union with hate.[3]

Love is the psychosis of normal people.[4]

Love is loneliness for two.[5]

What's so special about love? The dramas themselves offer an explanation, stating that "no hay Afecto, que más que el del Amor venza."[6] This line from Calderón would seem to echo Juan Luis Vives's assertion that "Love is the strongest of all emotions … [A]ll emotions proceed from it."[7]

But what is love? Not all the dramas agree on this point; however, they do at least agree on what love *isn't*. A negative definition of love may be found in the following exchange:

> OTAVIO: ¡Pluguiera al cielo!
>   Que la afición no es amor.
> ANTONIO: ¿Qué es?
> OTAVIO: Un tibio deseo
>   que está pintado en el alma
>   al temple de los afectos,
>   a quien cualquier accidente
>   (sea de tibieza o celos)
>   con ser los que le hacen más
>   le templan en ser lo menos.[8]

Here love is contrasted to a "lukewarm desire" called *afición* (affinity) that can be augmented or diminished by "any accident" such as jealousy.

So if love is not equivalent to *afición*, then what is it exactly? Continuing the previous exchange, Otavio declares:

> Tengo amor,
> que está al olio tan impreso
> en el corazón, donde
> fue toda afición bosquejo,
> que no le podrá borrar
> el Pintor más sabio, y diestro,
> ni de los celos las sombras,
> ni de la ausencia los lejos.[9]

In a beautiful metaphor, here he clarifies that *afición* was merely the ephemeral *bosquejo* (sketch or drawing) of the indelible oil painting that love would later become.

We find multiple positive definitions of love in the *comedias*, such as "todo amor es interior gozo,"[10] but also seemingly contradictory ones, such as: "Amor es todo invenciones,"[11] "Amor es miedo y posesión medrosa después que el bien alcanza,"[12] and "Es el amor deseo de un contento, que nunca llega a su dichoso estado."[13] The lady Laura gives an eloquent speech defining love:

> [E]l amor es un deseo
> engendrado en el alma, por los ojos,
> lince sin vista, que causando antojos
> las voluntades tiene por trofeo.
> Dulce amargura, muerte de recreo
> y general que tiene por despojos,
> cuerdas locuras, lágrimas y enojos,
> sin juzgar de lo hermoso, ni lo feo.
> Hijo del tiempo, y como el tiempo viejo,
> blanco apartado, donde locos tiran,
> declarado enemigo del consejo.
> Sagrado, donde ociosos se retiran,
> y de los ciegos, cristalino espejo,
> pues lo miran en él, y no se miran.[14]

This fuller, more complete definition of love is suitably ambivalent in its affective tenor.

Upon what is love based? How is it born? In what is it grounded? Elvira says to Don Tello:

Amor se funda en querer
lo que quiere quien desea,
que amor que casto no sea,
no es amor, ni puede ser.[15]

We note that chastity receives special emphasis here. Later in the same dialogue, we find the further clarification:

Nace amor de un gran deseo,
luego ya creciendo amor
por los pasos del favor,
al fin de su mismo empleo.[16]

These lines emphasize both the connection of love to virtue and its relationship to another one of the passions, namely desire.

In this account, love is born of desire, but grows with the steps of "favor" (presumably encouragement of the lover on the part of the beloved) until it surpasses the desire that was its original kernel. A more nuanced progression in the steps of love's evolution may be found in the following lines from Juan de Matos Fragoso's *La tía de la menor*:

[E]l amor
tomado desde el principio
es inclinación primero;
pasa después a cariño,
crece a deseo que enciende,
sube a llama que es peligro.
Siendo de estos accidentes
particulares motivos
la vista en la inclinación,
en el deseo el sentido,
en el cariño el afecto,
y en la llama el albedrío.[17]

Here we see a veritable hierarchy arranged like stair steps in ascending order of intensity: first inclination, then *cariño* or affection, then desire that becomes inflamed, and only then the fire of love, which quickly becomes a danger. Each of these steps corresponds to a different faculty of the human person: inclination corresponds to sight, "sense" (presumably the sense of touch) corresponds to desire, "affect" corresponds – etymologically as well – to affection, and finally the flame of love corresponds to the will. This explicit mention of the will implies important consequences for morality, as we shall see later.

How else is love portrayed or depicted? The colour most often mentioned as symbolic of love is deep purple: "una morada Violeta, por ser de amor color propia."[18] A line from a sacramental drama asks rhetorically, "¿cuándo Morado / color símbolo de Amor / no ha sido?"[19] The reasoning behind this colour symbolism, perhaps ironically, is that this is the colour of blood; love's further iconography, according to one *comedia* by Lope, includes depiction as a voracious wild beast that inspires fear: "el miedo fundo en que amor pintan rapaz."[20] This apparently violent, visceral imagery[21] only adds to the ambivalence of love's portrayal on the early modern Spanish stage.

How is love expressed? Options include by facial expression, a glance, a sweet voice, or overt physical affection. Calderón's *Eco y Narciso* includes the lines, "[con] cada suspiro, / que en efecto son aire, / camaleón de amor / se muda mi semblante."[22] Here the face becomes a chameleon of love that changes colour with every sigh of the beloved. One of the plays to thematize love, Calderón's *Amor, honor y poder*, declares, "son los ojos a veces, intérpretes del amor."[23] In this overtly metatheatrical metaphor, the play of love is acted by the eyes. The power of the voice to express love is found in the lines, "dulce voz de cariño, siendo un volcán allá dentro."[24] Note the contrast here between the sweet sound of the voice and the raging volcano inside the lover's breast. Physical affection[25] may be used to express love in the *comedias*, but most often such contact is limited to an embrace (or several).[26] The embrace might occur when lovers bid each other farewell,[27] but is not necessarily limited to that occasion. In extreme instances, love might be expressed through tears – even tears wept by men, as in the felicitous phrase, "lágrimas de amor que lloran / los hombres que quieren bien."[28] A common stereotype – but not a positive one – in early modern Spain was that the Portuguese were particularly sentimental and prone to crying, as in the line, "es al fin Portugués, y en amor se derritió."[29] This aspect of love goes against the macho self-image more typical of the early modern Spanish male. The problem with non-verbal communication, though, is that it is liable to be misinterpreted. We see this liability acknowledged in the lines, "No es ya la vez primera, prima[,] / que tu cariño vigilante, / halla un falso testigo / en mi semblante."[30] Facial expressions possess the capacity to "bear false witness."

These descriptions of love beg the question: love for whom? Various types of love mentioned in the *comedias* include love for parents or grandparents, love for children or siblings, love for other relatives or friends, and even love for travel companions. Love for parents is mentioned on the part of both male and female *comedia* characters, as in "de un hijo el amor digno"[31] or "de tus hijas el cariño te detenga."[32] Sometimes filial love relationships[33] are evoked precisely by their lack, as in the line, "apartadas crianzas tienen muy sin cariño el calor de los padres."[34] Here the early modern custom of sending children away from home – to be raised at court, for example, or in the home of a master to which they were apprenticed – is critiqued overtly as a system lacking in warmth that prevents the spontaneous generation of normal filial affection. Love for grandparents is evoked, even extending to the walls of their ancestral home, as when the Pilgrim says to the Demon about the Hospital in Calderón's *El primer refugio del hombre*: "Sus paredes reverencio, con el cariño de ser el Solar de mis Abuelos."[35] Walls hold memories, as this fond evocation of domestic (and by extension, salutary) space recalls.

Love for children receives an honoured place on the part of both fathers and mothers, as in the simple phrase "el digno amor de una madre."[36] Synonyms offered for this kind of love include both *affection* and *tenderness*.[37] Adjectives used to describe it are "sweet" and "pure."[38] This passage from Lope de Vega's *El castigo sin venganza* describes what happens to even the bravest warrior when his first child is born:

> [E]l bravo, el arrogante
> se deja sujetar del primer niño,
> que con dulce cariño,
> y media lengua muda, o balbuciente,
> teniéndole en los brazos, le consiente,
> que le tome la barba.[39]

Considering the fact that in this culture, the beard was considered to be a repository of male honour,[40] it is quite remarkable that the new baby is allowed to tug on its father's beard with impunity. Other characteristics of paternal love are to brag unceasingly about a child's exploits;[41] every parent who has ever interacted with other parents on the sidelines of an intermural soccer field can relate. However, parental love can also lead to discipline or correction, as when one character reports that "el cariño de padre cuidadoso me desvela en que la doctrina enmiende."[42] This dramatic character seems to recognize that the motivation behind the father's chastisement is actually care and even affection.

Love of siblings is also evoked in the dramas ("fraternal amor"),[43] along with the "natural" or biological love that seems to come with kinship ("el natural amor del parentesco").[44] This love may be extended to encompass unrelated individuals[45] who nonetheless grew up in the same household together.[46] The love of friends is also valued, as in "recíproco cariño, / que entre mí, y Rubén / mantuvo amistoso / lazo antiguo."[47] Even travel companions are accorded a special place in love's panoply: "de México a España, / hace amistad tan extraña, / que el cariño de un viaje / casi es deudo."[48] (If this seems strange to us, perhaps we ought to remember how long it took to journey from Mexico to Spain by boat!)

The fundamental rules seems to be that we come to love those whom we perceive to be most like ourselves,[49] whether because of shared nationality or some other trait. Love of one's countrymen in fact extends naturally to love of one's country itself, as in "el amor de la patria"[50] and "de la Patria el heredado cariño os llama."[51] Conversely, "hijos, al verse de su patria enajenados, y de su cariño ausentes"[52] will suffer hurt as a result of alienation from the familiar surroundings of home. In fact, the bonds of patriotism were believed to be so great that early modern people living in exile would feel a "natural" love for their compatriots even if their identity was unknown. For example, witness this speech by the Muslim Mudarra:

> Gozad lo que antes tuvisteis
> prisioneros afligidos,
> que aunque os da la libertad
> piadoso el corazón mío,
> nada os doy, pues solo os vuelvo
> lo mismo que habíais perdido.
> Válgame Alá, si supiera
> antes lo que hoy he sabido,
> que soy de estirpe Christiana
> de tan noble padre hijo,
> yo me vengara más presto,
> dando aquel traidor castigo,
> no en vano dentro del pecho
> para vengar tal delito,
> me daba la sangre voces:
> no acaso ha sido el cariño
> que hallan en mí los Christianos.[53]

This impassioned discourse from Juan de Matos Fragoso's appropriately titled *El traidor contra su sangre* just goes to show that blood runs thicker than water.

Love of one's country, in turn, extends readily to love for its ruler. Thus we find lines regarding this "natural" obligation of a subject like "el cariño que como a Príncipe os debo"[54] and "por la virtud, el cariño, y lealtad con que veneran a su Rey Esclarecido."[55] Here virtue, affection, and loyalty are conflated with "veneration" (an overtly religious term of adoration) for the illustrious King placed on a pedestal by some of the more blatantly propagandistic plays. The language of love is of course also employed in religious contexts defined more narrowly, such as love for the Virgin Mary in Agustín Moreto's *Nuestra Señora del Aurora*.[56]

In order to round out this picture of love in the *comedias*, we must address one glaring omission: romantic love does of course appear in these plays, but often not in the context of marriage. Occasionally we find affection mixed with convenience as a motive for marriage ("con quien casarse trataba por cariño, y conveniencia"),[57] but more frequently only the convenience aspect is mentioned. For example, one male character admits that "en Madrid desde Valencia, no de amor, de conveniencia he tratado un casamiento con doña Leonor."[58] He emphasizes pointedly that this will not be a marriage of love. In fact, whenever "convenience" is invoked as a rationale, it is most often juxtaposed to love or pleasure as its opposite.[59] At very least, a love that is grounded in the basis of convenience should not be counted as "fine" or delicate love, the kind that truly moves one's sensibilities.[60] This situation is so sad that we hear characters declare that guests should wear mourning attire (appropriate for a funeral) at the wedding.[61]

The single most important qualification for a spouse was, in fact, equality of lineage. One woman declares:

> Igual esposo me espera,
> que amor llanezas buscando,
> sangre igual bebe en mis ojos,
> sin ver que es grosero el vaso.[62]

Here she specifically hopes an illustrious bloodline will compensate for ugliness of figure. On the flip side, inequality of birth or social class inevitably leads to problems in this status-obsessed culture. For example, in one representative scenario,

> Resistió ella el casamiento,
> quizás habiendo conocido,
> cuánto en las desigualdades
> está violento el cariño:
> mas como las principales
> mujeres nunca han tenido
> propia elección, hizo ella
> de la suya sacrificio.
> Casóse forzada en fin
> de sus padres: ay delirio
> de la conveniencia, [¿]qué
> te falta para homicidio?
> Él con poca inclinación
> al estado recibido,
> y con poco gusto de ella,
> imaginad discursivo
> ahora vos, de qué humores
> compuesto naciera hijo,
> que nacería para ser concepto de amor tan tibio.
> Bien pensaron que yo fuera,
> como otros hijos han sido,
> la nueva paz de los dos,
> mas tan al revés lo vimos,
> que de los dos nueva guerra
> fui por afectos distintos,
> de amor, que engendré en mi madre,

> y de odio en el padre mío,
> contra la naturaleza,
> bien ni un instante me quiso,
> aborreciéndome aun cuando
> son los enfados hechizos.[63]

This sad tale of familial enmity began with an arranged marriage,[64] which the aristocratic woman resisted, to no avail. Finally ceding to her parents' wishes,[65] she married against her will, which her son (the speaker of these lines) later characterizes as equivalent to homicide on the part of his grandparents. From this love described as "lukewarm" at best, the child was born with tepid humours to match, according to Galenic psychology. He postulates that perhaps it was thought at the time of his birth that he would bring peace to this fray; alas, the opposite proved true, and he became the locus of his mother's love, but also of his father's hate. "Against nature" his father, he is certain, did not love him "even for an instant." So much for *happily ever after* …

Indeed, many plays seem so cynical on this point that it almost appears that anyone who actually marries for love will automatically be condemned to unhappiness. Marriage for love was so countercultural during this time period that the possibility was taken up, pondered, and then discarded as a recipe for disaster. This sentiment comes through in the lines:

> Amar lo imperfecto, es
> accidental y violento;
> lo violento no es durable …
> [U]n imperfecto esposo
> un martirio será eterno,
> que al paso de sus erradas
> acciones irá creciendo,
> y no importa que el amor
> venza los impedimentos,
> quite los inconvenientes,
> y perdone los defectos,
> pues nos dice el Castellano
> refrán, que es breve Evangelio,
> que quien por amores casa,
> vive siempre descontento.[66]

Later in the same play, the same speaker nuances this proverb:

> [Q]ue quien por amores casa,
> vive siempre descontento,
> según lo afirma el refrán;

… y es muy cierto,
cuando por amor se hacen
desiguales casamientos:
pero cuando son en todo
iguales los dos sujetos,
no hay, si el amor los conforma,
más paraíso en el suelo.[67]

Once again the most important characteristic to be sought in a mate is "equality" – presumably of social class or lineage. Love is not to be confused with comfort (as when a character clarifies, "es comodidad, no amor"),[68] and in fact true love seems to be almost reserved for the lower class.[69]

For the upper class, love is explicitly a contract – "es contrato natural amor, que confirma el trato"[70] – replete with all the niceties of notarial language.[71] In an effort to secure this contract, an individual's affection could be pawned like personal valuables that were mortgaged to secure a loan.[72] In this case, a female's advice to her male interlocutor is to forget the affection he left at the pawn shop and give up hope that it will ever possibly be redeemed:

[O]lvidad vuestro cariño,
que en los hombres es muy fácil.
¿Digo fácil? ¡Ay de mí!
Es pena más tolerable,
porque ellos pueden tener
sin culpa las variedades.[73]

She bitterly comforts him with the thought that his sorrow will be made tolerable by the fact that "variance" (i.e., unfaithfulness) is permitted in this society "without blame" to men. Such escapades on the part of husbands will be the cause of cruel heartbreak to their wives.[74]

A different – but equally bitter – consolation might be found in the culturally sanctioned assumption that marriage for love would not last anyway, because women are constitutionally incapable of fidelity: "¿Quién vio en mujeres jamás amor firme, y gloria cierta?"[75] In fact, in the "politics" of love, the *fueros* (ancient privileges that kings typically swore to uphold for each city) are supposedly more honoured by women in the breach than in the practice.[76] The downright misogyny of these male playwrights is difficult to stomach by today's standards, as in this description of a deceitful woman's tears:

[L]ágrimas de mujer,
yo hablo de las que engañan,
son en sucesos de amor

> pericones, y pendangas,
> que a todos manjares sirven.[77]

This colourful speech mixes slang[78] with words borrowed from other languages (*pendanga* seems to be a derivative of *pendenga*, a Portuguese word for *conflict*; the Spanish equivalent would be *pendencia*) to indicate that women's tears become the sauce that seasons every dish. Women are not alone in being targeted for criticism regarding fake performances of love, however; other lines accuse men of feigning love only to appear more "manly."[79] As a friend of mine commented recently, with all of these complications, it's a wonder heterosexual love ever happens!

Some explanation for this conundrum may be found in the specific actions love executes, such as making us blind, distorting our sight, or spurring and dragging us along. Cupid, god of love, was traditionally pictured as blind;[80] this myth appears as the reason why love's choice of objects might seem undiscriminating. In the immortal words of Shakespeare, "Love looks not with the eyes, but with the mind; / And therefore is wing'd Cupid painted blind."[81]

In a slight variation on this theme, love is the blindfold[82] covering the eyes of the lover, who thereby does not see the beloved's faults; in still another iteration, loves gilds the beloved's errors[83] so they will not become apparent. The experience of blind love is equated to being lost in a forest[84] or labyrinth such as the one that lends Cervantes's *El laberinto de amor* its name.[85] Love distorts the eyesight like reading glasses that make the text one is reading appear larger on the page.[86] Love is a painter who chooses to cast his subject in the best light.[87] Love spurs us on until it effectively whips our horses into a trot ("Anda el amor con espuelas"[88] and "amor te azota al trote"),[89] with the emphasis in all cases being on velocity[90] or speed. In one curious metaphor, love is compared to the swift hand of a clock:

> [E]s el amor en nosotras
> como mano de reloj,
> que solo se vio que anduvo
> puesto que la vuelta dio;
> pero no se ve cuando anda,
> porque corre tan veloz,
> que no le alcanza la vista,
> aunque le alcanza el dolor.[91]

Love drags[92] or sweeps[93] us along until we rein it in like a wild horse.[94] If we do not rein it in, an excess of love leads to being thrown off a cliff.[95] However, just at the point where we thought we had gone into free fall, love swoops down like a bird and bears us up on its wings.[96] Love's wings are fiery. It flies so fast, it even outpaces time ("el amor / con alas de fuego vuela / tan veloz, que deja atrás / al tiempo").[97]

Here we recall once more the god Cupid, who was often depicted with wings. Anyone who has ever received an old-fashioned Valentine's Day card will recall that Cupid is armed with a bow[98] and a quiver full of arrows (see figure 3).[99] Love's disdainful arrows[100] wrought in the forge of Vulcan[101] might take the shape of a miniature portrait[102] of the beloved sent as a token of favour and meant to be worn somewhere on the lover's body.[103] In a figurative transposition, Cupid's bow is said to be reflected in the arched shape of the beloved's eyebrows.[104] Occasionally love's arrows are given to some other archer[105] instead of Cupid, or else Cupid might come armed instead with a sword,[106] shield,[107] harpoon,[108] or net.[109] Even with such formidable weapons, however, sometimes love still misses its mark.[110]

Other imagery for love was not tied so closely to its iconographical depiction. Symbolic of love were the turtle doves[111] thought to mourn for each other when widowed.[112] The vine wrapping itself around the elm tree[113] was another image encountered frequently in lyric poetry.[114] In fact, nature itself was understood to be so permeated with love that even the flowers were enamoured of each other. Thus the King implores Estela:

> ¿No tienen amor las flores?
> ¿[N]o es este cardeno lirio
> el que en las selvas de Arcadia
> fue enamorado jacinto?
> ¿No es eclipse esta flor del Sol;
> y este ciprés Cipariso?
> ¿[N]o es Adonis esta planta,
> y este Narciso, Narciso?
> Pues si en la tierra las flores,
> si los peces en los ríos
> aman; ¿para qué te precias
> de libre, con pecho altivo?[115]

Specifically, love was associated with sunflowers[116] because they literally turn toward the sun. A related image saw love as a magnet[117] attracting the beloved like metal. Not just any metal, however – love was specifically likened to gold, the carats of which would serve as indicators of its quality.[118]

However, like gold, love must be refined[119] through fire.[120] Fiery imagery[121] for love abounds, with the experience of falling in love usually likened to one's heart being set ablaze.[122] All it takes is a spark ("centella de amor")[123] or perhaps some hot coals,[124] and suddenly love becomes a conflagration:

> De sola una vez a incendio
> crece una breve pavesa;
> de una vez sola un abismo

> sulfúreo volcán revienta;
> de una vez se enciende el rayo,
> que destruye cuanto encuentra;
> de una vez escupe horror
> la más reformada pieza;
> de una vez amor ¿qué mucho,
> fuego de cuatro maneras,
> mina, incendio, pieza, y rayo,
> postre, abrase, asombre, y hiera?[125]

Love makes the blood boil,[126] even if it starts out cold like a pitcher of ice water.[127] Love's kitchen contains an oven[128] warm enough to toast souls.[129] Alternatively, love strikes as lightning[130] or erupts like a volcano;[131] not suprisingly, the specific volcano mentioned in these Spanish dramas in the context of love is Mount Etna,[132] the one still active on the eastern coast of Sicily, which erupted in 1669. If love's volcano does not erupt on its own, then controlled explosions might be used to blast open the mine of a reluctant lover's breast.[133] Love is the gunpowder used to pry open a heart that had previously proved resistant ("amor en mi pecho mina de pólvora es").[134]

For make no mistake: love is war ("como es guerra civil Amor, nunca se desdeña de valerse del ardid").[135] According to legend, Cupid was so militant because he was the offspring not just of Venus, but also of Mars.[136] Not only Cupid, but also lovers themselves set out on the battlefield with military strategy. They armed themselves with weapons[137] for combat. As Fadrique admits,

> [C]omo amor
> es guerra, y en guerra fueron
> permitidos los ardides,
> creí, era bien usar de ellos.[138]

Specific historical resonances of wars sometimes appear in unexpected contexts in these plays, for instance alluding to the contemporaneous conflict in Flanders: "gasta el pecho a pedazos, guerra en la Flandes de amor arde por distintos lados, sin munición vive el fuego."[139]

Further historical specificity is attained in dramatic dialogue by allusion to new types of military technology, such as arrows fashioned from lead[140] instead of wood. Other substances mentioned are iron,[141] mercury, or quicksilver.[142] Some lines in these plays pause to comment on the evolution of technology used for warfare:

> ¡ … Amor usaba
> antes del Arco, y las Flechas,

porque la Pólvora, aún no
había ostentado su fuerza![143]

The implication is that if gunpowder had been invented by the ancient Greeks, then Cupid might have been depicted with a pistol or revolver instead of his traditional bow and arrows.

Not surprisingly, when love wounds its victim, that person falls sick as with a serious illness: "Un dolor, una ansia, una voluntad, y un melancólico amor, que cuando es enfermedad, es la enfermedad mayor."[144] Specific physical ailments mentioned in the context of love are a fever[145] (especially the quartan[146] variety), hernia,[147] and an itch[148] like that produced by scabies or mange.[149] According to courtesans – who, after all, ought to know – love is most certainly contagious.[150] What is worse, wounds of love are inoperable ("en heridas de amor el Cirujano mejor yerra"),[151] the result being that gaping sores are often simply plastered over with a different love ("poner sobre tu llaga un emplasto de otro amor").[152]

Being in love feels a bit like being drunk,[153] which eventually can lead to alcohol poisoning. In fact, poison[154] is a frequent metaphor for love or its effects ("El amor me da veneno").[155] As with some kinds of low-grade poison, one can build up a tolerance for it if it is introduced little by little.[156] The specific source of the poison might be a toxic plant[157] or perhaps the venom of a snake. Love itself is said to be a crafty aspid[158] or lurking viper[159] lying in wait, ready to bite the unsuspecting.[160] Alternatively love is said to be a basilisk,[161] a legendary creature who could kill with a single glance (see figure 4). When their capacity for creative analogy fails these playwrights, sometimes they refer to love simply as an unspecified monster, cruel and bloody,[162] whose appearance threatens prodigious events. Indeed, love is the world's "greatest monster" in Calderón's *El mayor monstruo del mundo*.[163]

In keeping with this realm of fantasy[164] and mythological creatures, love causes madness[165] and delirium,[166] positioning itself as the very antithesis of reason.[167] In the words of Shakespeare,

Lovers and madmen have such seething brains,
Such shaping fantasies, that apprehend
More than cool reason ever comprehends.[168]

Love is crazy enough to build towers on the water.[169] Love offers idolatrous human sacrifices[170] upon its high altar,[171] which makes love a heretic[172] deserving excommunication.[173]

Romantic love is paradoxical, for suddenly we descend from high to low, with a contrast between love's high altar and a lowly feeding trough ("pesebre de amor").[174] This constellation of imagery is not unusual in lyric poetry of the time, for example Lope de Vega's love poems to Elena Osorio.[175] But on this textual rollercoaster ride, soon we are raised on high again to love's splendid palace: "Así el alma toda, que era el Palacio de mi amor, dejó a Lisarda el mejor cuarto."[176] This gentleman's seemingly magnanimous posture is countered by terse, succinct statements such as simply "Amor es avaro" (love is greedy).[177]

Love is so greedy, in fact, that the lover wants to be with the beloved all the time,[178] even – or most especially – at night.[179] If he cannot be with her, then the next best option is to spend time alone so he can think about his beloved: "suele en su cuidado ser amor un Filósofo cansado, que busca soledades."[180] However, this "tired philosopher" ultimately gives up studying because he is too distracted by amorous pursuits.[181] He is so consumed by love that he wants to run out and tell everyone about it.[182] He finds it impossible to talk of anything else:

> [N]o es posible que sea
> buen cortesano el Amor,
> pues de ninguna manera
> habla más que una cosa,
> mezclando gusto, y tristeza.[183]

In speaking of love, the lover may speak plainly[184] or not so plainly, i.e. by employing elaborate conceits. Love has its own grammar: "en Gramática de amor saber distinguir es fuerza."[185] As with any grammar, even the most fluent speaker of love's language sometimes makes mistakes ("Esos son los solecismos de amor").[186] However, the discourse of love does at least promote ingenuity: "el ingenio, que es buen tercero del cariño."[187] Indeed, the most ingenious tropes of courtly discourse are said to have been inspired by love:

> El que más ansia ha tenido
> de mirarse señalado
> por su ingenio, y celebrado
> de Cortesano entendido,
> la principal causa ha sido
> amor, para que pretenda
> en una, y otra contienda
> de ingenio, por varios modos,
> verse aplaudido entre todos,
> porque su dama lo entienda.[188]

These elaborate feats of subtle ingenuity at the court of the Catholic Monarchs have been studied by Roger Boase in *The Secrets of Pinar's Game*.[189] In what would seem to be a direct echo of the emblems and *invenciones* Boase describes, we find in Calderón's *Lances de Amor y Fortuna* a clever explanation of a coat of arms painted on a shield with 4 S's for Love:

> Cuatro esses ha de tener
> el amor siendo perfecto:
> (Dios me saque de este aprieto:)
> por la primera ha de ser
> sabañón, que ha de comer,
> y pruébase esta verdad,
> en que la necesidad
> el respeto al amor pierde,
> que toda hermosura muerde,
> y masca toda deidad.
> Después de comer no hay duda,
> que ha de vestirse esta dama;
> En la segunda se llama
> sastre el amor, porque acuda
> a esta belleza desnuda,
> y el amante que no ha sido
> para dar plato, y vestido,
> aunque a su fineza pese,
> será a la tercera esse
> viendo, y callando, sufrido.
> Y para el que no sufriere
> tanta desdicha, y afán,
> es el amor sacristán,
> que le entierre, pues se muere,
> de donde claro se infiere,
> que todo amor ha tenido,
> o verdadero, o fingido
> las esses de este blasón,
> siendo el amor sabañón,
> sacristán, sastre, y sufrido.[190]

Calderón returned to this same *invención* in a different play, this time making the four alliterative S's stand for adjectives instead of nouns: "Cuatro esses ha de tener amor para ser perfecto: sabio, solo, solícito, y secreto."[191]

In the face of such intricate wordplay, we can only conclude with Agustín Moreto that "invencionero es amor."[192] Even love's pangs can be turned into flattery: "es sutil estratagema de amor, que una pena misma hacerse lisonja sepa."[193]

These clever plays on words and similar feats of ingenuity are so subtle and delicate, they cannot be touched for fear they might break:

> [A]mor palaciego es
> escaparate del alma,
> donde se ven por defuera
> juguetes de porcelana,
> trastos de imaginación,
> melindres de filigrana,
> retruécanos de cristal,
> y tiquis miquis de ámbar,
> que aunque se ven, no se tocan.[194]

The image here is of a curiosity cabinet with glass windows, so popular during this period when *Kunst-* and *Wunderkammern* were all the rage (see figure 5).

In keeping with fragile objects made of glass, the extreme delicacy of love's subject matter required lovers to be discreet: "el amor todo es cautela."[195] A rule of thumb to follow was that "en materias de amor siempre calla un Caballero."[196] The secrecy of love's proceedings is satirized with reference to the Inquisition's secret tribunals: "La inquisición es de Amor esta casa, porque siempre se hacen las causas secretas."[197] Modest love wants to hide, blushing, under a lady's large skirt.[198] The idea of hiding under a lady's skirt was nothing new to the Spanish court; in fact, a special term (*guardainfante*) was coined to signify a hoop skirt large enough to hide a pregnancy or even a prince underneath.[199]

As if these extremely specific details were not enough to clue us into the fact that we are in the realm of the royal court, in the *comedias* we find numerous references to the concept of courtly love as such, as in "Cortesano amor tenéis"[200] or "el amor Cortesano permite los galanteos."[201] The dramas are also quite clear on what courtly love does *not* permit – for example, when the Prince confesses to Félix: "mi amor, Félix, pasa de los límites corteses."[202] We even encounter precise definitions of courtly love, as in the lines "será tan cortés mi amor, que amaré sin esperanza, como los amores son de Palacio solamente una humana admiración."[203]

However, as time wears on we also begin to witness a breakdown of the courtly love paradigm, as when one character complains that "en materias de amor, esto de nombrar las partes es muy gran desatención."[204] The same old worn-out Petrarchan formulas such as enumerating parts of a woman's body begin to feel stale in the face of elaborate, newfangled Baroque conceits. Nonetheless, the spirit (if not the form) of courtly love lives on in the ideal that love cannot be forced: "es vil el amor que conseguido por fuerza quita a su dueño el merecer."[205] Isabel reinforces this sentiment in her speech to Crespo:

> [M]al aya
> el hombre que solicita

por fuerça ganar vn alma;
pues no aduierte, pues no mira,
que las victorias de amor,
no ay trofeo en que consistan;
sino en granjear el cariño
de la hermosura que estiman,
porque querer sin el alma
una hermosura ofendida,
es querer a una mujer
hermosa, pero no viva.[206]

This stark image could not be more vivid: love that is forced is like loving a corpse. The *comedias* are adamant on this point: "No sufre fuerzas amor."[207]

In fact, love that is forced could only ever possibly be characterized as vile or "villainous" love: "mal haya amor villano, que la fuerza del cariño la funda en la de los brazos."[208] Forcing love is likened to dragging a resisting cat into water.[209] In a humorous swipe at the universities, university-educated playwright Calderón de la Barca joked that since true love must arise spontaneously, wisdom in the affairs of love cannot be studied at university.[210] (I'm not sure I agree with him, considering the fact that many of my students seem to study little else.)

Paradoxically, given that love cannot be forced, somehow being in love is still about desire for conquest. A swaggering braggart echoes Caesar to announce his romantic prowess on stage: "César de amor, llegué, vi, y vencí."[211] The linguistic register employed to describe a campaign of wooing is the same one might use to describe a siege: "el amor cercados tiene estos muros con desvelos, y con balazos de celos."[212] A successful conquest in love is accomplished only by penetrating the fortress's walls ("tu amor asaltó esta muralla").[213] Victory is figuratively celebrated in a triumphal procession, replete with palm branches for the victor.[214]

Faced with this arduous process, we might well ask: is there an easier way? Can love be bought instead?[215] In early modern Spain, as in all times and places, in one sense "love" was for sale by prostitutes, whose profession was regulated and therefore officially tolerated during much of the early modern period.[216] We find traces of these transactions in the *comedias*, as in the line, "hallarás si de amor tratas, damiselas como natas a poco precio en tu tierra."[217] We must also consider the case of the high-class courtesan depicted in Lope de Vega's closet drama *La Dorotea* who leaves her lover Fernando in favour of the wealthy *indiano* Don Bela. Traces of this sort of situation, too, find their way into the dramas, as in the line "flecha del Amor, que disparada, en vez de plomo, de oro, viene armada."[218] But the *comedias* are almost uniformly insistent on the point that true love cannot be bought[219] with either wealth[220] or treasure.[221] Repeatedly, curious ekphrastic passages refer to disinterested love as "naked" and therefore genuine.[222] In fact, any effort to buy true love is compared to simony, which was the sin of buying or selling ecclesiastical offices: "comprar el amor, siendo infinito, es hacer simonía el apetito."[223]

However, just because love can't be bought does not mean it shouldn't be generous. Witness Inés's reproach to the *gracioso* Bretón: "O, qué mal tu amor se aliña[,] sintiendo tanto el gastar."[224] After all, gifts are one of love's primary languages ("es el Don idioma del cariño").[225] Love is referred to repeatedly in economic terms as a debt that must be repaid ("fuera deuda el amor, y tiranía el negarle").[226] Conversely, love is a loan not to be denied to a good creditor.[227] A lover's complaints are criticized as an oblique means of charging interest:

> El que no calla, procura
> llevar algún interés;
> que decir sus penas, es
> hacer del amor usura.[228]

Here the indiscreet lover is accused of turning love into usury (charging interest was still considered a sin by the Catholic Church during this time period).[229] "Mortgaging" or sacrificing one love to give priority to another was considered fraud.[230] Love cannot be bought, but it does demand tribute[231] like a vengeful deity,[232] sometimes exacting payment even in blood.[233] This tribute can take various forms:

> [S]on pensiones precisas
> de los vasallos de Amor,
> tributar a su divina
> Deidad inquietudes, ansias,
> divertimientos, envidias,
> anhelos, suspiros, quejas,
> lágrimas, melancolías,
> sentimientos, penas, llantos,
> porque en la gran Monarquía
> de sus tiranos imperios,
> no hay ventura sin desdicha.[234]

Even in a less overtly tyrannical[235] system, still love charges the equivalent of a mortgage instalment.[236] It mitigates this cynical picture somewhat to learn that love does not sue for non-payment ("nunca hizo Amor pleito de acreedores").[237]

Perhaps this decision to refrain from litigation reflects an acknowledgment that love is subject to unpredictable Fortune (see figure 6).[238] Love produces air in the form of sighs:

> Venid conmigo suspiros,
> ofreced viento a las velas,

si es que en los mares del fuego
bajeles de amor navegan.[239]

This air or wind[240] of Love's sighs in turn becomes the force powering the lover's boat.[241] When intensified, the air and wind combine with other elements to form a violent[242] storm.[243] Love becomes the tempestuous sea ("el Mar de Amor")[244] in which the lover's boat is tossed.[245] When someone sings to the lovesick, it sounds like the seductive song of a mermaid,[246] recalling the deadly Sirens whose temptation Odysseus avoided by lashing himself to his ship's mast. But not all of love's victims are so lucky. If one is not careful, love can end in proverbial shipwreck[247] for all involved.

This likelihood is enough to produce massive anxiety in love's adherents: "amor me hizo indiscreto con penas, desvelos, y ansias."[248] Love quickly becomes a veritable hell of apprehension.[249] In its more benign form, the pricks of love can feel like an internal tickling sensation,[250] which is nevertheless enough to make us come "unstitched" or unglued.[251]

Theoretically, true love cannot be mixed with fear: "no fuera posible, que mis afectos le miraran con cariño, si le miraran, temiendo"[252] (the reader will recall that biblical "love casts out fear").[253] But paradoxically, love can produce fear: "amor todo es miedos."[254] This is due to the fact that in picaresque fashion, love plays tricks[255] on us, catching us like a mouse in its trap ("Púsonos el queso amor, y dimos en ratonera").[256] One particularly vivid line refers to a kiss as love's "cheese": "El beso es el queso de los ratones de amor."[257] In an explicitly metatheatrical metaphor, love moves us around as pawns like the director of a farce: "quiere el Amor, / que haga hoy, de agrado, y rigor, / en su Farsa dos Papeles."[258]

Love's knots at first tie our necks together[259] like a necklace embedded with precious stones.[260] But then love's jewellery morphs into a yoke such as one would use to harness an ox or beast of burden.[261] Sometimes this yoke becomes heavy.[262] Ultimately the lover finds herself in chains[263] such as the ones used to keep a prisoner in bondage: "presa en los hierros de amor."[264] Alternatively, sometimes love itself becomes a prison,[265] while the chains are the lover's errors.[266] The pains of love are explicitly described as tortures[267] that must be borne silently.[268] Love can even lead to death.[269]

But short of death, is there an end to love? On the one hand, the *comedias* are filled with sappy Hallmark-card sentiments like the idea that true love endures forever.[270] Loyal love is said to be as strong or firm as crystal,[271] jasper,[272] or diamond,[273] in fact enduring even beyond death: "el verdadero amor es preciso que pase más allá de la muerte."[274] However, the *comedias* are not united on this point. We also find more pragmatic, realistic assertions such as "no hay amor que pase los umbrales del sepulcro"[275] in recognition of the fact that most human love is merely an earthly phenomenon. It can change its mind whimsically ("de amor la esquiva mudanza")[276] or fade eventually with time.[277] In a strikingly antisemitic image, love is pictured as unreciprocated[278] and therefore condemned to wander eternally like the Wandering Jew: "babeando se anda, hecho un Juan de Espera Amor."[279] This "drooling" Juan de Espera was a stereotyped figure condemned to perpetual wandering and hopeless waiting after having committed blasphemy against God.[280]

The flame of love eventually dies out,[281] especially from stubbornness ("muriendo con la terquedad del alma mi amor").[282] The ashes of love are said to be the vestiges of sins committed under its influence.[283] These ashes cover what was once a sumptuous palace, likened explicitly to the Alcázar of Seville:

> El fatal destrozo
> de un amor desengañado,
> cuyo Alcázar suntuoso
> ruinas de fuego sepultan,
> cenizas que ya son polvo.[284]

Ultimately absence and forgetfulness become love's tomb ("ausencia, y olvido / tumba de mi amor / ha sido").[285] Sometimes absence is sought as a cure for love deliberately: "ausencia, y tiempo le curen; porque nadie convalece de amor mejor, ni más presto, que un enamorado ausente."[286] But if the cure does not work – in a moment of acute self-awareness by Spain that it was a failed empire – love can turn out to be as big a disaster as Spanish colonies in the Caribbean: "Yo a quien ha hecho el rigor nuevo Caribe de amor."[287] In this case, the lover is not the only one who suffers; if love dies, then the pimp receives no reward for his services either ("de amor que muere, el alcahuete no espere tener derechos en nada").[288] True to their Celestinesque heritage, the *comedias* of course specify what some of these services are.[289]

However, even after it has died, a first love is never truly forgotten: "el primero amor, tarde, o nunca puede borrarse de un noble pecho."[290] The inevitable corollary is that love can be revived.[291] It can be patched or mended like a torn garment,[292] or rise from the ashes like the Phoenix.[293] In fact, the dramas go so far as to claim that this undead, zombie-like mythical bird is actually an apt symbol for love: "Símbolo del Amor es, el Fénix, que en blanda hoguera fuego nace … y fuego otra vez se engendra."[294]

As it turns out, nothing works to revive a dead or dormant love quite so well as jealousy ("suelen soplar los celos las cenizas de un amor").[295] In fact, a love that is *not* accompanied by jealousy is said to lack soul: "sin celos amor, es estar sin alma un cuerpo."[296] In one formulation, jealousy is said to unfold as merely the last of four phases in every love affair:

> [E]stas son las cuatro edades
> de cualquier amor, pues vemos

que en brazos del desdén nace,
crece en poder del deseo,
vive en casa del favor,
y muere en la de los celos.[297]

Other plays state more succinctly, "Muerte de amor son los celos."[298] Needless to say, this jealousy does have its negative side:

En este (ay Dios) tiempo que
la nave de amor sulcaba
espumas de nieve risas,
se levantó una tormenta
de celos a decir iba,
mas no fue solo de celos,
de traiciones, de mentiras,
de engaños, y falsedades.[299]

Here jealousy is seen pejoratively to lead to betrayal, lies, falsity,[300] and deceit.

Love's Achilles heel was always trust or confidence ("la confianza, que es la ruindad del cariño").[301] This vulnerability leads naturally to disillusionment: "desengañado de mi amor, mi afrenta veo."[302] In fact, in a rather picturesque turn of phrase, disillusionment is seen as the dessert course in love's feast:

Para postre desengaños
guisados por escarmientos,
que en la cena del amor
siempre es el plato postrero.[303]

This disillusionment results from treachery as vile as Judas's betrayal of Jesus.[304] In another colourful image borrowed from medieval bestiaries as well as zoological accounts of "New" World exotic animals and their habits, love is characterized as a wily crocodile who spits water on the ground to make its prey slip and fall:

Con falso, y cruel estilo
(si por el camino siente
pasajera alguna gente)
engañoso el cocodrilo
toma agua en la boca, y fiero
por donde ha de pasar,
la senda empieza a mojar
del mayor deslizadero.
Escóndese con aviso

natural; y así en tal caso
y en viéndolos cerca, al paso
sale a ellos de improviso.
Espántalos denodado,
huyen de él, valos siguiendo,
llegando al paso, y cayendo
en la senda que ha mojado.
Deteniéndose, es forzoso
les alcance su rigor:
de aquesta suerte tu amor,
(cocodrilo cauteloso)
persiguiéndome enojado,
como engañarme procura,
a pesar de tu hermosura,
peligro de mi cuidado,
imitando sus despojos,
de la manera que ves,
para que caiga a mis pies
ha echado el agua en tus ojos.[305]

This description of wildlife might sound fanciful, but at least the crocodile was a real animal. In other comparisons, love becomes the chimera, a monstrous beast from classical mythology (see figure 7):

[Q]uimera es mi amor sin duda,
mas considera, y repara,
que la quimera fue un monstruo,
cuyo cuello articulaban
tres cabezas de animales,
que eran, de león, de cabra,
y la otra de serpiente,
lo mismo en mi amor se halla:
mi amor es una quimera,
que tres cabezas la enlazan:
en la primera se muestra
la realeza, y fuerza extraña
con que me rendí a tus ojos,
y me consagré en tus aras:
en la segunda se advierte
la nobleza, y la prosapia
de mis honestos deseos,
que por tales incitaban:

la postrera es de serpiente,
porque en pena tan amarga,
todo el amor que encarezco,
todas las penas pasadas,
todos los justos deseos,
y todo el bien que esperaba
todo se acaba en serpiente,
porque en este amor el alma
solo ha sacado veneno,
pues solo disgustos saca.[306]

This complicated comparison takes the time to spin out each of its components separately – royalty, nobility, and bitterness, corresponding to each of the chimera's three heads.

The appearance of this mythical creature should have alerted us by now to the fact that much of what passes for love is merely a fantasy: "las ciegas fantasías de Amor, cuando más se defiendan, en aire se consuman."[307] In the words of a character named Diana, "amor todo es ilusiones."[308] Madrid, in particular, enjoyed a reputation as a place where what appeared to be love turned out to be nothing more than papier mâché.[309] A different iteration of the same idea is the notion that love is a magic spell.[310] This was, of course, an era when magic spells could be literal;[311] witness the following speech by Tancredo to Marcela:

Que estoy tal, que aun si pudiera
con algún fingido trato,
hacerte amar de Torcato,
el alma, y vida le diera.
Si hechizos supiera hacer,
o de la Nigromancia,
o que en algún monte había
hierbas de tan gran poder.
Al de la Luna, o Thesalia,
a Colcos señora fuera,
y al Templo olor ofreciera,
donde se adora a Acidalia.[312]

He swears he would even employ the dark arts of necromancy to influence her love life if he knew how.

This stance might at first seem generous and noble; but to contextualize, we find lines in the same play asking rhetorically whether love has ever been truly disinterested. Tancredo once again speaks to Marcela:

¿Ha tenido amante el mundo
que quiera sin interés?
¿Tú no ves que mi amor es
del primero amor segundo?
Después de aquel primer hombre,
di, sin interés alguno,
ha querido hombre ninguno,
ni amor ha tenido, nombre?
Unos quieren por casarse,
otros por enriquecer,
otros por tener mujer,
de quien servirse, y fiarse.
Cual por verse regalado,
cual por sola sucesión,
y cual por obligación,
y de su gusto forzado.
Cual por tema, o por mudanza,
cual por competidor;
en efecto no hay amor
que quiera sin esperanza.[313]

In fact, a King says of his own royal court that there is no love present without financial profit.[314]

According to these plays, Spain's current concept of love is dishonest ("el torpe, y deshonesto amor del Siglo")[315] to the point where love is viewed alternatively as a cheat,[316] a liar,[317] and a thief.[318] In another flagrantly ethnic insult, love is a *morisco* bandit hiding in the mountain ranges near Granada, waiting to pounce upon the unsuspecting traveller: "que en mitad del curso de su más florido tiempo amor no le saltease Monfí de los años tiernos."[319] After a successful robbery, the roadside bandit will of course pawn the loot. In the process, what used to be the sacred tokens of love are downgraded to second-hand merchandise[320] to be sold at the town fair:

Granjería común amor se ha hecho,
y de él hay feria franca dondequiera,
do[nde] cada cual atiende a su provecho.[321]

That is, of course, unless he has not already squandered love's tokens at gambling in love's seedy[322] casino (see figure 8). In the words of the Muslim character Alcuzcuz:

Ea, fulleros de amor,
que pues está puesto el naipe,

y os adivináis los juegos,
no hay para qué barajarle.[323]

Another character named Pedro develops this analogy in an extended comparison:

A los alcahuetes digo
que son de amor gariteros,
vaya al discurso al garito.
Pone un garitero casa,
el alcahuete es lo mismo,
los galanes son tahures,
y entran en ella infinitos.
De aqueste juego el tahur
que da palmadas, y gritos,
es el celoso, que siempre
celos son voces, y ruido.
El que pierde, y el que calla,
es tahur à lo Ministro,
que entra, y paga su dinero,
sin sentirlo, con-sentirlo.
El que juega sobre prenda,
es el amante novicio,
que saca del Mercader,
ya la joya, ya el vestido.
El que hace alicantina,
es el amante entendido,
que pierde, y dice, esto es hecho,
necio el que pierde continuo.
Sobre palabra, es aquel
que promete, y que cumplido
el plazo, paga: el galán
que sirve, por lo entendido,
con papeles estudiados,
es el fullero del vicio,
pues juega con cartas hechas.
Los mirones que han venido
a enfadar, sin dar provecho,
son los vecinos prolijos,
que del garito de amor
mirones son los vecinos.
Las barajas de este juego,
son las Damas, bien se ha visto

> ser todas ellas barajas;
> y para el barato digo,
> que cuando hay baraja nueva,
> tiene seguro el partido.[324]

Here ladies are viewed as no more important or valuable than a deck of cards for men to play with. It is of course not too much of a leap from there to call Venus, the goddess of love, a "public prostitute."[325]

In this swift spiral downward, love becomes a chemistry experiment,[326] a musical instrument to be manipulated,[327] and – finally – a theatre of tragedy.[328] In what might be seen as a literary precursor to José Espronceda's Romantic vision of disintegrating love in "El estudiante de Salamanca," the man who tries to grasp the woman he loves finds himself holding only a cadaver.[329] Baroque romantic love ends in a spectacularly bleak *memento mori* (see figure 9).[330] Little wonder, then, that at least one character claims not to give two shits about love.[331]

In this dystopian vision, the only type of love that seems a safe bet is self-love. In the words of Lucanor:

> ¡Qué pegado afecto al alma
> el del amor propio es,
> pues nunca le suena mal
> que haya quien le quiera bien![332]

Self-love was of course epitomized in the classical myth of Narcissus, which is the foundation for Calderón de la Barca's *Eco y Narciso*. In this play, the rhetorical question is posed, "¿qué hechizo, ni qué veneno más fiero, que su propio amor?"[333] Self-love also appears as an allegorical figure in the same playwright's *Lo que va del hombre a Dios*. In this sacramental drama, the allegorical figure of Culpa (Blame) says as Amor Propio moves toward her: "A la Culpa, ¿cuándo no se acerca el propio Amor?"[334]

This negative portrayal of self-love in the *autos sacramentales* is fairly consistent – witness lines such as "locos devaneos de mi Amor propio"[335] – but in contrast, the *comedias* are more indulgent toward this phenomenon, as is Saint Augustine.[336] A character in Francisco de Rojas Zorrilla's *Casarse por vengarse* heralds the reality of "uno no poder jamás desechar el amor propio, que es natural el primero";[337] this sounds like an admission that self-love is a natural instinct, and therefore hard to get rid of. No doubt knowing this, a demon summons self-love in a hagiographical play to come do his bidding, i.e., to lead a saint astray: "Llega tú ahora, Amor propio, por si abres algún resquicio."[338] Here the devil hopes that self-love will prove to be a point of vulnerability – a chink in the saint's armour.

This particular attempt to exploit a saint's weakness is obviously demonic, but there is an important sense in which even more routine love acts as the great equalizer:

> Que bien la Gentilidad
> llamaba Dios al amor,
> pues el más humilde honor
> iguala a la Majestad.[339]

This democratizing action by love could prove laudable in the moral realm, as could its propensity to restrain lovers from evil action.[340] This discussion of the (im)morality of love[341] leads to the obvious question: can we control this passion?[342]

The *comedias* differ on this point. Some lines state emphatically that love is not a choice:[343]

> No es amor elección, pues si lo fuera,
> nadie en el mundo aborrecido amara.
> No es voluntad, que nadie le rindiera,
> donde con voluntad no se pagara:
> no es razón, pues con ella se rijiera,
> no es gusto, pues sin él no se entregara.
> ¿Qué será donde falta (¡cielo injusto!)
> elección, voluntad, razón, y gusto?[344]

William Irvine echoes this view adamantly: "Falling in love is like waking up ... with a fever. We don't decide to fall in love, any more than we decide to catch the flu."[345]

However, adding nuance to this passive view of love as something that happens *to* us, we find descriptions of love as a kind of suffering to which we give in:[346]

> Sea amor, o sentimiento,
> nieve, ardor, llama, o ceniza,
> yo me abraso, yo me rindo
> a esta furia vengativa
> de amor, contra la quietud
> de mi libertad tranquila:
> y sin esperanza alguna
> de sosiego en mis fatigas,
> yo padezco en mi silencio.[347]

This type of silent, suffering love is elsewhere referred to as Platonic.[348] (This may not be our current understanding of Platonic love, but such was one reception of Plato's philosophy in Spain during this time period.)[349]

This last point brings us to the question of which (if any) philosophers of love Renaissance Spanish playwrights were familiar with. Specific philosophers and titles of their works are sometimes mentioned on stage. For example:

> Quiero reclinarme aquí,
> donde en Ovidio, mejor
> leeré el Remedio de Amor.[350]

Specific philosophical ideas about love may also be found here, such as the Platonic notion that love enters through the eyes ("Amor entra por los ojos").[351] This idea is spun out into the theory that love enters through the eyes, but then lodges in the soul:

> Presumo, que el amor es un deseo,
> engendrado en el alma, por los ojos,
> lince sin vista, que causando antojos
> las voluntades tiene por trofeo.[352]

Perhaps surprisingly, we also find references to such technical philosophical details as Plato's theory of the Forms[353] and his notion about the transmigration of souls.[354] There are also explicit allusions to subsequent theorists of love such as Aristotle,[355] but Plato appears to have been the favourite philosopher for many of these playwrights to quote in this context. Whether in reference to Plato's ideas about the harmony of the spheres[356] or his definition of love as a natural desire for beauty,[357] his concepts are not only repeated but often attributed to him by name as someone famous enough to be recognized outside the confines of academic erudition. Witness the following exchange from Lope de Vega's *Fuenteovejuna*:

> BARRILDO: Dijo el cura del lugar
>   cierto día en el sermón
>   que había cierto Platón
>   que nos enseñaba a amar;
>   que éste amaba el alma sola
>   y la virtud de lo amado.
> PASCUALA: En materia habéis entrado
>   que, por ventura, acrisola
>   los caletres de los sabios
>   en sus [a]cademias y escuelas.

This rejoinder by Pascuala sounds like an apologetic wink on the part of the playwright for letting himself get carried away with excessive touches of glittering erudition.

As if to make up for forcing the reader or spectator to wade through too much philosophy, there also appear hilarious burlesque scenes making fun of philosophical navel-gazing about love. Witness the lines of this comical *gracioso*:

> [N]o alcanzo yo los rodeos
> de Platónicos amores,
> que como siempre profeso
> el escuderico amor,
> el Filósofo no entiendo.[358]

In an even harsher (though humorous) condemnation, Carlos opines to Enrique that philosophers' digressions on love should be burned in an Inquisitorial auto-da-fé:

> Y así, al instante trata
> de entregar cuantos libros traje, al fuego,
> y despídeme luego
> los Maestros que he tenido,
> pues que tan poco a todos he debido,
> que no le han enseñado
> en tanto docto afán a mi cuidado
> cuestión de amor, que la desdicha mía
> alivie, siendo amor Filosofía.[359]

Burn the love treatises, he says, because they have not helped him anyway.

We shall give the last word to Ponlevi in Calderón's *La banda y la flor*, who exclaims to Celia: "Soy más práctico de amor que teórico."[360] The *comedias*, too, seem to be more interested in practising love than in concocting theories about it. (Is there a lab for this class?)

6

The Wounding Smell of Sorrow[1]

The emotion about a present evil is sadness.[2]

Tristitia omnis a Sathana [All sadness is from Satan].[3]

Sorrow carves riverbeds in our soul.[4]

Where there is sorrow there is holy ground.[5]

Sorrow in the *comedias* is dark like the night: "el entierro del Sol en la tristeza nocturna."[6] It is cold as the winter:

> [L]lega el hielo tirano,
> y con intensos rigores
> los pimpollos y colores
> cubre de tristeza y luto,
> porque hasta tener el fruto
> no están seguras las flores.[7]

Sorrow is a cup we must drink, "grande el vaso de ese dolor,"[8] except that its pangs overflow the glass:

> [Y]a el corazón con el dolor se ahoga,
> ya no caben las penas en el vaso.
> Ya la piedad por el amor aboga,
> ya me pone la soga a la garganta,
> y el verdugo dolor tira la soga.
> Ya el corazón tristes endechas canta,
> ya se deshace en lágrimas severo,
> y sangre vierte viendo sangre tanta.[9]

Sorrow pierces the heart[10] and breaks open the chest.[11] Sorrow is cumulative ("O qué mal podrá pasar mi tristeza, cada día se aumenta");[12] as psychologist Sherry Cormier confirms,

> Cumulative grief has a snowball effect. A new loss builds on the prior loss(es) and in some way reignites the pain, much like the reopening of a wound that has been held together with very fragile stitches. Losses you believed you'd grieved successfully come back in a haunting fashion.[13]

And sorrow is supremely democratic: "[¿]no hay en el Mundo grandeza, que sujeta a la tristeza, o a la lástima no esté?"[14] In response to this last, obviously rhetorical question asked on the *comedia* stage – everyone experiences sorrow; no one is exempt.

Sorrow's symptoms include sighing,[15] bowing one's head,[16] not raising one's gaze,[17] and turning away. These are not altogether different from the monastic malaise known to medieval writers as *acedia*: "Manifested in both somatic and psychological symptoms, such as fatigue, inertia, anxiety, despair, sadness, and boredom, symptoms of *akēdia* persisted well into the Middle Ages."[18] Robert Kaster explains,

> *Acedia* – most familiar as Sloth, the misleading label that it wears among the Seven Deadly Sins – was a debilitating affective state, embracing not just idleness but despair and sadness as well, which seemed to come into being as a distinct emotion in late antiquity and to pass out of existence again with the waning of the Middle Ages.[19]

We may surmise that *acedia* did not in fact disappear, but was merely transmuted or tranformed[20] into other emotions with similar symptoms but perhaps bearing a different name (or names).

On the early modern Spanish stage, a sad[21] or pale[22] face denoted sorrow, especially the eyes: "Y de su grave tristeza dieron los ojos señales."[23] (Philosopher Ludwig Wittgenstein once remarked, "Grief … is personified in the face.")[24] Sad eyes were said to be clouded,[25] until the "rain storm"[26] came in the form of tears.[27] On the one hand, weeping brings relief for sorrow;[28] but on the other, it can be difficult to stop: "es tanta su tristeza, que no deja de llorar."[29] Crying might normally be considered feminine (at least in some circles); psychoanalyst Susan Roos affirms in this regard, "permissions and support for emotional expression for men who are coping with significant, ongoing loss – or grief of any kind – are not sanctioned in quite the same way as they are for women."[30] But Lope de Vega assures us that "real men do cry":[31]

Las lágrimas de flaqueza
son lágrimas de mujer.
Mas las de rabia y tristeza
no es agua, fuego han de ser
lágrimas de fortaleza.[32]

Manly tears are here described as "tears of strength."

Weeping can be magnified into loud cries of lament: "Representarán sus llantos, su tristeza y desconsuelo."[33] Grief counsellor Stephen Levine describes the sound of this kind of sorrow: "A sound, nearly a moan, seeps from the broken heart and resonates through the throat and out of the body into song. The body is a sounding chamber. As our song deepens, it makes the heart audible, bringing a deeper knowing to the surface so we might hear it for ourselves."[34]

Laments in turn often become a funeral dirge.[35] In Tirso de Molina's *Los amantes de Teruel*, Drusila describes to her mistress the details of a funeral procession passing outside their window:

> Ponte a la ventana,
> y desde sus rejas
> mirarás, señora,
> la villa revuelta.
> Mujeres, y niños
> con lágrimas tiernas
> esta calle ocupan,
> y esas otras despueblan.
> Desde las ventanas
> arrancan de pena
> sus cabellos rubios
> dueñas y doncellas.
> Los viejos ancianos
> van con la terneza,
> en hebras de plata,
> ensartando perlas.
> Óyense supiros,
> que al aire penetran,
> hasta el eco mismo
> suspira en respuesta.
> Destempladas cajas
> de esto el compás llevan,
> que son en las muertes
> llanto de la guerra.
> Alrededor viene
> gente de la Iglesia,
> con capas de coro,
> y amarilla cera.
> Y haciendo sus voces
> con las cajas mezcla,
> los responsos mueven
> extraña tristeza.

Luego más abajo
se ve por la tierra
de Moros vencidos
rendidas banderas.
Y en hombros de nobles,
con armas, y espuelas,
un difunto armado
a usanza de guerra.
Alaridos tristes
del pueblo le cercan,
de que era bien quisto
muestras verdaderas.
Ya dicen las cajas,
que el entierro llega,
y el alma te dice
quién es el que entierran.[36]

Adele Tutter explains the importance of such funerary rituals for producing clo-sure in the bereaved:

Ceremony, rite, and prayer are distinguished by repetition, soothing the bereaved while recursively evoking their essential quality: their enduring and stable repetition over time. By structuring mourning within rituals, customs, and traditions that have been and will continue to be repeated, lives shaken by death and displacement gain a stabilizing ballast of performance, a sustaining matrix of continuity. Whether by the draping of the mirrors or by the periodic traveling of ancestral paths, their familiar sameness is a consolation, assuring secure links with past and future and thereby mitigating the devastation of our worlds and our selves.[37]

Mourning customs and rituals for this time period were fairly specific, and their particulars appear in lines of dialogue on stage. For example, Raymundo asserts to the Queen:

Justo es el luto, y el llorar es justo;
justo es el no lavar el rostro bello;
muy justa es la tristeza, y el disgusto;
el no tocarse, ni peinar cabello.[38]

Here the details of not washing the face or brushing the hair might surprise a mod-ern audience. It was very much assumed that a person in mourning would don special mourning attire ("ya el vestido y la cara, tristeza y semblante muda"),[39] with the specific colour worn most likely to be black.[40] All one's accessories must also be black, including stockings, plumed hats, and mantle or cloak: "calzas, plumas, y manto negro lleva, de algún antiguo amor tristeza nueva."[41] The longer the grief lasted, the longer these official mourning garments might be left on, even to the point of growing old with long use.[42]

The use of black to adorn one's body could extend likewise to the decoration of physical space. Witness one noble character's command to cover the walls of his palace with black cloth: "Cubrid de jerga negra mi palacio, fúnebres instrumentos imiten mi tristeza."[43] Requisite periods of mourning were observed by entire cities, which shut their doors and windows as a visible sign to show respect for the dead:

> Si entrando
> en la ciudad, no viste en sus vecinos,
> plazas, calles, ventanas, la tristeza,
> el luto y el dolor de la desdicha,
> ahora lo sabrás de mis palabras.[44]

The actual funeral rites[45] might include processions with music, as in "los blancos yelmos de negro luto, y den común tristeza con roncas lenguas las trompetas sordas."[46]

Now that we know how to identify sorrow, we might well ask: what does sorrow do? What are its effects? Sorrow suspends normal activities, as when the allegorical figure of Thought asks Human Ingenuity:

> ¿Qué tristeza,
> humano Ingenio del Hombre,
> en tu estudiosa tarea
> te tiene tan suspendido?[47]

As we see from this passage, sorrow produces lethargy[48] to the point where the person who experiences it does not feel like working.[49] Anna Gotlib confirms, "A sad person is one who dwells, one who (inappropriately) ruminates, one who refuses to move on – one who is stuck as a moral agent."[50]

Sorrow afflicts,[51] oppresses,[52] and assaults,[53] until it finally prostrates and vanquishes us. Thus Lesbia exhorts her mistress, "No así de una tristeza te dejes postrar, señora, y rendir."[54] Sorrow leaves us with no wish to speak.[55] Even if the sad person does want to talk, his sorrow might make speech impossible: "te oprima el llanto, y enmudezca la tristeza."[56]

The result of not speaking is an ominous silence.[57] The sad person becomes increasingly preoccupied[58] with racing thoughts ("A mil pensamientos llego, que me causan gran tristeza")[59] and the brooding of a sick imagination.[60] He or she rebuffs displays of physical affection[61] and flees from love,[62] or – conversely – craves company: "jamás de mi lado faltarás, porque lo que más deseo hoy en mis tristezas, es que tú me hagas compañía."[63]

But more typically, sorrow seeks solitude, with characters stating resolutely, "he menester soledad en que pasar la tristeza."[64] The stated purpose is to "fight" against sadness in this setting.[65] In fact, sorrow is thought to be a monster who feeds on solitude, as in these lines spoken by Rosimunda to Estela:

[E]s la tristeza
monstruo que en las soledades
de sí sola se alimenta.[66]

The result is utter isolation[67] and an inability to share one's cares and concerns with anyone: "no puede mi tristeza dar su cuidado a nadie."[68] Psychologist Sherry Cormier confirms the ever-present nature of this danger: "chronic loneliness can be a killer. Loneliness is linked to higher stress hormones and earlier mortality … Human connection leads to significant changes in brain functioning, while loneliness or social disconnection increases stress hormones and impairs executive functioning of the brain."[69]

What are some specific occasions for sorrow, its proximate causes? Sorrow is occasioned either by one's own problems or those of someone else. On the most banal level, sorrow might be experienced at the loss of something precious or valuable, such as an exquisite piece of jewellery.[70] Grief counsellor Stephen Levine confirms that loss is indeed central to sorrow: "our greatest disappointment is loss. Loss of loved ones, loss of love, loss of safety, loss of trust, loss of faith, loss of meaning, loss of youth, loss of life: loss of what we held precious."[71]

More serious sorrow might be caused by being forgotten by a loved one,[72] or by that loved once's absence[73] – for example, a soldier going off to war.[74] And then of course the soldier might never return, or the beloved might die by some other manner, as we see in lines about a character who seeks to "replace" a dead child with a slave who might prove to be some small consolation: "andáis buscando un esclavo … que pueda la tristeza consolaros, de un hijo que habéis perdido."[75] Psychoanalyst Susan Roos describes poignantly this kind of sorrow:

Activation of the fantasy [of the lost child] intensifies painful emotions, as the disparity between the fantasy and current living reality can be cruel and wounding. Attempts to manage the crushing discrepancy between fantasy and reality can be found in the writings of individuals whose lives are significantly compromised by chronic sorrow.[76]

Even if the beloved does not die, love might not be reciprocated, in which case the unreciprocating person is compared to a rock or stone (like marble), to snow or ice.[77] Sorrow might be caused by envy or jealousy, especially if a rival is luckier in love.[78]

Sorrow could also arise vicariously in response to other people's problems, such as the illness of a close friend or family member.[79] Sorrow was nearly always thought to be in order at the death of a good person, as with a sacramental drama's *loa* containing the line "ser de la muerte del Justo la señal, llanto y tristeza."[80] In extreme cases, the person grieving a loved one's death might succumb to sadness and follow that person to the grave, as when Fabricio says of Juana:

> Pasó en fin a mejor vida,
> y fue la tristeza tanta
> de su padre, que en tres días
> siguió sus tiernas pisadas.
> También murió.[81]

Here a father witnesses the untimely death of his daughter and, within three days, dies too.

But vicarious sorrow was not limited to witnessing the misfortune of a familiar person who is beloved. It might also be occasioned by seeing poverty or unhappiness suffered by anyone, whether that person was known well or not. We see this possibility in a question posed by a marginal character to the Marqués: "¿Quién duda, señor Marqués, que te haya dado tristeza la desdicha y la pobreza que en esta casa ves?"[82] This empathetic form of sorrow would become worse in proportion to the degree of suffering witnessed, particularly if that suffering included hunger and a lack of warm clothes.[83] The suffering was only compounded when combined with the perils of old age: "Pobreza, y tristeza, grillos de la edad dicen que son."[84] Exhaustion of course only made a perilous situation worse.[85] Grief counsellor Stephen Levine remarks on this correlation between sorrow and advanced years: "Unattended sorrow gradually displaces the joy of youth and adds to the diminishment of trust and hope."[86]

In general, sorrow might arise at any sudden change of status or surroundings, as in "de su nuevo estado procede la tristeza que le ha dado"[87] or "La tristeza en que vivo, viendo en mi bien tan súbita mudanza."[88] One character asks the Duke rhetorically who would *not* be sad at such a sudden change in stature:

> Duque, presagios no son,
> triste estáis, tenéis razón,
> que el mudar naturaleza,
> ¿a quién no causa tristeza?
> Y más a vos, que trocado
> habéis un ilustre estado
> por esta vil rustiqueza.[89]

This nobleman who once enjoyed a rich estate now has to content himself with rustic simplicity. A person's physical surroundings are seen in these plays to be crucial to mental health, as when a character who is used to greater luxury seems surprised at not feeling more depressed: "llaneza de esta humilde casería, era cosa que podía causarme mayor tristeza."[90]

Of the worse kinds of sadness we see characters experience, we might list sorrow at being vanquished or beaten; thus Isabel asks regarding a proud gentleman, "¿Tanto pudo la tristeza de verse vencido?"[91] Then there is sorrow at being imprisoned ("de su prisión ... su pena y larga tristeza"),[92] especially without cause: "Tristeza, señor, recibo, y justo desasosiego de verme preso sin causa."[93] Anyone deprived of liberty[94] long-term would feel sorrow; this might include prisoners of war, captives, and slaves. In this gallery of the sorrowful there figures also the desolation of exile[95] – "ay Valencia, patria mía, ¡con qué tristeza aquel día de tus murallas salí!"[96] – as well as the loss of one's home to invading conquerors.[97] A fascinating example of this type of sorrow is the cry of a Muslim character: "cantar Alhambra hanina, lleno de mortal tristeza: poner Cristianos su Cruz, y sus banderas por ella."[98] Here a Muslim reports being filled with "mortal sadness" at seeing the Christians reconquer Granada's Alhambra and fly their flags over the gorgeous Islamic palace.

This mention of the clash of civilizations between Muslims and Christians leads us to a consideration of the most intense kind of sadness described in early modern Spanish drama: spiritual sorrow. Characters report being moved to sorrow by gazing at an image and describe this experience in language redolent of devotion to sacred icons, as in "el alma llena de devoción de esta imagen, que enternece su tristeza."[99] Such devotion – which the Counter-Reformation officially upheld through the Council of Trent's revalidation of the Catholic Church's stance on icons and other sacred images[100] – was intended to foster a very specific emotion, namely the sorrow of repentance. We see this passion reflected explicitly in lines such as "es fuerza ir por la Penitencia, que es tristeza, y llanto"[101] and the more detailed confession by a penitent: "me mandaron entregar el mismo arrepentimiento. Éste ahora en mi tristeza, me pone aquel fiero yugo de mi conciencia, aspereza."[102]

However, the *comedias* caution against taking penitential sorrow to extremes. For example, this speech shows remarkable theological sophistication in juxtaposing Scriptural references to sorrow in the New and Old Testaments (the epistles of Saint Paul versus King Solomon's Ecclesiastes) to instruct the audience not to indulge in extreme sadness, but instead to entrust their souls joyfully to God:

> Escribe san Pablo, que la tristeza
> por Dios nunca se prohibe
> que a penitencia endereza
> el corazón en que vive.
> Mas la del mundo, es de suerte,
> que dice que engendra muerte,

> y allá dice Salomón,
> que humilla al fuerte varón,
> y el consuelo le divierte.
> Jamás a tristezas des
> tu alma, y tu alegre vida
> nos dice el Eclesiastés,
> vuelva en sí, y el llanto impida,
> pues sabe tan bien lo que es.
> Su alma a Dios encomiende,
> que es lo que ya se pretende,
> porque el llorar es sin fruto,
> allá el mundo vista el luto,
> acá en oración se entiende.[103]

The fact that these lines were written by Lope de Vega – not, like Calderón de la Barca, considered frequently to be a deep thinker, philosopher, or theologian – shows just how pervasive biblical discourse was in early modern Spanish culture and on the *comedia* stage.

Ideally, relief for spiritual sorrow would be brought about by consolatory rituals offered by the Church in the sacrament of penance, as when the dying Baldovinos asks his squire: "O mi criado leal, aliviado has la tristeza de mi congoja mortal. ¿Tráesme acaso confesor?"[104] I have studied this play (and others like it) in greater detail in my essay "Staging Penance: Scenes of Sacramental Confession in Early Modern Spanish Drama."[105]

What ultimately causes or brings sorrow or sadness? We have spoken already of sorrow's proximate causes, but not its ultimate ones. Some characters are said to suffer from a "natural" predisposition to melancholy, as in "Amón se muere de una grave tristeza, pensión que trae la naturaleza."[106] Here we see the Galenic legacy of humoral psychology. Such a humoral imbalance was often referred to specifically as melancholy.[107] However, in this play and others we see a deliberate attempt on the part of playwrights to differentiate occasional sadness from this more persistent malady. Marjory Lange, drawing upon English Renaissance material, articulates the distinction as understood within the period quite succinctly: "Melancholy builds upon false sorrow, imagined griefs."[108]

A similar understanding of this distinction is evidenced on the Spanish stage. For instance, witness the following exchange between King David and his son Amón:

> AMÓN: Calla, necio,
>   melancolía, y tristeza
>   los Físicos dividieron,

>   en que la tristeza es
>   causa de algún mal suceso;
>   pero la melancolía
>   de natural sentimiento;
>   y así, no podré decirlo.
> DAVID: ¿De qué nace el padecerlo,
>   cuando sea así? ¿A qué mal
>   no se aplica algún remedio?
> AMÓN: Ya me aplico yo el mejor.
> DAVID: ¿Cuál es?
> AMÓN: Sentir como siento.
> DAVID: Ése no es remedio, antes
>   es dar al mal más esfuerzos.[109]

Here the son rejects his father's attempt to remedy his ailment by claiming that melancholy is his natural predisposition, and thus there is nothing he can do about it.

Other plays go even further within this medical/moral discourse[110] to distinguish among various types or categories of sadness. The following speech on the topic of "Where does sadness come from?" illustrates once again a level of sophistication in talking about emotion that we might not have anticipated from a popular playwright such as Lope, who was neither a philosopher nor a theologian:

>   ¿De qué nace la tristeza?
>   Tu amigo soy.
> CÉSAR: Gran señor,
>   yo pienso que este rigor
>   es propia naturaleza.
>   Tres suertes hay de este mal,
>   ocio, tristeza, y la mía,
>   que es una melancolía,
>   y una enfermedad mortal.
>   Es el ocio suspensión,
>   en que está el mismo sentido
>   sin moverse detenido,
>   ni tener humana acción.
>   Es la tristeza, tener
>   por qué estar triste, que un hombre
>   sabe de su mal el nombre,
>   y viénese a entristecer.
>   La fiera melancolía

> es estar triste sin causa,
>
> digo, sin la que se causa
>
> de sangre como la mía.[111]

His distinction among lethargy, sadness, and melancholy – and especially his definition of melancholy as "sadness without cause" – could almost proceed straight
out of a textbook definition of clinical depression today.

But in this, Lope was a little ahead of his time. We are pulled forcefully back
to the more typical reality for the early modern period by popular notions such
as causation of sadness by witchcraft, incantations, or spells. This in itself is
not particularly surprising; what does give us pause is the attribution of spells
or enchantments by pagans to Christians, as when an ancient Roman (and
therefore pagan) character complains: "dicen que una gran tristeza que padece,
causada es de los hechizos de Cristianos."[112] In this line penned by a Christian
author we see a tolerance for complexity, a less black-and-white world view
than we might have anticipated in an age of Inquisitorial persecution of religious difference.

More orthodox views on sadness that nevertheless respect its spiritual quality[113] are of course expressed in the *autos sacramentales*, as when Lust is said to
"stain" and sadden Purity, the mother of joy.[114] A more specific instance of this
same scenario occurs in the secular drama when the sin of incest (or at least the
sexual attraction he feels toward his mother-in-law) fills Antioco with worry
and sadness: "Antioco enamorado de su madrastra enfermó de tristeza, y de
cuidado."[115] Ultimately the sorrow sin causes is about fear of losing one's salvation, as when King Henry VIII in Calderón's *La cisma de Inglaterra* laments an
omen of the heresy into which he has fallen: "Lutero la [carta] que sobre mi
cabeza puse … ¡qué tristeza! ¡Otro prodigio, otro agüero me amenaza! Muerto
soy, Santos Cielos."[116]

Other than the disheartening prospect of losing one's salvation, what are some
other potential dangers of sorrow? Being sad makes it virtually impossible to enjoy
anything,[117] a sentiment repeated often in the *comedias* – which, we should not
forget, were written precisely for the purpose of popular enjoyment. Grief counsellor Stephen Levine reiterates, "In the throes of acute grief … [w]e can barely
taste our food or see a sunset. What used to give us pleasure now holds none. The
mirrors of our heart are draped in sackcloth."[118]

In fact, the sorrowful person is estranged from all pleasure: "desde ayer le ha
dado una tristeza, que de todo placer le tiene ajeno."[119] The sad individual is
unable to laugh, even though characters recognize that laughter would be the best
way to cheer up.[120] In fact, sorrowful people are annoyed by cheerful activities, as
we see in the admonition: "no la envía colación, fiesta y grandeza porque quien
tiene tristeza, se cansa de la alegría."[121] Here we see advice not to send a sad person

pomp and festivities – or even breakfast! – due to an awareness that sad people tire quickly of joyful things.

When taken to an extreme, sorrow produces the feeling that seeing someone else's happiness only becomes torture for the sad individual: "el alegría ajena es tormento para el triste."[122] We see characters admitting this when they are asked by companions why recent festivities did not improve their mood:

> ARIAS: Buena la noche ha estado, ¿no alegró tu tristeza tanta gala, y belleza, que junta has admirado?
> ALEJANDRO: Antes con su alegría doblé, Don Arias, la tristeza mía.[123]

Another extended exchange between Don Diego and Leonor repeats the truism that melancholy is sadness without cause or occasion and contains a deliberate rejection by Leonor of Don Diego's plan to cheer her up:

> LEONOR: Toda melancolía
>   nace sin ocasión; y así es la mía,
>   que aquella distinción naturaleza
>   dio a la melancolía, y la tristeza;
>   y para ella los medios son más sabios
>   llorar los ojos, y callar los labios.
> DON DIEGO: Otros hay.
> LEONOR: ¿Qué?
> DON DIEGO: Aliviarla,
>   y ya que no vencerla, desecharla.
>   ¿Quieres esta noche
>   salir a ver la máscara, en un coche,
>   que hace Madrid, en generosas pruebas
>   de cuánto estima las felices nuevas
>   de la mayor victoria,
>   que ha de durar eterna a la memoria
>   del tiempo, en duras las minas grabada?
> LEONOR: No, que no puede divertirme nada
>   la común alegría,
>   que antes la pena mía
>   halló para afligirme nuevos modos,
>   viéndome triste, estando alegres todos.[124]

Here he offers her the chance to go out that evening in a horse-drawn carriage to see the masque being performed in Madrid to celebrate Spain's recent military victory. She politely refuses his offer, sure that the "common joy" will only make her feel worse.

In fact, sad people are often so thoroughly enmired in their sadness that they become convinced that all of nature participates in their gloom. Marjory Lange confirms that this is the case likewise in English Renaissance poetry, especially with reference to tears:

> Creating resemblances between water in nature – rivers, rain, and the like – and poets' tears is a significant, much-exploited development of the miscellaneous lyric, with its origins reaching back to antiquity. The Renaissance poet is particularly sensitive in identifying Earth's display of storms, floods and tides as a mirror of his grief.[125]

One such instance of the pathetic fallacy occurs in Spanish drama in a characterization of the lily flower as feeling sad.[126]

Sorrow produces oblivion in that sad characters tend to forget everything else ("el mar de la tristeza, que tanto cubre de olvido").[127] The Old Testament heroine Esther refers to this aspect of sorrow, likening the experience to being engulfed in a sea:

> El ver que me voy quedando sola
> entre enemigos de mi pueblo Hebreo,
> que el mar de mi tristeza, de ola en ola,
> me lleva al golfo en que morir me veo.[128]

She does not in fact die of this sadness; but in the moment, she feels like she will. According to medical opinion of the time, it was possible to die suddenly from extreme sadness: "muchos omes mueren subitamente de gran duelo," warns Juan de Aviñón in *Sevillana medicina* (1545).[129]

Sorrow also diverts the memory, as when Lisardo asks Enrico: "¿qué pena, o melancolía / os divierte la memoria?"[130] The one thing that cannot be forgotten by the sad person is sorrow's cause: "No puede tristeza tanta cubrirse jamás de olvido."[131] Memory can be a tricky thing, though, because often it is precisely the remembrance of some former good – now lost – that causes a person to become sad. We see this scenario in the lament, "La causa de mi tristeza en tus brazos fue memoria, sólo de perder la gloria."[132] A similar reaction can occur when visiting one's former home: "Haberme criado aquí, causa esta tristeza en mí y por eso voy llorando."[133] In these cases, most often characters do not wish to forget; instead they choose to nurse their grief, as in the following rant by Circe:

> Quien tiene de qué quejarse,
> ¡o cuánto en quejarse yerra[!],
> que la justicia del llanto
> hace apacibles las penas.
> Yo así mi tristeza quiero,
> que tampoco no me deba,
> que en repetirla procure
> hacer menor mi tristeza.
> Dejadme sola.[134]

This portrayal is similar to the sympathetic characterization of Circe in the recent classicizing novel by Madeline Miller.[135]

The real problem with sorrow is that it knows no limits: "no guarda la tristeza término cortesano."[136] A sad disposition turns so habitual that soon it becomes second nature.[137] This intuition on the part of early modern dramatists is confirmed by recent clinical findings that if it goes untreated for too long, so-called situational depression might become permanent and morph into clinical depression:

> [P]ersons who are suffering their first major depression are more likely to have recently undergone a significant stressor. Unfortunately, stressors (and the stress response) are implicated only in the first few episodes of depression. In the fourth depression or so, depression appears to take on a rhythm all its own, recurring no matter what is going on in the person's life. It has become "hard wired."[138]

Characters on stage express this worry quite directly: "Vamos, que quiero alegrarme, que si dura esta tristeza vendrá a ser naturaleza, y peligrosa a matarme."[139] Indeed, one character named Isabel exhorts her friend Leonor not to let this happen (she thus manifests an awareness of the possibility that it might):

> Leonor, aunque tu tristeza
> tanto te aflija enemiga,
> que de continua fatiga
> se ha hecho ya naturaleza,
> templa el tirano, sangriento
> influjo de su rigor,
> y aprenda de mi dolor
> a desechar el tormento.[140]

Even though she describes her friend's sadness as having already become second nature due to continuous fatigue, she still expresses hope that Leonor can moderate the "tyrannical, bloody influx of its rigour" and learn from Isabel's own example to exorcize the cause of her torment.

Characters such as Isabel show an awareness that sorrow destroys a person's health. It does this by upsetting the body's natural equilibrium: "Destemplan melancolías la salud, enfermo estás."[141] It withers or dries out the brain[142] (we might think here of Cervantes's famous description of the chivalrous madman Don Quijote: "se le secó el celebro").[143] In terms of specific physical symptoms, sorrow causes headache[144] and fever.[145] Sorrow weighs upon the heart. Grief counsellor Stephen Levine confirms: "Unresolved grief is like a low-grade fever. It flows in peaks and valleys. Sometimes it spikes into almost overwhelmingly afflictive emotions; at other times it lies almost dormant, nearly comatose, just beneath the surface, until a shadow crosses the heart and releases it."[146] In a similar description by a different author, "Grief is felt, sensed in the viscera of our bellies, the inner walls of our chests, the curve of our shoulders, the heaviness in our thighs. Grief is registered in our sinews and muscles. It feels labored, as though a great weight has settled on our chest or a heaviness has entered our bones."[147]

In another scene that bears comparison with *Don Quijote*, one stage character asks another the cause of his sadness and receives the reply that the emotion stemmed from something he read in a book:

CRISANTO: Yo tengo una gran tristeza,
    y ésta en mi imaginación
    carga tanto el corazón,
    que es en mi naturaleza.
CARPOFORO: ¿De qué esa tristeza pudo
    ocasionarse?
CRISANTO: Yo he sido
    inclinado a haber leído,
    y algunas cosas que dudo,
    me ponen en confusión
    de imaginar si es así
    lo que leí.[148]

In an example that rings true for most academics, this bookworm needs to take his nose out of his book.

In addition to weighing down the heart, sorrow does not allow the heart to breathe freely: "la extrañeza de una pena, una tristeza, no permita al corazón desahogos."[149] Sorrow blinds the eyes ("cegóme tristeza tanta")[150] and leads to insomnia ("que duermo mal a la noche, y que no tengo alegría").[151]

Alternatively – and this once again anticipates the textbook description of clinical depression – sorrow can cause one to sleep too much, as in the recommendation, "Dejadla, que siempre el sueño es de la tristeza dueño."[152] The result is a nifty little rhyme.

Sometimes sleep comes from exhaustion after a great sorrow has passed. This slumber is described as a "sweet" relief, a blessing, and a gift.[153] Once again in accordance with the clinical framework for depressive illness, sadness can also cause a lack of appetite.[154] We see this when Don Félix remonstrates with Teodor: "Come, por Dios, y deja la tristeza."[155] A fuller picture emerges from the following realization by Ginebra of what has gone wrong with her daughter Feliciana, whom she has been attempting to diagnose through a meticulous inventory of her symptoms:

> ¿Era aquella, Feliciana,
> la tristeza de estos días?
> [¿]El hallarte en los desvanes,
> suspirando, y escribiendo,
> y en la Iglesia, y calle, haciendo
> gestos, señas y ademanes?
> [¿]Por esto soñando hablabas,
> cintas y empresas traías,
> comiendo te suspendías,
> y en la cama vueltas dabas?[156]

It turns out that unbeknownst to her mother, Feliciana has secretly loved Torcato without her mother's blessing, and fears her reaction.

As we see from the above-quoted lines, a state of sorrow is difficult to hide from the people closest to us, who are likely to notice concrete changes in our behaviour or aspect. For example, sorrow can cause a person to neglect his or her physical appearance: "dejada del aliño, y la belleza, que fuera de la tristeza vives de ti descuidada."[157] In certain extreme cases, as we have seen, this neglect may extend to not attending to personal hygiene: "el no lavar el rostro bello, muy justa es la tristeza, y el disgusto, el no tocarse, ni peinar cabello."[158] Sorrow makes change more difficult because it reduces resilience, adaptability, and the capacity to stay flexible. One character shows an awareness of this aspect of sorrow with the rhetorical question, "¿Quién duda, que la tristeza con cualquier novedad más que se alivia, se aumenta?"[159]

At its peak potency, sorrow can lead to insanity[160] and even delirium.[161] Sorrow can produce violence ("intricado camino, que hay del llanto a la violencia")[162] or even death.[163] Characters express fear of this possibility[164] and assure one another that such a thing is possible: "no dudes que le mate la tristeza, invisible cuchillo a un desdichado."[165] Here sadness becomes an "invisible knife" stabbing the unfortunate person who falls victim to its treachery.

In fact, capitalizing (as they do) upon such extreme cases,[166] the *comedias* self-consciously exploit the potential for bizarre outcomes such as a character dying from sorrow:

> Desde el punto que Duarte
> oyó tan trágicas nuevas,
> de una tristeza cubrió
> el corazón, de manera
> que pasando a ser letargo
> la melancolía primera,
> desmintió, muriendo, a cuantos
> dicen, que no matan penas.[167]

Here Duarte's reported death allegedly provides "proof" that it is indeed possible to die from sadness.

Sorrow makes one self-centred or *ensimismado* (witness the accusation "a tu tristeza rendido vives solamente en ti")[168] to the point where even suicide is contemplated as a distinct possibility. One character menaces another with this likelihood if he does not provide the help the other requests: "si me desamparáis, según mi tristeza es fuerte, luego me daré la muerte."[169]

If such a fate is to be avoided, then some remedy for sorrow must be found. But are there any? Some dramatic characters assert bleakly that sorrow cannot be controlled,[170] even by a king.[171] One of them offers a curiously medicalized explanation for this:

> Bien sabéis la diferencia
> que hay de la melancolía
> a la tristeza; la mía
> tiene esa misma licencia.
> Que como es enfermedad,
> que nace de algún humor,
> manda en mí con más rigor,
> que mi propia voluntad.[172]

Here the familiar discourse of the humours provides a "way out" of having to exercise free will. Philosopher Jamie Lindemann Nelson expresses a similar perspective on sadness: "skepticism about whether it is appropriate to hold anyone accountable for her sadness as such, or for its absence or its specific character, suggests that sadness is not so much something you do, but rather something that happens to you."[173] This "passive" interpretation of sadness accords well with the prevalent early modern term used to designate the emotions, i.e., *passions*.

This "active vs. passive" debate as applied to emotions is definitely one instance where early modern English (Protestant) versus Spanish (Catholic) playwrights diverge. In the English Renaissance,

[f]uneral sermons were condemned … for their perceived connections with Catholicism (with the dangers of idolatry inherent in praising the dead) … Grief came to be perceived as entirely controllable by an effort of will – aided by faith – so consolation was largely a process of reminding the bereaved of their grounds for faith … [M]ourners should restrict grieving, since grief impedes healing.[174]

This was not so uniformly or dogmatically the case in Catholic Spain. However, although many Spanish characters speak on stage about the difficulty of conquering sorrow,[175] others seem to hold out the possibility – in agreement with their English counterparts – that sadness can be tempered or moderated.[176] They seem to answer what philosopher Anna Gotlib calls "the uncomfortable, yet morally vital, question: Are there limits to how, when, and to what extent one ought to be sad?"[177]

Some claim that sadness can be alleviated,[178] or even – in the best-case scenario – banished into exile where it will no longer be able to disturb the erstwhile sufferer.[179] Another option presented is to put the brakes on sadness[180] or simply to leave sorrow behind as one moves on.[181] Various therapeutic measures for sorrow are explored in the *comedias*, which accords with the popular entertainment aspect of this genre (the *comedia* itself might be seen as a form of therapy for the sorrowful). These possible therapies include things like taking a walk[182] to enjoy nature,[183] especially on the beach;[184] smelling sweet flowers;[185] going on a hunting expedition;[186] or even taking a nap.[187]

It is interesting to see here how early modern intuitions preceded postmodern scientific experiments. Psychologist Sherry Cormier notes, "being in nature promotes well-being: lowering blood pressure, increasing cancer-fighting cells, assisting with attention deficit symptoms, and easing depression and anxiety … [W]alking in nature quiets the brain and reduces ruminations and brooding."[188] Other pleasant diversions mentioned as antidotes to sadness in these plays include trout fishing or participating in knightly tournaments or jousts:

Podrás pescar con redaya
las truchas de este río,
o en cosas de mayor brío
tener la tristeza a raya.
Haz una justa, un torneo,
dente veinte mil ducados,
y otros veinte, estos gastados.[189]

We hear characters telling each other to try to "throw off" or "leave" their sadness behind ("trata de desechar esa tristeza"; "Deja la vana tristeza")[190] and not to "give way" to sorrow,[191] which implies they can exert some measure of control over it.

"Giving way" to sorrow was thought to occur partly through idleness, as I have explained more fully in my chapter on sloth in *Sins of the Fathers: Moral Economies in Early Modern Spain*.[192] We find evidence of this belief in the following exchange:

> ANTONIA: Traigo en la fantasía
> 　　una oscura Babilonia.
> 　　Y el ocio suele causar
> 　　melancolía y tormento.
> DOÑA BEATRIZ: Es dar al entendimiento
> 　　para tristeza lugar.[193]

Instead of wallowing in their sadness through idleness, characters are advised to distract their attention in another direction: "¡Extraña melancolía! Pues procure vuestra Alteza divertir esa tristeza."[194] One such diversion might involve the flatteries of being courted:

> Para remedio escogí
> decir a Fátima amores,
> para que saliesen colores,
> donde faltar las vi.
> Con este sobresalto
> tan extraño en su vergüenza
> el rostro de color falto,
> a cobrar color comienza,
> que de claveles esmalto.
> Que en esta melancolía
> un súbito desatino,
> remueve la fantasía,
> que bien Galeno divino
> este entimema decía.
> Que bien le siguió Platón,
> y Aristóteles también.[195]

These lines by Lope de Vega citing Galen, Plato, and Aristotle on melancholy once again show a more detailed knowledge of classical psychological theories than we might have expected from this popular playwright.

In lines that may hit a little closer to home for dramatists who were themselves "book men," some characters urge one another to avoid sadness by not being so nerdy and bookish:

> Causa tus estudios son,
> César, de tu gran tristeza.
> No escribas más, dale Atilio
> mis papeles, tu virtud
> estima ya tu salud,
> quiero que se ponga auxilio.[196]

Classical literature is mentioned as particularly dangerous for making a sad person worse.[197]

Instead of reading sad stories, stage characters advise one another to listen to music, sometimes offering to play an instrument or call a musician to perform for the benefit of the sad individual.[198] Alternatively, they might ask one another to sing[199] (which of course became the perfect excuse to work a little more music into the natural flow of a performance). Grief counsellor Stephen Levine strongly supports this form of therapy: "Singing opens other areas of the brain; it takes us to other hemispheres. Singing reinforces the spirit and enhances the quality of consciousness we call the heart."[200] There are times, however, when music only makes things worse, perhaps due to the jarring contrast between the "sweetness" of the song and the perceived bitterness of the person's sad situation.[201]

Sorrow in early modern Spain was very much believed to be contagious, as we see from the line "tu tristeza me deja receloso, quisiera que mostraras regocijo."[202] Conscious of this, many characters try to avoid contagion (as when Leonor begins a speech to Don Diego: "Por no darte pesar con mi tristeza").[203] They try to alleviate each other's suffering,[204] but they also attempt to evaluate whether each other's sorrow is appropriate or not. We see this assessment process in Flora's pronouncement "No digo, que tu tristeza no es justa"[205] and in the following speech by Claricia:

> Cese la injusta tristeza,
> alzad los ojos, alzadlos,
> que es principio de bajeza,
> los Caballeros, Reinaldos,
> como vos, mostrar flaqueza.[206]

Here Claricia exhorts Reinaldos to "cease" his "unjust" sadness.

Still other characters seek a similar evaluation by submitting their cases to each other's judgment: "Mirad, señor, si es justa mi tristeza; mirad si siento mi desdicha en vano."[207] I have studied similar instances in the "asking for advice" chapter of *Conscience on Stage: The* Comedia *as Casuistry in Early Modern Spain*.[208] The outcome of this arbitration is not always favourable; for instance, some characters judge each other's sorrow to be "excessive" ("[s]u excesivo dolor, ansia y tristeza").[209]

When sorrow is considered appropriate, however, it moves others to compassion, as when one character says of another that the person is "de su tristeza movida."[210] A scenario of empathy plays out in the theatre – as in some other genres of the period, such as the pastoral novel – when characters share one another's sorrows by recounting their woes.[211] As psychotherapist Alexander Lowen notes, "[t]he sharing of sorrow halves its pain."[212] Philosopher Anna Gotlib agrees:

[T]he horror, the permanent scarring, of some experiences might fall beyond our abilities to communicate – and yet … in our attempts at telling, we might nevertheless find some measure of endurance and meaning from the possibility of being heard, and seen, in our sorrow.[213]

Thus on the early modern stage, Estela encourages Aurora:

[D]escansa, pues, tu tristeza
conmigo que los pesares,
si se repiten, y cuentan,
pasan plaza de favores.[214]

Most of the *comedias* seem to offer hope that the sorrowful person can be consoled, as in "podrás venir con tus hijos a consolar la mayor tristeza y soledad que ha tenido corazón humano."[215] Here even the worst sorrow and solitude ever experienced by a human heart is said to be amenable to comfort. This act of consolation would most often be performed by a loyal friend,[216] although a servant might also be commanded to fulfil this important function:

FLORA: ¿Qué me manda vuestra Alteza?
FELISARDA: Que consueles mi tristeza.
FLORA: ¿Cómo, si en el alma está?[217]

Here the servant anticipates that all her efforts might not be enough to console her mistress. The potential failure of consolatory efforts is likewise reflected in the line, "Por más que solicitéis aliviar de mi tristeza la causa, mal la extrañeza de tanta pena podréis."[218] Here the cause of sorrow is perceived to be so "strange" that no attempts at consolation will alleviate it.

Even the best attempts at consolation could also backfire, as when Joachim says to his sons:

Hijos, vosotros sois mozos,
bien os está el alegría,
que yo la tristeza escojo
para mi cansada edad,
que es el alivio que tomo;
dejadme solo un momento,
que renováis mis enojos,
con decirme que me alegre.[219]

Here the old man complains that his sons' efforts to cheer him up produce more annoyance than beneficial effect. Humorously, the *comedias* also contain advice for what sort of consolatory effort is likely to be successful in each case, e.g., "Alabanzas en mujeres, ¿qué tristeza las resiste?"[220] Here women are misogynistically depicted as so vain that praise or flattery will always serve to lift their spirits.

One form of consolatory discourse is categorically prohibited in these plays: contradiction. This prohibition stemmed from the belief that contradicting a sad person led only to more sorrow; as the sad widow Ruth says to her mother-in-law Naomi: "Cuanto más me contradices, aumentas más mi tristeza."[221] The stubborn Ruth has made up her mind to leave her native Moab to follow Naomi back to her former home among the Israelites, and she warns that no one is going to be able to talk her out of it.

Instead of using words to console each other, sometimes *comedia* characters will instead offer a gift: "se iguala de ver una gala nueva, porque no hay tristeza a prueba del mosquete de una gala."[222] Here a new outfit or dress is said to be as effective as a musket (i.e., gun) at blowing sadness away. Money also proves remarkably effective at making sorrow flee: "El Oro aplacar hace la fiereza. Huye de él la tristeza."[223]

Even if there is no money to be had, good wishes still count for something:

A lo menos me debéis
que mil que tuviera os diera,
para que se disminuyera
la tristeza que tenéis.[224]

Here a character declares that he would give his friend 1,000 coins (denomination not specified) to cheer him up if only he had that kind of cash.

More conventionally, sympathy is expressed with the formulaic "pésame mucho," a phrase still often heard at Hispanic funerals around the world. Over time the phrase has been substantivized grammatically into a noun, as in "te envío el pésame, que con igual tristeza me han dado mis vasallos"[225] and "El Reino todo de tristeza lleno, a vuestra señoría envía el pésame."[226]

Similar to sympathy – but more effective – is empathy, which might be defined as accompanying someone in sadness: "le acompaño en la tristeza."[227] Empathy is most likely to be generated by perceived similarity to one's own situation: "las congojas que paso, la semejanza del caso ocasiona mi tristeza."[228] Empathy is said to be a mirror in which one character reflects another's pain:

> Si estáis triste, en la tristeza
> se entretendrá el alma mía,
> que ya a imitaros empieza,
> si alegre, hará mi alegría
> alarde de esa belleza.
> Seré, en fin, espejo fiel,
> que en todas ocasiones,
> sin colores, ni pincel,
> retrate hasta las acciones
> vuestras, mirándoos en él.[229]

Here one character provides a "faithful mirror" for the other's soul affliction.

Not surprisingly, characters ask each other for empathy, pleading with them to bear witness to their suffering so that they do not have to face it alone. This is the case when the Admiral implores Don Félix:

> Tristezas, don Félix, son,
> perdonad, que estoy de suerte,
> que todo me da la muerte
> todo pienso que es traición.
> No os espante mi aspereza,
> pues sois de mi mal testigo;
> sufrid, sufrid a un amigo
> efectos de una tristeza.[230]

He calls on his friend to bear witness to his pain and also to suffer it with him.

Sometimes bold characters even demand empathy from each other for themselves: "¿si os mueve ajena tristeza, cómo no sentís la mía?"[231] Here one character chastises another for being moved by someone else's sorrow, but not his own (which is perceived to hit closer to home). Others seem to reproach themselves for failing to commiserate with their loved ones: "¿Vos con tanta tristeza, y yo no muero? Poco siente quien os ama."[232] A truly empathetic person might choose to visit a friend in need (as in "Yo habiendo ahora sabido la tristeza que ha tenido Laura, me trujo mi amor a verla"),[233] but sometimes the best consolation is simply to listen sympathetically in silence ("Yo nada digo, porque temo aumentar tu tristeza").[234] Grief counsellor Stephen Levine extols silence's benefits:

> In silence, time and space are joined. Some moments seem longer than ever; others seem to have passed in a quite unaccustomed flash. We come to know ourselves and the world around us at a whole new level. All the truths are welcomed and invited into the heart of silence. We sit with the saints and the suicidal in the sacred cave of the heart, enveloped in the silence from which all that heals is born.[235]

What are some early modern Spanish emotion rules or scripts associated with sorrow? Renaissance sorrow was often hidden, perhaps in response to social constraints, as when Cenobia confesses, "Una oculta tristeza el corazón me oprime."[236] Servants were in general not supposed to show sorrow in front of their masters.[237] However, in certain circumstances sorrow might be a worthy response by a servant to seeing his master offended:

> También la tristeza es
> noble, y digno pensamiento
> de un leal que ve ofendido
> su señor.[238]

Leaders were not supposed to show sorrow in front of their subjects, as when a ruler is told, "el Reino también se cansa de verte en tanta tristeza."[239] The same held true for army captains, who were not to show sorrow in front of their soldiers: "Mucho ofende, señor, vuestra tristeza a todo vuestro ejército."[240] In this often too painfully apparent struggle between the socially acceptable facade and the awkward reality, characters urge one another to stop feeling sorrowful ("Deja aquella congoja, esa tristeza")[241] and challenge each other not to let themselves be overcome with emotion ("¿Tanto de una tristeza te dejas vencer?").[242] They command each other at least to put on a brave face ("Alza el rostro, que no es justo que muestres tanta tristeza"),[243] or else they might be accused of underestimating the value of their lives: "No estimes tu vida en poco, que así animas la tristeza."[244] But sometimes, on rare occasions, they give each other permission to show sorrow, as when Gonzalo Bustos says to his master: "No es falta de corazón mostrar, señor, tal tristeza, ni se nota a fortaleza el no sentir la pasión."[245] Modern-day translation: real men do cry. We even hear characters claim some potential advantages for sorrow, such as this emotion's being propitious for study: "es madre del estudio la tristeza."[246] Thus wise men are thought to be saddest, "los sabios son los de mayor tristeza,"[247] for they have studied the work of ancient philosophers (and amassed enough of their own life experience) to know that suffering and sorrow have been the fate of mankind since at least the curse of Original Sin placed upon Adam and Eve.

Douglas Abrams describes some possible advantages to sorrow:

New studies conducted by psychology researcher Joseph Forgas show that mild sadness can actually have a number of benefits that could reflect its value. In his experiments, people who were in a sad mood had better judgment and memory, and were more motivated, more sensitive to social norms, and more generous than the happier control group. People who are in a so-called negative state of sadness were more discerning about their situation, better able to remember details, and more motivated to change their situation. What is particularly interesting is that brief sadness might generate more empathy or generosity. Participants in the study played a game, part of which involved deciding how much money to give themselves and how much to give others. The sad participants gave significantly more to the other participants. While depression certainly collapses our circle of concern inward, the periodic feeling of sadness might widen it. Forgas concluded that sadness may have some benefit in our lives, which may be why people are drawn to music, art, and literature that makes them feel sad ... Sadness is in many ways the emotion that causes us to reach out to one another in support and solidarity.[248]

Self-styled "scientist of bereavement" George Bonanno confirms these impressions:

Sadness turns our attention inward so that we can take stock and adjust. When people are made to feel temporarily sad ... they become more detail-oriented ... People made to feel sad are also more accurate in the way they view their own abilities and performance and are also more thoughtful and less biased in their perceptions of other people ... [S]ad people show greater resistance to stereotypes when they make judgments about others ... [S]adness helps us focus and promotes deeper and more effective reflection.[249]

Indeed, in early modern terms, the consequence of sin's curse is that all joy ends in sorrow: "Toda mortal alegría viene a parar en tristeza."[250] Sorrow will always return periodically to afflict the human race.[251] This cyclical pattern conforms to Richard Solomon's opponent-process theory of emotion, in which any intense emotional state will be followed sequentially by its opposite.[252] Psychologist Sherry Cormier applies this model to grief specifically:

[H]ealing from grief is cyclical rather than linear. Grief ebbs and flows, much like the tide of an ocean that comes in and goes out. At times, the waves of grief are small and contained, but on other occasions they are large and often overwhelming but not necessarily crippling.[253]

By virtue of the fact that it is cyclical, sorrow will always serve as a precursor to joy: "Víspera de la alegría llamó un cuerdo a la tristeza."[254] We hear the voices of a few lucky characters such as Rogerio, who has recovered from past sadness: "Ya yo, señor, estoy bueno, y mi tristeza pasada, en contento convertida."[255]

Getting to that place, however, can feel like cramping while swimming a long distance or – even worse – like wading through quicksand: "el ausencia porfía, ¿quién vencerá su aspereza? Nadando va mi tristeza, por llegar a su alegría."[256] When it finally comes, though, the joy that comes out of sorrow is experienced as profound contentment: "podremos decir que es fruto de la tristeza el contento."[257] Prior sorrow only makes joy – when it does finally come – more intense: "no mereció tanta alegría quien antes no pasó tanta tristeza."[258] It is to this joy that we shall now turn.

7

Ode to Joy

Joy thou beauteous godly-lightning / Daughter of Elysium …[1]

In what gardens do joys grow?[2]

Bodies uncloth'd must be, / To taste whole joys.[3]

Joy is the gas in the car of life.[4]

Synonyms for joy in early modern Spanish drama include contentment, pleasure, liking, celebration, or solace. The music sung by the chorus in Calderón's sacramental play *El jardín de Falerina* beckons to Man: "Ven, Hombre, ven, donde todo es contento, alegría, agrado, festejo, solaz y placer."[5] Joy's characteristics include overflowing that cannot be contained, as in "no cabe en mí la alegría"[6] or "No sé dónde mi alegría puede caber en mi pecho."[7] Joy makes one's head explode with light.[8] It bathes one in pleasure: "en placer nos bañamos de esa divina alegría."[9] Joy is contagious, as we see in Lope de Vega's *El amigo hasta la muerte*, where the "friend to the death" of the play's title is the friend who shares in one's joys, "el que en los tiempos alegres se alegra con mi alegría"[10] – a tautology that is also a tongue-twister. As Mary Moschella reminds us, joy must be shared:

> Joy often arises in deep interpersonal connections and the experiences of loving and being loved. It may also arise in communities of resistance to evil or injustice. It is something that is deeper for being shared … Joy is rather more like the loaves and the fishes: when offered up and shared, it tends to multiply.[11]

"A cuantos veo quisiera repartir mi alegría,"[12] declares one character. In this passional arithmetic, pleasure doubles when joy is spread around.[13]

The colour of joy is almost universally red: "Colorado, que es señal de mi alegría."[14] It is sometimes contrasted with the green of hope.[15] If joy is feigned or "borrowed," it can still be signified by the red, for example, of a rose in bloom.[16] In fact, joy is often reflected in flowers, as in the parallelism "en los cristales bullicio, en las flores alegría, en los vientos suavidad, en las hojas armonía."[17] Sometimes trees cause joy as well, specifically when they are viewed as being "indicators of love."[18] In fact, entire gardens can be joyful, as in "la verde, hermosa alegría de este florido jardín."[19] The sounds of joy include babbling brooks[20] and birds singing,[21] specifically nightingales.[22] Marianne Meye Thompson reminds us that the characterization of nature as joyful stems directly from the Old Testament, as she makes reference to

> those passages where the natural creation – the sun, the pastures, and meadows – act or sing with joy (Pss. 19:5, 65:12–13). In response to the Creator or sovereign God, the natural world responds in joy … The trees "sing for joy" in the presence of the Lord who judges the earth.[23]

The season of joy is typically springtime[24] or perhaps summer,[25] with late-blooming flowers causing special joy because they seem an unexpected bonus: "flor tardía al dueño del jardín causa alegría."[26] Jürgen Moltmann relates the seasonality of joy to the rhythms of the Church's liturgical year:

> The Easter rejoicing embraces the whole groaning creation. Easter jubilation is also the joy of the earth as indicated in the Psalms of the Old Testament. Therefore we celebrate Easter in springtime, the European springtime, as a sign for the final spring of the new, eternal creation of all things.[27]

Another constellation of imagery for joy involves a golden light or aura.[28] This light's source is typically the sun or sunshine, as in "¿Cómo no sale el Sol de la alegría … ?"[29] or "os mostráis Sol de Polonia, y llenáis de resplandor y alegría todos esos Horizontes con tan divino arrebol."[30] For psychotherapist Alexander Lowen,

> our Sun … is the celestial flame, the spinning sphere whose rays make the earth fertile. When it shines, it lights up and warms the earth, setting in motion the dance of life. For many creatures waking to a bright, sunny day fills them with joy.[31]

Joy is the warmth of a rosy sunrise,[32] bathing the world in light,[33] which seems somehow uniquely appropriate to the atmosphere of the pastoral world.[34]

Joy is not exclusively experienced at daybreak, however; it can also make its presence felt at sunset[35] or even when the stars come out.[36] The pathetic fallacy might seem to be a danger here in certain passages that sound almost pantheistic in outlook, as when Timbreo exclaims to Rut (Ruth): "Todo muestra alegría, la fuente, el monte, el prado, los árboles, las aves, y los peces."[37] As Adam Potkay observes, "Joy breaks down the boundaries that separate self and other, humanity and nature. It bestows a glorious we-mode upon the earth."[38]

In a different play, Bato tries to cheer up the patriarch Ioachín (the Virgin Mary's father) with a lyrical hymn to the beauty of nature all around him:

Ea señor amoroso,
señor bueno, señor santo,
señor que en nobleza os pongo
al igual de aquellos Reyes,
que del soberano tronco
de Jesé tienen principio,
y de aquel divino Apolo,
que con el harpa a Saúl
sacó del pecho al demonio,
dad a este campo alegría,
y a vuestros pastores gozo,
volved los ojos a ver,
montes, prados y rastrojos,
cabañas, dehesas, fuentes,
huertas, viñas, pagos, pozos,
todo os ofrece sus frutos,
los montes altos, copiosos,
robustos robles, y encinas,
castaños, y sicomoros,
nogales, abetos, pinos,
jaras, enebros, madroños,
nísperos, y cornicabras,
alcornoques, murtas, ornos,
palmas, tejos, azebuches,
laureles, y zinamomos.
Los prados, hierbas, y flores,
tomillos, mastranzos, olmos,
narcisos, violetas, trebol,
lirios azules, y rojos,
las huertas, frutas famosas,
por el Junio caluroso,
la manzana envuelta en sangre,
y por otra parte en oro,
el rojo trigo las eras,
por la mitad del Agosto,
las blancas, y negras uvas,
a la entrada del Otoño,
las viñas que en anchas cubas,
rebose cociendo el mosto,

> mirad que os cantan las aves,
> los más celebrados tonos,
> que vio la solfa del mundo,
> des[pués] que Jubal famoso,
> puso a la cítara cuerdas,
> mano al órgano sonoro,
> y del martillo tomaron
> las voces estilo y modo,
> ea, señor, alegráos.[39]

The apparently endless rhetorical figure of *amplificatio* in this speech could almost be said to comprise an inventory of joy.

So much for joy in nature. How is joy expressed in people? On happy faces,[40] especially the eyes, as in "Mi alegría puedes mirar en mis ojos."[41] As Golden Age lexicographer Sebastián de Covarrubias explains, quoting St. Thomas Aquinas: "*laetitia* is when the soul is moved in such a way that it is forced out to the exterior and is clearly conspicuous in the face."[42] Theologian Jürgen Moltmann relates the joy upon faces to nothing less than the countenance of God: "In the Old Testament it is God's turning towards his people and his shining countenance that provokes joy."[43] In Juan Bautista Diamante's *Más encanto es la hermosura*, likewise, choruses of nymphs are said to be approaching with "sweet, festive signs" of joy on their faces.[44] Joy is thought to be written in the eyes[45] or even on the "paper" of the face.[46] It is said to be translated there from the heart[47] or the soul.[48]

Joy warms the heart so that it becomes tender, as in "Dadme, señora, esas plantas, que de alegría de veros, el corazón se enternece."[49] Paradoxically, Joy can produce tears as well.[50] For example, his mother Mary exclaims to the adolescent Jesus after finding him in the Temple at Jerusalem: "Tierna lloro, no de pesar, de alegría: ¡qué efecto tan milagroso!"[51] Sometimes joyful tears are bounteous enough to water the plants on the ground.[52] Enrique explains the difference between sad tears and happy ones:

> Natural es la razón,
> que en un mal acreditado,
> viéndose el pecho apretado,
> las expele el corazón:
> mas si de alegría son,
> como está el alma espaciosa,
> por todas partes rebosa
> las lágrimas en despojos,
> y así se sale a los ojos,
> la que fue perla a ser rosa.[53]

In this florid image, teardrops become pearls, which then morph into roses – perhaps representing the rosy cheeks of the joyful person. Tears bring catharsis, an Aristotelian dramatic concept[54] referenced obliquely in Calderón's *Céfalo y Pocris*.[55] Paradoxically, tears are also said to constitute the laughter of the eyes: "lágrimas de alegría son la risa de los ojos."[56]

How is joy expressed to others? Gaily coloured clothes reflect joy, as in the lilting description, "De alegría, y galas llenos, cual no se ha visto jamás, Caballeros."[57] One father on stage commands his daughter to dress joyfully.[58] If there is a perceived disconnect between a person's outward appearance and his inner state of mind, that disjunction is commented upon by other characters.[59] This might happen, for instance, during decreed periods of mourning when sumptuary laws prohibited the donning of lavish adornments.

Another way people could express joy to each other was by the (to this day) pervasive and culturally sanctioned practice of embrace, as when one character declares to another, "vengo hoy a transformar tu tristeza en abrazos y alegría."[60] Joy provides the occasion for effusive displays of affection such as kisses,[61] or even – in a custom less likely to be practised now (!) – the kissing of a perceived-to-be-socially-"superior" person's feet 1,000 times.[62] Joy provides cause for celebration[63] and congratulation,[64] especially (in a theatrical setting) by a group; witness the line spoken by a chorus: "Todos de nuestra alegría te damos el parabién."[65] A female character issues this invitation for female friends to join in a congratulatory dance: "amigas, cantadme mil parabienes, bailemos, que el alegría aquestos efectos causa; todos celebren mi dicha."[66] If no one else is around, however, dramatic characters see no problem with congratulating themselves; for example, "pues a mí mismo me doy parabién de mi alegría."[67]

What change(s) does joy effect? Joy is said to be a remedy for affliction, in a discourse invoking specifically medical language.[68] Joy provides a much-sought-after port in the storm.[69] Joy makes one forget sorrows, as in "vamos con una alegría a olvidar muchos pesares."[70] Indeed, joy is celebrated even more after sadness – "tras una grande pena luce más el alegría"[71] – perhaps because then it is not taken for granted. In this vein, we find traces in these plays of stints when the theatres were shut down by government decree for periods of public mourning, especially after a royal death. This is the case when Diana refers to "la alegría de las fiestas, / que estuvieron algún tiempo, / si no quitadas, suspensas."[72] From the playwrights' perspective, this soul-crushing paucity was also bad for business.

How is joy felt by the person experiencing it? Joy can come suddenly ("a mí de veros me ha dado una súbita alegría");[73] in fact, Adam Potkay theorizes that the surprise aspect of joy is central to its functioning:

The present or approaching good in which the mind most typically delights is a union or fulfillment that is not in our power to effect. It comes to us, and it tends to come as a surprise … The surprise of joy always signals some loss of agency.[74]

But we are reminded in the plays that sudden, excessive, or extreme joy can be hazardous to health: "como el pesar, también suele matar la alegría."[75] A person might lose consciousness or fall into a swoon, as in "temor de que el alegría no me cause algún desmayo."[76] A person might even die from the shock of too extreme a joy coming on too quickly.[77] By way of contrast, eighteenth-century poet Mary Robinson's Sappho cherishes "the pleasing torture of excessive joy."[78] Mary Clark Moschella describes the experience of joy as by definition very intense:

> The experience of joy is something intensely felt, perceived as an ancient memory bubbling up from deep inside even while it also feels given, from some great beyond, an experience so unexpected and profound that one can only try to take it in.[79]

The solution to joy's peril is to slow down and space it out, measuring out pleasure just a little bit at a time, as when one character commands another, "Tente, demos esta alegría más poco a poco al alma."[80] Alternatively, there might be an effort to "rein in" joyous impulses. This is the sentiment expressed by Rodrigo when he asks rhetorically:

> En tanto bien, pensamiento,
> ¿qué resta que desear,
> sino sólo refrenar
> los impulsos del contento?
> Que según del alma mía
> la capacidad excede,
> como la tristeza, puede
> matar también la alegría.[81]

Apparently, one can die of excessive joy, just like (as we saw earlier) one can die of a broken heart.

If not too sudden or excessive, joy promotes health, as in "mujer, la salud es la hermosura en virtud de su alegría y color."[82] Its conspicuous absence is noted, as in "la falta de salud, y de alegría no me permite que me huelgue tanto."[83] One character prays to God to restore his "healthful joy," which he admits to having lost through prevarication.[84] The joy of a sick person might be restored through a miraculous cure, such as that effected through being touched by a holy relic,[85] or – in a more secularized version of the miracles so characteristic of the romance genre – the mere presence of a person loved by the sick individual.[86]

Restored health is likened by analogy to the perfect state of wholeness first enjoyed by Adam and Eve in the Garden of Eden.[87] Joy extends life, as in

"Estoy con tanta alegría que aumentas la vida mía,"[88] and is more likely to be felt by the well-rested who are not grouchy. Thus Flora suggests to her mistress Climene:

> ¿No será mejor, señora,
> que esos aplausos celebre
> con sus lisonjas el sueño,
> en cuyo descanso vuelve
> a recibir la alegría
> con nueva alma?[89]

In other words: everything looks better after you've had a good night's sleep.

What brings or causes joy? In the first instance, good news, as in "guardándoos para la postre nuevas, que os den alegría."[90] A key concept important for this semantic field is *albricias*, or the ancient custom of giving a gift to the first person who brought a piece of good news. Messengers often ask for or request *albricias* from the hearer to whom they bring glad tidings; for example, "A pediros albricias mi alegría viene de las venturas de este día."[91] Later the term came to mean simply an exclamation indicating that great joy was felt upon hearing by the recipient of good news.

Other causes for joy might include simple quotidian pleasures such as a clean room,[92] a brisk walk,[93] or the satisfaction of useful work. Thus a character in Tirso de Molina's *La dama del olivar* summarizes his own personal recipe for contentment: "con la salsa dulce del trabajo, sustento mi alegría, sin miedo de la torpe apoplejía."[94] (*Apoplexy* was a catch-all medical term that referred to either a hemorrhage inside one of the body's organs or else the loss of blood circulation directed toward an internal organ.)

Joy was often associated with beauty, especially of a fresh young girl. For example, one father on the stage promises that his daughter's presence will bring joy to the beholder: "Llamo a una hija mía, que te dará mirándola alegría."[95] Joy is particularly associated with beauty that was previously lost but has now been restored, as in "alegría de la vida / que vuelve restituida / a su pompa la su belleza."[96] In fact, joy is a bit of a show-off, parading around to display beauty in all its glory: "hará mi alegría alarde de esa belleza."[97]

Upon the theme of restoration[98] the *comedias* play numerous variations. In this category we might include joy upon finding hidden treasure or else over reunion with a long-lost friend. As Adam Potkay puts it,

> Joy is an experience of reunion or fulfilment, of desire at least temporarily laid to rest, of a good thing that comes to pass or seems sure to happen soon … Joy is what we feel … in situations … in which what was lost is found; what was missed restored; what constrained is lifted; what we desire arrives.[99]

Theologian Jürgen Moltmann relates this constellation of topics to three related parables told by Jesus in Luke 15: "three well-known parables: about the widow's lost and found coin, about the lost and found sheep, which the shepherd carries on his shoulders home, and about the lost son, whom his father folds in his arms … These are parables of God's love for the lost and of God's joy in finding them."[100]

Some of this biblical discourse of joy finds its way into the *comedias*. For example, in one dialogue between the characters Juan and Lope, we hear soldiers rejoicing at finding treasure or plunder within the bowels of a galley ship:

> JUAN: ¿Tanto tesoro escondido
>   dentro de Galera había?
> LOPE: Dígatelo la alegría
>   de tus Soldados.[101]

In a different dialogue, Don Íñigo explains to Laura why he is so happy after reading a letter that has just arrived from Granada:

> LAURA: ¿De qué es, señor, la alegría?
>   Dame de ella parte, pues
>   tenerla por propia puedo.
> DON ÍÑIGO: De Granada he recibido
>   aqueste pliego, que ha sido
>   de Don Diego de Toledo,
>   un Caballero, de quien
>   en mis mocedades fui
>   amigo, y a quien debí
>   la vida, y honor también
>   en ciertas adversidades,
>   de que el silencio sea juez,
>   que se corre la vejez
>   de escuchar sus mocedades.
>   Pídeme que busque aquí
>   a un Don Félix de Toledo,
>   hijo suyo, a quien hoy puedo
>   pagar lo que a él le debí:
>   y aunque me puedo acordar
>   de él muy poco, nada haré
>   en hallarle, porque fue
>   la posada en que ha de estar,
>   según dice el sobrescrito,

> frente de la misma casa
> que dejé, esto es lo que pasa.
> LAURA: Y yo me huelgo infinito
> hoy de nueva semejante,
> por lo que a ti te ha alegrado.[102]

Here the reunion is not precisely with his old friend, but with the friend's son; even so, in extending to the son hospitality and protection, Don Íñigo will be able to repay a debt incurred years ago while still in his youth.

More reunions lie in store for spectators of the *comedia* stage, for happy reunions are known to be part and parcel of the comedic genre. These might include reunions with a spouse ("ya es entera la alegría, que tengo en ver a mi esposa")[103] or other family member ("te confieso el alegría, que ver mi hermana en tal lugar me daba").[104] Even reunion with a bastard child – who, in the end, is still a blood relation – might prove cause for joy on the *comedia* stage; consider the lines, "es milagro del cielo: cegóme tristeza tanta, y el alegría me ha dado la vista que me faltaba [del] hijo mío."[105] Illegitimacy is actually thematized in this play, called *El bastardo Mudarra*, by the notorious womanizer Lope de Vega (who himself had numerous illegitimate children).

In the absence of physical reunion, the receipt of a portrait might suffice: "Cuando el retrato pequeño a su original parece, es cuando alegría ofrece a los ojos de su dueño."[106] Here the type of portrait referenced was likely a miniature meant to be worn around the neck, such as the miniature portraits Sor Juana Inés de la Cruz exchanged with the viceroy's wife in colonial Mexico.[107]

Joy might also be experienced due to liberation from captivity, coming to the end of a long journey, or arriving in one's native country. The freed captive's joy is described in these plays as peerless: "cautivo escapado de algún bárbaro, ¿qué pueda competir con mi alegría?"[108] The joy of a long journey completed hovers between the pilgrim's lot and the mariner's *eureka* at sailing into port.[109] Play lines provide the opportunity for a little gratuitous patriotism when an exiled character remembers fondly how happy he was in Spain: "ver o dulce España donde me vi tan lleno de alegría, y por quien lloro ausente en tierra extraña."[110] These heart-warming lines appear in Lope de Vega's *La prisión sin culpa*: "ciudad, patria y casa y honra mía, me causa aquella alegría, que tras larga tempestad tiene el pájaro en el nido."[111] We are almost reminded here of the familiar children's ditty "in all the world, my nest is best."

Joy results from good fortune,[112] which some perceive as stemming from the favourable influence of the stars.[113] This might entail literal good luck, such as receiving a fair sum of money. Don Carlos declares, "los dobloncillos me dan / una intrínseca alegría,"[114] while another character states simply: "el alegría consiste en tener dineros."[115] Similar passages refer more specifically to silver,[116] amber-scented gloves, and a purse filled with 100 *escudos*.[117] In Lope de Vega's

Los torneos de Aragón, Marcela pronounces a paean to gold as an antidote for melancholy:

> Es del oro la nobleza
> tan antigua como el mundo,
> es del mundo la belleza,
> es nuestro padre segundo
> después de la naturaleza.
> Es hijo del sol hermoso,
> es antídoto dichoso
> contra la melancolía,
> es de la vista alegría,
> y a la salud provechoso.[118]

Entire cities such as Lisbon could bathe in this joyful, golden aura.[119] But true, lasting joy is greater than earthly riches, as we see in this exchange between the King and his rustic host, Fabio:

> FABIO: Seáis, señor, bien venido
>   a esta pobre casería.
> REY: Rica de tanta alegría,
>   podrá poner en olvido
>   las casas de Creso, y Midas.[120]

Here the avaricious King Midas is recalled as a negative *exemplum*.

In fact, the best joys are not terrestrial, but spiritual. In Potkay's assessment, "'Joy,' although it often involves a physical response, is more typically associated with goods intangible rather than tangible, spiritual rather than sensual."[121] Somewhat improbably, neuroscientist Antonio Damasio confirms this assertion:

> I assimilate the notion of spiritual to an intense experience of harmony, to the sense that the organism is functioning with the greatest possible perfection. The experience unfolds in association with the desire to act toward others with kindness and generosity. Thus to have a spiritual experience is to hold sustained feelings of a particular kind dominated by some variant of joy, however serene.[122]

Joy's "mother" is moral purity, according to this formula ("esa cándida pureza, Madre de alegría"),[123] especially exemplified by the virtue of chastity: "Es gloria, es alegría de un casto y libre pecho."[124] Joy is found in unstained honour, as when a character named Isabel laments nostalgically for

> un anciano padre mío,
> que otro bien, otra alegría
> no tuvo, sino mirarse
> en la clara Luna limpia
> de mi honor.[125]

For this dishonoured woman, the Derridian trace of previous joy is felt most poignantly in its current absence.[126]

What are some of joy's other enemies, along with loss of honour? Anything that obscures joy is a cloud casting shadows over the sun, as in "O nube de mi alegría, y del Sol que viendo estoy"[127] and "en parte mi alegría con este rigor se aniebla."[128] Worry is known to disturb joy ("¿Qué cuidado hoy turbará mi alegría?"),[129] as does the simple tedium of domestic cares: "domésticos cuidados hacen que el alma divierta de toda humana alegría tal vez sus libres potencias."[130] The implication here is that excessive chores should be avoided in order not to divert energy away from joy's capacity.

The cultural mechanisms in place to ensure that domestic tedium did not take over in Renaissance Spain included feast days, holy days, and *romerías*, or group pilgrimages to visit a saint's shrine.[131] The allegorical character of Furor describes the festive atmosphere surrounding a *romería* in one of Calderón's *autos sacramentales*:

> Que todos los concursos,
> de varias Romerías,
> tal vez en zelo empiezan,
> y acaban en delicia,
> el verse unos a otros
> conmueve a la alegría,
> la alegría al banquete,
> el banquete a la risa,
> la risa al baile, al juego,
> a la vaya, a la grita.[132]

But such spiritual occasions could also be taken advantage of by the cynical to lead pilgrims into temptation. Such is the case when the allegorical figure of Lascivia (Lust) beckons alluringly:

> Llegad, llegad, Peregrinos,
> adonde todo es deleite,
> alegría, y regocijo.[133]

This is a more cynical view of how joy might become twisted in the interest of lust.

Even without a pilgrimage to a saint's shrine, the saint's feast day could still be celebrated joyfully, as when one character says about a patron saint: "para mostrar alegría, cuando se celebra el día de su martirio y corona."[134] Here the feast day in question is the anniversary of the saint's martyrdom, after which a crown of eternal glory would be waiting in heaven as a reward. The feast day might also be the Sabbath,[135] reflecting Catholic Christianity's debt to Old Testament Judaism (although redefined as Sunday instead of Saturday, of course), or a more secularized holiday.[136] Don Felipe describes such a day with the lines:

> Digo que en gozosa muestra
> del alegría de todos;
> pues todos juntos quisieran
> significar los afectos
> en regocijos, y fiestas.[137]

This celebration might be an annual event (as with the promise "cada año os haré una fiesta, por señal de mi alegría"),[138] perhaps one costing lots of money;[139] for example, the start of the grape harvest, known as *la vendimia*: "el día que la Vendimia empieza es de alegría."[140] This would be an annual festival to which agricultural workers felt they were entitled. As one *campesino* protests to his boss: "¿Día / para todos de pública alegría, / quieres, Señor, que sea / para nosotros sólo de tarea?"[141] N.T. Wright comments upon the historical aspect of harvest season as a time for joy:

> The great divine action that produces victory over evil and rescue for God's people will be a mixture of new covenant (restoration after exile) and new creation (fresh harvests, producing bodily restoration) ... History and harvest go closely together. God's actions on behalf of his people will result in the renewal of the good creation.[142]

The communal aspect is important here, as Adam Potkay understands: "[I]ndividuals most often take joy not in themselves but, on the contrary, in temporarily losing themselves within some larger collective or social organism."[143] Meye Thompson concurs: "in Deuteronomy the people are called to rejoice on the occasion of festivals and when going to the temple, and they are called to rejoice in the company of others, a point underscored by their gathering together in the central sanctuary. Rejoicing is the activity and response of the people together."[144] Finally, theologian Miroslav Volf sums up this perspective:

> Joy is best experienced in community. Joy seeks company ... and the company of those who rejoice feeds the joy of each. Feasts and celebrations both express and nourish joy. As feasts and celebrations illustrate, though joy is irreducibly personal – nobody

can rejoice in my place! – joyfulness can also be an aura of a social space, whether a household or a larger community, so that when we enter such a space, we enter into joy, and, often, joy enters into us.[145]

Joy on such a public occasion would be expressed through music[146] and dance.[147] Some melodies were accompanied by song,[148] while others were performed on musical instruments (some stringed)[149] played by gallant musicians.[150] Specific instruments mentioned in the plays are tambourines,[151] trumpets, lyres and *albogues,* or woodwinds.[152] In one intriguing instance, a specific dance is mentioned, notably the *son* dance[153] performed in pairs to African rhythms imported from Spain's Caribbean colonies. Leaping motions[154] are also described, sometimes around bonfires. Witness the following exchange between Telemo and Severo:

> TELEMO: ¿Que regocijados vienen
>   los villanos?
> SEVERO: Dan al día
>   holocaustos de alegría.[155]

Holocaustos in this instance denoted joyful bonfires (the word did not yet bear its negative World War II–era connotations).

In addition to singing, dancing,[156] and the lighting of bonfires, public festivals would involve banquets[157] at tables[158] where guests were served steaming pots[159] full of food such as rice.[160] This food would have been accompanied by wine,[161] even for some of the youngest participants (although for small children, the wine would be diluted with water). Burlesque comedies[162] might be performed to contribute to the generally festive atmosphere. Much laughter[163] would ensue, and all would stay out late, finding themselves awake even in the middle of the night.[164] In the urban – as opposed to rural – version, the streets would overflow with ebullient crowds: "revientan las calles de alegría."[165] Merrymaking might spill over from streets into houses.[166] If the celebration was official, it might include either gun or cannon salutes: "hizo muestras de alegría, la artillería dispara."[167] In Calderón's sacramental play *El segundo blasón del Austria* we find the command, "Sube, pues, al Altar, y haga la alegría la salva a los Umbrales del Templo."[168] The *salva* was a shot of greeting (a bit of pomp and circumstance) that some artillery fired into the air, for example at the start of a parade or procession.

Exuberant artillery shots were not the only sounds indicative of joyful celebration. There was also loud acclaim by the populace.[169] The shouts of joyful celebrants are described as quite noisy,[170] signifying the communal rituals of praise and applause.[171] One stage direction stipulates: "Suena dentro gran grito de alegría entre los villanos."[172] N.T. Wright reminds us that this aural aspect of joy is biblical: "Nehemiah 12:43 … says, remarkably, that 'the joy of Jerusalem was heard far away'; joy was not simply a shared *feeling*; it was something that could be *heard*, from a long way off."[173]

This directive leads to a logical question: were there class connotations of joy? In the *comedias*, at least – which, we must recall from the circumstance of their performance in the *corrales*, were definitely a popular phenomenon – joy does seem to carry a certain lower-class association. A similar stage direction reads: "Suena dentro la Música, con alegría de Labradores."[174] A line from Agustín Moreto's *Los más dichosos hermanos* betrays a similar prejudice: "el vulgo alegre en saraos va delante, previniendo su alegría, y sus aplausos."[175]

Joy as a passion seems to have been connected in people's minds to the rhythms of rural life: "hoy festeja su padre el alegría en toda la serranía"[176] and "[t]odo el Campo es alegría."[177] Sometimes the people performing all this joyous behaviour are interpellated explicitly as shepherds.[178] But villagers also travelled from small towns to big cities for festivals; for example, the distance from Alcalá de Henares (birthplace of novelist Miguel de Cervantes) to the metropolis of Madrid was not too great to travel for a day trip.[179] The inevitable corollary to this class phenomenon was that excessive public joy was considered by the upper class to be vulgar; for example, one class-conscious character begs pardon: "Perdonadme si grosera incurriera mi alegría acaso en alborozo."[180] The boundaries of socially acceptable joy were delimited by concepts such as "immodesty" and "lack of composure."[181]

Such nuances of class distinction were delicately woven into the fabric of courtly existence. It was considered the duty of courtiers to bring joy to their monarch, especially if she was a lady surrounded by chivalrous gentlemen. We hear a funny version of this in a speech by a maid to her mistress:

> Señora mía,
> los Príncipes tus galanes,
> que andan hechos ganapanes,
> para traerte alegría
> por fiestas tienen contienda,
> que han de gastar dos millones,
> y yo les dije: Tontones,
> que destruís vuestra hacienda.
> Si hartarla queréis los tales
> de alegría verdadera,
> allí está una turronera,
> que da la libra a dos reales.[182]

Foreseeing that the gallants' contest to win the lady's favour will cost "two million" (the unit of currency is here left unspecified), the maid reports her advice to them:

"You're wasting your inheritance. If you really want to bring her joy, go buy some *turrones* (a kind of sweet candy still eaten in Spain today)."

Another courtly pastime thought to bring joy was the hunt. We find approving pronouncements such as the following:

> Noble ejercicio es la caza,
> ¿a quién no mueve, y obliga
> su milicia generosa? …
> ¿A quién no causa alegría
> esta lucha imaginada?[183]

This speech is notable for having been written by Calderón during the reign of King Philip IV, a monarch whom his *privado* the Count-Duke of Olivares notoriously kept occupied with hunting to prevent him from meddling in affairs of state.

Class preoccupations with passions such as joy extended to the use of emotion to convey signals of courtly favour or impending banishment. If a master did not look cheerfully upon his servants, it was thought to be a sure sign of his displeasure: "cuando el señor a quien sirve noche y día, le mira sin alegría, es señal de poco amor."[184] The clout that came with local power or authority brought joy to the person lucky enough to enjoy high social standing: "en Castilla el que es Adelantado, vive con alegría, porque es Señor de Dueñas, y Buendía."[185] Here the *adelantado* (governor or prefect) is described as joyful because he is lord over many ladies.

But according to the prevalent emotion scripts of this time period, those lords and ladies would have experienced – and expressed – joy differently. A gendered aspect to this passion quickly becomes apparent in the expectation that women were supposed to appear joyful before men: "es prudencia en la mujer, mostrar al hombre alegría."[186] This dictate carried over all the way into the twentieth century, as we see it pop up again in fascist propaganda designed to instruct the "proper" wife.[187]

Emotion scripts could also change the dynamics of intercultural interactions, such as between Spain and Africa or between Spain and France. In the first instance, a character is advised to put on a cheerful face as protection against the African Muslim: "así es razón que su venida muestre agradecido rostro y alegría; éste será quien la defienda y guarde del Africano Moro."[188] In a different historical drama, one character counsels another: "es de importancia que muestres, Marcela mía, a mi respuesta alegría para que la tenga Francia."[189] Here the passions of a whole country, namely France, are thought to depend upon the "proper" facial expression of one woman.

At this point we might well ask: is there a life-cycle factor? Is any one specific age of person more joyful than some others? Consistently we find the notion of joy connected to youth. Witness Joachim's (the Virgin Mary's father's) response to his children's youthful efforts to cheer him:

> Hijos, vosotros sois mozos,
> bien os está el alegría,
> que yo la tristeza escojo
> para mi cansada edad.[190]

A similar exchange occurs in Calderón's sacramental play *Las espigas de Ruth*, inspired by the Old Testament story of Jesus's Moabite ancestor Ruth. Here Ruth debates the propriety of rejoicing with her Israelite mother-in-law (who, like herself, is also a widow), Naomi:

> RUTH: Hacia aquí se acerca
>   el regocijo, y pues todos
>   con la Venida se alegran
>   de su Dueño, no en nosotras
>   reparen, que de sus Fiestas
>   nos desdeñamos, y así,
>   introducidas en ellas
>   la celebremos.
> NOEMÍ: En mí
>   será impropiedad, que vea
>   alegría.
> RUTH: Antes será,
>   como exceso de Fineza,
>   que en el Día del Señor,
>   que Criados le festejan,
>   no hay Canas que alegres, bien
>   a sus ojos no parezcan.[191]

Contrary to Ruth's opinion, Naomi assumes her old age to be ill-suited for joy, a sentiment affirmed in numerous passages.[192]

Joy, then, is the province of youth – especially of young love. The lyrics to a song meant to accompany Calderón's *Mujer, llora, y vencerás* capture the feeling: "esta varia alegría … es de Amor Galería."[193] Joy is occasioned by overtures of love being well received, as when the King says to Porcia: "Tanta es, Porcia, la alegría de ver que mi amor alientas."[194] The reverse gender scenario is also true, as when a woman exclaims, "Pues ¿qué será mi gusto y alegría, habiendo hallado un dueño tan gallardo?"[195] A lover who enjoys the favour of his beloved will of course rejoice, as when Lisardo confides to Don Félix:

> [Y] así, yo alegre, y contento,
> feliz, gozoso, y ufano
> con los favores estoy
> del bellísimo milagro
> que adoro, del Sol que sigo,
> y la Deidad que idolatro.[196]

A previously unfortunate lover was particularly joyous when his suit finally met with success[197] (as Saint Thomas Aquinas put it, joy "proceeds from the presence of the thing loved").[198] Lovers would be joyful at overcoming resistance to their union: "vencer la resistencia aumenta a los amantes la alegría."[199] After the wedding,[200] they would experience joy together as newlyweds ("la alegría, que da la boda a los recién casados"),[201] even if sadness or sorrow had reigned before.[202] Further joys were in store as they conceived children, although infant (and maternal) mortality rates were still high.[203] Surviving progeny would therefore become the apples of their parents' eyes. Upon finding Him "missing" in the Temple in Jerusalem, Jesus's Mother Mary in her Renaissance Spanish dramatic iteration addresses her teenage Child as: "Hijo, mi bien, mi alegría, mis celestiales despojos, mi perdido de mis ojos."[204]

Such were the occasions for joy within the microcosm of the individual family unit. More communal causes included weddings, military victories, coronations, the signing of peace treaties, liberation from captivity, and the overthrow of tyranny. Aleto gushingly describes the political effect of her wedding on the populace to his princess:

> Tienes, o Princesa mía,
> con tu alegre casamiento
> todo el reino tan contento,
> que lo muestra su alegría.
> No solos los caballeros
> celebran tu dulce boda
> mas la vulgar gente toda,
> de Plebeyos jornaleros.[205]

Similar joy would result from victorious entries into cities[206] and warriors' triumphs.[207] In the case of historical drama, these scenes were not necessarily limited to Spaniards or Christians. Thus we find historically accurate lines such as: "ahora el Cristiano huya, y el Moro en tanta alegría publicaba la victoria."[208]

However, other plays voiced out-and-out propaganda in favour of the Spanish monarchy, such as these lines praising King Philip II for his victory in the Netherlands:

¿Quién no llora de alegría
de ver que a los enemigos
se les quita de las manos
el hijo de Carlos Quinto?[209]

It is especially interesting here to note how one emotion script trumps another: soldiers are admonished to repress their pangs of lovesickness when they are supposed to be rejoicing instead in the triumph of winning a battle: "a un soldado infaman penas de amor. Muestra, señor, alegría, honra tu sangre, pues vienes victorioso."[210] Love pangs are vilified as "infamous" in this context, since they are resolutely subjugated to "higher-order" cultural values such as "honouring one's blood."

A ruler's coronation is considered grounds for rejoicing, as we see when a newly minted monarch confides to his brother: "mi coronación, mi amado hermano, ha sido para mí tanta alegría, que no es mayor … la ciudad que gano."[211] Here he declares his joy to be as large as an entire city. Early on in Juan de la Cueva's *Tragedia del príncipe tirano* a joyful character implores, "no cese el alegría de nuestra alegre elección, tenga fin la turbación."[212] Justin Crisp relates coronation ceremonies specifically to joy on a philosophical plane as well: "Joy is … the *crown* of the good life … [J]oy is the expression and manifestation of the good life, just as the crown is an expression and public manifestation of royal authority."[213]

Joy might be sparked by the liberation of a noble family like the Abencerrajes,[214] the subsequent slaughter of whom provided fodder for countless frontier ballads of the *romancero* tradition. The same could be true when an entire city was liberated, which is what happens in the fourth act of Juan de la Cueva's *La libertad de Roma por Mucio Cevola*. The play's stage directions read: "vuelve Cevola a Roma donde fue recibido con grande alegría."[215] Then the Roman citizen Publio Valerio proclaims: "Salgan juegos, celébrese la gloria de Mucio, muestren todos alegría, venga el Senado, vengan varias gentes, y denle su alabanza."[216] This general proclamation of joy doubtless resulted in gladiatorial contests.

Yet further cause for rejoicing could be found in the signing of peace treaties. For instance, in Francisco de Rojas Zorrilla's *Los tres blasones de España* we find the injunction, "Haya fiesta, haya alegría en aqueste verde prado, pues la tregua se ha jurado."[217] In general, peace brings joy,[218] reflected in metrical harmony.[219] A blessing pronounced onstage over a couple combines these ideas of contentment, pleasure, joy, peace and solace: "plegue a Dios que en contento, gusto, alegría y solaz gocéis los dos de la paz."[220]

Harmony among people was connected conceptually to – and thought to be influenced by – the harmony of the spheres, imagined in Neoplatonic terms as celestial music. We hear these ideas highlighted in this exchange between the allegorical figures of Ingenuity and Thought in Calderón's sacramental play *El día mayor de los días*:

> INGENIO: ¿Qué Misteriosa armonía,
>   Pensamiento, antes del Alba,
>   hace a la Noche más salva,
>   que pudiera hacer al Día?
> PENSAMIENTO: Es tan grande la alegría,
>   en que a su dulce, a su nuevo
>   Canto me pasmo, y me elevo.[221]

This harmony could extend even to cordial relations between nations, as evidenced by state visits when one set of rulers visited the court of another. This happens on the stage in Lope de Vega's *La nueva victoria del Marqués de Santa Cruz*. A formal letter written in prose is read out loud to welcome the arrival of the Prince and Princess of Savoy: "No se puede encarecer el alegría, que esta Corte ha sentido con la venida de sus Altezas, los Príncipes de Saboya."[222] Such an occasion would have been celebrated with knightly jousts and tournaments, with boons granted to the winners by the monarch. Seekers bold enough to ask for boons might even approach a king or queen directly; such is the case with the lines "Día que es todo alegría, / es día de hacer mercedes; / y pues como Reina puedes, / esta pretensión es mía."[223] The one who asks may well receive, for joy is marked by magnificent liberality: "es cosa maravillosa su alegría, y su liberalidad … [D]a todo cuanto tiene."[224]

But alas, these moments of reckless joy and abandon do not last forever. Especially as the seventeenth century advances, a sense of Baroque *desengaño* pervades many of these plays, and we begin to glimpse a teleology of joy in which every good thing must come to an end. Joy is fleeting: "al repartir las Viviendas, a espaldas de la alegría aposentó la tristeza."[225] Witness the lament of Leonor to Don Félix:

> Pero ¿cuándo una alegría
> donde empieza no acaba?
> ¡Qué breve es la edad del bien!
> ¡Quién en el mundo creyera,
> que el día del placer fuera
> la víspera del pesar![226]

Nowhere is this truer than with the joy of romantic love: "tahúr parece el amante, pues no dura su alegría."[227] Here the lover is likened to a gambler (see again figure 8) whose luck eventually runs out.

But so far we have spoken only of terrestrial joys. Joy is also very much a part of early modern Spanish religious devotion. As the allegorical figure of Faith sings in the *loa* (accompanying song) for Calderón's *El nuevo hospicio de pobres*, the goal is "Pues para que no todo sea serio, y tenga la alegría parte con la devoción."[228] One of the foci for joy within Catholic doctrine is the purity of the Virgin Mary, which is praised night and day in Lope de Vega's *El capellán de la Virgen*.[229] It was Mary, of course, who brought joy to the world (think of the Christmas carol by that name) with the birth of Jesus: "María que ha de dar a todo el mundo alegría."[230] Adam Potkay confirms the centrality of Christmas to the Christian experience of joy by making reference to "Christmas, the season in which joy springs from the partial fulfillment of a salvation prophecy and from the anticipation that the rest of the promise will be fulfilled."[231]

There are numerous other occasions for joyful celebration within the Christian experience, especially a moment like conversion which is believed to hold eternal significance. In Lope de Vega's overtly propagandistic *El bautismo del príncipe de Marruecos* (The Baptism of the Prince of Morocco), a character familiar with the event reports regarding the Prince's conversion:

Ya en cosas de Dios
están hablando los dos,
y él muestra grande alegría.
Caso ha sido milagroso …[232]

Other moments in the life of a Christan might not seem joyful to onlookers, but were often nonetheless experienced as joyful by true believers. A key case in point would be the instance of martyrdom, "que para la muerte fiera camine con alegría."[233] The undevout do not understand this kind of joy; to them it seems perverse. The Muslim Tariq in Lope de Vega's *El postrer godo de España* expresses astonishment at the firm faith of the Visigothic Christians:

Qué notable hechicería,
pues ¿cómo, que a morir van,
y van con tanta alegría?
Decid que los quiero ver,
porque no lo he de creer
menos que a mis propios ojos.[234]

But some pagan cultures too believed a noble death should be joyful. This belief system is reflected in a line from Juan Pérez de Montalbán's overtly classicizing

Segunda parte del Séneca de España, Don Felipe Segundo: "Amigos, nadie me llore, antes como los antiguos Griegos, mostrad alegría: pues hoy morirán conmigo."[235] Most royal subjects do not wish for such a leader.

But for early modern Catholic Spaniards, ultimately, true joy would come only at the end of time when Christ returned to establish His kingdom on earth: "aunque hacer el Firmamento alguna alegría aprueba, hasta el cumplimiento, no hay nunca alegría perfecta."[236] A passage of dialogue in Calderón's sacramental play *Los alimentos del hombre* asks explicitly the question of when this will happen:

> ADÁN: ¿Qué amanecer? ¿Qué esplendor
>   se puede, Invierno, esperar
>   en Noche tuya?
> INVIERNO: El que a dar
>   venga con su Resplandor,
>   como oíste, a la alegría,
>   que ve el Mundo su Arrebol
>   a la media Noche el Sol,
>   y la Estrella al medio Día.
> ADÁN: ¿Cuándo vendrá ese consuelo?
> INVIERNO: Cuando den Bellas Criaturas
> MÚSICA: Gloria a Dios en las Alturas,
>   y Paz al Hombre en el Suelo.[237]

The heaven imagined in this scene will be pure joy: "el cielo es todo alegría."[238] Adam Potkay confirms, "'Joy' is a keyword of Christian soteriology … [T]he joy of heaven will be like the most intense joy in life if that joy could not fade or be taken away … Anticipating the joy of an after-life brings with it a joy of its own."[239] But until then, we must languish with Fernando de Rojas's Pleberio *in hac lachrymarum valle* – in this valley of tears.[240] We hear multiple lines spoken on stage repeat obsessively the same question: "O Reino de alegría, ¿cuándo tras tantas penas te veremos?"[241]

Until that day comes, we are left with a few final questions. Can the passion of joy be controlled? If so, then what are we supposed to do with it? Psychotherapist Alexander Lowen states categorically: "One cannot make up one's mind to be joyful."[242] But a few characters on the stage are commanded to be joyful, which implies that it must be within their control to do so; for example, "Sentáos y toma alegría."[243] Theologian Justin Crisp comments on the paradox of this command:

> [A]n injunction to be joyful might seem ethically irresponsible and politically danger-
> ous, too close to peddling just one more religious opiate to the oppressed masses. To

enjoin human beings to 'rejoice always (!),' as does St. Paul (Phil. 4:4), might verge on a demand to be content with the *status quo*, to insist that one should be happy with whatever little one has and with any suffering that comes one's way and, thus, never question what material and social conditions have conspired to put one in one's place. As opiates do, such joy might, for a moment, minimally increase the quality of one's life, but it would do so to the detriment of the dis-content arguably necessary to motivate movements for substantial change.[244]

However, Crisp insists, there is a sense in which the command to rejoice is not devoid of validity, even in the biblical realm. Particularly when we start to think in terms of shared agency (part divine / part human), we begin to see how the responsibility for being joyful does lie at least partially with us: "[J]oy is genuinely our own response, and yet, it also comes to us as a gift – it is something in which we actively participate."[245] Meye Thompson sees joy as something that can be cultivated: "To cultivate … trust and confidence in God and God's goodness is to cultivate joy."[246] And N.T. Wright sees joy specifically as a virtue or habit one can exercise.[247] Miroslav Volf emphasizes the cognitive aspect of this emotion, suggesting that if we fail to rejoice at a certain situation, we might not be perceiving it correctly.[248]

In one ingenious image from a hagiographical drama, joys are said to be exchanged for terrestrial glories in some heavenly sort of Bank: "Tus glorias pones en Banco del cambio de tu alegría."[249] As this line comes from a hagiographical play, perhaps it means true heavenly joy will come only from renouncing earthly glories. But as much as Baroque *desengaño* means that sorrow is the reality for most of earth's temporal (and temporary) inhabitants, so the allegorical figure of Nature whispers a message of hope about the cyclical nature of things: "Víspera de la alegría llamó un cuerdo a la tristeza."[250] Sorrows are simply the dark vespers sung at night before the dawn of a fresh supply of joy.

8

Fear Itself

Fear is an inconstant pain.[1]

Our fears do make us traitors.[2]

The only thing we have to fear is fear itself.[3]

Fear envelops us like a cape or a mantle.[4] Fear is a gaping abyss.[5] Fear sprawls out,[6] ties us up,[7] and holds us prisoner[8] in a dark dungeon.[9] Fear besieges[10] and blinds.[11] Fear buffets the soul ("un miedo el alma combate")[12] but also the heart, tongue, and spirit: "miedo en nuestros corazones, lenguas y ánimo."[13] Fear makes us want to flee[14] with great speed[15] and figuratively puts wings on our feet.[16] The capacity for fear to get people moving gave rise to proverbial sayings such as:

> No hay espuela como el miedo,
> no hay viento como el peligro,
> no hay alas como el recelo.[17]

Fearful persons disperse to the four winds just as surely as soldiers who have been routed in battle.[18]

Persons fleeing from a particular danger might well end up living in exile.[19] A common place to seek refuge for Spaniards fleeing their homeland was Italy,[20] although Spain itself became a haven for exiles from other places such as Portugal.[21] The worst fear of a banished refugee would be the potential for dying abroad.[22]

Symptoms of fear include trembling,[23] shivering,[24] or twitching[25] with paroxysms like someone bitten by a tarantula.[26] Thus Mencía laments abjectly to Don Gutierre before he murders her in a case of utterly unjustified uxoricide:

> Miedo, espanto, temor, y horror tan fuerte
> parasismos han sido de mi muerte.[27]

The fearful person suffers chills[28] to the point of turning the blood cold,[29] or –
metaphorically speaking – having ice in one's pores.[30] In a curious early modern
medical notion, this apparent drop in body temperature was thought to be caused
by blood rushing from the limbs to some other part of the body such as the
soul: "Sangrarme del alma puedo, que a ella se fue de miedo cuánta en los brazos
tenía."[31] The result is an even odder image of "bleeding" the soul.

Other physiological responses to fear include profuse sweating ("me espantan
de suerte, que voy húmedo de miedo")[32] and a pale face ("el semblante pálido del
miedo").[33] Fear is said to be written on the face,[34] with hair standing on end,[35] as
predicted so famously by the Ghost of Hamlet's father:

> I could a tale unfold whose lightest word
> Would harrow up thy soul, freeze thy young blood,
> Make thy two eyes, like stars, start from their spheres,
> Thy knotted and combinèd locks to part,
> And each particular hair to stand on end,
> Like quills upon the fearful porpentine.[36]

The fearful person begins chewing on things nervously,[37] has trouble breathing,[38]
or even feels like he or she is choking.[39] Either the pulse becomes weakened[40] or
else the heart palpitates.[41] The stomach becomes upset[42] to the point of passing
gas[43] and ultimately being unable to control the bowels.[44] In the vein of scatalogi-
cally quixotic comedy, humorous lines from characters onstage report vile smells
as a result.[45]

Additional symptoms include a loss of sensation or numbness[46] as well as feeling "suspended" as if in mid-air.[47] Fear paralyzes its victims into inaction so that
the hands are still, not busy;[48] the same thing happens to the feet.[49] Fear makes
our steps unsteady[50] to the point of fainting or falling unconscious.[51] Deep sleep[52]
may ensue or else its opposite, insomnia ("que el Miedo no duerma"),[53] due to the
fact that all the senses are disturbed: "el miedo turba todos los sentidos."[54] The
fearful person finds himself running around in circles,[55] shouting – even though
making such a scene is considered shameful[56] – praying,[57] or being struck mute.[58]
The inability to speak is as much a result of being tongue-tied[59] as having words
catch in the throat.[60] Psychiatrist I.M. Marks confirms: "In humans as well as in
animals, two obvious behavioral expressions of fear present a striking contrast.
One is the tendency to freeze and become mute … The opposite is to startle,
scream, and run away from the source of danger."[61] Thus Porcia laments that she
is "buried" in silence and takes recourse to communicating with her glance when
words fail:

> Yo sepultada en silencio,
> y con el miedo confusa

hice lengua en los ojos,
por tener la lengua muda.[62]

Inability to speak, however, assumes thought content cannot be communicated; just as likely, a prior result of fear is forgetfulness, so that even one's thoughts keep getting lost. Witness the following exchange between Félix and Tomé:

FÉLIX: En tanto que subo, reza,
    Tomé, algunas oraciones.
TOMÉ: Pardiez que no se me acuerda
    con el miedo las que niño
    me enseñó mi buena abuela.[63]

Here Tomé admits to being so frightened, he has forgotten even the prayers his grandmother taught him when he was a child. Such a stunned state betokens idiocy ("soy idiota del miedo")[64] and loss of hearing to take in instruction ("¿para oír me impide mi propio miedo?").[65]

The natural response of the fearful person to this onslaught of physiological symptoms is to go into hiding,[66] such as crouching,[67] crawling beneath furniture,[68] climbing a tree,[69] or shutting oneself behind closed doors,[70] for example in a monastery where a fugitive[71] might request asylum.[72] Alternatively a fearful person might wear a mask[73] or don a disguise.[74] Further deceitful stratagems[75] might be elaborated, up to and including telling outright lies.[76]

Fear deceives not just others, but also the person who experiences it. It does this by creating illusions[77] and fanciful imaginations: "es del miedo fantasía"[78] and "finge estos fantasmas el miedo."[79] Thus one character declares that fantasy is a monster who engenders fear and then nurtures it: "mi loca y engañada fantasía, nace un monstruo, que al miedo después cría."[80] Fear dilutes joy[81] and replaces it with sorrow.[82] Fear diminishes hope[83] and causes one to lose confidence.[84] Fear is patently bad for one's health.[85] Fear is irrational[86] and ultimately causes insanity.[87]

Is it possible to die from fear? This option is explored in the plays more literally in the case of armies ("de su horror el ejército moría")[88] and more figuratively in the case of individuals not involved in combat through such expressions as "Me moriré de miedo"[89] or "estoy perdiendo mil vidas de miedo."[90] The fear of death, specifically, looms large in the imagination.[91] Douglas Abrams affirms, "Many psychologists say that the fear of death lies behind all other fears."[92] Exceptions to this rule are noted with admiration, as in the mention of legendarily stoic Romans who, it was believed, did not fear death: "No causa miedo en Corazón Romano Muerte cruel, ni áspero enemigo."[93] But this was the exception that proved the rule.

In addition to death, what were some things or entities early modern Spanish people feared? High up on the list was fear of the king, as in "aquel gran Rey de Toledo, de quien tiene España miedo."[94] This was especially true if they had done something wrong like breaking the law.[95] What people feared about the king was explicitly his anger (thought to inspire fear in even his most loyal subjects),[96] or just simply his annoyance.[97] If people felt this way about the king, then how much more so toward the Holy Roman Emperor! Thus an actor dressed as an Angel says to the stage version of Carlos V: "del Moro, Español, y el Africano seas el miedo, y la total ruina."[98] Fear of the king's power extended also to the king's spies: "Yo, que de espías del Rey es fuerza que miedo cobre, hasta las horas que veis, no quise salir."[99] This character is probably trying to hide something, and thus acutely conscious of being watched.

Fear could prove an understandable response to something so general as a threat: "miedo de una amenaza."[100] This threat might come from declared enemies[101] or, more generically, from criminals or delinquents.[102] (Fear of the delinquent survives to this day, in truisms such as "a liberal is someone who has not yet been mugged.")[103] Specific fears in Spanish Golden Age society involved thieves[104] or bandits,[105] known to lurk behind hills and in caves outside cities to waylay and rob the traveller. Thus Temor appears as an allegorical figure in the *loa* for an *auto sacramental* dressed as a pilgrim. The allegorical figure of Man asks concerning this figure, "¿Quién es aquel peregrino, / que parece que su sombra / le atemoriza y le asombra?"[106] Pilgrim garb was thought to be an appropriate outfit for Fear because pilgrims were often attacked by roadside bandits. Of course, the wealthier a person was to begin with, the more he or she might fear being robbed, as we are reminded in this dialogue between two *comedia* characters:

> IORAN: Piensa en que tienes gran dinero y joyas.
> BATO: Eso es miedo mayor, pues quien los tiene
>   está lleno de miedo, y de cuidados,
>   de ladrones, de hijos, y criados.[107]

The humorous conclusion these two characters reach is that one is in at least as much danger from grasping children and servants as from common robbers or thieves.

One of the most troubling aspects of fear is its recurring nature, which psychologists today might associate with PTSD. A character confesses, "Tengo un miedo apresurado, que con fatiga notoria es horror de la memoria."[108] The closest most non-veterans come to experiencing this sort of psychic trauma is the suffering induced by recurring dreams. These too appear in the *comedias*, as in "el miedo, que el sueño pudo ponerme"[109] and "las lumbres de mis desdichas presagas, cuando aquel sueño introdujo miedo al cuerpo, horror al alma."[110]

Some dreams were believed to contain omens, premonitions, or prophecies concerning future events. These are most often recognized in hindsight, as in "Ya de mi miedo miro el agüero cumplido";[111] but there is also a sense in which omens and fear feed on each other, so that only the person who is already fearful pays much attention to omens or (in)auspicious events: "duda, teme, desconfía, y está tan cerca del miedo, que se paga de accidentes, y se recela de agüeros."[112] The same could be true of oracles, specifically mentioned in the line, "miedo de un oráculo / que me ha representado en mil imágenes."[113]

The mention of oracles suggests the topic of the pagan gods, whose designs were famously communicated to human beings by the Oracle at Delphi. Pagan deities feature prominently in Calderón's mythological dramas. In one of these, the character Apolo relates:

[E]scuché,
a fuerza de guerra, clarines,
jubebas, y sacabuches,
en arriculados truenos,
que miedo, y horror infunden,
la voz se escuchó de Jove,
a cuyo tonante numen,
despavorido se esconde,
quien no temeroso huye.[114]

Here he describes how even the Olympians are rattled by the thunder of the mighty Jove.

Within a Christian context, angels or demons were more likely to be mentioned, as in "tendré de un Ángel miedo"[115] or "gran temor, y miedo eterno a unos dioses ministros del infierno."[116] These "gods" with a lower-case *g* were often conflated with demons by Christian humanists and colonizers alike. But demons per se were very much feared as powerful, physical presences in the early modern world, as I have shown in *Exorcism and Its Texts*.[117] For example, in one representative exchange two characters attempt to identify a menacing presence they are sensing and express fear that it is a demon come to wound them:

MERIAN: Demonio debe de ser.
DARDIN: Miedo tengo que nos hieran.[118]

Such demons would have been familiar to *comedia* audiences, even the illiterate, from sources such as the graphic paintings of Hieronymus Bosch, which are specifically referenced in the plays, including the title of one artwork in particular – namely, *The Temptation of Saint Anthony* (see figure 10).[119]

In fact, the general level of demonological knowledge was so sophisticated that at times specific demons' names are mentioned,[120] with playwrights thereby demonstrating a confidence that this esoteric lore will be recognized. Further precise demonological expertise is evidenced by the inclusion of details such as the propensity of demons to travel in legions just like soldiers in the Roman army (this detail, which appears in the gospels, "immediately links the demon possession … with a central technique of Roman imperial control of local subjects"[121]). Thus we overhear a character confessing his fear that a "legion of spirits" will emerge from a grave like a flock of jackdaws flying to sleep in the forest:

¿Qué pensaré, Ioran, que estoy temblando?
Ni doy azadonada que no piense
que ha de salir de esta mísera fosa
una legión de espíritus, cual suele
banda de grajos a dormir en bosque.[122]

The mention of a grave here evokes, similarly, the fear of ghosts, which is again expressed in specific terms by characters on stage (thus Don Juan asserts, "De algún muerto tiene miedo").[123] The fear of ghosts could only be exacerbated on a night like All Souls: "la noche de los difuntos no saco de puro miedo la cabeza de la ropa."[124] This fear could extend to specific beliefs about not eating the bread wreath or *rosca de difuntos*[125] left as an offering on early modern Spanish tombstones – even before "Old" World Spanish customs could be influenced in a direction opposite from the more typical transatlantic flow by the colonial Mexican Day of the Dead.[126]

Not all of the ghosts appearing on stage in the *comedias*, however, were actually meant to inspire fear. We find abundant references in humorous plays to "pretend" ghosts as well as tricks played upon friends to expose their superstition. In one of these scenes a character describes a routine whereby a sibling named Manfredo comes out at night with some sort of firecracker or other apparatus to make sparks fly in the dark, the intended result being to scare the unwitting observer: "Pasa las noches en ellas, cuando por ponerle miedo, sale mi hermano Manfredo echando de sí centellas."[127] The illusion of supernatural intervention could prove particularly effective when blaming practical jokes on the activity of poltergeists ("Diréle yo que es un duende, y tendrá de él miedo").[128] We find numerous dramatic references to these prankster devils or *duendes* that confirm ethnographers' findings about the persistence of folk superstition even today in Spain's countryside. One character alludes to "[e]l duendecillo que, nunca visto, acobarda; el miedo con que se guarda la viña sin viñadero."[129] Somehow, conveniently, these trickster demons are never seen, but they are blamed for all sorts of everyday blunders and/or mishaps.

Just as entertaining are the presumed remedies for fear inspired by these alleged supernatural entities, such as drinking a courage-inspiring potion: "esa jícara bella,

que en bebiéndola, con ella perderás el miedo al coco."[130] Here *coco* refers to a
bogeyman still invoked by Hispanic parents to scare their children into staying in
bed at night.[131] We also find references to more serious attempts to control fear
of the supernatural, such as magic. One theatrical magician boasts, "ya yo puedo
al Infierno poner asombro, y miedo, pues con tanto cuidado la Magia he estu-
diado."[132] The real-life version of his nefarious activities would likely have gotten
him into trouble with the Inquisition.

More orthodox means of controlling or repelling demons might include the
formal ritual of exorcism. Thus one *comedia* character brags to another, "Conmigo no tengas miedo, que yo sé bravos conjuros."[133] It is unlikely that this
comical figure would have been an official exorcist sanctioned by the Church.
References to key elements of the exorcism ritual in the dramas, however, do
show a degree of familiarity on the part of dramatists with the particulars
of this rite, even if their intent was to satirize it. One such element was the
sahumerio or suffumigation meant to (in Shakespeare's words) "fire out" the
fiend.[134] For example, one comically frightened male character wants a woman
to speak for him because she is either more courageous than he or else freshly
exorcized: "estoy hecho una basura, dígalo Inés, que tiene menos miedo, o está
sahumada."[135]

Another popular belief was that calling on a specific saint as advocate could
help a scared person to fend off fear: "¿Y no haya santo abogado del miedo que
un hombre tiene?"[136] We find bits and snatches of popular religious rituals such
as exorcism scattered throughout the *comedias* in piecemeal fashion, a haphazard
state of affairs that probably serves as a more or less accurate reflection of the
average person's degree of knowledge regarding esoteric or occult phenomena.
For instance, a character reports praying a Hail Mary after sneezing – and then
quickly covering his mouth – because a sneeze was thought by some people to be
the body's effort to expel a demon.[137] We still say "bless you!" when people sneeze
as a holdover vestige of this belief.

Fear of demons was inextricably tied to fear of illness during the early modern
period in Spain. Specific illnesses feared might include apoplexy[138] or fever.[139] But
people also might be afraid of no specific illness in particular, just generally anxious about falling sick. This anxious condition, then as now, was referred to by its
clinical name of hypochondria.[140] Patients were not the only ones to fear illness;
doctors, too, might fear being unable to cure certain conditions.[141] We should
not underestimate the fear involved with not knowing even the basics about how
devastating contagions like the plague were transmitted.

Medical illness, of course, was not the only way in which early modern people
could receive bodily harm. At least as frequently as people became sick, they were
injured in a fistfight or some other physical altercation. One character confesses
on stage his fear or "miedo de que algún amante loco me pegue un sopetón."[142]
Another strategizes about finding a secluded place to pray, away from danger of

falling into a quarrel.[143] The potential for this to happen was especially high in early modern Spain – as it continues to be in the United States – due to the proliferation of weapons of all kinds. We find references in the *comedias* to explicit fear of the sword,[144] short sword or cutlass,[145] halberd,[146] knife,[147] gun,[148] and harquebus[149] (a predecessor of the musket, which was the weapon responsible for Cervantes's loss of the use of his left hand in the Battle of Lepanto). It seems that early modern Spaniards were armed to the teeth. We hear pleas especially from women for gentlemen to put their weapons away for fear that an accident will happen or else some provocation to violence might occur (for instance, "¡Valerio, envaina, que me causas miedo, Jesús! ¿No ves que estoy preñada? Palpitaciones tengo").[150] Here a woman begs Valerio to put his sword back in its sheath because she is pregnant and he is scaring her so much that she experiences heart palpitations. Not surprisingly, we also find references to protective armour[151] to fend off potential attacks.

For we must not forget that early modern Spain was often at war, and its ethos was that of a warlike society. Characters on stage speak about their fear of war ("miedo de la guerra")[152] evoked by squadrons[153] of soldiers or the sight of the enemy's flag.[154] The sounds of battle[155] were deemed particularly fearsome, especially for the non-soldier.[156] However, official acts of war on the part of Spanish kingdoms' or cities' military leaders were not the only occasions for gentlemen to access their stockpiles of weapons and armour. Duels were painfully common and were in fact the preferred means of dealing with irresolvable disagreements. Duelling met with official approval, to the point where government officials publicized these events by announcing the date, time, and place when the challenger would meet his opponent.[157] If for whatever reason one of the two parties was not ready by that deadline, their combat might be delayed.[158] A female character describes in fearful tones the manner in which duellists would sally forth to meet each other:

> Entré … temerosa
> como suele el que sale a un desafío,
> que se recata de cualquier cosa.
> Desmayado el valor, difunto el brío,
> por puntos a las manos le miraba,
> temiendo el golpe del acero impío.
> A cada paso que adelante daba,
> o qué de veces me mató mi miedo,
> en mi pecho su estoque imaginaba …
> Ningún temor a mi temor se iguala.[159]

She describes looking over her shoulder, constantly worrying that the enemy's sword is about to strike.

Men also feared for their safety, and for this very reason seldom left the house without a sword.[160] However, possession of a sword could, as it were, cut both ways: lack of a weapon might leave a man feeling more exposed and/or vulnerable, but it could also be invoked as an excuse for not fighting if he was desperate to avoid altercation. We glimpse this possibility in the line "teniendo espada, no presumierais que os daba el perdón de miedo."[161] Here we see fear being rejected as an excuse for not facing up to one's manly obligations.

Not everyone who received a challenge to a duel accepted it, though; we find evidence of this refusal in the line "a persona desafío, y que si no saliera, y tiene miedo, le buscaré en [L]a Vega de Toledo."[162] This reference to a park called La Vega in the city of Toledo provides a telling detail about where a man might go to hide if he was looking to escape detection. A similar scene in Lope de Vega's *El sol parado* shows Medoro describing to the Maestre de Santiago a challenge to a duel sent to him by Gazuel the Brave, who is a Muslim:

> [S]i huyes
> por miedo de aceptar el desafío,
> y te escondes de verle cuerpo a cuerpo,
> este papel que aquí te envía, le firmes,
> y un capítulo escrito en vuestra lengua.[163]

Medoro here provides the Maestre with options such as a written response in case he is too afraid to accept the challenge and instead chooses to retreat into hiding.

The problem with hiding away from the centre of the city was that wild beasts inhabited the untamed countryside. "[T]engo miedo a las fieras,"[164] confesses one *comedia* character, with others offering more detail about the horror of the wild beast's visage.[165] Tofiño admits, "perdido vengo de miedo de los leones,"[166] while another male character recalls feeling fear at seeing a camel when he was a child.[167] Beltrán fears the fangs of a ferocious hunting dog: "[¿]Qué diablos tiene este galgo, / que hoy nos pone a todos miedo?"[168] One unusually honest character acknowledges being scared even of a little mouse.[169] The great exception, of course, to fear of savage animals was the culturally sanctioned contest against them which happened routinely in the bullfight. Tello boasts, "no tengo a Toros miedo"[170] – and in fact, in the face of a gallant *torero*, fear is attributed rather to the bulls instead.[171]

Apart from these idolized paragons of bravery, however, most (especially comical) everyday characters on the *comedia* stage admit – often humorously – to being wimps. They are afraid of the forest,[172] or even of a large garden,[173] especially if they are alone in the dark[174] during the night.[175] They fear even their own shadows,[176] let alone any loud, scary noise.[177] The most "lethal" fear is that they will find themselves in danger without anyone to come to their rescue in time.[178] S.J. Rachman confirms the impact of solitude on fear among soldiers: "most people appear to be more susceptible to fear when they are alone. When they were isolated, even experienced combat veterans performed badly and were far more inclined to surrender. Prolonged isolation had the effect of reinforcing the soldiers' fears and lessened their resistance."[179] Psychiatrist I.M. Marks explains the biological basis for this fear:

> The dangers of being alone without our fellows are numerous … Although being alone helps some small, cryptic species to avoid predators, in many others isolated animals are more likely to be killed by predators and may have more difficulty in finding food or obtaining the warmth generated by group huddling or activity, not to mention problems in finding a mate. Important mechanisms have evolved to keep conspecifics [members of the same species] attached to one another and to reestablish contact when it has been lost.[180]

And fearful early modern Spaniards might really, really need to be rescued – from a very bad storm, for example. Some villagers exclaim in a *comedia* by Calderón:

> 4TH VILLANO: ¡Qué ansia!
> 2ND VILLANO: ¡Qué miedo!
> AURELIO: ¿Qué súbita tempestad nos anochece tan presto?[181]

It is tantalizing to imagine that such dialogue on stage might have been accompanied by dramatic climatological sound effects. Another play by Lope offers a fairly detailed description of a storm:

> Comenzaron con esto las señales
> de oscura tempestad, que el miedo aumenta
> sonando de las ruedas celestiales,
> los quicios que la máquina sustentan,
> ocultos los terrestres animales,
> las aves que en el aire se alimentan,
> revolando entre negros torbellinos,
> bajaban a los árboles vecinos.
> Pegaba a la celeste artillería
> la cuerda el seco humor, y de los senos
> de las oscuras nubes escupía
> relámpagos de luz, de miedo truenos,
> pirámides el fuego resolvía.[182]

Given the imperfect tense of the verbs, this description would likely have taken the place of the storm's dramatic re-enactment.

Any storm would of course prove especially disturbing at sea – a frequent occurrence in this Age of Discovery when numerous galleons were lost due to shipwreck. We find references in the *comedias* to "miedo del mar soberbio"[183] including ones in which these playwrights cannot resist opportunities for rhyme, such as "de miedo de la mar, / aun no se atrevió a pasar."[184] Some characters report being so frightened of the sea that they experience seasickness merely from watching the tide roll in.[185] But that is nothing compared with the fear experienced by mariners on the voyage across the Atlantic Ocean to the Indies during Spain's most intense colonizing activity. Witness the following speech by a character named Sancho:

> En el monte de Sanlúcar,
> que mira verdes cabellos
> de sus pinos, en las aguas
> del mar de España soberbio,
> cuando parten a las Indias
> los navegantes modernos,
> que codiciosos del oro
> no ven los peligros ciertos,
> hay un gatazo, señor,
> que sentado en uno de ellos
> está diciendo: Tornau,
> tornau, sonando los ecos
> en las naves, con que muchos
> se desembarcan de miedo.[186]

He reports the evil omen of a gigantic cat whose "meow" sounds like "turn around" in Catalan – a warning issued to sailors to turn back before it's too late.

Even the seafarers who did not lose their nerve might repent of their decision to venture out, at least enough to prevent them from ever embarking again: "si llegó al puerto con vida, cobre al agua tanto miedo, que no se vuelva a embarcar."[187] We must not forget that in this still-superstitious age, mariners were not the only ones to consult astrologers or otherwise bow to the perceived will of the stars. One lady character laments, "consolada no puedo estar yo, sin tener miedo al influjo de mi estrella,"[188] while Beatriz complains to Rosarda "[d]el miedo que esos Planetas me dan."[189]

Stars and planets were thought to align or conjoin either auspiciously or in a menacing fashion, especially on key occasions such as the day of one's birth or marriage. They were thought to influence human affairs much like the goddess Fortune raised or lowered human beings on her wheel (see again figure 6).[190] A fall from power, for example by a king's *privado*, might be explained either as the result of envy[191] (always to be feared by those who enjoy favour) or as the simple consequence of reaching a lower rung[192] on that wheel. Ungrateful men, no matter how loyal, might be secretly awaiting an opportunity to stab their unsuspecting victim in the back.[193]

Greater than fear of death in this society was fear of losing one's reputation: "No es miedo, no, de la muerte, señor, el que me apasiona, sino miedo de la infamia que a vueltas de ella se compra."[194] Fear of notoriety might be phrased as "risk of losing fame."[195] Closely bound up with notions of reputation was of course the fraught concept of honour, which was made to carry so much cultural freight. Lucinda expresses a common concern when she says, "Tengo miedo, el honor que he de perder."[196] In one strikingly metaliterary moment, a character speaks to an actor playing the part of a playwright: "Imagino, que haces alguna Comedia, y vas de miedo del silbo, descartando borradores."[197] This line reflects a fear on the part of dramatists that the audience will whistle (our modern-day version might be more of a hiss) if they do not like the text of the play. This fear generates a proliferation of discarded rough drafts.

The sound of groundlings whistling in the *corrales* brings us to a political aspect to fear – one related to social class. Throughout the comedia corpus we see time and time again that fear is definitively a lower-class emotion. Consider this speech by Violante:

¡O! Cómo el miedo es villano,
pues en la misma inocencia
sabe esconder su contagio.[198]

Specifically, lower-class individuals might fear poverty[199] or hunger, particularly in times of scarcity like a siege.[200] In Marxist terms of class struggle, the poor fear the rich;[201] they are intimidated by displays of wealth such as arms and horses. For example, one higher-class character says to another: "ensillen su caballos, y armen luego, que quiero poner miedo a estos villanos."[202]

The lower classes who lack social power explicitly fear punishment, in particular if they have broken the law; this same fear is also expressed by noblemen, however.[203] An acute fear during this time period was the ever-present danger of being sent to row the king's ships as a galley slave[204] – effectively a death sentence, due to the fact that the oarsmen's ankles were chained together or to their posts, so that if the ship sank, the *galeotes* would sink with it. The plight of these condemned prisoners (sometimes criminals, but also prisoners of war) was made famous by an episode of *Don Quijote* in which the knight errant frees a group of galley slaves he sees in chains on the presumption that no one should suffer bondage against his free will.[205] This scene has often been interpreted as one of the most overtly subversive political passages in the world's first great modern novel.

Even upper-class characters express fear of running into trouble with the law, however, so we should not attempt to confine this particular fear within restrictive

boundaries of social status. The nobleman Don Félix confesses that he trembles at
the sound of the cry "halt, in the King's name":

> [J]usticia
> me pone tan digno miedo,
> que al decir "tenéos al Rey,"
> de pies, y de manos tiemblo.[206]

In fact, fear of governmental or judicial authority is often characterized as "noble"
in these plays, as in "Al noble miedo de la justicia se volvió a Toledo."[207] The fear
of justice or prosecution is one of the only fears to which a nobleman will freely
admit. We see this pattern in the lines, "ennobleciendo el delito, también la fuga
enoblezco; pues el miedo de los nobles, es de la justicia el miedo."[208] The mental
and verbal contortions are obvious as this aristocratic character conveniently quali-
fies terms such as "crime" and "flight" as "ennobled" simply because they reflect
fear of running into trouble with the law. Such fear might be obviated, however,
in a corrupt legal system by bribery or favouritism shown to relatives or friends by
judicial authorities. We find traces of these unsavoury practices in lines such as "es
mi amigo el Alguacil, no hay que tenerle miedo."[209]

Other fears confessed or admitted to by rich characters include a fear of popular
rebellion. Thus one feudal lord declares, "si no me acaba el miedo, iré a ver si mis
vasallos se rebelan."[210] (This fear extends also to kings.)[211] The rich might fear that
the poor will revolt, but still they do not want to show it. The aristocrat Constantino admonishes his companion, "Calla, cobarde, que es honrar esta canalla
mostrar tenerlos miedo. Cinquenta somos, y el valor que heredo basta."[212] This
line is a reference to the oft-debated question among Renaissance humanists of
whether virtue in general – or specific virtues, such as valour – could be inherited
through noble blood.[213]

Tyrants, especially, have ample cause to fear that they will be overthrown or
deposed: "no hay tirano sin miedo."[214] It is a commonplace of *comedia* criticism to
wonder just how far Lope de Vega's denunciation of tyrannicide extended in a historical drama such as *Fuenteovejuna*, where a mob of *villanos* assassinate the tyrant Fernán
Gómez, who has abused their women and disrupted their town's peaceful, rustic life.
Writing centuries later during the Spanish Civil War, the director of the travelling
student theatrical troupe La Barraca, Federico García Lorca, famously did away with
the Catholic Monarchs in his adaptation of the play to allow for a more definitively
subversive political reading. General Franco got the message, had him arrested and
executed by the Guardia Civil, and ordered his unmarked body to be thrown into a
mass grave. In the words of Lope himself, tyrants of all time periods have reason to
"tener al vulgo miedo, que señala con el dedo, y con la lengua amenaza."[215]

A dirty little secret buried deep within the *comedia* corpus is that the tyrant's
fear of the oppressed extends also to gender relations. In fact, one of the primary

reasons men keep women in subjection is that they are actually afraid of them.[216] Thus a male character refers to "estas las fieras mujeres, que ocasionaron mi miedo, éste el azote del hombre, el pasmo del Universo."[217] The deliberately named Lesbia offers a radical proposal:

> Y porque vean
> los hombres, que si se atrasan
> las mujeres en valor,
> y ingenio, ellos son la causa,
> pues ellos son quien las quita
> de miedo libros, y espadas,
> dispone, que la mujer
> que se aplicare inclinada
> al estudio de las letras,
> o al manejo de las armas,
> sea admitida a los puestos
> públicos, siendo en su patria
> capaces del honor que en guerra
> y paz más al hombre ensalzan.[218]

Here she accuses men of denying women the chance to study[219] or learn how to defend themselves with weapons out of fear that if they did so, women would surpass them in both intellect and physical strength. She proposes as an experiment that the tables be turned by educating women and then raising them to positions of public authority, where she is sure they will prove worthy of the honours men customarily garner for themselves, both in peace time and at war.

Misogynistic fear of women takes the form of accusing them of lying ("Eres la mujer primera que tiene miedo al mentir")[220] or even biting just like monkeys do when they are frightened.[221] Fearing virile or courageous women, men feel the need to put them in their place by instilling fear in *them* instead; one male character enjoins another, "pongámosle miedo a esta mujer de valor."[222] The cultural imperative in operation here is that men who admit to being afraid of women will be considered effeminate, "afeminados viles (si una mujer os causó tanto asombro, miedo tanto, tanto pasmo) … [M]ujer soy, que estas montañas defiendo."[223] This *mujer varonil*[224] deliberately plays upon such stereotypes to call men out as cowards while she defends her mountain range.

This strategy is clever, for she knows that men are *macho*; as Rodrigo Arias boasts, "Miedo en mí no tiene entrada."[225] Another male character confirms, "no soy hombre yo, que en mi vida mostré miedo."[226] He makes an exaggerated claim to never have shown fear – even once – in his life. Fear is the antithesis of manliness because it is perceived as weak and fragile (we can almost see here the puffed-up male thumping his chest with his fist, issuing a challenge to fate or the universe: "¿pero a mí se atreve el frágil, débil afecto del miedo?").[227]

By contrast – with the notable exception of the *mujer varonil* – women on stage are portrayed as fearful in general,[228] although some female characters would deny this assertion vehemently.[229] We find such categorical statements as "en la mujer es natural, la ley guarde del miedo"[230] and "la mujer más valiente, toda es miedo,"[231] indicating that even the most valiant woman is still undone by fright. Women fear men in a patriarchal society.[232] Diego says to Ana about an illicit portrait of a gentleman found to be in her possession:

> ¿Querrás decirme que fue
> de una amiga, que por miedo
> de su padre, o su marido,
> te le trajo a ti en secreto?[233]

He assumes the reason for the miniature portrait's[234] surreptitious delivery must be the lady's fear of repercussions from a father or husband who might prove overly zealous to defend the family's honour.

Women feared not just husbands and fathers, but also brothers in this warped system where female bodies were considered repositories of intangible cultural values. Celia confesses,

> [T]engo notable miedo
> a mi hermano, porque al fin
> como a padre le respeto;
> trata de casarme ahora,
> que para mi casamiento
> tiene treinta mil ducados.[235]

Here she expresses "notable" fear of her brother, who has stepped into a paternal role towards her in the absence of their father. He wants to marry her off, and for that purpose has brought a dowry of 30,000 ducats. She obviously does not like this idea, or else she would not express fear at the prospect.

Female characters on stage do express fear specifically of getting married, as when one woman says, "esos hombres me dan miedo, porque estoy temiendo el verme casada con uno de ellos."[236] But paradoxically, women also fear being lonely and single: "ha de tener miedo una sola mujer, de vivir sin compañía."[237] This fear might possibly be occasioned by perceived physical danger, as for example of being assaulted: "Mujer hay, que el ir a Misa sola, gran miedo le da."[238] A related fear might be of receiving unwanted sexual advances. Thus Pastrana expresses fear specifically that a man will pinch her and implores him to keep his hands to himself.[239] This (probably wise) precaution could extend to a more general fear of being harrassed, as when a girl admits fearfully, "mirad que soy niña y he miedo a los hombres que andan en la villa."[240] As the #MeToo movement indicates, this fear by women of unsolicited contact by men has unfortunately not diminished, even in our times.

We would do well to ask whether in addition to considerations of gender, there might also be an ethnic aspect to fear in play here. We begin to approach this topic somewhat generically through fear of rough geography[241] or unknown lands.[242] These more general fears degenerate quickly, however, into a fear specifically of "savages," as when Gila reports:

> Lo espantoso del traje,
> que me pudiera dar viendo un salvaje,
> o miedo, o desengaño,
> me picó más aprisa, que lo extraño.[243]

These "savages"[244] may seem like giants[245] or else normally tall human beings who nonetheless possess some monstrous feature of unnatural size.[246] Alternatively, they might simply be ugly;[247] regrettably, physical appearance has enjoyed a perceived correlation to moral virtue at least since Plato.[248] Unfortunately the superficiality of this assumption has still not disappeared from Western culture.

The most salient precise ethnic fear during this time period was undoubtedly the fear of Muslims by Spaniards. Thus we hear characters exhorting each other, "no os espantéis, amigos, no cobréis al Moro miedo."[249] One fearful character admits that with each step Muslims take, it feels like they are treading on his soul.[250] The concrete reason why Spaniards were so fearful of Muslims is that they dreaded being kidnapped and held captive for ransom like Cervantes, who languished in Algiers for five years.[251] Bruce Taylor quotes from a letter written by the citizens of Gibraltar in 1614 expressing their fear of being taken captive by Muslims:

> [T]he people felt secure "neither at night nor during the day, neither in bed nor at mealtimes, neither in the fields nor in our homes." Corsair assaults continued unabated, with dozens of people being carried away to North Africa each year and huge sums being required to ransom them from captivity.[252]

A character on stage named Jorge alludes to this fear explicitly:

> Tengo miedo
> si una vez con ella estoy
> que esclavo en Argel me quedo
> para siempre desde hoy.[253]

Here the fear of being "trapped" by a woman is likened humorously to slavery in Algiers.

Once kidnapped, one of the only strategies for survival to which Spaniards had recourse was to "turn Turk" and, as renegades, deny their Christian faith.[254] We hear traces of this anguishing dilemma in the lines spoken by a character named Padilla:

> [Y]a no sólo tengo miedo
> de cepo, cadena y grillos,
> sino de cantar el Credo.[255]

Here he confesses to being ashamed to sing the Apostles' Creed out of fear that he will be identified by his Muslim captors as a Christian. The obvious implication is that he, and characters like him, now experience a double fear that Muslims will discover they are really Christians and vice versa. Thus one theatrical "Muslim by profession" alludes to the "silencio que he tenido en callar que soy Cristiano, fue miedo de pensar que me tendrían por renegado."[256]

A renegade effectively brought upon himself the worst of both worlds: if he was found out, superiors of either faith would doubt his sincerity. To make his imposture more convincing, he would don Muslim clothing[257] and learn admirably well (in a way fans of good acting such as these playwrights would appreciate) how to speak Arabic and otherwise play the part.[258] Arrogant Muslim characters on stage seem aware of the effect their reputation for ruthless cruelty exerts over their Spanish enemies. Thus a Muslim character named Alima brags,

> [M]i fama solamente
> da tal miedo a los Cristianos;
> ved los soldados, que al mar
> corriendo van fugitivos.[259]

The awe of him apparently strikes such fear in Christian hearts that, rather than facing such a grim opponent, even soldiers with military training run scurrying back to sea.

A similar courage is expressed by Andalusian Muslims who are up against none other than the Maestre de Santiago, one of Spain's famed military orders of knights originally constituted by noblemen in the context of the Crusades: "Venga el Maestre [de Santiago] y sus cruces, que tanto miedo nos pone, veamos si descompone tantos Moros Andaluces."[260] Here a Muslim defies the Maestre to approach with his "crosses" (i.e., flags bearing the symbol of a red cross in the shape of a sword, which was the emblem of the Knights of Santiago [see figure 11])[261] to see whether he could disperse so many Andalusian Muslims.

In truth, however, we find almost as many lines in the *comedias* expressing defiance of Muslims as expressing fear of them; for example,

[¿]Qué hombre yo para miedo
de tres morillos villanos[?]
[Q]ue todas vuestras tres manos
cortaré con sólo un dedo.[262]

Here a Spaniard boasts hyperbolically that he can cut the hands off three "little Moors" without lifting more than one of his own fingers. Another Spaniard similarly exhorts another to place "tu silla sobre la cerviz cobarde del Africano, y su miedo postre a tu invencible espada."[263] This ekphrastic picture reminds us of contemporaneous artistic depictions of Santiago Matamoros (literally, the Moor-slayer), patron saint of Spain, appearing dressed as a knight on horseback and not flinching to inflict slaughter on Muslims (see figure 12). The political repercussions of such images produce ripple effects even within Spanish culture today. For example, one such depiction of Santiago Matamoros in the form of a statue was scheduled to be removed from public view in Santiago de Compostela (the shrine thought to house the relics of this saint) in the wake of Muslim terrorists' bombing of the Atocha train station in 2004.[264]

Another grand master of a different one of Spain's military orders, the Knights of Calatrava, is similarly said to inspire fear in his Muslim opponent:

Trajo las suyas el [Maestre] de Calatrava,
y el Moro a sus hazañas cobró miedo,
perdiendo la esperanza en que se hallaba.[265]

The fear of this famous warrior is apparently enough to cause the Muslim to lose hope. In addition to specific military orders, certain cities of Spain were considered powerful enough by Muslims to strike fear in their hearts; for example, Toledo:

Toledo,
aquella insigne ciudad,
que dio a España majestad,
y a toda el África miedo.[266]

This mention of "all Africa" is a bit exaggerated; in reality, most of Spain's African Muslim enemies were confined to a geographical area known as the Barbary Coast.[267]

However, there was also a danger of invasion by these Muslims' Ottoman allies in Turkey. Thus Santa Juana encourages Carlos:

Tendrá a tu buena fortuna,
y no imitadas hazañas

> tal miedo el Turco feroz,
> que volviendo las espaldas
> la Otomana multitud,
> pisarán después tus plantas
> las lunas, que enarboló
> la potencia Solimana.[268]

Here she predicts the "ferocious" Turk, upon seeing the unheard-of deeds of noble Spanish warriors – who will tread under their feet the moon symbol appearing on Turkish flags – will have no choice but to turn tail and flee.

The other great internal enemies Spaniards faced – in addition to Muslims, *moriscos*,[269] and their allies – were, of course, the Jews. Jews are depicted repeatedly in the *comedias* as fearful, to the point where this connection becomes a commonplace ("no fuera yo Judío a no temer";[270] "no fuera buen Judío, si no tuviera buen miedo,"[271] etc.). In fact, Jews are pictured as wailing in fear.[272] Specifically, Jews would fear the Inquisition ("miedo de la santa Inquisición"[273]), which was weaponized for the purpose of rooting out covert Judaizers in the wake of Spain's imminent decision to expel the Jewish people in 1492.

But aside from this specific phobia, Jews in the *comedias* are also portrayed as fearful in general, in a cultural move that undoubtedly participates in antisemitic propaganda fashioned for the theatre with the tools of emotional discourse. Jews are represented on stage as cowards who are fearful of charms or spells.[274] According to superstitious beliefs from this time period, these charms might be placed deliberately in the food of an individual to bewitch that person or gain control over his or her actions, especially to induce the victim toward romantic love or away from it (i.e., by causing impotence).[275]

A parallel belief – although this one could be accidental instead of deliberate – was the notion that someone could cast the "evil eye."[276] The results of *aojamiento* might include shrivelling up, falling ill, or even dying.[277] Whether or not early modern people believed in such superstitions – and there are alternative lines we could point to which present a more sceptical viewpoint[278] – nonetheless, the conflict between people groups signified by such accusations was all too real. A testament to this mutual hatred and suspicion may be found in lines spoken by a Jew to Madrigal (a Christian) by yelling out a window and cursing the target of his wrath:

> Mueras de hambre, bárbaro insolente,
> el cuotidiano pan te niegue el Dios,
> andes de puerta en puerta mendigando,
> échente de la tierra como a Gafo,
> agraz de nuestros ojos espantajo,
> de nuestra sinagoga asombro y miedo.[279]

The pronouncer of this curse condemns the "insolent barbarian" to go from door to door begging because God will deny him his daily bread (incidentally, *gafo* is still an insult hurled in Venezuela at someone considered to be dumb, stupid, or brutish).

Once Spain had rid itself of "internal" enemies – i.e., Jews and Muslims – it was time to look elsewhere for other foes to conquer. Just as heroes of Spain's Reconquest took up the mantle of Crusaders fighting infidels in the Holy Land, now that the Reconquest was completed, Spain's martial energies must be directed someplace else. Historically Spain had a long-standing interest in southern Italy, due both to hereditary claims of Aragon to Naples and Sicily and to Spain's self-nominated role as defender of the papacy (and, by extension, the Catholic faith). Thus a warlike Spaniard boasts on stage, "¿no soy yo quien puso a toda Italia miedo y quien con mi nombre puedo ponerle al mundo también?"[280] He thinks the mere mention of his name to be so intimidating that it will strike fear in the heart of the whole world.

Likewise, Portugal lived in perpetual fear of annexation by Spain – an eventuality that finally occurred during the reign of King Philip II. These events and their protagonists would have been readily recognizable to *comedia* audiences in lines such as "Pedro Arias fue quien puso con el nombre de Aragón miedo al Algarve confuso"[281] (the Algarve is the southernmost part of Portugal). During the rule of the Hapsburg monarchs, Spain extended its dominion northward in Europe as well, to the Low Countries;[282] the most famous echo of Spain's exploits in the Netherlands may be found in Lope de Vega's *Los españoles en Flandes*.

Spain's perennial rival on the Continent during this time period was, of course, France. We find traces of this perpetual enmity falling on both sides of the fear equation. A messenger from Rome harangues the French by taunting them about fearing the Spaniards:

¿Los Españoles teméis?
¿Miedo con vosotros puede?[283]

We must not forget it was also Spanish troops led by *el Gran Capitán* Gonzalo Fernández de Córdoba who had protected Pope Alexander VI (the Spaniard Rodrigo Borgia) from invasion by French troops led by King Charles VIII. But fear by the Spaniards of the French also shows up now and again, especially in the lines of French characters on stage. Thus a French general boasts of his prowess against Spain:

Sí, Monsieur, que si llega al Mediodía,
será rayo de Francia, y de la mía,
doblad esas banderas, y volvamos
contentos de haber puesto a España miedo.[284]

Spain's rivalry with France was too notorious to escape mention not just in historical dramas, but also in hagiographical plays such as this one (Lope de Vega's *Juan de Dios y Antón Martín*).

Not content with European conquests, during this time period Spain launched its colonial empire. The *comedias* contain a certain amount of propaganda favouring this enterprise. For example, Pillalonco, an Inca priest, delivers the following speech to Pillán, an Inca god:

> Cuéntame, Pillán divino,
> ¿quién es este famoso
> Capitán, que del Perú
> viene a Chile sobre el hombro
> del mar Antártico, dando
> tanto miedo a nuestro Polo,
> que los fieros Araucanos
> de Valdivia victoriosos
> los nunca vencidos pechos
> bañan en cobarde asombro?[285]

These admiring words placed in the mouth of an Indigenous person portray Spanish conquistadores as striking fear in the hearts of the "fierce," "never-before-beaten" Arawaks.

But this fairly obvious indoctrination of Indigenous people by their colonizers could only extend so far. Also reflected in some *comedia* lines is, conversely, Spaniards' own fear that Native peoples will kill them in resistance and revolt. For example, in Lope de Vega's *Los guanches de Tenerife y conquista de Canaria* one Spaniard tries to reassure another, "no hayas miedo tú que mueran nuestros Españoles hoy."[286] Spain itself had once been a colony of Rome, so Spaniards remembered what colonization felt like. In the play *Roma abrasada*, Lope de Vega took the opportunity to remember Spain's classical past. At one point the Parthian King Volgesio refers on stage to imperial eagles emblazoned by Romans on their paraphernalia: "a sus águilas el miedo / que tiene ahora la sujeta España."[287]

This image of a fearful Spain subject to Rome was somehow necessary for classicizing national mythology even though Old Christian Spaniards usually preferred to trace their lineage back to the Visigoths. (The Visigoths had played the part of warlike conquerors in their invasion and conquest of the Roman province of Hispania.) Thus we hear Don Alonso boast, "Godo soy, nací sin miedo."[288] Obviously ethnic identities can be put on and taken off at will according to the ideological agenda of the moment; the basic rule of this game for emotional discourse is that the winners will always boast of their prowess, while the losers will always seek to inspire sympathy. In its role of fostering patriotic propaganda, the *comedia* frequently imputes fear to "foreigners."[289] But in a remarkable moment of self-awareness, a Spanish character notes, "Admíranse los hombres, de amor al propio, y al extraño miedo."[290] We fear whatever seems strange to us. After all, xenophobia was the order of the day.

Which brings us to the moral connotations of fear versus valour. Fear bears a definitely negative moral valence (as in, "yo no puedo hacer virtud lo que miedo")[291] but also a pejorative common-sense one. This prejudice is voiced in stark phrases like "Es necio miedo"[292] or "Siempre es ignorante el miedo."[293] Fear is shameful[294] and therefore condemned by the courageous.[295] Characters accuse one another of fear to impute cowardice, as when the King retorts to Fortán: "Gentil excusa de miedo."[296] The act of fleeing, in particular, is condemned as cowardly, as in "nada es peor, que el huir de miedo"[297] and "¿cómo a sufrir me resuelvo la fuga cobarde, que el miedo aconseja?"[298] In contrast, the most honourable thing to do instead of fleeing is to stand and fight, even if it means dying in the attempt.[299]

If fear bears such negative moral connotations, this implies it can be avoided. Can fear, in fact, be controlled? S.J. Rachman asserts, "Fear seems to feed on a sense of uncontrollability: it arises and persists when the person finds himself in a threatening situation over which he feels he has little or no control."[300] Characters ask this very question for themselves ("¿cómo puedo yo este miedo perder al mal?")[301] or for a hypothetical other ("¿quién pudiera poner freno al miedo?").[302] We find characters who are determined to lose their fear[303] or else dismiss it.[304]

But fear can prove difficult to resist.[305] At best, it's a process, and is best expressed grammatically through use of the progressive tense.[306] Fear can be repaired[307] in the sense that someone can seek reassurance.[308] Fear can be deposed by someone talking you down off a high ledge or out of a tree limb.[309] Characters tell one another not to lose heart[310] but instead to trample mercilessly on their fear.[311]

Fear can be tempered,[312] mitigated,[313] consoled,[314] or remedied, particularly by turning one's thoughts in a different direction.[315] Psychologist S.J. Rachman confirms, "concentration of attention upon a distracting task in a situation of stress reduces anxiety."[316] One can free oneself from fear[317] or be freed therefrom by someone else.[318] Honour is said to be fear's antidote: "venza el honor al miedo."[319] These plays record some failures of these efforts at emotion regulation ("De esta templanza mal se asegura mi miedo");[320] but if actual fear management doesn't work, the rule is: fake it until you make it.[321]

Is fear ever justified? The *comedias* answer this question in the affirmative: "Es justo el miedo en tantas ocasiones, y no son ilusiones, y no son antojos."[322] In other words, there are times when fear can be entirely legitimate.[323] Characters sometimes use fear to spur each other on to action.[324] This leads us to a question: is there a good kind of fear? Social scientists claim that "mild fear may improve efficiency" as well as accuracy or precision.[325] Once again, these plays offer a similarly affirmative answer. "[E]l miedo … es en fin un Católico Cristiano"[326] – fear is a good Catholic Christian.

Why is that? A character named Pedro offers the insight that "Ese sólo es miedo honrado, que advirtiendo su justicia, temer a Dios es virtud."[327] Fear of God is honourable (and indeed, even virtuous) because God is just. It is proper to fear His righteous punishment, that is, to experience "miedo de los enojos de Dios."[328] As we saw at the outset of this chapter, *Temor* (Fear) appears as an allegorical figure dressed as a pilgrim in the *loa* for an *auto sacramental.* Man sees him and asks,

> ¿Quién es aquel peregrino,
> que parece que su sombra
> le atemoriza y le asombra?

What follows is a dialogue between Love and Fear:

> AMOR: El Temor de Dios divino,
> que siempre vive asustado
> de su justicia y rigor;
> llega y háblale: Temor.
> TEMOR: ¿Si soy a juicio llamado?
> AMOR: No temas; el Amor soy.[329]

In other words, the person who fears God properly does not have to fear punishment, because God is love. Fear of God logically extends to a holy fear of the Eucharist, which becomes Christ's body through the miracle of transubstantiation; from there it extends outward also to the other sacraments.[330]

Indeed, only a tyrant does not fear God; such a negative example is portrayed (and punished) in Lope de Vega's *El tirano castigado.*[331] The ultimate punishment such a person should fear is that of losing salvation.[332] In fact, the *comedias* seem to indicate that the sensation of guilt lies at the root of all fear ("siempre el miedo de la culpa nace").[333] This means, in consequence, that the only way out of feeling fearful is to obtain absolution for one's sins through the sacrament of reconciliation.[334] The relief of absolution – even if a specific, further penance is assigned by the priest – allows the conscience to rest in the security that one no longer needs to fear death.[335] Early modern Spanish dramas may well have deliberately stoked or exploited their audience's fears for dramatic effect, but at least they also offered effective antidotes.

9

That White Sustenance, Despair

So We must meet apart –
You there – I – here –
With just the Door ajar
That Oceans are – and Prayer –
And that White Sustenance –
Despair –[1]

One who despairs … abandons God.[2]

Despair is an extreme limit-point beyond other feelings, as when Abenzaide says to Juan Gómez: "es sentimiento, que en mí / pasa a desesperación."[3] It is like sorrow or sadness, but more exaggerated.[4] In *The Courage to Be*, theologian Paul Tillich writes that despair "is an ultimate or 'boundary-line' situation. One cannot go beyond it."[5]

Etymologically speaking, despair is the opposite of hope, and *comedia* playwrights enjoyed the rich resonance of this linguistic association.[6] A disconsolate[7] or despairing person lacks hope when there is simply none left,[8] because it has either been shattered[9] or buried.[10] In *Despair: Sickness or Sin?* Mary Louise Bringle defines despair as "the specific surrender of hope."[11]

Despair mourns the loss of hope by wearing mourning garments.[12] But really, despair bears a more fraught relationship to hope; things are seldom so simple and uncomplicated as merely "lack" or "loss." Despair begins when hope starts doubting, as in "no hay mayor tormento que la esperanza dudosa."[13] Despair comes when hope sounds false notes.[14] Despair is in fact only reached when there is no longer even a glimmer of light remaining: "¿Pues no me queda sombra de esperanza?"[15] Despair sounds a wake-up call to false hopes, pretence, and deceit.[16] Despair is a loss of trust or confidence and faith, as when the Demon asks of Divine Justice:

Si se concede término a esperanza,
¿a quién se le ha de dar? Que no la tiene:

> si por Fe, y Caridad favor se alcanza,
> para el profundo abismo se previene.
> Porque perdiendo ya la confianza,
> a desesperación tan grande viene,
> que diciendo, del Cielo desconfío,
> repudió la razón al albedrío.[17]

Here the Theological Virtues of Faith and Love have lost their erstwhile companion, Hope.

What are the characteristics of despair? Despair is blind, as in "ciega desesperación."[18] Despair is precipitous and hasty, "[p]recipitado anhelo de desesperación."[19] Despair throws caution to the wind.[20] It causes its victim to lose appetite, as in this dialogue with and concerning the melancholy Old Testament character Amón:

> AMÓN: Pues ¿qué puedo hacer?
> DAVID: Buscar
>   alegres divertimientos.
> IONADAB: De uno le decía yo ahora,
>   harto alegre.
> AMÓN: Ya está bueno:
>   todos cansan más que alivian,
>   porque como yo no tengo
>   gusto, se me vuelven todos
>   en más pena, porque es cierto
>   que en el humor que domina
>   se convierte el alimento.
> DAVID: Aunque en metáfora sea
>   eso que has dicho, yo quiero,
>   ya que de alimento hablas,
>   materialmente entenderlo:
>   ¿no es de desesperación
>   especie, que un hombre cuerdo
>   aun este humano tributo
>   se niegue a sí?
> IONADAB: Sí, por cierto;
>   yo que coma, y aun de todo
>   le estaba ahora diciendo,
>   pero no me entiende.[21]

Here the despairing Amón rejects various remedies suggested to him, including that he eat something to make himself feel better.

The suffering of despair is inexpressible, worse than martyrdom.[22] Even imprisonment is preferable: "de mejor gana estuviera con mi esperanza en prisión, que libre y desesperado."[23] This assertion is supported by a recent Israeli psychiatric study of despair and hope among released prisoners.[24] However, in "The Phenomenology of Despair," philosopher Anthony Steinbock considers despair to *be* a form of imprisonment, namely, temporal imprisonment in the present:

> [D]espair is oriented to the present … In despair, I am consumed not so much by the now, but by the absence of the future and the past … [D]espair confines us to the present and functions as a kind of imprisonment … Past and future are constricted to an overwhelming experience of a fixed present.[25]

This equation of despair with imprisonment was already current in the early modern period, as we see from the iron cage of despair encountered by the pilgrim in the Interpreter's house in John Bunyan's *Pilgrim's Progress*.[26]

Various colours are associated with this passion, each bearing a different resonance according to context. Despair is connected to the colour yellow: "el color amarillo, que jeroglífico es de la desesperación."[27] Some say the colour of despair is a dark, putrid green – presumably the rotten version of bright, green hope.[28] Another option is black, a colour associated with despair also in English, as in the phrase "black despair." This colour for despair is described specifically as the colour of mourning.[29] It can be flecked with gold, representing sadness.[30] Despair is further associated with specific plants, such as the broom shrub[31] or wallflower.[32] Despair is experienced during a bleak, dreary winter,[33] but the imagery associated with it is often more sinister than simply cold weather. It is the hidden rock causing a shipwreck[34] – an image all too familiar to mariners sailing to Spain's "New" World colonies. The allegorical figure of Despair appears holding an unsheathed dagger in Cervantes's *La casa de los celos*.[35] At some point, if left unchecked, despair becomes one's executioner.[36]

Where does despair come from? Despair results from cowardice, as in "tu cobardía es muerte de tu esperanza,"[37] or from weakness: "unas tristezas y ansias en el corazón, que a tal desesperación han traído mis flaquezas."[38] Despair can be the result of waiting eternally in suspense.[39] Foolish passion leads to despair,[40] as does jealousy[41] – for example, because a romantic rival has gained the upper hand.[42] Despair can be a consequence of prolonged hunger or being surrounded by enemies, as in a military siege:

No queda
otra esperanza a la vida,
que contraste dos violencias,
del hambre que nos desmaya,
y el contrario que nos cerca.[43]

Despair can result from losing one's homestead due to war.[44] Persistence is useless if accompanied by despair: "es inútil la porfía, donde falta la esperanza."[45]

A perhaps unanticipated context for despair that is peculiarly appropriate to the cultures of medieval and early modern Spain is that of revenge. Offences to one's honour could lead to desperate gambits to seek revenge, as when Doña Urraca describes the action of Rodrigo Díaz de Vivar, el Cid:

Con qué desesperación
quiere vengarse, de un tajo
le partió de arriba abajo
cabeza, riendas, y arzón,
al caballo de don Diego.[46]

Here the Cid wants to avenge himself of the affront he suffered at the hands of Diego Ordóñez de Lara, who destroyed the Cid's helmet with a sword, leaving his face and head bathed in blood. His response is to plunge his own sword into Don Diego's horse.

What, precisely, are despair's theological contours? First of all, the *comedias* are clear on one point: despair is a sin. As a Christian priest explains to a Muslim sultan's wife,

Es la desesperación
pecado tan malo y feo,
que ninguno, según creo,
le hace comparación.
El matarse es cobardía,
y es poner tasa a la mano
liberal del soberano
bien que nos sustenta y cría.
Esta gran verdad se ha visto
donde no puede dudarse,
que más pecó en ahorcarse
Judas, que en vender a Cristo.[47]

Here the holy Father points out to her that Judas's despair, which led him to suicide (see figure 13), was an even greater sin than betraying Christ.

Countless plays affirm this message. Despair is characterized as hellish,[48] inevitably leading to perdition. In reference to Thomistic theology, Rebecca DeYoung confirms in "The Roots of Despair" that "in despair, one counts oneself already among the damned."[49] This is true even within the paradigm of classical mythology. For example, Venus says to her son Eneas: "Hijo Eneas, ¿dónde vas? Con tal desesperación, a tu cierta perdición."[50]

But most of the time in the *comedias*, despair is portrayed as the emotion experienced by non-Christians in the last moment before death. An illustrative instance of this occurs when the dying Hiszentarif exclaims to the Christians around him:

> Ya
> en mi desesperación
> poco hay que vencer, Cristianos,
> pues ... pero en balde intentó
> decirlo el labio, si al pecho
> falta la respiración.
> *Stage direction: [Cae.]*[51]

The stage directions clarify that the actor is supposed to pretend to fall down dead at this precise moment.

Theologically speaking, despair is considered to be the sole unforgivable sin because despairing of God's mercy leads to damnation.[52] Mary Louise Bringle explains the theology behind this idea: "This type of sinful despair is finally 'unforgivable': not so much because God cannot or will not forgive it, as because it dully and obdurately refuses to embrace the possibility of forgiveness."[53] She further outlines the positions of various famous theologians with regard to this concept:

> Luther ultimately concurs with Thomas Aquinas and with Augustine in designating despair an unforgivable sin against the Holy Ghost. No offering of God's mercy will suffice to forgive us if we resolutely refuse to trust in the very possibility of our forgiveness ... To renounce the possibility of grace is to foreclose on the divine mercy with a presumptuous assumption that our own assessment of a situation is superior to God's.[54]

John McCloskey confirms this theology with reference to Christopher Marlowe's contemporaneous play *Faustus*: "It is the sin of despair which effects the catastrophe. No matter what the sin, repentance and salvation are always possible unless, through despair, man sins against the Holy Ghost."[55] Katherine Koller describes the sin of despair in greater detail with reference to the Despair Canto of Book I in Edmund Spenser's contemporaneous *Fairie Queene*:

> Despair was one of the great temptations at the hour of death. At this moment the devil tried to remove all hope of God's mercy, and by the enumeration of man's sins, by describing the miseries of this present life and stressing the just punishment man deserved, lead him to suicide. Satan, when death is near, casts before man's eyes a mist, that unless he take heed, he shall see nothing but the fierce wrath and terrible judgment of God and sin, desperation, death and hell … If the assault of the devil is successful he has won the battle for man's soul. By despairing of God's mercy and by self-murder, man has brought about his physical and spiritual death and the eternal damnation of his body and soul. The temptation of despair is explicit in the *Ars Moriendi* as one of the five great temptations at the hour of death. It was also discussed at length by St. Augustine, by the church fathers, by Catholic writers and in Spenser's own time by … Protestant writers … These writers also gave explicit instructions about the way to resist the temptation to despair. Refuse to argue with the devil; pray earnestly, remember the promises of God; trust in His mercy, think on Christ's forgiveness of Peter, of the thief on the cross; repeat the creed.[56]

Figure 14 shows a drawing that appears in a manuscript *Ars Moriendi* depicting artistically this temptation to despair.

To avoid this sin, believers are commanded to stay hopeful, despite their errors.[57] Satan himself despairs because he knows he is beyond salvation; thus Lucifer proclaims with saucy arrogance: "Mi misma desesperación, supuesto, que habiendo errado, de haber errado, no me arrepiento."[58] Bettie Doebler rehearses the recurrence of this motif in mythology as well as classics of world literature:

> Lucifer was … known throughout theological history as the primary type of one who had fallen unregenerate through sin to despair. Along with Phaeton from the classical tradition and … Judas, his place in typology was unchallenged. Lucifer frozen in the depths of Dante's *Inferno* is perhaps the most powerful allegorical image of the psychological nature of despair in all of literature.[59]

Harold Golder confirms that this characterization of Satan is echoed in John Milton's *Paradise Lost*, an epic poem contemporaneous with many of these Spanish plays: "It [despair] provides, in Milton's *Paradise Lost*, one of Satan's most powerful motives in rejecting a reconciliation with Heaven."[60] Milton's Satan invokes despair specifically in his rhetorical question, "Which way shall I fly Infinite wrath and infinite despair?"[61]

Demons intentionally tempt human beings to despair in order to effect their damnation, as when one woman expresses her awareness that "ya el demonio envuelto en mi flaqueza a desesperación tan grande incita mi loca y feminil naturaleza."[62] (This pejorative characterization of a "feminine nature" was of course penned by a male playwright.) Thus the allegorical figure of Furor commands Tierra about the human family he is giving her:

> Pues afligirla a que sea
> desesperación, para que
> caduca, y perecedera,
> de tu Cárcel temporal,
> pase a mi Cárcel eterna.[63]

This chilling line reflects demonic Furor's desire to imprison humanity eternally in hell.

Through the diabolical arts of magic and necromancy, specifically, Satan and his demons try to tempt human souls to renounce hope, as in Juan Ruiz de Alarcón's *La cueva de Salamanca*, about the legendary necromancer the Marquis of Villena: "Como el Marqués estudió esta diabólica ciencia, tuvo el infierno esperanza de su perdición eterna."[64]

The study of magic often led to the signing of a pact with the devil, written with the magician's own blood, in which he forfeited his soul[65] in exchange for earthly rewards. Demonic pacts in literature are not limited to male magicians, however; many witches and female magicians entered a similar agreement. For example, in Calderón's *Las cadenas del demonio*, Irene says to the Demon:

> [D]esesperación
> me hizo (de cólera tiemblo)
> salir de mí (de ira rabio)
> hasta (ahógame el aliento)
> decir, que en muerte, y en vida
> el alma le daré en precio
> a cualquiera que me dé
> la libertad que apetezco.[66]

Here she points specifically to despair as the emotion that compelled her to agree to this diabolical bargain.

The ultimate consequence of despair is succumbing to demonic possession, as we see in this dialogue between Saint Augustine and Satan, speaking through a female demoniac:

ENDEMONIADA: ¿Hablas[,] Agustín[,] conmigo?
AGUSTÍN: Contigo[,] villano ingrato.

> ENDEMONIADA: ¿Luego atrevimiento tienes
>   de argüir conmigo?
> AGUSTÍN: Aunque sabes
>   mucho, y tú mismo te alabes,
>   ¿por qué en este cuerpo vienes?
> ENDEMONIADA: Porque me ha dado lugar
>   con su desesperación.[67]

Here we see that despair gives entrance to the devil, who would otherwise not obtain permission from God to enter the body of a human being. In "The Left Hand of God: Despair in Medieval and Renaissance Tradition," Susan Snyder confirms the connection of despair to demonic possession as demonstrated in medieval texts:

> Chrysostom's second letter to Stagirius reveals that his correspondent was "possessed" by a demon who tempted him to lose his trust in God and to kill himself … The seventh-century *Poenitentiale Theodori* mentions both despair and suicide in the section on diabolical possession.[68]

But it is not necessary to sign a pact with the devil to despair at the moment of death. Any sinner (which includes all of humanity) could potentially lose hope at this crucial moment. The classic example of this pattern is Tirso de Molina's *El condenado por desconfiado*, the very title of which announces the reason for the sinner's condemnation. The fate of the desperate sinner has perhaps been made most famous by Mozart's operatic adaptation *Don Giovanni*, at the end of which the unrepentant Don Juan sinks through a trap door into the fiery pit of hell (see figure 15). This Enlightenment adaptation of Tirso's *El burlador de Sevilla* forms an interesting contrast to José Zorrilla's much longer play *Don Juan Tenorio*, written in Spain at the height of Romanticism. In this later version, the dead Inés comes back as a ghost to save Don Juan's soul by striking a bargain with God, which Don Juan accepts: either she can convince him to trust God's mercy, thereby escaping hell's fire, or else she will give up her own soul in order to save his. Most later consumers of the Don Juan myth do not realize how far this version strays from the original.

If Don Juan is the negative exemplar, then who is a positive model showing theatrical audiences how to deal with despair? The foremost exemplary figure offered from the Old Testament is Job, who even in his despair chose not to curse God and die (as even his own friends counselled him to do): "Bien ha engañado las señas de la desesperación, que así maldiciendo el día, maldijo el pecado Job."[69] Here we see that Job "deceived" despair by cursing sin instead. Other biblical models may be found in the *comedia* corpus, although most of these figures pale in comparison to this Old Testament hero.

Another biblical figure whose despair is justified within a *comedia* text is Amón, King David's son, who rapes his own sister Tamar. He asks to be left alone to cope with his despair privately: "dejadme a solas … mientras véis que me acompañan desesperación, tristeza, locura, imposibles, rabia."[70] This is a typical response to despair, as confirmed by gerontologist Melvin Kimble: "Despair grows and festers in isolation."[71] Unfortunately, Tamar's and Amón's story does not contain as edifying an outcome as Job's.

While despair does lead to damnation if it occurs at the moment of death, not all despair happens at such a crucial juncture. To what other things does despair lead, if the person experiencing it is not also dying? Despair leads to confusion[72] and lack of confidence.[73] It causes one to turn inward and retreat from the world: "me vuelvo a mi jardín primero, que ni peligros, ni esperanza quiero."[74] This line might remind us of Fray Luis de León's Horatian "Oda a la vida retirada."[75] Despair impedes resistance[76] and leads to discord.[77] Despair leads one to attempt vain actions,[78] leading to risk[79] and imprudent decisions, the consequences of which can be all too dangerous. Forensic psychiatrists who treat criminals (for example, murderers who have killed their parents) confirm that "recklessness … arises from despair … Individuals with the feeling that they have nothing to lose are prone to full-blown desperation. Thus, they are particularly dangerous."[80]

An article titled "Does Despair Really Kill?" appearing in the *American Journal of Public Health* defines a concept known as behavioural despair:

Behavioral despair consists of risky, reckless, and unhealthy acts that are self-destructive and reflect limited consideration of the future (e.g., high-risk sexual behaviors, gambling, self-harm, reckless driving, excessive spending, criminal activity, smoking, substance abuse, low physical activity).[81]

Some examples of imprudent decisions induced by despair in Golden Age *comedias* are trampling on things and then leaving suddenly, as when Elvira confesses: "En tal desesperación, todo lo atropello y dejo."[82]

This abrupt departure could take the form of exile,[83] including the self-imposed variety.[84] Despair might even drive someone to flee to the desert, as in "me voy sin esperanza alguna, de vivir a los desiertos y solitarios riscos."[85] In an article titled "On Navigating Despair," modern-day psychotherapists echo this metaphorical characterization: "[t]he people we interviewed had a difficult time articulating the experience and often used metaphors such as being in a swampland, on a cliff's edge, or in a desert with no way to escape the seeming peril."[86]

Despair provokes a shift in allegiances, from the earthly to the supernatural. This change might take the form of a lover's betrayal[87] or an act of war such as burning a village: "Ningunos bárbaros quedan, quememos su población, haga la desesperación lo que las fuerzas no pueden."[88] Here despair is referred to specifically as an emotional weapon.

Akin to burning a village in its devastation – albeit on an individual, as opposed to collective, scale – would be the similarly destructive action of rape, which we have already glimpsed in the biblical figure of Tamar. When this action is taken in Francisco de Rojas Zorrilla's *El más impropio verdugo por la más justa venganza*, it is tied explicitly within the play's discourse to the passion of despair. The rapist declares:

> Este ingrato despego,
> este desdén, este invencible fuego,
> y el no esperar mudanza,
> desesperaron tanto mi esperanza,
> que esta noche he intentado
> el último remedio a mi cuidado.
> Por ese Monasterio,
> donde el Cielo sólo tiene imperio,
> y despechado, y loco
> a nueva furia ahora me provoco;
> aunque es pretexto injusto
> a la violencia remitir el gusto,
> y gozar a Diana
> por fuerza, que el amor todo lo allana,
> en su propio aposento,
> que por una pared de este Convento
> tiene fácil la entrada.[89]

Within the context of Golden Age society, his purposed crime is made all the more outrageous by the fact that its setting is a monastery.

How is it that someone could fall so irretrievably under the force of this violent passion as to commit such horrific acts as raping a woman or burning an entire village? The plays are actually quite clear on this point. Despair deprives one of reason[90] and leads to madness.[91] In "Religious Despair in Medieval Literature and Art," Arieh Sachs confirms the traditional association of despair with insanity:

> An important aspect of this connection between despair and madness is the fact that desperate persons were supposed to be particularly prone to nightmares. Scenes of diabolical horror arose from their disturbed conscience, or, conversely, delicious visions of criminal pleasure; for the devil usually appeared in extremes of either pleasure or pain. Such people's reason having tottered, their

"imagination" was supposed to hold sway, providing them with hallucinatory objects of "fear."[92]

Despair was thought to lead to a swiftly changing – and, quite possibly, unbalanced – emotional state: "en la desesperación cabe mudanza tan nueva, que la pasión se desmaya."[93]

Despair leads inexorably to a desire for death,[94] particularly a death perceived as "noble," which is nonetheless condemned in the *comedias* as a vain wish.[95] Part of the reasoning behind this desire for death is that the desperate person does not wish to become a burden to others. One *comedia* character explains the passion of despair in precisely these terms: "por librarte de pensar mis daños, mi desesperación hará que pida, a la muerte remedio de mi vida."[96] In "Despair as a Cause of Death: More Complex Than It First Appears," epidemiologist and biostatistician Ana V. Diez Roux confirms that still today, deaths by overdose, suicide, or alcoholism among working-class people are typically referred to as "deaths of despair."[97]

Although suicide was considered to be an act of valour primarily in the classical world, vestiges of this mindset do linger in the *comedias*. The classic example would be Cervantes's tragedy *La Numancia*, which recounts an actual historical event where the Celtiberian inhabitants of the region of Soria committed collective suicide by jumping off a cliff rather than allowing themselves to be conquered by the invading Romans led by the general Scipio Africanus.[98]

The overwhelming majority of references to suicide in these plays, however, confirm that self-murder is forbidden by Catholic doctrine.[99] Here we might recall that medieval Italian poet Dante's second part of the seventh circle of Hell includes the Wood of the Suicides (*Inferno*, canto 13) where the two dogs who pursue victims – only to tear them apart – represent Poverty and Despair (see figure 16).[100] The quintessential biblical example of despair-induced suicide was of course thought to be Judas (see again figure 13).[101]

An important distinction is that suicide was not to be confused with martyrdom (although arguably, the result is the same).[102] Thus the King in Calderón's *El príncipe constante* is careful to clarify:

[L]a muerte sí, ésta te pido,
porque los cielos me cumplan
un deseo de morir
por la Fe, que aunque presumas,
que esto es desesperación,
porque el vivir me disgusta,
no es sino afecto de dar
la vida en defensa justa
de la Fe, y sacrificar
a él la vida, y alma juntas.[103]

Here the King asserts that although his desire for martyrdom might be misinterpreted by some as arising from despair, in truth his motivation is more noble: to defend the one true Faith.

While martyrdom is perhaps the most extreme example, despair can – in the best-case scenario – lead to brave acts that are still out of the ordinary.[104] Despair drives people to fight madly, which can sometimes gain them the victory: "desesperados, de manera peleaban, que parece que ponían en duda nuestra esperanza."[105] But perhaps wary of this possibility, playwrights are careful to distinguish between true courage (which is a virtue) and the sort of false courage that is only the result of despair. They make this distinction by asserting that "en archivos de la fama la desesperación no es valentía."[106] Lines such as this one only confirm my previous conclusions regarding the ambiguity of Fortitude along with the other Virtues.[107]

In fact, in this warlike culture obsessed with virile valour, despair is consistently presented as distinctly unheroic: "No es la desesperación digna de los nobles pechos."[108] It is beneath noble characters, as when Baldovino tells Carlos, "deja a viles pechos esa desesperación."[109] Likewise, a queen reproves her king:

Desesperarse en la pena,
no es acción digna de vos;
porque es dar a los sentidos
más poder, que a la razón.[110]

Here she instructs him to use reason to control his emotions, thereby not succumbing to the temptation to despair.

Moreover, one does not have to be royal or even noble in order to be portrayed as "rising above" this ignominious passion; it is enough merely to be wise: "Tanta desesperación es indigna de hombre sabio."[111] However, the opposite argument could also be made – that a person who lives without hope anyway is less likely to experience hurt when his hopes are dashed. Leonor voices this truism in the line, "El no vivir con esperanza alguna en todas las humanas pretensiones, hace menor el daño."[112]

In this formulation, despair is framed as discretion,[113] as in Lope de Vega's *El desconfiado*, the title of which – meaning "suspicious," "distrustful," or "lacking confidence" – could in some instances describe a despairing person. In seemingly hopeless situations, despair can seem justified, and *comedia* characters specifically seek to legitimize this passion: "mucha alición, y poco merecimiento engendró en mi pensamiento justa desesperación."[114]

Despair is the very stuff of tragedy,[115] which some scholars have argued was not written or performed often in Golden Age Spain because it was rejected forcefully by Catholic theologians in favour of redemption narratives.[116] The intuitive connection between tragedy and despair as exemplified in Shakespeare, Tennyson, Housman, Conrad, Shaw, O'Neill, and Arthur Miller has been explored in

William R. Brashear, *The Gorgon's Head: A Study in Tragedy and Despair*.[117] But even in plays that may fall short of being designated formally as tragedies, despair is presented as an all-too-human passion that is universal enough to permeate the human condition:

> ¡O verdugo del alma la esperanza!
> Quien sin desesperar un bien espera,
> no es hombre, es piedra.[118]

In other words, a person who has never felt despair must be as unfeeling as a rock.

If this is the case, and despair is universal, then what are its antidotes or remedies? We find characters on stage encouraging each other with remonstrances not to despair: "No tan presto desconfíes, que aun esperanza nos queda."[119] Characters pull each other successfully back from the brink, as in "no quise consentir en tu desesperación."[120]

But other lines offer the opinion that it is useless to advise someone in the throes of desperation ("Es, Sirene, error aconsejar a quien corre tras la desesperación")[121] because this passion is without remedy.[122] While it is considered impious to rejoice at the despair of another person[123] – an emotion that has a name only in German, namely *Schadenfreude* – sometimes characters do something even worse than smirk and gloat: they actually incite one another to lose hope.[124] Frondoso laments to Apolo that such is the situation:

> A tal desesperación
> he venido que he perdido
> mi sentido, mi vestido,
> mi cayado y mi zurrón.
> A todos parezco mal[;]
> nadie lo que soy arguye[;]
> mi propia sombra me huye[;]
> ¿quién ha visto pena igual?
> Por venganza o compasión
> aun no hay en mi mal testigos,
> los que me eran más amigos
> ya mis enemigos son.[125]

Here the speaker laments that even those who used to be his friends have now become his enemies.

The bottom line is this: despair takes over when consolation fails.[126] It comes when hope arrives too late, and thereby withers like a flower blooming when the season is too advanced to flourish (see figure 17).[127] This image might claim some universality, at least in the West, as a similar metaphor appears in a short story by the twentieth-century American novelist William Faulkner. The story is called "Dry September."[128]

The symbiotic, cyclical nature of hope and despair leads to paradoxical phrasing such as "desesperada esperanza,"[129] which in some instances playwrights enjoyed spinning out into full-blown oxymorons:

> Así corre mi esperanza
> con desesperada furia,
> tormenta de pensamientos
> en el mar de mis fortunas.[130]

In "An Existential Place of Pain," Nancy Scroggs confirms that despair can be experienced in cycles, especially in women.[131] The cyclical quality of this dynamic tension offers, perhaps, the only possible way out when despair is at its darkest. So the question becomes: how can black despair be transformed into what Emily Dickinson so memorably experienced as "that white sustenance" (see epigraph to this chapter)?

Perhaps true to the optimism of their comedic genre, the *comedias* proclaim that despair can change into hope: "lo que es hoy mortal desconfianza, y en desesperación el pecho viste, puede vestir mañana de esperanza."[132] Psychotherapist Denis O'Hara relates the cyclical nature of despair to a dialectic with hope. He refers to the classical myth of Persephone, whose despair at being dragged down into the underworld by the Lord of Hades was eventually mitigated by an agreement with him that she would spend half of each year above ground and half below.[133] Susan Snyder traces the portrayal of despair through the medieval period, noting that:

> It seems strange, perhaps, that the usual images express only the negative side of the despair paradox, but they are mainly redeemable states, in some cases even suggesting their opposites. Day must follow night, and barren winter must give way to spring. Dante had to go down into hell before he could rise to paradise ... The punishing, rejecting left hand of God may cast a man into everlasting fire, but it may also raise him up to heaven.[134]

In "Despair That Restores," psychotherapist Kirk Farnsworth similarly declares,

> An experience of despair which tears a man out of himself and forces him to question the meaning of his existence can be the trigger for a new and authentic way of life ... Since despair seems to point beyond itself, the pathway to hope can be forged through a valley of despair.[135]

While this positive valorization of despair would probably not have resonated with early modern audiences at the theatre, they would have at least intuited the interdependence of comedy and tragedy. If despair is the stuff of tragedy, then hope is invariably the stuff of its opposite, comedy – and modern-day gerontologists point specifically to the utility of humour in helping their patients cope with end-of-life despair:

> Comedy provides a way of transcending and coping with despair. Humor expresses a certain heroic defiance in the face of life's most challenging experience and provides a valuable resource for the celebration of life and the divine comedy of faith, hope and love.[136]

Let us thus turn now to hope as we explore the other half of this paradoxical symbiosis.

10

Hope against Hope

Hope is the passion for the possible.[1]

Hope deferred makes the heart sick.[2]

Hope is a dream of a person who is awake.[3]

"Hope" is the thing with feathers
That perches in the soul –
And sings the tune without the words –
And never stops – at all –.[4]

Hope appears as an allegorical figure in nearly a dozen *autos sacramentales* by Pedro Calderón de la Barca.[5] But how, in general, is hope defined in the context of early modern Spanish drama? The best definition of hope per se appears in Lope de Vega's *Los donaires de Matico*: "esperanza es la fe del bien que mi alma adora."[6] Hope is a cherished faith in something good. This definition is amplified by psychologist James Averill and his colleagues: "Hope is a sign of health, a fighting spirit, and faith that somehow good will triumph."[7]

This definition would seem to call for a host of positive adjectives to describe hope; and indeed, we find these words spoken abundantly on the early modern Spanish stage. Hope is described both as sweet[8] and as a force working sweet things,[9] as in "dulcísima esperanza, bien haya el dulce mar que te merece."[10] Hope is eternally cheerful,[11] secure,[12] and even saintly.[13] Hope is pictured as the stirrups in which a horseman places his feet as he rides ("en loca esperanza estribo").[14] But this mention of "crazy hope" allows us to glimpse its other side too.

Hope can be innocent and overly credulous, as when Francisca reproaches Fernando:

[C]rédula, pues, mi esperanza,
dos años merecí ser

(vos ausente, y yo mujer)
de la firmeza alabanza.[15]

She admonishes him that her gullible hope led her to wait for him faithfully during two years of absence. In situations such as this one, hope can seem vague and far off: "esa vaga, lejana esperanza."[16] Hope can feel empty like the wheel of a water mill that has dumped out all its water: "noria mi pensamiento, mas tales vasos alcanza los vacíos de esperanza, y los llenos de tormento."[17] When it fills up again, the substance filling its erstwhile empty spaces is sheer torment.

Hopes held by ignorant people[18] are characterized as foolish or implausible.[19] Either hope must be realistic, or else the hoper should adjust his or her expectations.[20] One should not waste effort hoping for impossible things.[21] Antti Lampinen remarks that in the ancient world, "Hope was to many Greeks a deeply dangerous sentiment, clouding the rational and realistic assessment of facts and causalities, and making both individuals and communities vulnerable."[22]

In terms of temporal orientation, hope is identified most typically with Christmas, as in Lope de Vega's *El nacimiento de Cristo* when the chorus says to the Virgin Mary:

Venga a las almas
con tu consentimiento
la esperanza,
de salir de tinieblas,
deba Abrahán la luz a tus entrañas.[23]

Mary's answer of "yes" to God brought hope of salvation to human souls. Later in the same play we again find hope being emphasized, along with faith and joy.[24]

Hope is also associated with springtime, particularly the months of April[25] and May:[26]

Aquí palabra os dio la Primavera,
que no verá vuestra esperanza Estío.
Creced las flores blancas, y encarnadas;
almendros, como crecen mis favores,
juntemos esperanzas bien fundadas,
que como en una cáscara dos flores
engendran dos almendras abrazadas,
abrazarán dos almas dos amores.[27]

This rosy vision of two young hearts entwined contrasts sharply with the "miserable" hope of worn-out old age: "O mísera esperanza de dos caducos viejos combatida."[28]

In fact, we find lines in which older people specifically draw their hope from the young, as in "suplirá vuestro valor la esperanza que a mí me niega la edad."[29] Hope rests in the younger generation, specifically sons who will become heirs, as in "mi hijo, mi Esperanza, y mi deseo, Dulce refugio al mal."[30] Later in the same play, Juan de la Cueva's *Los siete infantes de Lara*, Bustos caresses his son verbally with the words, "hijo ... ay dulce esperanza mía, vida a mi vejez cansada, gloria a esta alma."[31]

Childless men are urged to seek out good Spanish wives to bear them male children to solidify their legacy.[32] Entire nations such as Spain or Portugal looked to their valiant young princes[33] to defeat collective enemies and make their royal fathers proud.[34] Conversely, if a young man died, the hope of his whole family would suffer[35] – much more so if he was a prince, because succession to the throne might be placed in jeopardy.[36] Young noblemen killed in the flower of their youth on stage in the *comedias* (or at least warranting a report of their off-stage demise) include the Roman emperor Constantine[37] and conquistador Juan Pizarro (ca. 1511–1536) who accompanied his three brothers in the conquest of Peru.[38]

With its focus on the younger generation, hope looks forward towards happiness.[39] Time opens up new avenues for hope.[40] Hope's youth and glimmering freshness shine in numerous metaphors and similes, such as hope appearing as a ray of light[41] or hope shining like the sun. As Felisardo announces cheerily, "Pues yo con esta esperanza como el sol amanecí."[42] Hope is the sun shining through clouds of annoyance,[43] bringing warmth[44] and a rosy glow[45] like the sky at dawn. In the later hours, hope is moonlight that pierces the dark night: "es, amando, la esperanza, luz que de noche se ofrece, que desde lejos parece."[46]

In another variation, hope is the lighthouse ("la esperanza el farol")[47] guiding the mariner out of a storm ("esperanza en los tormentos").[48] Hope is compared to the Strait of Gibraltar, also referred to as "the columns of Hercules" (see figure 18), which offered Spanish imperial ships safe passage from the Atlantic Ocean to the Mediterranean Sea.[49]

In a constellation of nautical imagery, hope appears alternatively as a ship navigating the sea of love,[50] a tranquil gulf offering refuge from stormy seas,[51] or a timely wind filling one's sails.[52] In still another iteration, hope is the port[53] where a ship may dock after a long journey, such as the well-named Cape of Good Hope:

> La galera de mi amor,
> que cortando las espumas
> de imposibles, y de estorbos
> a vela, y remo procura
> llegar a buena esperanza.[54]

In lines evoking specifically religious imagery, hope is a sanctuary for cares.[55]

Sometimes, however, the ship does not make it to port, but instead suffers damage[56] from being tossed by the waves. Jealousy is mentioned as a specific identity for this tempest.[57] Even if the ship does arrive safely, sometimes it is not greeted with the warm welcome it had expected.[58] In this case, the ship's occupants are left gasping for breath, which – it turns out – is also a metaphor for hope.[59]

Hope is often termed "divine breath" ("divino aliento de mi esperanza")[60] or even just regular respiration;[61] like air, hope is deemed necessary for life: "¿Quién, ¡ay de mí! sin esperanza podrá?"[62] Hope sustains existence; the person who does not hope eventually forgets his or her identity.[63] Hope is a key ("O llave de mi esperanza")[64] that opens doors, especially doors into hearts.[65] In a particularly homely image, hope is the hook on which we hang our underwear:

> Para el adorno interior,
> colgadura es la esperanza,
> porque defiende el rigor
> del frío de la tardanza
> en el Invierno de amor.[66]

Here hope protects us from the cold just like warm long johns.

Hope is the garment with which a knight clothes himself when he wants to appear most gallant and dashing.[67] A knight in a jousting tournament always carried a shield emblazoned with his coat of arms. One particular knight's shield that is mentioned on stage bears the image of an anchor, specifically to symbolize hope: "Áncora pintada, Geroglífico, e Insignia, que le dan a la Esperanza."[68]

Hope's anchor is tied to especially rough ropes: "Las áncoras de esperanza en fuertes gúmenas cuelgan, y con los dientes herrados muerden."[69] The "iron teeth" of these ropes could bite into the skin of a sailor's hands if he was not careful. In one beautiful image, hope anchors the soul ("Ya tengo el alma a la esperanza asida");[70] but its ballast is not always so stable as it might seem. It can still jerk a lover around under water like a fish caught on a fishing line.[71] Perhaps as a visual signifier of this attachment, actual ribbons[72] were exchanged between lovers as a token of their affection. One lover thanks his beloved for giving him such a remembrance: "apenas me da palabras con que pueda agradecerte la esperanza de esta cinta, dulce prenda, lazo fuerte."[73]

More specific still are the green ribbons mentioned on numerous occasions that clearly signified hope due to the symbolism of their colour: "O cintas verdes, por mi bien halladas, si esperanza me dais del bien que os pido."[74] A character who has been deceived and therefore lost hope is specifically instructed to take off his green ribbon: "Quita esa cinta verde, que a quien engañan, la esperanza pierde."[75] In a literalization of this imagery, any hopeful person is said to be hanging on hope.[76]

The good news is, the same hope that can leave one hanging or suspended in mid-air (very helpful for enhancing the suspense of a *comedia*'s plot) can be used to encircle a fortress[77] or even to scale a wall. Like Ariadna's thread leading Theseus through the labyrinth, it can lead a knight to the iron bars through which his lady's hands might reach.[78] Multiple passages in the *comedias* conjure the mythical Theseus specifically in the context of hope:

> Diome la esperanza un hilo,
> con que en el viento fiado,
> entré en este laberinto
> por la puerta del engaño.
> Fui dando a sus salas vueltas,
> de la esperanza guiado,
> que es el mozo de los ciegos
> que rezan en los palacios.[79]

Hope is a reliable guide through the labyrinth,[80] even if one ends up literally "hanging by a thread."[81] In the language of Gracianesque *conceptismo*, this thread is identified explicitly as a lock of a lady's hair: "la esperanza prendada, presa de un cabello está."[82] Even when the lady's lover is left dangling, still he hangs onto hope like a convicted criminal wishing for a last-minute reprieve.

In a feat of Baroque ingenuity, however, this image takes an unexpected turn: suddenly hope is identified not with the strength of the rope, but instead with its weakness. The best hope for a man who is about to be hanged is that somehow, at the last moment, instead the rope will break. We see this exact scenario played out in the following speech:

> Puesta la soga al cuello
> sustenta la esperanza al condenado,
> y erizado el cabello
> mira si tiene algún amigo al lado,
> si se quiebra, o se enreda,
> o pasa el Rey, donde mirarle pueda.[83]

The condemned man waits there, hoping against hope that the rope will break, or get tangled, or else the king will pass by at that exact moment and decide to pardon him on a whim.

But this is of course only one variation on a theme. In other imaginings, hope is the thread that should be preserved at all cost, guarding it from being cut as if it were the only lifeline[84] attached to the waist of a rock climber or mountaineer. Women hold tremendous power in this equation, however; for they are often (in men's imagination) the ones standing on top of the mountain, peering over the cliff with a gigantic pair of scissors poised in mid-air. Ladies can sever the lifeline merely by spurning their suitors' advances. This scenario is envisioned in the phrase, "sale una hembra que corta la esperanza a sus deseos."[85]

Hope is not always pictured as tethered, however. Perhaps more frequently, hope soars freely like a bird on feathered wings.[86] This imagery goes back at least to the ancient Greek poet Pindar: "Towards the close of *Pythian* 8, Pindar paints an enthralling depiction of a young man soaring on the wings of hope."[87] Keely Elizabeth Heuer notes that even in the myth of Pandora, hope presumably had wings like the rest of her jar's contents, all the rest of which flew away.[88] This detail is still present in today's discourse, from Emily Dickinson's poem that forms one epigraph to this chapter to the metaphors employed by medical doctor Jerome Groopman: "[W]e are 'lifted by' hope, hope 'has wings.' Certainly, this sense of elevation was apparent at the bedside, as I observed patients, and in my own experience as a patient … [I]t involved a unique feeling state that was intensely visceral, sensed as a sharp upward shift in mood."[89]

Hope is symbolized specifically by the eagle, the only bird thought to fly high enough to get close to the sun: "Águila bella, del color de mi esperanza, que sólo un Águila alcanza ver el Sol que mira."[90] But sometimes hope is depicted instead as other flying creatures with weaker flight capacity,[91] or even wings that will melt like Icarus's did when they approach hope's object, which is the source of light and warmth. Thus Antonio pictures his love like a butterfly attracted to the flame of his beloved's flashing eyes:

> Amor con alas de hielo
> lleva la esperanza mía,
> cual mariposa a la llama,
> al sol de unos ojos bellos.[92]

In yet another variation on this "winged creature" motif, hope is a swan that sings as it dies: "es el cisne mi esperanza, que canta cuando se muere."[93] From this word picture we derive the still-extant phrase *swan song*. In a more positive picture, hope is the legendary phoenix, eternally reborn.[94] In this retelling, renewed hope arises from the ashes even stronger than the original version.[95]

It is not lost on these playwrights that hope, in addition to being a passion, is one of the three Theological Virtues (which are faith, hope, and love).[96] The three Theological Virtues are represented by three jewels in Calderón's auto *El pleito matrimonial*. In a different sacramental play, *Los alimentos del hombre*, they are pictured alternatively as specific flowers, namely lilies and roses: "Primavera le situará de sus Flores, significándose en ellas Fe, Esperanza y Caridad, Lirios, Rosas y Azucenas."[97] A different flower is chosen, however, to signify hope in God:

> Es la Esperanza en Dios
> la Flor de la Siempre-Viva,
> en metáfora de flores
> la más brillante, y más linda.[98]

The theological significance, of course, is that hope in God never dies.

Theological musings apart, hope is signified throughout the *comedia* corpus by the image of flowers in general, as in "estas flores que poseo, que esperanza mía son."[99] It is worth noting in this context that the goddess *Spes* was pictured holding a flower on coins minted under Rome's empire, which included Spain (see figure 19). Alternatively, hope is evoked by trees[100] and fruits,[101] or even nuts.[102] Nature in general nurtures hope, which is why Carlos so lyrically praises the countryside:

> Sólo el campo es el papel
> donde mi esperanza leo,
> y donde mira el cuidado,
> siguiendo el norte a su aguja,
> letras que a surcos dibuja;
> tosco el pincel del arado:
> y porque el discurso avive
> en sus rústicas lecciones,
> yo señalo los renglones,
> y el tiempo me los escribe;
> y con ser cuaderno bruto,
> desempeña mis congojas,
> pues siempre logro en sus hojas
> la seguridad del fruto.[103]

This word play on *hojas* – meaning both leaves of a tree and leaves of a book – would have delighted the conceptist heart of Quevedo or Gracián.

In a related set of extended metaphors, hope is sown like a seed[104] and then watered with the dew[105] of a lover's tears[106] until its leaves start to grow.[107] This hope will eventually be harvested, but not until the time is right. Thus the Comendador de Ocaña says to a beautiful village girl:

> Vi de tu labranza
> nacer al corazón verde esperanza.
> Venturoso el villano
> que tal Agosto ha hecho
> del trigo de tu pecho.[108]

He not so subtly speaks of her bosom as a field of wheat that some lucky villager has harvested in August when the crops grew ripe.

James Averill and his colleagues note the persistence of this agricultural lexical field in the discourse of hope still today:

> [H]ope as a vital principle is the most productive of the abstract metaphors. It has
> many extensions (subcategories) and lexical variations, including some common,

everyday expressions. For example, hope may be identified as a life principle (e.g., as the life blood of the soul). An extension of this life-sustaining theme is that hope is food or a remedy for ailments; so, too, is the identification of hope with environmental conditions (e.g., springtime) associated with the renewal of life. Finally, there is a set of conventional metaphors in which hope is itself treated as a life form, to be "nourished," "fostered," and the like.[109]

In this formulation, sometimes things turn out well for the farmer, and the harvest is doubled ("tu esperanza ya tiene doblado el fruto");[110] but unfortunately hope does not always come to fruition ("no ha de llegar mi esperanza a madurar").[111] In this case, it is said to have died on the vine ("Murió mi esperanza en flor").[112]

This flower which failed to bear fruit[113] will soon dry up and lose its petals.[114] Time's mutability may cause hope to wither,[115] in which case it is called "vain" ("mi esperanza vana").[116] (The ancient Greek poet Pindar thus refers to the "vain goal of empty hopes" in the case of the healer Asclepius, who tried to revive a corpse.)[117] Even if hope does yield fruit, the fruit does not always taste[118] good ("en mi esperanza mal fruto").[119] But as with plants, there is always the possibility that given the right conditions, even a withered and brown trunk – apparently dead – will suddenly begin to sprout new leaves.[120]

The association of hope with new life makes it not only the quintessentially Renaissance passion – in the etymological sense of Re-naissance as rebirth – but also the most common emotion evoked by the colour green. The biological logic behind this association is obvious: "¿Y no hay esperanza allí, / pues verdes las hojas son?"[121]

As the saying goes, "hope springs eternal," and for this reason hope appears specifically in connection to evergreen plants such as the myrtle bush: "el mirto cuando esperanza, que dicen que sin mudanza conserva eterno verdor."[122] Another plant or herb mentioned as evergreen – and thus eternally hopeful – is marjoram.[123] In one play we are led rapidly through the chain of associations of grass being green, horses eating grass, suitors feeding off of hope, and thereby being equated to horses: "caballos pretendientes, que sola esperanza pacen."[124] The implication is that suitors sustain themselves on an exclusive diet of hope, much like horses maintain a herbivorous regimen. This semantic field affords rife opportunities for clever banter, such as in the following dialogue, where hope – being green – becomes a salad:

JULIANA: Pues sírvate de ensalada
    la esperanza.
SERAFINA: Bien.
JULIANA: Supuesto,
    que es verde y tiene su azúcar,

> y su vinagre, si hay celos,
> y sea el primer plato
> la constancia, y yo te ofrezco
> si le admites, que este plato
> te sepa muy bien por nuevo.
> Para postre desengaños
> guisados por escarmientos,
> que en la cena del amor
> siempre es el plato postrero.[125]

Here a love affair's likely trajectory is compared ingeniously to sequential courses of a meal.

This resonance is repeated *ad nauseum* in the *comedias*, such as in the lines "Lo verde me dio esperanza"[126] and "de esmeraldas es, y creo, que el color de la esperanza os desagrade."[127] This visual semiotic code comprises the field of meaning around which Tirso's *Don Gil de las calzas verdes* is structured. This play (see figure 20) contains repeated references to the colour green and its symbolic resonance, as when Don Gil introduces himself as: "Don Gil de las calzas soy verdes, como mi esperanza."[128] The humorous antics of this green-stockinged gentleman find their more serious counterpart in Lope de Vega's *Santiago el Verde*,[129] in which this colour association is also evoked ("Esta esperanza llevo de Santiago el Verde").[130] Often when an actor wore a green costume, it was understood to signify hope.[131]

But other than run around in green tights, what does hope actually do? The *comedias* are quite specific on this point. Hope relieves[132] by alleviating doubt.[133] It improves a bad situation: "cada uno su mal mejora con la esperanza que alcanza, de que puede haber mudanza."[134] It lifts up[135] and revives the heart ("Con esa esperanza que me ofreces, resucita el corazón").[136] Hope does the heart good[137] and comforts the senses.[138] It offers consolation to souls: "almas, cuya esperanza es el consuelo más seguro."[139]

This consolation is described as delicious honey or nectar produced by flowers: "miel sabrosa de consuelos, que la esperanza entre sus flores labra."[140] Hope nourishes[141] and sustains the body[142] (but hope itself must also be nourished,[143] or else it will starve). Hope inspires confidence, fostering ingenuity and shrewd astuteness.[144] It paves the way to satisfaction, leading thereby to happiness. Thus Cupid promises, "yo haré que de amor la esperanza pase presto a ser dicha de amor."[145] Hope for the good conquers evil – "la esperanza del bien los males vence"[146] – as hope multiplies, with one hope leading to another, and so on.[147] Hope is always out there on the horizon,[148] beckoning us to follow after it.[149]

What did early modern Spanish people hope for, that they went to such great lengths to chase after? In general they hoped for bad situations to improve[150] or for restoration of a previous good, now lost ("esperanza de volver a restaurar lo perdido").[151] They hoped for good luck[152] or good health.[153] In bad enough situations, such as a shipwreck, they hoped merely for survival, "la esperanza de salvar la vida."[154] Women especially hoped for a good outcome in childbirth;[155] but sadly, not all their husbands shared this fond expectation.

In fact, some callous husbands actually wished for their wives' deaths, so that they could be free to marry someone else. In a clever intermedial pun on the green Cruz de Alcántara worn by the knights of this military order (see figure 21), Galindo reveals that every husband

[t]iene
siempre una verde esperanza
de enviudar, cuando no alcanza,
lo que a su estado conviene.[156]

In the rest of the speech he mentions other military orders – with their respective costumes – and explains how each one is appropriate to the unhappy husband who must now bear the "cross" of his unpleasant wife. Here early modern Spanish males' avarice[157] reaches new lows of depravity as they sit around waiting and hoping for their wives to die! This sounds like an inversion of the scenario satirized in 1941 by the playwright Joseph Kesselring in *Arsenic and Old Lace*[158] (in this play, devious old ladies poison their husbands slowly with arsenic by administering small doses to them daily in their meals).

Such desperate measures aside, early modern Spanish plays remind us constantly that persistent social problems such as poverty led many *pícaros* and other marginalized individuals to feel hopeless, as when a character laments, "en la pobreza mía me vi tan sin esperanza … hacienda no tenía."[159] Whole *comedias* such as Guillén de Castro's *El pretender con pobreza* thematized this dilemma. In this play, a character describes the painful process of pulling himself up by his bootstraps: "la vil pobreza, a la esperanza importuna, mi limitada fortuna sacó fuerzas de flaqueza."[160] We might recall profitably here that not all these dramatists were noble, and some of them – such as Lope de Vega – were constantly on the lookout for ways to improve their lot.

Hope seems especially vital to the miserable, fainting hearts who have nothing else to cling to: "O esperanza, notoria amiga de alentar los desmayados, aunque estén en miserias."[161] The author of these lines was none other than Miguel de Cervantes, who held onto hope through five years of captivity. Cervantes often gave voice to the marginalized and victims of oppression, as we see in another line in a different play by the same author: "felicísimo este día, pues en él toma fuerzas mi esperanza de ver mis Aduares mejorados, viendo a sus robadores castigados."[162] *Aduares* were Gypsy camps. Here Cervantes's love for justice shines through the centuries as we hear him speak approvingly of robbers being punished.

Of course, this was not always the case – far too often, as Don Quijote learned the hard way, justice was not served even by those in charge of administering it.[163] But up until the moment when the accused's sentence was pronounced by a judge or magistrate, there remained a reservoir of hope that perhaps even corrupt officials might be persuaded to do the right thing ("hasta oír la Sentencia, aun hay esperanza").[164] Cervantes's "rufián dichoso" Cristóbal de Lugo expresses the hope that good deeds will eventually find their reward:

> LUGO: Las ánimas me llevan cuanto tengo,
>   mas yo tengo esperanza que algún día
>   lo tienen de volver ciento por uno.
> MÚSICO 2: A la larga lo tomas.
> LUGO: Y a lo corto,
>   que al bien hacer jamás le falta premio.[165]

This pious sentiment – later echoed by Calderón repeatedly in *La vida es sueño* – reflects a trust in God that good works will receive their just reward.

Such pie-in-the-sky metaphysical speculations are, in general, limited to serious philosophical or hagiographical plays and *autos sacramentales*, however; most *comedia* characters are more concerned simply about feeding their bellies. A hope for food is manifested by Mauricia in the line: "Según eso, ¿esta tarde mal tendremos esperanza de que merendaremos?"[166] Stomach pangs unabated, she is left hoping wistfully for an afternoon snack.

For *campesinos* the availability of food was tied directly to the abundance or scarcity of crops. The dishonoured villager Peribáñez remembers nostalgically a former time when he could enjoy the fruits of his labour:

> Éstos son mi trigo, y heras.
> Con qué diversa alegría,
> o campos, pensé miraros
> cuando contento vivía,
> porque viniendo a sembraros,
> otra esperanza tenía.
> Con alegre corazón
> pensé de vuestras espigas
> henchir mis trojes.[167]

His fondest hope back in that time was to fill his granaries with wheat.

A good crop, however, was dependent upon rainfall to ensure successful growth. One commonly expressed hope in these plays is, consequently, a hope for rain. Queen Isabel the Catholic announces triumphantly onstage to King Fernando:

Milagrosa novedad.
Logróse vuestra esperanza:
ved que agua abundante y recia
riega la tierra.[168]

This "miracle" occurs after an apparition of the Virgin Mary in response to prayers for rain.

These prayers for rain reflect the fact that much of Spain's geography is not particularly well suited for agriculture, tending instead toward the grazing of livestock.[169] We find acknowledgments of this harsh reality in lines such as Faquín's overture to his superior:

Puesto que tan rico sea
su merced, y de esta aldea
no tenga mucha esperanza,
le juro que es buena hacienda
el ganado, así vacuno,
como ovejuno.[170]

Here he pleads with a rich man not to dismiss the importance of his village, which specializes in the cultivation of cattle and sheep.

Villagers often had to resort to such servile pleas for assistance, "esperanza de socorro."[171] Residual vestiges of the feudal system meant that they had to rely on wealthy or noble landowners for protection and defence.[172] They might hope for help[173] or rescue[174] from imprisonment,[175] or even from captivity by Muslim pirates such as Cervantes suffered. His ransom was organized by Trinitarian friars, which is why Cervantes chose to be buried in a Trinitarian monastery – where his humble, all-but-unmarked grave bearing the initials "M.C." was discovered only in 2015.[176]

Calderón gives voice to this same hope, "la Esperanza de que su Rescate venga," in his sacramental play thematizing captive redemption, *La redención de cautivos*.[177] The rescuers would be hopeful that their mission be successful, whether in the case of Spanish Christians captured by Muslim pirates or in the plight of prisoners of war.[178] Either way, the former captives would long to see their native land again: "por verte, España, cada día alas el alma, y la esperanza postas."[179] The exiled Lope de Vega was capable of imagining the suffering experienced by innocent victims who languished in prison: "Quien padece prisiones tan rigurosas / sin culpa, tenga esperanza que le ha de librar el cielo."[180] Sometimes these sufferers'[181] only hope was to await divine help.

For their part, soldiers would hope not to be killed in battle,[182] deriving some consolation from each small strategic advance: "un caballo, una lanza, y alguna corta esperanza de estas ganadas almenas."[183] In a campaign like the Reconquest of Granada, every horse, sword, and battlement made a difference. Military generals, in turn, bore the responsibility of not embarking upon hopeless missions. Thus a character in Calderón's *El sitio de Breda* declares, "es una fuerza invencible, y un sitio sin esperanza de victoriosa alabanza, que por armas no es posible tomarla."[184] With apologies to the defenders of the Alamo, it is never advisable to fight a battle you know you will lose.

If you know you are losing, sometimes the best strategy is to retreat swiftly, setting fire even to one's own army's barracks in order to slow down the enemy's pursuit.[185] This would have been perceived as extremely prejudicial to honour, however; a far preferable option was to keep hoping to win ("esperanza de que saldrá vencedor").[186] Hope of gain,[187] pleasure,[188] or conquest[189] could be a motivational factor, whether victory was desired over opposing troops or over a resisting woman's body.[190] The greater the victory aimed at, however, the less realistic was the hope of achieving it: "tanto más la victoria, cuanto menos la esperanza."[191]

This last example highlights the relationship of hope to ambition. The two are equated in the line, "esperas un grande Estado. La esperanza, y la ambición te meterán por su puerta."[192] Ambition might manifest itself as hope for employment,[193] hope for applause,[194] or even such a lofty hope as wishing for eternal fame.[195] In hagiographical or biblical dramas the hope to achieve sainthood[196] was viewed as a legitimate aspiration. Stage characters might hope to inherit a noble title ("esperanza de ser de una gran casa heredero"),[197] a principality,[198] or even a realm.[199]

These hopes might be achieved biologically by birth ("Esperanza de heredar al Rey su Padre"),[200] by merit ("quien tus huellas imita, de Reinar tenga esperanza"),[201] or even by treacherous usurpation, as when Juan admits: "De reinar tengo esperanza con traidora, o fiel acción."[202] Tyrannicide (or else pre-emptive suicide by a tyrant who has been condemned) has often been seen as cause for hope throughout world history. For example, as recounted by the ancient Roman historian Tacitus,

> Hope in the aftermath of Nero's death distinguishes the reactions of senators, *equites*, and the righteous members of the citizen body (*integra pars*) – these classes, Tacitus wishes us to believe, appreciated the situation from the standpoint of the impartial observer and saw in the death of Nero the beginning of a better era.[203]

The subversive potential of early modern Spanish stage plays to foment tyrannicide[204] has been studied by A. Robert Lauer.[205] Douglas Davies explains the near-universal political resonance of hope:

> Within the Jewish-Christian-Islamic worlds, and in ideological movements emerging from them, including Marxism, much is invested in anticipating a future state

of affairs. God's kingdom will come in some way or a socialist revolution will create a new world order of freedom from want, pain, hardship, and oppression. Hope becomes partnered with ideas of time and the future goal of perfection inspires the present moment of hope.[206]

Successful aspirers to political power might hope to govern a city[207] or conquer an empire ("la esperanza del Imperio que apeteces").[208] If not winning or conquering, at least they could hope for favourable truce terms.[209] Hope for an auspicious peace treaty[210] would have resonated with a Spain often at war. Sometimes peace treaties were brokered by strategic marriages,[211] a technique employed by courtiers and ladies-in-waiting hoping for advancement.[212] Then as now, the betrothal or engagement ring[213] became a symbol of this hope. The only hope for courtiers jostling for favour was often to displace someone else in the pecking order, as in one character's admission, "de que Carlos perdiese su privanza, encubrí mi esperanza."[214] *Privados* or favourites such as this Carlos (the ultimate example from this time period being the Conde-Duque de Olivares, favourite of King Philip IV [see once again figure 21])[215] were the dispensers of power[216] in a political economy perceived to be a zero-sum game.

In pursuit of such privilege, hopefuls[217] flocked to the royal court, even if this meant uprooting and moving away to a different city.[218] Aside from *privanza*, other perks sought after might be a dowry[219] or landed estate ("la vida en la sangre, la esperanza en la hacienda").[220] The goal was to amass ever-greater land holdings, even if it meant the death of a competitor. One such schemer confesses, "de su muerte espero resucitar mi esperanza, aumentar mi patrimonio."[221]

Failing any plans to kill off rivals, one could at least hope for disposable income, as with a young lady who is said to possess both beauty and riches: "fuera de su hermosura, tiene cinco mil de renta, y esperanza de otros cuatro."[222] Presumably she is set to inherit further *tierras*, which will generate additional annual income. Hope for wealth could inspire devious stratagems if the money was unscrupulously obtained.[223] Simply knowing a rich person was enough to make one hopeful, even if he was not known to be generous: "el rico, aunque no da, da esperanza, y se le fía."[224] Here we glimpse the subterfuge by which the wealthy knew how to leverage their social assets.

Whether it was a throne, a kingdom, a *privanza*, a favourable marriage, or that eternally sought-after quotient known as cash, hope usually aimed at a specific target.[225] This target might be an explicit prize[226] or reward.[227] Women hoped to be the belle of the ball,[228] while their suitors hoped to distinguish themselves as their cherished ladies' champions.[229] In a joust, for example, they might wear their ladies' colours[230] as a symbol of undying loyalty to a certain woman. If successful in the contest, they might obtain the laurel wreath[231] of victory or other tangible, wearable signs of hope, including a plumed hat with feathers (thought to be symbolic of hope's wings).[232] The real crown of victory, moreover, was a lady's favours bestowed after the public event, such as – for example – being granted entrance to her room.[233]

If, on the contrary, a jouster lost the contest, he might instead hope for reparation after this humiliation or offence to his honour. So one character proclaims with the phrase, "me queda más esperanza de cobrar mi honor."[234] How could this reversal be accomplished? The most frequent strategy, as we see in both Lope de Vega's *La venganza venturosa* and Calderón's *A secreto agravio, secreta venganza*, was through revenge.[235] Hope is said to make the blade of revenge sharper,[236] to the point where a crazy or unjustified hope becomes a poisonous dagger ("mi loca esperanza veneno, y puñal dorado").[237] If all else fails – revenge falters, and honour is lost – then the last hope of an unlucky gentleman was to wish for death.[238]

Right before death, however, he would want to confess. In the Catholic world view, pardon for sin could be obtained only from a confessor[239] officially licensed to administer the sacrament of penance. Without absolution from a priest, there could be no hope of pardon[240] for sin.[241] Hope for salvation[242] was ultimately based on God's mercy, not human works.[243] The good news was that for the repentant sinner, hope for eternal life[244] was possible even in Purgatory ("en el Purgatorio todavía hay esperanza"),[245] that divine waiting room where sin could still be purged (it's never too late). Douglas Davies explains that

> Christian hope became intertwined with fear in a complex religious ritual process involving prayers said for the dead at the Mass and the practice of gaining indulgences through pilgrimages or even through monetary purchase that allowed a degree of freedom from purgatory.[246]

Ultimately Catholics hoped to enter heaven, where all their hopes and dreams would some day come true.[247] Thus Francisco recounts the contents of his mystical experience:

> Soñaba que me iba al cielo
> y que en este hermoso vuelo
> iba mi esperanza asida
> a un hábito que formaba
> una senda hasta la gloria.[248]

Note once again the common element of hope as a ribbon or tie like the ones we have seen in previous passages. In an effort to share this beatific vision, missionaries sought to propagate the One True Faith ("en esperanza de propagación de Fe")[249] to the ends of the earth[250] with the tool of catechism.[251] On the reverse side, infidels or pagans are imagined in the *comedias* as hoping to convert eventually to the Catholic creed ("animó su esperanza de venir a ser Cristiano").[252]

Where does this hope come from, that it is powerful enough to inspire renegades to forsake their own cultural heritage? On this point the stage plays are unanimous: hope descends from heaven,[253] and is guided by it: "El cielo justo mueva mi lengua, y guíe mi esperanza."[254] So Vanegas says to Alima: "venga toda Bebería, que en Dios mi esperanza fundo, y no hay poder en el mundo contra aquel que en Dios confía."[255]

The specific quality of God's which is said to inspire most hope is His compassion: "aun nos queda Esperanza de que Dios se compadezca de nosotros."[256] God's compassion toward the human race was exemplified in the figure of Christ ("Cristo es mi bien, mi esperanza").[257] On the topic of Christ inspiring hope, we find an extended allusion to the Apostle Peter – who was, after all, a fisherman, but also became the first pope – walking on the water toward Jesus in the middle of a fierce storm:

> Aquel de los Pontífices supremos,
> Pedro, el mayor a nuestro Pedro santo
> mostró en el mar la misma confianza,
> que por llegar a quien amaba tanto,
> hizo la barca Amor, la Fe los remos,
> y entre la espuma intrépido se lanza;
> así conduce a Pedro la esperanza.[258]

Saint Peter's example would inspire this emotion, as could prayer to other saints for aid.[259]

The most direct access to Christ, however, was thought to be through His Mother the Virgin Mary. Thus *comedia* characters are instructed: "poned vuestra esperanza en María."[260] In a similar category, John the Baptist was the long-awaited prophet whose arrival would precede that of the Saviour whom he would announce.[261] Ironically, in this view, an excess of hope conceived as a virtue actually did damage to the Jewish people[262] because they were still waiting and hoping for a Messiah who had already come: "el Hebraísmo lo diga, a quien la Esperanza preso trae en su error."[263]

Even outside the Christian context, divine entities were routinely invoked as sources of hope. Pagan characters on stage might pray to Jove, king of the gods;[264] Mars, the god of war;[265] or other pagan deities ("tengo justa esperanza en los Dioses").[266] In ancient Rome, Hope actually *was* a deity (see again figure 19):

> Roman *Spes* was worshipped as a goddess. The earliest temple, devoted to *Spes Vetus* ('old Hope'), was located on the Esquiline, at the highest point on the east side of the city … and it is dated as early as 477 BC … The name avoided confusion with another temple of *Spes* built, at a later stage, by A. Atilius Calatinus during the first Punic war in the mid-3rd cent[ury] BC.[267]

All hope in mere mortals, as opposed to deities, is necessarily destined to fail – "¡o vana siempre en hombres la esperanza!"[268] – which is why supernatural entities (then as now) are needed.

Characters even philosophize onstage, advising their audiences not to place hope in unreliable, terrestrial things: i.e., women and dice.[269] Some playwrights hypothesize that hope is not affected by the stars;[270] but hope does act as a prophet foretelling future events,[271] much like astrologers tried to do by reading messages in the sky. The ancient Romans likewise practised divination by reading auspices (this language is repeated in the line, "con verde auspicio prognosticó su esperanza")[272] or omens,[273] which are also mentioned in these plays in the context of hope. Hope is figured as the canvas on which a painter crafts a picture of things to come: "figura amor, en … esta pintura del lienzo de mi esperanza."[274] A wise hope, however, should keep silent instead of opting for bold expression, just like dangerous prophecies were better kept under wraps.[275]

For the trouble with prophecies is that their outcome cannot not be controlled, try as one might; in like fashion, we find an ongoing debate transpiring on the *comedia* stage about whether hope can be controlled or not. This question is intimately tied up with the related discourse of whether a specific hope is permissible, implying that hope *can* be controlled by permitting or rejecting its advances. For example, we hear one character raise a series of rhetorical questions: "¿No son decentes los ruegos? La esperanza, ¿quién dirá que no es lícita?"[276]

Characters on stage are constantly evaluating whether their own hope is just, right, or ethical, as with the assertion, "Justa mi esperanza fue, porque a la virtud se incline."[277] The same goes for whether it is legitimate to give someone else hope, as in the assertion by Isabel that "Quien da esperanza no injuria, y la esperanza es favor."[278] We hear characters giving themselves a pep talk to take courage and regain hope ("volved, esperanza, al pecho, no os vais"),[279] or alternatively asking each other for encouragement to reinforce it: "Rodrigo, dame los brazos, hijo, esfuerza mi esperanza."[280] Characters urge one another not to lose hope, on the grounds that surely the tide will turn at the next revolution of Fortune's wheel (see once again figure 6).[281]

Indeed, in the area of this passion much of the *comedias'* didactic content centres around the organic and cyclical imagery already mentioned. Hope can be sewn like a seed[282] and cultivated[283] unless its ground is a wasteland, "esperanza tan baldía."[284] Hope can be fed to keep it alive for a time ("ufano, y desvanecido, alimenté la esperanza algún tiempo")[285] or nursed back to health like a convalescent ("convalecer a mi esperanza quiero").[286] Hope can be animated or revived by human contact, as in "deseaba verte para animar mi esperanza."[287] Hope can be revived through encouraging words[288] or letters,[289] or even by animated shouts heard from a distance.[290] It can be controlled in the positive sense that one can resolve to direct one's steps toward it: "A que esperanza me encamino, y me resuelvo."[291]

Such are the positive ways to control hope; but what about on the negative end of the spectrum? Once again, at this intersection of ethics with emotion, the plays indicate substantial room for volitional agency.[292] Hope can be suspended voluntarily, as in the line "mi esperanza hasta otra ocasión es fuerza suspenderla y dilatarla."[293] The problem with this strategy, however, is that hope deferred runs the risk of going amok ("peligra la esperanza en la dilación del premio").[294]

Latin Silver Age poet Statius, whose *silvae* were imitated directly by Spanish Baroque poet Francisco de Quevedo, called hope the "heaviest of mortal cares when long deferred."[295] A postponed hope becomes an affliction: "no se ejecuta mi deseo, que aflije diferida la esperanza."[296] Instead of clinging to it, one can choose to cease and desist, as in "no más amor desde hoy, de mi esperanza desisto."[297] One can distance oneself[298] from hope until it can be renounced.[299]

Hope can be blocked[300] or impeded (Don Juan complains, "¡Que el paso a mi esperanza impiden!"),[301] for one can close the doors to hope: "cerrarme todas las puertas a la esperanza,"[302] thereby denying it entrance.[303] Hope can be cut short[304] or trampled on,[305] as by a horse;[306] or hope can be raised, only to be dashed to pieces again.[307] Reprehending someone often produces the effect of destroying their hope and self-confidence.[308]

In the face of such concerted opposition, in some way most comic stage characters still continue to hang onto hope,[309] if only by a thread. In a variation on this theme, in Aristophanes's classical comedy, hope is likened to a flotation device when the character Paphlagon declares, "There's but a splinter of hope keeping me afloat."[310] Hanging onto hope is equated to not losing sight of it, or somehow managing to keep it within view ("Quedé yo con la Esperanza, sin que de vista la pierda").[311] On the flip side, loss of hope tends to happen when it seems most far off: "mas por ahora la esperanza anda muy lejos."[312] To stay realistic, hope needs to see its object face to face.[313]

Even with these precautions in place, however, hope can begin to grow faint[314] or thin ("tu esperanza enflaquecía").[315] It then becomes smaller or diminished, "Menguando va mi esperanza."[316] This happens daily from invidious gossip: "La envidia, y murmuración te harán luego compañía; tu esperanza cada día sentirá diminución."[317] A faint hope runs lightly without deep breaths.[318] It can fall easily to the ground.[319] Shattered hopes can lead to such bitter disappointment that the hopeless sufferer even begins to weep tears of blood: "Mi mal lograda esperanza sangre por mis ojos llora."[320]

But these scenarios are for good, valid, or legitimate hopes. What about illegitimate ones? In "Hypothesis: There Is Hope," C.R. Snyder writes,

Sophocles portrayed hope as a human foible that only served to stretch out suffering (centuries later, Nietzsche uttered a virtually identical damnation of hope). Plato chastised those who listen to the voice of hope, calling it a "foolish counselor." Euripides labeled it as a "curse upon humanity." Francis Bacon, in a culinary analogy, said, "Hope is a good breakfast, but a bad supper." Similarly, Benjamin Franklin warned, "He that lives upon hope will die fasting." This common view held that hope was all illusion, lacking substance. It seduced humankind with a false promise. Perhaps the most succinct summary of the cynicism about hope was rendered by Shakespeare in *The Rape of Lucrece*, as he wrote, "And so by hoping more they have but lesse."[321]

The distinction between "good" and "bad" hope was being made already by the ancient Romans:

[T]his might explain the cult or quasi-cult titles *sancta* and *bona*, applied to *Spes* in some of the personifications … [N]ot all *Spes* is positive, but by specifying the "good" kind, suppliants may seek to separate themselves out from the ordinary run of mortals who hope fruitlessly, unwittingly attracting the attentions of the "bad" kind of hope.[322]

As these great thinkers intuited, the negative side of hope is that it can prove presumptuous[323] or vain,[324] for example in the case of falling in love with a person of a different culture or faith. This was said to happen specifically when a Christian woman became enamoured of a Muslim man.[325] Illegitimate hope produces suffering ("¿tantos años de sufrir tras una experiencia vana?"),[326] which in turn causes hope to lose its lustre. Thus Hiszentarif announces to the Spaniards: "De vuestra esperanza vana llegó el último desdoro, Castellanos."[327] Paradoxically, however, hope still shines brightly enough to blind the one who follows it.[328]

Hope can be destroyed[329] or killed by violence[330] or absence,[331] or even by a single word from the mouth of one's beloved: "Esforzaba mi esperanza, y derribóla, sola una palabra."[332] Hope can be undone by impatience[333] or lack of gratitude.[334] Hope can be shot down just as surely as with the use of bullets[335] or cannonballs in theatrical allusions to new military technologies. More old school are the references to pulling the rug out from under it, or – in the case of Samson – pulling down the columns of the Philistines' banqueting hall.[336] The Emperor Nero makes a similar threat in Lope de Vega's *Roma abrasada*:

SÉNECA: Cuatro columnas en quien apoya esta esperanza Roma.
NERO: Derribárélas yo.[337]

This was the same cruel emperor who, according to legend, played the fiddle as Rome burned.

Ultimately hope expires after being assaulted by wave after wave, "últimamente la esperanza expira en competencia de montañas de olas."[338] The last hope for a lost hope is to die: "pasando mi esperanza desde perdida a difunta."[339] Right before hope dies, however, there is a final paroxysm ("Aquí llegó mi esperanza al último parasismo")[340] and then a last breath ("aquí mi esperanza muerta exhaló el último soplo").[341] Some hopes essentially die before they are even fully born: "a Dios perdida esperanza, antes muerta que nacida."[342]

A dead hope is entombed[343] in forgetfulness: "da sepulcro de olvido a una esperanza, que yace en la cuna donde nace."[344] If it is cremated instead of buried, oblivion arises from hope's ashes ("muriendo la esperanza, nace de sus cenizas el olvido").[345] All that is left of a dead hope are relics,[346] like pieces of a dead saint's body or clothing.

Hope can be lost[347] in whole or in part,[348] especially by a person who is already disillusioned.[349] A lost hope can potentially be found, however;[350] but failing that, absence or distance from the unattainable beloved can provide some relief.[351] Lost hope must be recovered from like an illness or a wound, as in "yo a sanar de una esperanza."[352] Alexandre Johnston affirms the hurtful nature of hope, according to the ancient Greek poet Pindar: "Particularly when it merges with a bitter and painful *eros*, *elpis* may bind, hurt, or wound the mental organs and the body."[353] Once recovery from this kind of wounding hope is achieved, the numbly hopeless person will at least feel no pain: "ya quien no tiene esperanza, por lo menos no le alcanza un dolor."[354]

Even if hope is not lost altogether, it staggers or flounders like a ship battered by a storm.[355] Hope can wither[356] from the frost[357] or else shrivel up like a dead flower:

> Con qué justa razón a la esperanza
> dieron nombre de flor, pues que la imita
> en que tan brevemente se marchita,
> que tiene entre las hojas la mudanza.[358]

Anticipating Bob Dylan's song "Blowing in the Wind,"[359] like dried leaves, dead hopes are blown about by the winds of change unless they somehow manage to retain their fuller shape: "Si el viento de la mudanza, en flor mi esperanza deja."[360]

For this age of Baroque *desengaño*, hope is an illusion in which no one should believe: "No hay que creer en finezas de la esperanza, pues parece, que obligan, y sólo engañan."[361] Hope can tell lies ("mintió mi esperanza");[362] in this upside-down world, the only viable options for hope are to deceive ("Engañóme mi esperanza")[363] or be deceived.[364] Sometimes this deceit is welcome[365] – even pleasant – to those fleeing from truth. But the *comedias* warn that those who live off of hope are merely flattering their torment: "Quien vive de la esperanza lisonjea su tormento."[366] In the eyes of the ancient Spanish Roman author Seneca – so important an influence for Renaissance Neostoics like Francisco de Quevedo – "hope constitutes a dangerous emotion for the Stoic philosopher, one that feeds on constant anguish and therefore urges him on to forsake tranquility."[367] Hope thus appears as a chimera [see once again figure 7],[368] a shadow,[369] or a dream.[370] To anticipate the title of the great epic film of the American Confederacy, one can wake up someday to find hope "gone with the wind": "el viento se ha llevado mi esperanza."[371]

It is essential to distinguish legitimate hope from fantasy, as when one character asserts, "La buena esperanza alabo, pero no la fantasía."[372] Such fantasy is often generated especially by pride,[373] as in cases where hope pretends to boast a courage[374] that isn't really there. Some hopes are crazy and foolish ("¡Ay necio fin de una esperanza loca!"),[375] so they will be defrauded,[376] in which case those who feel them might just decide to euthanize or put them to death.[377] People can still cling to dead hopes by remembering them fondly, as at a funeral ("las exequias celebro a una difunta esperanza").[378]

Legitimate or sturdy hope should not be built like a castle in the air, "como quien en el aire funda toda su esperanza";[379] it should not be constructed like a tower[380] or pyramid.[381] In a variation on this imagery, one should not build houses of feathers for the winds of hope to come and blow away.[382] As one character warns,

> Pues fabricar la esperanza
> sobre el vano fundamento
> de la nieve, sombra, y viento,
> despojos de la mudanza,
> ¿paréceos a vos cordura?[383]

This rhetorical question obviously begs for the answer, "no."

Examples of such faulty "engineering" would include building one's hopes on false friends.[384] Hope is fragile and can vanish quickly (as Aurora laments: "¡qué presto ha desvanecido mi esperanza!"),[385] disappearing in an instant or a single day.[386] Hope might be fed by the continuous mutability of Fortune ("la continua mudanza del tiempo me da esperanza"),[387] but this cuts both ways; it can experience the downward part of the cycle of Fortune's wheel [see once more figure 6] as well as its rise: "Tu bien se acaba ya, ya tu Esperanza defraudó la Fortuna, con mudanza."[388] In one particularly striking image, Time tries to bargain with Hope and "talk her down" ("el tiempo regatea a la esperanza").[389]

The stuff of hope is highly flammable,[390] so that it often goes up in smoke: "en humo se nos fuera la esperanza de tener libertad."[391] For this reason it is not advisable to have only one hope, known today as "putting all of one's eggs into one basket": "qué necios son los que no tienen más que una esperanza."[392] It is better to die than to live without hope;[393] for without hope, even a strong mountain might come tumbling down.[394] Having said that, however, some *comedias* aver that hope does indeed have an expiration date.[395] Others demur on this point, claiming that hope ends only with death ("solamente el morir es el fin de la esperanza")[396] – or not even then; this belief reflects the philosophical view that hope is immortal ("¡ay esperanza inmortal!").[397]

Be that as it may, there is such a thing as a desperate hope,[398] also referred to as one's last hope ("postrera esperanza")[399] or, better still, hope against hope ("Creer contra la Esperanza, a la Esperanza").[400] This means one hopes against all odds[401] – perhaps invoking Saint Rita, patron saint of lost causes – even against one's own best interest.[402] Kazantzidis and Spatharas theorize, "The desire for possible rather than probable or likely outcomes and, thus, the element of uncertainty that characterizes hope, may also explain why affective hope is proverbially 'the last to die.'"[403] In this vein, Laurel Fulkerson explains why in ancient Roman religion, Hope was the perfect goddess to pray to *last*:

> [I]t seems to be in precisely those moments when it looks like the other gods have let you down that you might want to turn to Hope. So this "last-chance" goddess might ironically share features with certain other personifications, such as Robigo, the goddess of wheat-rust, who might avoid your crops if you appease her.[404]

Such desperate hope is not dissuaded by evidence to the contrary[405] of what is wished for. This hope cannot be taken from us ("La esperanza no os la puedo yo quitar");[406] for like its counterpart among the Theological Virtues (Love), according to this view, hope never fails: "al faltar todo, nunca la esperanza falta."[407] The appearance of Hope's companion Theological Virtue here – which is also one of the passions – prompts us to ask: what about hope's relationship to the other passions? We shall end this chapter by considering how hope acts in conjunction with love, along with some of the other emotions treated in this study.

Love without hope is hell ("amar sin esperanza es el infierno de amor")[408] because hope is essentially what keeps love alive: "no hay muerte de amor, si hay esperanza."[409] Desire cherishes hope of one day being fulfilled,[410] for hope is the guiding light or North Star of desire.[411] This relationship of hope to desire goes back at least as far as Lucretius, who called *spes* or hope "the one thing, the more of which we have, the more our breasts burn with terrible desire."[412]

Hope fixates on its object like a mariner looks to the North Star for guidance[413] until, ultimately, it arrives safely to port.[414] Hope resists fear,[415] knowing that fear can cut short hope's flight;[416] only when hope is lost does fear begin to rise.[417] This had been the case for the ancient Roman poet Ovid living in exile:

> Fear typically threatens to obliterate hope … [F]ear regularly proves stronger than hope, especially as time goes by and Ovid's longed-for return to Rome or transfer to another place is not achieved … Ovid essentially identifies Augustus with fear, since both threaten to crush his hopes.[418]

In this Ovidian tradition, the *comedias* confirm that hope can be dried up or choked out by fear:

De mil colores el temor se muda,
sécase por momentos la esperanza,
que la imaginación que el daño alcanza,
del verde tronco la color desnuda.[419]

In this set of images, hope is the wilted flower (see once again figure 17), while fear is the sharp thorn.[420]

Hope and courage enjoy a synergistic, reciprocal relationship: hope infuses us with courage,[421] which in turn inspires more hope.[422] This feedback loop is especially active in the context of battles[423] or affronts.[424] Hope makes light of dangers,[425] for it is intrepid like Pallas Athena, the warrior queen of gods: "la Esperanza la Divina Palas es, cuyos Trofeos hacen vencer los peligros, y desperdiciar los riesgos."[426] It is possible for hope to drown in sorrow;[427] but normally, hope alleviates sorrow or melancholy instead, as when one character announces, "Templo el dolor con la esperanza."[428] Hope redefines sorrow[429] to the point where it cannot be recognized. Hope causes us to sing[430] with joy ("con la esperanza me alegro").[431]

Such is the relationship of hope to the other passions; but what about hope's relationship to the other virtues? (For we must remember – like Courage, Hope is both a virtue and a passion.)[432] Some downtrodden Renaissance stage characters have lost hope in justice;[433] but for others, hope in justice is founded in law,[434] whether through lawsuits[435] or simply by the power of the king[436] to administer punishment or reward.[437] Andreas Michalopoulos notes that hope in justice had been invested in kings and emperors at least since imperial Rome:

During the imperial times *spes* became closely associated with the (deified) *princeps* and his qualities as the leader of the empire. Beginning with Augustus, hope was transformed into an extension of the personality of the emperor and stood for the promise of prosperity for the Roman people embodied by a charismatic leader.[438]

Justice is a Cardinal Virtue; but by way of contrast, Hope as a Theological Virtue is a pillar sustaining Faith.[439] Hope is said to be the daughter of patience ("la paciencia es hija de la esperanza")[440] in what is probably a direct reference to Romans 5:3–4: "We glory also in tribulations, knowing that tribulation worketh patience; and patience trial; and trial hope."[441] Hope earns merit only when accompanied by patience,[442] which rules it and keeps it in line.[443] Hope fosters perseverance ("La esperanza mucho alcanza, si esperando persevera"),[444] which is not technically one of the Cardinal or Theological Virtues; but it is traditionally associated with integrity and virtuous behaviour. It is also part of hope's genealogy in Romans 5.[445] As Lope de Vega put it in his aptly titled *Porfiando vence amor*, "quien tiene esperanza, en tanto que el bien no alcanza muy justamente porfía."[446]

In conclusion, then, hope has more connections to other emotions than any other passion, and also more connections to specific virtues. It thus serves to round out and bind together all the previous chapters of this study.

11

Conclusion: The Soul's Theatre

[T]he passions … are both the soul's theater and the soul of theater.[1]

Catharsis on the street is not recommended.[2]

The previous nine chapters have studied the fundamental passions identified by Aquinas and the Scholastics, except the two (anger and courage) which I have studied elsewhere.[3] But is it really that simple? Do all the emotions portrayed on the early modern Spanish stage fit this pattern?

As usual with the study of early modern culture, it's messier than that. In the course of my investigation, I have found multiple instances on stage when one emotion is mistaken for another. One example would be the line "la contingencia de ser odio lo que veo que es cariño,"[4] or its mirror opposite, "el que cariño juzgaba, es rencor."[5] So which is it? Is the emotion in question loving affection, or hateful rancour?

We also find confessions like "en mí el agrado es rigor, que en mí el cariño, es crueldad; que es odio, la voluntad,"[6] which seem to redefine emotions by moulding them to fit the countours of a particular stage character. The same thing happens when passions are adjusted to fit them to a specific case:

> [H]ay impiedad, que es cariño;
> que hay rigor, que es agasajo;
> y injuria, que es beneficio.[7]

So some impiety is actually affection; rigour can really be attentiveness; and injury can be beneficial.

On the one hand, these Scholastically trained playwrights seem to acknowledge that theoretically, the passions are supposed to be distinct: "al dividir las luces de las sombras, siendo apartar tristeza, y alegría, Obra primera del primero Día."[8] God divided sadness from joy just as He divided light from darkness on the first day of Creation. But on multiple other occasions we hear characters struggling to define emotions, as in the question "¿Es lo que en el alma siento amor, o agradeci-miento?" or in the exchange:

DON LOPE: [¿]Y esa es piedad, o cariño[?]
JUAN GÓMEZ: No sé.[9]

Here a character admits he has no idea how to classify a given emotion.

Similar examples could be multiplied ad infinitum. We hear characters making subtle distinctions between shades of colour on the emotional spectrum, such as "no presumas, que de quejoso se pasa a vengativo mi amor, que no tanto se desmanda contra el cariño el enojo"[10] or "partido el amor, aunque infinito / deja de ser amor, y es apetito."[11] Other characters comment that an emotion changes hue the moment it is "forced."[12] One emotion might masquerade as another, as in "lo que ira le parece, es quinta esencia de amor,"[13] or "llegando el desengaño, no hay amor, que no sea odio."[14] One emotion is said to be a sign of another, deeper, underlying sentiment.[15]

Frequently one character will contrast his or her emotions with someone else's, as in "mi amor es natural, y su amor es contingencia."[16] Characters debate with one another, differentiating among various subgroups or categories of a given feeling.[17] Characters measure the weight of various passions ("en iguales balanzas su amor, sus desconfianzas, y sus penas estarán")[18] and provide alternative classifications for them.[19]

We witness emotions morphing into one another, as in "lo que fue amor, es enojo"[20] or "quiero ... hacer ánimo del miedo."[21] This is especially true in the case of an abandoned woman, whose previous affection toward her lover now suddenly turns to hate.[22] This abrupt change of tune is the same thing that happens in Shakespeare's *Coriolanus* when the titular character announces, "wrath o'erwhelm'd my pity."[23] In fact, the speed of emotional change occurring on stage is often astounding, as when Alfonso laments:

Ayer favorecido,
¿hoy preso? ¿Hoy sin estado?
Ayer causando envidia, ¿hoy escarmiento?
¿Tan presto se ha ofendido?
¿Tan cerca está (cuidado)
la voluntad del aborrecimiento?[24]

This type of sudden reversal or *peripeteia* is the stuff of dramatic art.

A central question here is whether characters can control their emotions or foster this sort of metamorphosis of one passion into another. As one painfully honest character admits, "desde el odio al cariño no es fácil de hallar la senda."[25] The pathway from hatred to love is not easy to find. Occasionally we do witness individual steps along this path leading from one emotion to another. In fact, sometimes we find a whole series of emotions that turn out to form a thread or chain of connected passions ("del yerro al castigo, pasa del castigo al odio").[26] Witness here the language of moral instruction in lines such as "ha privilegiado de mi enojo mi cariño"[27] or "haciendo mérito del desahogo, y cariño del desprecio."[28]

However, we also find characters acknowledging real limits to this capacity for change.[29] Often, instead of changing their feelings, characters will instead reach deep inside themselves to find – and then reveal – emotions long hidden, perhaps even to themselves: "no sé, qué reverencial respeto, qué interior cariño, qué ignorado amor, qué afecto no conocido, qué oculta veneración."[30] Or sometimes this same process might happen in reverse: characters may work hard to bury or deny their feelings if they judge them to be wrong. Freud would be delighted to hear the exact language of repression used to describe this process: "¡O quiera amor, que yo pueda reprimir mis sentimientos!"[31]

This infinitely messy picture brings us to an important theme of my previous monograph: ambiguity.[32] There are often no clean or neat distinctions possible in the study of emotions, but instead only endless permutations and combinations. This is not the case of a living scholar (myself) imposing a postmodern viewpoint on authors who have long been dead and gone; this was in fact the stance of Juan Luis Vives, Spain's great humanist who was also a great theorist of the emotions, to the point where he is now recognized by many to have been the founder of modern psychology. Here's what he says:

> Some emotions thrive in the company of others, some are curbed and kept in check by others. Love causes envy, hatred, or anger when somebody hates or harms something dear to us. Anger gives rise to the desire of and the joy in revenge. Whoever loves something hopes that it will take place so he may enjoy it and fears it might never happen. If it happens, he rejoices; if what he expects does not happen, he becomes sad … [A] great joy can be spoiled by sadness, jealousy is weakened by compassion or fear and grief is taken away by another grief. Pain and sadness can be removed by fear.[33]

As his modern translator Carlos Noreña observes,

> Emotions to Vives are not atomic units isolated from each other. They are rather constellations and mixtures of parts which interact constantly, reinforcing or weakening neighboring emotions. Such blendings of emotions result in complex emotional responses which defy our attempt to impose on them sharp definitions and clearly cut taxonomies.[34]

My personal favourite example of emotional ambiguity comes straight out of Vives's *The Passions of the Soul*: "gladiators who were wounded under the armpits, frequently died laughing."[35] Apparently their bodies could not tell the difference between being tickled and being stabbed.

Characters might experience two or more different and conflicting emotions, for instance, when they are acting in two or more different capacities simultaneously, for example when one female character recalls: "supe a un mismo tiempo en el corazón guardar el odio como ofendida, como amante la piedad, como noble el pundonor."[36] Kimberlé Crenshaw would call this crossover among various social roles "intersectionality."[37] A similar example occurs in this speech by the Emperor Federico:

> Entre al amor, y venganza
> turbado el corazón late,
> y en dos afectos a un tiempo
> me siento osado, y cobarde.[38]

Note the similar phrase "a un (mismo) tiempo" uniting these two passages.

Some emotions are frequently paired together, but we do not necessarily perceive conflict between them. For example, in Calderón's sacramental drama *La púrpura de la rosa*, Alegría and Tristeza are both allegorical figures dressed as ladies, each with her own musical chorus. Presumably the symmetry of this pairing would have appealed to the Renaissance's classicizing sensibilities; I have discussed the physical staging of similar pairs of Virtues and Vices previously.[39]

We could amass examples likewise from the more "secular" *comedias*, such as "yo confuso entre esperanza y miedo"[40] or "estoy entre amor y miedo haciendo discursos varios."[41] Don Juan says to Don Alonso:

> [E]n dos iguales líneas
> los dos extremos toquéis
> del pesar, y la alegría.[42]

Here the *comedia* audience is cued visually to imagine Don Alonso situated at the midpoint between joy and sorrow, even if the two emotions are not embodied in allegorical figures as they would be in the *auto sacramental*.

But relations between conflicting emotions are not always so sanguine – for if we think about it, that would make for a boring play. Instead, we often find characters caught between two emotions perceived to be polar opposites, as when Lisidoro reports:

> [L]idiaron mis ansias
> aquel repetido duelo
> a que siempre están retados
> amor, y aborrecimiento.[43]

In fact, "duels" between contrasting emotions seem to have been a favourite device of this playwright, Calderón de la Barca, who made this agonistic scenario even more explicit in his *Duelos de Amor y Lealtad*. In this play, the two emotions of love and loyalty are pictured as being measured on a scale: "Amor, y lealtad, pudieron en porfiadas balanzas, tener suspenso mi afecto con acciones encontradas; pero al amor se añadió, para que vencedor quedara, la parte de la piedad."[44] Love wins out over loyalty only because pity is added to love's side of the scale. The theme of the measuring scale[45] is repeated in Calderón's *El Faetonte*:

> [E]n dos balanzas
> de amor, y lástima, el fiel,
> a pesar de amor, declina
> a la lástima.[46]

Here pity wins out over love.

Alternatively, instead of using a figurative scale, sometimes characters merely weigh competing emotions in either hand, as in "en una mano el amor, y en otra el rigor presente."[47] Still another variation is to have one emotion serve as the measure of another.[48] Other playwrights, not content to stage a contest between only two emotions, throw in a third one just to keep things interesting; such is the case with Juan Pérez de Montalbán's *Amor, lealtad y amistad*. In this play, a different verdict is reached: "aunque es el amor tan grande, está la amistad primero."[49] In this playwright's view, friendship wins out over either love or loyalty.

In addition to the duel, another metaphor used to convey the notion of a contest among the passions is the idea of a lawsuit: "callaron duda, y amor, que eran sus dos abogados."[50] Here love and doubt act as counsel for the prosecution versus counsel for the defence. Yet another metaphor still is that of an all-out battle: "con miedo, y amor estoy lidiando, en ver su hermosura."[51] This "lid" could signify anything from a joust to open warfare. A synonym for this word was, of course, *batalla*. As the King admits,

> Siento temor,
> con el amor en batalla:
> y cuanto el amor me anima,
> tanto el amor me acobarda.[52]

He confesses that love produces two results in parallel: courage and cowardice, in equal measure.

One thing is certain: normally no truce was possible between conflicting emotions. One passion must lose, and another one must win.[53] Harsh language of violent struggle reflects this uncomfortable reality; for example,

"[¡]con qué ansia, resistencia, y repugnancia el cariño pisa la concupiscencia!"[54] Here love literally "steps on" or tramples lust. At the end, the losing side must concede to the victor: for instance, "al fin se rinde la esperanza al miedo."[55] Hope gives way to fear. We should recall that in late medieval and early modern times, it was still customary for the leader of one army to concede victory to his opponent.

However, occasionally in these plays it is possible to find a third term or *aporia* between two extremes, as in "Luego entre amor, y crueldad no será crueldad, ni amor el destierro."[56] Banishment seems to be an acceptable compromise between love and cruelty. A similar example might be "cielos quieran que halle un medio … entre el cariño, y la ofensa."[57] Here we find the specific language of the midpoint or median, which I have already studied in *Ambiguous Antidotes*.[58] In still another variation, two emotions can be joined with a hinge to allow them to alternate ("aquel Sacramento era Bisagra de su Poder, y Amor").[59] Here the sacrament of the Eucharist allows God to manifest alternately His love and His might.

Not only God, but regular human characters on stage could sometimes combine opposing passions into a single emotional stance, as in "su amor con su dolor juntar supo."[60] The zoological example of the bee demonstrated being "stung" with both love and hate:

> Una abeja es pequeñita,
> que tiene dos aguijones
> de amor y aborrecimiento.
> … ¡[Q]ué bien se esconde![61]

In a fascinating analogy, the same was actually thought to be true of Cupid's arrows (see again figure 3). As Cupid himself confesses to his mother Venus:

> Ya sabes, madre, y señora,
> que el amor tiene dos flechas,
> una de plomo, otra de oro:
> la de plomo es cosa cierta,
> que causa aborrecimiento,
> hiriendo a Dafne con ella:
> y con la de oro algún Dios,
> ten por segura la fuerza,
> porque al supremo poder
> no puede haber resistencia.[62]

Apparently Cupid could distinguish between his two arrows producing love and hate because one was made of gold, the other of lead.

Still further instances of ambiguity with regard to the passions in the *comedias* were the cases where one and the same emotion could mean opposite things for two different characters. For instance, in a sacramental drama Culpa says of Man: "su pena es mi alegría"[63] (his sorrow is my joy). Once again the metaphor of the scale or balance is resurrected to express equivalency between their two perspectives: "queden en igual balanza mi alegría, y vuestra pena, mi gusto, y vuestro dolor."[64] This play of perspectivism is something we normally associate more with the novelistic genre than with stage plays. But perhaps that is one critical assumption we ought to revise.

In fact, sometimes characters discuss these tensions overtly, as in the following exchange:

> LOPE: Siempre, Manrique, parece
> que al paso que yo estoy triste,
> tu estás contento, y alegre.
> MANRIQUE: Y dime, ¿cuál es mejor,
> en pasiones diferentes,
> la alegría, o la tristeza?
> LOPE: La alegría.
> MANRIQUE: Pues qué quieres,
> ¿que deje yo lo mejor
> por lo peor? Tú que tienes
> la tristeza, que es la mala,
> eres quien mudarte debes,
> y pasarte a la alegría,
> pues será más conveniente,
> que el ir yo de alegre a triste,
> venir tú de triste a alegre.[65]

Here two characters actively debate which passion is preferable, with joy winning out over sadness. Manrique then urges Lope to change his mood – i.e., control his emotions – because they have already established that it's better to be joyful than to mope.

Even when they do not debate the advantages or disadvantages of different emotional states with each other, characters will often debate within themselves by employing the dramatic convention of a monologue or aside. Witness the following speech by Argenis:

> ¡Válgame el Cielo! ¿Qué enigmas,
> qué confusiones son éstas?
> Juntos favor, y rigor,

risa, y llanto, gloria, y pena,
gusto, y pesar, vida, y muerte,
sólo en Argenis se engendran,
pues si el bien, y el mal tan juntos
andan, y el uno se templa
con el otro, yo confuso
entre alegría, y tristeza,
porfiaré, porque también
entre dos causas opuestas,
la misma que me acobarda
es la misma que me alienta.[66]

Soliloquies such as this one have been identified as "thimotic moments" by my former doctoral student Yoandy Cabrera.[67] A similar instance occurs in a speech by César to Serafín:

Aunque es mi dicha inmensa
en servirte, y agradarte,
no sé qué oculta tristeza
se ha apoderado del alma,
que más a llorar me fuerza,
que a cantar, y no sé cómo
en un corazón se avenga
el gusto, y pesar a un tiempo.[68]

These speeches show a remarkable degree of interiority and self-awareness for a genre previously thought to be lacking in subjective content.[69]

In fact, these *comedia* characters show such a sophisticated level of emotional intelligence that they deliberately use one emotion as a "cure" or antidote for another: "se atreva de sus pasiones, curando con el amor la tristeza."[70] Synonyms for "cure" include "take away,"[71] "moderate,"[72] and "banish."[73] Once again the discourse of battle is deliberately employed; one emotion is said to serve as a "shield" against another's assaults.[74] Alternatively, one emotion might steal another's sword.[75] Sometimes, however, a passion's designated antidote fails:

REY: ¿Es posible, que no sepa
    yo en qué te dar alegría?
AMINTA: Nada, pues, de mis pesares
    tus cariños no me alivian.[76]

This failed attempt at emotional therapy nonetheless tells us how early modern people would go about trying to re-establish passional equilibrium.

It should come as no surprise to scholars of early modern Spanish theatre that according to the medieval Scholastic mentality – behind which Saint Thomas Aquinas was arguably the driving force – the passions were organized into pairs of affects, for example "dos afectos, tan contrarios, y distintos, como son odio, y amor."[77] A signal word for the intrusion of the Scholastic mindset into *comedia* discourse is the word "contraries," as in "dos contrarias proposiciones opuestas, del rencor, y amor"[78] and "amor, y poder con fuerza, y dolor, son dos contrarios."[79] Some synonymic adjectives for this word are "encontrados" and "opuestos," as in this speech by a Demon:

> Afectos más poderosos,
> más encontrados, y opuestos,
> pues son el amor y el odio,
> tan postrado, tan rendido,
> tan sujeto, y tan penoso
> me tiene.[80]

In accord with the Baroque love of paradox, these pairs of passions sometimes swap characteristics.[81] This paradox packs a punch because, of course, these passions were viewed as opposites.

The persistence of Scholastic taxonomies for organizing the passions in the *comedias* and *autos sacramentales* begs the question: what is the perceived relationship of the passions to virtue and vice? What is the ethical valence or tenor of these emotions?

It turns out that these plays have quite a lot to say about whether emotions are virtuous or vicious. "Good" emotions are characterized explicitly as such ("afectos tan buenos"),[82] but they also receive a plethora of positive adjectives to describe them, including honest,[83] decent,[84] noble,[85] innocent,[86] perfect,[87] pure,[88] and chaste.[89] "Bad" emotions likewise are called ugly, vicious,[90] illegitimate,[91] shameful,[92] indecent,[93] crude,[94] criminal,[95] and disordered.[96] Again, a Baroque sensitivity to paradox is evident in transformations[97] or combinations[98] of one emotion deemed to be negative with a companion emotion perceived to possess redeeming qualities.

The *comedias* also contain references to specific emotions that are equated to either virtue or vice. For example, in "La virtud, que está de amor en la llama derritiendo el corazón"[99] love is portrayed as a virtue; but in "en un hidalgo penar / se queja el amor de vicio / cuando se puede quejar"[100] love is connected to vice. Clearly "hay Amor que es Virtud, y Amor que es vicio."[101] Notice too that specific emotions are called "sins" or "errors," as in "el pecado que hace por amor"[102] and "perdona este yerro amor de mi cólera."[103]

So how does one decide? What makes an emotion sinful? What keeps an affect innocent? Often in these plays the moral valence of a passion is tied directly to its concrete effects in terms of the action it inspires. For example, "aquel amor que es honesto, es el que es perfecto amor"[104] – i.e., for love to be perfect, it must be honest. A similar example might be "amor da espíritu, da valor, y los sujetos mejora" (love animates us, gives us courage and makes us better) or even, in a direct quotation from 1 Corinthians 13:7, "el amor todo lo sufre"[105] (love suffers all things). In fact, love counsels moderation even when meting out punishment: "castigo pide la ofensa, y el amor pide templanza."[106] On the flip side, a negative criterion for love would be "no es verdad el amor que hace violento"[107]: true love is not violent. Similarly, love must be forgiving: "no es perfecto amor el que no perdona faltas."[108] True love is not lascivious either.[109]

This criterion for determining the (un)ethicality of emotions seems relatively straightforward: emotions are only sinful if they lead to negative or sinful actions. But is this really the essence of Catholic Christianity as early modern Spaniards understood it? After all, Jesus consciously separated feelings from actions in the Sermon on the Mount:

> You have heard that it was said to them of old: Thou shalt not kill ... But I say to you, that whosoever is angry with his brother shall be in danger of judgment ... You have heard it said to them of old: Thou shalt not commit adultery. But I say to you, that whosoever shall look on a woman to lust after her, hath already committed adultery with her in his heart.[110]

These commands by Christ audaciously legislate emotional content, thereby holding His followers to a higher standard.

So – can emotions be chosen? Renaissance debates about free will[111] made conscious volition a prerequiste for sinning. And it turns out that discussions of emotion in these plays are also rife with terms for "free will" and its synonyms. For example, Celia declares:

> [E]l amor
> procede del albedrío,
> libre me da Dios el mío
> para amar, o aborrecer.[112]

Here she rehearses the doctrine of free will and claims her own freedom to choose whether to love or to hate.

But the plays (and their authors) appear far from uniform on this point. We find nuances such as "el amor no es elección, sino influjo"[113] – love is not exactly a choice, more like an influence – combined with outright denials like "el amor no tiene voto"[114] (love does not have a vote). To make matters even more confusing, we find complaints such as "el amor tiene en mí cautivo el libre albedrío"[115] (love holds free will captive). Huhh? Do we exercise free will when it comes to our emotions, or not?

Upon further examination, it becomes clear that early modern Spanish drama is obsessed with this question. The razor-thin subtleties about the passions explored (and exploded) on stage are worthy of the medieval Scholastics. Apparently a passion such as love is free of intention ("libre está amor del intento"),[116] but instead occurs as an accident: "amor es accidente, que en el sentido se engendra."[117]

This conception of the passions as accidental or contingent was so popular during this time period that it has lent a title to the foremost Spanish-language scholarly contribution on this topic, *Accidentes del alma*.[118] William MacLehose offers a useful explanation of how this model for generating emotions evolved:

> Medieval theories of the accidents of the soul consist of a synoptic fusion of Platonic and Aristotelian thought, transmitted through the Islamic natural philosophers, particularly Avicenna and Averroës. The medical tradition in the twelfth- and early thirteenth-century west at first followed the description of the motions or movements of the soul found in Haly Abbas's *Pantegni*: six accidents of the soul were identified, both arising from and consequently affecting the physiology of the body. Joy, sadness, fear, anger, anxiety and shame were all associated with the vital spirit, which either moved outward from the heart to the extremities or, in the case of fear, centripetally from the extremities to the heart. The heart-centered model received greater complexity in Avicenna's influential treament of the subject in his *De anima*. With Avicenna's views on psychology, which gain prominence only in the thirteenth century in the west, we find a closer connection between the accidents of the soul and the brain, cognition and perception.[119]

So we see that when the word "accident" occurs to describe an emotion in the drama of early modern Spain, the playwright is self-consciously employing a technical term that elite members of his audience would likely have recognized. The notion of passions as accidents appears, for example, in this speech recited on stage by Ángela to Estefanía:

> [E]l rigor encoje el brío,
> y el amor extiende el brazo,
> porque son pasiones propias,
> y no están en nuestras manos.[120]

"They are not in our hands" – this sounds an awful lot like Pontius Pilate washing his hands symbolically to absolve himself of any responsibility for Jesus's death.

A key concept here is that of "inclination." A character named Laura says to her father as she defends the right to choose her own marriage partner:

> La inclinación, padre mío,
> es efecto natural,
> que no manda el albedrío.[121]

She appears to be carving out a space for emotions to work apart from free will. And she is not the only one to make these claims; in a similar instance, Beatriz says to Don Felipe:

> El remedio del amor,
> es, considerar, que pende
> la inclinación de un influjo,
> que domina, aunque no vence.[122]

Now, this is about as clear as mud – "the inclination of an influence that dominates but does not win"?? The difficulty here is conceptual, not linguistic. No amount of effort expended attempting to improve the translation can change the fact that these related ideas are all muddled up.

There are plenty of instances where characters do try to sort through the various confusing strands of this Scholastic debate, such as

> La Voluntad es lo mismo
> que un acto de amor; lo fundo,
> en que siempre que apetezco,
> o determino, lo admito
> como bien.[123]

Here *appetite*, *determination*, and *granting admission* (or entrance) to love are parsed separately as distinct strands of the process of "willing" to love someone. Sometimes love's phases are described differently, or else additional steps are added to make the process of falling in love sound even more complex:

> No hay edad para el amor,
> porque la voluntad es
> la potencia que primero
> usa el hombre, y más entero
> usa el discurso después:
> y como haya en tierna edad
> voluntad esta pasión,

> cuando es poca la razón,
> lleva más la voluntad.[124]

However, these intricate speeches prove to be more the exception than the rule. Normally characters limit themselves to simple, staccato, provocative pronouncements such as "amor es voluntad"[125] or "No tiene elección mi amor, ni albedrío mi tristeza."[126] Whether the audience agrees with such warnings and disclaimers will likely determine whether they feel much sympathy for these characters.

On balance, I would like to be able to say that while there is no consensus, the scales are tipped at least slightly in favour of Renaissance individualism and free will over determinism. (This will come as no surprise to readers of my previous monographs.)[127] As the stage character Saint Teresa of Ávila asks rhetorically to the demon:

> ¿Pues por qué me he de rendir
> a aqueste tirano, haciendo
> esclavo acá a mi albedrío
> de este yerro de mi afecto?[128]

She at the same time recognizes the possibility of committing an "error of affect" but nonetheless asserts the freedom of her will[129] or *albedrío* not to subject itself to passion's tyranny.

The language of casuistry is key here; for example, "Que el errar una elección de amor, está contingencia."[130] Does this mean that to love is a choice – and thereby prone to error – but said error can be excused by contingency or circumstance? Perhaps the emotion of love itself cannot be chosen; but even still, it does not colonize the self entirely: "en el peso de ese amor atado, libre la voluntad, y entendimiento."[131] In such lines it is impossible not to see a split, conflicted, or divided "self" like the one described aptly by George Mariscal.[132] The interior struggle shown here sounds exhausting: "me abraso, yo me rindo a esta furia vengativa de amor, contra la quietud de mi libertad tranquila."[133] Here the subject admits to giving in to love, but only after what amounts to a protracted struggle.

Emotions conceived as "accidents of the soul" can nevertheless change the valence of moral actions. Specifically, the passions are often invoked as an excuse when a character's deeds have turned out to be less than praiseworthy. We find casuistical mitigations like "de perdón son dignos yerros en amor fundados"[134] or "no hay delito que deba llamarse delito, cuando es amor quien le gobierna."[135] Evidently an emotion such as love can excuse error, blame, and punishment.[136] In fact, in a direct parody of the Catholic Church, love is said to offer a general pardon or indulgence (mercy conferred by the Church in its capacity to shorten the length of time a sinner spends in Purgatory): "mi amor este indulto le concede"[137] (see figure

22). This joke became so conventionalized that instead of employing the technical term *indulto* it was enough simply to reference the Church: "en amorosos delitos, mi amor siempre pide Iglesia."[138]

But once more we find ourselves returning to actions, perhaps because they are more concrete, and thus we feel we are standing on less slippery ground. What about the morality of emotions themselves? Over and over again in these dramas we find comments to the effect that the moral valence of a given emotion depends on its source; for example, one character admonishes another, "es tu amor hijo de tu vanidad."[139] Presumably this love is not the good kind of love because it stems from vanity. In an even more chilling example, witness the following exchange:

> MARQUÉS: Pues yo que abrasar me vi,
>   palabra mezclada en fuego
>   de ser su esposo la di;
>   tomóla, gocéla, y luego,
>   la olvidé, y la aborrecí.
> CARDENIO: Eso es muy propio de amor
>   que se funda en apetito.[140]

This woeful tale of love turned sour is diagnosed as the result of love grounded in appetite (i.e., sexual desire).

Sometimes the two can be quite difficult to tell apart – "amor y liviandad no se apartan por un dedo"[141] – or, alternatively, your emotions might stem from someone else's will being imposed on you ("este amor, y este cuidado nace de ajeno albedrío").[142] An external source for an emotion might be a parent or, more generically, the Fates.[143] An extreme alternative for displacing guilt was to blame the stars: "Esto de amor ha de ser por confrontación de Estrellas."[144] Specifically, the stars were said to "dispose"[145] or "incline"[146] lovers towards each other. At very least, the stars were thought to intensify an existing passion.[147] In a convenient irony, the stars could be blamed whether a love affair turned out well or badly.[148]

In fact, there is an instructive parallel between Spanish Golden Age preoccupation with astrology[149] and early modern Spanish understandings of the passions. The Church's problem with judicial astrology ultimately rested on the conundrum of free will, as Calderón dramatized so memorably in *La vida es sueño*. Time and again we hear characters exclaiming in tones of exasperation that they were dragged along by the force of irresistible passion, as when the King says to the Admiral:

> Ya sabéis
> la violencia de mis ansias;
> ya os dije, que mi albedrío

> no es mío, y que me le arrastra
> esta pasión poderosa.[150]

This graphic image goes back to the etymology of the word *passion* as suffering (the reader will recall that Greek *pathē* were involuntary in human beings, to the point where ancient Greek and Roman religious cults built shrines to different emotions as deities). Even this piece of lore recovered by Renaissance Spanish playwrights from their classical inheritance pops up now and again in the drama:

> Los afectos humanos, Beatriz bella,
> tal vez arrebató fuerza divina,
> porque vienen atentos a una estrella,
> que superior, ilustra, y predomina:
> y aunque es verdad, que no se vencen de ella
> con tal poder, ya que no fuerza, inclina,
> que pierden libertad, discurso, y brío
> el alma, la razón, y el albedrío.
> No es amor elección, pues si lo fuera,
> nadie en el mundo aborrecido amara,
> no es voluntad que nadie la rindiera,
> donde con voluntad no se pagara:
> no es razón, pues con ella se rigiera,
> no es gusto, pues sin él no se entregara,
> ¿qué será donde falta (¡cielo injusto!)
> elección, voluntad, razón y gusto?
> ¿Qué será, pues, violencia semejante,
> sino fuerza, rigor, y tiranía
> de amor[?][151]

Here the force of human affects is attributed to manipulation by a "divine force." As Spanish humanist Juan Luis Vives stated in *De Anima et Vita*, the *passions* are so called "because the soul is passively submitted to their blows and buffets."[152]

If emotions can depend on something so unchangeable as the stars, then how can we go about fixing them? Stage characters can often be overheard asking God or heaven for help ("El cielo mi amor corrija").[153] Some lines seem to indicate that emotions can be put on or taken off like clothes,[154] or at least mitigated somewhat ("mi amor mitigo").[155] Even extremely powerful emotions have certain boundaries, limits, or constraints.[156] But this tiny sliver of an opening for free will to resist the determinism of the Fates or stars is only that: a tiny sliver. This minuscule *agujero* left Spanish Golden Age playwrights hanging, holding in their hands a theological problem which they never stopped scrambling to try to resolve.

And that's where the role of the theatre comes in. It just so happens that the theatrical space was the perfect venue for sorting out precisely these types of issues. In recent years, researchers have begun to emphasize the "performative aspect of emotion … [Late medieval and early modern] emotions … were seen not as internal states of mind but rather 'as patterned behaviors and performances.'"[157] As Philippa Maddern, editor of *Performing Emotions in Early Europe*, explains:

> The study of the history of emotions can be nuanced and enriched by attention to performance, since our emotions, sometimes considered to be "internal" features of ourselves, are anticipated and produced through certain bodily acts and naturalized gestures … [W]e understand emotions to emerge from and be articulated through bodily practices and stylized acts … [W]e … explore the performance of emotion, believing that such performance is not a single act but a repetition and ritual. We examine cases where that which, traditionally, may have been considered an internal essence of emotion is actualized and understood through a sustained set of acts, rituals, and stylizations – in this sense, "performance."[158]

Previously, sociologist Erving Goffman had argued as early as the 1950s and '60s that

> individuals' behaviors always involve the presentation of self to audiences of others. In making a dramatic presentation, individuals use a cultural script of ideologies, values, and norms, along with staging props (wardrobes, spacing, and objects), to present the self not only dramatically but also strategically.[159]

Social historian Peter Burke acknowledges literary criticism's debt to Goffman, noting the obvious synergy between "emotional scripts" and theatrical scripts:

> Theatrical metaphors pervade recent discussions of emotions in a manner reminiscent of Erving Goffman's analyses of everyday life in the 1950s and 1960s. Where Harré speaks of the "emotional repertoire" and Sousa of "paradigm scenarios," Wierzbicka refers to what she calls the "emotional scripts" available in a given culture, an idea parallel to that of "code." She also talks about emotional "scenarios."[160]

Relevant here too is William Reddy's concept of "emotives," emotional utterances that act like John Austin's "performatives,"[161] transforming the self and others as they are expressed.[162] Reddy stipulates that these speech acts have "(1) descriptive appearance, (2) relational intent, and (3) self-exploring and self-altering effects."[163] He further theorizes that "An 'emotional regime' is the ensemble of prescribed *emotives* together with their related rituals and other symbolic practices … Every political regime is supported by an emotional regime."[164]

As if these confluences between emotions and theatricality or performativ-
ity were not sufficient, we could gather instances of representative early modern
authors who conflated the two. For example, Walter Charleton urged his ideal
reader to relate what he has read in his book *Natural History of the Passions* (1674)
to what he has "daily observed within the theatre of [his] own breast."[165] We might
recall that in early modern Europe, the mind itself was viewed as a sort of theatre,
specifically a "memory theatre" that could be constructed to aid with mnemonic
tasks.[166] Finally, as Jennifer Low and Nova Myhill suggest, a further layer of meaning is added by the use of printing language in early modern antitheatrical tracts
to describe what happens in the performance of plays:

> The word "impressions" suggests a sympathetic relationship between player and play-
> goer greater than the mere experience of seeing or hearing, in which the minds of the
> spectators actually receive the "impressions of the mind" imprinted by the counterfeit
> emotions of the actors. The language of printing that appears with some frequency
> in antitheatrical tracts, as well as the concurrent suggestion that the audience will
> imitate what they see on stage in a startlingly literal way, implies that the process that
> Gosson envisions in *Plays Confuted in Five Actions* is a literal reforming of the specta-
> tors' minds into the mental shape "counterfeited" by the actors.[167]

This "reforming of the spectators' minds" is the process that interests us here.

Within the past decade or so, scholars of early modern English drama have begun
to describe the social role of theatre as a laboratory for teaching people how to read
emotions on other human beings' faces, in their body language, through their tone
of voice, etc. As Steven Mullaney observes, "the drama of post-Reformation England served as a kind of affective laboratory."[168] In the words of Bridget Escolme,
"the early modern theatre is a place where audiences went to watch extremes of
emotion and to consider when those extremes became excesses."[169] As Mullaney
had argued twenty years previously,

> As a forum for the representation, solicitation, shaping, and enacting of affect in
> various forms, for both the reflection and ... the reformation of emotions and their
> economies, the popular stage of early modern England was a unique contemporane-
> ous force ... [I]t certainly served as a prominent affective arena in which signifi-
> cant cultural traumas and highly ambivalent events ... could be directly or indirectly
> addressed, symbolically enacted, and brought to partial and imaginary resolution.[170]

A concrete example in the Senecan tradition would be the ways in which "images
of anger performed on the stage shaped contemporary thinking on revenge."[171]

What if plays, like novels, are "cultural artifacts that instantiate social passions,
rather than merely describing them"?[172] In their mantra about the historicity of
texts and the textuality of history,[173] the New Historicists have been insisting since

the 1980s that texts can be powerful enough to influence the course of real-world events. But how does this influence actually work?

Here we must turn to recent developments in nueroscience to understand the brain mechanisms behind the scenes in theatre's laboratory. Lisa Perfetti notes that

> A recent approach to emotion combining cognitive science with literary criticism argues that people understand what they are feeling by appraising how their feelings match emotion prototypes, or stories about emotion.[174]

The theatre offers precisely such models or prototypes. Key scenes "work as instructional systems, teaching readings of the passions attentive to social relation and degree … [T]hese scenes negotiate ongoing concerns about the social management of emotion."[175]

This role for theatre is confirmed by none other than Juan Luis Vives, the greatest Spanish Renaissance theorist of the passions:

> [C]ompassion is mostly aroused by sight … Those, however, who are guided by thought, are more moved by a story but would be hardly touched if the event had taken place in their very presence. Quintilian says: "The same words and the same sound draw our emotions more when expressed by a stage character." While we listen to them the emotion is reinforced by our fantasy and thought. The same disaster rouses our emotions more with the help of the actor's artistry. The likelihood of our being touched by the story is increased by the emphasis upon the gravity of the suffering, by realizing how undeserving the victim is, how much more entitled to good than to evil things … The audience is admonished to think of their children, wives, most precious possessions, themselves, and the common fate of humanity.[176]

Let us see how this laboratory experiment functions in terms of both actors and audience.

In the context of *Hamlet*, Irmgard Maassen refers to "what early modern theatre writing called a 'passion,' a piece of rhetoric or a performance highly charged with emotion."[177] Michael Hattaway explains, "Elizabethan players probably thought of their task as having to render scenes, rather than create characters, to remember their lines and be in the right spot at the right time to deliver a 'passion' (Elizabethan for a passionate speech) or to perform a piece of business."[178] Thomas Rist confirms early modern usage of this word in this way: "Indeed, a literary composition (if sufficiently emotional) was a 'passion.'"[179]

The use of *passion* as a technical term in a theatrical context may shed fresh light on familiar passages such as Hamlet's speech about the players:

> Is it not monstrous that this player here,
> But in a fiction, in a dream of passion,

Could force his soul so to his own conceit
That from her working all his visage wan'd,
Tears in his eyes, distraction in's aspect,
A broken voice, and his whole function suiting
With forms to his conceit?[180]

The word *passioning* could also be used as a verb in a dramatic context in early modern England, as in Julia's lines in Shakespeare's *Two Gentlemen of Verona*:

For I did play a lamentable part;
Madam, 'twas Ariadne, passioning
For Theseus' perjury and unjust flight.[181]

Further insight into the emotional engagement of early modern actors may be gained by attention to one further technical term: "personation." As Emma Rhatigan explains,

[T]he early modern term "personation" ... was just coming into use in the early seventeenth century ... At the same time, however, it remains important to distinguish between the personal investment in a part ... and the "personation," the eliding of self and part, that the revellers would have seen in the actors who performed ... [T]he process of "personation" involved actors becoming "physical incarnations" of the characters they were playing.[182]

Charles Whitney confirms: "The word 'personation' appeared about this time to denote such individualized acting soliciting greater emotional engagement."[183]

If this acting technique sounds familiar, it should. Arguably, early modern theatre practitioners were anticipating the methods of Russian director Constantin Stanislavsky (1863–1938), the famed "inventor" of what came to be known as "method acting." Stanislavsky's method acting involves generating emotion to portray a character through the process of remembering one's own emotions: "[T]he Stanislavsky method ... [is one] in which actors recall gestures, movements, and other expressions of an emotion they have felt strongly in the past in order to evoke those feelings once again."[184]

Stanislavsky's method was not, of course, entirely new; previously, in the nineteenth century, psychologist William James had posited that actors who play emotional scenes must of necessity experience the corresponding feeling.[185] What *is* new in theatrical criticism written after the post-structuralists is the extension of Stanislavsky's ideas not just to the actors, but also to their audience (we might recall here that Lope de Vega's *Arte nuevo* advises playwrights to create characters with affects strong enough to transform both actor and audience).[186] Keith Oatley and Mitra Gholamain participate in this trend:

[N]ot only do many actors follow Stanislavski's injunctions to draw on their autobiographical experience to give their performances emotional authenticity, but the
audience (or readers) draw from their memories consciously or unconsciously as they
respond to the movements and turns of the story.[187]

It is to this "deep acting" on the part of the audience that we shall turn now.

Jonas Liliequist writes in the context of early modern Sweden that "[a] good
night at the theatre could be judged by its capacity to bring tears to its audience."[188] In their introduction to *Shakespearean Sensations: Experiencing Literature
in Early Modern England,* Katherine Craik and Tanya Pollard agree: "men and
women respond to plays … not only with their minds and souls but also with
their hearts, hands, viscera, hair, and skin."[189] In an essay for Craik's and Pollard's
fascinating volume, Matthew Steggle analyzes the early modern phenomenon of
audience applause:

> Applause … speaks . . to the uneasy dividing lines between free will and the effects
> of passion, between individual psychology and group dynamics … [S]uch para-
> doxical events as … changing fashions in clapping … and applause coerced from
> an audience by vain Roman emperors … [make it] more and more apparent that
> applause does indeed have a complex cultural history, and provides only an uncer-
> tain access to the state of mind of those who make it. At the same time, by its very
> nature, it remains somehow suspect and undignified, the product of uncontained
> emotion.[190]

Much like the canned laughter heard in the background on today's television sit-
coms, early modern plays included "prompts"[191] for certain emotions as well as an
"explicit modelling of cues to the viewer's ideal response."[192]

These prompts and cues might encourage spectators' emotional identification or disidentification with stage characters' feelings. While unfortunately
there are no surviving actors' manuals from the Golden Age in Spain,[193] we can
extrapolate from such now-obsolete disciplines as quirology (hand language)
to approximate what would have constituted a readable figurative code of
gesture:

> A lo largo de los siglos XVII y XVIII, la quirología sería uno de los códigos estiliza-
> dos de los que se servirían los intérpretes para transmitir determinados afectos a un
> público educado visual y patéticamente en tales convenciones y que, por lo tanto,
> podría descifrarlas sin apenas esfuerzo.[194]

A public educated both visually and emotionally: this was the goal of early modern
playwrights and producers of plays.

According to legal philosopher Martha Nussbaum – who also manifests a serious interest in the arts – a spectator at a theatrical performance feels emotions of the following types:

1. Emotions toward characters: (a) sharing the emotion of a character by identification, (b) reacting to the emotion of a character.
2. Emotions toward the "implied author," the sense of life embodied in the text as a whole: (a) sharing that sense of life and its emotions through empathy, (b) reacting to it, either sympathetically or critically. These emotions operate at multiple levels of specificity and generality.
3. Emotions toward one's own possibilities. These, too, are diverse and operate at multiple levels of specificity and generality.
4. Emotions of exhilaration and delight at coming to understand something about life or about oneself.[195]

Similarly, William Beeman describes a theatrical phenomenon he labels the "phatic" dimension of spectator engagement: "The audience by being an audience undergoes a changed cognitive state. They are engaged in 'framed behaviour' with the performer, in which every communicative element of the event becomes performatively significant."[196] He continues, "performance frames allow members of society the freedom to suspend the normal structures of social life and enter into alternative 'subjunctive' structures."[197]

This notion of frames might make us think of what "frames" are normally used for: namely, to surround or encase a painting – or a mirror. Here we must recall that Lope de Vega calls theatre a "mirror of life" in his *Arte nuevo de escribir comedias en este tiempo* (1609).[198] And what exactly are mirrors used for? Here we might be tempted to jump with Alice in Wonderland into the looking glass, going back even further in time, to remember that "Seneca … changed his judgements in favour of retaliation by looking in a mirror, to see how ugly anger made him."[199] Does the theatre provide this mirror for its audience?

I would argue that it does, but not just as a result of spectators' engagement with the actors. Spectators respond not only to prompts from actors, but also to cues from fellow audience members. In *Communal Justice in Shakespeare's England: Drama, Law, and Emotion*, Penelope Geng posits that "playgoers chiefly patronized the theatres for the pleasure of participating in fiction-making as members of an emotional community."[200] She explains,

Emotional contagion in the theatre ensured that what was felt by an individual was potentially reciprocated and amplified by another. This experience of being connected to others through a shared, theatrical experience fostered intersubjective empathy.[201]

This topic of "intersubjective empathy" is crucial to theatre's role in educating the emotions. Here once again we must return to the pioneering work of Shakespeare scholar Steven Mullaney, who writes of theatre's "affective technologies."[202] Geng describes how this works:

> Audiences are given the chance to calibrate their emotional reactions to the spectating characters ... These opportunities for emotional appraisal, which the form of theatrical performance makes urgently possible, test audiences' capacity for empathy.[203]

Nussbaum makes the perceptive observation that the very physical shape of the classical amphitheatre allowed spectators to see each other's emotions:

> Even the arrangement of the theater contributed to this emphasis: instead of being seated in the dark, in seeming isolation from one another, gazing ahead at an illuminated spectacle – as in many modern performances – spectators, seated in the sunlight, saw across the staged action the faces of their fellow citizens. The performances were occasions for deep emotion; tales abound of intense emotional reactions on the part of the audience, including pregnant women whom the tragic action precipitated into labor.[204]

Theatre serves as a potent form of socialization[205] because "our emotion systems may require something like calibration."[206]

Lest we be tempted to think that these modern-day critics are imposing onto early modern drama the trappings of an anachronistic world view, Katherine Rowe summarizes the position put forth in William Davenant's pro-theatre tract "A Proposition for Advancement of Moralitie by a New Way of Entertainment of the People" (1653):

> The face-to-face arena of the theater ... promotes a stable economy and polity through competitive public scrutiny; playgoing ratifies the standing and virtue of each civil gentleman who puts his capacity to govern his passions on display.[207]

Roughly 100 years later, listen to Jean-François Marmontel describing the experience of going to the theatre in eighteenth-century France:

> Imagine five hundred mirrors sending to one another the light that they reflect, or five hundred echoes of the same sound: this is the image of a public moved by the ridiculous or pathetic. It is there most especially that the example is contagious and powerful. One laughs first at the impression that the risible object makes, one receives in the same way the direct impression that a touching object makes; but what is more, one laughs at laughing, one cries as well at crying; and the effect of these repeated

emotions goes very often to the point of convulsive laughter or to suffocating pain. Now, it is especially among the people, those without seats, that this kind of electricity is sudden, strong, and rapid.[208]

One wonders if these "groundlings" ever fainted suddenly or had to be held up by their companions, since they were not lucky enough to have a seat to sink into! Lest we object that these testimonies apply only to early modern England and Enlightenment France, witness a similar commentary by Juan Luis Vives, describing cases presented in the theatre: "Tenderness of heart makes people merciful and sympathetic to the point of feeling sorry even for those who deserve their calamities, as when children and women feel sorry for thieves and parricides, even if they are only punished with a beating."[209]

This last example raises the issue of incongruity of spectator response, which does not always match the one a performance's creators intended to evoke (this happens in my classroom every time I show clips from silent black and white horror films of the 1920s and '30s with their melodramatic organ music – my students are not the least bit frightened, but instead laugh at these old films as "cheesy"). Here it is important to remember that staged or cinematic portrayals often refract, instead of represent, lived experience.[210] Steven Mullaney describes a "spatial and perspectival irony that alienates members of the audience from their own affective responses, making them occupy multiple and contradictory points of view":[211]

> [T]he affective intelligence of such scenes is lodged in the incongruity that develops from its contradictory internal and external points of view … Perspective by incongruity … is an inherently *dramaturgical* way of glimpsing something that might otherwise be impossible to apprehend.[212]

Let us observe concretely how this works in practice. Because the application of these ideas to Renaissance Spanish drama is a brand-new endeavour – and additionally, because most readers of this book will not have a detailed knowledge of the convoluted plot lines even of the most popular *comedias* – instead we shall illustrate the emotional responses of early modern audiences with reference to two Shakespeare plays that most of us remember from high school: *Hamlet* and *Macbeth*. These two examples will illustrate emotional identification and disidentification on the part of the audience, respectively.

In the second act of *Hamlet*, the prince describes the First Player's performance of mourning:

> […] He would drown the stage with tears
> And cleave the general ear with horrid speech,
> Make mad the guilty and appall the free,

Confound the ignorant, and amaze indeed
The very faculties of eyes and ears.[213]

Maassen writes regarding this speech: "Enacted emotion, such as the First Player's performance of mourning, is highly effective; whether dissembled or not, it works to produce 'real' feeling in the audience, thus defying all possibility to dismiss it as merely hypocritical, delusory, or staged."[214]

We must recall here that the audience for this play-within-a-play were the members of the Danish royal court. The subsequent "Mouse Trap," a minidrama called *The Murder of Gonzago* (an eerily familiar tale of murderous treachery) which Hamlet orders the players to perform so that he can watch his uncle's – that is, his father's presumed murderer's – reactions, has been analyzed by Stephen Laqué:

> The passions can be manipulated and put to use by representation – and theatre is a form of representation which is particularly suited to evoking "things which are usually joined with the passions." By assuming the roles of theatre-manager and stage director Hamlet is thus also becoming something one might call an "experimental philosopher" in a Cartesian vein who investigates the ways in which representation can "excite or displace" the passions.[215]

This, then, is an instance in which Althusserian interpellation[216] of audience members works like it's supposed to: the spectators respond to cues or prompts from the author via the actors, who use words, gestures, and tone of voice to elicit certain feelings from the audience.

In *Macbeth*, though, arguably we see the opposite outcome. For Kathleen Rowe, "*Macbeth* … dramatizes the government of affect in the context of shifting loyalties":[217]

> For the audience … our privileged access to Macbeth's tyrannical passions confirms the honor and good sense of those who flee … [O]ur intimacy with Macbeth's bloody passions has the effect of glossing positively what otherwise looks like disloyalty and inconstancy.[218]

Bruce R. Smith agrees, while simultaneously extending this argument to two of Shakespeare's other plays:

> [T]he ultimate effect of the suffering represented in *[The Rape of] Lucrece* and *King Lear* might have been, not an excitation of pity and fear or terror or despair, but an act of self-control. In keeping with medical regimes of bodily control and the tenets of stoicism, these works … challenged early modern readers and audiences to remain unmoved, even as they also invited sympathy for sufferers in the fictions. Allison P. Hobgood reaches a similar conclusion regarding the

experience of fear in *Macbeth*: she argues for 'a titillating gamble' … that trains the audience in self-control by exciting and exorcising the very passions that threaten to overwhelm.[219]

In other words, audiences could just as easily disidentify emotionally with characters portrayed onstage as identify with them. This is a considerably more sophisticated and complex dynamic than the merely straightforward, simple Aristotelian notion of *mimesis*.

But these are not, of course, entirely new insights. Even though Aristotle and the ancients did not enjoy the advantage of our access to the latest developments in neuroscience, still they intuitively grasped the psychic power of theatre. Since the dawn of Western civilization, theatre's detractors and proponents have both warned against – and extolled the value of – drama's capacity for soul instruction, or *psychagogia*.[220] Witness this speech by Socrates in Plato's *Republic*:

> Even the best of us when we listen to a passage from Homer or from a tragedy in which a grieving hero is represented as dragging out his sorrows in a long speech and people sing and beat their breasts – then, as you know, we delight in surrendering ourselves.[221]

Aristotelian catharsis purges emotions, but it does this by first deliberately arousing them. Richard Sorabji observes: "Aristotle's definitions are carefully designed to bring out the interconnection among … emotional states. In the law courts the orator can stop the judges feeling pity if he can convert pity to fear, indignation, or envy."[222] Could this be the pedagogical function of theatre: to convert or transform less desirable into more desirable emotions? After all, "Aristotle … maintained that teaching people to feel joy and grief at the right things is the crucial function of education."[223] My former teacher Victoria Kahn describes the Renaissance reception of Aristotle's *Poetics*:

> In the early modern period, the pleasures of tragedy were primarily interpreted in ethical terms: tragedy instructed about virtue and vice both in its explicit plot and in its cathartic effect, by which it purged or moderated those passions that hindered ethical action.[224]

In order to understand this mechanism fully, we must attempt to re-enter the Renaissance medical mindset according to which "plays did … alter an audience's humoral balance."[225]

According to Italian poet and literary critic Giambattista Guarini, comedy possessed the ability to purge melancholy.[226] This idea crops up in Shakespeare's *The Taming of the Shrew* (1593–94). A messenger who introduces the play tells a character named Sly to watch a comedy as a remedy for his sadness:

For so your doctors hold it very meet,
Seeing too much sadness hath congealed your blood,
And melancholy is the nurse of frenzy.
Therefore they thought it good you hear a play
And frame your mind to mirth and merriment,
Which bars a thousand harms, and lengthens life.[227]

Similar ideas were anticipated in Stephen Gosson's *Playes Confuted in Five Actions* (1582)[228] and then repeated in the Prologue to Thomas Dekker's *If it be not good, the Diuel is in it* (1612),[229] Thomas May's comedy *The Heire* (1622),[230] and even Thomas Hobbes's *Elements of Law* (1640).[231] Francis Bacon called literature in general "a plectrum to play men's souls with."[232] Particularly relevant in this regard is the case of Sir William Davenant, who in the aforementioned "Proposition for Advancement of Moralitie by a New Way of Entertainment of the People" (1653) requested state support for a public stage, "a theatrical 'Academy' of moral entertainments. His theater would provide an arena for the professional instruction and management of the passions roiling Cromwell's uneasy populace."[233]

In a quirky twist, eighteenth-century French physician Philippe Pinel developed a so-called moral treatment for insanity using theatre:

Moral treatment meant, first of all, gentleness, and, secondly, the use of a "theatrical apparatus" to break down the delusions of the patient. Pinel understood theater in precisely the same terms as Diderot, as a mimetic illusion capable of circumventing reason by working directly on the imagination.[234]

Thus we see that both ancient and early modern defenders of theatre (as well as the occasional keeper of an insane asylum!) glimpsed the dramatic art's potential to foster emotional education.

It has taken centuries and, in some cases, millennia for the fields of neuroscience and psychology to demonstrate *why* it works. By far some of the most productive work in this area has been done in reference to child psychology. Scholars from multiple disciplines have long recognized that "[children's] play centrally involves role playing, and is thus a development of empathy."[235] Patrick Hogan also refers to a child's "play" with a story and posits that his theory of the relationship between emotion and narrative could affect our views of artistic creation, not just aesthetic response:

It seems likely that authors incorporate autobiographical material even in entirely nonautobiographical works (for example, in filling out characters in historical novels) through just such a process. Certainly, biographical criticism has given us many examples of this sort … [A child's] retellings support not only our account of aesthetic response, but a parallel account of artistic creation.[236]

Even before the stage of maturation suitable for role-play,

> [E]ach child increasingly finds and becomes subject to a socially available reper-
> toire of emotion-acts: love, jealousy, anger, fear in all their variety of forms and
> degrees of expression. Sarbin (1986) calls this socially acknowledged way of doing
> an emotion the "dramatistic," in contrast to the "dramaturgical" where an indi-
> vidual might also adopt and set aside emotion-acts called for in more routine or
> ritualistic fashion, expressing caring emotions appropriate to a nurse or sad ones
> as a mourner.[237]

With this researcher's use of explicitly theatrical terminology, it becomes apparent that theatre replicates an interaction so primal as a mother's affective attunement to her newborn infant. Nussbaum gravitates toward this analogy:

> The "subtle interplay" between baby and parent is crucially mediated by play with
> narratives and images, as the child too becomes able to imagine another person's
> experience. During the ambivalence crisis, narrative play provides the child with sev-
> eral distinct benefits. First of all, spending time in narrative play has already given her
> ways of understanding the pain that her destructive wishes would inflict on others,
> and therefore of taking their full measure. At the same time, narratives have given
> nourishment to curiosity, wonder, and perceptual delight, strengthening her ability to
> see other people in noninstrumental and even non-eudaimonistic ways, as objects of
> wonder in their own right. This assists her in her own reparative efforts. Furthermore,
> this same wonder and delight give her ways of relating to her own sometimes fright-
> ening and ambivalent psychology: she becomes interested in understanding it, rather
> than fleeing from it and pushing it underground … This project of understanding, in
> turn, militates against depression and helplessness, feeding her interest in living in a
> world in which she is not perfect or omnipotent. Finally … by dressing imperfection
> in a pleasing and playful shape, narrative play can undercut primitive shame at all
> that is human, helping a child to attain a certain forbearance and even joy about the
> lives of imperfect beings.[238]

We must mention here Jerrold Levinson's theory of "shadow object proposal":
"that 'objects of response' in fiction are not characters, but 'real' individuals or phenomena from the subject's life experience, ones resembling the persons or events
of the fiction, and of which the fiction puts the subject covertly or indirectly in
mind."[239] There is an obvious link here to the reader-response theory of Hans Robert Jauss and Wolfgang Iser which became so popular in the 1980s:[240] "the 'realization' (or concretization) of the literary work is entirely personal to the reader and it
is to a great extent the result of recruiting personal memories."[241] Hogan clarifies:
"the priming of … episodic memories is not the most important source of literary
emotion. Rather, it is the activation of emotional memories."[242]

It is now clear from cutting-edge research in the field of neuroscience that this activation of emotional memories happens through the mediation of something in our bodies called mirror neurons. Mirror neurons were discovered in 1996 by Giacomo Rizzolati, Leonardo Fogassi, Vittorio Gallese and their collaborators at the Institute of Neurosciences at the University of Parma. Jean-Michel Oughourlian explains what they are:

> [T]here exist, in the frontal motor areas of the brain, mirror neurons that become activated by the sight of an action performed by another human being and that light up, as seen with a PET-scan (positron emission topography), in the person who witnesses an action in exactly the same manner as they do in the person who performs it. These neurons in the motor and premotor areas remain silent in the presence of a movement done by a nonhuman or nonanimal.[243]

Two of these same scientists, Rizzolatti and Sinigaglia, in their explanation of this concept, elaborate on Antonio Damasio's concept of the "as-if-body-loop":

> [O]bservation of the faces of others expressing an emotion would activate the mirror neurons of the premotor cortex. These neurons would then send a copy of their activation pattern ... to the somatosensory areas and the insula. The activation of these areas, analogous to what occurs when the observer spontaneously expresses that emotion ("as if"), would be at the root of our understanding of the emotive reactions of others.[244]

The consequences of these new developments in brain science are only just beginning to be spun out for theatre. As Rizzolatti and Sinigaglia recount,

> In an interview some time ago, the great theatrical director ... Peter Brook commented that with the discovery of mirror neurons, neuroscience had finally started to understand what has long been common knowledge in the theatre: the actor's efforts would be in vain if he were not able to surmount all cultural and linguistic barriers and share his bodily sounds and movements with the spectators, who thus actively contribute to the event and become one with the players on the stage. This sharing is the basis on which the theatre evolves and revolves, and mirror neurons, which become active both when an individual executes an act and when he observes it being executed by others, now provide this sharing with a biological explanation.[245]

This potential activation of emotional memories has important ramifications for democracy, due to what Tylus calls "theater's ability to socialize citizens"[246] and what Rowe refers to as the "role of the theater in disseminating knowledge of the passions ... [t]eaching civic virtue to a wide audience."[247]

In *The Secret History of Emotion: From Aristotle's "Rhetoric" to Modern Brain Science*, Daniel Gross predicts: "a moral society where sympathy predominates will also be a literate society where the dramatist and the rhetorician play an important role."[248] Legal philosopher Martha Nussbaum likewise postulates,

> All societies, then, need something like the spirit of tragedy and the spirit of comedy – the former shaping compassion and the sense of loss, the latter indicating ways to rise above bodily disgust in a spirit of delighted reciprocity … Tragic spectatorship cultivates emotional awareness of shared human possibilities, rooted in bodily vulnerability.[249]

As my readers will no doubt already have intuited, the placement of such high stakes on the theatrical wager amounts to nothing less than a defence of the arts.

Notes

1. Introduction: Can Feelings Be Wrong?

1 Robert Hemfelt et al., *Love Is a Choice: The Groundbreaking Book on Recovery for Codependent Relationships* (Nashville: Thomas Nelson, 1991).

2 See Hélène Cixous, "The Laugh of the Medusa," trans. Keith Cohen and Paula Cohen, *Signs* 1.4 (1976): 875–93; and Georges Bataille, *L'erotisme* (Paris: Minuit, 2011).

3 Julia Kristeva, *Powers of Horror: An Essay on Abjection*, trans. Leon Samuel Roudiez (New York: Columbia University Press, 1982).

4 While this book purports to study only early modern Spain, points of contact with other geographical areas, historical periods, and cultures have been noted where relevant.

5 Paul Johnson, *Affective Geographies: Cervantes, Emotion, and the Literary Mediterranean* (Toronto: University of Toronto Press, 2021).

6 Richard Meek and Erin Sullivan, "Introduction," in *The Renaissance of Emotion: Understanding Affect in Shakespeare and His Contemporaries*, ed. Richard Meek and Erin Sullivan (Manchester: Manchester University Press, 2015), 1–22, at 3.

7 Brian Cummings and Freya Sierhuis, "Introduction," *in Passions and Subjectivity in Early Modern Culture*, ed. Brian Cummings and Freya Sierhuis (Farnham: Ashgate, 2013), 3.

8 Cummings and Sierhuis, "Introduction," 3.

9 Jon Elster, *Alchemies of the Mind: Rationality and the Emotions* (Cambridge: Cambridge University Press, 1999), 48.

10 Jan Plamper, *The History of Emotions: An Introduction*, trans. Keith Tribe (Oxford: Oxford University Press, 2015), vii.

11 Plamper, *The History of Emotions*, 281. See "Feeltank Chicago," http://feeltankchicago .net/01.html.

12 Peter N. Stearns and Carol Z. Stearns, "Emotionology: Clarifying the History of Emotions and Emotional Standards," *American Historical Review* 90.4 (1985): 813–36.

13 Barbara H. Rosenwein, *Emotional Communities in the Early Middle Ages* (Ithaca: Cornell University Press, 2006).

14 William M. Reddy, *The Navigation of Feeling: A Framework for the History of Emotions* (Cambridge: Cambridge University Press, 2001).

15 Christian Ankowitsch, *Generation Emotion* (Berlin: BTV, 2002).

16 Marion Muller, *"These Savage Beasts Become Domestick": The Discourse on the Passions in Early Modern Europe* (Trier: Wissenschaftlicher Verlag, 2004), 10.

17 "[N]euroscientist Antonio Damasio recently proposed a distinction between emotions and feelings … For Damasio, when an organism encounters a stimulus capable of triggering an emotion, the emotion consists of the actual physical response of the organism as it is mapped and modified by the brain. This is a process that can become, but does not necessarily become, conscious. Emotionally competent stimuli in fact can be detected while bypassing attention and thought. Often – but again, not always – attention and thought are subsequently turned on these stimuli, but emotions are modifications of the body that are autonomous from conscious thought and attention. Feelings, on the other hand, are 'largely constituted by the perception of a certain body state' or 'the perception of the body state forms the essence of a feeling.' Feelings require a level of awareness and attention, awareness that is based on mental maps of the body's physical state. Emotions are changes in the state of the body, which the brain maps and which can then become the basis for feelings" (Ariel Ducey, "More Than a Job: Meaning, Affect, and Training Health Care Workers," in *The Affective Turn: Theorizing the Social*, ed. Patricia Ticineto Clough and Jean O'Malley Halley [Durham: Duke University Press, 2007], 187–208, at 191, quoting Antonio Damasio, *Looking for Spinoza: Joy, Sorrow, and the Feeling Brain* [New York: Harcourt, 2003], 55, 89).

18 Lone Bertelsen and Andrew Murphie, "An Ethics of Everyday Infinities and Powers: Félix Guattari on Affect and the Refrain," in *The Affect Theory Reader*, ed. Melissa Gregg and Gregory J. Seigworth (Durham: Duke University Press, 2010), 138–57, at 140, citing Antonio Damasio, *Looking for Spinoza* (New York: Vintage, 2004), 28.

19 Plamper, *The History of Emotions*, 11.

20 Brian Massumi, *Parables for the Virtual: Movement, Affect, Sensation* (Durham: Duke University Press, 2002), 61.

21 Lawrence Grossberg et al., *Affect's Future: Rediscovering the Virtual in the Actual* (Durham: Duke University Press, 2010), 316.

22 Louise d'Arcens, "Affective Memory across Time: The Emotive City of Christine de Pizan," in *Ordering Emotions in Europe, 1100–1800*, ed. Susan Broomhall (Leiden: Brill, 2015), 85–104, at 86.

23 Reddy, *The Navigation of Feeling*, 94.

24 Daniel Goleman, *Emotional Intelligence: Why It Can Matter More than IQ* (London: Bloomsbury, 1996), 6.

25 Meek and Sullivan, "Introduction," 11.

26 Penelope Gouk and Helen Hills, "Toward Histories of Emotions," in *Representing Emotions: New Connections in the Histories of Art, Music and Medicine*, ed. Penelope Gouk and Helen Hills (London: Ashgate, 2005), 15–34, at 16–17, quoting the *OED*.

27 Jonathan Ree, "Mixed Emotions: Keeping Them In and Getting Them Out," *Los Angeles Times* (Book Review Section), 2 May 2000, 1ff., at 1.

28 Thomas Dixon, *From Passions to Emotions: The Creation of a Secular Psychological Category* (Cambridge: Cambridge University Press, 2003), 13.

29 Louis C. Charland and R.S. White, "Anatomy of a Passion: Shakespeare's *The Winter's Tale* as Case Study," in *Ordering Emotions*, ed. Broomhall, 197–224, at 198, citing Thomas Dixon, "'Emotion': The History of a Keyword in Crisis," *Emotion Review* 4 (2012): 338–44.

30 Dixon, *From Passions to Emotions*, 109.

31 Dixon, *From Passions to Emotions*, 112.

32 Dixon, *From Passions to Emotions*, 233.

33 "Generally speaking, 'passion' was the common word used to denote what is nowadays classified as 'emotion'" (Muller, *"These Savage Beasts,"* 10).

34 Gail Kern Paster, *Humoring the Body: Emotions and the Shakespearean Stage* (Chicago: University of Chicago Press, 2014), 10.

35 *Webster's New Collegiate Dictionary* (Springfield, MA: G. & C. Merriam, 1976).

36 Timothy Mitchell, *Passional Culture: Emotion, Religion, and Society in Southern Spain* (Philadelphia: University of Pennsylvania Press, 1984), 2.

37 Elena Carrera, "Anger and the Mind–Body Connection in Medieval and Early Modern Medicine," in *Emotions and Health, 1200–1700*, ed. Elena Carrera (Leiden: Brill, 2012), 95–146, at 96.

38 Dixon, *From Passions to Emotions*, 41, 46.

39 Javier Villa-Flores and Sonya Lipsett-Rivera, "Introduction," in *Emotions and Daily Life in Colonial Mexico* (Albuquerque: University of New Mexico Press, 2014), 1–14, at 2.

40 See Hilaire Kallendorf, "The Demon as Scapegoat" in *Exorcism and Its Texts: Subjectivity in Early Modern Literature of England and Spain* (Toronto: University of Toronto Press, 2003), 140–8.

41 Agneta H. Fischer, *Emotion Scripts: A Study of the Social and Cognitive Aspects of Emotion* (Leiden: DSWO Press, 1991), 86.

42 Plamper, *The History of Emotions: An Introduction*, 14.

43 Charles Michel, "Les bons et les mauvais esprits dans les croyances populaires de l'ancienne Grèce," *Revue d'Histoires e Litteratures Religeuses* new series 1 (1910): 193–215, 202–3.

44 Hilaire Kallendorf and Craig Kallendorf, "Catharsis as Exorcism: Aristotle, Tragedy, and Religio-Poetic Liminality," *Literary Imagination* 14.3 (2012): 296–311.

45 "[T]he Stoic notion of *apatheia* called for the sage's freedom from all *pathe*, the four perturbations of delight, lust, distress, and fear" (George W. McClure, *Sorrow and Consolation in Italian Humanism* [Princeton: Princeton University Press, 1990], 5).

46 Muller, *"These Savage Beasts,"* 117. She cites John M. Rist, *Stoic Philosophy* (Cambridge: Cambridge University Press, 1969), 25–6.

47 Muller, *"These Savage Beasts,"* 117.

48 Sebastián de Covarrubias Orozco, *Tesoro de la lengua castellana* (Madrid: Luis Sánchez, 1611), 46.

49 Paster, *Humoring the Body*, 10.

50 Dixon, *From Passions to Emotions*, 41, 46.

51 Erin Sullivan, "The Passions of Thomas Wright: Renaissance Emotion across Body and Soul," in *The Renaissance of Emotion*, ed. Meek and Sullivan, 25–44, at 37.

52 Juan Luis Vives, *The Passions of the Soul: The Third Book of* De Anima et Vita, trans. Carlos G. Noreña (Lewiston: Mellen, 1990), 2.

53 Dixon, *From Passions to Emotions*, 40.

54 Ben Anderson, "Modulating the Excess of Affect: Morale in a State of 'Total War,'" in *The Affect Theory Reader*, ed. Gregg, and Seigworth, 161–85, at 163.

55 Lucía Díaz Marroquín, *La retórica de los afectos* (Kassel: Reichenberger, 2008), 160–1, quoting Ignacio de Loyola, *Ejercicios espirituales*, in *Obras completas de San Ignacio de Loyola*, ed. Ignacio Iparraguirre (Madrid: Biblioteca de Autores Cristianos, 1963), 1.

56 Díaz Marroquín, *La retórica de los afectos*, 189.

57 I am paraphrasing him a bit here – his actual comment was, "El lenguaje nunca es inocente." See "'El lenguaje nunca es inocente,' según Juan Goytisolo, *El País* (1 December 1984), https://elpais.com/diario/1984/12/02/cultura/470790008 _850215.html.

58 Lope de Vega, *Rimas sacras*, in *Obras poéticas*, ed. José Manuel Blecua (Barcelona: Planeta, 1989), 297.

59 Dixon, *From Passions to Emotions*, 21–2, 29.

60 Paster, *Humoring the Body*, 10.

61 Saint Teresa's poem reads: "Nada te turbe, / nada te espante / todo se pasa; / Dios no se muda, / la paciencia / todo lo alcanza. / Quien a Dios tiene / nada le falta / solo Dios basta." This poem was resurrected recently for English-speaking readers in Teresa of Avila, *Let Nothing Disturb You* (Notre Dame, IN: Ave Maria Press, 2008).

62 On *ataraxia* see Elena del Río Parra, "La suspensión como acto estético en las letras áureas," *RILCE* 26.1 (2010): 157–67, at 157. On Neostoicism in the

Renaissance see Mark Morford, *Stoics and Neostoics: Rubens and the Circle of Lipsius* (Princeton: Princeton University Press, 1991). On Neostoicism in Spain see Henry Ettinghausen, *Francisco de Quevedo and the Neostoic Movement* (Oxford: Oxford University Press, 1972).

63 Dixon, *From Passions to Emotions*, 65, citing Albert Hirschman, *The Passions and Interests: Political Arguments for Capitalism before its Triumph* (Princeton: Princeton University Press, 1997).

64 See *Politics and the Passions, 1500–1850*, ed. Victoria Kahn et al. (Princeton: Princeton University Press, 2006).

65 Jan Plamper, *The History of Emotions*, 246.

66 Grossberg et al., "Affect's Future," 311.

67 Alan Eppel, *Sweet Sorrow: Love, Loss and Attachment in Human Life* (London: Karnac, 2009), 43.

68 Simo Knuuttila, "Medieval Theories of the Passions of the Soul," in *Emotions and Choice from Boethius to Descartes*, ed. Henrik Lagerlund and Mikko Yrjönsuuri (Dordrecht: Kluwer, 2002), 49–83, at 51.

69 Raphaële Garrod, "Conceptual Eclecticism and Ethical Prescription in Early Modern Jesuit Discourses about Affects: Suárez and Caussin on Maternal Love," in *Ordering Emotions*, ed. Broomhall, 180–96, at 192.

70 Philippa Maddern et al., "Introduction: Performing Emotions in Medieval and Early Modern Worlds," in *Performing Emotions in Early Europe*, ed. Philippa Maddern et al. (Turnhout: Brepols, 2018), xiii–xxx, at xvii.

71 Pierre Payer, *The Bridling of Desire: Views of Sex in the Later Middle Ages* (Toronto: University of Toronto Press, 2016), 52–3.

72 C.C.W. Taylor, "Emotions and Wants," in *The Ways of Desire*, ed. Joel Marks (Chicago: Precedent, 1986), 217–31, at 217.

73 Simo Knuuttila, "Medieval Theories," 51.

74 Pierre Payer alerts us to a potential pitfall here: "The concupiscence that is the material component of original sin must not be confused with the natural concupiscence that is simply the desiring, appetitive aspect of the lower sense part of the soul" (Payer, *The Bridling of Desire*, 48).

75 Henrik Lagerlund and Mikko Yrjönsuuri, "Introduction," in *Emotions and Choice*, ed. Lagerlund and Yrjönsuuri (Dordrecht: Kluwer, 2002), 1–28, at 15, in reference to the Franciscan John of La Rochelle (1200–1245).

76 Knuuttila, "Medieval Theories," 61.

77 Knuuttila, "Medieval Theories," 58.

78 Thomas Aquinas, *Summa theologiae*, online edition, Corpus Thomisticum (Fundación Tomás de Aquino, 2013), "Prima secundae," quaestiones 22–48. http://www.corpusthomisticum.org/sth2022.html. Nicholas Lombardo estimates that "[w]hen Aquinas finished the *Prima secundae* of the *Summa theologiae* in 1271, questions 22–48 probably constituted the longest sustained discussion of the passions ever written" (Nicholas E. Lombardo, "Emotions and Psychological

Health in Aquinas," in *Emotions and Health, 1200–1700*, ed. Elena Carrera [Leiden: Brill, 2012], 19–46, at 19).

79 Elena Carrera, "Introduction," in *Emotions and Health*, ed. Carrera, 1–17, at 15.

80 Lombardo, "Emotions and Psychological Health," 21.

81 For my treatment of courage see Hilaire Kallendorf, "Fleeting Fortitude," in *Ambiguous Antidotes: Virtue as Vaccine for Vice in Early Modern Spain* (Toronto: University of Toronto Press, 2017), 69–83. For my treatment of anger see Hilaire Kallendorf, "Angry Young Murderers," in *Sins of the Fathers: Moral Economies in Early Modern Spain* (Toronto: University of Toronto Press, 2013), 133–51.

82 Christopher Allen, "Painting the Passions: The *Passions de l'Âme* as a Basis for Pictorial Expression," in *The Soft Underbelly of Reason: The Passions in the Seventeenth Century*, ed. Stephen Gaukroger (London: Routledge, 1998), 79–111, at 90.

83 Alejandro Cañeque, "The Emotions of Power," 101.

84 Alonso López Pinciano, *Philosophia antigua poética*, ed. José Rico Verdú (Madrid: Fundación José Antonio de Castro, 1998), 54–6.

85 Eduardo Ruiz Jaren, *Oliva Sabuco: filosofía y salud* (Madrid: Manuscritos, 2009), 13.

86 Carlos G. Noreña, *Juan Luis Vives and the Emotions* (Carbondale: Southern Illinois University Press, 1989), 173.

87 Thomas Wright, *The Passions of the Minde in Generall* (London: Valentine Simmes, 1604), 4.

88 Muller, *"These Savage Beasts,"* 187–8; she quotes Roger Smith, "Self-Reflection and the Self," in *Rewriting the Self: Histories from the Renaissance to the Present*, ed. Roy Porter (London: Routledge, 1997), 52. She further cites Peter Harrison: "Indeed, the seventeenth century generally finds it difficult to articulate an epistemology in which God does not play some indispensable role" (Peter Harrison, "Reading the Passions: The Fall, the Passions, and Dominion over Nature," in *The Soft Underbelly of Reason*, ed. Gaukroger, 49–78, at 68).

89 William Childers, "Hispanic Casuistry Studies: Room to Grow," *Hispanic Review* 79.2 (2011): 317–26.

90 Franco Moretti, *Distant Reading* (London: Verso, 2013), 48–9.

91 Moretti, *Distant Reading*, 48.

2. The Impure: Disgust

1 Mette Hjort and Sue Laver, "Introduction," in *Emotion and the Arts*, ed. Mette Hjort and Sue Laver (New York: Oxford University Press, 1997), 3–19, at 17.

2 P. Devlin, "Morals and the Criminal Law," in *Morality and the Law*, ed. R. Wasserstrom (Belmont, CA: Wadsworth, 1971), 24–48, at 40.

3 Colin McGinn, *The Meaning of Disgust* (Oxford: Oxford University Press, 2011), 6–7.

4 Calderón, *El pastor fido*, auto sacramental. All quotations from early modern Spanish plays are taken from the database Teatro Español del Siglo de Oro (TESO), distributed by ProQuest, unless otherwise noted. Spelling has been modernized.

5 As one *bella mal maridada* (beautiful young woman married to an older man) laments:

> Condenada a eterno llanto
> con un viejo he de vivir,
> con sangre quiero teñir
> canas que me ofenden tanto.
> ¿Yo he de tener cada punto
> en su nieve sepultado
> un deseo mal logrado
> de un gusto casi difunto?
> Yo triste que ayer nací,
> ¿he de peinar mis cabellos
> para quien, asida de ellos,
> me tiene junto de sí?
> ¿Yo he de tener por mi dueño,
> y dar el alma, y la mano
> a un Rey, que como tirano
> goza este mundo pequeño?
> Yo, ¿será justo que alabe
> lo que me cause disgusto?
> ¿Y que bese scrá justo
> boca que a tierra me sabe?   (Guillén de Castro, *El desengaño dichoso*, Acto 3)

6 TELLO: Eso si tened
> disgusto en amor tan llano,
> placeres de amor fingidos
> que siempre sois, advertid,
> como vinos de Madrid:
> aguados, y mal medidos.   (Lope de Vega, *Querer la propia desdicha*, Acto 2)

7 Lope de Vega, *El rey sin reino*, Acto 2. Carolyn Korsmeyer writes regarding this "surfeit" disgust: "Some foods disgust with their immediate taste or smell, and others disgust when they are presented in excess or surfeit. Too much rich, sweet cheesecake, for example, begins to cloy and then to revolt" (Carolyn Korsmeyer, *Savoring Disgust: The Foul and the Fair in Aesthetics* [Oxford: Oxford University Press, 2011], 64).

8 Sally Planalp, *Communicating Emotion: Social, Moral and Cultural Processes* (Cambridge: Cambridge University Press, 1999), 91.

9 Patrick Colm Hogan, *Affective Narratology: The Emotional Structure of Stories* (Lincoln: University of Nebraska Press, 2011), 148.

10 De la propia manera
que un gusto quita la vida,
un disgusto la alimenta,
que hay venenos tan crueles,
que por no perder la esencia
de su efecto, en no matar
logran su naturaleza.　　　　　(Juan Bautista Diamante, *El defensor del Peñón*, Jornada 1)

Colin McGinn confirms, "A poisonous substance will … be the most disgusting of all" (McGinn, *The Meaning of Disgust*, 67).

11 Daniel Goleman, *Emotional Intelligence: Why It Can Matter More than IQ* (London: Bloomsbury, 1996), 7. The part of the brain controlling this "primordial attempt" is called the insula. Carolyn Korsmeyer describes its function: "The insula is … implicated in the control of taste aversion and the perception of nauseating tastes, supporting the speculation that the emotion of disgust evolved from protective taste responses" (Korsmeyer, *Savoring Disgust*, 19).

12 Calderón, *La señora y la criada*, Jornada 2. Carolyn Korsmeyer reiterates in the context of aesthetics, "Disgust … has a striking corporeal character; its signature marker is nausea" (Korsmeyer, *Savoring Disgust*, 3).

13 The "natural" antipathy of the four elements is described in Calderón's one-act auto sacramental *La vida es sueño*.

14 Lope de Vega, *La Filisarda*, preliminares (dedication by Lope to Don Juan Antonio de Vera y Zúñiga). I discussed this phenomenon in a previous book: "Supposedly a branch of rosemary placed above a door's lintel could prevent snakes and scorpions from entering one's house" (Hilaire Kallendorf, *Ambiguous Antidotes: Virtue as Vaccine for Vice in Early Modern Spain* [Toronto: University of Toronto Press, 2017], 23).

15 Calderón, *Primero soy yo*, Jornada 2.

16 Matilde says to the queen:

¿Qué mandáis, señora?
Perdido traes el color;
¿qué disgusto puede haber,
que se atreva a tu hermosura?　　　　　(Agustín Moreto, *La fortuna merecida*, Jornada 1)

17 Las colores de mi gusto
(no pienso que las querréis)
las de mi rostro podréis
trasladar, de mi disgusto,
que la vergüenza, y el susto
ya de colores se esmalta.　　　　　(Lope de Vega, *La mayor virtud de un rey*, Jornada 2)

18 Charles Darwin, *The Expression of the Emotions in Man and Animals* (London: John
    Murray, 1872), 257.
19 CONSTANZA: Templemos las congojas
        de algún disgusto importunas.   (Lope de Vega, *El villano en su rincón*, Acto 3)

20 FLAMINIA: Yo no hablaba con el gusto
        que solía, y si me hablaban,
        en mi suspensión notaban
        la razón de mi disgusto. (Lope de Vega, *Muertos vivos*, Acto 1)

21 Thomas Dixon, *From Passions to Emotions: The Creation of a Secular Psychological
    Category* (Cambridge: Cambridge University Press, 2003), 167.
22 Juan Bautista Diamante, *Santa Teresa de Jesús*, Jornada 2.
23 Calderón, *Los cabellos de Absalón*, Jornada 1.
24   Negro, y blanco son
        colores de mi disgusto,
        lo negro muestra tristeza,
        lo blanco, mi suerte en él.   (Lope de Vega, *Los porceles de Murcia*, Acto 1)

25 TELLO: Volverse a Alcalá imagina
        sin hablarle mi despecho.
    PEREJIL: Déjalo para otro día,
        que ahora no querrá la Guarda.
    TELLO: ¿Qué Guarda?
    PEREJIL: ¿Qué? La Amarilla,
        que tiemblo de ella.
    TELLO: ¿Por qué?
    PEREJIL: Yo la tengo antipatía,
        porque es del color del miedo.
                                (Agustín Moreto, *El valiente justiciero*, Jornada 2)

    This resonance for the colour yellow persists to this day in phrases such as "lily-
    livered coward," where the liver is associated with the condition of jaundice, which
    causes the skin to turn yellow.
26 SARAY: Cantar una a disgusto,
        es rabiar en armonía.   (Antonio Zamora, *Judas Iscariote*, Jornada 2)

27 RODRIGO: Mi aliento
        le destempló el instrumento.
    FARFÁN: En eso verás cuál es,
        pues los como tú animales

tienen cierta antipatía
con la música, y poesía.   (Guillén de Castro, *La justicia en la piedad*, Jornada 1)

28 ALEJANDRO TO LÁZARO: Pretendo,
     que cierto disgusto sepas;
     todas las noches que salgo,
     canta este hombre, y me pesa
     de que en esta calle cante.   (Calderón, *Nadie fíe su secreto*, Jornada 2)

29 MISENO: Es poeta Caballero;
     no temáis; hará por gusto
     versos.
        OCTAVIO: Con mucho disgusto
     los de Nise considero.
     Temo, y en razón lo fundo,
     si enhiesto da, que ha de haber
     un Don Quijote mujer
     que dé qué reír al mundo.   (Lope de Vega, *La dama boba*, Acto 3)

30 Lope de Vega, *La resistencia honrada, y Condesa Matilde*, Jornada 1.

31 PEDRO DE URDEMALAS: Dicen que la variación
     hace a la naturaleza,
     colma de gusto y belleza
     y está muy puesto en razón.
     Un manjar a la contin[u]a
     enfada, y un solo objeto
     a los ojos del discreto
     da disgusto, y amohina.
     Un solo vestido cansa,
     en fin con la variedad
     se muda la voluntad,
     y el espíritu descansa.   (Cervantes, *Pedro de Urdemalas*, Jornada 3)

32 Calderón, *Mujer, llora, y vencerás*, Jornada 1.
33 Lope de Vega, *Los comendadores de Córdoba*, Jornada 1.
34 Lope de Vega, *La inocente Laura*, Acto 1.
35 Tirso de Molina, *El melancólico*, Acto 2.
36 Calderón, *La siembra del Señor*, auto sacramental.
37 DON FREY DIEGO DE TOLEDO: Y pues con vos, que es, parece,
       este disgusto, sepamos,
         ¿qué causa ha habido para él?
     GOBERNADOR DE ZAMORA: Mucha …

Ya os acordaréis, señor,
de aquel infeliz caso
de Monsalve.
Don Frey Diego de Toledo:
Sí me acuerdo,
que no es muy para olvidado.
GOBERNADOR DE ZAMORA: Pues habiendo él muerto, y yo,
puesto preso a su contrario
en casa de Don Luis, su primo,
por querer así, evitando
más disensiones, obviar,
que llegasen a las manos
Diego Mazariegos, y un
hijo del difunto anciano,
que a vengar dicen, que vino
su afrenta, un día, de tantos
como hubo en el intermedio,
nos amaneció fijado
un cartel, en que, valido
de los Fueros Castellanos,
que del honor en demanda
quieren no se niegue campo
a cuantos le pidan, siendo
Caballeros Hijos de algo:
A público desafío
le llamaba; con que usando
de la templanza, con que debe en semejantes casos
mediar la Justicia, quise
componerlos, y ajustarlos,
sin sangre.   (Antonio Zamora, *Mazariegos y Monsalves*, Jornada 2)

38 CLARA: Yo voy vestida a mi gusto;
este ornato es más hermoso
para el gusto de mi Esposo,
que el otro le dio disgusto …
No ha de quedar cosa en mí,
que huela a ser vanidad;
cabellos a Dios atad,
ya que os desatáis de mí.
Id en buena hora, cabellos,
a ser prisiones de Cristo.   (Lope de Vega, *El serafín humano*, Acto 2)

39 FABRICIO: Eso excede
        de lo que entonces fue común disgusto,
        yo hablo de las galas, y el lacayo.
     OCTAVIO: De pensar en las calzas me desmayo.
        Muero de risa en ver con el toldillo
        que se quitaba muy a lo discreto,
        después de entrado el Rey, el sombrerillo,
        para engendrar de sí mayor concepto.
     FABRICIO: Costoso era, por Dios, el vestidillo.
     OCTAVIO: La maleta, y las postas en efecto
        le deslucieron, llegaron baúles,
        con galas blancas, nácares y azules.   (Lope de Vega, *Del mal lo menos*, Acto 1)

40 RICARDO: Yo llegué, Casandra mía,
        a cierta casa de juego,
        donde hallé en conversación,
        seis o siete Caballeros.
        Rogáronme que jugase;
        jugué por entretenerlos,
        que por no darte disgusto,
        ha días que ya no juego.
        Gané quinientos escudos,
        enviaron por dineros,
        dije que yo volvería,
        mas fue por librarme de ellos.
        Con el gusto del ganar,
        que es dulce cosa, en efecto,
        bajé la calle del Prado,
        libre de tal pensamiento.
        Vuelvo el rostro, y veo tras mí
        venir tres hombres de aquellos,
        que miran, juzgan, y asisten
        en semejantes sucesos.
        Todos tres con falsa risa,
        quitándose los sombreros,
        me dan del haber ganado
        mil parabienes diversos.
        Yo con igual cortesía,
        sin cubrirme, lo agradezco,
        mas ellos me hacen cubrir,

> y así me dice el más necio:
> Vuestra merced nos dejó
> de su valor satisfechos,
> y así a servirle venimos,
> y en toda ocasión lo haremos.
> Ahora vamos a ver
> ciertas damas sin dineros,
> vuestra merced nos los preste,
> que a la noche nos veremos.
> Nunca doy de lo que gano,
> respondí a los tres riendo:
> fuera de la mesa, o casa,
> donde otras veces pierdo.
> Allá nos podremos ver,
> mas ¿por qué te canso en esto?
> Pues se resuelve en que juntos
> mano a la espada pusieron.   (Lope de Vega, *El castigo del discreto*, Acto 1)

41 Lope de Vega, *La mal casada*, Acto 1.

42 Peter N. Stearns and Deborah C. Stearns, "Historical Issues in Emotions Research: Causation and Timing," in *Social Perspectives on Emotion*, ed. William M. Wentworth and John Ryan, vol. 2 (Greenwich, CT: JAI, 1994), 239–66, at 243–4.

43 Peter Stallybrass and Allon White, *The Politics and Poetics of Transgression* (Ithaca: Cornell University Press, 1986), 191.

44 Tirso de Molina, *El condenado por desconfiado*, Jornada 1.

45 Martha Nussbaum, *Upheavals of Thought: The Intelligence of Emotions* (Cambridge: Cambridge University Press, 2001), 347.

46   De tu disgusto, mi Lisardo, tengo
> el que es razón, en lo demás que toca
> a vender a tu padre aquella hacienda,
> respondo, que aunque soy pobre, y tan pobre
> que no tengo más renta, era bajeza;
> siendo reliquias de tan noble padre,
> y ya como solar de su hidalguía,
> borrar con ella el nombre de Montanos;
> y así por ningún precio puedo ahora
> servir al Senador.   (Lope de Vega, *Los bandos de Sena*, Acto 1)

47 Lope de Vega, *Los peligros de la ausencia*, Acto 2.

48 Lope de Vega, *El perro del hortelano*, Acto 1.
49 Lope de Vega, *El testigo contra sí*, Acto 2.
50 Lope de Vega, *El hombre de bien*, Acto 1.
51 Nussbaum, *Upheavals of Thought*, 629.
52 See A. Robert Lauer, "Honor / Honra Revisited," in *A Companion to Early Modern Hispanic Theater*, ed. Hilaire Kallendorf (Leiden: Brill, 2014), 77–90.
53 Calderón, *Bien vengas mal*, Jornada 3.
54 Juan de Matos Fragoso, *El yerro del entendido*, Jornada 2.
55 Tirso de Molina, *Del enemigo el primer consejo*, Jornada 1.
56 Tirso de Molina, *Amor, privanza y castigo*, Acto 1.
57 REY: Don Álvaro, vuelve en ti;
      advierte que esa caída
      si da peligro a tu vida
      me ha de dar la muerte a mí.
      Nunca yo me coronara,
      si me había de costar tal disgusto, tal pesar,
      nunca yo a ser Rey llegara;
      pues no hay Reino, no hay blasón
      mayor al que quiere bien
      que estar gozando de quien
      es dueño de su afición.
      Si con mi pena te obligo
      esta afición galardona,
      que no quiero la corona
      si he de perder tal amigo.

      (Tirso de Molina, *Próspera Fortuna de Don Álvaro de Luna, y adversa de Ruy López de Avalos, primera parte*, Jornada 3)

58 Lope de Vega, *El ejemplo de casadas y prueba de la paciencia*, Acto 3.
59 Lope de Vega, *Los pleitos de Inglaterra*, Acto 1.
60 Lope de Vega, *El amante agradecido*, Acto 2.
61 Lope de Vega, *El príncipe despeñado*, Acto 1.
62 Lope de Vega, *El castigo sin venganza*, Acto 1.
63 Lope de Vega, *Hay verdades que en amor*, Acto 1.
64 Lope de Vega, *El cuerdo en su casa*, Acto 2.
65 Patrick Colm Hogan, *What Literature Teaches Us about Emotion* (Cambridge: Cambridge University Press, 2011), 242.
66 Juan de Matos Fragoso, *Con amor no hay amistad*, Jornada 3.
67 Martha Nussbaum, *Hiding from Humanity: Disgust, Shame, and the Law* (Princeton: Princeton University Press, 2004), 111.
68 Juan de Matos Fragoso, *Con amor no hay amistad*, Jornada 3.

69 For a recent study of comic interludes or *entremeses* that do subversively present divorce as an acceptable or even desirable option for women trapped in unhappy marriages, see chapter 1, "Women and Domestic Violence in Early Modern Spain," of Tania de Miguel Magro, *Staging Violence: Gender and Social Control in Jácaras and Entremeses* (London: Routledge, 2021), 35–50.

70 Luis Quiñones de Benavente, *El murmurador*, entremés.

71 Lope de Vega, *La mal casada*, Acto 3.

72 Lope de Vega, *La necedad del discreto*, Jornada 2.

73 Lope de Vega, *Castelvines y Monteses*, Jornada 1.

74 Robert Rawdon Wilson, *The Hydra's Tale: Imagining Disgust* (Calgary: University of Alberta Press, 2002), xiii.

75 Francisco de Rojas Zorrilla, *Casarse por vengarse*, Jornada 2.

76 Lope de Vega, *El remedio en la desdicha*, Acto 3.

77 Antonio Zamora, *No hay deuda que no se pague, y convidado de piedra*, Acto 1.

78 Agustín Moreto, *El desdén con el desdén*, Jornada 1.

79 See Melveena McKendrick, "The 'Mujer Esquiva.' A Measure of the Feminist Sympathies of Seventeenth-Century Spanish Dramatists," *Hispanic Review* 40.2 (1972): 162–97.

80 Agustín Moreto, *Santa Rosa del Perú*, Jornada 1.

81 Hogan, *What Literature Teaches Us about Emotion*, 240–1.

82   Taurina to Giroto:

Tan menos Giroto es justo
dar a una mujer disgusto
por ser un hombre robusto.

(Lope de Vega, *Las batuecas del Duque de Alba*, Acto 1)

83 Susan Miller, *Disgust: The Gatekeeper Emotion* (New York: Routledge, 2013), 180.

84 Lope de Vega, *Después que el famoso César*, loa.

85 Lope de Vega, *No son todos ruiseñores*, Jornada 1.

86 Lope de Vega, *La fuerza lastimosa*, Jornada 1.

87 Lope de Vega, *El hijo de los leones*, Acto 2.

88 Korsmeyer, *Savoring Disgust*, 74.

89 Lope de Vega, *Lo que hay que fiar del mundo*, Acto 3.

90 Martha Nussbaum, *Political Emotions: Why Love Matters for Justice* (Cambridge, MA: Harvard University Press, 2015), 262.

91 Lope de Vega, *El favor agradecido*, Acto 2.

92 On these renegades from the Christian faith see Bartolomé and Lucile Bennassar, *Los cristianos de Alá: la fascinante aventura de los renegados* (Madrid: Nerea, 2001).

93 Miller, *Disgust: The Gatekeeper Emotion*, 154.

94 Hogan, *Affective Narratology*, 148.

95 Lope de Vega, *El Amete de Toledo*, Acto 3.

96 Miller, *Disgust: The Gatekeeper Emotion*, 13.

97 Lope de Vega, *El bobo del colegio*, Acto 2.

98 For example, Galician novelist Alfredo Conde writes ironic footnotes in which he comments about the untranslatability of certain Galician words into Castilian Spanish (Alfredo Conde, *El griffón* [Madrid: Alfaguara, 1987]).

99 Tirso de Molina, *Averígüelo Vargas*, Jornada 3.

100 Lope de Vega, *El mejor maestro, el tiempo*, Acto 1.

101 Juan de Matos Fragoso, *El genízaro de Ungría*, Jornada 2.

102 Lope de Vega, *El príncipe perfecto*, Acto 3.

103 No quiero estorbar tu gusto,
pero advierte que tenemos
los Españoles que habemos
probado ya su disgusto.
Dos veces se han atrevido
a esta Isla con su armada,
y dos veces de su espada
nos habemos resistido.
Tenemos la vez tercera
por la gente que nos falta,
cuya roja sangre esmalta
toda esa blanca ribera.
Hoy hemos de consultar
a nuestro Dios sobre el caso,
el más peligroso paso
es de esa laguna al mar.
Irán cincuenta soldados
en guarda tuya, y la harán,
bañándote, aunque estarán
lejos del agua alojados.
(Lope de Vega, *Los guanches de Tenerife, y conquista de Canaria*, Acto 1)

104 Lope de Vega, *El ejemplo de casadas y prueba de la paciencia*, Acto 1.

105 Calderón, *El año santo de Roma*, auto sacramental.

106 Juan Bautista Diamante, *Pasión vencida de afecto*, Jornada 1.

107 See Hilaire Kallendorf, "Pride & Co.," in *Sins of the Fathers: Moral Economies in Early Modern Spain* (Toronto: University of Toronto Press, 2013), 15–44.

108 Antonio Zamora, *La poncella de Orleans*, Jornada 1.

109 McGinn, *The Meaning of Disgust*, 121.

110 Hogan, *Affective Narratology*, 148.

111 William Ian Miller, *The Anatomy of Disgust* (Cambridge, MA: Harvard University Press, 1997), 36.

112 See Hilaire Kallendorf, *Ambiguous Antidotes: Virtue as Vaccine for Vice in Early Modern Spain* (Toronto: University of Toronto Press, 2017), 4, figure 1.

113 Calderón, *Lo que va del hombre a Dios*, auto sacramental.

114 Calderón, *No hay cosa como callar*, Jornada 3.

115 Nussbaum, *Political Emotions*, 18. Robert Wilson, drawing upon Jean-Paul Sartre, ventures the hypothesis that "disgust arises inevitably out of a mucoid world in which slime invokes essentially ambiguous states of being, indeterminate or caught between definite states" (Wilson, *The Hydra's Tale*, 44).

116 McGinn, *The Meaning of Disgust*, 80.

117 Cervantes, *Los baños de Argel*, Jornada 1.

118 Nussbaum, *Upheavals of Thought*, 220.

119 Calderón, *La aurora en Copacabana*, Jornada 2.

120 On the cruelty of Almanzor according to Christian chroniclers, see Ana Echevarría Arsuaga, "El azote del año mil: Almanzor, según las crónicas cristianas," in *Los protagonistas del año mil* (Actas del XIII Seminario sobre Historia del Monacato, 2–5 de Agosto de 1999) [Madrid: Centro de Estudios del Románico, 2000], 91–116). For a less biased view, see Virgilio Martínez Enamorado, "Héroe o villano. Guerrero o mecenas. Almanzor en la historiografía española moderna y contemporánea (siglos XVI–XXI)," *Boletín de la Real Academia de Córdoba de Ciencias, Bellas Letras y Nobles Artes* 81.143 (2002): 199–214.

121 Juan de la Cueva, *Los siete infantes de Lara*, Acto 1.

122 Calderón, *Amar y ser amado, y divina Filotea*, auto sacramental.

123 Calderón, *La vacante general*, auto sacramental.

124 Henry Kamen explains the difference between edicts of grace and edicts of faith. In an edict of grace, Inquisitors preached a sermon in the district being visited, held up a crucifix and made the congregation raise their right hands and swear an oath to support the Inquisition. They then recited a list of heresies and invited those who wished to discharge their consciences to come forward and denounce themselves or others. If they came forward within the "grace period" (30–40 days), they would be absolved and "reconciled" to the Church without suffering serious penalties. The edicts of faith omitted the grace period (Henry Kamen, *The Spanish Inquisition: A Historical Revision*, 4th ed. [New Haven: Yale University Press, 2014], 232–3). This is in fact the origin of the phrase "grace period" which we still use today.

125 Calderón, *El orden de Melchisedech*, auto sacramental.

126 Wilson, *The Hydra's Tale*, 56.

127 Calderón, *Las órdenes militares*, auto sacramental.

128 Miller, *Disgust: The Gatekeeper Emotion*, 66.

129 Calderón, *No hay instante sin milagro*, auto sacramental.

130 Calderón, *El mágico prodigioso*, Jornada 1.

131 Calderón, *El nuevo hospicio de pobres*, auto sacramental. "Manjares" is a reference to the Eucharist.

132 Juan Bautista Diamante, *Santa Teresa de Jesús*, Jornada 3.

133 For example, see Freddy Domínguez, "From Saint to Sinner: Sixteenth-Century Perceptions of 'La Monja de Lisboa'," in *A New Companion to Hispanic Mysticism*, ed. Hilaire Kallendorf (Leiden: Brill, 2010), 297–322.

134 On *acedia*, see Stanley W. Jackson, "*Acedia* the Sin and Its Relationship to Sorrow and Melancholia in Medieval Times," *Bulletin of the History of Medicine* 55.2 (1981): 172–85. Jackson writes: "By the late fourth century A.D. the Christian Church had come to use the term 'acedia' to designate a constellation of feelings and behaviors which were considered unusual, undesirable, and indicative of a need for remedial attention. In the words of John Cassian (c. 360–435 A.D.) it was a 'weariness or distress of heart,' 'akin to dejection'" (172).

135 Juan Bautista Diamante, *Santa Maria Magdalena de Pazzi*, Jornada 3.

136 Agustín Moreto, *El esclavo de su hijo*, Jornada 1.

137 Calderón, *El diablo mudo*, auto sacramental.

138 Lope de Vega, *El último godo*, Jornada 1.

139 Nussbaum, *Upheavals of Thought*, 582.

140 Antonio de Solís, *Eurídice y Orfeo*, Jornada 1.

141 Agustín Moreto, *El lindo Don Diego*, Jornada 2.

142 Juan Bautista Diamante, *Amor es sangre y no puede engañarse*, Jornada 1.

143 Juan Bautista Diamante, *Amor es sangre y no puede engañarse*, Jornada 1.

144 Guillén de Castro, *Las mocedades del Cid, comedia primera*, Acto 3.

145 Calderón, *El lirio y la azucena*, auto sacramental.

146   Desde que Lidoro envió
          a tratar la boda, vio
          cuánta repugnancia hubo
          en vos, y que sólo atenta
          al bien común del Estado,
          habíais cedido.

                    (Antonio Zamora, *Amar es saber vencer, y el arte contra el poder*, Acto 1)

147 Agustín Moreto, *Primero es la honra*, Jornada 3.

148 McGinn, *The Meaning of Disgust*, 60.

149 Antonio Zamora, *El hechizado por fuerza*, Jornada 1.

150 Miller, *Disgust: The Gatekeeper Emotion*, 111.

151 Calderón, *Dar tiempo al tiempo*, Jornada 2.

152 Calderón, *Antes que todo es mi dama*, Jornada 2.

153 Juan Pérez de Montalbán, *Como amante y como honrada*, Jornada 2.

154 See Bessel van der Kolk, *The Body Keeps the Score: Brain, Mind, and Body in the Healing of Trauma* (New York: Penguin, 2015).

155 Calderón, *Del secreto a voces*, Jornada 3.

156 Juan Pérez de Montalbán, *Amor, lealtad y amistad*, Jornada 3.

157 Calderón, *A secreto agravio, secreta venganza*, Jornada 3.

158 Jonathan Dollimore, *Death, Desire and Loss in Western Culture* (New York: Routledge, 1998), 252.

3. Question Your Desires

1 Juan Luis Vives, *The Passions of the Soul: The Third Book of* De Anima et Vita, trans. Carlos G. Noreña (Lewiston: Mellen, 1990), 19–20. William Irvine provides contemporary corroboration for this point in rather graphic terms: "[I]t is possible for a single desire to give rise to thousands or even millions of these instrumental desires. Desires … are like microorganisms dropped into a warm, nutrient-rich pond. Left to their own devices, they will reproduce until the pond is a fetid swamp" (William B. Irvine, *On Desire: Why We Want What We Want* [Oxford: Oxford University Press, 2005], 283).

2 Sir Walter Raleigh, quoted in Annette C. Baier, "The Ambiguous Limits of Desire," in *The Ways of Desire*, ed. Joel Marks [Chicago: Precedent, 1986], 39–61, at 43.

3 Thomas Hobbes, *Leviathan*, ed. R. Tuck (Cambridge: Cambridge University Press, 1991), 54.

4 William Shakespeare, *A Midsummer Night's Dream*, in *The Complete Works of William Shakespeare* (New York: Gramercy, 1975), I.1 p. 154.

5 Agustín Moreto, *Antioco y Seleuco*, Jornada 1.

6 Agustín Moreto, *Antioco y Seleuco*, Jornada 1.

7 Lope de Vega, *La bella Aurora*, Acto 1.

8 Lope de Vega, *San Nicolás de Tolentino*, Acto 1.

9 Lope de Vega, *El laberinto de Creta*, Acto 3.

10 Taxonomies for different types of desire are often quite elaborate: "Aristotle … divides desire (*orexis*) into three distinct forms that can be seen to map onto the reasoning, spirited and appetitive parts of Plato's tripartite division of the soul. Aristotle agrees with Plato that reason gives rise to desire, specifically desire for good, which he consistently calls *boulesis*. He also agrees with Plato that there are two specific kinds of non-rational desire: spirited or passionate desire (*thumos*) and appetitive desire (*epithumia*)" (George Kazantzidis and Dimos Spatharas, "Introductory: 'Hope,' *Elpis, Spes*: Affective and Non-Affective Expectancy," in *Hope in Ancient Literature, History, and Art*, ed. George Kazantzidis and Dimos Spatharas [Berlin: De Gruyter, 2018], 1–31, at 14).

11 This succinct definition seems far preferable to some of the confusing attempts at definition offered by philosophers. For example, Felipe de Brigard writes with regard to the Greek *nostos* (desire or longing): "Philosophers often think of desire as naming a somewhat disjointed group of mental states, including wanting, wishing, craving, and preferring – states that are often referred to as pro-attitudes. Philosophical

theories of desire also disagree as to whether the essence of desire is some kind of disposition to act, a certain kind of pleasure brought about by the satisfaction of desire, or its anticipation" (Felipe de Brigard, "Nostalgia and Mental Simulation," in *The Moral Psychology of Sadness*, ed. Anna Gotlib [London: Rowman & Littlefield, 2017], 155–81, at 166).

12 Juan Pérez de Montalbán, *La ganancia por la mano*, Jornada 3.

13 "sellos de amor en sus rosas, por armas de mis deseos" (Juan Pérez de Montalbán, *La ganancia por la mano*, Jornada 2).

14   Dulce amor, dulce deseo,
     saliendo vais de mantillas,
     que hacer al alma cosquillas,
     ya pasa de ser empleo.

(Juan Pérez de Montalbán, Segunda parte del Séneca de España,
Don Felipe Segundo, Jornada 1)

The mention of *mantillas* or veils used by women raises the spectre of the mysterious *tapadas*. On these elusive *tapadas* see Laura R. Bass and Amanda Wunder, "Veiled Ladies of the Early Modern Spanish World: Seduction and Scandal in Seville, Madrid, and Lima," *Hispanic Review* 77.1 (2009): 97–146.

15 "en el mar de amor estoy, los remos son tus deseos" (Juan Pérez de Montalbán, *La ganancia por la mano*, Jornada 2).

16 "una hermosura encubierta se mira con el deseo" (Agustín Moreto, *Primero es la honra*, Jornada 2).

17 Juan Pérez de Montalbán, *El divino portugués San Antonio de Padua*, Jornada 2.

18 Francisco de Rojas Zorrilla, *Los áspides de Cleopatra*, Jornada 1.

19 Juan de Matos Fragoso, *Amor, lealtad y ventura*, Acto 1.

20 Guillén de Castro, *El nacimiento de Montesinos*, Acto 1.

21 "podrá tan gran deseo almas de hielo encender" (Lope de Vega, *Lo cierto por lo dudoso*, Acto 2).

22 "Leonor, sartén de mi deseo" (Lope de Vega, *Los peligros de la ausencia*, Acto 2).

23 "el deseo que te aflije" (Calderón, *La torre de Babilonia*, auto sacramental).

24 "por ella mitigo las fiebres de mi deseo" (Juan Ruiz de Alarcón, *La cueva de Salamanca*, Acto 2).

25 "¿Qué infierno como un deseo?" (Lope de Vega, *La noche de San Juan*, Acto 2). This idea might derive at least tangentially from Saint Augustine. As Hannah Arendt explains his thought on this point, "All desire craves its fulfillment, that is, its own end. An everlasting desire could only be either a contradiction in terms or a description of hell" (Hannah Arendt, *Love and Saint Augustine*, ed. and trans. J.V. Scott and J.C. Stark [Chicago: University of Chicago Press, 1996], 32).

26 Some examples of *autos sacramentales* where Desire appears in the list of characters as an allegorical figure are Calderón's *Las espigas de Ruth*, *La humildad coronada de las plantas*, *El pastor fido*, *La nave del mercader*, and *A tu prójimo como a ti*.

27 The stage directions for one play read: "sale el Hombre, y el deseo de gala con las joyas" (Calderón, *La nave del mercader*, auto sacramental). This portrayal is supported by the further characterization of Desire as a spendthrift; in the same play Hombre (Man) admits of his Talents: "Mi deseo los gastó en alhajas que llevó en humo." Here his Desire spent his talents on jewels which were soon (like the title of the famous film about the American Civil War) "gone with the wind."

28 Amor says of Desire in one of these plays, "A ser Deseo noble, no fuera villano el vestido" (Calderón, *La nave del mercader*, auto sacramental).

29 Calderón, *La nave del mercader*, auto sacramental.

30 Calderón, *A tu prójimo como a ti*, auto sacramental. The rest of the quotations in this paragraph are from this same play unless otherwise noted.

31 "estando acá su deseo, quizá tal vez consentido" (Calderón, *A tu prójimo como a ti*, auto sacramental).

32 Mundo says: "si engañado una vez al deseo miro, él traerá tras sí a su Dueño" (Calderón, *A tu prójimo como a ti*, auto sacramental). Later Man realizes he is lost: "ya que perdido me veo, seguir deja mi deseo, un perdido a otro perdido" (Calderón, *A tu prójimo como a ti*, auto sacramental).

33 "al deseo tiene el Mundo divertido" (Calderón, *A tu prójimo como a ti*, auto sacramental).

34 "el que una vez tiene el deseo perdido, aunque oiga a la Gracia, desprecia el auxilio" (Calderón, *A tu prójimo como a ti*, auto sacramental).

35 "¿qué al Hombre le faltara, si alcanzara su deseo?" (Calderón, *A tu prójimo como a ti*, auto sacramental).

36 Man declares: "he de seguir esta vez los rumbos de mi deseo, gozando el Mundo, gozando de los públicos Festejos" (Calderón, *A tu prójimo como a ti*, auto sacramental).

37 "estás, deseo, en las delicias del Mundo" (Calderón, *A tu prójimo como a ti*, auto sacramental).

38 "no hay Gusto para mí, estando, deseo, sin ti" (Calderón, *A tu prójimo como a ti*, auto sacramental).

39 "mi deseo, que ya estoy sin la agonía que de alcanzarle tenía" (Calderón, *A tu prójimo como a ti*, auto sacramental). Catherine Belsey theorizes, "Desire is by definition unfulfilled: you want what you don't have. Desire is predicated on absence" (Catherine Belsey, *Desire: Love Stories in Western Culture* [Oxford: Blackwell, 1994], 136).

40 Calderón, *Amor, honor y poder*, Acto 1.

41   HOMBRE: ¿Quién te enmendó?

     DESEO: ¿Quién pudo, sino tu arrepentimiento?

                              (Calderón, *A tu prójimo como a ti*, auto sacramental)

42 "el deseo tanto anticipa las horas" (Calderón, *Casa con dos puertas mala es de guardar*, Jornada 2).

43 "muchas ansias del deseo" (Lope de Vega, *Amar, servir y esperar*, Jornada 2); "Con mil ansias el deseo me trae aquí" (Agustín Moreto, *Hasta el fin nadie es dichoso*, Jornada 3).

44 "Mira que ofende la dilación al deseo" (Calderón, *La sibila del Oriente*, Jornada 3); "es fuerza que al deseo le dé la esperanza enfado" (Calderón, *Cuál es mayor perfección*, Jornada 3).

45 "en vuestra ausencia el deseo siglos de pena tendrá" (Guillén de Castro, *El curioso impertinente*, Acto 2).

46 Guillén de Castro, *Las mocedades del Cid, comedia primera*, Acto 2.

47 "largas son las horas del deseo, parece que de plomo van calzadas" (Agustín Moreto, *La confusión de un jardín*, Jornada 1).

48 "la ambición de mi deseo" (Calderón, *El alcalde de Zalamea*, Jornada 3).

49 "el deseo licencioso en aspirar" (Antonio Solís, *Triunfos de amor y fortuna*, loa).

50 "Gran deseo de Reinar me da voces en el pecho" (Lope de Vega, *El hijo de Reduán*, Acto 3); "deseo por llegar a ser de Castilla Rey" (Lope de Vega, *El piadoso aragonés*, Acto 2).

51 "sin freno el deseo, sin ley la ambición" (Antonio Zamora, *Ser fino y no parecerlo*, Acto 1).

52 "Un necio deseo tengo" (Calderón, *La dama duende*, Acto 1).

53 "ambicioso, brevemente hoy con la vida, bárbaro, perdieras el deseo atrevido, e imprudente" (Calderón, *Los cabellos de Absalón*, Jornada 2).

54 "grillos, echad el temor a los pies, cuando el deseo se arroja por las ventanas" (Calderón, *Los cabellos de Absalón*, Jornada 2).

55 "dando al mar aljófar puro, y al joven dulce deseo" (Lope de Vega, *Amar, servir y esperar*, Jornada 2).

56 "tiemple la edad el deseo" (Lope de Vega, *Roma abrasada*, Acto 1).

57 "el oído del deseo abre la puerta al engaño" (Lope de Vega, *La ventura sin buscarla*, Acto 2).

58 "El Caballero encantado en la peña del deseo" (Lope de Vega, *Los palacios de Galiana*, Acto 3).

59 One character reports, "Fingimos conversación de diferentes materias (disfraz que toma el deseo para engañar la modestia). Decíamos nuestro amor con equívocas sentencias" (Francisco de Rojas Zorrilla, *Progne y Filomena*, Jornada 1).

60 "mientras queriendo más guardas ponerle intentan, se enciende más su deseo, y crece el daño" (Agustín Moreto, *No puede ser*, Jornada 1).

61 "los asombros de mi pertinaz deseo" (Juan Bautista Diamante, *Santa Teresa de Jesús*, Jornada 2).

62 "Insaciable deseo" (Calderón, *No hay instante sin milagro*, auto sacramental).

63 "cuanto te pida el deseo más avaro y codicioso" (Calderón, *El mágico prodigioso*, Jornada 2).

64 "es gigante el deseo" (Lope de Vega, *Los bandos de Sena*, Acto 1).

65 Calderón, *Darlo todo y no dar nada*, Jornada 3.

66 Eugene Goodheart, *Desire and Its Discontents* (New York: Columbia University Press, 1991), 2–3. Anna Clark describes deliberate portrayals of excessive desire in ancient Greek drama: "Playwrights, artists and philosophers experimented with representations of excessive sexual desire to explore the limits of the human experience. Often, they did not depict *how* people were *supposed* to behave, or even how they actually behaved sexually – instead they represented sexual desire as excess, as fantasy, frightening, or funny. The comic playwright Aristophanes satirically depicted politicians with gaping anuses who voraciously craved sex with other men. The tragic playwright Euripides told how sexual desire, fate and ambition destroyed families and dynasties" (Anna Clark, *Desire: A History of European Sexuality* [New York: Routledge, 2008], 16–17).

67 "como hay parte de deseo, y este deseo lastima, parece efecto de amor, porque apetece, y aspira" (Agustín Moreto, *El desdén con el desdén*, Jornada 1).

68 "la pena de este deseo" (Calderón, *La exaltación de la Cruz*, Jornada 1).

69 Stephen Levine, *Unattended Sorrow* (Emmaus, PA: Rodale, 2005), 175.

70 "que de ser tuya, el deseo llegue a estar desesperado" (Juan Bautista Diamante, *El cerco de Zamora*, Jornada 1).

71 "necia resistencia ha de llegar a violencia de mi amoroso deseo" (Lope de Vega, *Lo que ha de ser*, Jornada 3).

72   Ya vuestra hermosura he visto
       que, astrólogo el deseo,
       por dos estrellas que mira,
       sabe quién es el sujeto.   (Juan de Matos Fragoso, *El yerro del entendido*, Acto 1)

73 "guiado de mi deseo, y de la noche ayudado" (Calderón, *Amor, honor y poder*, Jornada 3).

74 Alternatively, hope is desire's North Star: "siendo al imán del deseo la esperanza el norte fijo" (Calderón, *En esta vida todo es verdad y todo mentira*, Acto 1).

75 For a scientific explanation of this phenomenon, see Anjan Chatterjee, *The Aesthetic Brain: How We Evolved to Desire Beauty and Enjoy Art* (Oxford: Oxford University Press, 2014). In the case of physical attractiveness, asserts psychologist David Buss, "Beauty may be in the eyes of the beholder, but those eyes, and the minds behind the eyes, have been shaped by millions of years of human evolution … [S]tandards of attractiveness are not arbitrary – they reflect cues to youth and health, and hence to reproductive value. Beauty is not merely skin-deep. It reflects internal reproductive capabilities" (David M. Buss, *The Evolution of Desire* [New York: Basic Books, 2016], 86, 111).

76 "tu hermosura, bello imán de mi deseo" (Calderón, *El Faetonte*, Jornada 2).

77 "adoróla por instantes, porque una ajena hermosura la hace el deseo más grande. Esquiva la halló a sus ruegos" (Francisco de Rojas Zorrilla, *Progne y Filomena*, Jornada 3).

78 "¿cómo, retrato, engañas al deseo?" (Agustín Moreto, *Primero es la honra*, Jornada 3).

79 "a donde alcanzan los ojos, es donde llega el deseo" (Juan Bautista Diamante, *El sol de la sierra*, Jornada 2). Desire can also be moved, however, by the sound of a lovely voice: "Vuestra voz movió el deseo de veros" (Agustín Moreto, *Lo que puede la aprehensión*, Jornada 3).

80 "el deseo tiene tantos ojos prevenidos" (Agustín Moreto, *La fingida Arcadia*, Jornada 2).

81 "Argos es de mi vida su deseo" (Francisco de Rojas Zorrilla, *Peligrar en los remedios*, Jornada 3). Argos is a many-eyed giant in Greek mythology.

82 "Centinela es el deseo, que el campo de amor corre" (Francisco de Rojas Zorrilla, *No hay amigo para amigo*, Jornada 2).

83 "contemplando en estas puertas, Alfeo, y vuelto en lince el deseo, estas ventanas mirando" (Lope de Vega, *El robo de Dina*, Acto 3).

84 "siempre fue sutil el ingenio del deseo" (Juan Pérez de Montalbán, *El hijo del serafín, San Pedro de Alcántara*, Jornada 1).

85 Thus Hianisbe says to the lady (Dama):

> [U]n deseo
> es lince, que penetrar
> los mares sabe, y fingir
> a los ojos el objeto
> más apartado, y secreto.   (Calderón, *Argenis y Poliarco*, Jornada 3)

86 Doña Juana De Madrid describes this process:

> [L]a soledad, y el deseo
> representándole especies
> ciegas a mi pensamiento,
> llena la imaginativa
> de entes de razón diversos,
> que obrando, como fingiendo,
> los vi como verdaderos.   (Francisco de Rojas Zorrilla, *Lo que quería ver el Marqués de Villena*, Jornada 2)

87 Alejandro says to Don Arias:

> Pintor el deseo,
> dio a la memoria pinceles,
> al pensamiento colores,
> con que desmintió lo ausente.   (Calderón, *Nadie fíe su secreto*, Jornada 1)

88 "vuestra imagen copio, siendo el pincel mi deseo, y el lienzo mi voluntad" (Tirso de Molina, *Amar por arte mayor*, Acto 1).

89 "con el buril del deseo impreso en el corazón" (Francisco de Rojas Zorrilla, *No hay amigo para amigo*, Jornada 2). A *buril* was an instrument used by engravers to inscribe metal or stone.

90 "sospecho que desde Moro a Gentil, apóstata mi deseo, hoy pasa, adorando a Palas en la hermosura de Venus" (Calderón, *El gran príncipe de Fez*, Acto 1). Here "Gentil" is a synonym for *pagan*, like the gods of Greek and Roman antiquity were to the Christians.

91 "la polilla del deseo me gasta el pecho a pedazos" (Francisco de Rojas Zorrilla, *No hay amigo para amigo*, Jornada 1).

92 "en sangrientos raudales vertió la vida, por donde bebió el deseo" (Antonio Zamora, *La poncella de Orleans*, Jornada 1).

93 Antonio Zamora, *Siempre hay que envidiar, amando*, Jornada 2.

94 "la sed del deseo" (Antonio de Solís, *El Doctor Carlino*, Jornada 1).

95 "no reposa mi deseo" (Calderón, *Mañana será otro día*, Jornada 2); "no descansa un deseo" (Lope de Vega, *La mayor victoria*, Jornada 2). Conversely, a hypothetical person with no desire is said to look well-rested instead of haggard: "¡qué descansado está el Hombre, que sin deseo se ve!" (Calderón, *La nave del mercader*, auto sacramental).

96 Émile Durkheim, *Suicide: A Study in Sociology*, trans. John A. Spaulding and George Simpson (New York: Free Press, 1951), 247.

97 As Mundo says, "aunque el Hombre esté dormido, su deseo nunca duerme" (Calderón, *La nave del mercader*, auto sacramental).

98 Calderón, *La nave del mercader*, auto sacramental. The character of Queen Isabel la Católica recounts on stage an instance when her dream contained desires:

> A España oprimida vi
> del Africano, y Hebreo,
> sueños son de mi deseo,
> ¿si serán verdades? (Lope de Vega, *El mejor mozo de España*, Acto 1)

A recurring revenge dream likewise is recounted in the line: "Tanto vengarle deseo, que durmiendo muchas veces sueño, que doy muerte al reo" (Lope de Vega, *El piadoso veneciano*, Acto 3). William Irvine confirms that desires do influence the content of dreams: "If we sleep, we temporarily subdue our desires – unless we dream, in which case our dreams will likely be shaped by our desires" (Irvine, *On Desire*, 1). Catherine Belsey agrees: "Desire … generates dreams, and constitutes their meaning" (Belsey, *Desire*, 208).

99 Jean-Michel Oughourlian, *The Genesis of Desire*, trans. Eugene Webb (East Lansing: Michigan State University Press, 2010), 26.

100 [E]l deseo,
> monstruo que de lo imposible
> se alimenta, vivo fuego
> que en la resistencia crece,
> llama que la vive el viento,
> disimulado enemigo
> que mata a su propio dueño,
> y en fin deseo en un hombre
> que sin Dios y sin respeto

> lo abominable, lo horrible
> estima por sólo serlo.   (Calderón, *El purgatorio de San Patricio*, Acto 1)

101 Hianisbe says to the Lady (Dama): "amor, donde no hay cosa, que el deseo de gozar no facilite, y disponga" (Calderón, *Argenis y Poliarco*, Jornada 2).

102 "amante a quien ruega su mismo deseo" (Calderón, *También hay duelo en las damas*, Jornada 2).

103 Carlos declares, "Los deseos Tarantela de amor corren muy a prisa" (Juan Bautista Diamante, *No aspirar a merecer*, Jornada 2). On the *tarantella*, a manic dancing frenzy thought to be brought on by the bite of a tarantula spider, see Laura Biagi, "Spider Dreams: Ritual and Performance in Apulian Tarantismo and Tarantella" (PhD dissertation, New York University, 2004).

104 "prisa me da el deseo, date prisa" (Tirso de Molina, *Quien habló, pagó*, Jornada 3).

105 "parezca, que va sin ti tu deseo" (Juan Bautista Diamante, *Alfeo y Aretusa*, Jornada 2).

106 "dilatando su deseo" (Agustín Moreto, *Industrias contra finezas*, Jornada 2). On *dilatio* in the *comedia* see Hilaire Kallendorf, "*Dilatio*, Deferral, and *Différance*," in *Conscience on Stage: The* Comedia *as Casuistry in Early Modern Spain* (Toronto: University of Toronto Press, 2007), 192–8.

107 "te veo, entre estas soledades afligido, ciegamente abrasándome el deseo; estoy, como en los aires suspendido" (Agustín Moreto, *Los hermanos encontrados*, Jornada 2).

108 Goodheart, *Desire and Its Discontents*, 6.

109 "te despeñe así el deseo" (Tirso de Molina, *La Santa Juana*, Acto 1).

110 "llevado en las alas del deseo" (Calderón, *La crítica del amor*, Jornada 1).

111 Calderón, *El mayor encanto, amor*, Jornada 2.

112 "del deseo, que me incita, y del gozo que me mueve" (Calderón, *El cordero de Isaías*, auto sacramental).

113 "es el deseo para las promesas fácil, donde se sembraron gustos arrepentimientos nacen" (Lope de Vega, *La vida de San Pedro Nolasco*, Jornada 3).

114 Lope de Vega, *Contra valor no hay desdicha*, Acto 2.

115 "sin que ande a caza … de razones mi deseo" (Calderón, *No hay cosa como callar*, Jornada 3).

116 "Mi deseo … tiene a la razón por defensa" (Guillén de Castro, *El nacimiento de Montesinos*, Acto 1).

117 "¿De qué sutiles razones, deseo, os queréis valer?" (Juan Ruiz de Alarcón, *Los favores del mundo*, Acto 2).

118 Calderón, *Cada uno para sí*, Jornada 2. Other lines by the same author indicate that desire never tells the truth: "mintió el deseo; mas ¿cuándo dijo verdad el deseo?" (Calderón, *El mayor encanto, amor*, Acto 1).

119 Lope de Vega, *El piadoso aragonés*, Acto 1.

120 Belsey, *Desire*, 71.

121 "suspiros, que habéis salido por el hilo del deseo, del alma su laberinto" (Francisco de Rojas Zorrilla, *Sin honra no hay amistad*, Jornada 3).

122 "resbalóse la voz por el deseo" (Francisco de Rojas Zorrilla, *Los áspides de Cleopatra*, Jornada 1).

123 "pártase el alma, parta, y el deseo la rija" (Lope de Vega, *La pobreza estimada*, Acto 2).

124 "en hombros de mi deseo mudó casa mi memoria" (Lope de Vega, *La mayor virtud de un rey*, Jornada 1).

125 "¡o qué a prisa piensa un vehemente deseo, que no hay más, que lo que piensa!" (Calderón, *Hado y divisa de Leonido y Marfisa*, Jornada 3).

126 Lope de Vega, *La ventura sin buscarla*, Acto 2.

127 "una pena pueda más cuando le aprieta un deseo" (Guillén de Castro, *Los mal casados de Valencia*, Acto 2).

128 Calderón, *Los empeños de un acaso*, Jornada 3.

129 "ya que tan solo me veo, y herido, salvar deseo la vida" (Calderón, *El encanto sin encanto*, Jornada 3).

130 "me queda el deseo de viandas, y de bebidas diversas" (Calderón, *Lo que va del hombre a Dios*, loa for auto sacramental). Psychological counsellor Stephen Levine notes ironically, "We rarely notice the effect of desire until we find ourselves leaning into the refrigerator" (Levine, *Unattended Sorrow*, 178).

131 Hilaire Kallendorf, "That Gnawing Hunger: The Plus Size of Gluttony," in *Sins of the Fathers: Moral Economies in Early Modern Spain* (Toronto: University of Toronto Press, 2013), 112–32. William Irvine notes rather grimly, "Four of the seven deadly sins (envy, gluttony, lust, and greed) directly involve desire, and the remaining three (sloth, wrath, and pride) can do so indirectly" (Irvine, *On Desire*, 198).

132 "sólo le ha faltado a mi deseo el postre que te dio la mulatilla" (Lope de Vega, *El premio del bien hablar*, Acto 1).

133 "en una empanada tenemos nuestro deseo" (Antonio de Solís, *Un bobo hace ciento*, Jornada 1).

134 "le ha de vencer el deseo de gustar de su Maná" (Calderón, *El arca de Dios cautiva*, auto sacramental).

135 "deseo de más oro y plata" (Lope de Vega, *El marido más firme*, Acto 3).

136 "deseo aumentar mi hacienda" (Lope de Vega, *El robo de Dina*, Acto 2).

137 "veo abrasarse mi deseo por hacer esta conquista" (Guillén de Castro, *Las mocedades del Cid, comedia segunda*, Acto 1).

138 Thus Lucindo says of Prince Polidoro:

> [S]e empeñó
> en venir (con el pretexto
> de la guerra) a militar
> de parte de su deseo.   (Antonio de Solís, *Las amazonas*, Jornada 1)

139 Lope de Vega, *Roma abrasada*, Acto 3.

140 Juan Bautista Diamante, *Lides de amor y desdén*, Acto 1.

141 Thus a character addresses the Divinity: "yo por mí no deseo Triunfos, Laureles, ni Empresas, sino por Ti" (Calderón, *El santo Rey Don Fernando, segunda parte*, auto sacramental).

142 "es volver atrás mi primer deseo, pues ha de perder la Patria" (Calderón, *Dicha y desdicha del nombre*, Jornada 1).

143 Lope de Vega, *Las cuentas del Gran Capitán*, Acto 1.

144 Calderón, *La aurora en Copacabana*, Jornada 2. On homesickness and longing for home see De Brigard, "Nostalgia and Mental Simulation."

145 One character advises the other concerning the advantages of this system: "contentos los dos, podrás tú el deseo conseguir de fundar el Mayorazgo, sin la pena de elegir" – i.e., without confronting the dilemma of having to choose which son will receive a greater share of the inheritance (Calderón, *El gran mercado del mundo*, auto sacramental).

146 One character describes himself thus: "cuando infeliz deseo sólo vivir ignorado" (Calderón, *La fiera, el rayo y la piedra*, Jornada 2).

147 "de ninguno acompañado deseó verse Crisanto, y halló alivio en la soledad" (Calderón, *Los dos amantes del cielo*, Jornada 3).

148 Lope de Vega, *El mejor mozo de España*, Acto 1. This thirst has been explored recently in Ian Leslie, *Curious: The Desire to Know and Why Your Future Depends on It* (New York: Basic Books, 2014).

149 "el deseo de saber ese enigma" (Calderón, *El Faetonte*, Jornada 2).

150 Roger Shattuck, *Forbidden Knowledge: From Prometheus to Pornography* (New York: St. Martin's, 1996).

151 One character gives the example of how the price of tomatoes rose after they were prohibited during an outbreak of plague:

> Y el ejemplo te he [de] dar,
> que en los tomates contemplo,
> y de paso has de notar,
> que te hablo con un ejemplo,
> como soy tan ejemplar.
> Por la peste prohibieron,
> nadie a ochavo los quería;
> y cuando faltar los vieron,
> tanto el deseo crecía,
> que a real de a ocho valieron.   (Agustín Moreto, *De fuera vendrá*, Jornada 1)

152 For example, "malparió cierta Romana con el deseo de ver un monstruo, y no se atrever a llegar" (Lope de Vega, *Si no vieran las mujeres*, Jornada 1). For more on early modern monsters, see Elena del Río Parra, *Una era de monstruos: representaciones de lo deforme en el Siglo de Oro español* (Madrid and Frankfurt: Iberomericana, 2003).

153 Michel Foucault, *Language, Madness, and Desire*, ed. Philippe Artières et al., trans. Robert Bononno (Minneapolis: University of Minnesota Press, 2015), 93–146, at 146.

154 "No ignoraréis cuánto ha sido siempre curioso el deseo" (Calderón, *La fiera, el rayo y la piedra*, Jornada 2).

155 Calderón, *De una causa dos efectos*, Jornada 1.

156 "Un Doctísimo Hebreo tiene Jerusalén, cuyo deseo siempre ha sido estudioso" (Calderón, *El mayor monstruo del mundo*, Acto 1).

157 "Deseo yo leer Latín, dezid, ¿no me enseñaréis?" (Tirso de Molina, *Marta la piadosa*, Acto 2).

158 We see this dynamic in the following exchange:

> SILVIA: Ya sabe que en la mujer el deseo de saber …
> BATULO: Es una alhaja civil.   (Calderón, *El Faetonte*, Jornada 2)

159 "pasiones del deseo en mujeres como yo se criaron para el pecho" (Agustín Moreto, *La fingida Arcadia*, Jornada 2).

160 "Lo que desprecié deseo, / que es niño amor, y apetece / hoy lo que ayer aborrece" (Tirso de Molina, *Segunda parte de Santa Juana*, Acto 3).

161 Lope de Vega, *La primera información*, Jornada 2.

162 Juan Bautista Diamante, *Santa Teresa de Jesús*, Jornada 2.

163 For example, "el lauro me está esperando del martirio que deseo" (Juan Pérez de Montalbán, *El divino portugués San Antonio de Padua*, Jornada 3).

164 "Ya deseo perder por ti la vida" (Lope de Vega, *La carbonera*, Jornada 1).

165 "libertar a mi padre, por quien con noble codicia, deseo en cambio dichoso, dar por la suya mi vida" (Juan de Matos Fragoso, *El traidor contra su sangre*, Jornada 2).

166 "el deseo de haber de morir con él" (Calderón, *El segundo blasón de Austria*, auto sacramental). Elaine Hatfield and Richard Rapson note that pacts of "love suicide" are still common in Japan: "Love suicides in Japan have been an institution since the end of the seventeenth century. In plays and stories, the suicide pacts were dramatized with sensational effect – the journey together to the chosen place, the leaving behind forever of familiar scenes, the agonizing mental conflicts, the last tender farewell. In Japanese thought suicide is not ignoble. It is the final vindication of what a person believes. When it is glorified by frustrated love, it becomes a sublime tragedy" (Elaine Hatfield and Richard Rapson, *Love, Sex, and Intimacy: Their Psychology, Biology, and History* [New York: HarperCollins, 1993], 35).

167 For a synthesis of Aristotle's views on the desire for revenge, see Giles Pearson, "Species of Desire II: *Thumos* (Retaliatory Desire)," in *Aristotle on Desire* (Cambridge: Cambridge University Press, 2012), 111–39.

168 Jonathan Dollimore has written an entire book on the convergence of death (Thanatos) with desire (Eros), noting that "There is even an equivalence between eros and death: Hades, the god of death; Dionysus, the god of eros – these are one and the same" (Dollimore, *Death, Desire and Loss*, 5).

169 For Senecan influence on Renaissance drama in general, see Gordon Braden, "Senecan Tragedy and the Renaissance," *Illinois Classical Studies* 9.2 (1984):

277–92; and more recently, Susanna Braund, "Haunted by Horror: The Ghost of Seneca in Renaissance Drama," in *A Companion to the Neronian Age* (Oxford: Wiley-Blackwell, 2013), 425–43. For a study of Seneca's influence on the Neostoicism of early modern Spanish poets like Francisco de Quevedo, see Henry Ettinghausen, *Francisco de Quevedo and the Neostoic Movement* (Oxford: Oxford University Press, 1972).

170 Lope de Vega, *Los palacios de Galiana*, Acto 3. A similar sentiment is expressed in a different line from the same play: "un gran deseo de hacer en mi enemigo venganza" (Acto 2).

171 Lope de Vega, *El hombre por su palabra*, Acto 1.

172 Calderón, *El indulto general*, auto sacramental. On Lust see Hilaire Kallendof, "Lusty Lads and Luscious Ladies," in *Sins of the Fathers*, 74–96.

173 "miren lo que hace un deseo de boda libidinoso" (Agustín Moreto, *De fuera vendrá*, Jornada 3).

174 Thus Filomena objects: "Amor llamas al deseo torpe" (Juan Bautista Diamante, *Jupiter y Semele*, Acto 1).

175 "Noche, que has dado lugar a cuanto intenta el deseo: noche, cuyo rostro feo suele el amor desear" (Lope de Vega, *Las cuentas del Gran Capitán*, Acto 2).

176 "ni en mi vida me dio más dulce deseo de su amorosa conquista" (Lope de Vega, *Si no vieran las mujeres*, Jornada 1).

177 Lope de Vega, *Los peligros de la ausencia*, Acto 2.

178 "con los amores que les enseña el deseo tienen (el ser) por trofeo de una mujer vencedores" (Lope de Vega, *La mayor virtud de un rey*, Jornada 3).

179 "sólo el galanteo que aspira a deseo hace lícito el favor" (Agustín Moreto, *La cautela en la amistad*, Jornada 2).

180 Juan Pérez de Montalbán, *Amor, privanza y castigo*, Acto 2.

181 Juan de Matos Fragoso, *Amor, lealtad y ventura*, Jornada 3. The *suerte* is a technical term for one of the "acts" or phases of a bullfight.

182 Elena Lombardi explicitly addresses desire's temporality: "Comparing the three versions of desire with respect to time, we can say that desire-as-loss secludes itself in the past (the desired object is unattainable, thus excluding the possibility of satisfaction); desire-as-lack defers its happening to the future (the desired object stands as a promise / sign of satisfaction); desire-as-fulfilment actualizes itself in the present, whereby the past (the longed for object of desire) coalesce[s]" (Elena Lombardi, *The Syntax of Desire: Language and Love in Augustine, the* Modistae, *Dante* [Toronto: University of Toronto Press, 2007], 12).

183 Calderón, *El golfo de las sirenas*, Acto 1.

184 Belsey, *Desire*, 27–8, referencing Maurice Blanchot's *The Writing of the Disaster*.

185 Sociologist Ann Swidler recalls, "For the courtly tradition, love was … a sudden and certain passion ('love at first sight')" (Ann Swidler, *Talk of Love: How Culture Matters* [Chicago: University of Chicago Press, 2001), 112.

186 Francisco de Rojas Zorrilla, *La traición busca el castigo*, Jornada 1.

187 "Es el amor deseo de un contento, / que nunca llega a su dichoso estado" (Agustín Moreto, *No puede ser*, Jornada 1).

188 "como haya conseguido mi deseo, nada a mi vida le falta" (Calderón, *Mañana será otro día*, Jornada 3).

189 Levine, *Unattended Sorrow*, 180. Pornography scholar Z. Patterson's comment about the process of surfing for porn on the internet seems relevant here: "The user constantly shifts on to new images – and in this process, new delays – in an endless slippage of desire in which part of the pleasure derives from habitual repetition and habitual deferral" (Z. Patterson, "Going On-Line: Consuming Pornography in the Digital Era," in *Porn Studies*, ed. L. Williams [Durham, NC: Duke University Press, 2004], 104–23, at 109).

190 "por lograr su deseo, perderá la libertad" (Juan Ruiz de Alarcón, *Las paredes oyen*, Acto 3).

191 Calderón, *La niña de Gómez Arias*, Acto 1.

192 "con la privación crece el deseo" (Juan Ruiz de Alarcón, *La industria y la suerte*, Acto 3).

193 "la resistencia, Don Juan, con la competencia encienden más mi deseo" (Juan Ruiz de Alarcón, *La industria y la suerte*, Acto 1).

194 Lope de Vega, *Castelvines y Monteses*, Jornada 1.

195 Calderón, *La aurora en Copacabana*, Acto 1.

196 Calderón, *Las espigas de Ruth*, auto sacramental.

197 Calderón, *La piel de Gedeón*, auto sacramental.

198 "en batalla civil mi esposo con su deseo trabaron dudosa lid" (Francisco de Rojas Zorrilla, *La traición busca el castigo*, Jornada 2).

199 "en vano lo deseo" (Calderón, *Agradecer y no amar*, Jornada 2).

200 Juan Bautista Diamante, *Santa Teresa de Jesús*, Jornada 1.

201 Oughourlian, *The Genesis of Desire*, 22. Eugene Goodheart agrees: "The gap between desire and its object is insurmountable. Indeed, it is the very gap that nourishes and sustains desire, because its satisfaction would be its extinction. It may even court rejection, since denial only increases desire. Desire is committed to permanent revolution, to an enduring disappointment as a way of guaranteeing its survival" (Goodheart, *Desire and Its Discontents*, 3).

202 "bien creo que hubiera vuestro deseo, antes de hablarme, quedado en silencio sepultado" (Calderón, *Los dos amantes del cielo*, Jornada 1).

203 "quiere atajar el Señor el curso a vuestro deseo, el vuelo a vuestra intención" (Calderón, *La torre de Babilonia*, auto sacramental).

204 "Lo que se mira imposible entibia cualquier deseo" (Agustín Moreto, *El Cristo de los milagros*, Jornada 3).

205 Calderón, *El castillo de Lindabridis*, Jornada 3.

206 Thus Astrea refers to "En mí un difunto deseo" (Calderón, *Ni Amor se libra de Amor*, Jornada 3).

207 "el pasado deseo de mi apetencia cesó" (Calderón, *El nuevo hospicio de pobres*, auto sacramental).

208 "Viuda quedo de un deseo, / póngase luto el amor" (Juan Pérez de Montalbán, *Lo que son los juicios del cielo*, Jornada 3).

209 In this regard, Wilhelm Hofmann and Loran Nordgren point out that "Public health figures suggest that 40% of deaths in the United States each year are associated with behaviors that are at least partially attributable to the way people deal with desires such as those for unhealthy foods, tobacco, alcohol, unprotected sex, aggressive urges, and illicit drugs" (Wilhelm Hofmann and Loran F. Nordgren, "Introduction," in *The Psychology of Desire*, ed. Wilhelm Hofmann and Loran F. Nordgren [New York: Guilford, 2015], 1–13, at 2).

210 Agustín Moreto, *La fuerza de la ley*, Jornada 1.

211 Agustín Moreto, *Los jueces de Castilla*, Jornada 2.

212 Agustín Moreto, *Industrias contra finezas*, Jornada 2.

213 "el no lograr mi deseo me tiene con pena extraña" (Guillén de Castro, *La humildad soberbia*, Acto 3). William Irvine addresses this possibility, but assures us that our brains are wired to find a way around it: "When we form a chain of desire, there is always a chance that some of the links in the chain will be broken – that we will discover that we cannot fulfill them and thereby ascend the chain. When this happens, we experience frustration, and the feeling of frustration pushes us to find a detour around the broken link. We do this by using our intellect to forge new links to our chain – that is, we generate new instrumental desires, the fulfillment of which will enable us to circumvent the broken link and allow us once again to ascend the chain we have formed" (Irvine, *On Desire*, 88). Jean-Michel Oughourlian's view of this situation is far less sanguine: "The mechanism of mimetic desire can impel us toward beings or objects that are increasingly difficult to obtain and that will seem all the more seductive to us the more inaccessible they are. Coming up against a rival who obstructs it, insatiable desire can become endlessly intensified, becoming a gnawing pain, a self-alienation, a hopeless enslavement. Thus one can arrive at the most acute and terrifying form of passional pathology … Every obstacle, even if only dreamed, feeds desire" (Oughourlian, *The Genesis of Desire*, 25, 29).

214 "quien tiene amor, cuando logra sus deseos" (Juan Pérez de Montalbán, *La ganancia por la mano*, Jornada 2).

215 "ver si la ocasión con el deseo hacen en el camino algún empleo" (Calderón, *A secreto agravio, secreta venganza*, Acto 1). On occasion as a circumstance of sin see Fernando Plata, "On Love and Occasion: A Reading of the 'Tale of Inappropriate Curiosity,'" in *Cervantes and Don Quixote* (Proceedings of the Delhi Conference on Miguel de Cervantes), ed. Vibha Maurya and Ignacio Arellano (Hyderabad: Emesco, 2008), 195–210.

216 "la ocasión, habiendo a tiempo llegado en que pueda mi deseo hacer el feliz empleo, tantos años esperado" (Calderón, *A secreto agravio, secreta venganza*, Acto 1).

217 Casuistry may be defined as case morality. On casuistry in early modern Spain see
      Kallendorf, *The Comedia as Casuistry*, and Elena del Río Parra, *Cartografías de la
      conciencia española en la Edad de Oro* (Mexico City: Fondo de Cultura Económica,
      2008). For a more general overview of European casuistry see Albert R. Jonsen and
      Stephen Toulmin, *The Abuse of Casuistry: A History of Moral Reasoning* (Berkeley:
      University of California Press, 1990); and more recently, Carlo Ginzburg and
      Lucio Biasiori, eds., *A Historical Approach to Casuistry: Norms and Exceptions in
      Comparative Perspective* (London: Bloomsbury, 2018).

218 Lope de Vega, *No son todos ruiseñores*, Acto 1.

219 "Las circunstancias son, qual, quando, por que, en que lugar, enque tiempo, con que
      instrumentos, quantas vezes" (García López de Alvarado, *Breve compendio de confessión*
      [Venice: Juan Maria Bonelli, 1552], 3; quoted in Kallendorf, *The* Comedia *as Casuistry*, 10).

220 Calderón, *El galán fantasma*, Acto 1.

221 Calderón, *Psiquis y Cupido*, loa for auto sacramental.

222 Guillén de Castro, *El desengaño dichoso*, Acto 3.

223 "que yo empiece a coger el fruto de mi deseo" (Agustín Moreto, *La fingida Arcadia*,
      Jornada 3).

224 On this classical poem which was a source for both Garcilaso and Góngora, see
      Baerbel Becker-Cantarino, "'Vana Rosa,' from Ausonius to Góngora and Gryphius,"
      Revista Hispánica Moderna 37.1/2 (1972/73): 29–45.

225 "hallando el claro puerto a mi deseo" (Francisco de Rojas Zorrilla, *Casarse por
      vengarse*, Jornada 3).

226 Tirso de Molina, *Segunda parte de Santa Juana*, Acto 2.

227 "si el amor es deseo, cuanto más presto se alcanza se estima después en menos"
      (Tirso de Molina, *Esto sí que es negociar*, Jornada 1).

228 Juan Ruiz de Alarcón, *Examen de maridos*, Acto 3.

229 Agustín Moreto, *Industrias contra finezas*, Jornada 2.

230 According to cultural materialist Jonathan Dollimore, the common misperception
      that the moral valences of desire are mostly negative is due to the "Christian belief that
      man, through transgressive desire, brought death into the world" (Jonathan Dollimore,
      Death, Desire and Loss in Western Culture [New York: Routledge, 1998], xix).

231 Calderón, *Darlo todo y no dar nada*, Jornada 3.

232 Wilhelm Hofmann et al., "Desire and Desire Regulation," in *The Psychology of
      Desire*, ed. Hofmann and Nordgren, 61–81, at 61.

233 "el natural deseo, y voluntad de la Carne" (Calderón, *Los misterios de la misa*, auto
      sacramental). Anna Clark notes, "During the Middle Ages, the Church denounced
      fornication, but municipal authorities believed desire was natural. So they set up
      official municipal brothels, where women who sold sex were supposed to work as
      prostitutes" (Clark, *Desire*, 12). William Irvine is less than sanguine about giving in
      to these so-called natural desires, however: "Many 'natural' desires are parasitic: they
      take up residence in us without being invited, and while within us, try to hijack our

plan for living. We should work to rid ourselves of these desires, much as we would try to rid ourselves of a tapeworm" (Irvine, *On Desire*, 282).

234 "el lícito deseo" (Tirso de Molina, *La Santa Juana*, Acto 1).

235 "decente, y justo el deseo" (Juan Bautista Diamante, *El cerco de Zamora*, Jornada 1).

236 "Yo tu buen deseo estimo" (Juan Bautista Diamante, *El cerco de Zamora*, Jornada 1).

237 "No es sino justo deseo" (Calderón, *El mayor monstruo del mundo*, Jornada 3).

238 "tu piadoso deseo levanta el alma" (Lope de Vega, *La limpieza no manchada*, Acto 1).

239 "un leal deseo no sabe presumir caso tan feo" (Agustín Moreto, *El mejor amigo, el rey*, Jornada 1).

240 Eráclito declares proudly, "pues no hay más ambición para mí, ni deseo más digno, que el de ser quien soy" (Calderón, *En esta vida todo es verdad y todo mentira*, Jornada 3).

241 Dama 1 exclaims, "es mérito desear" (Calderón, *La aurora en Copacabana*, Acto 1).

242 Calderón, *Fortunas de Andrómeda y Perseo*, Jornada 3.

243 "no es bien dilatar, Moro, tu noble deseo" (Juan Bautista Diamante, *Santa María del Monte, y convento de San Juan*, Jornada 1).

244 "Yo aspiro a cuanto deseo" (Calderón, *Las cadenas del demonio*, Jornada 2).

245 "noble deseo de ver mundo" (Antonio Zamora, *El custodio de la Ungría, San Juan Capistrano*, Jornada 1). This type of desire is the subject of Beth E. Notar, *Displacing Desire: Travel and Popular Culture in China* (Honolulu: University of Hawai'i Press, 2006).

246 "cuanto me prometió mi deseo" (Calderón, *Guárdate de la agua mansa*, Jornada 1).

247 "porque eligiese en su varias lides, árbitro el deseo, de cuál de las dos se agrada" (Calderón, *Basta callar*, Jornada 1).

248 A Queen asserts, "Yo creo que el Médico mejor es el deseo" (Lope de Vega, *El mayor imposible*, Jornada 3).

249 Juan Pérez de Montalbán, *El divino portugués San Antonio de Padua*, Jornada 2.

250 "es atrevido un deseo" (Calderón, *Las tres justicias en una*, Jornada 3).

251 "no hay riesgo que amague donde hay deseo que alienta" (Antonio Zamora, *La poncella de Orleans*, Jornada 3). *Amagar* means *to threaten*.

252 Calderón, *Agradecer y no amar*, Jornada 1.

253 Juan Bautista Diamante, *Santa María del Monte, y convento de San Juan*, Jornada 3.

254 "mi honesto deseo" (Lope de Vega, *La noche de San Juan*, Acto 1); "a justos y honestos fines encamine su deseo" (Juan Ruiz de Alarcón, *Mudarse por mejorarse*, Acto 3).

255 "este heroico sentimiento … este Cristiano deseo" (Juan Pérez de Montalbán, *Lo que son juicios del cielo*, Jornada 3).

256 "tan santo deseo" (Juan Pérez de Montalbán, *El divino portugués San Antonio de Padua*, Jornada 1).

257 A Muslim character expresses this desire in an odd mix of religious registers: "señor, a Alá bendigo. Hoy se ha cumplido mi mayor deseo, que fue vivir en tierra de Cristianos" (Lope de Vega, *La envidia contra la nobleza*, Acto 3). William Irvine describes a similar experience in the life of Thomas Merton: "Merton's desire to

convert to Catholicism … is a classic example of a spontaneous desire: 'All of a sudden, something began to stir within me, something began to push me, to prompt me. It was a movement that spoke like a voice'" (Irvine, *On Desire*, 17, quoting Thomas Merton, *The Seven Storey Mountain* [San Diego: Harcourt Brace, 1948], 236).

258 The desire to pursue a religious vocation leads one pious woman to disguise herself: "El deseo de ser Monja le dio atrevimiento y fuerzas para disfrazarse" (Tirso de Molina, *La Santa Juana*, Acto 2).

259 "un buen deseo antes obliga, que ofende" (Guillén de Castro, *La fuerza de la sangre*, Jornada 3).

260 Tirso de Molina, *La reina de los reyes*, Jornada 1.

261 Jean Leclercq, *The Love of Learning and the Desire for God: A Study of Monastic Culture*, trans. Catharine Misrahi (New York: Fordham University Press, 1982), 67–8.

262 Beatriz relies on this truism in her reply to the *gracioso* Mosquito: "Mosquito, no puedo abrirte, sabe Dios si lo deseo, porque se llevó Don Juan la llave" (Calderón, *El escondido y la tapada*, Jornada 3).

263 "no te ofendía mi amor, ni era indigno mi deseo" (Calderón, *Nadie fíe su secreto*, Jornada 2).

264 "Tuvo disculpa el deseo de un yerro desatinado" (Agustín Moreto, *La traición vengada*, Jornada 3).

265 Calderón, *De una causa dos efectos*, Jornada 3.

266 Francisco de Rojas Zorrilla, *Los trabajos de Tobías*, Jornada 2.

267 Arendt, *Love and Saint Augustine*, 23.

268 "es antojo del deseo" (Francisco de Rojas Zorrilla, *El más impropio Verdugo por la más justa venganza*, Jornada 3); "es azar de mi deseo" (Juan Bautista Diamante, *El Hércules de Ocaña*, Jornada 1).

269 "me arrastra mi deseo, cómplice en el peligro" (Calderón, *El Conde Lucanor*, Jornada 3); "El deseo es el mayor peligro de cuantos rije la vida" (Juan Bautista Diamante, *Alfeo y Aretusa*, Jornada 1).

270 "el que rinde los sentidos al deseo, no habrá peligro que evite" (Juan Bautista Diamante, *Alfeo y Aretusa*, Jornada 1).

271 "Anda el deseo en competencia del honor" (Lope de Vega, *Amar sin saber a quién*, Jornada 3). A specific context in which honour is placed in jeopardy by desire is the much-debated issue of clandestine marriage: "si me desposo esta noche a fuerza de mi deseo, será de mi honor infamia" (Lope de Vega, *Amar, servir y esperar*, Jornada 3).

272 "con este deseo, esta ansia, este desvelo, este estudio (mejor diré esta ignorancia)" (Calderón, *El día mayor de los días*, auto sacramental).

273 "Tuyo es el traidor deseo" (Calderón, *La piel de Gedeón*, auto sacramental).

274 "a lo irracional del gusto, y a lo bruto del deseo" (Calderón, *No siempre lo peor es cierto*, Jornada 1). Deborah Tolman decries this stereotype about desire: "In our worst scenarios, we think of desire as a kind of selfish, exploitative monster, as a force that demands its bearer find satisfaction at the expense of or without concern for someone else. Desire is uncivilized. It is all about individual needs and has

nothing to do with relationships" (Deborah L. Tolman, *Dilemmas of Desire: Teenage Girls Talk About Sexuality* [Cambridge, MA: Harvard University Press, 2002], 13). Tolman argues in favour of a healthier concept of desire that would not be considered "brutish" or socially unacceptable for teenage girls.

275 "morir me veo a manos de mi bárbaro deseo" (Agustín Moreto, *La fingida Arcadia*, Jornada 3). The most extreme example of "barbaric" desire may well be the rape and other sexual violence perpetrated against women in the context of warfare. See *Brutality and Desire: War and Sexuality in Europe's Twentieth Century*, ed. Dagmar Herzog (Basingstoke, Hampshire [UK]: Palgrave Macmillan, 2009).

276 The allegorical figure of Faith exclaims, "¡Qué ingrato ha mostrado su deseo, pues con tal baldón le ultraja!" (Calderón, *Psiquis y Cupido*, loa for auto sacramental).

277 Calderón, *Primero y segundo Isaac*, auto sacramental.

278 Lope de Vega, *La mayor victoria de Alemania de Don Gonzalo de Córdoba*, preliminares.

279 "algún deseo inhumano" (Agustín Moreto, *Antioco y Seleuco*, Jornada 2).

280 "Hoy en su muerte veré satisfecho mi deseo" (Calderón, *La gran Zenobia*, Jornada 3).

281 "deseo ya la muerte de Leonida mi esposa" (Lope de Vega, *La ilustre fregona*, Jornada 2).

282 "Nerón deseó que fuese toda Roma una cabeza, para que cortarla pudiese" (Lope de Vega, *El hombre por su palabra*, Acto 1).

283 "verás cómo ejecuta su muerte y nuestro deseo una dracma de cicuta" (Lope de Vega, *El hijo de Reduán*, Jornada 3). *Cicuta* is hemlock, the poison Socrates famously drank to commit suicide.

284 "con qué prisa deseo, con qué gusto verle al villano envuelto con su sangre" (Guillén de Castro, *El desengaño dichoso*, Acto 2).

285 "son los meses años, un martirio del deseo, y una imaginada gloria, verdugo de la memoria" (Calderón, *Amor, honor y poder*, Jornada 2).

286 "quiere amor que el deseo a la razón se anteponga" (Lope de Vega, *Por la puente, Juana*, Acto 3).

287 "suele un loco deseo engañar una desdicha" (Lope de Vega, *Amar, servir y esperar*, Jornada 2).

288 "el deseo poco cuerdo" (Calderón, *Amigo amante y leal*, Jornada 2).

289 Lope de Vega, *Lo cierto por lo dudoso*, Acto 3.

290 Pindar, *Nemean* 11, quoted in Alexandre Johnston, "'Poet of Hope': *Elpis* in Pindar," in *Hope in Ancient Literature*, ed. Kazantzidis and Spatharas, 35–52, at 38.

291 "¿Si es delirio del deseo?" (Calderón, *Duelos de amor y lealtad*, Jornada 1).

292 Juan Pérez de Montalbán, *El divino portugués San Antonio de Padua*, Jornada 2.

293 Calderón, *Guárdate del agua mansa*, Jornada 3.

294 Arthur Schopenhauer, *The World as Will and Representation* [1819/1844], trans. E.F.J. Payne, 2 vols. (New York: Dover, 1966), ll. 580, 573.

295 Irvine continues, "Around the world, rising levels of affluence have not translated into increased levels of personal satisfaction. In particular, the citizens of affluent nations enjoy a level of material well-being unimaginable to their great-

grandparents. Even those citizens labeled impoverished by government statisticians have antibiotics, reliable contraception, CD players, Internet access, and indoor plumbing. But although they 'have it all' compared to their ancestors, they remain dissatisfied" (Irvine, *On Desire*, 106, 5).

296 "¡Si es fantasma del deseo!" (Calderón, *Amado y aborrecido*, Jornada 2).

297 "quimérico te engañe tu deseo" (Tirso de Molina, *Los lagos de San Vicente*, Acto 3).

298 Sigismundo asks Auristela, "Cielos santos, ¿es ilusión del deseo?" (Calderón, *Afectos de odio y amor*, Jornada 2).

299 "vase en humo el deseo" (Lope de Vega, *San Nicolás de Tolentino*, Acto 2).

300 Belsey, *Desire*, 155.

301 "infeliz mi deseo, venga siempre trayendo un pesar tras sí" (Calderón, *Fuego de Dios en el querer bien*, Jornada 2).

302 "me va matando el deseo" (Agustín Moreto, *El valiente justiciero*, Jornada 1).

303 "alguna ocasión forzosa dio lugar a un mal deseo" (Guillén de Castro, *Los mal casados de Valencia*, Acto 1).

304 As when Narciso admits, "equívoco mi deseo extraños discursos fragua" (Calderón, *Eco y Narciso*, Jornada 3).

305 "¡O bajeza del deseo!" (Agustín Moreto, *El desdén con el desdén*, Jornada 1).

306 "porque inquietó a mi esposa con torpe, indigno deseo, le quitara yo la vida" (Antonio de Solís, *Eurídice y Orfeo*, Jornada 3).

307 "ni que un descortés deseo insta en querer con violencia cautivar mi voluntad" (Antonio Zamora, *Cada uno es linaje aparte, y los Mazas de Aragón*, Jornada 2).

308 "los visajes, y ademanes, que hacen por cumplir su vil deseo" (Luis Quiñones de Benavente, *El murmurador*, entremés).

309 The King says to his son the prince: "perdona, hijo, al deseo, que no pensé que tan feo cupiera en mi edad" (Lope de Vega, *Nadie se conoce*, Jornada 3).

310 "malicioso el deseo, no será bien que fabrique siniestramente el concepto" (Juan Bautista Diamante, *Amor es sangre y no puede engañarse*, Jornada 2).

311 Agustín Moreto, *El desdén con el desdén*, Jornada 1.

312 "ya me ofende el hacer público su mal deseo" (Guillén de Castro, *La humildad soberbia*, Acto 1).

313 "los envidiosos que con mal deseo hablan de los ausentes" (Lope de Vega, *El valiente Céspedes*, Acto 2).

314 "su esposa te da deseo, y a mí su esposo también" (Lope de Vega, *El marido más firme*, Acto 2).

315 "mi deseo mis ofensas ha inventado" (Calderón, *El mágico prodigioso*, Jornada 2).

316 "aquel traidor, capaz de tan mal deseo" (Guillén de Castro, *Los mal casados de Valencia*, Acto 2).

317 "la fuerza tirana de un torpe deseo" (Juan Bautista Diamante, *Ir por el riesgo a la dicha*, Jornada 1).

318 "condolida veo, ni alivio en mi prisión, ni en mi deseo" (Juan Ruiz de Alarcón, *La cueva de Salamanca*, Acto 3). As Jonathan Dollimore notes, this characterization of

desire echoes the Stoics such as Seneca: "desire or passion is the great evil: to desire
is to be unfree, conflicted, miserable, futile" (Dollimore, *Death, Desire and Loss*, 24).
We might recall also that Jacques Lacan considers the human subject to be forever
trapped inside a cage built with the materials of desire and language.

319 "defenderme en vano intento: deseo, ya estoy vencida" (Calderón, *Amor, honor y
       poder*, Acto 1).

320 "por solo el menor deseo que te ofenda y te fatigue" (Calderón, *El mágico prodigioso*,
       Jornada 2).

321 "sitiar la veo de uno, y otro deseo" (Calderón, *El mayor encanto, amor*, Jornada 2).

322 "me asaltó el deseo" (Agustín Moreto, *Hasta el fin nadie es dichoso*, Jornada 1).

323 Calderón, *Las manos blancas no ofenden*, Jornada 1.

324 "el deseo injusto, que en el amor es delito" (Guillén de Castro, *El vicio en los
       extremos*, Jornada 3).

325 "pues en su modestia creo, que no cupiera deseo que a tal maldad le inclinase" (Lope
       de Vega, *Guardar y guardarse*, Acto 2).

326 Juan Bautista Diamante, *Santa Teresa de Jesús*, Jornada 1.

327 Juan Pérez de Montalbán, *Cumplir con su obligación*, Jornada 3.

328 On contemporaneous perceptions of Muslim culture as effete or feminized,
       especially in the context of Islamophilic King Enrique IV's "Arabized, effeminate"
       court, see Thomas Devaney, "Virtue, Virility, and History in Fifteenth-Century
       Castile," *Speculum* 88.3 (2013): 721–49.

329 The answer to this question may well depend on what kind of desires we are talking
       about in a given instance. Psychologists distinguish between *volitive* desires, which
       can be controlled, and *appetitive* desires, which cannot: "volitive desires … [are]
       wants and wishes … and appetitive desires … [are] yearnings and cravings" (Utpal
       M. Dholakia, "Three Senses of Desire in Consumer Research," in *The Psychology
       of Desire*, ed. Hofmann and Nordgren, 407–31, at 409). A useful distinction here
       might be between the appetitive desire of being hungry in general versus the volitive
       desire of being hungry for chocolate cake.

330 Lope de Vega, *La ilustre fregona*, Jornada 1.

331 Irvine, *On Desire*, 186, quoting Bhikkhu Bodhi, *The Noble Eightfold Path: Way to
       the End of Suffering* (Seattle: BPS Pariyam, 2000), 33). The "Third Noble Truth" of
       Buddhism states that the secret to finding contentment is to eliminate all desire (Joel
       Marks, "Introduction: On the Need for Theory of Desire," in *The Ways of Desire*, ed.
       Marks, 1–16, at 6).

332 Oughourlian, *The Genesis of Desire*, 27.

333 "Symposia were not just the place for the satisfaction of every desire – for food,
       drink, sex, beautiful sights and sounds, and the cultural riches provided in the after-
       dinner entertainment – but also a place where the men and young boys who were
       traditionally present would learn how to regulate their desires in the appropriate
       manner. The heady mix of drink, beautiful young boys, flute girls and music was
       seen as a productive testing ground for the development of virtue, since it aroused

the very desires that could threaten the social order and provided an appropriate context for their regulation" (Frisbee C.C. Sheffield, *Plato's* Symposium*: The Ethics of Desire* [Oxford: Oxford University Press, 2006], 4–5).

334 Lope de Vega, *El caballero de Olmedo*, Acto 1.

335 Marks, "Introduction," 8.

336 Clark, *Desire*, 11.

337 Calderón, *De un castigo tres venganzas*, Jornada 2.

338 Lope de Vega, *El desprecio agradecido*, Jornada 2.

339 Lope de Vega, *Barlan y Josafa*, Acto 2.

340 Antonio de Solís, *El amor al uso*, Jornada 2.

341 This opinion is echoed in recent work done by psychologists: "[A]n approach that has proven effective is to undermine the hedonic simulations that motivate appetitive behavior, for example by mindfulness or reappraisal. Once a person recognizes the potential harm that these simulations can do in motivating unhealthy consumption, they can learn various strategies that make them less compelling. As a result, these simulations increasingly lose their control over behavior, such that they arise and dissipate with little effect" (Esther K. Papies and Lawrence W. Barsalou, "Grounding Desire and Motivated Behavior," in *The Psychology of Desire*, ed. Hofmann and Nordgren, 36–60, at 54).

342 "permitir no creo de dilación un punto a mi deseo" (Calderón, *El mágico prodigioso*, Jornada 3).

343 "fue alentar mi deseo, para que más presto vaya" (Calderón, *Mañanas de abril y mayo*, Acto 1).

344 "estímulo del deseo" (Juan Bautista Diamante, *Amor es sangre y no puede engañarse*, Jornada 1).

345 "Más con eso incitas mi deseo" (Juan Bautista Diamante, *Amor es sangre y no puede engañarse*, Jornada 3).

346 "logra tan dichoso empleo; encamina este deseo; resucita esta esperanza" (Guillén de Castro, *El perfecto caballero*, Acto 2).

347 "reprima la fuerza del deseo" (Lope de Vega, *No son todos ruiseñores*, Acto 1).

348 Juan Pérez de Montalbán, *La ganancia por la mano*, Jornada 3.

349 Irvine, *On Desire*, 19, 11.

350 Irvine, *On Desire*, 99.

351 "ajusto mis deseos al amor como al olvido" (Agustín Moreto, *La traición vengada*, Jornada 1).

352 "por corregir el deseo" (Antonio Solís, *El alcázar del secreto*, Jornada 1).

353 "Reñirle tan loco error y reducir su deseo" (Lope de Vega, *El marido más firme*, Acto 3).

354 Lope de Vega, *Los palacios de Galiana*, Acto 3. William Irvine advocates this approach: "satisfaction can best be gained not by working to satisfy the desires we find within us but by selectively suppressing or eradicating our desires" (Irvine, *On Desire*, 6).

355 Calderón, *Sueños hay que verdad son*, auto sacramental.

356 Juan Pérez de Montalbán, *A lo hecho no hay remedio, y príncipe de los montes*, Jornada 2.

357 Irvine, *On Desire*, 6.

358 "como se satisficiera deseo de un gusto lleno con otro manjar ajeno" (Calderón, *El hombre pobre todo es trazas*, Acto 1).

359 Calderón, *Guárdate de la agua mansa*, Jornada 3.

360 "un día que ha querido cazar con más diligencia el deseo, no ha topado caza ninguna, aunque sea penetrando las entrañas" (Calderón, *Eco y Narciso*, Jornada 1).

361 Pedro commands, "detén al deseo la rienda" (Tirso de Molina, *Don Gil de las calzas verdes*, Acto 1).

362 This capability is expressed in the negative: "suelto el freno de honor a mi deseo" (Francisco de Rojas Zorrilla, *Casarse por vengarse*, Jornada 3).

363 "no se le dé al deseo rienda, con que desbocado se precipite soberbio" (Francisco de Rojas Zorrilla, *Abrir el ojo*, Jornada 2).

364 "de este observado freno he roto los alacranes, por detener mi deseo" (Francisco de Rojas Zorrilla, *La traición busca el castigo*, Jornada 2). *Alacranes* in modern Spanish means scorpions; this likely refers to a part of the bit or muzzle of a horse that stings it around the mouth when the rider or driver pulls up sharply on the reins.

365 Lope de Vega, *El guante de Doña Blanca*, Acto 3.

366 "a vuestro cortés deseo licencia de hablar le doy" (Calderón, *Cómo se comunican dos estrellas contrarias*, Jornada 2).

367 "has de templar tu deseo" (Juan Pérez de Montalbán, *El valiente Nazareno*, Jornada 3).

368 Antonio Zamora, *Mazariegos y Monsalves*, Jornada 1.

369 "Así mi deseo allano" (Francisco de Rojas Zorrilla, *Progne y Filomena*, Jornada 2).

370 "en un Convento es notorio / que templara este deseo" (Francisco de Rojas Zorrilla, *Lo que son las mujeres*, Jornada 1).

371 "haz Cruces a tu deseo" (Juan Pérez de Montalbán, *El sufrimiento premiado*, Jornada 2). *Hacer cruces* means making the sign of the cross, a ritual used to ward off demonic attack. For a discussion of the extended use of demonic possession and exorcism metaphors in the context of desire and love madness, see Hilaire Kallendorf, "Love Madness and Demonic Possession in Lope de Vega," *Romance Quarterly* 51.3 (2004): 162–82.

372 Irvine, *On Desire*, 119.

373 Juan Ruiz de Alarcón, *Las paredes oyen*, Acto 1.

374 As with Pigmaleón's plea, "Dad lugar breve rato a mi deseo" (Calderón, *La fiera, el rayo y la piedra*, Jornada 2).

375 Agustín Moreto, *Antioco y Seleuco*, Jornada 3.

376 Antonio Zamora, *Siempre hay que envidiar, amando*, Jornada 2. Anjan Chatterjee describes the relationship between desire and action: "Desire drives us to act. The chemical currency for desire is dopamine. The brainstem sends dopamine to parts of the striatum to motivate us to act on our desires" (Chatterjee, *The Aesthetic Brain*, 110).

377 Calderón, *Los dos amantes del cielo*, Jornada 3.

378 Antonio Zamora, *El hechizado por fuerza*, Jornada 2.

379 Antonio Solís, *La gitanilla de Madrid*, Jornada 1.

380 Juan Bautista Diamante, *Amor es sangre y no puede engañarse*, Jornada 3. As Eugene Goodheart theorizes, "Desire is an emotional shuttle which depends upon a conflict of emotion" (Goodheart, *Desire and Its Discontents*, 5).

381 "sufrir me deje entre enemigas violencias, de deseo, y de cuidado, entre esperanzas, y penas" (Juan Bautista Diamante, *Triunfo de la paz y el tiempo*, Acto 1).

382 Dollimore, *Death, Desire and Loss*, xx.

383 Irvine, *On Desire*, 100.

384 "dará mi albedrío licencias a mi deseo" (Calderón, *La niña de Gómez Arias*, Jornada 3).

385 "indigno cautiverio, que rendirle su albedrío ¿[a] quién no manda su deseo?" (Agustín Moreto, *El desdén con el desdén*, Jornada 1).

386 Calderón, *Darlo todo y no dar nada*, Jornada 3.

387 Calderón, *El pastor fido*, auto sacramental.

388 "¿De manera que el deseo de gozarme os hizo fuerza, y no el merecerlo yo?" (Juan Ruiz de Alarcón, *El desdichado en el fingir*, Acto 1).

389 "Yo esforzaré mi deseo a quererle cuanto pueda" (Francisco de Rojas Zorrilla, *Donde hay agravios no hay celos*, Jornada 1).

390 "ese deseo te incita" (Lope de Vega, *El saber puede dañar*, Acto 3).

391 "nunca su deseo, siguiendo sus apetitos, deje de instarle" (Calderón, *La nave del mercader*, auto sacramental).

392 The allegorical figure of Deseo says of Hombre: "yo, que su deseo soy, a ir por aquí le inclino" (Calderón, *La nave del mercader*, auto sacramental).

393 Calderón, *La nave del mercader*, auto sacramental.

394 I have treated the topic of free will in the dramas separately in my essay "Free Will a Fortress: The Self in Spanish Renaissance Drama," in *The Self in Premodern European Thought*, ed. José Luis Bermúdez and Catherine Conybeare (Cambridge University Press, forthcoming). A previous essay of mine that treats the topic of free will within different generic parameters – namely Cervantes's prose – is Hilaire Kallendorf, "Lycanthropy and Free Will: The Female Werewolf in Cervantes' *Persiles*," *eHumanista: Journal of Medieval and Early Modern Iberian Studies* 42 (2019): 1–19.

395 "Maldito sea el deseo, que me obligó para intentar el daño" (Lope de Vega, *Los peligros de la ausencia*, Acto 3).

396 "tiene prendas Carlos para ponerle deseo, como con Fénix las tuvo para abrasarte de celos" (Lope de Vega, *Servir a buenos*, Acto 3). On costumes for Lust and the other Seven Deadly Sins, see Hilaire Kallendorf, "Dressed to the Sevens, or Sin in Style: Fashion Statements by the Deadly Vices in Spanish Baroque *Autos Sacramentales*," in *The Seven Deadly Sins: From Communities to Individuals*, ed. Richard Newhauser (Leiden: E.J. Brill, 2007), 145–82.

397 "Es retórico rodeo, para que con mayor deseo me escuches" (Lope de Vega, *Si no vieran las mujeres*, Jornada 2).

398 Agustín Moreto, *Los más dichosos hermanos*, Acto 2.

399 Francisco de Rojas Zorrilla, *Lo que son mujeres*, Jornada 2.

400 "Cada paso que el deseo da, se retira otro paso el temor" (Calderón, *Ni Amor se libra de Amor*, Jornada 3).

401 "amor se puede enseñar pero puédese guiar de la esperanza el deseo" (Lope de Vega, *El laberinto de Creta*, Acto 3).

402 "deseo, que logró tus esperanzas" (Calderón, *A tu prójimo como a ti*, auto sacramental).

403 "se adelanta mucho quien pone el deseo más allá de la esperanza" (Calderón, *Basta callar*, Jornada 1).

404 "tengo vivo el deseo en una muerta esperanza" (Agustín Moreto, *El Cristo de los milagros*, Jornada 3).

405 *Oxford English Dictionary*, https://www.oed.com/.

406 "Vivir sin deseo, Alfeo, no puede ser, mas se pide en el deseo templanza" (Juan Bautista Diamante, *Alfeo y Aretusa*, Jornada 1).

407 The four Cardinal Virtues are Justice, Fortitude, Prudence, and Temperance. I explained their name in an earlier book: "St Thomas Aquinas … [was] the main Christian thinker who called the Virtues 'Cardinal' because they were the hinges of a moral life" (Hilaire Kallendorf, *Ambiguous Antidotes: Virtue as Vaccine for Vice in Early Modern Spain* [Toronto: University of Toronto Press, 2017], 178).

4. The Problem of Hate

1 Robert Burton, "Of the Moouing Faculty," in *Anatomy of Melancholy* (London: 1621), 38.

2 Milan Kundera, *Immortality* (New York: Grove Weidenfeld, 1990), 24.

3 Donald L. Carveth, "Psychoanalytic Conceptions of the Passions," in *Freud and the Passions*, ed. John O'Neill (University Park: Pennsylvania State University Press, 1996), 25–51, at 36.

4 "de este hombre el odio fiero" (Lope de Vega, *La prisión sin culpa*, Acto 2); "el odio cruel" (Tirso de Molina, *El castigo del penséque*, Acto 2); "hoy con odio tan profundo me arrojas de ti" (Lope de Vega, *La Santa Liga*, Acto 1).

5 "obstinado mi aborrecimiento" (Antonio Zamora, *El lucero de Madrid, y divino Labrador san Isidro*, Acto 1); "tras el odio pertinaz" (Lope de Vega, *Carlos quinto en Francia*, Acto 1); "ese necio rencor, que ha vinculado por mayorazgo suyo el odio porfiado, de quien huyo" (Francisco de Rojas Zorrilla, *El más impropio verdugo por la más justa venganza*, Jornada 2).

6 Juan de la Cueva, *Tragedia del príncipe tirano*, Acto 1.

7 "En faltando el honor hay odio eterno" (Lope de Vega, *El príncipe perfecto*, Acto 3).

8 Daniel Lord Smail, "Hatred as a Social Institution in Late-Medieval Society," *Speculum* 76 (2001): 90–126, at 94.

9 Calderón, *Psiquis y Cupido*, auto sacramental.

10 "hay razón que a odio le iguale, y nadie más triste es" (Calderón, *Auristela y Lisidante*, Jornada 2); "dulcemente suena a mi odio, porque triste suena, la voz de tanta militar Sirena" (Calderón, *La exaltación de la cruz*, Jornada 2).

11 Calderón, *El pintor de su deshonra*, auto sacramental.

12 Smail, "Hatred as a Social Institution," 108–9.

13 "Juan Carvajal tiene a mi hermana afición, y contra el odio mortal que sustenta mi opinión / casarse en secreto intenta" (Tirso de Molina, *La prudencia en la mujer*, Jornada 1).

14 Calderón, *Fineza contra fineza*, Acto 1.

15 Juan de Matos Fragoso, *El traidor contra su sangre*, Acto 1.

16 Calderón, *Psiquis y Cupido*, auto sacramental.

17 Calderón, *El lirio y la azucena*, auto sacramental.

18 Tirso de Molina, *La mejor espigadera*, Jornada 3.

19 Lope de Vega, *El mayordomo de la duquesa de Amalfi*, Acto 1.

20 Agustín Moreto, *El licenciado Vidriera*, Jornada 1.

21 "el odio es tan rudo, que nunca entiende por señas" (Francisco de Rojas Zorrilla, *Nuestra Señora de Atocha*, Jornada 2).

22 "póneme una cara, en que el odio me declara, que concibe contra mí" (Lope de Vega, *La batalla del honor*, Acto 2).

23 "Si me aborrecieres tanto, que llores de odio, o de espanto" (Francisco de Rojas Zorrilla, *Los trabajos de Tobías*, Jornada 2).

24 Lope de Vega, *El hombre de bien*, Acto 3.

25 Antonio de Solís, *Las amazonas*, Jornada 1.

26 Calderón, *Psiquis y Cupido*, auto sacramental.

27 Juan Bautista Diamante, *Santa Juliana*, Jornada 1.

28 Lope de Vega, *El Nuevo Mundo, descubierto por Cristóbal Colón*, Acto 3.

29 Juan de la Cueva, *La libertad de Roma por Mucio Cevola*, Acto 3.

30 "llegó a mi pasado odio la ocasión de su venganza" (Calderón, *Mujer, llora, y vencerás*, Jornada 3).

31 "Pues ¿qué delito mayor, si hay odio entre dos hermanos que atropella cualquier ley?" (Agustín Moreto, *El valiente justiciero*, Jornada 3).

32 Juan Pérez de Montalbán, *Despreciar lo que se quiere*, Jornada 1.

33 Lope de Vega, *Castelvines y Monteses*, Jornada 1.

34 Calderón, *Psiquis y Cupido*, auto sacramental.

35 "teme un odio mortal, porque todos quieren mal a quien sus delitos sabe" (Juan Ruiz de Alarcón, *Los favores del mundo*, Acto 3).

36 Juan Ruiz de Alarcón, *Examen de maridos*, Acto 3.

37 Juan Ruiz de Alarcón, *Mudarse por mejorarse*, Acto 3.

38 Smail, "Hatred as a Social Institution," 95.

39 Smail, "Hatred as a Social Institution," 123.

40 Tirso de Molina, *La dama del olivar*, Acto 2.

41 Juan de la Cueva, *La libertad de España por Bernardo del Carpio*, Acto 4.

42 Juan de Matos Fragoso, *El traidor contra su sangre*, Jornada 2.

43 Tirso de Molina, *La venganza de Tamar*, Jornada 3.

44 Tirso de Molina, *La venganza de Tamar*, Jornada 2.

45 Tirso de Molina, *Esto sí que es negociar*, Jornada 2.

46 "Confesó, que había mentido, por tener al Cardenal envidia, y odio mortal, y de su error convencido. Fue en público castigado" (Lope de Vega, *El cardenal de Belén*, Acto 3).

47 Antonio Zamora, *Mazariegos y Monsalves*, Jornada 1.

48 Juan de la Cueva, *La constancia de Arcelina*, Acto 3.

49 Francisco de Rojas Zorrilla, *Progne y Filomena*, Jornada 1.

50 Francisco de Rojas Zorrilla, *Persiles y Sigismunda*, Jornada 3. Aristotle differentiates hatred from anger by saying that anger is an emotion felt only towards individuals, while hatred is felt toward groups or classes of people (Aristotle, *Rhetoric* 2.4, 1892a1–14, in *The Rhetoric and the Poetics of Aristotle*, trans. W.R. Roberts [New York: Modern Library, 1954]; discussed in David Konstan, "Hatred," in *The Emotions of the Ancient Greeks: Studies in Aristotle and Classical Literature* [Toronto: University of Toronto Press, 2006], 185–200, at 185–6). In medieval culture, this distinction had morphed a bit; Daniel Smail differentiates the two related emotions thus: "'Hatred' … was a conventional term of medieval secular jurisprudence used to describe an enduring public relationship between two adversaries. 'Anger,' in contrast, was generally used to describe a short-term and hence repairable rage, something that could break out between members of a kin group, real or fictive, who normally love each other – brothers and sisters, parents and children, lords and vassals, or God and his people. In moral literature, hatred was typically paired with love, whereas anger was paired with patience" (Smail, "Hatred as a Social Institution," 90–1).

51 Calderón, *La vida es sueño*, auto sacramental.

52 Tirso de Molina, *La venganza de Tamar*, Jornada 3.

53 Francisco de Rojas Zorrilla, *El profeta falso Mahoma*, Jornada 2.

54 Juan Bautista Diamante, *Amor es sangre y no puede engañarse*, Jornada 1.

55 G.H. Katzman, "Neurobiological and Psychological Mechanisms Explaining How Hatred Is Programmed into the Minds of Children," *Open Pediatric Medicine Journal* 3 (2009): 58–60.

56 Tirso de Molina, *La prudencia en la mujer*, Jornada 1.

57 Calderón, *Fineza contra fineza*, Jornada 2.

58 Tirso de Molina, *El castigo del penséque*, Acto 3.

59 "tanto puede el odio cuando inclina la enemistad si a descendientes pasa" (Tirso de Molina, *Ventura te dé Dios, hijo*, Jornada 1).

60 "el odio de nuestros nobles linajes, sin razón de parte vuestra" (Juan Bautista Diamante, *Santa María Magdalena de Pazzi*, Jornada 1).

61 Juan Bautista Diamante, *Santa María Magdalena de Pazzi*, Jornada 1.

62 Calderón, *El Faetonte*, Acto 1.

63 "nació / obligado a aborrecerme por odio de su linaje" (Lope de Vega, *Los enemigos en casa*, Acto 1). This characterization contrasts somewhat with the medieval French one described by Daniel Smail; in the archival documents he examines, "hatred was considered a formal right to which a victim's kinfolk were naturally entitled and which, like any right, they could cede or remit at will" (Smail, "Hatred as a Social Institution," 100).

64 Konstan, "Hatred," 194.

65 Lope de Vega, *Los enemigos en casa*, Acto 1.

66 Lope de Vega, *Don Lope de Cardona*, Acto 1.

67 Lope de Vega, *Castelvines y Monteses*, Jornada 1.

68 Smail, "Hatred as a Social Institution," 91, 94, citing Albertanus of Brescia, *Liber consolationis et consilii*, ed. Thor Sundby (London, 1873), 102–20.

69 Agustín Moreto, *Hasta el fin nadie es dichoso*, Jornada 1.

70 Karl Figlio, "The Dread of Sameness: Social Hatred and Freud's 'Narcissism of Minor Differences,'" in *Psychoanalysis and Politics: Exclusion and the Politics of Representation*, ed. Lene Auested (London: Karnac, 2012), 7–24, at 13–14.

71 Calderón, *El rey don Pedro en Madrid*, Jornada 3.

72 Calderón, *Sueños hay, que verdad son*, auto sacramental.

73 Calderón, *Afectos de odio y amor*, Acto 1.

74 Lope de Vega, *El más galán portugués Duque de Braganza*, Acto 3.

75 Juan de Matos Fragoso, *El genízaro de Ungría*, Jornada 2.

76 Lope de Vega, *Los españoles en Flandes*, Acto 3.

77 Howard Thurman, *Jesus and the Disinherited* (Boston: Beacon 1996), 74.

78 Patricia T. Clough, "The Affective Turn: Political Economy, Biomedia, and Bodies," in *The Affect Theory Reader*, ed. Melissa Gregg and Gregory J. Seigworth (Durham: Duke University Press, 2010), 206–25, at 223, citing Sara Ahmed, "Affective Economies," *Social Text* 79 (2004): 117–39. See also Sally Frances Reid and Russell G. Smith, "Regulating Racial Hatred," *Trends & Issues in Crime and Criminal Justice* (Australian Institute of Criminology) (February 1998): 1–6.

79 Calderón, *Sueños hay que verdad son*, auto sacramental. On the irony of Jews, who have often been the target of racial hatred, being the haters in turn of other ethnic groups, see Ami Pedahzur and Yael Yishai, "Hatred by Hated People: Xenophobia in Israel," *Studies in Conflict & Terrorism* 22 (1999): 101–17. Gypsies are still the victims of hate crimes throughout Europe. For a representative example of a hate crime against Gypsies in England in 2003 see George Monbiot, "Acceptable Hatred," *The Guardian* (4 November 2003).

80 Lope de Vega, *Roma abrasada*, Acto 3.

81 Figlio, "The Dread of Sameness," 19.

82 Lope de Vega, *La serrana de la vera*, Acto 3.

83 Francisco de Rojas Zorrilla, *Sin honra no hay amistad*, Jornada 1.

84 Lope de Vega, *Los locos de Valencia*, Acto 1.

85 Francisco de Rojas Zorrilla, *Lo que son mujeres*, Jornada 3.

86 Lope de Vega, *Los tres diamantes*, Jornada 1.

87 Agustín Moreto, *El poder de la amistad*, Jornada 3.

88 Lope de Rueda, *Eufemia*, Escena 5.

89 Juan Luis Vives, *The Passions of the Soul: The Third Book of* De Anima et Vita, trans. Carlos G. Noreña (Lewiston: Mellen, 1990), 7.

90 Class struggle remains a source of intergroup social hatred today, as we see in Gerry Mooney, "The 'Broken Society' Election: Class Hatred and the Politics of Poverty and Place in Glasgow East," *Social Policy and Society* 8.4 (2009): 427–50.

91 Lope de Vega, *Los Benavides*, Jornada 3.

92 Lope de Vega, *La carbonera*, Jornada 1.

93 The mixed feelings of Hungarian early modern subjects toward their ruler, the Emperor Sigismund, in the fifteenth century is the topic of Katalin Szende, "Between Hatred and Affection: Towns and Sigismund in Hungary and in the Empire," in *Sigismund von Luxembourg. Ein Kaiser in Europa* (Tagungsband des internationalen historischen und kunsthistorischen Kongresses in Luxemburg 8.-10. Juni 2005) (Mainz am Rhein: Verlag Philipp von Zabern, 2006), 199–210.

94 Lope de Vega, *El gran duque de Moscovia, y emperador perseguido*, Acto 3.

95 Calderón, *Fieras afemina amor*, Jornada 1.

96 Two examples are "desdeñado / él de ella y en eterno odio, y despecho / vive" (Juan de la Cueva, *La constancia de Arcelina*, Acto 2); and "La pena, el odio, el áspero desvío, / con que soy de Eliodora desdeñado" (Juan de la Cueva, *El infamador*, Acto 2).

97 Juan Bautista Diamante, *Pasión vencida de afecto*, Jornada 1.

98 "cuán mal defendido está hoy de la razón del odio, el afecto paternal" (Juan Bautista Diamante, *Pasión vencida de afecto*, Jornada 3).

99 Lope de Vega, *El valor de las mujeres*, Acto 1.

100 Venganza, aborrecimiento,
son de primero lugar,
que bastan a derribar,
el más seguro contento.   (Lope de Vega, *La serrana de la vera*, Acto 2)

101 Mari J. Matsuda, "Public Response to Racist Speech: Considering the Victim's Story," in *Words That Wound: Critical Race Theory, Assaultive Speech and the First Amendment*, ed. Mari Matsuda et al. (Boulder: Westview, 1993), 17–52, at 24.

102 "hijo de Cosdroas nací en tan enemigo instante, que su odio, y mi desdicha nacieron de un parto iguales" (Calderón, *La exaltación de la cruz*, Jornada 3).

103 "más crédito consigue / que amor, aborrecimiento" (Juan Bautista Diamante, *Amor es sangre, y no puede engañarse*, Jornada 2).

104 "es tan difícil amar / sobre un aborrecimiento" (Francisco de Rojas Zorrilla, *Los bandos de Verona*, Jornada 1).

105 Calderón, *La señora y la criada*, Jornada 1.

106 Agustín Moreto, *Hasta el fin nadie es dichoso*, Jornada 1.

107 Lope de Vega, *La historia de Tobías*, Acto 1.

108 Calderón, *Los tres mayores prodigios*, Jornada 1.

109 Some exploration of the synergy between these two emotions is offered in Paul Ian Steinberg and John S. Ogrodniczuk, "Hatred and Fear: Projective Identification in Group Psychotherapy," *Psychodynamic Practice* 16.2 (2010): 201–5.

110 Vives, *The Passions of the Soul*, 75, 77.

111 Calderón, *El indulto general*, auto sacramental.

112 Calderón, *Las tres justicias en una*, Jornada 1.

113 Calderón, *Fineza contra fineza*, Acto 1.

114 Lope de Vega, *La Reina Juana de Nápoles*, Acto 2.

115 Calderón, *Auristela y Lisidante*, Jornada 3.

116 "Foreo, nuestro padre, desamparada ya nuestra inocencia, nos trató el odio de su mismo yerro" (Antonio Zamora, *Áspides hay basiliscos*, Jornada 1).

117 Izzeldin Abuelaish and Neil Arya, "Hatred – A Public Health Issue," *Medicine, Conflict and Survival* (2017), DOI: 10.1080/13623699.2017.1326215.

118 Antonio de Solís, *Las amazonas*, Jornada 2.

119 Lope de Vega, *La nueva victoria del Marqués de Santa Cruz*, Jornada 1.

120 Lope de Vega, *Por la puente Juana*, Acto 1.

121 Lope de Vega, *Los palacios de Galiana*, Acto 3.

122 Calderón, *En esta vida todo es verdad y todo mentira*, Jornada 2.

123 "Disimularme conviene el odio que la ha cobrado por si el padre está avisado" (Lope de Vega, *El postrer godo de España*, Acto 2).

124 "Pero si olvida el odio, y el disgusto que tiene con Galafre el de Toledo" (Lope de Vega, *Los palacios de Galiana*, Acto 1).

125 Juan de la Cueva, *La muerte de Ajax Telamón, sobre las armas de Aquiles*, Acto 3.

126 Juan de la Cueva, *Tragedia de la muerte de Virginia y Appio Claudio*, Acto 1.

127 Juan Bautista Diamante, *El jubileo de la Porciúncula*, Jornada 1.

128 Aurel Kolnai, *On Disgust* (Chicago: Open Court, 2004), 106. This view of emotions as "commitment devices" is echoed in Robert Frank, *Passions within Reason: The Strategic Role of the Emotions* (New York: W.W. Norton, 1988).

129 Juan Bautista Diamante, *Amor es sangre y no puede engañarse*, Jornada 1.

130 Lope de Vega, *Santiago el verde*, preliminares.

131 Lope de Vega, *El mayordomo de la Duquesa de Amalfi*, Jornada 3.

132 "Aplaca el odio del Rey, que no se aplacó jamás" (Juan de la Cueva, *La libertad de España por Bernardo del Carpio*, Acto 3).

133 Lope de Vega, *Carlos quinto en Francia*, Acto 1.

134 COUNT PARIS: Templado está ya mi odio.

 ALEJANDRO ROMEO: No llega tu enmienda a tiempo.

                 (Francisco de Rojas Zorrilla, *Los bandos de Verona*, Jornada 3)

135 "Apagar hizo aquel odio, que ardiendo en nobles centellas tuvo" (Francisco de Rojas Zorrilla, *Los bandos de Verona*, Jornada 1).

136 Smail 99, citing Archives Départementales des Bouches-du-Rhône 381E 86, fol. 36v, 29 May 1354.

137 Lope de Vega, *Carlos quinto en Francia*, Acto 3.

138 Lope de Vega, *Los enemigos en casa*, Acto 1.

139 Juan Bautista Diamante, *Pasión vencida de afecto*, Jornada 1.

140 Juan de Matos Fragoso, *El traidor contra su sangre*, Acto 1.

141 Tirso de Molina, *Privar contra su gusto*, Acto 1.

142 Antonio de Solís, *La gitanilla de Madrid*, Jornada 1.

143 Tirso de Molina, *El árbol del mejor fruto*, Acto 2.

144 "a Céspedes aborrezco, de suerte, que sobran causas para el odio que le tengo" (Juan Bautista Diamanate, *El Hércules de Ocaña*, Jornada 3).

145 "el motivo que a ellos les da el odio natural de este aborrecido pueblo" (Juan Bautista Diamante, *Cumplirle a Dios la palabra*, Jornada 1).

146 "bastante sea el del odio natural, que en nuestras naciones reina" (Juan Bautista Diamante, *El defensor de el Peñón*, Jornada 1).

147 Lope de Vega, *El capellán de la Virgen*, Acto 1.

148 Sophia Menache, "Love of God or Hatred of Your Enemy? The Emotional Voices of the Crusades," *Mirabilia* 10 (2010): 1–20, at 19.

149 Juan de la Cueva, *El infamador*, Acto 2.

150 Lope de Vega, *La fábula de Perseo*, Acto 1.

151 Juan de la Cueva, *La constancia de Arcelina*, Acto 1.

152 Juan de la Cueva, *El infamador*, Acto 3.

153 Lope de Vega, *Los enemigos en casa*, Acto 1.

154 Lope de Vega, *La firmeza en la desdicha*, Acto 2.

155 Paul Vitz and Philip Mango, "Kleinian Psychodynamics and Religious Aspects of Hatred as a Defense Mechanism," *Journal of Psychology and Theology* 25.1 (1997): 64–71, at 68. Later in the same article they nuance their position a bit: "Obviously, the patient does not have the freedom to stop hating in the sense of easily or suddenly abandoning pathological structures built up over many years. But, as stated, patients do have the freedom to begin to stop hating" (68).

156 Catullus, *Odi et amo: The Complete Poetry of Catullus*, trans. Roy Arthur Swanson (Stuttgart: Macmillan, 1959). The line "Odi et amo" appears in Poem 85, addressed to Lesbia.

157 Nathaniel Hawthorne, *The Scarlet Letter* (New York: Barnes & Noble, 2003), 244.

158 Sara Ahmed, "The Organisation of Hate," *Law and Critique* 12 (2001): 345–65, at 351–2.

159 C. Fred Alford, "Hatred Is the Imitation of Love," in *The Psychology of Hate*, ed. J. Sternberg (Washington, DC: American Psychological Association, 2005), 235–54, at 239. He continues: "Hatred has many qualities analogous to love; it establishes a connection between the hater and his or her world, giving meaning and purpose to life, and so providing an experience of transport and transcendence in being lifted up by hate to a higher and purer realm" (241).

160　H. Guntrip, "Early Perceptions of the Schizoid Problem," *in Personal Relations Therapy: The Collected Papers of HJS Guntrip* (New York: Jason Aronson, 1994), 39–62, at 45.

5. Loneliness for Two (a.k.a. Love)

1　Simone Weil, *Love in the Void: Where God Finds Us*, ed. Laurie Gagne (Walden, NY: Plough, 2018), 29.

2　Dante Alighieri, "Poem XX," in *The New Life (La Vita Nuova)*, trans. Dante Gabriel Rossetti, Project Gutenberg, www.gutenberg.org.

3　Peter Gay, *The Cultivation of Hatred* (New York: W.W. Norton, 1993), 198. This quotation by Gay echoes an earlier one by William James: "The closest human love incloses a potential germ of … hatred" (William James, in James Jacques Barzun, *A Stroll with William James* [Chicago: University of Chicago Press, 1983], 25).

4　Sigmund Freud, quoted in Brian Magee, *The Philosophy of Schopenhauer* (Oxford: Clarendon, 1983), 217.

5　Ulrich Beck and Elisabeth Beck-Gernsheim, *The Normal Chaos of Love* (Cambridge: Polity, 1995), 190.

6　Calderón, *El indulto general*, loa for auto sacramental.

7　Juan Luis Vives, *The Passions of the Soul: The Third Book of* De Anima et Vita, trans. Carlos G. Noreña (Lewiston: Mellen, 1990), 24.

8　Francisco de Rojas Zorrilla, *Los áspides de Cleopatra*, Jornada 1.

9　Francisco de Rojas Zorrilla, *Los áspides de Cleopatra*, Jornada 1.

10　Calderón, *El gran teatro del mundo*, loa for auto sacramental.

11　Lope de Vega, *El galán de la Membrilla*, Acto 1.

12　Lope de Vega, *Los embustes de Zelauro*, Acto 1.

13　Agustín Moreto, *No puede ser*, Jornada 1.

14　Juan Pérez de Montalbán, *Amor, lealtad y amistad*, Jornada 1.

15　Lope de Vega, *El mejor alcalde, el rey*, Acto 2.

16　Lope de Vega, *El mejor alcalde, el rey*, Acto 2.

17　Juan de Matos Fragoso, *La tía de la menor*, Jornada 2.

18　Calderón, *El postrer duelo de España*, Jornada 1.

19　Calderón, *El año santo en Madrid*, auto sacramental.

20　Lope de Vega, *El desconfiado*, Acto 3.

21　Jean-Michel Oughourlian declares starkly, "the mechanisms that feed either love or violence are really the same" (Jean-Michel Oughourlian, *The Genesis of Desire*, trans. Eugene Webb [East Lansing: Michigan State University Press, 2010], 39).

22　Calderón, *Eco y Narciso*, Jornada 2. Elaine Hatfield and Richard Rapson quote Peter Ustinov as privileging this means of expressing love in his maxim, "Love is … a tender look which becomes a habit" (Elaine Hatfield and Richard Rapson, *Love, Sex, and Intimacy: Their Psychology, Biology, and History* [New York: HarperCollins, 1993], 109).

23　Calderón, *Amor, honor y poder*, Acto 1.

24 Agustín Moreto, *El desdén con el desdén*, Jornada 1. Elaine Hatfield and Richard
    Rapson note, "French psychophysiologist Susana Bloch and her colleagues …
    argued that not just joy but also passionate love ('eroticism') and companionate
    love ('tenderness') are associated with different breathing patterns and sounds.
    Mothers often coo or croon softly with their mouths held near the infant's head.
    They speculated that such tender maternal sounds become the forerunners of the
    breathing patterns and sounds associated with love" (Hatfield and Rapson, *Love, Sex,
    and Intimacy*, 109).

25 Francis Weller explains how physical affection releases the so-called love hormone,
    oxytocin: "the hormone oxytocin, often called the 'love hormone,' is released
    when we are touched and held or when we engage with someone who cares"
    (Francis Weller, *The Wild Edge of Sorrow: Rituals of Renewal and the Sacred Work of
    Grief* [Berkeley: North Atlantic, 2015], 14). Elaine Hatfield and Richard Rapson
    speculate regarding the psychic origins of physical intimacy in romantic attachment:
    "After birth, mothers instinctively try to re-create the security of the womb. Mothers
    kiss, caress, fondle, and embrace their infants; they cradle them in their arms. In the
    womb, neonates hear the steady drumbeat of the mothers' heart – beating
    at 72 beats per minute. After birth, mothers instinctively hold their babies with
    their heads pressed against their left breasts, closest to the maternal heart …
    [I]n adulthood, these same kisses, tender caresses, and embraces continue to provide
    security for men and women – unconscious of their early origins" (Hatfield and
    Rapson, *Love, Sex, and Intimacy*, 110–11).

26 "en el éxtasis de amor iba repitiendo abrazos" (Francisco de Rojas Zorrilla, *Casarse
    por vengarse*, Jornada 2).

27 "al vernos abrazar al despedirnos, con tal cariño" (Calderón, *Hado y divisa de
    Leonido, y de Marfisa*, Jornada 3).

28 Calderón, *A secreto agravio, secreta venganza*, Jornada 2.

29 Juan Pérez de Montalbán, *El divino portugués San Antonio de Padua*, Jornada 2.

30 Juan Bautista Diamante, *Amor es sangre, y no puede engañarse*, Jornada 2.

31 Calderón, *Las tres justicias en una*, Jornada 1.

32 Calderón, *Fieras afemina amor*, Jornada 1. Peter Gay writes regarding love toward
    parents, "There are those who never undergo the great experience of loving anyone
    other than mother or father; in the nineteenth century, this was the fate of some
    notable men and women, a fate often masquerading as filial duty" (Peter Gay, *The
    Tender Passion* [New York: Oxford University Press, 1986], 21). Alan Eppel reports
    that "[i]n the psychoanalytic view all love is transference love, an unconscious
    yearning for the first object of love, the mother" (Alan Eppel, *Sweet Sorrow: Love,
    Loss and Attachment in Human Life* [London: Karnac, 2009], 17).

33 Ulrich and Elisabeth Beck remark (in the context of the current breakdown of
    marriage as an institution) concerning filial love, "The child becomes the last
    remaining, irrevocable, unique primary love object" (Beck and Beck-Gernsheim,
    The Normal Chaos of Love, 37). More has been written about maternal than paternal

love, beginning with Aristotle: "Aristotle … identified maternal love as the paradigm of friendship: it was selfless, and this selflessness was grounded in a conscious and rational goodwill towards one's offspring. Aquinas highlighted these two features of selflessness and rationality in his commentary on the *Nicomachean Ethics*. He identified maternal love with benevolent love or friendship – *amicitia* or *amor benevolentiae* – characterised by goodwill towards another for his or her own sake. By contrast, concupiscence (*amor concupiscentiae*) used the object of one's affection: one wished someone well for the good – pleasure or usefulness – one hoped to gain for oneself by means of that person" (Raphaële Garrod, "Conceptual Eclecticism and Ethical Prescription in Early Modern Jesuit Discourses about Affects: Suárez and Caussin on Maternal Love," in *Ordering Emotions in Europe, 1100–1800*, ed. Susan Broomhall [Leiden: Brill, 2015], 180–96, at 184). Francesco Alberoni distinguishes the experience of mothers from the experience of fathers in this regard: "the birth of a child is always a true and proper experience of falling in love for the mother. All her interests, all her cares, all her anxieties are focused on the child … The mother constantly falls in love with her child. And not only when he is young, but also when he is grown, when he is an adult. Every so often, she sees him, she looks at him with astonished, passionate eyes, recognizing the fact that he is with her … This is not a question of seeing in the adult the child who is no longer there. No, she sees the adult just as she used to see the child; she looks at him and falls in love with what he is today" (Francesco Alberoni, *Falling in Love*, trans. Lawrence Venuti [New York: Random House, 1983], 51, 141).

34 Calderón, *En esta vida todo es verdad, y todo mentira*, Acto 1.

35 Calderón, *El primer refugio del hombre, y probática piscina*, auto sacramental.

36 Calderón, *Las tres justicias en una*, Jornada 1.

37 "Con qué paternal cariño, con qué amor, con qué terneza" (Calderón, *El gran príncipe de Fez*, Jornada 3).

38 "Válgame Dios lo que obliga el puro amor paternal" (Juan de Matos Fragoso, *El hijo de la piedra*, Jornada 3).

39 Lope de Vega, *El castigo sin venganza*, Acto 1.

40 This connection of beards with honour may contain a trace of Spain's Jewish heritage. Cyrus Adler et al. write in this respect, "The modern Oriental cultivates his Beard as the sign and ornament of manhood: he swears by his Beard, touching it. The sentiment seems to have been the same in Biblical times. According to the Egyptian and Assyrian monuments, all western Semites wore a full, round Beard, evidencing great care … To mutilate the Beard of another by cutting or shaving is, consequently, considered a great disgrace" (Cyrus Adler et al., "Beard," in the Jewish Encyclopedia, http://www.jewishencyclopedia.com).

41 "Si mi madre apasionada, con amor, y sin cordura, me alabó sobradamente[,] el afecto da disculpa. ¿Cuándo el amor de los padres hizo fe?" (Calderón, *Fortunas de Andrómeda y Perseo*, Jornada 3).

42 Agustín Moreto, *La fuerza del natural*, Jornada 2.

43 Agustín Moreto, *El parecido*, Jornada 2.

44 Juan Pérez de Montalbán, *Como amante y como honrada*, Jornada 2.

45 "suele hacer el amor un segundo parentesco" (Calderón, *El alcalde de sí mismo*, Jornada 1).

46 "en dos que se crían juntos un linaje de cariño" (Agustín Moreto, *Antioco, y Seleuco*, Jornada 1).

47 Antonio Zamora, *Judas Iscariote*, Jornada 2.

48 Agustín Moreto, *El lindo Don Diego*, Jornada 1.

49 "el cariño que engendra la semejanza" (Calderón, *Hado y divisa de Leonido, y de Marfisa*, Jornada 2).

50 Agustín Moreto, *Primero es la honra*, Jornada 2.

51 Calderón, *De una causa dos efectos*, Jornada 1.

52 Calderón, *El segundo Scipión*, Jornada 1.

53 Juan de Matos Fragoso, *El traidor contra su sangre*, Jornada 3.

54 Juan Bautista Diamante, *Amor es sangre, y no puede engañarse*, Jornada 2.

55 Calderón, *Los misterios de la Misa*, loa for auto sacramental.

56 "Aquí la gozan, en donde con tal cariño la aplauden, que guía la devoción un bello rico Estandarte" (Agustín Moreto, *Nuestra Señora del Aurora*, Jornada 3).

57 Calderón, *Hado y divisa de Leonido, y de Marfisa*, Jornada 1.

58 Juan de Matos Fragoso, *Con amor no hay amistad*, Acto 1.

59 "el contrapesar mi amor el gusto a la conveniencia" (Calderón, *La púrpura de la rosa*, loa).

60 "no es fino amor, amor que se funda en conveniencias" (Francisco de Rojas Zorrilla, *Donde hay agravios no hay celos*, Jornada 2).

61 "lutos vestid de dolor, que una boda sin amor no es mal paño para lutos" (Juan Pérez de Montalbán, *Los amantes de Teruel*, Jornada 3).

62 Calderón, *El Rey Don Pedro en Madrid, e Infanzón de Illescas*, Jornada 1.

63 Calderón, *Las tres justicias en una*, Jornada 1.

64 Elaine Hatfield and Richard Rapson remind us that arranged marriage was the norm for many centuries in the West and still is the standard in many Eastern cultures: "Marriage-for-love represents an ultimate expression of individualism, a concept that in premodern religious, traditional, and authoritarian societies was considered … dangerously sinful and traitorous. Today, some nations (such as China, India and the Arab countries) still consider 'being in love' the worst possible reason for getting married. Individuals do not personally choose to marry other individuals; marriages are arranged by family members and go-betweens, the assumption being that the only sensible approach is for families to marry their offspring into other families" (Hatfield and Rapson, *Love, Sex, and Intimacy*, 2–3).

65 Peter Gay notes that arranged marriages lasted well into the nineteenth century, even among the bourgeoisie: "Parents' preoccupation with monetary security or social ascent could clash with their children's imperious desire for emotional fulfillment" (Gay, *The Tender Passion*, 98). But he notes that there was some stratification even within this social group: "the uppermost or most tradition-bound within the bourgeoisie – old

commercial clans, rich and anxious parvenus, patrician Catholics, orthodox Jews –
were more likely than their less proud or prosperous fellow-bourgeois to treat marriage
negotiations as affairs of state rather than as affairs of the heart" (100).

66 Juan Ruiz de Alarcón, *Examen de maridos*, Acto 3.

67 Juan Ruiz de Alarcón, *Examen de maridos*, Acto 3.

68 Juan Pérez de Montalbán, *Don Florisel de Niquea*, Jornada 3.

69 "es hábito de amor gozar más, quien vale menos" (Calderón, *Con quien vengo,
    vengo*, Jornada 1). William Jankowiak confirms this social-class aspect of love
    during the European Middle Ages: "Whatever meaning courtly love held for the
    individual, it also served to establish social boundaries between the cultural elite
    and the peasantry. Whereas the latter enjoyed the crudities of sexual bantering, the
    elite, especially its women, preferred to deemphasize the erotic in favor of romantic
    imagery. In this way the earthy language of eros … was replaced by the high-flown
    language of romance and gentility" (Jankowiak, "Introduction," 12).

70 Calderón, *A Dios por razón de estado*, auto sacramental.

71 "el contrato de amor ha de ser *in solidum*, y no *de mancomún*" (Agustín Moreto, *De
    fuera vendrá*, Jornada 2). The legal phrase *de mancomún* indicates that the contract
    has been approved by two or more individuals. The satirical topos of love as a
    contract is carried to greater lengths in the following passage:

> [E]s de mi dulce conquista,
> despacho donde el amor
> paga, como fiel deudor
> favores a letra vista;
> es una firme escritura,
> a donde la voluntad
> da fianzas de verdad,
> e hipoteca la hermosura;
> es receta que recibe
> el alma para sus males,
> con que da ciertas señales,
> de que cobra gusto, y vive;
> es libranza que aceptó
> el alma para pagar:
> pues en llegando a firmar
> lo que debe confirmó;
> es cédula, que aunque breve
> remata cuentas de amor
> entre el desdén, y el favor.
>
> (Juan Pérez de Montalbán, *La deshonra honrosa*, Jornada 1)

72 "en fe de la palabra de esposo, empeñé el cariño" (Calderón, *Cuál es mayor perfección*,
    Jornada 2).

73 Agustín Moreto, *El lindo Don Diego*, Jornada 3.

74 "hacen en los más honrados pechos al amor rendidos, aborrecibles maridos agravios tan declarados" (Guillén de Castro, *El perfecto caballero*, Acto 2).

75 Guillén de Castro, *El conde de Irlos*, Acto 1.

76 "[E]n políticas de amor, / suelen tener unos fueros / las Damas, que obligan más, / que el guardarlos, el romperlos" (Calderón, *Los empeños de un acaso*, Jornada 1).

77 Juan Bautista Diamanate, *Cuánto mienten los indicios, y el ganapán de desdichas*, Jornada 2.

78 *Pericones* could mean either hand-held fans (*abanicos*), which women used to wield coquettishly, or else a kind of traditional dance, sometimes performed by a man with a woman, popular in Argentina and Uruguay. If the latter, it is at least possible that a conversation or even an argument could resemble the back-and-forth movements of a pair of dancers. But interestingly, this particular kind of dance would often include a pause where the dancers would stop to exchange lines of rhymed dialogue on amorous or funny topics; these dialogues came to be known as *relaciones*. Given the dramatic context of the lines from the play, it seems appropriate to favour this meaning for the word.

79 "un hombre gentilhombre, / si está con una mujer, / su amor suele encarecer, / solo por parecer hombre, / porque el amor y afición / muestran que un hombre lo es" (Juan Pérez de Montalbán, *La ganancia por la mano*, Jornada 1).

80 "Es error pensar, que Amor, siendo ciego, guíe bien" (Calderón, *El año santo de Roma*, auto sacramental). Semir Zeki explains that neurologically speaking, love actually *is* blind: "one feature of mentalizing in terms of the 'theory of mind' is to distinguish between self and others, with the potential of ascribing different sets of beliefs and desires to others and to oneself. To obtain an imagined unity-in-love, so that the self and the other are merged, this process of mentalizing, and thus distinguishing between self and the other, must be rendered inactive or at any rate less potent. But such judgment is also often suspended with the trust that develops between individuals and certainly with the deep bonding that develops between a mother and her child. Here, then, is a neural basis … for saying that love is blind" (Semir Zeki, *Splendors and Miseries of the Brain: Love, Creativity, and the Quest for Human Happiness* [Chichester: Wiley-Blackwell, 2009], 141).

81 William Shakespeare, *A Midsummer Night's Dream*, in *The Complete Works of William Shakespeare* (New York: Gramercy, 1975), 153–74, I.1, p. 155.

82 "la venda de los ojos del amor" (Calderón, *Amar y ser amado, y divina Philotea*, auto sacramental).

83 "tus yerros doró amor" (Calderón, *Afectos de odio y amor*, Jornada 3); "los del amor son los más dorados yerros" (Calderón, *El Faetonte*, Acto 1).

84 "ando en las selvas de amor, a lo de escudero andante" (Calderón, *Peor está que estaba*, Jornada 3).

85 "Ya en el ciego laberinto te metió el amor cruel, ya no puedes salir de él" (Cervantes, *El laberinto de amor*, Jornada 1).

86 "Hay antojos del desdén, y hay antojos del amor; los de amor, hacen mayor el cuerpo de lo que ven" (Agustín Moreto, *El poder de la amistad*, Jornada 2).

87   Amor, que es pintor, conforma
        dos luces, que en mí tenéis,
        si hoy aquesta luz me veis,
        y por eso me estimáis,
        cuando a otra luz me veáis
        quizá me aborreceréis.   (Calderón, *La dama duende*, Jornada 3)

88 Juan Pérez de Montalbán, *Cumplir con su obligación*, Jornada 1.

89 Agustín Moreto, *El lego del Carmen*, Jornada 1.

90 "el veloz curso del amor suspenden" (Calderón, *El alcalde de sí mismo*, Jornada 3).

91 Juan Pérez de Montalbán, *La toquera vizcaína*, Jornada 3.

92 "Cielos, mucho me arrastra el cariño" (Agustín Moreto, *Industrias contra finezas*, Jornada 2).

93 "Un desordenado amor me lleva, arrastra, y destierra" (Calderón, *Afectos de odio y amor*, Jornada 2).

94 "es fuerza ya en este conocimiento tirar al amor la rienda" (Juan Bautista Diamante, *Santa Teresa de Jesús*, Jornada 2).

95 "amando / Desenfrenadamente, al fin terrible / los trujo Amor, a su muerte / despeñando" (Juan de la Cueva, *La constancia de Arcelina*, Acto 2).

96   [D]iérame el amor sus alas,
        volara abrasado, y ciego,
        pues quien al viento se entrega,
        alas de viento navega,
        y las de amor son de fuego.   (Calderón, *A secreto agravio, secreta venganza*, Acto 1)

97 Calderón, *Bien vengas mal*, Jornada 2.

98 "Ten[,] amor[,] el arco quedo" (Juan Pérez de Montalbán, *A lo hecho no hay remedio, y príncipe de los montes*, Jornada 2).

99   [E]l más pernicioso trasto,
        que vio amor en su armería,
        entre las flechas, y rayos
        de su munición.   (Calderón, *Afectos de odio y amor*, Jornada 2)

John Alan Lee explains that "[i]n ancient Greek mythology, the arrows of Eros are shot through the eyes of the lover" (John Alan Lee, "Love-Styles," in *The Psychology of Love*, ed. Robert J. Sternberg and Michael L. Barnes [New Haven: Yale University Press, 1988], 38–67, at 42).

100 "De amor tirano las flechas, hechas de desdén" (Juan de Matos Fragoso, *El yerro del entendido*, Jornada 2).

101 "En la fragua de Vulcano, fabrica el amor sus flechas al manso suave fuego de mil apacibles quejas" (Juan Bautista Diamante, *Triunfo de la paz y el tiempo*, Acto 1).

102		"No me mintió el harpón de fuego, que amor flechó en su retrato" (Calderón, *Los tres afectos de amor: piedad, desmayo y valor*, Jornada 1).

103		Such miniature wearable portraits and their use as props in early modern Spanish stage plays are described in Laura Bass, *The Drama of the Portrait: Theater and Visual Culture in Early Modern Spain* (University Park: Penn State University Press, 2008).

104		"me estáis cegando con flechas de amor que arrojan de vuestras cejas los arcos" (Francisco de Rojas Zorrilla, *No hay amigo para amigo*, Jornada 1).

105		For example, Sagittarius: "Noviembre a su Sagitario de amor le ha dado las flechas, hurtándolas a su aljaba" (Calderón, *Fieras afemina amor*, loa).

106		"con el acero de amor te dio en el alma la herida" (Francisco de Rojas Zorrilla, *No hay amigo para amigo*, Jornada 1).

107		"espadachines de amor, broqueleros de la muerte" (Luis Quiñones de Benavente, *Los cuatro galanes*, entremés). An *espadachín* was a man who was dexterous with a sword or *espada*. A *broquelero* was a person who fashioned shields for either defence or heraldic purposes. By extension, the word could refer to a fighter who often used a shield.

108		"Hiere amor el corazón con el dorado harpón" (Cervantes, *Pedro de Urdemalas*, Jornada 2); "Harpón de Amor, que disparó de su Aljaba" (Calderón, *El castillo de Lindabridis*, Jornada 3). An interesting variation on this image is "de mi amor hace fisga" (Juan de Matos Fragoso, *El amor hace valientes*, Jornada 3). A *fisga* was a three-pronged harpoon used to spear large fish.

109		[A]mor cruel
		cansado del arco y flecha,
		trocó al aljaba la red.							(Calderón, *Los lances de Amor y Fortuna*, Acto 1)

110		"Tiró al blanco el amor, mas erró el tiro" (Juan Pérez de Montalbán, *A lo hecho no hay remedio, y príncipe de los montes*, Jornada 3).

111		"tórtolas tiernas … símbolos de amor" (Calderón, *Fineza contra fineza*, Jornada 2).

112		"de amor llenos se arrullen como palomos, pues todos pájaros somos" (Juan de Matos Fragoso, *El hijo de la piedra*, Jornada 3).

113		"¡Ay triste olmo desasido del cariño de la vid!" (Francisco de Rojas Zorrilla, *Los trabajos de Tobías*, Jornada 2).

114		See, for example, Francisco de Quevedo, "*Farmaceutria* o medicamentos enamorados," in *Silvas*, trans. Hilaire Kallendorf (Lima: Universidad Nacional Mayor de San Marcos, 2011), 115–21, at 118. The relevant stanza reads:

> Mira la vid que a Baco soberano
> la boca regaló y honró las sienes,
> cómo sirve de grillos en el llano
> a los pies de los olmos que mantienes.
> ¡Ay, cómo los enlaza! ¡Ay, si hiciese
> Amor que ansí mi Aminta me ciñese!

Quevedo further employs the image of the widow turtle dove in his first *silva*, "Exequias a una tórtola que se quejaba viuda, y después se halló muerta" (89–90).

115 Calderón, *Amor, honor y poder*, Jornada 2.

116 "Girasol de vuestro amor, siguiendo las luces claras de tanto Sol" (Calderón, *De las tres justicias en una*, Jornada 2).

117 "¿cómo el amor de tu pecho no me atrae como imán?" (Guillén de Castro, *Progne y Filomena*, Acto 2).

118 "fue solo para probar los quilates del cariño" (Antonio Zamora, *Ser fino y no parecerlo*, Jornada 3); "he de ver patente los quilates de amor finos que publicáis" (Juan de Matos Fragoso, *La devoción del Ángel de la Guarda*, Jornada 2).

119   [M]i amor arrogante
   mármol, jaspe, oro, arrebol
   ha de ablandar al crisol
   cincel, buril, y diamante.   (Calderón, *Antes que todo es mi dama*, Jornada 2)

120 "el Amor todo es Fuego" (Calderón, *La cura y la enfermedad*, auto sacramental).

121 "el amor con llama de fuego ardiente, libres voluntades rinde" (Calderón, *Judas Macabeo*, Jornada 2).

122 "Amar, señora, es tener inflamado el corazón, con un deseo de ver a quien causa esta pasión" (Agustín Moreto, *El desdén con el desdén*, Jornada 2).

123 Juan Bautista Diamante, *El Hércules de Ocaña*, Jornada 2.

124 "mi amor en vivos carbones arde" (Juan Pérez de Montalbán, *Olimpa y Vireno*, Jornada 2).

125 Calderón, *El alcalde de Zalamea*, Jornada 2.

126 "aunque la sangre pudiera amor, cumpliendo el adagio, hacer que sin fuego hierva" (Calderón, *El Conde Lucanor*, Jornada 2).

127 "haciendo el amor ardiente a un cántaro de agua fría" (Calderón, *La crítica del amor*, Jornada 2).

128 "salamandra de mi amor, vengo a vivir en tu ardor" (Agustín Moreto, *La fuerza de la ley*, Jornada 2). The *salamandra* is a traditional wood-burning stove. It derives its name from the legend that salamanders could survive fire, which probably started because salamanders sometimes emerged from logs when they were thrown onto the fire.

129 "Morillo de la propia chimenea de la cocina de amor, donde las almas se tuestan" (Juan Bautista Diamante, *El defensor del peñón*, Jornada 1). Sociologist Theodore Kemper connects the "warm" feeling of love to actual physical warmth: "the physiological condition that allows for bodily warmth also matches the emotional disposition of warmth toward others" (Theodore D. Kemper, "Love and Like and Love and *Love*," in *The Sociology of Emotions: Original Essays and Research Papers*, ed. David D. Franks and E. Doyle McCarthy [Greenwich, CT: JAI, 1989], 249–70, at 265).

130 "¡qué ardiente el Rayo es de Amor!" (Calderón, *El castillo de Lindabridis*, Jornada 2); "es rayo amor, y abrasa cuanto toca" (Calderón, *La cisma de Inglaterra*, Jornada 2).

131 "en ira, y rabia envuelto, soy un ardiente Volcán; mi amor es el Fuego, y tu desprecio la
     Nieve" (Calderón, *El veneno y la triaca*, auto sacramental). This metaphor re-emerges in
     the nineteenth century in a florid statement by Richard Kräfft-Ebing: "love unbridled
     is a volcano that burns down and lays waste all around it" (Richard Kräfft-Ebing,
     Psychopathia Sexualis [1886], 12th ed. [New York: G.P. Putnam's Sons, 1965], 12).

132 "Etna, pues, de mi amor" (Calderón, *La banda y la flor*, Jornada 1).

133 "que en mí reviente no sé qué callada mina, que amor en el alma enciende" (Calderón,
     Guárdate de la agua mansa, Jornada 2); "la mina, que amor ingeniero, tiene abierta
     contra la plaza de mis vanas altivezes" (Calderón, *Apolo y Climene*, Jornada 2).

134 Calderón, *El astrólogo fingido*, Acto 1.

135 Calderón, *El monstruo de los jardines*, Jornada 2. Peter Gay comments on
     aggression as one of love's components: "In a situation in which customs and
     the laws made man the master, libidinal expressiveness was rarely untainted by
     aggression, exhibiting an urge to wound or control, dominate or destroy, or just
     to show one's strength, thus exorcising the fear of one's weakness" (Gay, *The
     Tender Passion*, 106).

136 "amor vendado, hijo de Marte, y Venus ha nacido" (Calderón, *Peor está que estaba*,
     Jornada 2).

137 "envainando en su amor mismo de entrambas garras los corvos alfanjes" (Juan Pérez
     de Montalbán, *Don Florisel de Niquea*, Jornada 1). An *alfanje* was a weapon like the
     sabre but shorter, wider, and with a more curved shape.

138 Calderón, *De una causa dos efectos*, Jornada 2.

139 Francisco de Rojas Zorrilla, *No hay amigo para amigo*, Jornada 1.

140 "amor le hirió para mí, con las saetas de plomo" (Cervantes, *El rufián dichoso*,
     Acto 1); "jamás halle en su aljaba flechas de plomo amor con que tirarme"
     (Cervantes, *Pedro de Urdemalas*, Jornada 1).

141 "en las entrañas lleva el hierro de amor agudo que hasta en el alma se ceba"
     (Cervantes, *Pedro de Urdemalas*, Jornada 2).

142 "hieres[,] amor[,] como azogue penetrante y bullicioso" (Cervantes, *El laberinto de
     amor*, Jornada 2).

143 Calderón, *Dicha y desdicha del nombre*, Jornada 2.

144 Juan Pérez de Montalbán, *La toquera vizcaína*, Jornada 1. Peter Gay notices the
     prevalence of this imagery still in the nineteenth century: "they treated love as …
     an infection, a contagion that the novelist can only record" (Gay, *The Tender
     Passion*, 169). Roy Baumeister and Sara Wotman note that empirically speaking,
     according to their scientific study, love seems to produce illness only if it is not
     reciprocal: "When love is successful and reciprocal, people appear to benefit from
     it. Participants in the study who enjoyed positive, reciprocal love relationships
     showed good general health (better than people who were not in love), elevated
     self-confidence, and less activity by natural killer (NK) cells in the immune system, a
     pattern that is apparently linked to good health. Indeed, people who enjoyed mutual
     and reciprocal love reported unusually long times since they had last had a sore

throat, a cold, or a hangover. Love, it appears, is good for you – if the love is mutual. Unrequited love, however, had effects that differed substantially from the effects of reciprocal love. The positive effects of love on health and the immune system were missing among people whose love was not mutual. Moreover, people experiencing unrequited love showed higher levels of depression and tension, and they were significantly more likely to report a recent hangover than other people. Thus, once again, love is only beneficial if it is mutual, and unrequited love seems to be linked to some pathological patterns that are not found with reciprocal love" (Roy F. Baumeister and Sara R. Wotman, *Breaking Hearts: The Two Sides of Unrequited Love* [New York: Guilford, 1992], 8–9).

145 "de noche, y de madrugada me embiste de amor la fiebre" (Cervantes, *La entretenida*, Jornada 2).

146 "cuartanas de amor al mayor león sujetan" (Juan Pérez de Montalbán, *La deshonra honrosa*, Jornada 1).

147 "llamó al amor Averroës Hernia, un humor, que hila las tripas" (Agustín Moreto, *El desdén con el desdén*, Jornada 1).

148 "Una comezón de amor, que me está despedazando" (Juan Bautista Diamante, *El negro más prodigioso*, Jornada 2).

149 "rasca, rasca la memoria; pero advierte, que es el amor una sarna, que porque la rasquen, pica; y duele cuando la rascan" (Juan Bautista Diamante, *El Hércules de Ocaña*, Jornada 2).

150 "bien dijo un discreto Cortesano, que era contagio el amor, pues en la acción más acaso su veneno comunica" (Calderón, *Antes que todo es mi dama*, Jornada 1).

151 Juan Pérez de Montalbán, *Amor, lealtad y amistad*, Jornada 1.

152 Juan de Matos Fragoso, *Los indicios sin culpa*, Jornada 3.

153   DANTEA: ¿Qué es amor?
       TESTUZ: En el mundo es un licor,
       que hace lo mismo que el vino,
       pues cuantos aman entiendo
       que están borrachos a igual.
       Y con su dama es un mal
       que se les quita durmiendo.

                   (Agustín Moreto, *Industrias contra finezas*, Jornada 1)

154 "que se reduzca mortal en ponzoña irracional la ponzoña del amor" (Francisco de Rojas Zorrilla, *Los áspides de Cleopatra*, Jornada 1).

155 Juan Pérez de Montalbán, *Amor, lealtad y amistad*, Jornada 1.

156 "este veneno amoroso, este amor que se introdujo en el alma poco a poco" (Juan Pérez de Montalbán, *Despreciar lo que se quiere*, Jornada 2).

157 "verás como con maña devorativa siembro de amor la cizaña, para que no nazca neguilla" (Juan de Matos Fragoso, *El yerro del entendido*, Acto 1). The *neguilla* is a corn cockle plant.

158 "cauteloso áspid ... de amor" (Calderón, *El Faetonte*, Jornada 3).

159 "siendo basilisco Amor, víbora sangrienta" (Calderón, *No hay cosa como callar*, Jornada 1).

160 "pisa, pisa con tiento las Flores, que dice el Amor, que anda el Áspid en ellas" (Calderón, *El divino Orfeo*, auto sacramental).

161 "basilisco de amor" (Calderón, *El médico de su honra*, Acto 1); "desusado basilisco, / del veneno de su amor, / usó con tal artificio" (Calderón, *Auristela y Lisidante*, Jornada 1).

162 "Amor es monstruo sangriento, cruel, y desenfrenado" (Calderón, *El Rey Don Pedro en Madrid, e Infanzón de Illescas*, Jornada 3).

163 "el mayor monstruo del mundo que te amenaza prodigios, es mi amor" (Calderón, *El mayor monstruo del mundo*, Acto 1).

164 Francesco Alberoni theorizes that the realm of love is by definition a realm of fantasy, independent of its literary contexts: "When the most simple and unaware person falls in love, he (or she) is forced to use the language of poetry, religion and myth in order to express himself" (Francesco Alberoni, *Falling in Love*, trans. Lawrence Venuti [New York: Random House, 1983], 16). But on a less ethereal note, Anna Clark states that in seventeenth-century France the "pornographic *L'Ecole des Filles* sardonically noted that the source of women's spiritual, beautifully elevated thoughts and fantasies about love was really the fire of lust, coming from their genitals" (Clark, *Desire*, 107).

165 "¿Cuándo no es locura amor?" (Calderón, *El alcalde de sí mismo*, Jornada 3). Drawing upon clearly Platonic precedents, a concrete example of this kind of mad love is described by the teacher Diógenes to the notoriously crazy Alejandro Magno: "De desordenado amor parece este afecto, hijo" (Calderón, *Darlo todo y no dar nada*, Jornada 3). Sociologist Guy Oakes theorizes that love by its very nature is a type of madness: "Because the logic of love departs so radically from the logic of existing institutions, the lovers' intentions seem irresponsible and absurd, and the lovers themselves are perceived as irrational, immoral, or even mad" (Guy Oakes, "Eros and Modernity: Georg Simmel on Love," in *The Sociology of Emotions*, ed. Franks and McCarthy, 229–48, at 237). Semir Zeki explains the neurobiology behind this phenomenon: "sexual arousal (and orgasms), at least in women, de-activate considerable parts of the cortex ... This is perhaps not surprising, given that humans often take 'leave of their senses' during sexual arousal, perhaps even inducing them to conduct that they might later, in more sober mood, regret" (Zeki, *Splendors and Miseries of the Brain*, 139).

166 "Es una furia, un delirio de amor" (Calderón, *El alcalde de Zalamea*, Jornada 2).

167   [U]n capricho de amor, no es argumento,
        que se funda en razones,
            y la pasión de amor toda es pasiones.

                              (Calderón, *De una causa dos efectos*, Jornada 2)

Elaine Hatfield and Richard Rapson report a similar conception of love as reported by an interviewee: "Love is irrational. Whether you call it a mental illness or sublime spirituality, you behave in love in ways that do not represent your own true best interests, ways that deflect from the goals you've built your life around, even if the deflection is slight" (Hatfield and Rapson, *Love, Sex, and Intimacy*, 55). Peter Gay observes, "That love is irrational is, certainly, not a new insight. Stendhal had memorably imaged that old truth in his master metaphor of crystallization; Balzac had stated it tersely when he said that 'the more one judges, the less one loves'; Wilkie Collins had put it melodramatically in his novel *Basil* when he has his unfortunate hero muse, after he has fallen in love for the first time, at first sight, 'Prudence, duty, memories and prejudices of home, were all absorbed and forgotten in love'" (Gay, *The Tender Passion*, 91). Finally, Semir Zeki explores the neurobiology behind love's irrationality: "We are often surprised by the choice of partner that someone makes, asking futilely whether they have taken leave of their senses. In fact, they have. Love is often irrational because rational judgments have been suspended or no longer applied with the same rigour" (Zeki, *Splendors and Miseries of the Brain*, 141).

168 Shakespeare, *A Midsummer Night's Dream*, V.1.4–6, p. 169.

169 "de delirios un Amor, que en Agua sus Torres funda" (Calderón, *El divino Orfeo*, auto sacramental).

170 "vive amor idolatrado de este humano sacrificio" (Calderón, *El pintor de su deshonra*, Jornada 2).

171 "adorar una sombra del Amor, por Ídolo de su Altar" (Calderón, *El castillo de Lindabridis*, Jornada 3).

172 "amor … es un Hereje" (Calderón, *Antes que todo es mi dama*, Jornada 3). A humorous line from a different play declares that although heretical, love is at least an erudite heretic:

> No hay ley que el amor entienda
> que es un Hereje Letrado,
> que entiende mal la escritura.
>
> (Juan Pérez de Montalbán, *El sufrimiento premiado*, Jornada 2)

This kind of erudite or learned heretic who misinterprets Scripture is being held up in contrast to some of the rustics investigated by the Inquisition who could not read, but instead merely repeated popular heresies or superstitions they had heard from others.

173 "Que confesarla querías: ¿es tu amor excomunión de participantes?" (Juan Pérez de Montalbán, *La ganancia por la mano*, Jornada 2). This playful parody traces its origins back through medieval French love poetry to the classical Latin author Ovid: "The worship of the god Amor had been a mock religion in Ovid's *Art of Love*. The French poet [the anonymous author of the twelfth-century *Concilium in Monte Romarici*] has taken over this conception of an erotic religion with a full understanding of its flippancy, and proceeded to elaborate the joke in terms of the only religion he knows – medieval Christianity. The result is a close and impudent parody of the practices of the Church, in which Ovid becomes a *doctor egregius*

and the *Ars Amatoria* a gospel, erotic heterodoxy and orthodoxy are distinguished, and the god of Love is equipped with cardinals and exercises the power of excommunication" (C.S. Lewis, *The Allegory of Love* [Oxford: Oxford University Press, 1959], 20).

174 Calderón, *El escondido y la tapada*, Jornada 2.

175 Several of Lope de Vega's love poems to Elena Osorio, such as the sonnets "Suelta mi manso," "Querido manso mío," and "Vireno, aquel mi manso regalado," contain a pastoral analogy in which he is the shepherd and she is a sheep eating out of his hand. For an extended discussion of these and other of his literary creations into which he weaves autobiographical material – most notably *La Dorotea* – see Alan S. Trueblood, *Experience and Artistic Expression in Lope de Vega* (Cambridge, MA: Harvard University Press, 1974).

176 Calderón, *El escondido y la tapada*, Jornada 1.

177 Calderón, *El castillo de Lindabridis*, Jornada 3.

178 "quejoso vive el amor de los instantes que pierde" (Calderón, *A secreto agravio, secreta venganza*, Jornada 2).

179 "amor, de quien fue cómplice el oscuro manto de la noche" (Calderón, *Antes que todo es mi dama*, Jornada 1); "la noche siempre en sus sombras ampara hurtos de amor" (Calderón, *La estatua de Prometeo*, Jornada 2). An interesting corollary to this idea is that love never sleeps ("Siempre duerme poco amor") (Calderón, *Bien vengas mal*, Jornada 1).

180 (Calderón, *El alcalde de sí mismo*, Jornada 3).

181   El que más desvanecido
         del ingenio que alcanzó,
         se dio a sus estudios, dio
         sus estudios al olvido,
         en habiendo amor tenido;
         y solo a su dama atento,
         hace discursos al viento,
         porque tibiamente adora
         quien por su dama, señora,
         no pierde el entendimiento.   (Calderón, *De una causa dos efectos*, Jornada 3)

182 "No es grande amor, amor que guarda silencio" (Calderón, *Bien vengas mal*, Jornada 1).

183 Calderón, *El galán fantasma*, Jornada 2.

184 "Aquí sí que no hay rodeos, invenciones, ni tramoyas, sino amor Cristiano viejo, que habla con toda llaneza" (Juan Pérez de Montalbán, *Cumplir con su obligación*, Jornada 1).

185 Calderón, *Auristela y Lisidante*, Jornada 2. A similar phrase appears in the line, "en Gramáticas de Amor los sirvientes más leales son personas que padecen" (Calderón, *Gustos y disgustos son no más que imaginación*, Jornada 2). Ross Knecht – in the

tradition of Wittgenstein – makes much of this connection in *The Grammar Rules of Affection*: "Love too is a language-game" (Ross Knecht, *The Grammar Rules of Affection: Passion and Pedagogy in Sidney, Shakespeare, and Jonson* [Toronto: University of Toronto Press, 2021], 52).

186 Calderón, *El maestro de danzar*, Jornada 3.

187 Antonio Zamora, *Siempre hay que envidiar, amando*, Jornada 2. Similar lines are "¡O amor, qué ingenioso eres!" (Juan Pérez de Montalbán, *La doncella de labor*, Jornada 2) and the simple request "Déme ingenio, amor" (Calderón, *La crítica del amor*, Jornada 1).

188 Calderón, *De una causa dos efectos*, Jornada 3.

189 Roger Boase, *The Secrets of Pinar's Game: Court Ladies and Courtly Verse in Fifteenth-Century Spain* (Leiden: Brill, 2017).

190 Calderón, *Lances de Amor y Fortuna*, Jornada 3.

191 Calderón, *Ni Amor se libra de Amor*, Jornada 3.

192 Agustín Moreto, *La cautela en la amistad*, Jornada 2.

193 Calderón, *Mañanas de abril y mayo*, Jornada 2.

194 Calderón, *Las manos blancas no ofenden*, Jornada 3.

195 Calderón, *Amor, honor y poder*, Acto 1.

196 Calderón, *Amado y aborrecido*, Acto 1.

197 Calderón, *Antes que todo es mi dama*, Jornada 3.

198 "De mi color bien mi amor dar la pollera quisiera" (Calderón, *No hay burlas con el amor*, Jornada 2). The *pollera* is a large one-piece skirt worn during traditional festivities in Spanish-speaking Latin America. The style originated, however, with peasant dress from Spain's southern region of Andalucía.

199 The hoop skirt was large enough to hide an inconvenient pregnancy. On the *guardainfante* see Amanda Wunder, "Women's Fashions and Politics in Seventeenth-Century Spain: The Rise and Fall of the *Guardainfante*," *Renaissance Quarterly* 68.1 (2015): 133–86.

200 Calderón, *El hombre pobre todo es trazas*, Jornada 2.

201 Calderon, *Los tres afectos de amor: piedad, desmayo y valor*, Jornada, 2. Courtly love received its classic definition by C.S. Lewis: "love of a highly specialized sort, whose characteristics may be enumerated as Humility, Courtesy, Adultery, and the Religion of Love. The lover is always abject. Obedience to his lady's lightest wish, however whimsical, and silent acquiescence in her rebukes, however unjust, are the only virtues he dares to claim. There is a service of love closely modelled on the service which a feudal vassal owes to his lord … The whole attitude has been rightly described as 'a feudalisation of love'" (Lewis, *The Allegory of Love*, 2). Baumeister and Wotman invoke the conventions of courtly love, albeit ironically, to explain their notion of "falling upward" (i.e., falling in love with someone more desirable than one's self): "The notion of romantic love has its roots in the medieval traditions of courtly love, and the prototype for such love involved falling upward: Typically, a knight or minor noble would fall in love with a lady of higher status … As depicted

in the songs and poems of the era, this love remained sexually unconsummated (indeed, the ladies in such stories were often already married, although their husbands may have been away on crusade or at war). Some stories went so far as to allow the man to sleep in the same bed with his beloved lady without having sex, because of his high esteem for her and their mutual dedication to chastity and virtue. One suspects that practice may have departed from theory on occasion, of course" (Baumeister and Wotman, *Breaking Hearts*, 26).

202 Calderón, *Amigo amante y leal*, Jornada 2.

203 Calderón, *Cómo se comunican dos estrellas contrarias*, Jornada 2.

204 Agustín Moreto, *El caballero*, Jornada 2.

205 Calderón, *La niña de Gómez Arias*, Jornada 3.

206 Calderón de la Barca, *El alcalde de Zalamea*, Jornada 3.

207 Juan Pérez de Montalbán, *Despreciar lo que se quiere*, Jornada 2.

208 Calderón, *El pintor de su deshonra*, Jornada 3.

209 "Veamos quién lleva el gato / al agua del cariño" (Antonio Zamora, *Siempre hay que envidiar, amando*, Jornada 3).

210 "A ciencias de voluntad las hace el estudio agravio, porque amor para ser sabio no va a la Universidad" (Calderón, *Casa con dos puertas mala es de guardar*, Acto 1).

211 Calderón, *Argenis y Poliarco*, Jornada 3.

212 Juan Pérez de Montalbán, *Amor, lealtad y amistad*, Jornada 1.

213 Juan Pérez de Montalbán, *El divino portugués San Antonio de Padua*, Jornada 2.

214 "Victoria por mi amor, suya es la palma" (Juan Pérez de Montalbán, *A lo hecho no hay remedio, y príncipe de los montes*, Jornada 3).

215 William Jankowiak answers resoundingly in the negative: "Unlike lust, love cannot be bought (or for that matter, arranged, anticipated, or outlawed). If there is an attempt to buy it, love is invalid" (William Jankowiak, "Introduction," in *Romantic Passion: A Universal Experience?* ed. William Jankowiak [New York: Columbia University Press, 1995], 1–19, at 8).

216 See Mary Elizabeth Perry, "Deviant Insiders: Legalized Prostitutes and a Consciousness of Women in Early Modern Seville," *Comparative Studies in Society and History* 27.1 (1985): 138–58. The Catholic argument for legalizing prostitution was made by none other than Saint Thomas Aquinas, who argued that prohibiting prostitution "would result in the pullulation of sexual passions and abuses" (quoted in Anna Clark, *Desire: A History of European Sexuality* [New York: Routledge, 2008], 70).

217 Juan de Matos Fragoso, *Los indicios sin culpa*, Jornada 3. *Natas* refers to a creamy dessert.

218 Calderón, *Mujer, llora, y vencerás*, Jornada 1.

219 "el amor verdadero no es interesado amor" (Calderón, *Cómo se comunican dos estrellas contrarias*, Jornada 2); "amor, si busca interés, no se puede amor llamar" (Juan Pérez de Montalbán, *El divino portugués San Antonio de Padua*, Jornada 2). Recent anthropological work in Africa, however, has found the opposite to be true there: "the dichotomy of love and money, or of pure gift versus interested

commodity, is not natural. Rather it is a historical effect of particular economic transformations. Interpreted in this way, the question then becomes not whether love and money are opposed but rather how the divisions between the two are socioculturally produced and managed and what the potential consequences are for intimate relations ... By contrast, *fitiavina* is part of long-standing cultural practices that explicitly treat affect and exchange as mutually constitutive and distributed across social networks ... In *fitiavina*, love and material support are ideally fused ... [W]omen expect to receive material resources from their lovers" (Jennifer Cole, "Love, Money, and Economies of Intimacy in Tamatave, Madagascar," in *Love in Africa*, ed. Jennifer Cole and Lynn Thomas [Chicago: University of Chicago Press, 2009], 109–34, at 112, 113, 117). In modern-day Nigeria, Daniel Jordan Smith finds a similar pattern: "Young unmarried women use the phrase 'no romance without finance' to signal to their female peers that they are savvy about men and their motives and to assert agency by announcing plainly that they intend to benefit materially from any man with whom they have sex" (Daniel Jordan Smith, "Managing Men, Marriage, and Modern Love: Women's Perspectives on Intimacy and Male Infidelity in Southeastern Nigeria," in *Love in Africa*, ed. Cole and Thomas, 157–80, at 164–5).

220 "amor no se paga con riquezas" (Francisco de Rojas Zorrilla, *Donde hay agravios no hay celos*, Jornada 1).

221 "No se ha de pagar amor con tesoros" (Juan Pérez de Montalbán, *El divino portugués San Antonio de Padua*, Jornada 2).

222 "sin interés pintan en cueros a Amor" (Juan de Matos Fragoso, *Callar siempre es lo mejor*, Acto 1); "está en cueros amor, eso mejor le está al vino" (Agustín Moreto, *El licenciado Vidriera*, Jornada 2).

223 Juan Pérez de Montalbán, *El hijo del serafín, San Pedro de Alcántara*, Jornada 1.

224 Juan de Matos Fragoso, *Callar siempre es lo mejor*, Jornada 3. *Aliñar* means to season a dish with spices or condiments.

225 Calderón de la Barca, *El año santo en Madrid*, auto sacramental.

226 Agustín Moreto, *El poder de la amistad*, Jornada 1.

227 "Desperdicio es, no hacer muchos préstamos de amor a quien tan puntualmente los paga" (Calderón, *Fuego de Dios en el querer bien*, Jornada 3).

228 Agustín Moreto, *La fuerza del natural*, Jornada 2.

229 "Usury was controversial because a verse in the Old Testament specifically prohibited it between brothers, that is, co-religionists ('Thou shalt not lend to thy brother to usury') [Deuteronomy 23:19]" (Hilaire Kallendorf, *Sins of the Fathers: Moral Economies in Early Modern Spain* [Toronto: University of Toronto Press, 2013], 66).

230 "es de amor estelionato, hipotecarla a otra deuda" (Calderón, *La crítica del amor*, Jornada 2). *Estelionato* refers to fraudulent or deceptive business practices regarding contracts. It usually occurs when someone attempts to sell or mortgage the same goods or property twice by not revealing to the second buyer the details of the

first transaction. *Hipoteca* means pawning valuables for a sum of money, with the valuables to be returned when the loan is repaid.

231 "¿hermosa Astrea, ingrato tu pecho altivo, ha de negarle al amor tributo?" (Calderón, *La hija del aire, segunda parte*, Acto 1).

232 "al amor rindiendo juntos, como a deidad, y Monarca holocaustos, y tributos" (Juan de Matos Fragoso, *Con amor no hay amistad*, Acto 1).

233 "Quien pensara que esta boca de tanto amor obligada, pagara tributo en sangre" (Guillén de Castro, *El conde de Irlos*, Acto 2).

234 Calderón, *La desdicha de la voz*, Jornada 1.

235 "Amor tirano" (Calderón, *Las cadenas del demonio*, Jornada 3).

236 "con mi amor, y mi enemigo pagaré al alma censo" (Juan Pérez de Montalbán, *La ganancia por la mano*, Jornada 2). On the *censo* see Elvira Vilches, "Doing Things with Money in Early Modern Spain," in *A Companion to the Spanish Renaissance*, ed. Hilaire Kallendorf (Leiden: Brill, 2019), 508–30, at 515. Vilches writes, "People from all walks of life took *censos* or mortgage contracts to finance crops, acquire property, or obtain loans. During economic downturns landowners sold their land to a cathedral or monastery; in exchange, they received a sum of money and entered into a perpetual lease or *censo*" (515).

237 Calderón, *Mujer, llora, y vencerás*, Jornada 1.

238 "como amor es fortuna, sujeto viva a mudanzas" (Calderón, *La crítica del amor*, Jornada 3).

239 Calderón, *A secreto agravio, secreta venganza*, Acto 1.

240 "viento en popa del amor, corrí los inciertos mares" (Calderón, *Casa con dos puertas mala es de guardar*, Acto 1).

241 "rendido el zozobrado bajel de amor, a uno, y otro embate, sufrió uno, y otro vaivén" (Calderón, *No siempre lo peor es cierto*, Jornada 1).

242 "en el de mujer parece que está violento el cariño" (Calderón, *El monstruo de los jardines*, Jornada 3).

243 "deshechas borrascas del Amor, y la Fortuna" (Calderón, *Mujer, llora, y vencerás*, Jornada 1).

244 Calderón, *El castillo de Lindabridis*, Jornada 3.

245 "Yo así apacible juzgué del mar de amor, pero apenas reconocí sus halagos cuando sentí sus violencias" (Calderón, *Casa con dos puertas mala es de guardar*, Jornada 2).

246 "Mi pena alivia, Nise, y Sirena del Mar de mi amor serás" (Calderón, *La banda y la flor*, Jornada 3).

247 "cesen las confusas olas, que en náufrago amor espero" (Juan Bautista Diamante, *Amor es sangre, y no puede engañarse*, Jornada 2).

248 Calderón, *La desdicha de la voz*, Jornada 3.

249 "si fuego de aprehensión tiene quien ama, amor, y Infierno todo es uno mismo" (Calderón, *Antes que todo es mi dama*, Jornada 1).

250 "su amor me hacía mil cosquillas en el alma" (Juan Pérez de Montalbán, *La deshonra honrosa*, Jornada 3).

251 "pienso señor, que se os descose el amor" (Agustín Moreto, *Primero es la honra*, Jornada 2).

252 Calderón, *También hay duelo en las damas*, Jornada 2.

253 1 John 4:18.

254 Calderón, *Basta callar*, Jornada 2.

255 "el hombre más libre de las burlas de amor sale herido, cojo, y casado" (Calderón, *La crítica del amor*, Jornada 3).

256 Francisco de Rojas Zorrilla, *No hay amigo para amigo*, Jornada 2.

257 Agustín Moreto, *El desdén con el desdén*, Jornada 1.

258 Calderón, *Dicha y desdicha del nombre*, Jornada 2.

259 "Nudos de amor enlacen vuestros cuellos" (Calderón, *Argenis y Poliarco*, Jornada 3).

260 "Preciosísimo Rubí, en los engarces de Amor, de su Divina cadena sois el mejor eslabón" (Calderón, *Fieras afemina amor*, Intermedio after Jornada 3).

261 "rendido prisionero, de la coyunda de amor, el carro tiré de Venus" (Calderón, *La crítica del amor*, Jornada 2). A *coyunda* is a thick cord or rope used to tie oxen to the yoke.

262 "montes de dificultades son, que amor en mis hombros pone" (Agustín Moreto, *El secreto entre dos amigos*, Jornada 2).

263 "Cadenas son de Amor tan Nobles Lazos" (Calderón, *El árbol del mejor fruto*, auto sacramental).

264 Calderón, *Auristela y Lisidante*, Jornada 2.

265 "las prisiones de amor no se rompen fácilmente" (Calderón, *La hija del aire, primera parte*, Jornada 3).

266 "tu amor es la cárcel fuerte, las cadenas son mis yerros" (Calderón, *La devoción de la Cruz*, Acto 1).

267 "no apretéis tanto el cordel, que en el tormento de amor confieso, que quiero bien" (Calderón, *Amor, honor y poder*, Acto 1).

268 "no hay tristeza en amor, como sufrir, y callar" (Calderón, *Argenis y Poliarco*, Jornada 3).

269 "de un árbol mismo cortan la muerte, y amor sus flechas" (Calderón, *El galán fantasma*, Jornada 2).

270 "era eterno su cariño, para descansar en él" (Juan de Matos Fragoso, *El hijo de la piedra*, Acto 1). Sociologist Ann Swidler notes the disjunction of this rosy-coloured view with the reality reported by her research subjects: "the belief that real love lasts forever does not describe the world. My interviewees would be the first to insist that love dies all the time" (Ann Swidler, *Talk of Love: How Culture Matters* [Chicago: University of Chicago Press, 2001], 133). In this postmodern age, one is tempted to associate the unrealistic slogan "Love Never Dies" with the uncanniness of zombies or vampires; this motto, after all, appeared on the posters for *Bram Stoker's Dracula* (1992) directed by Francis Ford Coppola (Catherine Belsey, *Desire: Love Stories in Western Culture* [Oxford: Blackwell, 1994], 91).

271 Elvira to Don Fernando: "si mi amor fue cristal, fue firme cristal de roca" (Juan Bautista Diamante, *Santa María del Monte, y convento de San Juan*, Jornada 2).

272 "como amante, da mi brazo asunto al bronce, y mi amor materia al jaspe" (Juan de
    Matos Fragoso, *El amor hace valientes*, Jornada 3).

273 "con amor no hay diamante, que no se parta por medio" (Juan Pérez de Montalbán,
    Don Florisel de Niquea, Jornada 3).

274 Calderón, *El alcalde de sí mismo*, preliminares.

275 Juan Pérez de Montalbán, *El valiente más dichoso, Don Pedro Guiral*, Jornada 3.

276 Juan de la Cueva, *El degollado*, Acto 3. Oughourlian confirms: "many men and
    women attribute to love a capricious, ephemeral, and volatile character. They
    also tend to believe that love can withdraw as easily as it came, in an instant, that
    its lifetime is inherently limited so that there is no point in trying to preserve
    it; and that to try to do so would only increase love's eventual disappointment
    and exhaustion and hasten the disenchantment to which, by its very nature, it is
    condemned" (Oughourlian, *The Genesis of Desire*, 147).

277 "siempre es el más tierno / el más reciente cariño" (Antonio de Solís, *Eurídice y
    Orfeo*, Jornada 1).

278 Peter Gay argues that lack of reciprocity is actually almost necessary in order for love
    to flourish; once love is reciprocated, it loses its charm: "love must feed precisely on
    absences, on misunderstandings, on the indifference of the other, even on disdain; and it
    will rapidly and irreparably cool when it is reciprocated" (Gay, *The Tender Passion*, 79).

279 Calderón, *Agradecer y no amar*, Jornada 3.

280 On the stereotyped figure of Juan de Espera see "El mito visto por Doré" in a blog
    for *National Geographic* magazine: https://historia.nationalgeographic.com.es/a
    /judio-errante-mito-eterna-culpabilidad_12248/6.

281 "Cubierta está mi cabeza de ceniza, que un amor desatinado, si es fuego, solo deja en
    galardón cenizas" (Calderón, *Los cabellos de Absalón*, Jornada 2).

282 Calderón, *Mujer, llora, y vencerás*, Jornada 2.

283 "son los pecados frías cenizas del fuego que encendió amor" (Calderón, *Los cabellos
    de Absalón*, Jornada 2).

284 Calderón, *Mujer, llora, y vencerás*, Jornada 3.

285 Calderón, *Amar y ser amado, y divina Philotea*, Jornada 1.

286 Calderón, *De una causa dos efectos*, Jornada 3.

287 Calderón, *La niña de Gómez Arias*, Jornada 3.

288 Calderón, *El astrólogo fingido*, Acto 1.

289 "alcahuetes de amor terceros dulces, que deshacen enojos, y hacen nudos ciegos"
    (Juan Pérez de Montalbán, *La ganancia por la mano*, Jornada 2).

290 Calderón, *Fuego de Dios en el querer bien*, Jornada 1.

291 "Vuelva a vivir la ya difunta llama de mi amor" (Juan Bautista Diamante, *El sol de la
    sierra*, Jornada 2).

292 "a vejezes de Amor procuro echar un remiendo" (Calderón, *Dicha y desdicha del
    nombre*, Jornada 1).

293 "Fénix mi amor renace en sus enojos" (Juan Pérez de Montalbán, *Los templarios*,
    Jornada 2).

294 Calderón, *Fieras afemina amor*, loa.

295 Calderón, *El astrólogo fingido*, Acto 2.

296 Calderón, *Luis Pérez el gallego*, Jornada 1.

297 Calderón, *No siempre lo peor es cierto*, Jornada 1.

298 Calderón, *La devoción de la Cruz*, Jornada 2.

299 Calderón, *Basta callar*, Jornada 1.

300 Ross Knecht observes, "Love is distinguished from pain in that it is subject to trial and judgment. We identify a feeling as love only when it endures, when it persists in spite of obstacles, when it is borne out by devotion and fidelity. If it fails to do these things, we say that it is false, or a different thing altogether: a passing fancy or an adolescent infatuation" (Knecht, *The Grammar Rules of Affection*, 13).

301 Calderón, *El maestro de danzar*, Jornada 3.

302 Agustín Moreto, *La traición vengada*, Jornada 3.

303 Francisco de Rojas Zorrilla, *Lo que quería ver el Marqués de Villena*, Jornada 2.

304 "habéis sido Judas de amor, que besáis, y vendéis" (Calderón, *La niña de Gómez Arias*, Jornada 3).

305 Juan de Matos Fragoso, *Callar siempre es lo mejor*, Acto 1.

306 Juan Pérez de Montalbán, *La ganancia por la mano*, Jornada 3.

307 Calderón, *Celos aun del aire matan*, Jornada 1. Peter Gay argues that this is not necessarily a bad thing: "love contains an admixture of revived memories, old fantasies, perennial needs. It need not be self-destructive: to supply in fantasy what reality embodies only imperfectly, if at all, is to generate pleasure and to sustain morale" (Gay, *The Tender Passion*, 66).

308 Juan de Matos Fragoso, *De los indicios sin culpa*, Acto 1. Baumeister and Wotman describe the process by which unrequited love exposes the illusions on which said love was founded: "[U]nrequited love can expose the illusion of rationality and optimality that may surround love … [L]ove may foster a partly illusory sense of understanding the partner, whereas unrequited love may bring disillusionment and a sense of not understanding the partner, and may even reveal that one never understood the other at all. The powerful feeling of intimacy and mutual understanding is revealed, in retrospect, to have been illusory" (Baumeister and Wotman, *Breaking Hearts*, 72, 179–80). Peter Gay comments about this common feature of love in reference to Don Juan: "Don Juan, that widely envied machine of conquest, must have been battling some deep-seated neurotic malaise, whether disappointment with the reality of woman, homosexual panic, or fear of fiasco [i.e., impotence]. The facility with which such an unstable, helplessly restless lover crystallizes woman after woman and lives in a continuous fever of ever-changing illusions betrays his need for a self-deception far more treacherous than the occasional idealization of the loved object that accompanies the normal madness that is love" (Gay, *The Tender Passion*, 90).

309 "Madrid todo es trampa fiera, todo engaño conocido, todo amor papel batido, y toda mujer costera" (Juan Pérez de Montalbán, *Despreciar lo que se quiere*, Jornada 1).

310 "mi amor es un encanto, que el discurso limita" (Juan Pérez de Montalbán, *La ganancia por la mano*, Jornada 3).

311 Love potions have long been a staple of literature and other forms of artistic production, such as opera (think Wagner's *Tristan und Isolde*). Love spells are still prevalent in Africa: "Such preparations entailed the combination and application of various animal, plant, and store-bought products to make a man or woman irresistibly attractive or guard a lover's affection from interlopers" (Lynn M. Thomas and Jennifer Cole, "Introduction: Thinking through Love in Africa," in *Love in Africa*, ed. Cole and Thomas, 1–30, at 7).

312 Juan Pérez de Montalbán, *El sufrimiento premiado*, Jornada 3.

313 Juan Pérez de Montalbán, *El sufrimiento premiado*, Jornada 3.

314 "en la Corte donde he estado no hay amor sin granjería, y el interés se ha usurpado en mi Reino" (Cervantes, *La casa de los celos, y selvas de Ardenia*, Jornada 2).

315 Calderón, *La primer flor del Carmelo*, auto sacramental.

316 Calderón, *La dama duende*, Jornada 2.

317 "si ya no es que Amor me dé tan equívocas palabras, que sean mentira al oírlas" (Calderón, *El segundo Scipión*, Jornada 1).

318 "Dignamente ladrón / al amor le llaman" (Calderón, *De un castigo tres venganzas*, Jornada 2).

319 Cervantes, *La gran sultana, doña Catalina de Oviedo*, Jornada 1. *Monfí* (from the Arabic word meaning "exiled") was the name given to *moriscos* hiding in the mountain ranges of the Kingdom of Granada during the sixteenth and seventeenth centuries; they were known primarily as bandits.

320 "que tanta perfección alhaja viniese a ser del Baratillo de amor" (Calderón, *Los dos amantes del cielo*, Jornada 3). An *alhaja* was a metal object used for adornment, often decorated with inlaid pearls or precious stones. *Baratillo* refers to cheap used or second-hand merchandise.

321 Cervantes, *La casa de los celos, y selvas de Ardenia*, Jornada 2.

322 "villano grosero mi amor, con bárbaros modos" (Calderón, *Mujer, llora, y vencerás*, Jornada 3). Baumeister and Wotman explore the figurative sense in which love is a gamble: "To the would-be lover, the situation offers a wide range of possible outcomes, from bliss to despair, and so the episode resembles a gamble or an adventure. Would-be lovers may suffer acutely when they lose the gamble; but on the whole it was probably worth a try" (Baumeister and Wotman, *Breaking Hearts*, 202). Catherine Belsey theorizes, "Love and gambling are compulsive, unpredictable, thrilling, dangerous. What is at stake is a loss" (Belsey, *Desire*, 78–9).

323 Juan Bautista Diamante, *Santa María del Monte, y convento de San Juan*, Jornada 2.

324 Calderón, *Luis Pérez el gallego*, Jornada 2.

325 "Venus, pública ramera, delitos hizo de amor" (Calderón, *El Joseph de las mujeres*, Jornada 1).

326 "¡cuánto ignora, cuánto yerra el que químico de amor, vive de hacer experiencias!" (Calderón, *La niña de Gómez Arias*, Acto 1).

327 "en los órganos de amor, sé yo tocar bien las teclas" (Juan Bautista Diamante, *El jubileo de la Porciúncula*, Jornada 1).

328 "A Dios teatro funesto donde mi primer amor representó sus afectos" (Calderón, *El monstruo de los jardines*, Jornada 3).

329 "quiero tomar solamente el desengaño. Cadáver de amor ha sido esa dama" (Calderón, *La niña de Gómez Arias*, Jornada 3).

330 "triste, y discursivo, está de esqueleto vivo desengañando su amor" (Calderón, *El mágico prodigioso*, Jornada 2). In this play the *memento mori* is more literal than figurative: the devil creates a phantom in the shape of Justina, whom Cipriano embraces, only to find himself in the arms of a skeleton.

331 "no daré por cuanto amor hay en el Mundo, dos higas" (Calderón, *No hay burlas con el amor*, Jornada 2). This is my own very loose translation. *Dar higas* meant "giving the finger" to someone by holding the thumbs up between the pointer and middle fingers of both hands separately. Saint Teresa of Ávila famously used this gesture in her *Libro de la Vida* to "give the finger" to the devil. For the phallic origins of this gesture, see Sherry Velasco, "Vision, Vulnerability, and the Provocative 'Higas' in Lope de Vega's *Santa Teresa de Jesús*," in *Women Warriors in Early Modern Spain* (A Tribute to Bárbara Mujica), ed. Susan L. Fischer and Frederick A. de Armas (Newark: University of Delaware Press, 2019), 221–40.

332 Calderón, *El Conde Lucanor*, Jornada 1.

333 Calderón, *Eco y Narciso*, Jornada 2.

334 Calderón, *Lo que va del hombre a Dios*, auto sacramental.

335 Calderón, *El primer refugio del hombre, y probática piscina*, auto sacramental.

336 As Hannah Arendt glosses Augustine on this topic, "The right kind of self-love (*amor sui*) does not love the present self that is going to die but that which will make him live forever … He loves himself as God loves him, hating everything he has made in himself, and loving himself only insofar as he is God's creation. What he loves in himself is exclusively God's goodness, the Creator" (Hannah Arendt, *Love and Saint Augustine*, ed. and trans. J.V. Scott and J.C. Stark [Chicago: University of Chicago Press, 1996], 26, 91).

337 Francisco de Rojas Zorrilla, *Casarse por vengarse*, Jornada 2.

338 Agustín Moreto, *Santa Rosa del Perú*, Jornada 2.

339 Calderón, *Amor, honor y poder*, Acto 1.

340 "me detiene en Rosarda la rémora del cariño" (Calderón, *Los tres afectos de amor, piedad, desmayo y valor*, Jornada 3). A *rémora* is a marine fish that adheres forcefully to floating objects. People used to believe that it was strong enough to stop a boat. Figuratively the word came to mean any obstacle that impedes progress or makes something more difficult.

341 C.S. Lewis reminds us that perceptions of love's morality have changed drastically over the centuries: "A nineteenth-century Englishman felt that the same passion – romantic love – could be either virtuous or vicious according as it was directed towards marriage or not. But according to the medieval view passionate love

itself was wicked, and did not cease to be wicked if the object of it were your wife" (Lewis, *Allegory of Love*, 13–14). Saint Augustine differentiated between moral and immoral love by using two different Latin words, *caritas* and *cupiditas*: "Augustine's term for … wrong, mundane love that clings to, and thus at the same time constitutes, the world is *cupiditas*. In contrast, the right love seeks eternity and the absolute future. Augustine calls this right love *caritas*" (Arendt, *Love and Saint Augustine*, 17).

342 Kenneth and Karen Dion posit that individual answers to this question will be determined by whether the person involved can be classified as "internally controlled" or "externally controlled" with regard to their personal efficacy as a causal agent: "[persons who are] internally controlled tend to view events that affect them as being under their personal control; they regard themselves as being the captain of their fate. Externally controlled people, on the other hand, are more likely to see events affecting them as being beyond their personal control and due to such forces as luck, fate, powerful others, and so on" (Kenneth L. Dion and Karen E. Dion, "Romantic Love: Individual and Cultural Perspectives," in *The Psychology of Love*, ed. Sternberg and Barnes, 264–89, at 266).

343 Baumeister and Wotman confirm: "love cannot be summoned or created on demand, any more than it can be erased or prevented on demand" (Baumeister and Wotman, *Breaking Hearts*, 122). Ulrich and Elisabeth Beck agree: "No one can decide to fall into or out of love … Love … cannot be aimed at, invoked or coerced into existence nor can any institution restrict it. It simply happens, strikes [like] lightning or dies out according to laws which are not open to individual or social control" (Beck and Beck-Gernsheim, *The Normal Chaos of Love*, 179, 198). Dion and Dion observe that the very language we use to talk about the experience of romantic love removes agency: "that romantic love is regarded as an experience in which one loses control is illustrated by the phrases used to describe it: one 'falls in love,' one is 'swept off one's feet,' or one is 'head over heels in love'" (Dion and Dion, "Romantic Love," in *The Psychology of Love*, ed. Sternberg and Barnes, 273). Ann Swidler discusses the question of whether love is a choice or not in light of her findings from interviewing live subjects living near San José, California: "One way to think of love is as a voluntary choice. Then the question is whom one loves and why, and what one gives and receives in a relationship. One chooses well; gets a good deal; is more or less contented, satisfied, happy, and so forth. The other way to think about love is as a commitment, a bond that is no longer purely voluntary, if it ever was. If love is a commitment then it is given and received. Sometimes the emotional punch of the word 'love' comes from its power to signify a relationship beyond choice – one in which the normal expectation of reciprocity need not apply. At other times love signifies the ultimate choice, based on the unsurpassed virtues of the beloved" (Swidler, *Talk of Love*, 26).

344 Calderón, *El hombre pobre todo es trazas*, Jornada 2.

345 William B. Irvine, *On Desire: Why We Want What We Want* (Oxford: Oxford University Press, 2005), 12.

346 Sharon Brehm comments on the fact that this more active view of love is the one espoused by Saint Teresa of Ávila, for whom love was "an arrow shot by the will" (Sharon Brehm, "Passionate Love," in *The Psychology of Love*, ed. Sternberg and Barnes, 232–63, at 243).

347 Agustín Moreto, *El desdén con el desdén*, Jornada 1.

348 "amando sin esperanza, es Platónico mi amor" (Tirso de Molina, *Del enemigo el primer consejo*, Jornada 1).

349 See Susan Byrne, *Ficino in Spain* (Toronto: University of Toronto Press, 2015).

350 Calderón, *Los dos amantes del cielo*, Jornada 1.

351 Calderón, *Fieras afemina amor*, intermedio between Jornadas 2 and 3.

352 Juan Pérez de Montalbán, *Amor, lealtad y amistad*, Jornada 1.

353   No espero
    que se pueda borrar amor primero,
    enseña la moral Filosofía,
    que una forma donde otra forma habita
    no se puede estampar tan fácilmente.   (Calderón, *Peor está que estaba*, Jornada 2)

354 Witness Diego's lines:

    [Y]o en vos, hermoso dueño, imaginaba,
    y tanto en vos mi amor me tranformaba,
    que en vos el alma más, que en mí vivía.

                                       (Calderón, *Bien vengas mal*, Jornada 1)

355 "para prueba de que en lo vegetable anima Amor, el ejemplar dé" (Calderón, *El pastor fido*, auto sacramental).

356 Barrildo speaks the lines:

    El mundo de acá y de allá,
    Mengo, todo es armonía,
    Armonía es puro amor,
    porque el amor es concierto.

                        (Lope de Vega Carpio, *Fuenteovejuna*, in *Antología
                        de autores españoles antiguos y modernos*, vol. I *Antiguos*, ed.
                        Antonio Sánchez-Romeralo and Fernando Ibarra
                    [Hoboken, NJ: Prentice Hall, 1972], 296–346, Act I, pp. 303–4).

357 MENGO: ¿Qué es amor?
    LAURENCIA: Es un deseo
        de hermosura.   (Lope de Vega, *Fuenteovejuna*, Act I, pp. 303–4)

358 Calderón, *De un castigo tres venganzas*, Jornada 1.

359 Calderón, *De una causa dos efectos*, Jornada 2.

360 Calderón, *La banda y la flor*, Jornada 2.

6. The Wounding Smell of Sorrow

1 This chapter title adapts the phrase "the wounding smell of sadness" from Teresa Brennan, *The Transmission of Affect* (Ithaca: Cornell University Press, 2004), 44. Philosopher Andrea Westlund clarifies a subtle difference between sorrow and sadness: "In common speech, sorrow and sadness may be used interchangeably. I will, however, draw a distinction … Sadness is widely recognized as one of the relatively few basic, cross-culturally recognizable, emotions. It is often characterized by philosophers and psychologists as a painful appraisal of a situation as involving permanent, irrevocable loss. Psychologists have argued that sadness has at least two distinctive functional roles: it promotes reflectiveness in the wake of a loss, thus allowing the one who suffered the loss to recuperate and refocus, and it facilitates interpersonal help-seeking interactions, thus allowing them to secure the support they need. One might argue that sadness has epistemic value, insofar as it reveals what matters to us, or is meaningful to us … Sorrow, as I understand it, shares … features with sadness but differs qualitatively in at least three ways. Sorrow is more temporally extended than sadness (sadness may be fleeting, but not sorrow), has a greater intensity (sadness can be mild, but sorrow cannot), and is unambiguously painful (sadness may be tinged with pleasure, as in the case of nostalgia and other 'lyrical' emotions, but sorrow may not). Sorrow, thus understood, is a fitting response to significant and profound losss, the loss of things that are of great importance or deeply meaningful to us, including (though not limited to) the loss of a beloved person" (Andrea C. Westlund, "Untold Sorrow," in *The Moral Psychology of Sadness*, ed. Anna Gotlib [London: Rowman & Littlefield, 2017], 21–41, at 25, 26). For purposes of this chapter, however, I use the two words interchangeably, as she indicates is acceptable in common speech.

2 Juan Luis Vives, *The Passions of the Soul: The Third Book of* De Anima et Vita, trans. Carlos G. Noreña (Lewiston: Mellen, 1990), 7. Philip Bachelor differentiates among sadness, sorrow, and related emotions thus: "As a group of emotions, sorrow includes grief (including anguish and despair) and sadness (including pensiveness) … Sadness is a state of unhappiness, which is considered to be less intense and severe than grief. At the more intense end of the sorrow spectrum, grief may be characterized by a greater degree of emotional pain and anxiety" (Philip Bachelor, *Sorrow and Solace: The Social World of the Cemetery* [Amityville: Baywood, 2004], 118). John Harvey offers further clarification: "grief is the more private and mourning the more public, socially-approved response … [B]ereavement may be seen as the composite of private grief and public mourning" (John H. Harvey, *Give Sorrow Words: Perspectives on Loss and Trauma* [Philadelphia: Brunner / Mazel, 2000], 26).

3 Martin Luther, quoted in Darrin M. McMahon, *Happiness: A History* (New York: Atlantic Monthly Press, 2006), 173.

4 Francis Weller, *The Wild Edge of Sorrow: Rituals of Renewal and the Sacred Work of Grief* (Berkeley: North Atlantic, 2015), 1.

5 Oscar Wilde, "De profundis," Project Gutenberg, www.gutenberg.org.

6 Tirso de Molina, *Adversa fortuna de Don Álvaro de Luna, segunda parte*, Jornada 3.

7 Lope de Vega, *Las bizarrías de Belisa*, Jornada 2. Counselor Francis Weller confirms, "Grief takes us below the surface of our ordinary lives, dropping us into a world the color of a raven's wings. It is the night world, an encompassing surround of darkness and mystery" (Weller, *The Wild Edge of Sorrow*, 122).

8 Antonio Zamora, *El lucero de Madrid, y divino Labrador san Isidro*, Jornada 3.

9 Juan Pérez de Montalbán, *Lo que son los juicios del cielo*, Jornada 3.

10 "El dolor, con la flecha del cariño, me atraviesa el corazón" (Antonio Zamora, *El lucero de Madrid, y divino Labrador san Isidro*, Jornada 3).

11 "Pues señor, ¿Vuestra Alteza en tan mísero estado de tristeza? Rompa el dolor el pecho" (Calderón, *El príncipe constante*, Jornada 2).

12 Lope de Vega, *El más galán portugués, Duque de Berganza*, Acto 2.

13 Sherry Cormier, *Sweet Sorrow: Finding Enduring Wholeness after Loss and Grief* (Lanham, MD: Rowman & Littlefield, 2018), 110.

14 Calderón, *Lo que va del hombre a Dios*, auto sacramental.

15 "por vivir inmortal en tu tristeza, has hecho naturaleza, el suspirar y sentir" (Francisco de Rojas Zorrilla, *Casarse por vengarse*, Jornada 2).

16 "al último suspiro le ve inclinar la cabeza, cubriéndose de tristeza uno y otro Luminar" (Calderón, *A Dios por razón de Estado*, auto sacramental).

17 "la tristeza, con que apenas del suelo alza los ojos" (Lope de Vega, *La viuda casada y doncella*, Acto 3).

18 John Gale, "Response to Part I: The Relics of Absence," in *Grief and Its Transcendence: Memory, Identity, Creativity*, ed. Adele Tutter and Léon Wurmser (New York: Routledge, 2016), 51–63, at 54.

19 Robert Kaster, *Emotion, Restraint, and Community in Ancient Rome* (Oxford: Oxford University Press, 2005), 12.

20 I am alluding here to the theoretical framework, based upon the ideas of Marxist critic Raymond Williams, for my book *Sins of the Fathers: Moral Economies in Early Modern Spain* (Toronto: University of Toronto Press, 2013). In that volume, I showed how the medieval framework of the Seven Deadly Sins sometimes persisted, was at other times discarded, and at still other times was transformed, transmuted, or replaced during the Renaissance in combination with its main rival in terms of taxonomies for organizing sin: the Decalogue, or Ten Commandments. Thus my study was divided into three parts: Residue, Transformation, and Emergence.

21 "Cubierta tiene la cara de una tristeza mortal" (Lope de Vega, *Don Lope de Cardona*, Acto 3); "en tu rostro señales veo de tristeza, y pena" (Lope de Vega, *El primer Fajardo*, Acto 2).

22 "la pálida tristeza que enfadosa gualdas siembra en su cara" (Tirso de Molina,
    La venganza de Tamar, Jornada 2). *Gualdas* are a type of yellow, flowering, fruit-
    producing plant.

23 Calderón, *Argenis y Poliarco*, Jornada 2.

24 Ludwig Wittgenstein, *Remarks on the Philosophy of Psychology*, vol. 2, ed. G.H.
    von Wright and Heikki Nyman, trans. C.G. Luckhardt and M.A.E. Aue (Oxford:
    Blackwell, 1980), §570.

25 "en tus luces soberanas puso nubes de tristeza" (Guillén de Castro, *El nacimiento de
    Montesinos*, Acto 1).

26 "¿Pero de qué es la tristeza? Que fulminan esos ojos un diluvio de cristal" (Tirso de
    Molina, *Amar por arte mayor*, Acto 2).

27 "de cuya tristeza sus lágrimas me informaron" (Calderón, *De un castigo tres
    venganzas*, Jornada 2).

28 "quiero retirarme con tristeza a consolarme, que aun es consuelo llorar" (Lope
    de Vega, *El divino africano*, Acto 3); "¿Hay mayor desahogo a una tristeza, que
    lágrimas?" (Calderón, *Mujer, llora, y vencerás*, Jornada 1).

29 Lope de Vega, *El mejor alcalde, el rey*, Acto 2.

30 Susan Roos, *Chronic Sorrow: A Living Loss* (New York: Routledge, 2002), 54.

31 The reference here is to a chapter title of Cliff Richey and Hilaire Richey Kallendorf,
    Acing Depression: A Tennis Champion's Toughest Match (Washington, DC: New
    Chapter, 2010): "Real Men Do Cry," 227–35.

32 Lope de Vega, *El testimonio vengado*, Jornada 1.

33 Lope de Vega, *Roma abrasada*, Acto 3.

34 Stephen Levine, *Unattended Sorrow* (Emmaus, PA: Rodale, 2005), 183. A recent
    study of a culture where loud lamentation is still practised is Tova Gamliel, *Aesthetics
    of Sorrow: The Wailing Culture of Yemenite Jewish Women*, trans. Naftali Greenwood
    (Detroit: Wayne State University Press, 2014).

35 "en sonora música la pena, puesta en fúnebre metro la alegría, prosiga, dulce Esposa,
    la harmonía de la aflicción llorada" (Calderón, *Amar y ser amado, y divina Filotea*,
    auto sacramental).

36 Tirso de Molina, *Los amantes de Teruel*, Jornada 3.

37 Adele Tutter, "Prologue: Give Sorrow Words," in *Grief and Its Transcendence:
    Memory, Identity, Creativity*, ed. Adele Tutter and Léon Wurmser (New York:
    Routledge, 2016), xxxviii.

38 Lope de Vega, *El favor agradecido*, Acto 2.

39 Lope de Vega, *El llegar en ocasión*, Acto 1.

40 "sirviese el llanto amargo, y negro luto, y la tristeza que en tu pecho reina, para el
    que ya murió" (Lope de Vega, *El favor agradecido*, Acto 2).

41 Lope de Vega, *La vengadora de las mujeres*, Acto 3. Since the Golden Age,
    apparently Spanish customs have changed less than one might predict.
    Ethnographer Jane Collier reports according to interviews she conducted in
    the Spanish village of Los Olivos in Andalusia in the 1960s and then again in

the 1980s, "Mourning requirements did seem excessive in the 1960s. At that time, villagers summarized full mourning dress, or 'heaviest' mourning (*luto más pesado*), with the phrase 'veil and shawl' (*velo y manto*) … [A] woman in heaviest mourning, such as one who had recently lost a husband or parent, was expected to wear a black dress with long sleeves, heavy black stockings, a large square black veil, and over all, the heavy wool *mantón*. After a few months, a woman could shed her *mantón* when in her own home, but was expected to wear this costume every day, during the hot summers as well as the cold winters. Later, after the required period of deepest mourning had passed, a woman could begin to don 'lighter' black clothes. She could substitute a black sweater or crocheted shawl (*manto* or *toca*) for the heavy, blanketlike *mantón* and a smaller round veil for the large square one. As the mourning period neared its end, she could finally abandon her veil and begin to wear a short-sleeved black dress and clear stockings" (Jane Fishburne Collier, *From Duty to Desire: Remaking Families in a Spanish Village* [Princeton: Princeton University Press, 1997]), 183–4).

42 "un vestido negro y viejo, porque es vieja mi tristeza" (Lope de Vega, *El dómine Lucas*, Acto 1). Ethnographer Jane Collier reports according to interviews she conducted in the Spanish village of Los Olivos in Andalusia in the 1980s: "In the old days, people told me, women wore black clothes for several years after the death of a close relative" (Collier, *From Duty to Desire*, 177).

43 Tirso de Molina, *La vida de Herodes*, Acto 2. Normally, when its inhabitants were not in mourning, the palace walls would be covered with colorful tapestries, as we see by implication in this line about the transformation that occurs after the period of mourning is over: "de lutos a las galas, ayer desnudas paredes de tristeza apenas blancas, y hoy de brocados y sedas tan compuestas" (Guillén de Castro, *La fuerza de la costumbre*, Jornada 1).

44 Lope de Vega, *El secretario de sí mismo*, Acto 3.

45 "exequias a mi tristeza" (Lope de Vega, *Guardar y guardarse*, Acto 3).

46 Lope de Vega, *Las grandezas de Alejandro*, Acto 1.

47 Calderón, *El día mayor de los días*, auto sacramental.

48 "es tanta mi tristeza, que para nada me aliento" (Lope de Vega, *El labrador venturoso*, Jornada 1).

49 "[¿]tú, Belisa hermosa, sola en casa, y retirada, en tu tristeza ocupada, y en tu ocupación ociosa?" (Juan Ruiz de Alarcón, *Todo es ventura*, Acto 3).

50 Anna Gotlib, "The Topographies of Sadness," in *The Moral Psychology of Sadness*, ed. Gotlib, 1–17, at 6.

51 "la tristeza … con cuánto rigor os aflige" (Calderón, *Antes que todo es mi dama*, Jornada 1).

52 "la tristeza que me oprime el alma" (Lope de Vega, *Amor secreto hasta celos*, Acto 2).

53 "ahora asaltado de esta enfadosa tristeza" (Tirso de Molina, *El melancólico*, Acto 2).

54 Calderón, *Afectos de odio y amor*, Jornada 3.

55 "Vuestra tristeza he notado, en que no me hablais con gusto" (Lope de Vega, *La noche de San Juan*, Acto 1); "le ha caído dentro del alma tan mortal tristeza, que cuando va conmigo no me habla" (Lope de Vega, *La quinta de Florencia*, Jornada 1).

56 Lope de Vega, *De ello dirá*, Acto 3.

57 "no hay tristeza en amor, como sufrir y callar" (Calderón, *Argenis y Poliarco*, Jornada 3).

58 "como entraba divertido en mi tristeza no os vi" (Calderón, *De un castigo tres venganzas*, Jornada 1).

59 Lope de Vega, *El perro del hortelano*, Acto 3.

60 "todas son cosas que finge la fuerza de la tristeza, la imaginación de un triste" (Lope de Vega, *El caballero de Olmedo*, Acto 3).

61 "¡Jesús, qué tristeza tienes! Ni me hablas ni me abrazas" (Lope de Vega, *Los Benavides*, Jornada 1).

62 "si es escondida llama amor, bien mi tristeza huye de él" (Calderón, *Las manos blancas no ofenden*, Jornada 2).

63 Calderón, *Basta callar*, Jornada 3.

64 Lope de Vega, *El ruiseñor de Sevilla*, Acto 2.

65 "Deseo quedar solo, que peleo con mis tristezas a solas" (Tirso de Molina, *Cautela contra cautela*, Jornada 2).

66 Calderón, *El Conde Lucanor*, Jornada 2.

67 "yo de Nápoles también falto, porque una grande tristeza me tiene tan retirado, que en esta vecina Quinta lloro" (Calderón, *El pintor de su deshonra*, Jornada 3).

68 Calderón, *Fortunas de Andrómeda y Perseo*, Jornada 1.

69 Cormier, *Sweet Sorrow*, 81, 100.

70 Witness the following exchange:

> LEONARDO: ¿Qué tienes, que así has estado
>   divertida en mil enojos?
> MARÍA: Si hoy delante de mis ojos
>   una joya me ha faltado,
>   ¿he de tener alegría?
>   Y aun pienso que fue el perderla
>   por tener el gusto en ella.
> LEONARDO: ¿Tales extremos, María?
>   ¿Qué joya era?
> MARÍA: Era el Cupido
>   de diamantes.
> LEONARDO: ¿Que eso pasa?
>   Búsquese en toda la casa:
>   y si se hubiera perdido,
>   más joyas tenéis, en quien
>   valor, y arte se acrisola,
>   porque no estaba ésta sola.

> MARÍA: Ésta sola quise bien.
> LEONARDO: Tanto tu pecho sintió,
>   que te pudiese faltar,
>   que no me has dado lugar
>   para que lo sienta yo:
>   ya tanto tu llanto obliga,
>   que por darte gusto luego
>   he de buscar a Don Diego,
>   que de la joya me diga.   (Calderón, *El astrólogo fingido*, Jornada 3)

71 Levine, *Unattended Sorrow*, 176.
72 As in this speech by Climene:

> ¡O quién pudiera decir
> a voces, que mi tristeza
> es ver que hay para mí olvidos,
> cuando hay para otra finezas!   (Calderón, *Apolo y Climene*, Acto 1)

73 "después que vives ausente, mucha su tristeza, y pena es" (Calderón, *Argenis y Poliarco*, Jornada 2).
74 "conocí su tristeza, cuando a la guerra partí" (Lope de Vega, *El castigo sin venganaza*, Acto 3).
75 Lope de Vega, *La esclava de su galán*, Jornada 2.
76 Roos, *Chronic Sorrow*, 27.
77 "Mira si es harta causa de tristeza amar a un mármol, a una nieve, a un hielo" (Juan Pérez de Montalbán, *La toquera vizcaína*, Jornada 1).
78 "la tristeza de verte con Nise, celos me presenta" (Juan Pérez de Montalbán, *La ganancia por la mano*, Jornada 3); "Envidia, que en tristeza te consumes, deja el dolor que te transporta, y mueve" (Juan de la Cueva, *El viejo enamorado*, Acto 1).
79 This concern is voiced in the question, "¿Qué es la tristeza? ¿Tiene salud vuestra hija?" (Juan Ruiz de Alarcón, *El desdichado en el fingir*, Acto 3).
80 Calderón, *Los misterios de la Misa*, loa for auto sacramental.
81 Lope de Vega, *Quien todo lo quiere*, Jornada 2.
82 Tirso de Molina, *Cautela contra cautela*, Jornada 2.
83 "Vino a verse en fin tu padre en tan notable tristeza de ver mi necesidad, hambre, desnudez y pena" (Lope de Vega, *La mocedad de Roldán*, Acto 2).
84 Lope de Vega, *Las flores de Don Juan, y rico y pobre trocados*, Acto 1.
85 "la noche es toda tristeza … [H]ambre, cansancio y pereza me combaten a porfía" (Lope de Vega, *El amete de Toledo*, Acto 3).
86 Levine, *Unattended Sorrow*, 14. As Marjory Lange points out, however, even if old age brings more sadness, it also comes with less ability to express it because tears eventually dry up due to "a fundamental aspect of the aged nature – that of increased bodily desiccation … An elderly woman could be more lachrymate on account of her gender or less because of age" (Marjory E. Lange, *Telling Tears in the English Renaissance* [Leiden: E.J. Brill, 1996], 29–30).

87 Lope de Vega, *Porfiar hasta morir*, Acto 3.

88 Lope de Vega, *La octava maravilla*, Acto 2.

89 Tirso de Molina, *Esto sí que es negociar*, Jornada 2.

90 Lope de Vega, *El mejor alcalde, el rey*, Acto 1.

91 Lope de Vega, *El mejor mozo de España*, Acto 1.

92 Tirso de Molina, *Marta la piadosa*, Acto 1.

93 Lope de Vega, *Barlan y Josafá*, Acto 1.

94 "en ese extremo le han puesto tristeza, y melancolía, viéndose sin libertad" (Calderón, *El alcalde de sí mismo*, Jornada 3).

95 On the sadness of exiles see Anna Gotlib, "Memory, Sadness, and Longing: Exile Nostalgias as Attunement to Loss," in *The Moral Psychology of Sadness*, ed. Gotlib, 183–205. In this essay she writes of "the losses of home, of community, of culture, of language, and sometimes, of self that exiles (in which category I am including immigrants, refugees, migrants, and others forced to leave or leaving by desperate choice) know all too well" (183). She continues, "[E]xiles are largely defined by memory, longing, and time – and their relationship to them. To be an exile is to be, in important ways, cut off from the past not just geographically, but socially, epistemically, even narratively … [E]xile nostalgias can differ, depending on when they occur in the migration process. They might manifest as retrospective longing, sadness, and loss, preventing any meaningful efforts at assimilation; they might manifest as a prospective effort at integrating the longing for one's past and the realities of one's present; they might be some combination of the two" (194).

96 Lope de Vega, *El amete de Toledo*, Acto 1.

97 This kind of sorrow, accompanied by shame, on the part of Indigenous peoples is described in Donna Merwick, *The Shame and the Sorrow: Dutch-Amerindian Encounters in New Netherland* (Philadelphia: University of Pennsylvania Press, 2006).

98 Lope de Vega, *Los esclavos libres*, Acto 1. *Hanina* means servant girl; here the word is used as an adjective to signify Granada's subservience to its Christian conquerors.

99 Tirso de Molina, *La celosa de sí misma*, Acto 1.

100 For a discussion of Counter-Reformation treatises written for the express purpose of guiding artists toward appropriate ways to depict supernatural phenomena, see Hilaire Kallendorf, "Depicting Demons: Counter-Reformation Restraints and Baroque Representations," *The Center & Clark Newsletter* of the William Andrews Clark Memorial Library and the UCLA Center for Seventeenth and Eighteenth Century Studies (Spring 2001).

101 Calderón, *La vacante general*, loa for auto sacramental.

102 Lope de Vega, *El príncipe despeñado*, Acto 3.

103 Lope de Vega, *La campana de Aragón*, Acto 2. The Scripture reference is to 2 Corinthians 7:10: "For godly grief produces a repentance that leads to salvation and brings no regret, but worldly grief produces death."

104 Lope de Vega, *El marqués de Mantua*, Acto 2.

105 Hilaire Kallendorf, "Staging Penance: Scenes of Sacramental Confession in Early Modern Spanish Drama," in *Casuistry and Early Modern Hispanic Literature*, ed. Marlen Bidwell-Steiner and Michael Scham (Leiden: Brill, 2022), 176–201.

106 Calderón, *Los cabellos de Absalón*, Jornada 1.

107 "cruel de mi gran melancolía, éste el fin de mi alegría" (Calderón, *Con quien vengo, vengo*, Jornada 1). King Philip II of Spain was thought to suffer from melancholy, to the extent that his reign was considered by many to be a "melancholic age." See Roger Bartra, *Melancolía y cultura. Las enfermedades del alma en la España del Siglo de Oro* (Barcelona: Anagrama, 2021).

108 Lange, *Telling Tears*, 44.

109 Calderón, *Los cabellos de Absalón*, Jornada 1.

110 For further conflations of medical with moral discourse in the theatre of this time period, see Hilaire Kallendorf, "La virtud como metáfora médica en el drama español de la Edad Moderna," *eHumanista: Journal of Medieval and Early Modern Iberian Studies* 39 (2018): 105–21.

111 Lope de Vega, *La quinta de Florencia*, Jornada 1.

112 Calderón, *Los dos amantes del cielo*, Jornada 2.

113 For an engaging study of spiritual sorrow in an early modern English context, see Gary Kuchar, *The Poetry of Religious Sorrow in Early Modern England* (Cambridge: Cambridge University Press, 2008).

114 "Tú, Lascivia, has de viciar esa Cándida Pureza, Madre de alegría: veamos si hay mancha que la entristezca" (Calderón, *La primer flor del Carmelo*, auto sacramental).

115 Lope de Vega, *El castigo sin venganaza*, Acto 2.

116 Calderón, *La cisma de Inglaterra*, Jornada 1.

117 "Tengo una tristeza ahora que ese gusto me suspende" (Lope de Vega, *Los locos por el cielo*, Acto 1); "Con ocasión de tristeza, Flora, de gusto me privo" (Lope de Vega, *La Filisarda*, Acto 1).

118 Levine, *Unattended Sorrow*, 89.

119 Lope de Vega, *La niña de plata*, Acto 2.

120 "Si no te ríes, imposible es tu tristeza de divertir" (Calderón, *La señora y la criada*, Jornada 2).

121 Calderón, *El alcalde de sí mismo*, Jornada 1.

122 Tirso de Molina, *La peña de Francia*, Acto 3.

123 Calderón, *Nadie fíe su secreto*, Jornada 3.

124 Calderón, *No hay cosa como callar*, Jornada 2.

125 Lange, *Telling Tears*, 71.

126 "el lirio con su tristeza" (Lope de Vega, *El mejor maestro el tiempo*, Acto 2).

127 Lope de Vega, *El halcón de Federico*, Acto 2.

128 Lope de Vega, *La hermosa Ester*, Acto 1.

129 Juan de Aviñón, *Sevillana medicina* [1545], trans. Nicolás Monardes (Seville: Sociedad de Bibliófilos Andaluces, 1885), 305.

130 Juan de Matos Fragoso, *El yerro del entendido*, Acto 1.

131 Lope de Vega, *Los torneos de Aragón*, Acto 1.

132 Lope de Vega, *Lo que hay que fiar del mundo*, Acto 2.

133 Lope de Vega, *La envidia de la nobleza*, Acto 1.

134 Calderón, *El mayor encanto amor*, Jornada 2.

135 Madeline Miller, *Circe* (New York: Little, Brown & Co., 2018).

136 Tirso de Molina, *La mejor espigadera*, Jornada 1.

137 "mi pena va conmigo … Mi tristeza ya no es pasión, sino naturaleza" (Calderón, *Agradecer y no amar*, Jornada 1).

138 Roos, *Chronic Sorrow*, 169.

139 Lope de Vega, *La serrana de Tormes*, Acto 2.

140 Antonio Zamora, *Mazariegos y Monsalves*, Jornada 3.

141 Lope de Vega, *El castigo sin venganaza*, Acto 2.

142 "la tristeza marchita con la salud que te falta" (Tirso de Molina, *La venganza de Tamar*, Jornada 2).

143 Miguel de Cervantes, *Primera parte del ingenioso hidalgo don Quijote de la Mancha*, in *Obras completas*, ed. Florencio Sevilla (Madrid: Castalia, 1999), 145–320, ch. I, at 153.

144 "el dolor de cabeza, / que ocasiona mi tristeza, / y me aprieta el corazón" (Tirso de Molina, *No hay peor sordo*, Jornada 3). Interestingly, modern-day ethnographers in Nicaragua have reported encountering headache among the Native people there as a symptom of grief (Paul C. Rosenblatt, "Diversity in Human Grieving: Historical and Cross-Cultural Perspectives," in *Exploring Grief: Towards a Sociology of Sorrow*, ed. Michael Hviid Jacobsen and Anders Petersen [London: Routledge, 2020], 37–51, at 41).

145 "no como, ni duermo, perdido estoy de llanto, y de tristeza, parezco sin reposo un abrasado enfermo" (Lope de Vega, *La buena guarda*, Acto 1).

146 Levine, *Unattended Sorrow*, 5.

147 Weller, *The Wild Edge of Sorrow*, 98.

148 Calderón, *Los dos amantes del cielo*, Jornada 2.

149 Calderón, *Dar tiempo al tiempo*, Jornada 2. Curiously, "in Chinese medicine, the lungs are the organ of grief" (Cormier, *Sweet Sorrow*, 41).

150 Lope de Vega, *El bastardo Mudarra*, Acto 3. As this sensation is described by grief counsellor Stephen Levine, "when our grief is undeniable, we move like a blind person through a maze, feeling our way forward, slowly" (Levine, *Unattended Sorrow*, 60).

151 Juan Pérez de Montalbán, *Segunda parte del Séneca de España, Don Felipe Segundo*, Jornada 1. Grief counsellor Stephen Levine confirms, "Unattended sorrow disturbs sleep and infects our dreams" (Levine, *Unattended Sorrow*, 4).

152 Tirso de Molina, *La mejor espigadera*, Jornada 1.

153 "dulce sombra, y regalado sueño, que suele suceder a una tristeza" (Lope de Vega, *El soldado amante*, Acto 1).

154 Grief counsellor Steven Levine agrees: "Unattended sorrow affects our appetite, whether in the form of overeating or self-starvation" (Levine, *Unattended Sorrow*, 5).

155 Lope de Vega, *La doncella Teodor*, Acto 1.

156 Juan Pérez de Montalbán, *El sufrimiento premiado*, Jornada 1.

157 Calderón, *Mañanas de abril y mayo*, Acto 1.

158 Lope de Vega, *El favor agradecido*, Acto 2.

159 Calderón, *Hado y divisa de Leonido y Marfisa*, Jornada 3.

160 "estaba perdiendo el seso de tristeza pura" (Lope de Vega, *Laura perseguida*, Acto 2); "Muriendo estoy de tristeza, confuso, loco y turbado" (Lope de Vega, *El príncipe perfecto, parte segunda*, Acto 2).

161 "Ya más que tristeza es delirio la suya" (Calderón, *El secreto a voces*, Jornada 2).

162 Calderón, *También hay duelo en las damas*, Jornada 3.

163 "Traigo una tristeza en mí, que acabar mi vida aguarda" (Lope de Vega, *Servir a buenos*, Acto 1).

164 "ha estado siempre con la más grave tristeza que vi en mi vida; yo temo que, melancólico, muera" (Calderón, *El alcalde de sí mismo*, Jornada 2).

165 Lope de Vega, *El bastardo Mudarra*, Acto 2.

166 On the Baroque aesthetics of hyperbole as exemplified by "extreme" or limit-cases of conscience see Elena del Río Parra, *Cartografías de conciencia española en la Edad de Oro* (Mexico City: Fondo de Cultura Económica, 2008).

167 Calderón, *El príncipe constante*, Jornada 2.

168 Francisco de Rojas Zorrilla, *No hay amigo para amigo*, Jornada 1.

169 Lope de Vega, *Los embustes de Zelauro*, Acto 3.

170 "No tiene elección mi amor, ni albedrío mi tristeza" (Calderón, *La banda y la flor*, Jornada 1).

171 "Para oprimir la tristeza, no hay en los Reyes poder" (Lope de Vega, *El despertar a quien duerme*, Acto 1).

172 Lope de Vega, *Quien todo lo quiere*, Acto 1.

173 Jamie Lindemann Nelson, "Sadness, Sense, and Sensibility," in *The Moral Psychology of Sadness*, ed. Gotlib, 53–67, at 54.

174 Lange, *Telling Tears*, 111, 114, 116.

175 "Mal se rinde una pasión, mal se vence una tristeza" (Calderón, *El mayor monstruo del mundo*, Jornada 2).

176 "Aquí a templar la tristeza de tus pensamientos vienes" (Calderón, *Argenis y Poliarco*, Jornada 2).

177 Gotlib, "The Topographies of Sadness," 11.

178 "Holgárame de aliviar alguna tristeza mía" (Lope de Vega, *El mejor maestro, el tiempo*, Acto 1).

179 "hoy resuscite la alegría que ha muerto su tristeza, destierre su dolor, su luto quite" (Lope de Vega, *El príncipe perfecto, parte primera*, Acto 1).

180 "Si quieres poner freno a la tristeza, o Rey, que te molesta estos días, parte al campo" (Lope de Vega, *El príncipe despeñado*, Acto 3). Notice that here the king is advised to go take some fresh air in the country, getting away from the court, as a way to practice self-care.

181 This is the advice offered in the line, "Deja, Lucinda, esa tristeza, deja ese enojoso humor, alegra el rostro" (Lope de Vega, *El ruiseñor de Sevilla*, Acto 1).

182 Here is some salutary advice from grief counsellor Stephen Levine: "Walking, much like singing, steadies the mind. When we place one foot in front of the other, we can feel the body lean and sway as we move forward. The first steps may be slow, but gradually we find our gait. Though we may require effort to break our inertia, our willingness to move is soon required. At first, we find the mind doing the walking; then the body soon takes over, and with that, our thoughts are free to flow. With each step, as the mind gradually begins to note the sensations in each footfall, we reenter and become present in our body. We can feel the muscles lift the foot, swing it forward, then place it back on the ground, noting the moment when both feet touch the earth before the next foot rises to the challenge. When we attend to the moment-by-moment sensations that accompany each step, it is as though we are learning to walk all over again. We can imagine what it must have been like to take our first steps as a toddler. It's a sense of accomplishment and freedom rarely rivaled in the years that follow" (Levine, *Unattended Sorrow*, 102–3).

183 Calderón, "hoy, por vencer esta tristeza, salió al campo su belleza" (*El escondido y la tapada*, Jornada 1); "Pues puédente divertir tu tristeza estos jardines" (Calderón, *El príncipe constante*, Acto 1).

184 "vine a tan fiera tristeza, que a las orillas del mar salía" (Lope de Vega, *El caballero del Sacramento*, Acto 3).

185 "[de] las varias flores los regalados olores, que alegran toda tristeza" (Juan de la Cueva, *La muerte de Virginia y Appio Claudio*, Acto 1).

186 "la Primavera, suelen divertirme a ratos del cuidado, y la tristeza, porque la caza arrebata todas las tristezas nuestras" (Tirso de Molina, *Adversa fortuna de Don Álvaro de Luna, segunda parte*, Jornada 1).

187 "la Reina mi señora, divirtiendo la pasión de su tristeza, se rindió al sueño" (Calderón, *Gustos y disgustos son no más que imaginación*, Jornada 1).

188 Cormier, *Sweet Sorrow*, 104.

189 Lope de Vega, *Laura perseguida*, Acto 2.

190 Calderón, *De una causa dos efectos*, Jornada 2; Lope de Vega, *La inocente Laura*, Acto 2.

191 "Mal hace vuestra Alteza en dar tanto lugar a una tristeza" (Calderón, *El galán fantasma*, Acto 1).

192 Hilaire Kallendorf, "Loath to Call It Sloth: The Plus Side of *Pereza*," in *Sins of the Fathers*, 97–111.

193 Lope de Vega, *Los comendadores de Córdoba*, Jornada 2.

194 Tirso de Molina, *Quien habló, pagó*, Jornada 2.

195 Lope de Vega, *La viuda casada y doncella*, Acto 2.

196 Lope de Vega, *La quinta de Florencia*, Jornada 1.

197 "de Roma el fuego, o aquel del Troyano amante mayor tristeza me dan, no quisiera haberlo oído" (Lope de Vega, *El postrer godo*, Acto 2).

198 "Hija, querría que viniese un músico a alegrar tu tristeza" (Lope de Vega, *El ruiseñor de Sevilla*, Acto 2).

199 "Inés, cantad, que así en parte podré aliviar mi tristeza, y mi pesar: Cantad tono triste" (Calderón, *Luis Pérez el gallego*, Jornada 2).

200 Levine, *Unattended Sorrow*, 182.

201 "[de] la música no tengo alivio alguno, antes Flora de mi tristeza el extremo se aumenta con la dulzura de sus cláusulas" (Calderón, *Amado y aborrecido*, Jornada 3).

202 Lope de Vega, *Los palacios de Galiana*, Acto 1.

203 Calderón, *No hay cosa como callar*, Jornada 2.

204 "Sintiendo el Rey la extraña tristeza que padece … su hermana, y pretendiendo aliviarla" (Calderón, *Amado y aborrecido*, Jornada 3).

205 Calderón, *El postrer duelo de España*, Jornada 2.

206 Lope de Vega, *Las pobrezas de Reinaldos*, Acto 1.

207 Lope de Vega, *Los peligros de la ausencia*, Acto 3.

208 Hilaire Kallendorf, "Asking for Advice: Class, Gender, and the Supernatural," in *Conscience on Stage: The* Comedia *as Casuistry in Early Modern Spain* (Toronto: University of Toronto Press, 2007), 108–42.

209 Juan de la Cueva, *Comedia del príncipe tirano*, Acto 2.

210 Calderón, *Amado y aborrecido*, Jornada 2.

211 Psychologist Sherry Cormier asserts, "when survivors don't have to engage in emotional constipation, but instead have the freedom to tell and retell their story about the loss or trauma to caring companions and listeners, the potential for growth is even greater" (Cormier, *Sweet Sorrow*, 63).

212 Alexander Lowen, *Joy: The Surrender to the Body and to Life* (New York: Arkana, 1995), 141.

213 Gotlib, "The Topographies of Sadness," 9.

214 Calderón, *Amigo amante y leal*, Jornada 2.

215 Lope de Vega, *El piadoso veneciano*, Acto 2.

216 "consuelo en su tristeza, como un amigo fiel para amor" (Lope de Vega, *Servir a buenos*, Acto 1).

217 Lope de Vega, *La Filisarda*, Acto 1.

218 Calderón, *El postrer duelo de España*, Jornada 1.

219 Lope de Vega, *La madre de la mejor*, Acto 1.

220 Tirso de Molina, *No hay peor sordo*, Jornada 1.

221 Tirso de Molina, *La mejor espigadera*, Jornada 3.

222 Tirso de Molina, *La santa Juana*, Acto 2.

223 Juan de la Cueva, *El Infamador*, Acto 1.

224 Lope de Vega, *El bobo del colegio*, Acto 2.

225 Lope de Vega, *El amigo por fuerza*, Acto 2.

226 Lope de Vega, *La hermosura aborrecida*, Acto 2.

227 Tirso de Molina, *Los lagos de San Vicente*, Acto 2. However, empathy in the *comedias* is not always effective, as we seen in the line, "Todo su acompañamiento para mi tristeza es viento" (Lope de Vega, *El amigo por fuerza*, Acto 2).

228	Tirso de Molina, *Doña Beatriz de Silva*, Acto 2.

229	Tirso de Molina, *El melancólico*, Acto 2.

230	Lope de Vega, *Guardar y guardarse*, Acto 3.

231	Juan Ruiz de Alarcón, *La manganilla de Melilla*, Acto 2.

232	Calderón, *La cisma de Inglaterra*, Jornada 2.

233	Calderón, *Casa con dos puertas mala es de guardar*, Jornada 2.

234	Calderón, *La redención de cautivos*, auto sacramental.

235	Levine, *Unattended Sorrow*, 137.

236	Calderón, *La gran Cenobia*, Jornada 2.

237	"Tristeza en los vasallos / y viendo presente el dueño, / más parece obstinación, / que noble arrepentimiento" (Juan Pérez de Montalbán, *Amor, privanza y castigo*, Acto 1).

238	Calderón, *De un castigo tres venganzas*, Jornada 1.

239	Lope de Vega, *Lo que ha de ser*, Jornada 1.

240	Tirso de Molina, *Siempre ayuda la verdad*, Jornada 3.

241	Juan de la Cueva, *El saco de Roma y muerte de Borbón*, Acto 3.

242	Calderón, *La púrpura de la rosa*, auto sacramental.

243	Lope de Vega, *La desdichada Estefanía*, Acto 2.

244	Juan Pérez de Montalbán, *La deshonra honrosa*, Jornada 3.

245	Juan de la Cueva, *Los siete infantes de Lara*, Acto 2.

246	Lope de Vega, *La mayor victoria de Alemania de Don Gonzalo de Córdoba*, preliminares.

247	Lope de Vega, *La prueba de los ingenios*, Acto 3.

248	Douglas Abrams in Dalai Lama, Desmond Tutu, and Douglas Abrams, *The Book of Joy: Lasting Happiness in a Changing World* (New York: Avery, 2016), 110–11.

249	George Bonanno, *The Other Side of Sadness: What the New Science of Bereavement Tells Us* (New York: Basic Books, 2009), 31.

250	Lope de Vega, *El animal de Ungría*, Acto 1.

251	Thus Teodosia laments, "la tristeza que poseo de nuevo me ha entristecido" (Juan de la Cueva, *Tragedia del príncipe tirano*, Acto 3).

252	Richard L. Solomon, "The Opponent-Process Theory of Acquired Motivation," *American Psychologist* 35 (1980): 691–712.

253	Cormier, *Sweet Sorrow*, 76.

254	Calderón, *El diablo mudo*, auto sacramental.

255	Tirso de Molina, *El melancólico*, Acto 3.

256	Lope de Vega, *Por la puente, Juana*, Acto 2.

257	Lope de Vega, *Los melindres de Belisa*, Acto 1.

258	Lope de Vega, *El Amor enamorado*, preliminares.

7. Ode to Joy

1	Friedrich Schiller, "An die Freude" (German ode, 1786, later used by Beethoven in choral finale of 9th symphony), English translation by the Schiller Institute, https://archive.schillerinstitute.com/transl/schiller_poem/ode_to_joy.pdf.

2　William Blake, *Visions of the Daughters of Albion* (1793), The William Blake Archive, http://www.blakearchive.org/search/?search=joys%20grow.

3　John Donne, Elegy 19, https://www.poetryfoundation.org/poems/50340/to-his -mistress-going-to-bed.

4　Christian Center billboard, Ocean County, New Jersey, quoted in Adam Potkay, *The Story of Joy: From the Bible to Late Romanticism* (Cambridge: Cambridge University Press, 2007), 224.

5　Calderón, *El jardín de Falerina*, auto sacramental.

6　Calderón, *La desdicha de la voz*, Jornada 1.

7　Lope de Vega, *La corona merecida*, Acto 2.

8　"Podrá poner mi alegría luminarias en el seso" (Lope de Vega, *El padrino desposado*, Jornada 3).

9　Lope de Vega, *La madre de la mejor*, Acto 2.

10　Lope de Vega, *El amigo hasta la muerte*, Acto 1.

11　Mary Clark Moschella, "Calling and Compassion: Elements of Joy in Lived Practices of Care," in *Joy and Human Flourishing: Essays on Theology, Culture, and the Good Life*, ed. Miroslav Volf and Justin E. Crisp (Minneapolis: Fortress, 2015), 97–126, at 101, 107.

12　Lope de Vega, *Los peligros de la ausencia*, Acto 3.

13　"Repartida la alegría, el gusto suele doblar" (Calderón, *Nadie fíe su secreto*, Jornada 3).

14　Lope de Vega, *El verdadero amante*, Acto 1.

15　"Lo verde me dio esperanza, y lo carmesí alegría" (Lope de Vega, *El mejor mozo de España*, Acto 1).

16　"Pon la rosa carmesí de mi prestada alegría" (Lope de Vega, *El remedio en la desdicha*, Acto 1).

17　Calderón, *Casa con dos puertas mala es de guardar*, Jornada 3.

18　"Son sus árboles y flores indicios de amor; alegría me han causado" (Lope de Vega, *La locura por la honra*, Acto 2).

19　Guillén de Castro, *Cuánto se estima el honor*, Jornada 1.

20　"Dame algún contento ahora, infunde al alma alegría con esa corriente fría, y con esa voz sonora" (Tirso de Molina, *El condenado por desconfiado*, Jornada 3).

21　"sólo los amores de las parleras aves me causan alegría, cuando aparece el día" (Lope de Vega, *El Perseo*, Acto 2).

22　"Trinaban los alegres ruiseñores" (Lope de Vega, *El Amor enamorado*, preliminares) and "muéstrame el árbol o flor donde te causa alegría este galán ruiseñor" (Lope de Vega, *El ruiseñor de Sevilla*, Acto 3).

23　Marianne Meye Thompson, "Reflections on Joy in the Bible," in *Joy and Human Flourishing*, ed. Volf and Crisp, 17–38, at 21, 22.

24　"Yo he visto la Primavera dar a este campo alegría" (Lope de Vega, *El hijo de los leones*, Acto 2).

25　"jazmines, ya entre aljofares y escarchas dando al verano alegría" (Lope de Vega, *La traición bien acertada*, Jornada 1).

26 Lope de Vega, *Los trabajos de Jacob*, Jornada 1.

27 Jürgen Moltmann, "Christianity: A Religion of Joy," in *Joy and Human Flourishing*, ed. Volf and Crisp, 1–16, at 7. He expounds further: "It is a remarkable fact that the great Christian festivals are not distributed throughout the year but take place in the first half and are concentrated on the spring. The spring of the new year begins with the winter solstice, comes alive at Easter in the flowers and trees, and reaches its full flowering at Whitsun or Pentecost. This is … a way of showing that with the coming of Christ into this world, his death and resurrection, and the outpouring of the divine Spirit the spring of eternal life begins for human beings, all living beings, and the earth" (8–9).

28 "os vi en la puerta Dorada del oro de mi alegría" (Lope de Vega, *La madre de la mejor*, Acto 2).

29 Lope de Vega, *Las almenas de Toro*, Acto 3.

30 Calderón, *La vida es sueño*, Jornada 2. These lines are spoken of a person whose beauty is thereby compared to that of the sun.

31 Alexander Lowen, *Joy: The Surrender to the Body and to Life* (New York: Arkana, 1995), 9.

32 "amanezca el Alba de mi alegría" (Lope de Vega, *La envidia de la nobleza*, Acto 2).

33 "sale el Sol, y de alegría se baña el mundo" (Lope de Vega, *Don Gonzalo de Córdoba*, Jornada 1).

34 "Alegráos, pastores, ya viene el albor, tened alegría, que ya viene el día" (Lope de Vega, *El cardenal de Belén*, Acto 3).

35   Lindabridis aquella,
        que con hermoso Arrebol
        da a los Campos alegría,
        sin que le haga falta al Día
        irse ya poniendo el Sol:
        ¡qué hermosa es! (¡Valedme Cielos!)   (Calderón, *El castillo de Lindabridis*, Jornada 1)

36 "fiestas ordena el cielo, y de alegría le presta sus estrellas el dorado manto del cielo" (Lope de Vega, *La limpieza no manchada*, Acto 3).

37 Tirso de Molina, *La mejor espigadera*, Jornada 1.

38 Potkay, *The Story of Joy*, 1.

39 Lope de Vega, *La madre de la mejor*, Acto 1.

40 "Muestra en el rostro alegría" (Tirso de Molina, *Santo y sastre*, Acto 2).

41 Juan Pérez de Montalbán, *Cumplir con su obligación*, Jornada 1.

42 "Laetitia vero dicitur, quum ita mouetur animus, ut etiam ad exteriora egrediatur, & maxime in vultu conspiciatur" (Sebastián de Covarrubias, *Tesoro de la lengua castellana* [Madrid: Luis Sánchez, 1611], entry for *gozo*, p. 445).

43 Moltmann, "Christianity: A Religion of Joy," 3.

44 "En coros las bellas ninfas, con dulces festivas señas de alegría en los semblantes, hacia nosotros se acercan" (Juan Bautista Diamante, *Más encanto es la hermosura*, Jornada 2).

45 "la soberana alegría que amor escribe en mis ojos" (Lope de Vega, *El amigo por fuerza*, Acto 3).

46 "en el papel de su cara vi muchas veces escrita una alegría al mirarla" (Agustín Moreto, *El licenciado vidriera*, Jornada 1).

47 "a los ojos traslada su alegría el corazón" (Lope de Vega, *Servir con mala estrella*, Acto 2).

48 "el alma se sale a los ojos de alegría" (Antonio Zamora, *Cada uno es linaje aparte, y los Mazas de Aragón*, Jornada 3).

49 Calderón, *Cómo se comunican dos estrellas contrarias*, Jornada 3.

50 "también hay lágrimas de alegría" (Calderón, *A secreto agravio, secreta venganza*, Acto 1).

51 Gullén de Castro, *El mejor esposo*, Jornada 3.

52 "dos mil bendiciones le echan, todos lloran de alegría, y de sus lágrimas riegan el suelo" (Lope de Vega, *El rey sin reino*, Acto 1). In this case joyful tears are accompanied by 2,000 blessings.

53 Francisco de Rojas Zorrilla, *Casarse por vengarse*, Jornada 1.

54 See Hilaire Kallendorf and Craig Kallendorf, "Catharsis as Exorcism: Aristotle, Tragedy, and Religio-Poetic Liminality," *Literary Imagination* 14.3 (2012): 296–311.

55 "Vaya, vaya de Mojiganga, de alegría, y de pesar, que quien llora con placer, siente bien" (Calderón, *Céfalo y Pocris*, Jornada 3).

56 Francisco de Rojas Zorrilla, *Los encantos de Medea*, Jornada 2.

57 Lope de Vega, *El mejor mozo de España*, Acto 2.

58 "Hija, ponte muy bizarra, que estimo más tu alegría, que si me entrara este día de oro un millón" (Lope de Vega, *El ruiseñor de Sevilla*, Acto 3).

59 For example, "no era semejante el hábito, y su alegría. Que trae luto" (Lope de Vega, *El mármol de Felisardo*, Acto 2).

60 Tirso de Molina, *La vida de Herodes*, Acto 3.

61 "los besará con alegría" (Calderón, *La hija del aire*, Acto 1).

62 "vamos presto a darle las gracias de mi vida y alegría, los pies mil veces tengo de besarle" (Lope de Vega, *El santo negro Rosambuco de la ciudad de Palermo*, Acto 2).

63 Ingenio to África:

> ¿Cómo, África hermosa, el día
> de tan grande sentimiento
> en Tierra, Agua, Fuego, y Viento,
> celebras con alegría?
> ¿Qué causa te mueve?　　(Calderón, *A Dios por razón de estado*, auto sacramental)

64 One character says to his wife, "Enhorabuena mujer mía, salga el sol de mi alegría" (Lope de Vega, *Los embustes de Zelauro*, Acto 1); another says to a relative, "Yo que como parte soy de tu sangre, y tu alegría, tanta tengo de tu bien; parabién te doy" (Lope de Vega, *La victoria de la honra*, Acto 3).

65 Calderón, *El nuevo hospicio de pobres*, auto sacramental.

66 Tirso de Molina, *Quien no cae no se levanta*, Acto 2.

67 Lope de Vega, *De ello dirá*, Acto 1.

68 "halla igualmente su medicina el enfermo, su alegría el afligido, el mísero su remedio, el sediento su agua" (Calderón, *El origen, pérdida y restauración de la Virgen del Sagrario*, Acto 1).

69 "me guía en este mar de aflicción al puerto del alegría" (Cervantes, *Los baños de Argel*, Jornada 1).

70 Juan Bautista Diamante, *El defensor del Peñón*, Jornada 1.

71 Lope de Vega, *De ello dirá*, Acto 2.

72 Calderón, *Sueños hay, que verdad son*, loa for auto sacramental.

73 Lope de Vega, *Dios hace reyes*, Acto 3.

74 Potkay, *The Story of Joy*, 10, 25. One might think here of C.S. Lewis's autobiography, *Surprised by Joy* (New York: HarperOne, 2017).

75 Juan de Matos Fragoso, *El genízaro de Ungría*, Jornada 3.

76 Lope de Vega, *Los comendadores de Córdoba*, Jornada 3.

77 "suele un grande placer, y una súbita alegría quitar la vida" (Lope de Vega, *Porfiando vence amor*, Jornada 3).

78 Mary Robinson, sonnet sequence *Sappho and Phaon* [1796], quoted in Potkay, *The Story of Joy*, 156.

79 Moschella, "Calling and Compassion," 97–126, at 99.

80 Lope de Vega, *Los prados de León*, Acto 1.

81 Juan Ruiz de Alarcón, *Los pechos privilegiados*, Acto 1.

82 Lope de Vega, *Guardar y guardarse*, Acto 1.

83 Lope de Vega, *El ruiseñor de Sevilla*, Acto 1.

84 "supiera cantar, Señor, tus Piedades, pidiéndote que me vuelvas la alegría saludable, que en mi prevaricación perdí" (Calderón, *La cura y la enfermedad*, auto sacramental). This line echoes the Bible verse "restore unto me the joy of my salvation" (Psalm 51:12).

85 "de la mano una espina que traía, curéle, y con alegría de verse curado, y sano, va por todo el Monasterio" (Lope de Vega, *El cardenal de Belén*, Acto 3).

86 "yo espero que restaure su alegría y salud vuestra presencia" (Tirso de Molina, *El melancólico*, Acto 3).

87 "a la primera alegría de su salud reduciendo todos los Hijos de Adán" (Calderón, *Lo que va del hombre a Dios*, auto sacramental).

88 Lope de Vega, *El ruiseñor de Sevilla*, Acto 3.

89 Calderón, *Apolo y Climene*, Jornada 2.

90 Tirso de Molina, *La lealtad contra la envidia*, Acto 3.

91 Calderón, *Eco y Narciso*, Jornada 1.

92 "un aposento, en quien es tapicería, la limpieza, y la alegría, que es donde vive el contento" (Lope de Vega, *Al pasar del arroyo*, Acto 3).

93 "no hay alegría que iguale al caminar con el día" (Lope de Vega, *El hamete de Toledo*, Acto 3).

94 Tirso de Molina, *La dama del olivar*, Acto 2.

95 Lope de Vega, *Los muertos vivos*, Acto 3.

96 Calderón, *El médico de su honra*, Acto 1.

97 Tirso de Molina, *El melancólico*, Acto 2. *Alarde* means a military review or parade; figuratively, the term is used to express the notion of ostentatious display or show.

98 In the context of political restoration, Adam Potkay traces some uses of the word *joy* in the titles of sermons and broadsides celebrating the Restoration of the British monarchy after the fall of Oliver Cromwell's commonwealth. The Restoration was "publicly acclaimed … with the liberal use of 'joy' in dozens of sermons and broadsheet pamphlets (e.g. *England's day of joy and rejoicing … or, the True Manner of proclaiming Charles the Second King of England*)" (Potkay, *The Story of Joy*, 89).

99 Potkay, *The Story of Joy*, book blurb, vii.

100 Moltmann, "Christianity: A Religion of Joy," 9.

101 Calderón, *Amar después de la muerte*, Jornada 3.

102 Calderón, *Antes que todo es mi dama*, Jornada 1.

103 Agustín Moreto, *Antioco y Seleuco*, Jornada 1.

104 Lope de Vega, *El premio del bien hablar*, Acto 2.

105 Lope de Vega, *El bastardo Mudarra*, Acto 3.

106 Lope de Vega, *El mayorazgo dudoso*, Jornada 3.

107 See also Laura Bass, *The Drama of the Portrait: Theater and Visual Culture in Early Modern Spain* (University Park: Penn State University Press, 2008).

108 Lope de Vega, *El leal criado*, Acto 2.

109 "camino incierto halló peregrino el día, ni vio con más alegría roto marinero el puerto" (Lope de Vega, *Amar, servir y esperar*, Acto 1).

110 Lope de Vega, *Jorge Toledano*, Acto 2.

111 Lope de Vega, *La prisión sin culpa*, Acto 3.

112 "el alegría de veros con tal bonanza" (Lope de Vega, *El sembrar en buena tierra*, Acto 3). *Bonanza* here means prosperity or else a new development deemed favourable either economically or socially. Theologian Miroslav Volf comments upon this aspect of joy: "joy wells up in me when I see myself or those for whom I care as having had a good fortune or having been blessed. For instance, I rejoice over a bonus but not over getting regular pay" (Miroslav Volf, "The Crown of the Good Life: A Hypothesis," in *Joy and Human Flourishing*, ed. Volf and Crisp, 127–35, at 129).

113 "Amigos, hoy es el día que amanece en mí alegría, hoy me da favor mi estrella" (Lope de Vega, *La bella malmaridada*, Jornada 2).

114 Lope de Vega, *La buena guarda*, Acto 1.

115 Lope de Vega, *Los habladores*, entremés.

116 "sumas de granas de plato, y oro que te causará alegría" (Lope de Vega, *Servir con mala estrella*, Acto 2).

117 "El oro causa alegría, guantes de ámbar, y un bolsillo de cien escudos" (Lope de Vega, *Don Gonzalo de Córdoba*, Jornada 1).

118 Lope de Vega, *Los torneos de Aragón*, Acto 3.

119		Lisboa en esta alegría
		en dos extremos está
		de grandeza, y de riqueza,
		todo es hermosura, y oro.						(Lope de Vega, *El príncipe perfecto*, Acto 2)

120	Lope de Vega, *Con su pan se lo coma*, Acto 1.

121	Potkay, *The Story of Joy*, 5.

122	Antonio Damasio, *Looking for Spinoza: Joy, Sorrow, and the Feeling Brain* (Orlando: Harcourt, 2003), 284.

123	Calderón, *La primer flor del Carmelo*, auto sacramental. This line refers to moral purity as typified by the Virgin Mary.

124	Lope de Vega, *La bella Aurora*, Acto 1.

125	Calderón, *El alcalde de Zalamea*, Jornada 3.

126	The trace is a critical category I employed in *Conscience on Stage* which is equally applicable here: "The French word *la trace* can be translated variously as 'footprint,' 'mark,' 'trail,' or 'clue.' Ajay Heble relates it to both Ferdinand de Saussure's concept of the sign and Sigmund Freud's theory of memory, but attributes the term primarily to Derridian deconstruction: 'It is the name Derrida gives to the absences, the relations of difference, that are involved in the production of the sign'" (Hilaire Kallendorf, *Conscience on Stage: The* Comedia *as Casuistry in Early Modern Spain* [Toronto: University of Toronto Press, 2007], 39, quoting Ajay Heble, "Trace," in *Encyclopedia of Contemporary Literary Theory*, ed. Irena R. Makaryk [Toronto: University of Toronto Press, 1997], 646–67).

127	Lope de Vega, *Los melindres de Belisa*, Acto 3.

128	Lope de Vega, *La viuda valenciana*, Acto 2.

129	Calderón, *Primero soy yo*, Jornada 1.

130	Agustín Moreto, *La traición vengada*, Jornada 1.

131	N.T. Wright traces these early modern Spanish customs at least as far back as New Testament times: "Paul also envisaged something more. The 'celebrations' of *Kyrios Caesar* took place in public, as whole towns would be given over to days and seasons of festivals involving processions, music and dancing, feasting and drinking, and ultimately sacrifices and prayers at the relevant shrines" (N.T. Wright, "Joy: Some New Testament Perspectives and Questions," in *Joy and Human Flourishing*, ed. Volf and Crisp, 39–61, at 57).

132	Calderón, *A María el corazón*, auto sacramental.

133	Calderón, *El año santo de Roma*, auto sacramental.

134	Lope de Vega, *El capellán de la Virgen*, Acto 3.

135	"en este Fiat del Sábado, envuelta la alegría mayor, que pudo tener" (Calderón, *La devoción de la Misa*, loa for auto sacramental).

136	"para que tan festivo día, tenga el cumplimiento de alegría que merece" (Calderón, *La vacante general*, auto sacramental).

137	Calderón, *Guárdate de la agua mansa*, Jornada 2.

138 Lope de Vega, *El remedio en la desdicha*, Acto 1.
139 "si conforme lo que siento hubiera de mostrar el alegría, poco era en fiestas desprender mi hacienda" (Lope de Vega, *La traición bien acertada*, Jornada 3).
140 Calderón, *La viña del Señor*, auto sacramental.
141 Calderón, *El árbol del mejor fruto*, auto sacramental.
142 Wright, "Joy: Some New Testament Perspectives and Questions," 44.
143 Potkay, *The Story of Joy*, 10.
144 Meye Thompson, "Reflections on Joy in the Bible," 34.
145 Volf, "The Crown of the Good Life," 132–3.
146 "Gran música, y alegría, suena en la puerta Real" (Lope de Vega, *La niña de plata*, Acto 1). Neuroscientist Antonio Damasio describes having experienced "the continuous musical line of our minds ... a humming that turns to all-out singing when we are occupied by joy" (Damasio, *Looking for Spinoza*, 3).
147 "en fe de cuya alegría a cantar, y bailar vuelvo" (Calderón, *El gran mercado del mundo*, auto sacramental).
148 "envueltas en la alegría, cantando, y bailando" (Juan Bautista Diamante, *Alfeo y Aretusa*, Jornada 2).
149 "templar las ya sonoras cuerdas de plata, en señas de alegría" (Juan Bautista Diamante, *Cumplirle a Dios la palabra*, Jornada 3).
150 "vengan luego con instrumentos, músicos galanes, celebraremos todos la alegría" (Tirso de Molina, *La malcontenta*, Acto 1).
151 "Grita, y alegría dentro, y canten con sonajas" (Lope de Vega, *Las flores de Don Juan, y rico y pobre trocados*, Acto 1). Technically the *sonaja* is a pair of circular metallic disks hung on a metal wire; the tambourine is made with multiple *sonajas*.
152 "su Monarca la juren las demás islas; y en su alegría voces sean albogues, trompas y liras" (Antonio Zamora, *Áspides hay Basiliscos*, Jornada 1). The Basque *alboka* (*albogue* in Spanish) is a woodwind instrument consisting of a single reed, two small diameter melody pipes with finger holes, and a bell (traditionally made from the horn of an animal native to the region).
153 "Y haga el son cosquillas a la alegría" (Guillén de Castro, *El mejor esposo*, Jornada 2). The music for the *son* could be sung but was often played on African bongo drums.
154 "A dar saltos de alegría, vamos de aquí, Caballeros" (Lope de Vega, *El mármol de Felisardo*, Acto 2) and "el saltar, el bailar, y el alegría" (Lope de Vega, *La madre de la mejor*, Acto 2).
155 Juan Ruiz de Alarcón, *El dueño de las estrellas*, Acto 1.
156 For psychotherapist Alexander Lowen "dancing is the most natural activity on joyful occasions" (Lowen, *Joy: The Surrender to the Body and to Life*, 2).
157 N.T. Wright sees in joyful banqueting a clearly biblical echo: "right through the Bible the idea of a great feast is one of the central ways in which joy is expressed in family or community" (Wright, "Joy: Some New Testament Perspectives and Questions," 42).
158 "Para mayor alegría, coman conmigo a mi mesa" (Lope de Vega, *La corona merecida*, Acto 3).

159 "no hay alegría donde no hay olla" (Antonio Zamora, *El lucero de Madrid, y divino Labrador San Isidro*, Acto 1).

160 This detail is expressed in the negative when Tireo says: "no / permite la austeridad / la alegría del arroz" (Antonio Zamora, *Ser fino y no parecerlo*, Acto 1).

161 "del vino el alegría quita la melancolía" (Lope de Vega, *Argel fingido y renegado de amor*, Acto 2).

162 "Alguna cosa burlesca, que tenga mucha alegría" (Agustín Moreto, *El desdén con el desdén*, Jornada 2).

163 "Risa, que es alegría, y fiesta" (Calderón, *La vacante general*, loa for auto sacramental).

164 "fuera con más risa y alegría, a estar despierta a media noche" (Lope de Vega, *La primera información*, Jornada 2).

165 Lope de Vega, *Arauco domado por el excelentísimo señor Don García Hurtado de Mendoza*, Acto 1.

166 "Día de tan común alegría, cuyo luzimiento pasa por las puertas de tu casa" (Calderón, *La desdicha de la voz*, Jornada 1).

167 Lope de Vega, *Los españoles en Flandes*, Acto 2.

168 Calderón, *El segundo blasón del Austria*, auto sacramental.

169 "justo es, que dé muestras de su común alegría, justo es, que de nuestra fiesta la aclamación oiga altiva" (Calderón, *El segundo Scipión*, Jornada 3).

170 "hacen dentro ruido, dando voces en señal de alegría" (Guillén de Castro, *Las mocedades del Cid, comedia segunda*, Acto 3).

171 "Cuanto a la suma alegría que gozéis de aplausos llena, recibid la enhorabuena" (Calderón, *El Faetonte*, Jornada 2).

172 Lope de Vega, *El príncipe despeñado*, Acto 2.

173 Wright, "Joy: Some New Testament Perspectives and Questions," 43.

174 Calderón, *Las espigas de Ruth*, auto sacramental.

175 Agustín Moreto, *Los más dichosos hermanos*, Jornada 3.

176 Tirso de Molina, *La gallega Mari Hernández*, Acto 1.

177 Calderón, *La torre de Babilonia*, auto sacramental.

178 "Pastores, tanta alegría celébrese de mil modos, cantad, bailad, pues a todos alcanza" (Lope de Vega, *El nacimiento de Cristo*, Acto 3).

179 "¡Si de Alcalá te veniste sólo a gozar la alegría que Madrid hace este día!" (Juan Ruiz de Alarcón, *Las paredes oyen*, Acto 1). It is significant that this line occurs in a play by Alarcón because he is one of the later dramatists. The royal court for the Kingdom of Castile was not located in Madrid until well into the sixteenth century.

180 Calderón, *El gran príncipe de Fez*, Jornada 2. *Alborozo* was intense joy or rejoicing expressed with shouts, gestures, or other actions.

181 "que los tonos teniendo en sí dulzura, y alegría notable, jamás llegan a descompostura, ni inmodestia" (Luis Quiñones de Benavente, *El Abadeguillo*, entremés, preliminares).

182 Agustín Moreto, *Industrias contra finezas*, Jornada 1.

183 Calderón, *Luis Pérez el gallego*, Jornada 1.

184 Lope de Vega, *El piadoso veneciano*, Acto 1.

185 Calderón, *Céfalo y Pocris*, Jornada 1.

186 Lope de Vega, *El bobo del colegio*, Acto 3.

187 See, for example, "Recuerdos TV: Anuncio coñac soberano (Machista)" (https://www.youtube.com/watch?v=F49If5qxKC4) and "Parentesco en el Franquismo: mujer, sexismo y familia" (https://www.youtube.com/watch?v=l7SPQHvalfQ), both examples of Franco-era television propaganda. Thanks to Yoandy Cabrera for finding these YouTube video clips.

188 Lope de Vega, *Los comendadores de Córdoba*, Jornada 3.

189 Lope de Vega, *Los torneos de Aragón*, Acto 1.

190 Lope de Vega, *La madre de la mejor*, Acto 1.

191 Calderón, *Las espigas de Ruth*, auto sacramental.

192 "mi edad ya no es capaz de alegría" (Guillén de Castro, *Los enemigos hermanos*, Jornada 1).

193 Calderón, *Mujer, llora, y vencerás*, Jornada 2.

194 Agustín Moreto, *Primero es la honra*, Jornada 2.

195 Lope de Vega, *Argel fingido y renegado de amor*, Acto 1.

196 Calderón, *Antes que todo es mi dama*, Jornada 1.

197 "Un amante desdichado, pierde el seso de alegría, cuando ve que su porfía llega al puerto deseado" (Lope de Vega, *Sembrar en buena tierra*, Acto 3).

198 Quoted in Potkay, *The Story of Joy*, 75.

199 Juan Ruiz de Alarcón, *Mudarse por mejorarse*, Acto 3.

200 "que se hagan estas bodas con grande alegría todas" (Lope de Vega, *El molino*, Jornada 3).

201 Lope de Vega, *Castelvines y Monteses*, Jornada 3.

202 "pienso que el alegría del dichoso casamiento hará que mude aposento tan triste melancolía" (Lope de Vega, *Del mal lo menos*, Acto 2).

203 For example, "parió una niña, y de suerte nos limitó el alegría, que interpuso sólo un día del nacimiento a la muerte" (Guillén de Castro, *Cuánto se estima el honor*, Jornada 2).

204 Guillén de Castro, *El mejor esposo*, Jornada 3.

205 Guillén de Castro, *Comedia del príncipe tirano*, Acto 1.

206 "Sus hijos, como supieron, que victorioso venía, con música, y alegría a recibirle salieron" (Calderón, *La exaltación de la Cruz*, Jornada 1).

207 "el alegría que mis triunfos repetía" (Calderón, *El verdadero Dios Pan*, auto sacramental).

208 Lope de Vega, *Los Ramírez de Arellano*, Acto 1.

209 Lope de Vega, *Los españoles en Flandes*, Acto 1.

210 Lope de Vega, *Quien todo lo quiere*, Jornada 2.

211 Lope de Vega, *La campana de Aragón*, Acto 2.

212 Juan de la Cueva, *Tragedia del príncipe tirano*, Acto 2.

213 Justin E. Crisp, "Introduction: A Bright Sorrow," in *Joy and Human* Flourishing, ed.
     Volf and Crisp, vii–xviii, at xiv–xv.
214 Rustán says to the king:

> No te puedo decir el alegría,
> gran señor, que mostraban en Granada,
> cuando el pregón la libertad decía
> de aquella noble sangre disfamada,
> tu vida, pienso, que por tantos siglos dilatada,
> respeto de las muchas bendiciones
> que alcances a dos mil generaciones.   (Lope de Vega, *Pedro Carbonero*, Acto 3)

215 Juan de la Cueva, *La libertad de Roma por Mucio Cevola*, Acto 4.
216 Juan de la Cueva, *La libertad de Roma por Mucio Cevola*, Acto 4.
217 Francisco de Rojas Zorrilla, *Los tres blasones de España*, Jornada 1.
218 "Ya es todo paz, y alegría" (Lope de Vega, *El Duque de Humena*, baile).
219 "Será sin duda en métrica alegría, que aquí cuanto se escucha es armonía" (Calderón,
     El Faetonte, Jornada 3).
220 Lope de Vega, *El soldado amante*, Acto 3.
221 Calderón, *El día mayor de los días*, auto sacramental.
222 Lope de Vega, *La nueva victoria del Marqués de Santa Cruz*, Jornada 2.
223 Agustín Moreto, *El caballero del Sacramento*, Jornada 2.
224 Cervantes, *El vizcaíno fingido*, entremés.
225 Calderón, *Duelos de amor y lealtad*, Jornada 3.
226 Calderón, *Cada uno para sí*, Jornada 1.
227 Juan Ruiz de Alarcón, *Las paredes oyen*, Acto 3.
228 Calderón, *El nuevo hospicio de pobres*, loa for auto sacramental. For a more joyful
     interpretation of Calderón's sacramental plays than the one propagated in past
     generations by more traditional scholarship – which has tended to view this
     playwright as severe and sombre – see Rasmus Vangshardt, "The *Theatrum Mundi*
     of Celebration. Pedro Calderón de la Barca and the World Theatre as Aesthetic
     Theodicy," Ph.D. dissertation, University of Southern Denmark, 2021.
229 "con qué divina alegría / dicen de noche y de día, / viva la santa pureza" (Lope de
     Vega, *El capellán de la Virgen*, Acto 2).
230 Lope de Vega, *La madre de la mejor*, Acto 1.
231 Potkay, *The Story of Joy*, 61.
232 Lope de Vega, *El bautismo del príncipe de Marruecos*, Acto 3.
233 Lope de Vega, *El soldado amante*, Acto 1.
234 Lope de Vega, *El postrer godo de España*, Acto 3.
235 Juan Pérez de Montalbán, *Segunda parte del Séneca de España, Don Felipe Segundo*,
     Jornada 3.
236 Calderón, *La devoción de la Misa*, loa for auto sacramental.
237 Calderón, *Los alimentos del hombre*, auto sacramental.

238 Tirso de Molina, *Santo y sastre*, Acto 3.

239 Potkay, *The Story of Joy*, 17, 41, 90.

240 On Pleberio's lament in *Celestina* following the suicide of his daughter Melibea, and this biblical reference in particular, see Luis Galván, "'Valle de lágrimas' y lugares de la gloria: la *Celestina* y el Salmo 83/84," *Celestinesca* 28 (2004): 25–32.

241 Lope de Vega, *San Nicolás de Tolentino*, Acto 3.

242 Lowen, *Joy: The Surrender to the Body and to Life*, 11.

243 Lope de Vega, *El ruiseñor de Sevilla*, Acto 3.

244 Crisp, "Introduction," viii.

245 Crisp, "Introduction," xiii.

246 Thompson, "Reflections on Joy in the Bible," 36.

247 "In the letters of Paul, 'joy' takes second place only to 'love,' *agapē*. The fact that these, and seven others, are part of the 'fruit of the Spirit' (Gal. 5:22–23) does not mean they somehow grow spontaneously without moral or spiritual effort. They are virtues, to be practiced. But they are not, of course, self-generated. For Paul, the spirit creates the conditions for the new human characteristics to come to birth" (Wright, "Joy: Some New Testament Perspectives and Questions," 49–50).

248 "Since joy has a moral dimension, rejoicing can be an obligation (for instance, a command of God, as in the Hebrew Bible and in the New Testament). True, we have little control over feelings of joy; as a rule, they simply well up inside us when we perceive that some unowed good has happened to us or to those we care for. But we do have significant control over how we construe a situation and whether we are properly attentive to these unowed goods. The command to rejoice presupposes a belief that objectively a given situation ought rightly to be construed as good. Absence of joy can then amount to an untruthful rendering of that situation" (Volf, "The Crown of the Good Life," 131–2).

249 Lope de Vega, *El santo negro Rosambuco de la ciudad de Palermo*, Acto 2.

250 Calderón, *El diablo mudo*, auto sacramental.

8. Fear Itself

1 Baruch Spinoza, *Ethics* 3p18s2, in *Improvement of the Understanding: Ethics and Correspondence of Benedict de Spinoza*, trans. Robert Harvey Monro Elwes (Washington, DC: M.W. Dunne, 1901), p. 178.

2 William Shakespeare, *Macbeth*, in *The Complete Works of William Shakespeare* (New York: Gramercy, 1975), 1045–70, IV.2.6, at p. 1062.

3 Franklin D. Roosevelt, first inaugural address delivered on the steps of the U.S. Capitol building during the Great Depression, 4 March 1933, https://www.youtube.com/watch?v=rIKMbma6_dc.

4 "de cuyas negras sombras pende la capa del miedo" (Lope de Vega, *La ocasión perdida*, Jornada 3).

5 "los abismos del miedo" (Juan de Matos Fragoso, *Amor, lealtad y ventura*, Acto 1).

6 "el miedo me arrellanó" (Juan Bautista Diamante, *La Reina María Estuarda*, Jornada 1).

7 "me tiene asido el miedo" (Agustín Moreto, *El secreto entre dos amigos*, Jornada 3).

8 "yo prisionera de mi miedo" (Calderón, *La nave del mercader*, auto sacramental). This characterization of fear may go back to Seneca (*Ep.* 5.7–8), for whom fear of possible calamities could become like the chains of prisoners (George Kazantzidis and Dimos Spatharas, "Introductory: 'Hope,' *Elpis, Spes*: Affective and Non-Affective Expectancy," in *Hope in Ancient Literature, History, and Art*, ed. George Kazantzidis and Dimos Spatharas [Berlin: De Gruyter, 2018], 1–31, at 2).

9 "vivían en cárceles del miedo tenebrosas" (Agustín Moreto, *La confusión de un jardín*, Jornada 1).

10 "de miedo cercado" (Agustín Moreto, *La confusión de un jardín*, Jornada 1).

11 "el susto que a todos cerca, el miedo que a todos turba, el pavor que a todos ciega" (Calderón, *Fortunas de Andrómeda y Perseo*, Jornada 1).

12 Calderón, *El origen, pérdida y restauración de la Virgen del Sagrario*, Jornada 3.

13 Lope de Vega, *El cerco de Santa Fe*, Jornada 1.

14 "con el miedo se huyeron" (Lope de Vega, *El animal de Hungría*, Acto 2).

15 "me está dando prisa el miedo" (Antonio Zamora, *Mazariegos y Monsalves*, Jornada 2).

16 "alas me pone en los pies el miedo, para volar. Con más razón le pintaran con ellas" (Lope de Vega, *Angélica en el Catay*, Acto 2).

17 Lope de Vega, *El juez en su causa*, Jornada 2.

18 "Recogieron las trompetas algunos de los Soldados, esparcidos con el miedo de la rota" (Juan Bautista Diamante, *El cerco de Zamora*, Jornada 1).

19 "nada me obliga, sino el asombro, y el miedo, a ir donde prófuga, y vaga viva sin Patria" (Calderón, *El maestrazgo de Toyson*, auto sacramental).

20 "Con miedo de la justicia me trajo consigo a Italia" (Lope de Vega, *El blasón de los Chaves de Villalba*, Acto 2).

21 "Diéramos a este mancebo, que huyendo de Portugal viene de miedo mortal" (Lope de Vega, *El más galán portugués Duque de Braganza*, Acto 3).

22 "tengo miedo de morir en Reino extraño" (Lope de Vega, *El perseguido*, Jornada 1).

23 "va temblando de miedo" (Calderón, *El amor, honor y poder*, Acto 1).

24 "toda erizada al espanto, toda estremecida al miedo" (Juan Bautista Diamante, *Alfeo y Aretusa*, Jornada 2).

25 "de puro miedo están con perlesía los calzones" (Antonio Zamora, *Duendes son alcahuetes, alias el foleto, segunda parte*, Acto 1). *Perlesía* is a muscular weakness, sometimes caused by old age, accompanied by tremors.

26 "me quedo atarantado de miedo" (Luis Quiñones de Benavente, *El tiempo*, entremés).

27 Calderón, *El médico de su honra*, Jornada 2.

28 "¿de qué tembláis, miedo frío?" (Tirso de Molina, *La prudencia en la mujer*, Jornada 2); "estoy con el miedo resfriado" (Lope de Vega, *El perseguido*, Jornada 2); "me tiene helada el miedo" (Lope de Vega, *La fábula de Perseo*, Acto 3).

29 "Tu miedo mi sangre enfría" (Juan Ruiz de Alarcón, *La cueva de Salamanca*, Acto 2).

30 "en sus poros, hielos de miedo fugitivo" (Lope de Vega, *Las pobrezas de Reinaldos*, Acto 1).

31 Tirso de Molina, *La mujer por fuerza*, Jornada 1. David Gentilcore, using early modern Italian sources, reports a slight variation on this symptom: "Fright 'struck the limbs' and drove the blood to the heart. It caused the monthly bleeding [i.e., menstruation] to stagnate … Bloodletting was the common remedy for fright, to counter the blood blockage, as well as remedies to re-establish the menses … The effects of fear are … explained in terms of the blood. It undergoes a stoppage at the moment of the event. When it resumes movement thereafter its flow is slower, its colour lighter and its consistency more watery. When the fright is particularly intense, or is not dealt with in time, it can lead to *feluspersu* (*fiele, sperso*; literally, shed bile), which is the discharge of bile into the blood" (David Gentilcore, "The Fear of Disease and the Disease of Fear," in *Fear in Early Modern Society*, ed. William G. Naphy and Penny Roberts [Manchester: Manchester University Press, 1997], 184–208, at 197, 199). More recent (i.e., modern as opposed to early modern) sources still speak about how "mobilisation of sugar in the blood energised the muscles for flight" (Joanna Bourke, *Fear: A Cultural History* [London: Virago, 2005], 69).

32 Juan Ruiz de Alarcón, *La manganilla de Melilla*, Acto 3.

33 Calderón, *El castillo de Lindabridis*, Jornada 1.

34 "¿traigo escrito acaso yo, que tengo miedo en la frente?" (Juan Bautista Diamante, *El defensor del Peñón*, Jornada 3).

35   Y el dudoso temor me desengaña,
        cuando me puso un miedo en cada pelo
        el triste horror, y en cada poro un hielo.

                            (Lope de Vega, *El Amor enamorado*, preliminares)

36 William Shakespeare, *Hamlet*, in *The Complete Works of William Shakespeare* (New York: Gramercy, 1975), 1071–1112, I.5, at 1078.

37 "De una sábana mordía con el miedo" (Guillén de Castro, *El Conde Alarcos*, Jornada 1).

38 "el miedo no me deja respirar" (Lope de Vega, *Castelvines y Monteses*, Jornada 3).

39 "te aflijas tanto, que sea miedo el ahogo" (Antonio Zamora, *Ser fino y no parecerlo*, Jornada 3).

40 "me despulsa el miedo" (Lope de Vega, *Castelvines y Monteses*, Jornada 3). Drawing upon early modern Italian sources, David Gentilcore reports a slight variation on this symptom: "Women also requested a prescription [i.e., from a medical doctor] against fright for afflictions like heart constriction, anxiousness and fearfulness" (Gentilcore, "The Fear of Disease," 197).

41 "Ya del pecho cobarde, el pulso tibio, el miedo palpitante" (Antonio Zamora, *Siempre hay que envidiar, amando*, Jornada 1). S.J. Rachman confirms this aspect of fear using clinical data: "one can observe the heart rate of phobic patients double from 70 to 140 beats per minute within seconds of their approaching a fear-

provoking stimulus or situation" (S.J. Rachman, *Fear and Courage* [New York: W.H. Freeman, 1978], 284–5).

42 "para beber el Agua, no es el miedo buen Anís" (Calderón, *La piel de Gedeón*, auto sacramental). Anise seed (the spice in licorice candy) contains digestive properties and is still used to make herbal tea. During the early modern period it was thought to contribute to better digestion and as such was added to drinking water or other beverages.

43 "van hinchados del viento, que yo de miedo les doy" (Tirso de Molina, *Averígüelo Vargas*, Jornada 1).

44 "¿qué me hará de quien distilando está de puro miedo pez Griega?" (Tirso de Molina, *El Aquiles*, Acto 1). *Pez griega* was a term used to refer to the excrement of newborn babies. Psychiatrist I.M. Marks adds, "Soldiers under bombardment may vomit, defecate, or become so paralyzed with fear that they fail to take shelter" (I.M. Marks, *Fears, Phobias, and Rituals* [New York: Oxford University Press, 1987], 4).

45 "todos con miedo tal, que tomo que habemos de oler mal desde aquí" (Cervantes, *La gran Sultana, Doña Catalina de Oviedo*, Jornada 3). In his role of novelist as opposed to dramatist, Cervantes likewise employed scatalogical imagery in the service of slapstick humour. One notorious example is the episode in Part I of *Don Quijote* (chapter 20) when Sancho is scared by a mysterious noise and empties his bowels in close proximity to his master, who catches a whiff of the outcome. On possible connections of this episode to Rabelais see Ricardo Padrón, "The Problem of Sancho's Shit," *Arcade: Literature, the Humanities, & the World* (blog post), http://arcade.stanford.edu

46 "el sobresalto, y el miedo le quitaron el sentido" (Guillén de Castro, *Don Quijote de la Mancha*, Jornada 3).

47 "entre susto y miedo, allí equivocado el aliento; pues nos suspendía el susto" (Juan de Matos Fragoso, *La tía de la menor*, Acto 1). For other valences of "soul suspense" in the early modern period in Spain see Elena del Río Parra, "*Suspensio Animi*, or the Interweaving of Mysticism and Artistic Creation," in *A New Handbook to Early Modern Hispanic Mysticism*, ed. Kallendorf, 391–410. Working with early modern Italian sources, David Gentilcore lists the symptoms of the Italian equivalent of *susto*, which is *paura*: "tiredness, lack of appetite, insomnia, unease, abulia, paleness, nervous imbalance, paralysis, fevers, intestinal worms, cessation of the menses and, in children, an interruption of growth" (Gentilcore, "The Fear of Disease," 199).

48 "será la vez primera que el miedo juegue de manos, pues siempre las tuvo quedas" (Calderón, *Bien vengas mal*, Jornada 3).

49 "los pies me tiene asidos de miedo" (Lope de Vega, *El príncipe despeñado*, Acto 3).

50 "En las sombras de mi miedo tropezando voy" (Calderón, *El Conde Lucanor*, Acto 1).

51 "me falta el corazón, y me desmayo de miedo" (Cervantes, *La gran Sultana, Doña Catalina de Oviedo*, Jornada 2).

52 "el miedo tal vez suele causar sueño profundo" (Cervantes, *La entretenida*, Jornada 1).

53 Juan Bautista Diamante, *Triunfo de la paz y el tiempo*, zarzuela (one act only). Psychiatrist I.M. Marks observes, "Fear that continues for a long time leads to tiredness with difficulty in sleeping and bad dreams" (Marks, *Fears, Phobias, and Rituals*, 4).

54 Guillén de Castro, *El pretender con pobreza*, Jornada 3.

55 "Cipriano turbado, y Clarín turbado, dando vueltas con miedo" (Calderón, *El mágico prodigioso*, Jornada 3).

56 "Eres notable; ¿es posible, que tu miedo tan grandes estruendos hace, que dés voces?" (Calderón, *Mañanas de abril y mayo*, Jornada 3).

57 "Al miedo doy su oración" (Francisco de Rojas Zorrilla, *No hay ser padre siendo rey*, Jornada 3).

58 "mi voz absorta, helada, y muda, a miedo, espanto, novedad se entrega" (Calderón, *El Purgatorio de San Patricio*, Jornada 2).

59 "cuando quiera hablar, atara mi lengua el miedo" (Lope de Vega, *Los embustes de Zelauro*, Acto 1).

60 "el miedo se me ha puesto a la garganta" (Guillén de Castro, *Los enemigos hermanos*, Jornada 3); "a los pesares del alma les cierra el miedo la boca" (Guillén de Castro, *El perfecto caballero*, Acto 2).

61 Marks, *Fears, Phobias, and Rituals*, 4.

62 Cervantes, *El laberinto de amor*, Jornada 3.

63 Lope de Vega, *El galán de la membrilla*, Acto 2.

64 Lope de Vega, *La serrana de Tormes*, Acto 1.

65 Agustín Moreto, *Los hermanos encontrados*, Jornada 1.

66 "ese villano, que estaba de miedo de tanto asombro escondido entre unas ramas" (Calderón, *El gran príncipe de Fez*, Acto 1).

67 "Yo hincando el par de rodillas con más miedo que vergüenza" (Tirso de Molina, *Doña Beatriz de Silva*, Acto 3).

68 "Yo me entro con un miedo como yo debajo de este bufete" (Francisco de Rojas Zorrilla, *Los bandos de Verona*, Jornada 2).

69 "metíme en un alcornoque de miedo de su amador" (Tirso de Molina, *El Aquiles*, Acto 2). The *alcornoque* is the cork oak tree.

70 "el miedo cierre nuestras puertas" (Juan de la Cueva, *La libertad de Roma, por Mucio Cevola*, Acto 3).

71 Howard Thurman offers this reminder in the context of racial justice: "Fear is one of the persistent hounds of hell that dog the footsteps of the poor, the dispossessed, the disinherited" (Howard Thurman, *Jesus and the Disinherited* [Boston: Beacon 1996], 36).

72 This is the case with a character who recounts the following tale: "vida tenía el que me tuvo por muerto; con este miedo, señor, tomé un ábito de lego en un monasterio santo" (Lope de Vega, *El gran Duque de Moscovia, y emperador perseguido*, Acto 3).

73 "de máscara puedo hablar, y verla sin miedo" (Lope de Vega, *La imperial de Otón*, Acto 1). Counsellor Stephen Levine ponders the meaning of more figurative

"masking": "We long for identity and will often take on even uncomfortable masks, not to hide our faces, but because we fear we have no true face" (Stephen Levine, *Unattended Sorrow* [Emmaus, PA: Rodale, 2005], 200).

74 "Pierde de esta vez el miedo, que como disfrazado vas seguro" (Lope de Vega, *La serrana de Tormes*, Acto 3).

75 "por más que invente el miedo estratagemas" (Lope de Vega, *La mayor victoria de Alemania de Don Gonzalo de Córdoba*, preliminares).

76 "el miedo os miente fábulas de torpe error" (Tirso de Molina, *La lealtad contra la envidia*, Acto 2); "Siempre el miedo es testigo mentiroso" (Lope de Vega, *Las aventuras de Don Juan de Alarcos*, Jornada 1).

77 "¡Si es ilusión del temor!" (Calderón, *Los hijos de la Fortuna Teágenes y Cariclea*, Jornada 2); "pone el miedo ilusiones de noche" (Lope de Vega, *La envidia de la nobleza*, Acto 3).

78 Calderón, *Los hijos de la Fortuna Teágenes y Cariclea*, Jornada 2.

79 Antonio Zamora, *Duendes son alcahuetes, y el espíritu foleto, primera parte*, Jornada 2.

80 Lope de Vega, *La fuerza lastimosa*, Jornada 2.

81 "siempre aguando mi alegría, el temor desconfiado" (Tirso de Molina, *El pretendiente al revés*, Acto 1).

82 "en poder de mi miedo, triste, y solo sin él quedo" (Calderón, *A tu prójimo como a ti*, auto sacramental).

83 "¡ay de mí, triste! Que el miedo crece, y desmengua la esperanza" (Cervantes, *El laberinto de amor*, Jornada 3).

84 "Con miedo, y desconfianza sigo un imposible empleo" (Agustín Moreto, *El Cristo de los milagros*, Jornada 3).

85 "el miedo, que a la salud hace agravio" (Tirso de Molina, *El amor médico*, Acto 1).

86 "En cada paso que doy, un miedo, un temor me priva de la razón" (Juan de Matos Fragoso, *El hijo de la piedra*, Jornada 2).

87 Doña Ana admits, "Con el miedo perdí el tino" (Juan de Matos Fragoso, *Con amor no hay amistad*, Jornada 3).

88 Agustín Moreto, *La fuerza de la ley*, Jornada 1.

89 Calderón, *Los lances de Amor y Fortuna*, Jornada 2.

90 Calderón, *El Conde Alarcos*, Jornada 3.

91 "imágenes del miedo de la muerte cruel que me amenaza" (Lope de Vega, *La amistad pagada*, Jornada 3).

92 Douglas Abrams in The Dalai Lama, Desmond Tutu, and Douglas Abrams, *The Book of Joy: Lasting Happiness in a Changing World* (New York: Avery, 2016), 163. Joanna Bourke agrees: "The fear of death and dying is a constant presence in history (for some commentators it is at the core of every fear)" (Bourke, *Fear: A Cultural History*, xi).

93 Juan de la Cueva, *La libertad de Roma, por Mucio Cevola*, Acto 2.

94 Lope de Vega, *El primer Rey de Castilla*, Acto 1.

95 "son ladrones, y tienen al Rey gran miedo" (Lope de Vega, *La hermosura aborrecida*, Acto 3).

 96 "La ira del Rey, aunque sea con el Traidor, pone miedo al Leal" (Calderón, *El nuevo hospicio de pobres*, auto sacramental).

 97 Thus a Captain says, "tengo al Rey, y a sus enojos miedo" (Lope de Vega, *Las famosas asturianas*, Acto 3).

 98 Cervantes, *La casa de los celos y selvas de Ardenia*, Jornada 3.

 99 Juan Ruiz de Alarcón, *Los favores del mundo*, Acto 3.

100 Calderón, *El laurel de Apolo*, Acto 1.

101 "un enemigo menos a quien tener miedo" (Calderón, *El alcalde de Zalamea*, Jornada 2).

102 "el miedo del Delinquente" (Calderón, *Los alimentos del hombre*, auto sacramental).

103 Bourke, *Fear: A Cultural History*, 335.

104 "estos ladrones salieron haciendo la gente huir, que por miedo de morir la antigua lealtad perdieron" (Lope de Vega, *El leal criado*, Acto 2).

105 "este destierro, donde (según dicen) todo es horror, asombro y miedo, a causa de los Bandidos que en él andan" (Calderón, *A tu prójimo como a ti*, auto sacramental). Most likely "destierro" is a typographical error in the early printed version; *desierto* would make more sense in this context. The first word means "exile," while the second means "desert."

106 Calderón, *El año santo de Roma*, loa for auto sacramental.

107 Lope de Vega, *La historia de Tobías*, Acto 3.

108 Agustín Moreto, *Hacer del contrario amigo*, Jornada 2.

109 Cervantes, *El gallardo español*, Jornada 2.

110 Calderón, *La cisma de Inglaterra*, Jornada 2.

111 Lope de Vega, *El arenal de Sevilla*, Acto 1.

112 Juan Pérez de Montalbán, *Amor, privanza y castigo*, Acto 1.

113 Lope de Vega, *Adonis y Venus*, Acto 2.

114 Calderón, *Apolo y Climene*, Jornada 3.

115 Lope de Vega, *La historia de Tobías*, Acto 3.

116 Lope de Vega, *Bamba*, Jornada 1.

117 See Hilaire Kallendorf, "A Force Within: The Importance of Demonic Possession for Early Modern Studies," in *Exorcism and Its Texts: Subjectivity in Early Modern Literature of England and Spain* (Toronto: University of Toronto Press, 2003), xiii–xix.

118 Lope de Vega, *La mocedad de Roldán*, Acto 3.

119 "tentaciones, pensar puedo que al mismo San Antón le diera miedo" (Agustín Moreto, *El valiente justiciero*, Jornada 3).

120 "sin que me cause miedo de Astarot el engaño" (Calderón, *Las cadenas del demonio*, Jornada 3). Astarot was the Great Duke of Hell, forming an evil trinity with Beelzebub and Lucifer. This demon was probably named after Astarte, a Near Eastern goddess.

121 Warren Carter, "Cross-Gendered Romans and Mark's Jesus: Legion Enters the Pigs (Mark 5:1–20)," *Journal of Biblical Literature* 134.1 (2015): 139–55, at 144–5.

122 Lope de Vega, *La historia de Tobías*, Acto 3.

123 Lope de Vega, *El vaquero de Morana*, Acto 1.

124 Lope de Vega, *La dama boba*, Acto 3.

125 "una rosca de difuntos, que no la comen de miedo" (Agustín Moreto, *El mejor amigo, el rey*, Jornada 2).

126 On similar Old World customs predating Mexico's Day of the Dead rituals, see Stanley Brandes, "Sugar, Colonialism, and Death: On the Origins of Mexico's Day of the Dead," *Comparative Studies in Society and History* 39.2 (1997): 270–99.

127 Lope de Vega, *El Argel fingido y renegado de amor*, Acto 1.

128 Cervantes, *El viejo celoso*, entremés.

129 Guillén de Castro, *El perfecto caballero*, Acto 2.

130 Agustín Moreto, *Santa Rosa del Perú*, Jornada 3.

131 The etymology of this term may derive from the coconut or calabash gourd which, when pierced with three holes to drain the juice out of it, came to resemble a grinning face due to the holes in the shell.

132 Calderón, *El mágico prodigioso*, Jornada 3.

133 Lope de Vega, *Arcadia*, Acto 1.

134 "Till my bad angel fire my good one out" (William Shakespeare, Sonnet CXLIV, https://www.poetryfoundation.org/poems/50651/sonnet-144-two-loves-i-have-of-comfort-and-despair). I explained the significance of this procedure in my first book: "The original context was a description of an exorcistic procedure called (suf) fumigation, in which the demoniac was forced to inhale fumes from brimstone and poisonous herbs" (Kallendorf, *Exorcism and Its Texts*, 144).

135 Juan Pérez de Montalbán, *Lo que son juicios del cielo*, Jornada 3.

136 Tirso de Molina, *El castigo del penséque*, Acto 3.

137 "yo dije Ave María al estornudo de miedo. Tapóme la boca entonces" (Juan Bautista Diamante, *Santa María Magdalena de Pazzi*, Jornada 3).

138 "miedo de la torpe apoplejía" (Tirso de Molina, *La dama del olivar*, Acto 2).

139 "Miedo más que todos a la menor calenturilla" (Lope de Vega, *La historia de Tobías*, Acto 3).

140 "no puedo, venciendo el usado miedo de hipocondrias fantasías" (Calderón, *Hado y divisa de Leonido y Marfisa*, Jornada 2).

141 "los Señores Doctores miedo tuvieron para no ser de servicio en la curación" (Calderón, *La cura y la enfermedad*, auto sacramental).

142 Lope de Vega, *La mayor virtud de un rey*, Jornada 1. A *sopetón* is a strong, sudden blow with the hand.

143 "así puedo rezar doquiera sin miedo de pendencia" (Cervantes, *Pedro de Urdemalas*, Jornada 2).

144 "Tengo a sus espadas miedo" (Lope de Vega, *La carbonera*, Jornada 2).

145 "desnudando un alfanje, mucho mayor que Toledo, que pudiera poner miedo al gran Príncipe de Orange, te apuntaba al morrión" (Juan Pérez de Montalbán, *El valiente más dichoso, Don Pedro Guiral*, Jornada 3). The *alfanje* was a cutlass or short sword, similar to the sabre but shorter, wider, and more curved. The *morrión* was the part of a helmet that covered a knight's face.

146 "yo, deseándome hallar en todo sin que me dé miedo una, y otra alabarda" (Calderón, *Afectos de odio y amor*, Jornada 3). The *alabarda* was a medieval weapon similar to a lance whose point was traversed by a blade, sharp on one side and with the form of a half moon on the other.

147 "me estremezco todo: como cuando vi un cuchillo, qué miedo es el que te cobro" (Calderón, *Las tres justicias en una*, Jornada 3).

148 "con miedo de algún tiro" (Lope de Vega, *La cortesía de España*, Acto 2).

149 "¿miedo tienes a arcabuz?" (Lope de Vega, *La resistencia honrada*, Jornada 1).

150 Tirso de Molina, *Quien no cae no se levanta*, Acto 2.

151 "perderán el miedo a un coselete" (Agustín Moreto, *De fuera vendrá*, Jornada 1). The *coselete* was a light breastplate made of leather, worn by infantry soldiers; metonymically the word could also refer to the soldier who wore it.

152 Juan de Matos Fragoso, *El marido de su madre*, Acto 1. Psychiatrist I.M. Marks describes this fear as realistic even for soldiers: "Most soldiers are fearful at some stage of fighting, between 5% and 20% to the point of involuntary urination and defecation. Of veterans returning from the Spanish Civil War, only 9% said that they never experience fear in action" (Marks, *Fears, Phobias, and Rituals*, 406).

153 "Temblando quedo, qué cosa para mí ver un esquadrón volante" (Juan Pérez de Montalbán, *Los templarios*, Jornada 2).

154 Witness the following exchange in which several battle flags are described:

> DALÍ: Más de una vez la ocasión
> me ha quitado de gran presa,
> la roja Cruz de Manresa,
> y de San Jorge el Pendón;
> ¿qué dicen de aquel Toledo?
> FRANCISCO: A llevar el Virrey fue;
> no hay, Dalí, por qué te dé
> su Ángel blanco, y azul miedo.   (Lope de Vega, *Los cautivos de Argel*, Jornada 1)

155 "la ostentación, y el ruido de las armas … miedo es todo" (Guillén de Castro, *Los enemigos hermanos*, Jornada 2); "el eco … de voces y armas, confieso que tengo miedo" (Lope de Vega, *El cerco de Santa Fe*, Jornada 2).

156 "como Letrado sois, seréis cobarde" (Tirso de Molina, *Santo y sastre*, Acto 3).

157 "Un desafío es, no tengáis miedo, que el Rey me dio licencia que fijase unos carteles" (Lope de Vega, *La desdichada Estefanía*, Acto 1).

158 "esto en desengaño baste de que no puede ser miedo, pediros que se dilate nuestro duelo" (Calderón, *Los empeños de un acaso*, Jornada 2).

159 Juan Pérez de Montalbán, *Lo que son juicios del cielo*, Jornada 3.

160 Witness the confession, "Yo sin espada salí y tengo un poco de miedo" (Lope de Vega, *La escolástica celosa*, Jornada 1).

161 Calderón, *Mañanas de abril y mayo*, Jornada 3.

162 Lope de Vega, *El labrador venturoso*, Jornada 2.

163 Lope de Vega, *El sol parado*, Acto 3.

164 Calderón, *Los tres mayores prodigios*, Jornada 1.

165 "habiéndote dado esta fiera tanto miedo, vuelves, no digo al peligro, sino al horror del aspecto" (Calderón, *En esta vida todo es verdad y todo mentira*, Jornada 2).

166 Lope de Vega, *El guante de Doña Blanca*, Acto 1.

167 "su bestial grandeza, que cierto no me ha puesto tanto miedo un Camello que vi cuando niño" (Lope de Vega, *Laura perseguida*, Acto 2).

168 Lope de Vega, *El Amete de Toledo*, Acto 3. A *galgo* is a greyhound.

169 "a mí me pone miedo un ratón" (Juán Pérez de Montalbán, *El valiente Nazareno*, Jornada 1).

170 Lope de Vega, *El caballero de Olmedo*, Acto 3.

171 "alanceador galán y cortesano, de quien hombres y toros tienen miedo" (Lope de Vega, *El caballero de Olmedo*, Acto 2).

172 "el miedo grave de esta áspera arboleda" (Lope de Vega, *Los embustes de Zelauro*, Acto 3).

173 "¿que es grande el jardín, y que a solas tendrás miedo?" (Lope de Vega, *El soldado amante*, Acto 2).

174 "tengo con la grande oscuridad de mí misma asombro, y miedo; válgame Dios, que temblando estoy" (Calderón, *La dama duende*, Jornada 2). Fear of the dark is reported as far back as by the Greek physician Galen (131–201 AD) (Allan V. Horwitz and Jerome C. Wakefield, *The Loss of Sadness* [Oxford: Oxford University Press, 2007], 61). Alain Corbin describes vividly the transition during the nineteenth century away from fear of the dark as new technologies made nighttime activities more feasible: "fear of the dark was much more intense during the limited suffrage monarchy [in France] than at the end of the century. Gas and then electricity gradually modified the customs and rhythms of the city by night; they gave security and allowed new journeys to be made; they created ways of displaying the body and postures which made people forget the fascination formerly exercised by the masks suddenly revealed by a chance shaft of light. The bourgeois woman, who had gradually dared to take possession of the public space of the 'good districts,' now no longer feared to show herself on café terraces in the evening. Night life was reoriented, as was behaviour in public places" (Alain Corbin, *Time, Desire and Horror: Towards a History of the Senses*, trans. Jean Birrell [Cambridge: Polity, 1995], 10).

175 "Nunca he conocido el miedo como en esta noche oscura" (Guillén de Castro, *El desengaño dichoso*, Acto 2). S.J. Rachman quotes Napoleon's exclamation, "I have very rarely met with two o'clock in the morning courage" (Rachman, *Fear and Courage*, 87).

176 "el miedo ahora a mi sombra misma por cualquier parte temo" (Lope de Vega, *La boba para los otros, y discreta para sí*, Acto 2).

177 "sólo pretendéis dar miedo con voces y amenazas tan furiosas, ministros del temor" (Lope de Vega, *Amor, pleito y desafío*, Jornada 2). Psychiatrist I.M. Marks explains, "Fear is … shown to sounds that are part of the threat display of conspecifics [members of the same species]. Samurai warriors gave terrifying grunts as they cut down their opponents. Many other mammals give harsh, intense threat sounds like barks and roars" (Marks, *Fears, Phobias, and Rituals*, 50).

178 "quedó libre así del letal miedo, de que nadie a socorrerle venga" (Calderón, *El diablo mudo*, auto sacramental).

179 S.J. Rachman, *Fear and Courage* (New York: W.H. Freeman, 1978), 84.

180 Marks, *Fears, Phobias, and Rituals*, 51.

181 Calderón, *Hado y divisa de Leonido y Marfisa*, Jornada 1.

182 Lope de Vega, *La boba para los otros, y discreta para sí*, Acto 3.

183 Lope de Vega, *El bautismo del Príncipe de Marruecos*, Acto 1.

184 Lope de Vega, *El Duque de Viseo*, Acto 1.

185 "Enfermar mirando del mar la orilla, dicen que es miedo del mar" (Lope de Vega, *La prisión sin culpa*, Acto 1).

186 Lope de Vega, *El desprecio agradecido*, Jornada 3.

187 Lope de Vega, *El piadoso aragonés*, Acto 1.

188 Calderón, *La desdicha de la voz*, Jornada 3.

189 Lope de Vega, *El alcalde mayor*, Acto 1.

190 In defiance of these potentially malign influences, one imprisoned character boasts, "preso quedo; ni al mal, ni a la fortuna tengo miedo" (Calderón, *El príncipe constante*, Acto 1).

191 "No hayas miedo que derribe tan justa privanza envidia" (Lope de Vega, *Los trabajos de Jacob*, Jornada 2).

192 "el miedo de venir a humilde estado" (Lope de Vega, *El cuerdo loco*, Acto 1).

193 "Son los hombres tan ingratos, / que hacen al amor más fijo / temeroso de sus tratos" (Juan Pérez de Montalbán, *Olimpa y Vireno*, Jornada 3).

194 Juan Pérez de Montalbán, *El mariscal de Virón*, Jornada 3.

195 "huye el riesgo de mi fama" (Agustín Moreto, *Trampa adelante*, Jornada 3).

196 Lope de Vega, *El hombre de bien*, Acto 2.

197 Calderón, *Para vencer a Amor, querer vencerle*, Jornada 2.

198 Francisco de Rojas Zorrilla, *Peligrar en los remedios*, Jornada 3.

199 "[T]engo miedo, que el dinero no se cobre" (Lope de Vega, *Juan de Dios y Antón Martín*, Acto 3). Joanna Bourke describes fear of poverty as particularly prevalent during the nineteenth and early twentieth centuries in England and America: "fear of destitution was a visceral emotion, expressing itself in the roaring protest of the stomach or goosebumps on the skin … [I]ncreased state provision of welfare instigated by the Liberals in the 1890s did not eradicate the fear of poverty: it merely diluted its intensity. Dread of hunger or the cold might have diminished but fears associated with social status grew. Rather than trembling about the effects of absolute privation, people shuddered to think about the consequences of *relative*

impoverishment, such as being rehoused in a rougher area or forced to sell a prized possession" (Bourke, *Fear: A Cultural History*, 27). Fear of poverty is also expressed in the *comedias* by means of its opposite, i.e., the idea that money brings courage. As one character puts it, "¿Pues no es cosa bien extraña, que tenga miedo, y doblones, siendo cosas tan contrarias?" (Francisco de Rojas Zorrilla, *No hay ser padre siendo rey*, Jornada 2).

200 "pues soy soldado, tal, que a la hambre sola tengo miedo, ya el cerco es acabado" (Cervantes, *El gallardo español*, Jornada 3).

201 As one rich character says, "el vulgo me tiene miedo, mi riqueza es infinita" (Juan Pérez de Montalbán, *Amor, privanza y castigo*, Acto 3). This is one fear that persists still today: "Fear circulates within a wealthy economy of powerful interest groups dependent upon ensuring that we remain scared" (Bourke, *Fear: A Cultural History*, 358–86).

202 Lope de Vega, *El remedio en la desdicha*, Acto 2.

203 "miedo del Castigo" (Juan de la Cueva, *La libertad de España por Bernardo del Carpio*, Acto 2).

204 "¿Estos Redentores deja por miedo de que le entreguen a las galeras del Rey?" (Lope de Vega, *La vida de San Pedro Nolasco*, Jornada 2). Interestingly, in this line the specific fear described is the suspicion that the *Redentores* or Redemptionist friars who often organized the ransom for captives might turn the prisoner over to become a galley slave. The slave in question leaves the company of friars – who might otherwise help him – out of fear that they will instead effectively betray his trust.

205 Don Quijote exclaims upon seeing the galley slaves in their chains, "¿Cómo gente forzada? … ¿Es posible que el rey haga fuerza a ninguna gente?" (Miguel de Cervantes, *Primera parte del ingenioso hidalgo don Quijote de la Mancha*, in *Obras completas*, ed. Florencio Sevilla [Madrid: Castalia, 1999], 145–320, ch. XXII, at p. 207).

206 Calderón, *También hay duelo en las damas*, Jornada 2.

207 Calderón, *Cada uno para sí*, Jornada 2.

208 Calderón, *Hado y divisa de Leonido y Marfisa*, Jornada 3.

209 Cervantes, *El rufián viudo, llamado Trampagos*, entremés.

210 Guillén de Castro, *Dido y Eneas*, Jornada 3.

211 Thus Celio remarks, "Un Rey a su vasallo miedo tiene" (Lope de Vega, *La fe rompida*, Acto 2).

212 Tirso de Molina, *El árbol del mejor fruto*, Acto 1.

213 See Hilaire Kallendorf, "Class Trumps Sex: The (En)gendering of Virtue," in *Ambiguous Antidotes: Virtue as Vaccine for Vice in Early Modern Spain* (Toronto: University of Toronto Press, 2017), 145–63.

214 Lope de Vega, *Dios hace reyes*, Acto 2.

215 Lope de Vega, *Los locos de Valencia*, Acto 1.

216 Jonathan Dollimore, referencing the work of Camille Paglia, asserts that "men's fear of women is natural, even rational, and biologically (anatomically) grounded"

(Jonathan Dollimore, *Death, Desire and Loss in Western Culture* [New York: Routledge, 1998], xxiii).

217 Antonio de Solís, *Las amazonas*, Jornada 1.

218 Calderón, *Afectos de odio y amor*, Acto 1.

219 Peter Gay notes that this limiting of women's opportunities by men continued well into the nineteenth century: "men are, and have for untold centuries been despots. They have degraded women into household drudges, into slaves to their children, into sick nurses; they have kept women ignorant lest, literate and eager for more education, they neglect the tasks to which masculine selfishness has condemned them" (Peter Gay, *The Tender Passion* [New York: Oxford University Press, 1986], 63).

220 Lope de Vega, *De quien todo lo quiere*, Jornada 2.

221 "las mujeres, y las monas, no han de conocer el miedo, que en conociéndole muerden" (Tirso de Molina, *La mujer por fuerza*, Jornada 2).

222 Lope de Vega, *El piadoso veneciano*, Acto 1.

223 Tirso de Molina, *La lealtad contra la envidia*, Acto 2.

224 The classic study of the *mujer varonil* is Melveena McKendrick, *Women and Society in the Spanish Drama of the Golden Age: A Study of the* Mujer Varonil (Cambridge: Cambridge University Press, 1974).

225 Juan de la Cueva, *La muerte del Rey Don Sancho, y reto de Zamora por Don Diego Ordóñez*, Acto 3.

226 Guillén de Castro, *El pretender con pobreza*, Jornada 2.

227 Antonio Zamora, *El custodio de la Ungría, San Juan Capistrano*, Jornada 1. A World War II–era study of psychiatric casualties in the Women's Auxiliary Air Force repeated these stereotypes: "Men, on the other hand, submit to a sterner social and emotional code. They have, therefore, a greater need to preserve their self-esteem by the development of a more complex disguise or escape mechanism" (S.I. Ballard and H.G. Miller, "Psychiatric Casualties in a Women's Service," *British Medical Journal* [3 March 1945]: 193–4; quoted in Bourke, *Fear: A Cultural History*, 207–08).

228 The stereotype of women as fearful persisted at least through World War II. Attempts to "justify" women's "natural" fearfulness from that period are fascinating; for example, "Women were assumed to be less capable of calculating the 'mathematical probability' of escaping harm and their bodies were said to be frailer, making them particularly susceptible to panic if bombs dropped when they were menstruating, lactating or experiencing menopausal crisis" (Bourke, *Fear: A Cultural History*, 243).

229 One female character boasts, "no he visto, aunque mujer, de qué color es el miedo" (Lope de Vega, *El honrado hermano*, Acto 2).

230 Tirso de Molina, *La Santa Juana*, Acto 2.

231 Lope de Vega, *La mayor victoria*, Jornada 2.

232 "una dama de verle está rendida, que por miedo de padres y parientes le quiere ver secreta, y escondida" (Lope de Vega, *Los torneos de Aragón*, Acto 2).

233 Calderón, *Bien vengas mal*, Jornada 1.

234 On miniature portraits used as actual props in stage plays, see Laura Bass, *The Drama of the Portrait: Theater and Visual Culture in Early Modern Spain* (University Park: Penn State University Press, 2008).

235 Lope de Vega, *Santiago el verde*, Acto 1.

236 Agustín Moreto, *El lego del Carmen*, Jornada 1.

237 Tirso de Molina, *La mujer por fuerza*, Jornada 2.

238 Juan Ruiz de Alarcón, *La cueva de Salamanca*, Acto 2.

239 "Estése quedo, aparte, que me da miedo, no pellizque, mal aya él, sea cortés, si tiene amor" (Tirso de Molina, *Marta la piadosa*, Acto 2).

240 Lope de Vega, *Los prados de León*, Acto 1.

241 "leguas peñascosas, si a la vista deleitosas, gigantes que ponen miedo. A los pies para subirlas, y al tiento para bajarlas" (Tirso de Molina, *Amar por arte mayor*, Acto 1).

242 Perejil asks his master, "¿Y hacia dónde, señor, nos encaminas? Porque yo tendré miedo en Filipinas" (Agustín Moreto, *El valiente justiciero*, Jornada 3).

243 Juan Pérez de Montalbán, *A lo hecho no hay remedio, y príncipe de los montes*, Jornada 2.

244 For a real-life example of one early modern "savage" or "wild man" who suffered from hypertrichosis – i.e., long hair growing over most of his face and body – see M.A. Katritzky, "Literary Anthropologies and Pedro González, the 'Wild Man' of Tenerife," in *Medical Cultures of the Early Modern Spanish Empire*, ed. John Slater et al. (Burlington: Ashgate, 2014), 107–28.

245 "[L]a tengo más miedo que al Gigante" (Juan Pérez de Montalbán, *Don Florisel de Niquea*, Jornada 2); we might note that giants were standard fare for the romances of chivalry on which this play was based.

246 For example, "Un ojo, que el verle pone miedo, mayor que el otro mucho más que un dedo" (Juán Pérez de Montalbán, *Los templarios*, Jornada 3). Here one of the person's eyes is described as "monstrously" larger than the other. For early modern perceptions of the monstrous, see Elena del Río Parra, *Una era de monstruos: representaciones de lo deforme en el Siglo de Oro español* (Madrid and Frankfurt: Iberoamericana / Vervuert, 2003).

247 "ay Dios, todavía me da miedo su fealdad, el cabello se me eriza" (Juan Ruiz de Alarcón, *La cueva de Salamanca*, Acto 2).

248 See my comments about this tendency in an interview for a blog post on portrayals of characters with disabilities by Rachel Knight, "Misrepresentation in Pop Culture" (16 December 2020), https://liberalarts.tamu.edu/blog/2020/12/16/misrepresentation-in-pop-culture/.

249 Francisco de Rojas Zorrilla, *Nuestra Señora de Atocha*, Jornada 2.

250 "Siguiendo voy entre estos olivares los arrogantes Moros con tal miedo que no dan paso sin pisarme el alma" (Lope de Vega, *El sol parado*, Acto 1).

251 On Cervantes's captivity see María Antonia Garcés, *Cervantes in Algiers: A Captive's Tale* (Nashville: Vanderbilt University Press, 2005).

252 Bruce Taylor, "The Enemy Within and Without: An Anatomy of Fear on the Spanish Mediterranean Littoral," in *Fear in Early Modern Society*, ed. Naphy and Roberts, 78–99, at 79.

253 Lope de Vega, *Jorge Toledano*, Acto 2.

254 See Bartolomé Bennassar and Lucile Bennassar, *Los cristianos de Alá: la fascinante aventura de los renegados* (Donostia [Spain]: Nerea, 2001).

255 Lope de Vega, *La doncella Teodor*, Acto 2.

256 Lope de Vega, *Los esclavos libres*, Acto 3.

257 One Spanish character describes the experience of "passing for" a Muslim in the Andalusian town of Martos in the province of Jaén (we must recall that Spain's southernmost region of Andalusia was the last to fall to the Christians in the centuries-long process of Reconquest):

> Vime en Martos con muy gran
> miedo, y sucedió también,
> que siendo polvo de sen,
> remanecí soliman.
> Y el traje Moro me dio
> con la vida, esta gran presa.　　　　　(Tirso de Molina, *La reina de los reyes*, Jornada 2)

258 On the notion of "passing" or impersonating another nationality, see Barbara Fuchs, *Passing for Spain: Cervantes and the Fictions of Identity* (Champaign: University of Illinois Press, 2003).

259 Juan Ruiz de Alarcón, *La manganilla de Melilla*, Acto 3.

260 Lope de Vega, *El sol parado*, Acto 3.

261 Famous knights of this order from this time period included the Spanish Baroque poet Francisco de Quevedo.

262 Lope de Vega, *El hijo de Reduán*, Acto 2.

263 Calderón, *El origen, pérdida y restauración de la Virgen del Sagrario*, Jornada 3.

264 "Church to Remove Moor-Slayer Saint," *BBC News Online*, 3 May 2004, http://news .bbc.co.uk/2/hi/europe/3680331.stm.

265 Tirso de Molina, *La reina de los reyes*, Jornada 2.

266 Lope de Vega, *Pobreza no es vileza*, Acto 1.

267 "Quiero ver la bizarría de este que con miedo nombro, de este espanto, de este asombro de toda la Berbería" (Cervantes, *El gallardo español*, Jornada 1). The phrase "Barbary Coast" was current in Europe from the sixteenth to the early nineteenth century to denote coastal regions of North Africa inhabited by Berbers. Today this land is encompassed by Morocco, Algeria, Tunisia and Libya.

268 Tirso de Molina, *La Santa Juana*, Acto 3.

269 It is important to recall that Spain's *moriscos* (Muslims who had been forcibly converted to Christianity) were not formally expelled until 1609. See Benjamin Ehlers, *Between Christians and* Moriscos*: Juan de Ribera and Religious Reform in Valencia, 1568–1614* (Baltimore: Johns Hopkins University Press, 2006).

270 Tirso de Molina, *La prudencia en la mujer*, Jornada 2.

271 Calderón, *El socorro general*, auto sacramental.

272 "aquestas voces que oís, las dan Judíos de miedo" (Cervantes, *Los baños de Argel*, Jornada 3). This stereotype persisted during World War I: "during the air raids on London, Jews were singled out for expressing excessive terror. They were said to lack the 'British' tradition of conquering adversaries, of bulldog endurance" (Bourke, *Fear: A Cultural History*, 217).

273 Cervantes, *La cueva de Salamanca*, entremés.

274 "Algún Judío tendrá miedo a los encantos, que yo creo en Jesucristo" (Juan Ruiz de Alarcón, *La cueva de Salamanca*, Acto 2).

275 "no hayas miedo que te den hechizos en lo que comas" (Lope de Vega, *La pastoral de Jacinto*, Acto 1). See Ruth Behar, "Sexual Witchcraft, Colonialism, and Women's Powers: Views from the Mexican Inquisition," in *Gender and Witchcraft*, ed. Brian P. Levack (New York: Routledge, 2001), 218–44.

276   Confiésote, gran señor,
         que tuve miedo mil veces
         de no aojarla, y que le hacía
         las higas de siete en siete.   (Lope de Vega, *La hermosa Alfreda*, Acto 1)

277 See "Tratado del aojamiento," *Estudios de Historia de la Ciencia y de la Técnica* 20 (2001): 177–211.

278 For example, "No tengas miedo a las supersticiones de los hombres" (Lope de Vega, *El triunfo de la humildad y soberbia abatida*, Acto 2).

279 Cervantes, *La gran Sultana, Doña Catalina de Oviedo*, Jornada 1.

280 Juan Pérez de Montalbán, *El mariscal de Virón*, Jornada 2.

281 Lope de Vega, *El sol parado*, Acto 1. Pedro Arias de Ávila was a Spanish soldier who led the first large Spanish expedition to the mainland of the "New" World, where he was named governor of Panama and Nicaragua. He founded Panama City. For a new, exciting digital humanities project funded by the Spanish government that incorporates archaeological findings from colonial Panama, see "An ARTery of EMPIRE: Conquest, Commerce, Crisis, Culture and the Panamian Junction (1513–1671)" (ArtEmpire), http://www.upo.es.

282 Thus we find references to "el miedo, y temor de Flandes, a la presunción de España" (Calderón, *El sitio de Bredá*, Acto 1).

283 Juan de la Cueva, *El saco de Roma y muerte de Borbón, y coronación de nuestro invicto Emperador Carlos Quinto*, Acto 1.

284 Lope de Vega, *Juan de Dios y Antón Martín*, Acto 1.

285 Lope de Vega, *Arauco domado por el excelentísimo señor Don García Hurtado de Mendoza*, Acto 1.

286 Lope de Vega, *Los guanches de Tenerife y conquista de Canaria*, Acto 2.

287 Lope de Vega, *Roma abrasada*, Acto 1.

288 Lope de Vega, *El primer rey de Castilla*, Acto 1.

289 "¿Que ponga un forastero gentilhombre a Caballeros Catalanes miedo?" (Lope de Vega, *No son todos ruiseñores*, Jornada 3).

290 Lope de Vega, *La resistencia honrada*, Jornada 2.

291 Calderón, *Las tres justicias en una*, Jornada 2.

292 Calderón, *La banda y la flor*, Jornada 2.

293 Tirso de Molina, *La fingida Arcadia*, Jornada 2.

294 Thus Carrillo voices the admonition, "Acaba ya de temer, que es vergüenza tanto miedo" (Lope de Vega, *Los enemigos en casa*, Acto 1).

295 "no crea que yo puedo tener tan bajo miedo, que mi valor condene" (Calderón, *A secreto agravio, secreta venganza*, Jornada 2).

296 Calderón, *El Rey Don Pedro en Madrid, y infanzón de Illescas*, Jornada 2.

297 Calderón, *Hado y divisa de Leonido y Marfisa*, Jornada 2.

298 Juan Bautista Diamante, *Jupiter y Semele*, Acto 1.

299 "Soldados, volved, amigos; no os postre el infame miedo, que si es vergüenza la fuga, valor es matar muriendo" (Juan Bautista Diamante, *El remedio en el peligro*, Jornada 3).

300 Rachman, *Fear and Courage*, 50.

301 Calderón, *El Tuzaní del Alpujarra*, Jornada 2.

302 Juan Pérez de Montalbán, *Como amante y como honrada*, Jornada 1.

303 "a perder me determino de una vez el miedo a tanto imaginado peligro" (Calderón, *Para vencer a Amor, querer vencerle*, Jornada 2).

304 "Despido el torpe miedo, cobro aliento" (Juan de la Cueva, *Comedia del príncipe tirano*, Acto 4).

305 Ana confesses, "Mal resisto a este miedo" (Guillén de Castro, *El pretender con pobreza*, Jornada 2).

306 "iré dejando el miedo" (Juan Bautista Diamante, *El negro más prodigioso*, Jornada 2); "ya le voy perdiendo el miedo" (Agustín Moreto, *El lego del Carmen*, Jornada 3).

307 "pongamos a este miedo, a este peligro, y a esta desdicha un reparo" (Calderón, *El pintor de su deshonra*, Jornada 3).

308 "a consultar, qué medios puedo usar, que me aseguren de este miedo" (Calderón, *La serpiente de metal*, auto sacramental).

309 "dichoso seré si le quito el miedo" (Guillén de Castro, *La fuerza de la costumbre*, Jornada 2); "ya puedo hablar con vos, y deponer el miedo" (Calderón, *Saber del mal, y el bien*, Jornada 2).

310 "Desecha, Sulpicio, el miedo, no te falte el corazón" (Juan de la Cueva, *La libertad de Roma, por Mucio Cevola*, Acto 3).

311 "bien puedo atropellar cualquier miedo" (Lope de Vega, *Los enemigos en casa*, Acto 1).

312 "tiemple aquesto tus enojos, no pase el miedo adelante" (Cervantes, *El gallardo español*, Jornada 2).

313 "vuestra compañía, me dice que mitigue el miedo" (Lope de Vega, *El esclavo de Roma*, Acto 2).

314 "Cuando le escucho, Octavio, consuelo mucho mi miedo y dificultad" (Lope de Vega, *La francesilla*, Acto 2).

315 "El remedio del miedo estando a solas, es pensar otra cosa diferente" (Lope de Vega, *La historia de Tobías*, Acto 3).

316 Rachman, *Fear and Courage*, 82. Military psychologists during World War II also recognized the importance of distraction: "the most important thing men should do in a fearful situation was to engage in 'purposeful or manipulative activity.' Diversion was crucial" (Bourke, *Fear: A Cultural History*, 211).

317 "te librarás de este miedo" (Cervantes, *Los baños de Argel*, Jornada 1).

318 "os socorréis del miedo a mis manos" (Juan Bautista Diamante, *El Hércules de Ocaña*, Jornada 2).

319 Lope de Vega, *El labrador venturoso*, Jornada 3.

320 Juan Bautista Diamante, *El Hércules de Ocaña*, Jornada 1.

321 "fiados en ser muchos, disimularon el miedo" (Juan Bautista Diamante, *El Hércules de Ocaña*, Jornada 2); "con capa de virtud, muchos encubren su miedo" (Juan Bautista Diamante, *Ir por el riesgo a la dicha*, Jornada 1). For a discussion of the "cape" or "mantle" of virtue see Hilaire Kallendorf, "(Not Just) the Veneer of Virtue," in *Ambiguous Antidotes*, 164–7.

322 Guillén de Castro, *Progne y Filomena*, Acto 1.

323 "natural es la defensa; pero es legítimo el miedo" (Juan de Matos Fragoso, *Con amor no hay amistad*, Jornada 2).

324 "estuvo quedo, y después piquéle yo con las espuelas del miedo" (Guillén de Castro, *Don Quijote de la Mancha*, Jornada 3).

325 Rachman offers a specific example from the World War II era: "in one of the U.S. Air Force studies, it was found that 50 percent of the airmen reported that fear sometimes improved their efficiency" (Rachman, *Fear and Courage*, 60). In combat situations more generally, "fear could stimulate attention, sharpen judgement and energise combatants. Fear kept men alert and more 'combat effective'" (Bourke, *Fear: A Cultural History*, 389).

326 Calderón, *Antes que todo es mi dama*, Jornada 3.

327 Guillén de Castro, *La fuerza de la costumbre*, Jornada 1.

328 Calderón, *El arca de Dios cautiva*, loa for auto sacramental. This is the same fear evoked in a famous sermon by John Donne containing the line, "It is a fearfull thing to fall into the hands of the living God" (quoted in Bettie Anne Doebler, *Rooted Sorrow: Dying in Early Modern England* [London: Associated University Presses, 1994], 212).

329 Calderón, *El año santo de Roma*, loa for auto sacramental.

330 "el miedo que el Sacramento pone a quien sus leyes quiebra" (Lope de Vega, *Los comendadores de Córdoba*, Jornada 3). The specific sacrament referenced here is holy matrimony.

331 The dramatic tyrant must confess, "Soy un tirano, que no tuvo al cielo miedo; soy un bárbaro inhumano" (Lope de Vega, *El tirano castigado*, Acto 3). A. Robert Lauer has done a study of tyrranicide plays titled *Tyrannicide and Drama* (Wiesbaden: Franz Steiner, 1987).

332 "no haya miedo que en el cielo halle cerrada la puerta" (Guillén de Castro, *Las mocedades del Cid, comedia primera*, Acto 3).

333 Lope de Vega, *La boba para los otros, y discreta para sí*, Acto 1.

334 "Ya no tengo a culpas miedo después de la absolución, libre de las culpas quedo" (Lope de Vega, *Lucinda perseguida*, Acto 2).

335 "puedo perder a la Muerte el miedo, si con tímida Conciencia procuro hacer Penitencia" (Calderón, *La cura y la enfermedad*, loa for auto sacramental).

9. That White Sustenance, Despair

1 Emily Dickinson, "I Cannot Live with You" (640), poets.org/poem/i-cannot-live-you-640, accessed 22 July 2020.

2 Søren Kierkegaard, *Purity of Heart Is to Will One Thing*, trans. Douglas Steere (New York: Harper and Brothers, 1938), 132.

3 Juan Bautista Diamante, *El defensor del Peñón*, Jornada 3.

4 Witness the following exchange between Carlos, Conde de Urgel, and Polilla:

> CARLOS: Polilla, mi desazón
>   tiene más naturaleza: este pesar no es tristeza,
>   sino desesperación.
> POLILLA: ¿Desesperación, señor?
>   Que te enfrenes te aconsejo,
>   que tiras algo a bermejo.
> CARLOS: No burles de mi dolor.
> POLILLA: ¿Yo burlar? ¿Esto es templarte?
>   Mas tu desesperación,
>   ¿qué tanta es a esta sazón?
> CARLOS: La mayor.
> POLILLA: ¿Cosa de ahorcarte?
>   ¿Qué sino poco te ahoga?
> CARLOS: No te burles, que me enfado.
> POLILLA: Pues si estás desesperado,
>   ¿hago mal en darte soga?
>
> (Agustín Moreto, *El desdén con el desdén*, Jornada 1)

5 Paul Tillich, *The Courage to Be* (New Haven: Yale University Press, 1952), 54.

6 "de toda esperanza desespero" (Juan de la Cueva, *La muerte de Virginia y Appio Claudio*, Acto 4); "a espaldas de tu esperanza va mi desesperación" (Antonio Zamora, *Ser fino y no parecerlo*, Acto 1).

7 "el desconsuelo de no haber otra esperanza" (Calderón, *El maestro de danzar*, Jornada 2).

8   VIOLANTE: Está menguante mi luna,
      con que esperanza ninguna
      me ha quedado, pues ya vi
      conjurados contra mí
      la Estrella, el Sol y la Luna.   (Calderón, *Las tres justicias en una*, Jornada 3)

9 "Hecha pedazos está con mi esperanza en el suelo" (Lope de Vega, *El postrer godo de España*, Acto 2).

10 "Hoy hizo fin mi deseo. Hoy enterré mi esperanza" (Lope de Vega, *El vellocino de oro* [one act only]).

11 Mary Louise Bringle, *Despair: Sickness or Sin? Hopelessness and Healing in the Christian Life* (Nashville: Abingdon Press, 1990), 34.

12 "Desesperarme pensé, corté luto a mi esperanza" (Tirso de Molina, *Doña Beatriz de Silva*, Acto 1).

13 Lope de Vega, *El ruiseñor de Sevilla*, Acto 2.

14 "mal puede mi esperanza cantar en tan falsas cuerdas" (Lope de Vega, *El secretario de sí mismo*, Acto 1).

15 Lope de Vega, *El vellocino de oro*, [one act only]).

16 "ay despertador reloj del engaño de mi vida, esperanza y pretensión" (Lope de Vega, *El servir con mala estrella*, Acto 3).

17 Agustín Moreto, *El esclavo de su hijo*, Jornada 2.

18 Calderón, *Fineza contra fineza*, Jornada 3. Despair is also said to make characters blind. For example, consider the following speech by Don Juan:

      Ya el fuego que me abrasa,
      ladrón cruel de mi feliz sosiego,
      a desesperación violenta pasa,
      dejándome más ciego,
      con lo imposible de enmendar mi daño,
      no pudiendo encontrar el desengaño.
                    (Agustín Moreto, *Santa Rosa del Perú*, Jornada 2)

19 Calderón, *La hija del aire, segunda parte*, Jornada 3.

20 "la desesperación ha dado muerte al cuidado" (Juan Ruiz de Alarcón, *Ganar amigos*, Acto 3).

21 Calderón, *Los cabellos de Absalón*, Jornada 1.

22   Si vos, teniendo esperanza,
      padecéis tantos martirios,
      el que está desesperado

de un bien como el que ha perdido,
decidme qué sentirá;
mas no lo digáis, amigo;
el que lo sintió lo diga,
que otro no sabrá decirlo.   (Lope de Vega, *La Reina Juana de Nápoles*, Acto 2)

23 Juan Ruiz de Alarcón, *La cueva de Salamanca*, Acto 3.

24 Efrat Vignansky et al., "Despair Will Hold You Prisoner, Hope Will Set You Free: Hope and Meaning among Released Prisoners," *Prison Journal* 98.3 (2018): 334–58.

25 Anthony J. Steinbock, "The Phenomenology of Despair," *International Journal of Philosophical Studies* 15.3 (2007): 435–51, at 449.

26 John Bunyan, *Pilgrim's Progress* [1676] (Virginia Beach: CBN University Press, 1978), 26–7.

27 Calderón, *La lepra de Constantino*, loa for auto sacramental.

28 "le visto de verde oscuro, que es esperanza perdida" (Lope de Vega, *El verdadero amante*, Acto 1).

29 "el negro luto es color de mi esperanza" (Lope de Vega, *El perseguido*, Jornada 2). Black is contrasted to the green of hope: "dejando el color verde funda en negro su esperanza" (Tirso de Molina, *La fingida Arcadia*, Jornada 3).

30   [N]egras plumas, mosqueadas
      de átomos de oro a los visos
      del Sol, desesperación,
      y tristeza, afectos míos,
      publicaba en los colores de lo negro, y lo pajizo.

                              (Calderón, *De una causa dos efectos*, Jornada 1)

31 "Con su desesperación la retama, aunque la pierde" (Lope de Vega, *El mejor maestro, el tiempo*, Acto 2).

32   También lo dicen las flores,
      y lo parecen mejor
      los efectos de amor,
      en sus distintos colores.
      ¿Ay más desesperación
      que la de aquel alelí?   (Lope de Vega, *El mejor maestro, el tiempo*, Acto 2)

   Alelí is a stock flower of a light peach colour.

33 "Nació mi esperanza en vano, Sol de invierno" (Lope de Vega, *La mayor virtud de un rey*, Jornada 1).

34 This image appears in a speech by Alejandro to Nise:

      Turbó el imán del deseo,
      y ya de todo perdido
      el norte de la esperanza,

> dio por escollo en el risco
> de la desesperación,
> donde roto, y desunido,
> entregó al mar por despojos,
> los desmayados sentidos,
> que entre la espuma quedaron,
> buscando para el peligro
> de las ondas de su llanto,
> las tablas de los suspiros.　　　　(Agustín Moreto, *La fuerza de la ley*, Jornada 1)

35 The figure is described thus: "Es la desesperación esta espantosa figura, sobre todas cuantas son" (Cervantes, *La casa de los celos*, Jornada 2).

36 This image appears in multiple plays, including in the lines "de mi furor muerte me dará el verdugo de mi desesperación" (Calderón, *La hija del aire, primera parte*, Acto 1) and "¿no hay cordel que sea verdugo de mi desesperación?" (Tirso de Molina, *Quien no cae no se levanta*, Acto 2).

37 Lope de Vega, *La villana de Xetafe*, Acto 3.

38 Lope de Vega, *La buena guarda*, Acto 1.

39 "con no matarme nunca siempre matándome está; una desesperación" (Juan Bautista Diamante, *El sol de la sierra*, Jornada 2).

40 "esta necia pasión es ya desesperación" (Calderón, *Gustos y disgustos son no más que imaginación*, Jornada 2).

41 "recelo feroz en el potro de mis celos a mi desesperación" (Juan de Matos Fragoso, *Callar siempre es lo mejor*, Jornada 3).

42 "Desesperación, nacida de que otro tenga esperanza" (Antonio Zamora, *Viento es la dicha de amor*, Jornada 2).

43 These lines are spoken by the allegorical figure of Oído in Calderón's *Amar y ser amado, y divina Filotea* (auto sacramental).

44 "de mi pobre hacienda no le quedaba esperanza, respeto de tantas guerras" (Lope de Vega, *Si no vieran las mujeres*, Jornada 2).

45 Lope de Vega, *La mayor virtud de un rey*, Jornada 3.

46 Guillén de Castro, *Las mocedades del Cid, comedia segunda*, Acto 3.

47 Cervantes, *La gran Sultana*, Jornada 3.

48 "cuando al infierno bajar ves mi esperanza del cielo" (Lope de Vega, *El postrer godo de España*, Acto 1).

49 Rebecca K. DeYoung, "The Roots of Despair," *Res Philosophica* 92.4 (2015): 829–54, at 832.

50 Juan de la Cueva, *La muerte de Ajax Telamón, sobre las armas de Aquiles*, Acto 1.

51 Antonio Zamora, *El lucero de Madrid, y divino labrador San Isidro*, Jornada 3.

52 "dejada la vida, perdió para siempre la esperanza del cielo" (Lope de Rueda, *Camila*, coloquio, Acto 1).

53 Bringle, *Despair: Sickness or Sin?*, 66.

54 Bringle, *Despair: Sickness or Sin?*, 71.

55 John C. McCloskey, "The Theme of Despair in Marlowe's *Faustus*," *College English* 4.2 (1942): 110–13, at 112.

56 Kathrine Koller, "Art, Rhetoric, and Holy Dying in the *Fairie Queene* with Special Reference to the Despair Canto," *Studies in Philology* 61.2 (1964): 128–39, at 133–4.

57 Such injunctions include "pecadores, vivid con esperanza: no os desconfíe vuestro error, mortales" (Agustín Moreto, *El lego del Carmen*, Jornada 3); and "espera en Dios, porque más le enoja quien de su Amor desespera, y su Piedad" (Calderón, *El diablo mudo*, auto sacramental).

58 Calderón, *La primer flor del Carmelo*, auto sacramental.

59 Bettie Anne Doebler, *Rooted Sorrow: Dying in Early Modern England* (London: Associated University Presses, 1994), 113.

60 Harold Golder, "Bunyan's Giant Despair," *Journal of English and Germanic Philology* 30.3 (1931): 361–78, at 363.

61 John Milton, *Paradise Lost* (London: Routledge, 1905), Book IV, line 74, p. 70.

62 Lope de Vega, *La buena guarda*, Acto 2.

63 Calderón, *La redención de cautivos*, auto sacramental.

64 Juan Ruiz de Alarcón, *La cueva de Salamanca*, Acto 3.

65 "Un alma que sacrifico a la desesperación" (Tirso de Molina, *Los lagos de San Vicente*, Acto 2).

66 Calderón, *Las cadenas del demonio*, Jornada 1.

67 Lope de Vega, *El divino africano*, Acto 3. I have discussed this play in greater detail in Hilaire Kallendorf, "Saint = Exorcist: Calderón's *Las cadenas del demonio* and Lope's *El divino africano*," in *Exorcism and Its Texts: Subjectivity in Early Modern Literature of England and Spain* (Toronto: University of Toronto Press, 2003), 117–25.

68 Susan Snyder, "The Left Hand of God: Despair in Medieval and Renaissance Tradition," *Studies in the Renaissance* 12 (1965): 18–59, at 51–2.

69 Calderón, *El gran teatro del mundo*, auto sacramental.

70 Tirso de Molina, *La venganza de Tamar*, Jornada 2.

71 Melvin A. Kimble, "Human Despair and Comic Transcendence," *Journal of Religious Gerontology* 16.3–4 (2004): 1–11, at 3.

72 "que me admires lleno de confusiones, no irrites a mi desesperación" (Calderón, *Apolo y Climene*, Jornada 2).

73 "Quisiera también poner algún cuadro de esperanza, pero mi desconfianza dice que se ha de perder" (Lope de Vega, *Los ramilletes de Madrid*, Acto 2).

74 Lope de Vega, *Los ramilletes de Madrid*, Acto 2.

75 Luis de León, "Vida retirada," in *Poesías*, ed. Javier San José Lera (Alicante: Biblioteca Virtual Miguel de Cervantes, 2008).

76 "También desesperación es, no tratar resistir la fuerza de una pasión" (Calderón, *De una causa dos efectos*, Jornada 1).

77 "la desesperación es madre de las discordias" (Francisco de Rojas Zorrilla, *No hay ser padre siendo rey*, Jornada 3).

78   CONSTANCIO: … [V]erás que en vano me aguardas.
     ENIO: Eso es desesperación.   (Calderón, *Las armas de la hermosura*, Jornada 2)

79 "el fin de la esperanza, que es donde suele haber riesgo" (Juan Bautista Diamante, *Jupiter y Semele*, Acto 1).

80 Marc Hillbrand and John L. Young, "Instilling Hope into Forensic Treatment: The Antidote to Despair and Desperation," *Journal of the American Academy of Psychiatry and the Law* 36 (2008): 90–4, at 90, 92.

81 Lilly Shanahan et al., "Does Despair Really Kill? A Roadmap for an Evidence-Based Answer," *American Journal of Public Health* 109.6 (2019): 854–8, at 855.

82 Lope de Vega, *El labrador venturoso*, Jornada 1.

83 "habemos de vivir mientras que el cielo nos quita la esperanza, y el consuelo de volver a la patria deseada" (Lope de Vega, *La mayor virtud de un rey*, Jornada 1).

84 "adonde presumo yo que pase una triste vida. Que la desesperación le hizo dejar su tierra" (Lope de Vega, *Los Porceles de Murcia*, Acto 3).

85 Lope de Rueda, *Armelina*, Scena 5.

86 Brittney Beck et al., "On Navigating Despair: Reports from Psycho-Therapists," *Journal of Religion and Health* 44.2 (2005): 187–205, at 189.

87 "de mi mudanza fue causa el desesperar" (Juan Ruiz de Alarcón, *El semejante a sí mismo*, Acto 3).

88 Tirso de Molina, *Escarmientos para el cuerdo*, Acto 3.

89 Francisco de Rojas Zorrilla, *El más impropio verdugo por la más justa venganza*, Jornada 1.

90 "una desesperación de amor priva de razón" (Lope de Vega, *El Argel fingido y renegado de amor*, Acto 2).

91 "quitáronmele tan presto que con desesperación loco le vine siguiendo" (Lope de Vega, *El bobo del colegio*, Acto 3).

92 Arieh Sachs, "Religious Despair in Medieval Literature and Art," *Medieval Studies* 26 (1964): 231–56, at 253.

93 Juan Bautista Diamante, *El sol de la sierra*, Jornada 3.

94 "Dejadme morir a manos de mi desesperación" (Calderón, *Llamados y escogidos*, auto sacramental). These lines are spoken by the allegorical figure of Synagoga, obviously designed to represent the Jewish faith.

95 "la desesperación vana de morir noble" (Calderón, *Primero soy yo*, Jornada 1).

96 Lope de Vega, *Lo que ha de ser*, Jornada 2.

97 Ana V. Diez Roux, "Despair as a Cause of Death: More Complex Than It First Appears," *American Journal of Public Health* 107 (2017): 1566–7, at 1566.

98 Miguel de Cervantes, *Numancia*, ed. Robert Marrast (Madrid: Cátedra, 1968).

99 "es desesperación valiente, y no es Católico quien porque quiere morir muere" (Calderón, *El origen, pérdida y restauración de la Virgen del Sagrario*, Jornada 2).

100 See Robert Pinsky, "Dante's Canto XIII: The Wood of the Suicides," *Boston Review*, https://bostonreview.net/archives/BR18.1/dante.html.

101 For a discussion of medieval reception of the suicidal Judas figure, see Moshe Barasch, "Despair in the Medieval Imagination," *Social Research* (1999): 565–76.

102 The Baroque English poet John Donne made this argument most forcefully in *Biathanatos* (1608). Rowland Wymer makes the following nuanced assessment of Donne's position: "[T]here is no real moral difference between acts of omission and acts of commission, between allowing oneself to be killed and actually killing oneself. It all depends on the motivation. Some martyrdoms may have been undertaken for selfish reasons, some suicides for holy ones … [F]or Donne, Christ was the great example of a 'pure' suicide, a self-chosen death entirely for the glory of God" (Rowland Wymer, *Suicide and Despair in the Jacobean Drama* [New York: St. Martin's, 1986], 18).

103 Calderón, *El príncipe constante*, Jornada 3.

104 "sea atrevimiento, o sea desesperación" (Calderón, *La gran Cenobia*, Jornada 3).

105 Lope de Vega, *Quien todo lo quiere*, Jornada 3.

106 Calderón, *El origen, pérdida y restauración de la Virgen del Sagrario*, Jornada 2.

107 See Hilaire Kallendorf, "Fleeting Fortitude," in *Ambiguous Antidotes: Virtue as Vaccine for Vice in Early Modern Spain* (Toronto: University of Toronto Press, 2017), 69–83.

108 Lope de Vega, *El amigo por fuerza*, Acto 2.

109 Lope de Vega, *Los torneos de Aragón*, Acto 1.

110 Agustín Moreto, *Primero es la honra*, Jornada 3

111 Lope de Vega, *El vellocino de oro*, Acto 1.

112 Lope de Vega, *La mayor virtud de un rey*, Jornada 1.

113 "pienso que soy discreto por no tener esperanza" (Lope de Vega, *El desconfiado*, Acto 3).

114 Juan Ruiz de Alarcón, *Las paredes oyen*, Acto 1.

115 "aquí dio fin mi tragedia, aquí en sombra mi esperanza con triste luto y sangrienta dio fin al acto postrero" (Lope de Vega, *Por la puente, Juana*, Acto 3). For a study that connects tragedy more explicitly to the passion of sorrow in the context of classical theatre, see Charles Segal, *Euripides and the Poetics of Sorrow* (Durham: Duke University Press, 1993).

116 This view is being revised currently with the recovery of more Spanish Renaissance tragedies than scholars had previously recognized. See Margaret Rich Greer, "Spanish Golden Age Tragedy: From Cervantes to Calderón," in *A Companion to Tragedy*, ed. Rebecca Bushnell (London: Blackwell, 2005), 351–70.

117 William R. Brashear, *The Gorgon's Head: A Study in Tragedy and Despair* (Atlanta: University of Georgia Press, 2008).

118 Lope de Vega, *La gallarda toledana*, Acto 1.

119 Calderón, *La viña del Señor*, auto sacramental.

120 Lope de Rueda, *Armelina*, Escena 5.

121 Calderón, *El castillo de Lindabridis*, Jornada 3.

122 "no queda el menor / viso a la enmienda de tanta / necia desesperación" (Antonio Zamora, *Judas Iscariote*, Jornada 3).

123 "en la desesperación de un Príncipe despojado jamás la piedad ferió" (Tirso de Molina, *La lealtad contra la envidia*, Acto 2).

124 "ahora a casarse sentenciado con Feliciana, así Marcela incite su desesperación" (Juan Pérez de Montalbán, *El sufrimiento premiado*, Jornada 3).

125 Lope de Vega, *Adonis y Venus*, Acto 3.

126 "la desesperación / que tengo en el corazón / a no hallar consuelo en ti" (Lope de Vega, *El servir con mala estrella*, Acto 3).

127 "Gallarda empresa, a fe mía, esperanza tardía, que se marchita después. Que este pajizo color significa en su mudanza desesperada esperanza, que un tiempo fue verde flor" (Lope de Vega, *El padrino desposado*, Jornada 2).

128 See Edmond L. Volpe, "Dry September: Metaphor for Despair," *College Literature* 16.1 (1989): 60–5.

129 Antonio Zamora, *Siempre hay que envidiar, amando*, Jornada 1.

130 Lope de Vega, *Contra valor no hay desdicha*, Acto 3.

131 Nancy Scroggs et al., "'An Existential Place of Pain': The Essence of Despair in Women," *Issues in Mental Health Nursing* 31.7 (2010): 477–82, at 480.

132 Lope de Vega, *Amar sin saber a quién*, Jornada 2.

133 Denis J. O'Hara, "Psychotherapy and the Dialectics of Hope and Despair," *Counselling Psychology Quarterly* 24.4 (2011): 323–9, at 324–5 and 328.

134 Snyder, "The Left Hand of God," at 59.

135 Kirk E. Farnsworth, "Despair That Restores," *Psychotherapy: Theory, Research and Practice* 12.1 (1975): 44–7, at 46.

136 Melvin A. Kimble, "Human Despair and Comic Transcendence," *Journal of Religious Gerontology* 16.3–4 (2004): 1–11, at 1.

10. Hope against Hope

1 Søren Kierkegaard, quoted in J.J. Godfrey, *A Philosophy of Human Hope* (Dordrecht: Martinus Nijhoff, 1987), p. 29.

2 Proverbs 13:12.

3 Aristotle, *Categories*, in *The Basic Works of Aristotle*, Oxford translation, ed. R. McKeon (New York: Random House, 1941). Quoted in James R. Averill et al., *Rules of Hope* (New York: Springer, 1990), 53.

4 Emily Dickinson, "'Hope' is the Thing with Feathers" (314), https://www.poetryfoundation.org/poems/42889/hope-is-the-thing-with-feathers-314. Woody Allen famously wrote a parody of this poem in his 1975 collection of comic pieces titled *Without Feathers*: "How wrong Emily Dickinson was! Hope is not 'the thing with feathers.' The thing with feathers has turned out to be my nephew. I must take

him to a specialist in Zurich" (quoted in Niall W. Slater, "Up from Tragicomedy: The Growth of Hope in Greek Comedy," in *Hope in Ancient Literature, History, and Art*, ed. George Kazantzidis and Dimos Spatharas [Berlin: De Gruyter, 2018], 85–110, at 85).

5 These include *Amar y ser amado, y divina Filotea*, *El Arca de dios cautiva*, *El cordero de Isaías*, *El cubo de la almudena*, *La humildad coronada de las plantas*, *El nuevo hospicio de pobres*, *El nuevo palacio del Retiro*, *Las órdenes militares*, *La redención de cautivos*, *El segundo blasón del Austria*, and *El Santo Rey Don Fernando, primera parte*.

6 Lope de Vega, *Los donaires de Matico*, Jornada 2.

7 Averill et al., *Rules of Hope*, v.

8 "Así que ya estaba muerta, ánimo, dulce esperanza" (Juan Pérez de Montalbán, *La toquera vizcaína*, Jornada 3).

9 "que funde ya mi esperanza en ella su dulce empleo" (Juan Ruiz de Alarcón, *Examen de maridos*, Acto 3).

10 Lope de Vega, *La primera información*, Acto 1.

11 "a ofrecerte el fruto de aquella flor, siempre en mi esperanza alegre" (Calderón, *El amor, honor y poder*, Jornada 3).

12 "vuestra esperanza afianzada tuvo de vuestro amparo" (Antonio Zamora, *El lucero de Madrid, y divino Labrador San Isidro*, Jornada 3).

13 "Hagamos lo mismo ahora con una santa esperanza, que es la que de Dios alcanza altos efectos, señora" (Lope de Vega, *La madre de la mejor*, Acto 1).

14 Lope de Vega, *El caballero del milagro*, Acto 3.

15 Tirso de Molina, *La lealtad contra la envidia*, Acto 3.

16 Calderón, *El segundo Scipión*, Jornada 2.

17 Lope de Vega, *Al pasar del arroyo*, Acto 1. Donald Lateiner notes that "Conventional epithets for Greek *elpis*, hope, are *kenos*, empty or *typhlos*, blind – undesirable characteristics" (Donald Lateiner, "*Elpis* as Emotion and Reason [Hope and Expectation] in Fifth-Century Greek Historians," in *Hope in Ancient Literature*, ed. Kazantzidis and Spatharas, 131–49, at 132).

18 "Esperar, que en la ausencia sea constante Amor, es esperanza de ignorante" (Tirso de Molina, *Marta la piadosa*, Acto 1).

19 "no os aliente, Duque, tan necia esperanza, de mi piedad abusando" (Antonio Zamora, *La poncella de Orleans*, Jornada 3). Similarly, the ancient Roman historian "Tacitus compares adulation, the prime motivation of the Roman majority for bestowing their support on their preferred imperial candidate, to 'foolish hope'" (Sophia Papaioannou, "'A Historian Utterly without Hope': Literary Artistry and Narratives of Decline in Tacitus' *Historiae* I," in *Hope in Ancient Literature*, ed. Kazantzidis and Spatharas, 213–32, at 224).

20 "presumir el pensamiento otro fin que se ajuste a la esperanza, que fuera lo demás atrevimiento" (Lope de Vega, *No son todos ruiseñores*, Jornada 2).

21 A negative example of this may be seen in the line, "Hoy nuestra esperanza vana quiere un imposible hacer" (Lope de Vega, *La gallarda toledana*, Acto 2).

22 Lampinen, "Against Hope?," 293.

23 Juan Bautista Diamante, *El nacimiento de Cristo*, zarzuela, Acto 1.

24 "¡Con qué notable alegría, con qué fe, con qué esperanza al santo portal caminan!" (Lope de Vega, *El nacimiento de Cristo*, Acto 3).

25 "Donde su luz alcanza, va ya reverdeciendo la esperanza del Abril" (Antonio Zamora, *El hechizado por fuerza*, Jornada 3).

26 "[F]ebrero loco flores para Mayo siembra, que quiere que su esperanza dé fruto a la primavera" (Lope de Vega, *Las paces de los reyes*, Acto 2).

27 Lope de Vega, *No son todos ruiseñores*, Jornada 2.

28 Lope de Vega, *La serrana de Tormes*, Acto 1.

29 Juan Bautista Diamante, *Pasión vencida de afecto*, Jornada 1.

30 Juan de la Cueva, *Los siete infantes de Lara*, Acto 4. Accordingly, Bettie Doebler states regarding Elizabeth Stuart, the "Winter Queen" of Bohemia, around the time of the Thirty Years' War: "the death of her son prefigured the death of most of her hopes" (Bettie Anne Doebler, *Rooted Sorrow: Dying in Early Modern England* [London: Associated University Presses, 1994], 241).

31 Juan de la Cueva, *Los siete infantes de Lara*, Acto 4.

32 "si tú quieres tener sucesor, que pueda hacer cierta tu esperanza sola, busca mujer Española, y toma mi parecer" (Lope de Vega, *La doncella Teodor*, Acto 1).

33 "qué mar, qué tierra no asombra aquel valiente Felipe, cuya esperanza no hay gloria de toda la antigua historia" (Lope de Vega, *La mayor victoria de Alemania de Don Gonzalo de Córdoba*, preliminares).

34 "gloria a su padre Real, y esperanza a Portugal de otras hazañas mayores" (Tirso de Molina, *Averígüelo Vargas*, Jornada 1). Spain and Portugal were united into one Spanish monarchy under King Philip II.

35 This is the sentiment expressed in the line, "un hijo pierdes, y en él la esperanza de mi Casa, el Jordán de mi vejez" (Antonio Zamora, *Judas Iscariote*, Acto 1).

36 This is the dilemma of the ruler who laments, "sin esperanza os gobierno de sucesión venturosa" (Agustín Moreto, *Hasta el fin nadie es dichoso*, Jornada 2).

37 Constantine served as Roman emperor from 306 to 337 AD. The emperor Constantine's death is mourned in the lines:

> Al César Constantino,
> habéis, bárbaros, muerto; y al camino
> saliéndole tiranos,
> la esperanza quitáis a los Romanos,
> del más noble mancebo
> que vio en sus ojos coronado Febo.
>
> (Tirso de Molina, *El árbol del mejor fruto*, Acto 1)

38 A similar grief is expressed in philosophical terms with the epitaph, "mozo de la primavera humana, murió Juan Pizarro (o vana esperanza de los hombres)" (Tirso de Molina, *La lealtad contra la envidia*, Acto 2).

39 Such a forward-facing outlook is expressed in the line, "logrará nuestra unión tener más cerca de la dicha la esperanza" (Antonio Zamora, *El hechizado por fuerza*, Jornada 1).

40 "esperad a que abra el tiempo camino a nueva esperanza" (Antonio Zamora, *Mazariegos y Monsalves*, Jornada 1).

41 "es de la Esperanza la luz que va sucediendo a Oración" (Calderón, *Amar y ser amado, y divina Filotea*, auto sacramental). Note that here hope is experienced after prayer.

42 Lope de Vega, *El castigo del discreto*, Acto 2.

43 "tal vez tras nubes de enojos, de esperanza el sol se ve" (Cervantes, *El gallardo español*, Jornada 2).

44 The "fire" of hope is indeed so warm that this lover never wants the night to end: "Noche a quien llamaron fría, siendo mi esperanza fuego, ven esta vez a mi ruego, y nunca amanezca" (Tirso de Molina, *Siempre ayuda la verdad*, Jornada 2). James Averill and his colleagues affirm this resonance for hope as still current: "As heat, hope may help 'thaw' or animate behavior" (Averill et al., *Rule of Hope*, 59).

45 "la esperanza es el crisol de tanto hermoso arrebol" (Calderón, *La señora y la criada*, Jornada 1).

46 Calderón, *El amor, honor y poder*, Jornada 2.

47 Tirso de Molina, *Averígüelo Vargas*, Jornada 3.

48 Juan Ruiz de Alarcón, *Mudarse por mejorarse*, Acto 2.

49 This specific geographical reference appears in the line, "nunca a las columnas Españolas llegara con mi nave mi esperanza … yo que estoy en la tormenta fiera" (Lope de Vega, *La cortesía de España*, Acto 3). Interestingly, a similar image appears in the comic drama *Wasps* by Aristophanes, in which hope "is a passage, a crossing, the strait of the Hellespont (implicitly of course dangerous and uncertain, the very opposite of 'firm')" (Slater, "Up from Tragicomedy," 90).

50 "Yo en mi esperanza embarcado, el mar de amor discurría" (Juan Ruiz de Alarcón, *La amistad castigada*, Acto 2).

51 "En golfos de la esperanza voy sulcando mar inquieto" (Agustín Moreto, *El parecido*, Jornada 1).

52 "todas las velas tendiendo al viento de mi esperanza" (Lope de Vega, *El laberinto de Creta*, Acto 2).

53 "salgas del golfo de tus desdichas al puerto de tu esperanza" (Tirso de Molina, *La peña de Francia*, Acto 3).

54 Tirso de Molina, *Averígüelo Vargas*, Jornada 3.

55 "Bien pensaba yo tener en tu esperanza sagrado, donde acoger mi cuidado" (Lope de Vega, *Ello dirá*, Acto 3).

56 "La Nave pues de mi esperanza rota" (Lope de Vega, *Las aventuras de Don Juan de Alarcos*, Jornada 3).

57 "celos que combaten la casi rota chalupa de mi burlada esperanza" (Tirso de Molina, *Averígüelo Vargas*, Jornada 3). In Spain a *chalupa* is a small covered raft or boat with two boards for sails.

58 "Así por este mar del mundo incierto, / Contenta mi esperanza navegaba: / Perdonóla la mar, matóla el puerto" (Lope de Vega, *El premio del bien hablar*, Acto 3).

59 "aunque a precio del susto de su desmayo, aun da esperanza su aliento" (Antonio Zamora, *Todo lo vence el Amor*, Jornada 3). James Averill et al. offer a slight variation

of this image with hope as air: "Hope … has an airy, ephemeral quality" (Averill et al., *Rule of Hope*, 65).

60 Antonio Zamora, *Amar es saber vencer, y el arte contra el poder*, Acto 1.

61 "¡Esperanza, alienta!" (Antonio Zamora, *Cada uno es linaje aparte, y los Mazas de Aragón*, Acto 1); "esperanza te ha podido alentar" (Calderón, *El encanto sin encanto*, Jornada 3).

62 Lope de Vega, *El Genovés liberal*, Acto 1.

63 "La vida estriba en esperanza alguna; quien no llega a esperar de sí se olvida" (Juan Pérez de Montalbán, *El hijo del serafín, San Pedro de Alcántara*, Jornada 1).

64 Tirso de Molina, *El mayor desengaño*, Acto 2.

65 "mi esperanza, sin poder yo resistirla, ha abierto puerta en mi pecho" (Agustín Moreto, *Lo que puede la aprehensión*, Jornada 1).

66 Agustín Moreto, *Industrias contra finezas*, Jornada 3.

67 "Ahora partió de la esperanza vestido, que a esta empresa le llevó tan gallardo" (Lope de Vega, *El perseguido*, Jornada 2).

68 Calderón, *El castillo de Lindabridis*, Jornada 3.

69 Lope de Vega, *De cosario a cosario*, Acto 1. A *gúmena* is a thick rope used to tie the anchor of a ship.

70 Guillén de Castro, *El Conde de Irlos*, Acto 2. Psychologists C.R. Snyder and David Feldman seize upon this image: "Anchors are rituals, institutions, places, or mechanisms that serve as stable foundations that we can count on over the years … [A]nchors have the paradoxical effect of freeing the mind. Instead of weighing one down … anchors provide a stable launching pad for producing agentic and pathways thoughts about goals" (C.R. Snyder and B. David Feldman, "Hope for the Many: An Empowering Social Agenda," in *Handbook of Hope*, ed. C.R. Snyder [San Diego: Academic Press, 2000], 389–412, at 402, 403).

71 "un amante entretenido tras la esperanza se va como el pez que asido está río abajo" (Lope de Vega, *La pobreza estimada*, Acto 1).

72 Thus Fedra asks Floriano, "¿qué hiciste de aquella cinta que de esperanza te di?" (Lope de Vega, *Los locos de Valencia*, Acto 2).

73 Lope de Vega, *Contra valor no hay desdicha*, Acto 1.

74 Lope de Vega, *Los Ponces de Barcelona*, Acto 1.

75 Lope de Vega, *El príncipe perfecto*, Acto 1.

76 "Ay hermana, de tu esperanza colgado me tienes" (Guillén de Castro, *El perfecto caballero*, Acto 2).

77 "enlazan el muro de tu firmeza los lazos de su esperanza" (Tirso de Molina, *La villana de la Sagra*, Jornada 2).

78 "que fuese aquel caballero por un listón de esperanza a las rejas de tu huerto" (Lope de Vega, *El caballero de Olmedo*, Acto 1). On the significance of these iron bars or *rejas* through which lovers communicated, see Faith Blackhurst, "The Mediation of Love *por las rejas* in El *Quijote*," paper presented at the XXVI Congreso Internacional de Literatura y Estudios Hispánicos (17–19 June 2020).

79 Lope de Vega, *El servir con mala estrella*, Acto 3. Another play that mentions defeating the Minotaur with hope and patience is Lope de Vega's *La mayor victoria de Alemania de Don Gonzalo de Córdoba*: "éste con el Minotauro con Esperanza, y Paciencia" (Jornada 3).

80 For a study of the labyrinth motif in the *comedias* and its connection to casuistry, see Hilaire Kallendorf, "Splitting Hairs or Finding Threads: The Labyrinth as Metaphor for Moral Dilemma in the *Comedia*," in *DOCTA Y SABIA ATENEA. Studia in honorem Prof. Lía Schwartz*, ed. Sagrario López Poza et al. (A Coruña: Universidade da Coruña, 2019), 339–58.

81 "Si la esperanza me diera sólo un cabello a que asirme" (Juan Ruiz de Alarcón, *El semejante a sí mismo*, Acto 2).

82 Lope de Vega, *El mejor alcalde, el rey*, Acto 1.

83 Lope de Vega, *Quien todo lo quiere*, Acto 1. This commonplace is repeated in the shorter line, "esperanza de ahorcado, que la tiene en el cordel" (Lope de Vega, *Los comendadores de Córdoba*, Jornada 1).

84 "primero que a mi esperanza hubiera cortado el hilo" (Tirso de Molina, *El condenado por desconfiado*, Jornada 2).

85 Lope de Vega, *La dama boba*, Acto 3.

86 "Ligero pensamiento de amor, pájaro alegre que viste la esperanza de plumas, y alas verdes" (Tirso de Molina, *La venganza de Tamar*, Jornada 1).

87 Alexandre Johnston, "'Poet of Hope': *Elpis* in Pindar," in *Hope in Ancient Literature*, ed. Kazantzidis and Spatharas, 35–52, at 50.

88 Keely Elizabeth Heuer, "The Face of Hope: Isolated Heads in South Italian Visual Culture," in *Hope in Ancient Literature*, ed. Kazantzidis and Spatharas, 297–327, at 297.

89 Jerome Groopman, *The Anatomy of Hope* (New York: Random House, 2004), 193.

90 Calderón, *Amar después de la muerte*, Jornada 2.

91 "Vuela mi estrecha y débil esperanza con flacas alas" (Cervantes, *La entretenida*, Jornada 1).

92 Lope de Vega, *El mayordomo de la Duquesa de Amalfi*, Acto 1.

93 Calderón, *Amigo, amante y leal*, Jornada 1.

94 "esperanza que nace y muere tan fácilmente, que más que esperanza Cisne, parece esperanza Fénix" (Calderón, *Amigo, amante y leal*, Jornada 1).

95 This sentiment is displayed in the following passage by Fabricio:

> Sobre dejar la esperanza
> el que ama, era concepto
> de un discreto, harto discreto,
> esta aguda semejanza.
> Hay unos dardos atados
> al brazo con un cordel,
> que vuelven más recio a él,
> señor, después de tirados.
> Así de quien tiene amor,

> con esperanzas ajenas,
> salen a veces las penas,
> y vuelven con más furor.
>
> (Lope de Vega, *El mayordomo de la Duquesa de Amalfi*, Acto 2)

96 Derived from St. Paul's famous passage in 1 Cor. 13:13: "And now there remain faith, hope, and charity, these three" (http://www.drbo.org/chapter/53013.htm).

97 Calderón, *Los alimentos del hombre*, auto sacramental.

98 Calderón, *El segundo blasón del Austria*, auto sacramental. The "siempre-viva" flower is known in Latin as *gomphrena globosa* and in English as the bachelor button.

99 Francisco de Rojas Zorrilla, *Sin honra no hay amistad*, Jornada 2.

100 "el árbol de tu esperanza ya se consiente marchito" (Francisco de Rojas Zorrilla, *No hay ser padre siendo rey*, Jornada 3).

101 "los verdes tributos de tu esperanza mejores, brotando olorosas flores, rindiendo sabrosos frutos" (Guillén de Castro, *El perfecto caballero*, Acto 2).

102 Thus Pedro compares his aborted hopes to almonds picked prematurely:

> Rendido en fin a la suerte,
> preso aherrojado, y desnudo
> me despedí de mi esposa
> con dulcísimos arrullos,
> y lloré de nuestro amor
> el recién cortado fruto:
> pues como el almendro suele,
> siendo del Mayo preludio,
> morir a manos de un aire,
> antes de ver el capullo
> de la flor, que es la camisa
> con que abriga el almendruco,
> así mi verde esperanza,
> cuando con tan triste anuncio,
> lo jarifo amancillado,
> y lo enamorado mustio.
>
> (Juan Pérez de Montalbán, *El valiente más dichoso, Don Pedro Guiral*, Jornada 3)

103 Agustín Moreto, *La misma conciencia acusa*, Jornada 1.

104 "quiero sembrar mis esperanzas un día, por ver si cojo alegría después de tanto penar" (Lope de Vega, *El mejor maestro, el tiempo*, Acto 2).

105 "rocío, pues, de tan seca mudanza, la hierba de su esperanza reverdece al gusto mío" (Lope de Vega, *El hidalgo Bencerraje*, Acto 2).

106 "por mitigar tantos enojos, regaba mi esperanza con mis ojos" (Francisco de Rojas Zorrilla, *Casarse por vengarse*, Jornada 1).

107 "las hojas creciendo va, de tu florida esperanza" (Lope de Vega, *El genovés liberal*, Acto 1).

108 Lope de Vega, *Peribáñez y el Comendador de Ocaña*, Acto 1.

109 Averill et al., *Rule of Hope*, 57.

110 Lope de Vega, *El perseguido*, Jornada 3.

111 Lope de Vega, *La Reina Juana de Nápoles*, Acto 2.

112 Francisco de Rojas Zorrilla, *No hay amigo para amigo*, Jornada 2.

113 "llorara esperanza flor que nunca llegó a dar fruto" (Tirso de Molina, *La huerta de Juan Fernández*, Jornada 2).

114 "ya se enoja, dulce señora, mi amor, pues tal esperanza en flor, él la marchita, y despoja" (Lope de Vega, *La ocasión perdida*, Jornada 2).

115   [E]sta prolija esperanza,
           que tan verde ha de durar,
           que ni el tiempo la ha de ahajar,
           ni marchitar la mudanza.

        (Francisco de Rojas Zorrilla, *No hay amigo para amigo*, Jornada 2)

116 Lope de Vega, *Servir a buenos*, Acto 3.

117 Pindar, *Nemean* 8.44–45, quoted in Johnston, "'Poet of Hope," 43.

118 "¿son estas colores verdes de la esperanza que pierdes el mal sazonado fruto?" (Lope de Vega, *El verdadero amante*, Acto 1).

119 Lope de Vega, *El mayorazgo dudoso*, Jornada 1.

120 "hoy quiere mi ya marchita esperanza volverse a vestir de verde" (Francisco de Rojas Zorrilla, *Los áspides de Cleopatra*, Jornada 3).

121 Lope de Vega, *El mejor maestro, el tiempo*, Acto 2.

122 Lope de Vega, *El premio de la hermosura*, Acto 3.

123 "la mejorana, que de esperanza se viste" (Lope de Vega, *La octava maravilla*, Acto 2).

124 Lope de Vega, *Sembrar en buena tierra*, Acto 1.

125 Francisco de Rojas Zorrilla, *Lo que quería ver el Marqués de Villena*, Jornada 2.

126 Lope de Vega, *El mejor mozo de España*, Acto 1.

127 Calderón, *Agradecer y no amar*, Jornada 2.

128 Tirso de Molina, *Don Gil de las calzas verdes*, Acto 3.

129 Santiago el Verde is an actual saint whose feast day is 1 May. See Elsa Graciela Fiadino, "El juego festivo en *Santiago el Verde* de Lope de Vega," in *Actas del V Congreso de la Asociación Internacional Siglo de Oro* (Münster, 20–24 de julio de 1999), ed. Christoph Strosetzki (Münster: Vervuert Verlagsgesellschaft, 2001), 575–82.

130 Lope de Vega, *Santiago el Verde*, Acto 2.

131 "¿Ya no sabes que es de verde la esperanza que perdí, que nunca me la vestí?" (Lope de Vega, *El verdadero amante*, Acto 1). We might think here likewise of the Caballero del Verde Gabán in Cervantes' *Don Quijote* (part II, ch. XVI) (Miguel de Cervantes, *Segunda parte del ingenioso hidalgo don Quijote de la Mancha*, in *Obras completas*, ed. Florencio Sevilla [Madrid: Castalia, 1999], 321–508, at 361–4).

132 "amor, ya hallaste camino, para que entre la esperanza a fabricar tus alivios" (Antonio de Solís, *Las amazonas*, Jornada 2).

133 "de alivio mis dudas, vamos donde las consuele mi última esperanza" (Calderón, *No hay instante sin milagro*, auto sacramental).

134 Calderón, *El secreto a voces*, Jornada 1.

135 "mi esperanza me levanta" (Lope de Vega, *La francesilla*, Acto 1). As George Kazantzidis and Dimos Spatharas remark in reference to the ancient world, "The extent to which individuals, groups of individuals, or indeed mankind (as Pandora's ambiguous myth indicates) find solace in hope suggests their degree of displeasure with their present situation" (George Kazantzidis and Dimos Spatharas, "Introductory: 'Hope,' *Elpis, Spes*: Affective and Non-Affective Expectancy," in *Hope in Ancient Literature*, ed. Kazantzidis and Spatharas, 1–31, at 1–2). They note that the myth of Pandora was first recounted by Hesiod.

136 Antonio Zamora, *Cada uno es linaje aparte, y los Mazas de Aragón*, Acto 1.

137 "Darásle a mi corazón sumo bien, con la esperanza de tan dichosa ocasión" (Guillén de Castro, *Progne y Filomena*, Acto 1).

138 "Llega tú ahora, extrema Esperanza, para confortarle en todos sus Sentidos" (Calderón, *A tu prójimo como a ti*, Acto 1).

139 Lope de Vega, *San Nicolás de Tolentino*, Acto 3.

140 Tirso de Molina, *La villana de la Sagra*, Jornada 3.

141 "le alimenta la esperanza" (Calderón, *Los hijos de la Fortuna Teágenes y Cariclea*, Jornada 2).

142 Ariadna says, "Vengo animando la esperanza para que sustente al cuerpo" (Lope de Vega, *El laberinto de Creta*, Acto 2).

143 "la esperanza con que dura, ¿de qué parte se alimenta?" (Agustín Moreto, *Primero es la honra*, Jornada 2).

144 "Ya encamina mi astucia, mi esperanza" (Juan Bautista Diamante, *No aspirar a merecer*, Jornada 2).

145 Antonio Zamora, *Todo lo vence el Amor*, Jornada 3.

146 Lope de Vega, *El leal criado*, Acto 1.

147 "una esperanza enseñe el camino a otra" (Calderón, *El maestro de danzar*, Jornada 3).

148 "la Esperanza nunca se quede atrás, que la Esperanza es siempre la que adelante va" (Calderón, *El Santo Rey Don Fernando, segunda parte*, auto sacramental).

149 "Fuerza es ir tras mi esperanza" (Calderón, *La estatua de Prometeo*, Jornada 2).

150 "Creo que tiene esperanza, que te ha de ver enmendar" (Lope de Vega, *Los embustes de Fabia*, Jornada 2).

151 Antonio Zamora, *La poncella de Orleans*, Jornada 1.

152 "me da esperanza de que tendré buena suerte" (Guillén de Castro, *Las mocedades del Cid, comedia primera*, Acto 3).

153 "al Pobre la Esperanza de la Salud, y la Vida" (Calderón, *El primer refugio del hombre, y probática piscina*, auto sacramental).

154 Juan Ruiz de Alarcón, *La amistad castigada*, Acto 2.

155 "lo ha parido; logróse bien su esperanza" (Guillén de Castro, *El nacimiento de Montesinos*, Acto 3).

156 Lope de Vega, *Sembrar en buena tierra*, Acto 1.

157 See Hilaire Kallendorf, "Greed Breaks the Bag," in *Sins of the Fathers: Moral Economies in Early Modern Spain* (Toronto: University of Toronto Press, 2013), 45–73.

158 Joseph Kesselring, *Arsenic and Old Lace* (New York: Dramatists Play Service, 1969).

159 Guillén de Castro, *El perfecto caballero*, Acto 1. For a scholar who situates the picaresque genre within broader cultural discourses like the *arbitristas'* treatises recommending governmental solutions to social problems such as poverty and ubiquitous begging, see Anne J. Cruz, *Discourses of Poverty: Social Reform and the Picaresque Novel in Early Modern Spain* (Toronto: University of Toronto Press, 1999).

160 Guillén de Castro, *El pretender con pobreza*, Jornada 3.

161 Cervantes, *La entretenida*, Jornada 2.

162 Cervantes, *El gallardo español*, Jornada 3.

163 Consider, for example, the episode of the *galeotes* (I, 22) in Miguel de Cervantes, *Primera parte del ingenioso hidalgo don Quijote de la Mancha*, in *Obras completas*, ed. Sevilla, 145–320, at 207–10. On justice in Cervantes, see Musisi Kiwanuka, "The Eternal Quest: Justice and Don Quixote in Sixteenth Century Spain," *Penn History Review* 16.2 (2009): 31–50.

164 Calderón, *El pleito matrimonial*, auto sacramental.

165 Cervantes, *El rufián dichoso*, Acto 1.

166 Luis Quiñones de Benavente, *La maya*, entremés. Donald Lateiner comments on the biological evolutionary basis for hope: "Human beings developed *hopes* that energize them for hunting fat, protein, and sugars" (Lateiner, "*Elpis* as Emotion and Reason," 131).

167 Lope de Vega, *Peribáñez y el Comendador de Ocaña*, Acto 2.

168 Tirso de Molina, *La reina de los reyes*, Jornada 1.

169 On the power struggles between farmers and ranchers, especially with regard to enclosure laws, see Robert B. Ekelund et al., "Rent Seeking and Property Rights' Assignments as a Process: The Mesta Cartel of Medieval-Mercantile Spain," *Journal of European Economic History* 26.1 (1997): 9–35.

170 Lope de Vega, *El hijo de los leones*, Acto 1.

171 Calderón, *Mujer, llora, y vencerás*, Jornada 3.

172 "padre de la patria, en esperanza que la defienda" (Lope de Vega, *El honrado hermano*, Acto 2).

173 "lejana Esperanza de su Auxilio" (Calderón, *Duelos de amor y lealtad*, Jornada 2).

174 "os mantiene la Esperanza, de que seréis socorridos" (Calderón, *Duelos de amor y lealtad*, Jornada 2).

175 "a un preso esa esperanza anime" (Lope de Vega, *El mayorazgo dudoso*, Jornada 2).

176 See "Creen haber hallado los restos óseos de Miguel de Cervantes y su esposa," Agencia EFE, https://www.youtube.com/watch?app=desktop&v=3ZpLT8VMkiE; and "Encuentran los restos de Miguel de Cervantes," https://www.youtube.com/watch?app=desktop&v=p9PJ_Wz6uGg.

177 Calderón, *La redención de cautivos*, auto sacramental.

178 "De su ejército lo entiendo porque le mueve esperanza de librar a su señor" (Lope de
      Vega, *Mirad a quién alabáis*, Acto 3).

179 Lope de Vega, *Virtud, pobreza y mujer*, Acto 2. A *posta* (like the English *post*) was
      a waystation on the mail route where couriers could leave their tired horses and
      mount fresh ones.

180 Lope de Vega, *El laberinto de Creta*, Acto 2. Lope's thoughts on exile might possibly
      have been influenced by the similar experience of his poetic predecessor Ovid,
      for whom "in his exilic poetry, hope, *spes salutis*, stands as 'the poet's most reliable
      companion and unfailing partner, along with love and nostalgia for his friends
      and family back in Rome" (Andreas Michalopoulos, quoted by Kazantzidis and
      Spatharas, "Introductory: 'Hope,'" 18).

181 On spiritual suffering in the absence of God's intervention see Gerald Vann, *The
      Pain of Christ and the Sorrow of God* (Oxford: Blackfriars, 1949).

182   Del verde la Esperanza
          en eterna alabanza
          de Soldados, de espíritu tan fuerte,
          que … batallen con la muerte.   (Calderón, *Las órdenes militares*, auto sacramental)

183 Lope de Vega, *El primer Fajardo*, Acto 3. An *almena* was a battlement or merlon (the
      upper edge of a castle wall that looks like teeth).

184 Calderón, *El sitio de Breda*, Acto 1.

185 This is the situation described in the line, "No le quedaba al Francés recurso ya
      de esperanza; y marchando a toda prisa, sus cuarteles desampara, pegando fuego"
      (Agustín Moreto, *De fuera vendrá*, Jornada 1).

186 Juan Ruiz de Alarcón, *Examen de maridos*, Acto 1.

187 "esperanza de ganancia" (Lope de Vega, *Las grandezas de Alejandro*, Acto 2).

188 "esperanza de placer" (Lope de Vega, *Las aventuras de Don Juan de Alarcos*, Jornada 3).

189 "si allí le aguardaras, el fin de tu esperanza conquistaras" (Lope de Vega, *El laberinto
      de Creta*, Acto 1).

190 Thus a woman reports a successful defence of her chastity, "Puso los ojos en mí, mas
      perdiendo la esperanza de vencer mi honesto pecho, noble sangre, intención casta"
      (Lope de Vega, *El príncipe despeñado*, Acto 3).

191 Juan Ruiz de Alarcón, *El semejante a sí mismo*, Acto 2.

192 Lope de Vega, *La inocente Laura*, Acto 1. Bettie Doebler emphasizes this connection
      in relation to Macbeth: "The witches and their embodiment of his ambitions in
      their prophecies become an early focus for his imagination. And once he has shared
      that demonic hope with Lady Macbeth she becomes the goad to ambition and
      murder that he needs to allow the forces of evil to overcome him" (Doebler, *Rooted
      Sorrow*, 175).

193 "es inútil mi venida, y diligencia, perdida la esperanza de mi empleo" (Calderón,
      Agradecer y no amar, Jornada 2).

194 "si la esperanza de hallar aplauso en vos los anima" (Juan Ruiz de Alarcón, *La
      amistad castigada*, Acto 1).

195 "Valiente Almohaditen, esperanza, que de tu nombre habrá por mil edades memoria" (Lope de Vega, *La desdichada Estefanía*, Acto 1).

196 "hazéos santo; pintáos justo; ¿dónde está la esperanza, por quien a tantos desnudos vestistes, y de comer distes?" (Lope de Vega, *La historia de Tobías*, Acto 1); "esperanza de que a tanto has de llegar como el santo" (Lope de Vega, *La resistencia honrada y Condesa Matilde*, Jornada 2).

197 Juan Ruiz de Alarcón, *Examen de maridos*, Acto 2.

198 "ser Príncipe de Aragón puede alentar mi esperanza" (Lope de Vega, *El piadoso aragonés*, Acto 2).

199 "la esperanza del Reino, que ha perdido" (Lope de Vega, *El juez en su causa*, Jornada 3).

200 Calderón, *El veneno y la triaca*, auto sacramental.

201 Juan de Matos Fragoso, *La devoción del Ángel de la Guarda*, Jornada 1.

202 Tirso de Molina, *La prudencia en la mujer*, Jornada 2.

203 Papaioannou, "'A Historian Utterly Without Hope,'" 221.

204 "el ruego del tirano no se alcanza, las armas dan esperanza, y las tomaremos luego" (Lope de Vega, *El rey sin reino*, Acto 2).

205 A. Robert Lauer, *Tyrannicide and Drama* (Wiesbaden: Franz Steiner, 1987).

206 Douglas Davies, *Emotion, Identity, and Religion* (Oxford: Oxford University Press, 2011), 192. Natalla Tsoumpra extends these ideas into the realm of current political discourse: "In the 21st century the discourse of hope persists across what has often been described as a 'left-wing' or 'progressive' agenda … Barack Obama appealed to his voters through a rhetoric of hope; Alexis Tsipras' political campaign before the Greek elections of January 2015, and the referendum held in July 2015, was inspired by the idea of a hopeful resistance against the political crisis; Jeremy Corbyn's campaign for the Labour party leadership in the UK also promoted the idea of hopeful politics against the conservative and austerity-oriented agenda of the Tories" (Natalia Tsoumpra, "The Politics of Hopelessness: Thucydides and Aristophanes' *Knights*," in *Hope in Ancient Literature*, ed. Kazantzidis and Spatharas, 111–29, at 111).

207 "esperanza de verla Gobernadora de Milán, o de Pavía" (Tirso de Molina, *Santo y sastre*, Acto 2).

208 Tirso de Molina, *Del enemigo el primer consejo*, Jornada 3. Michael Paschalis explains the special connection of hope to empire: "*Spes* was worshipped as a goddess in Republican times and beginning with Augustus it became a monopoly of the emperor as an imperial virtue. The *Spes Augusta* represented the promise of prosperity for the Roman people and the capacity of the emperor to ensure it … In the *Aeneid* there is a direct and strong link between *spes* and Trojan future, settlement in Italy, establishment of the Roman race and growth of the Roman empire till the Augustan Age" (Michael Paschalis, "*uestras spes uritis*: Hope and Empire in Virgil's *Aeneid*," in *Hope in Ancient Literature*, ed. Kazantzidis and Spatharas, 171–82, at 171, 172).

209 "vuestra embajada, de la tregua que deseo, se asegure la esperanza" (Juan de Matos Fragoso, *El traidor contra su sangre*, Acto 1).

210 "tiene resolución Deidamia de que a Ceylán libre vuelva, en esperanza de que, haciendo confianza de ella, las Paces podrán capitularse mejor" (Calderón, *Duelos de amor y lealtad*, Jornada 2).

211 "tan cierta esperanza de ser vuestro amado esposo" (Juan Ruiz de Alarcón, *Los pechos privilegiados*, Acto 1).

212 "tienen tus criadas todas en la esperanza sus bodas, y en la Corte sus pasiones" (Juan Ruiz de Alarcón, *Las paredes oyen*, Acto 1).

213 "este anillo, esfera de mi esperanza" (Tirso de Molina, *No hay peor sordo*, Jornada 2).

214 Juan Pérez de Montalbán, *El mariscal de Virón*, Jornada 1.

215 For a biography of Gaspar de Guzmán, Conde-Duque de Olivares, see John Elliott, *The Count-Duke of Olivares: The Statesman in an Age of Decline* (New Haven: Yale University Press, 1989).

216 "sabéis su poder, y su privanza; tened de grandes premios esperanza" (Lope de Vega, *Amor, pleito y desafío*, Jornada 2).

217 "ya en gastar han dado la esperanza en la Corte pretendientes" (Lope de Vega, *Servir a señor discreto*, Acto 2).

218 "algún premio se dejó llevar de esta confianza, en cuya noble esperanza desde Toledo mudé su casa a la Corte" (Calderón, *Cada uno para sí*, Jornada 1).

219 "la esperanza, que en su dote había puesto" (Lope de Vega, *Las flores de Don Juan, y rico y pobre trocados*, Acto 2).

220 Lope de Vega, *Los ramilletes de Madrid*, Acto 2.

221 Tirso de Molina, *La vida de Herodes*, Acto 2.

222 Lope de Vega, *No son todos ruiseñores*, Jornada 3.

223 "De tu esperanza homicida colegir tu engaño puedes, pues para que rico quedes" (Tirso de Molina, *Santo y sastre*, Acto 1).

224 Agustín Moreto, *La fuerza de la ley*, Jornada 3.

225 "es bien que tenga la esperanza, que los justos en tan firme blanco emplean" (Lope de Vega, *El robo de Dina*, Acto 1).

226 "el alma de las victorias, es la esperanza del premio" (Calderón, *Fieras afemina amor*, Jornada 1).

227 "el fin de la Esperanza es el galardón" (Calderón, *El Santo Rey Don Fernando*, auto sacramental).

228 "perdí la esperanza que traía de lucir" (Calderón, *Amado y aborrecido*, Jornada 3).

229 Thus Lisareo declares, "si consigo la esperanza de Campeón, de Aurora un mundo pondré sujeto a sus plantas" (Juan Bautista Diamante, *Más encanto es la hermosura*, Jornada 1).

230 "tengo puesta en Blanca mi esperanza, con las colores y versos, y divisas de las cañas" (Juan Ruiz de Alarcón, *Examen de maridos*, Acto 3). On the tradition of jousting knights wearing their ladies' colours, see Roger Boase, "Ludic Dimensions of Courtly Love at the Court of Isabel *la Católica*," in *A Companion to the Queenship of Isabel* la Católica, ed. Hilaire Kallendorf (Leiden: Brill, 2023), 158–95.

231 "tu gente, poca, y valerosa, de la esperanza del laurel sedienta" (Agustín Moreto, *La fuerza de la ley*, Jornada 1).

232 "ni se ponga en el bonete pluma, o señal de esperanza" (Lope de Vega, *El hijo de Reduán*, Acto 2).

233 "merecí que de favores coronase mi esperanza, dándome, a riesgo del padre, en su mismo cuarto entrada" (Calderón, *También hay duelo en las damas*, Jornada 3).

234 Lope de Vega, *El juez en su causa*, Jornada 2.

235 "la esperanza de cobrar el honor con la venganza" (Lope de Vega, *La venganza venturosa*, Acto 2); "con tanta venganza me llenasteis la esperanza" (Calderón, *A secreto agravio, secreta venganza*, Acto 1). Antti Lampinen notes that "Hope for revenge, especially in the Roman literature, is a theme thoroughly enmeshed with the ideologies of the empire and the fear of the subaltern that can be approached with post-colonial theories in mind" (Antti Lampinen, "Against Hope? The Untimely *Elpis* of Northern Barbarians," in *Hope in Ancient Literature*, ed. Kazantzidis and Spatharas, 275–95, at 292).

236 "viene, esperanza, dad filos a mi venganza" (Tirso de Molina, *La vida de Herodes*, Acto 2).

237 Calderón, *A secreto agravio, secreta venganza*, Acto 1.

238 "(o triste caso) que aun de morir me falta la esperanza" (Juan Pérez de Montalbán, *Lo que son juicios del cielo*, Jornada 3).

239 "le miramos repartir la esmeralda al Confesor, por la esperanza feliz que en él tuvo" (Calderón, *La vacante general*, auto sacramental).

240 "esperanza de la medra, y del perdón" (Calderón, *El segundo Scipión*, Jornada 1).

241 "no habita la esperanza en el injusto pecho del pecador" (Cervantes, *El rufián dichoso*, Jornada 2).

242 "¿tal podrá en la hora angustiada del morir tener alguna esperanza de salvarse?" (Cervantes, *El rufián dichoso*, Jornada 2).

243 "siempre tengo esperanza, en que tengo de salvarme, puesto que no va fundada mi esperanza en obras mías, sino saber que se humana Dios" (Tirso de Molina, *El condenado por desconfiado*, Jornada 2).

244 "la Esperanza de que volveré a vivir de nuevo" (Calderón, *Lo que va del hombre a Dios*, auto sacramental).

245 Tirso de Molina, *Antona García*, Acto 1.

246 Davies, *Emotion, Identity, and Religion*, 193.

247 "soy el Cielo, en quien la esperanza está cerca de ser cumplimiento" (Calderón, *La cura y la enfermedad*, auto sacramental).

248 Lope de Vega, *El rústico del cielo*, Acto 1. For real-life accounts of mystical visions of heaven and hell during this time period in Spain's empire, see Hilaire Kallendorf, "Visions in the Service of Virtue: Rhetorical Mysticism in Motolinía's *Memoriales*," in *The Franciscans in Colonial Mexico*, ed. Thomas Cohen et al. (Norman: University of Oklahoma Press / American Academy of Franciscan History, 2021), 33–55.

249 Calderón, *La aurora en Copacabana*, Jornada 2.

250   La Católica esperanza,
        que los Pontífices tengan,
        de que el Universo esté

    todo entero a su Obediencia,

    cuando a un Pastor, y a un Rebaño

    se reduzcan las Ovejas.   (Calderón, *Los misterios de la Misa*, auto sacramental)

251 Thus the allegorical figure of Esperanza identifies herself, "Yo, que he sido su Esperanza, y la doy de que podrán catequizarse algún día" (Calderón, *El nuevo palacio del Retiro*, auto sacramental).

252 Lope de Vega, *El bastardo Mudarra*, Acto 3.

253 "del cielo bajaba la esperanza, y me decía, sirve, Jacob, y espera" (Lope de Vega, *El robo de Dina*, Acto 2). These lines refer to Jacob's dream of angels ascending and descending a ladder stretching to heaven. The "service" he is commanded in the vision to perform may allude to his serving Laban for seven years to win Rachel, only to be given her sister Leah as a wife instead. He then served and waited seven more years to obtain Rachel (Genesis 29:18–30).

254 Guillén de Castro, *El perfecto caballero*, Acto 3.

255 Juan Ruiz de Alarcón, *La manganilla de Melilla*, Acto 3.

256 Calderón, *La redención de cautivos*, auto sacramental.

257 Lope de Vega, *Los locos por el cielo*, Acto 3.

258 Lope de Vega, *El desprecio agradecido*, preliminares. This dedicatory poem to Don Francisco de la Cueva y Silva, "habiendo hecho una Información en Derecho a la limpia Concepción de la Virgen nuestra Señora," refers to contemporaneous debates about the Immaculate Conception of Mary.

259 "De tu salud la esperanza ponen el santo" (Juan Ruiz de Alarcón, *Todo es ventura*, Acto 3).

260 Tirso de Molina, *La reina de los reyes*, Jornada 3.

261 "El Profeta que esperaban los siglos viene conforme a la esperanza divina, dando a los desiertos voces el sobre escrito divino" (Lope de Vega, *La limpieza no manchada*, Acto 1).

262 "la Esperanza es la que más daño hace al Hebreo" (Calderón, *Amar y ser amado, y divina Filotea*, auto sacramental).

263 Calderón, *Amar y ser amado, y divina Filotea*, auto sacramental.

264 "no temáis, que en Jove tengo esperanza, que este mal hará mudanza, con el fin que deseáis" (Juan de la Cueva, *La libertad de Roma por Mucio Cevola*, Acto 4).

265 "Yo tengo en Marte esperanza, que tendrá Roma victoria" (Lope de Vega, *El honrado hermano*, Acto 3).

266 Lope de Vega, *Contra valor no hay desdicha*, Acto 3.

267 Kazantzidis and Spatharas, "Introductory: 'Hope,'" 24.

268 Lope de Vega, *La primera información*, Jornada 2.

269 "quien en la mujer, y el dado puso esperanza, ¿qué espera?" (Lope de Vega, *Las flores de Don Juan, y rico y pobre trocados*, Acto 2).

270 "la esperanza a nadie limitaron las estrellas" (Juan de Matos Fragoso, *La devoción del Ángel de la Guarda*, Jornada 1).

271 "mi prolija esperanza es profeta de mi bien" (Francisco de Rojas Zorrilla, *No hay amigo para amigo*, Jornada 1).

272 Lope de Vega, *Contra valor no hay desdicha*, Acto 1. This was the case likewise in ancient Greece: "In Book 8 [of Thucydides] we find out that when the news of the disaster in Sicily reached Athens, the people grew angry at those who encouraged their hopes by means of oracles and divinations … '[T]hey were furious at the oracle-mongers, seers, and anyone whose divinations had made them hope that they would capture Sicily'. After irrational passion then, what incited the Athenian hopes for Sicily was divination and oracle-mongering, practices about which Thucydides often phrases his scepticism, and whose interpretation cannot be relied upon. That superstition is not a reliable guide for hope is painfully evident in the case of Nicias too throughout the Sicilian expedition" (Tsoumpra, "The Politics of Hopelessness," 119).

273 "que lo que cantan aquí de nuestra esperanza sea agüero tan venturoso, que vais a contarlo a Grecia" (Lope de Vega, *Las mujeres sin hombres*, Acto 2). A similar hope was placed in the predictive power of dreams in ancient Rome: "the reason that people would consult the dream interpreter who would be armed with Artemidorus' handbook is precisely in order to find out how the predictive power of dreams would relate with their hopes and fears about the future" (Kostas Vlassopoulos, "Hope and Slavery," in *Hope in Ancient Literature*, ed. Kazantzidis and Spatharas, 235–58, at 236).

274 Lope de Vega, *El castigo del discreto*, Acto 1.

275 On the dangerous political import of some contemporaneous prophecies see Richard Kagan, *Lucrecia's Dreams: Politics and Prophecy in Sixteenth-Century Spain* (Berkeley: University of California Press, 1990).

276 Francisco de Rojas Zorrilla, *Lo que son mujeres*, Jornada 2.

277 Lope de Vega, *El gran Duque de Moscovia, y emperador perseguido*, Acto 1.

278 Lope de Vega, *El gran Duque de Moscovia, y emperador perseguido*, Acto 1.

279 Lope de Vega, *La vengadora de las mujeres*, Acto 2.

280 Guillén de Castro, *Las mocedades del Cid, comedia primera*, Acto 1.

281 "que tengas esperanza, que habrá muy presto mudanza en tu fortuna cruel" (Lope de Vega, *Virtud, pobreza y mujer*, Acto 2).

282 "Sembré esperanza, y favor, vuestro triste labrador" (Lope de Vega, *Los muertos vivos*, Acto 2).

283 "labradora soy de amor, mis esperanzas cultivo mientras que méritos siembro" (Juan de Matos Fragoso, *El hijo de la piedra*, Jornada 2).

284 Lope de Vega, *El molino*, Jornada 2. *Baldía* refers to farmland that is not cultivated.

285 Calderón, *Las tres justicias en una*, Jornada 1.

286 Francisco de Rojas Zorrilla, *Entre bobos anda el juego*, Jornada 1. Conversely, hope itself has been demonstrated by medical doctors to have the power to heal physical ailments: "positive emotions, including hope, are part of all forms of healing" (C.R. Snyder, "Hypothesis: There Is Hope," in *Handbook of Hope*, ed. Snyder, 3–21, at 4).

287 Antonio de Solís, *Un bobo hace ciento*, Jornada 1.

288 Witness the Conde de Irlos: "Las palabras de tu boca resucitan mi esperanza" (Guillén de Castro, *El Conde de Irlos*, Acto 1).

289 "Como quien viene con sola la esperanza de tus cartas" (Lope de Vega, *La mal casada*, Acto 3).

290 "escuché estas voces, que blandamente ruidosas, alimentar solicitan una esperanza animosa" (Juan Bautista Diamante, *Ir por el riesgo a la dicha*, Jornada 2).

291 Guillén de Castro, *El curioso impertinente*, Acto 2.

292 Here the early modern Spanish material forms a contrast to ancient Greek views: "in Greek thought, *elpis* (and its motivational aspects) is more commonly something that one resorts to when adversities limit one's ability to exert control over one's own life … [I]n Greek thought scripts of *elpis* are commonly associated with situations in which individuals have a sense of limited self-efficacy and thus typically emphasize the external conditions which restrain personal agency" (Kazantzidis and Spatharas, "Introductory: 'Hope,'" 9–10).

293 Calderón, *Primero soy yo*, Jornada 1. On *dilatio* see Hilaire Kallendorf, "*Dilatio*, Deferral, and *Différance*," in *Conscience on Stage: The* Comedia *as Casuistry in Early Modern Spain* (Toronto: University of Toronto Press, 2007), 192–7.

294 Juan Bautista Diamante, *Jupiter y Semele*, zarzuela.

295 Statius, *Thebaid* 2.321, quoted in Augoustakis, "Quaenam spes hominum?" 203. For a study of Quevedo's imitation of Statius, see Hilaire Kallendorf and Craig Kallendorf, "Conversations with the Dead: Quevedo and Statius, Annotation and Imitation," *Journal of the Warburg and Courtauld Institutes* 63 (2000): 131–68.

296 Lope de Vega, *La limpieza no manchada*, Acto 2.

297 Lope de Vega, *La firmeza en la desdicha*, Acto 1.

298 "Cuando te alejes de esta esperanza imposible" (Lope de Vega, *La niña de plata*, Acto 3).

299 "renuncian la esperanza, la fe niegan" (Agustín Moreto, *El caballero*, Jornada 3).

300 "haciendo que Ángela a entrambos cierre el paso a la esperanza, desviar este empeño" (Calderón, *Cuál es mayor perfección*, Jornada 2).

301 Agustín Moreto, *El Cristo de los milagros*, Jornada 3.

302 Calderón, *La aurora en Copacabana*, Jornada 3.

303 "¿con qué confianza daré paso a mi esperanza?" (Guillén de Castro, *Las mocedades del Cid, comedia primera*, Acto 1).

304 "Y labrando en la Mamora un fuerte, casi invencible, cortar esperanza y pasos, a Moros y Pichelingues" (Tirso de Molina, *Marta la piadosa*, Acto 2).

305 "otro dueño amado en tiempo te ha aventajado, que tu esperanza atropella" (Tirso de Molina, *Los amantes de Teruel*, Jornada 1).

306 "un caballo atropella lo mejor de mi esperanza" (Lope de Vega, *La hermosa Ester*, Acto 3).

307 "¿para otro desaire la despiertas la esperanza?" (Antonio Zamora, *No hay deuda que no se pague, y convidado de piedra*, Acto 1).

308 "mira mi desconfianza, cuán lejos de la esperanza me deja la reprehensión" (Juan
       Bautista Diamante, *La Reina María Estuarda*, Jornada 1).

309 "Está el pobre desdichado de su bajeza corrido, de su esperanza colgado" (Guillén de
       Castro, *La verdad averiguada, y engañoso casamiento*, Jornada 1).

310 Aristophanes, *Knights*, quoted in Slater, "Up from Tragicomedy," 87.

311 Calderón, *El nuevo hospicio de pobres*, auto sacramental.

312 Calderón, *El sacro Parnaso*, auto sacramental.

313 "la esperanza, y posesión se han de ver siempre a la cara" (Agustín Moreto, *La
       traición vengada*, Jornada 1).

314 "desmaya, Tancredo, en mí las fuerzas de mi esperanza" (Juan Pérez de Montalbán,
       El sufrimiento premiado, Jornada 2).

315 Tirso de Molina, *Los lagos de San Vicente*, Acto 3.

316 Lope de Vega, *La prueba de los ingenios*, Acto 2.

317 Lope de Vega, *La inocente Laura*, Acto 1.

318 "solo en perezoso aliento da de su vida esperanza" (Juan Bautista Diamante, *No
       aspirar a merecer*, Jornada 1).

319 "Cayó mi esperanza en tierra, con tu triste nueva" (Lope de Vega, *El príncipe
       despeñado*, Acto 2).

320 Guillén de Castro, *Las mocedades del Cid, comedia segunda*, Acto 3.

321 Snyder, "Hypothesis," 4. Nick Fisher notes that "it is characteristic of Greek
       ideas to take a less positive view of hope in general: hope, though emotionally
       appealing, leads people astray into rash decisions and failure" (Fisher, "Hope and
       Hopelessness," 70).

322 Fulkerson, "*Deos speravi*," 166.

323 "me llevó la esperanza a la mayor pretensión" (Lope de Vega, *La sortija del olvido*,
       Acto 2). Kazantzidis and Spatharas point out the risks of excessive hope: "Too much
       hopefulness may either sedate or, conversely, lead to unreflective, precarious, or
       foolhardy action" (Kazantzidis and Spatharas, "Introductory: 'Hope,'" 9).

324 "mi esperanza es vana, pues no puede alguna vez mejorarse mi fortuna" (Calderón,
       El príncipe constante, Jornada 2).

325 "con vano pensamiento, y esperanza enamoróse de un Alarbe Moro contra la ley de
       Dios" (Lope de Vega, *El primer rey de Castilla*, Acto 2).

326 Lope de Vega, *La ingratitud vengada*, Acto 3. The suffering induced by hope had
       been a topic in Virgil's *Aeneid*: "Virgil was of course aware that *spes* can play some
       grave tricks with people's minds, but he reserves its negative side (mostly) for Aeneas'
       enemies" (Kazantzidis and Spatharas, "Introductory: 'Hope,'" 28).

327 Antonio Zamora, *El lucero de Madrid, y divino Labrador San Isidro*, Jornada 3.

328 As Publio Valerio affirms when he warns Tarquinio, "Oye, Tarquinio, y deja más
       razones, y esa vana esperanza que te ciega, pues no saldrás con tales pretensiones"
       (Juan de la Cueva, *La libertad de Roma por Mucio Cevola*, Acto 1). Interestingly for
       this play, which is set in the classical world, in the culture of ancient Rome "often
       madness is nourished by 'hope' itself: in the opening of *Annals* 16.1 Tacitus hints

at Nero's mental deterioration by stating that the emperor was 'deluded' by his vanity … [T]his delusional state is clearly linked to the emperor's 'inane hopes' … Similarly, Suetonius (*Nero* 31) uses the word *furor* to describe the madness kindled by the hope of a vast hidden treasure in North Africa" (Kazantzidis and Spatharas, "Introductory: 'Hope,'" 17).

329 "No es mucho, amor, que procures que mi esperanza destrocen" (Tirso de Molina, *La huerta de Juan Fernández*, Jornada 3).

330 "No quiero hacer violencia a mi esperanza" (Francisco de Rojas Zorrilla, *Persiles y Sigismunda*, Jornada 2).

331 "tirana violencia, que has disparado la ausencia, para matar la esperanza" (Antonio Zamora, *Cada uno es linaje aparte, y los Mazas de Aragón*, Jornada 2).

332 Lope de Vega, *La gallarda toledana*, Acto 3.

333 "haces morir la esperanza a manos de la impaciencia" (Lope de Vega, *El vaquero de Morana*, Acto 1).

334 "tanta ingratitud os ha deshecho, loca esperanza mía" (Lope de Vega, *La mayor virtud de un rey*, Jornada 3).

335 "más que los vientos corren, balas que esperanza borren" (Tirso de Molina, *Escarmientos para el cuerdo*, Acto 2).

336 "¿que hallara un Sansón tan fuerte, el templo de mi esperanza?" (Lope de Vega, *El ausente en el lugar*, Acto 1).

337 Lope de Vega, *Roma abrasada*, Acto 3.

338 Lope de Vega, *El desprecio agradecido*, Jornada 3.

339 Calderón, *El pintor de su deshonra*, Jornada 1.

340 Calderón, *El Conde Lucanor*, Jornada 2.

341 Agustín Moreto, *La cautela en la amistad*, Jornada 2.

342 Calderón, *El postrer duelo de España*, Jornada 3.

343 "Alto desengaño mío, apercebid sepultura a mi esperanza, que ya indicios de muerta da" (Tirso de Molina, *Esto sí que es negociar*, Jornada 1).

344 Calderón, *Argenis y Poliarco*, Jornada 2.

345 Calderón, *La cisma de Inglaterra*, Jornada 1.

346 "quedaban de mi esperanza unas reliquias pequeñas" (Guillén de Castro, *El Conde de Irlos*, Acto 3).

347 "casi ofuscada del recio encuentro, perdí con el fuste la esperanza" (Juan Bautista Diamante, *Más encanto es la hermosura*, Jornada 1).

348 "pierde alguna, y no toda la esperanza" (Francisco de Rojas Zorrilla, *Progne y Filomena*, Jornada 3).

349 "la pobre mujer estaba ya desahuciada de esa esperanza" (Antonio Zamora, *No hay deuda que no se pague, y convidado de piedra*, Acto 1).

350 "Perdida esperanza mía, albricias, que ya os hallé" (Lope de Vega, *Por la puente, Juana*, Acto 3).

351 "Para quien sin esperanza padece, tiene Cupido el alivio de las ausencias" (Antonio Zamora, *Amar es saber vencer, y el arte contra el poder*, Jornada 2).

352 Francisco de Rojas Zorrilla, *Los áspides de Cleopatra*, Jornada 3.

353 Johnston, "'Poet of Hope,'" 50–1.

354 Juan de Matos Fragoso, *La devoción del Ángel de la Guarda*, Jornada 1.

355 "ya mi esperanza, si no se pierde, zozobra" (Juan Bautista Diamante, *Santa Teresa de Jesús*, Jornada 3).

356 "siempre llevo marchito el tronco de una esperanza" (Antonio Zamora, *Siempre hay que envidiar, amando*, Jornada 2).

357 "marchite un fuerte hielo su esperanza" (Lope de Vega, *El gallardo catalán*, Jornada 1).

358 Lope de Vega, *Lo cierto por lo dudoso*, Acto 2.

359 Bob Dylan, "Blowin' in the Wind," song on album *Finjan Club* (1962), https://www.youtube.com/watch?v=MMFj8uDubsE.

360 Antonio Zamora, *Siempre hay que envidiar, amando*, Jornada 3.

361 Antonio Zamora, *Todo lo vence el Amor*, Jornada 2. This attitude may echo the ancient Roman author Ovid, for whom the Narcissus myth illustrated the principle of simulacrum: "spem sine corpore amat" (Ovid, *Metamorphosis* 3.417, quoted in Kazantzidis and Spatharas, "Introductory: 'Hope,'" 18). Such illusions or simulacra are still important, however, since without them we "forfeit our humanity": "[Man's] suffering is limited only by his hope; take away his hope, as Hecuba's was taken, and he forfeits his humanity, destroyed by the hideous gap between his illusion and the intolerable reality" (William Arrowsmith, introduction to the Chicago translation of Euripides's *Hecuba* [1958], quoted in Nick Fisher, "Hope and Hopelessness in Euripides," in *Hope in Ancient Literature*, ed. Kazantzidis and Spatharas, 53–84, at 54).

362 Juan Pérez de Montalbán, *A lo hecho no hay remedio, y príncipe de los montes*, Jornada 3.

363 Calderón, *El mayor encanto, amor*, Acto 1. Andreas Michalopoulos comments on the Latin poet Ovid's similar attitude toward hope: "Ovid realizes that hope is futile and illusory and he acknowledges its power to deceive and make someone believe that they can actually materialize their wishes … His sole provider of hope, the only person that can bring Ovid back to Rome, is Augustus, the offended god who is thousands of miles away and whose priority is certainly not Ovid's recall from exile" (Andreas N. Michalopoulos, "Hope Dies Last at Tomis," in *Hope in Ancient Literature*, ed. Kazantzidis and Spatharas, 183–96, at 192, 193).

364 "Ay esperanza engañada, tan despacio conservada, y tan a prisa perdida" (Tirso de Molina, *El castigo del penséque*, Acto 2).

365 "La verdad huyo, a la esperanza pido engaños que alimenten mi deseo" (Juan Pérez de Montalbán, *Las paredes oyen*, Acto 1).

366 Juan de Matos Fragoso, *El yerro del entendido*, Acto 1.

367 Antony Augoustakis, "*Quaenam spes hominum*? Dashed Hopes in Statius' *Thebaid*," in *Hope in Ancient Literature*, ed. Kazantzidis and Spatharas, 197–212, at 200. On Quevedo's Neostoicism see Henry Ettinghausen, *Francisco de Quevedo and the Neostoic Movement* (Oxford: Oxford University Press, 1974).

368 "Ea, alegres quimeras, de una esperanza, que fundé en el viento" (Agustín Moreto, *La fortuna merecida*, Jornada 1).

369 "¿es sombra vana el esperanza mía?" (Tirso de Molina, *Los amantes de Teruel*, Jornada 2).

370 Elisa laments, "Mi esperanza ha sido un sueño, ¡ay de mi corta ventura!" (Lope de Vega, *El mármol de Felisardo*, Acto 2).

371 Lope de Vega, *El divino africano*, Acto 1. The movie *Gone with the Wind*, directed by Victor Fleming and produced by David O. Selznick, was released on 17 January 1940. Starring Vivien Leigh as Scarlett O'Hara and Clark Gable as Rhett Butler, it won the Academy Award for Best Picture.

372 Lope de Vega, *La hermosa Alfreda*, Acto 2.

373 "¿Pues qué esperanza vuestro orgullo engaña?" (Calderón, *El origen, pérdida y restauración de la Virgen del Sagrario*, Jornada 2).

374 "la menor esperanza finge brío" (Guillén de Castro, *El Narciso en su opinión*, Jornada 2).

375 Calderón, *Nadie fíe su secreto*, Jornada 3.

376 "vi defraudada mi esperanza tan del todo" (Cervantes, *El gallardo español*, Jornada 1).

377 "quiero a mi loca esperanza dar en el mar sepultura" (Calderón, *Peor está que estaba*, Acto 1).

378 Calderón, *El pintor de su deshonra*, Jornada 1.

379 Calderón, *La nave del mercader*, auto sacramental.

380 "Fundé mil torres de viento / en una flaca esperanza" (Lope de Vega, *Quien más no puede*, Acto 1).

381   ¿Será justo que entonces mi esperanza,
         que fue por ti pirámide en el viento
         caiga por la región de tu mudanza,
         lastimando su mismo fundamento?   (Lope de Vega, *La hermosa fea*, Acto 3)

382 "toda la casa es plumas como es la esperanza viento" (Lope de Vega, *Jorge toledano*, Acto 2).

383 Tirso de Molina, *Segunda parte de Santa Juana*, Acto 2.

384 "¿éstos los amigos son, en quien mi esperanza fundo? Sólo son ya los amigos para convites y fiestas" (Lope de Vega, *Los bandos de Sena*, Acto 3).

385 Juan Ruiz de Alarcón, *La amistad castigada*, Acto 1.

386 "¡Ah Dios, qué dulce esperanza gané y perdí en un solo día!" (Juan Ruiz de Alarcón, *Los favores del mundo*, Acto 2).

387 Calderón, *La gran Cenobia*, Acto 1.

388 Juan de la Cueva, *El degollado*, Acto 1.

389 Calderón, *El primer refugio del hombre, y probática piscina*, auto sacramental.

390 "su esperanza y mi opinión es como estopa en la llama" (Lope de Vega, *La escolástica celosa*, Jornada 1). *Estopa* refers to linen used in the manufacture of cords and fabric.

391 Cervantes, *La gran sultana*, Jornada 3.

392 Calderón, *El pintor de su deshonra*, Jornada 1.

393 "menos mal es morir, que vivir sin esperanza" (Calderón, *La gran Cenobia*, Jornada 3).

394 "Con esperanza sufre desengaños un monte, que a faltarle la esperanza, ya se rindiera al poso de los años" (Calderón, *Eco y Narciso*, Jornada 2).

395 "caduca esperanza" (Calderón, *El alcalde de sí mismo*, Jornada 3); "ya expiró mi esperanza" (Calderón, *De una causa dos efectos*, Jornada 3).

396 Lope de Vega, *El saber puede dañar*, Acto 3.

397 Lope de Vega, *El cuerdo loco*, Acto 2.

398 "Desesperada esperanza, el loco intento mudad" (Juan Ruiz de Alarcón, *Examen de maridos*, Acto 1).

399 Calderón, *El encanto sin encanto*, Jornada 3.

400 Calderón, *Primero y segundo Isaac*, auto sacramental.

401 "contrapuesto al ocaso logra la esperanza mía" (Guillén de Castro, *Las mocedades del Cid, comedia segunda*, Acto 3).

402 "es contra mi poder, sí, Leonido, mi esperanza, pues es contra mi interés" (Calderón, *En esta vida todo es verdad y todo mentira*, Jornada 3).

403 Kazantzidis and Spatharas, "Introductory: 'Hope,'" 8.

404 Laurel Fulkerson, *Deos speravi* [*Miles* 1209]: Hope and the Gods in Roman Comedy," in *Hope in Ancient Literature*, ed. Kazantzidis and Spatharas, 153–69, at 166.

405 "hablando con la Esperanza, te apartas de la evidencia" (Calderón, *Amar y ser amado, y divina Filotea*, auto sacramental).

406 Juan Ruiz de Alarcón, *Mudarse por mejorarse*, Acto 1.

407 Lope de Vega, *El Duque de Viseo*, Acto 3. The more familiar phrase is "love never fails" (1 Corinthians 13:8).

408 Calderón, *El hombre pobre todo es trazas*, Acto 1.

409 Calderón, *El Conde Lucanor*, Jornada 2.

410 "Albricias, alma, que aun tienen esperanza mis deseos" (Calderón, *Ni Amor se libra de Amor*, Acto 1).

411 "siendo al imán del deseo la esperanza el norte fijo" (Agustín Moreto, *La fuerza de la ley*, Jornada 1).

412 Lucretius, *De rerum natura* 4.1089–90, quoted and translated in Kazantzidis and Spatharas, "Introductory: 'Hope,'" 18.

413 "Es norte de mi esperanza" (Guillén de Castro, *Los enemigos hermanos*, Jornada 1).

414 "llegó mi esperanza al puerto" (Juan Bautista Diamante, *Más encanto es la hermosura*, Jornada 3).

415 "A mi esperanza nada le asusta" (Antonio Zamora, *El custodio de la Ungría, San Juan Capistrano*, Jornada 3).

416 "Allí es Troya, allí el temor corta a la esperanza el vuelo" (Juan Ruiz de Alarcón, *Mudarse por mejorarse*, Acto 3).

417 "al fin se rinde la esperanza al miedo" (Lope de Vega, *Los tres diamantes*, Jornada 1).

418 Michalopoulos, "Hope Dies Last," in *Hope in Ancient Literature*, ed. Kazantzidis and Spatharas, 183–96, at 188–9. On the reception of Ovid in Renaissance Spain, see

Marina Brownlee, *The Severed Word: Ovid's* Heroides *and the* Novela Sentimental (Princeton: Princeton University Press, 1990).

419 Lope de Vega, *El hidalgo Bencerraje*, Acto 2.

420 "Entre esperanza, y temor, que uno da flor, y otro espinas" (Lope de Vega, *Los muertos vivos*, Acto 3).

421 "va contra ti en mi brío, una esperanza, y pelea con muy ventajosos filos" (Antonio Zamora, *Ser fino y no parecerlo*, Jornada 2).

422 "la esperanza de tu pecho heróico" (Lope de Vega, *Los Ramírez de Arellano*, Acto 1).

423 "Sin Esperanza, ninguna lidiara, pues ella, es cierto, que da el ánimo" (Calderón, *El cordero de Isaías*, auto sacramental).

424 "da lugar al sentimiento, y esperanza a tu esquiva y dura afrenta" (Juan de la Cueva, *La muerte de Virginia y Appio Claudio*, Acto 1).

425 "El peligro, gran señora, no es nada, cuando interesa mi deseo la esperanza" (Agustín Moreto, *Lo que puede la aprehensión*, Jornada 2).

426 Calderón, *El cordero de Isaías*, auto sacramental.

427 "no se anegue en la pena la esperanza" (Lope de Vega, *El arenal de Sevilla*, Acto 3).

428 Juan Bautista Diamante, *Santa Juliana*, Jornada 1.

429   Las penas con esperanza
       de salir de ellas un día,
       no son penas.   (Lope de Vega, *Los palacios de Galiana*, Acto 1)

430 "que a Dios fió, cuando al Aire le arrojó su Esperanza y Fe, logrando viene, y cantando también" (Calderón, *Los alimentos del hombre*, auto sacramental).

431 Guillén de Castro, *La fuerza de la sangre*, Jornada 2.

432 For my previous treatment of Courage, among other virtues, see once more Hilaire Kallendorf, "Fleeting Fortitude," in *Ambiguous Antidotes: Virtue as Vaccine for Vice in Early Modern Spain* (Toronto: University of Toronto Press, 2017), 69–83. As stated previously, I have not covered Courage again in the present volume because it was already treated elsewhere. Hope, on the other hand, was not one of the virtues I chose to explore in *Ambiguous Antidotes* or anywhere else before now.

433 "¿Qué esperanza tener en Justicia puede?" (Calderón, *Los alimentos del hombre*, auto sacramental). On social justice in early modern Spanish stage plays, see *Social Justice in Spanish Golden Age Theatre*, ed. Erin Alice Cowling et al. (Toronto: University of Toronto Press, 2021).

434 "esperanza tengo que en viéndote Rey, has de amparar nuestra ley" (Tirso de Molina, *La prudencia en la mujer*, Jornada 2).

435 Thus Lisardo counsels Celio:

       No haremos nada
       si lo llevas a tal Chancillería,
       con las mil y quinientas, que en los pleitos
       pagará dos mil veces la esperanza,
       de que después se hará mejor venganza.

                          (Lope de Vega, *La venganza venturosa*, Acto 3)

436 "sólo en vuestra justicia la esperanza. Justicia, Rey, justicia" (Juan Ruiz de Alarcón, *Ganar amigos*, Acto 3).

437 "en mi Rey tengo esperanza, que premiando mis servicios, castigue al torpe Manuel de Sossa" (Tirso de Molina, *Escarmientos para el cuerdo*, Acto 3).

438 Michalopoulos, "Hope Dies Last," 190.

439 "ten en el Cielo esperanza, que es Columna de la Fe" (Calderón, *Los encantos de la Culpa*, auto sacramental).

440 Lope de Vega, *El gran Duque de Moscovia, y emperador perseguido*, Acto 1.

441 Romans 5:3–4, Douay-Rheims Bible, http://www.drbo.org/chapter/52005.htm. The Douay-Rheims version is a translation from the Latin Vulgate and thus the closest thing we have in English to the text that Renaissance Spanish playwrights would have most likely consulted.

442 "persevera, que no tiene la esperanza mérito sin la paciencia" (Calderón, *El jardín de Falerina*, auto sacramental).

443 "verdad es que la esperanza mil imposibles alcanza, regida de la paciencia" (Lope de Vega, *El gallardo catalán*, Jornada 3).

444 Lope de Vega, *El mejor maestro, el tiempo*, Acto 2.

445 The New International Version of the same verses reads: "We also glory in our sufferings, because we know that suffering produces perseverance; perseverance, character; and character, hope" (Romans 5:3–4, New International Version, https://biblehub.com/niv/romans/5.htm).

446 Lope de Vega, *Porfiando vence amor*, Jornada 2.

11. Conclusion: The Soul's Theatre

1 John O'Neill (ed.), *Freud and the Passions* (University Park: Pennsylvania State University Press, 1996), back cover.

2 Tim Newton, "The Sociogenesis of Emotion: A Historical Sociology?" in *Emotions in Social Life*, ed. Gillian Bendelow and Simon J. Williams (London: Routledge, 1998), 60–80, at 75.

3 For my treatment of Anger see Hilaire Kallendorf, "Angry Young Murderers," in *Sins of the Fathers: Moral Economies in Early Modern Spain* (Toronto: University of Toronto Press, 2013), 133–51. For my treatment of Courage or Fortitude see Hilaire Kallendorf, "Fleeting Fortitude," in *Ambiguous Antidotes: Virtue as Vaccine for Vice in Early Modern Spain* (Toronto: University of Toronto Press, 2017), 69–83.

4 Calderón, *El cordero de Isaías*, loa for auto sacramental.

5 Calderón, *En esta vida todo es verdad, y todo mentira*, Jornada 3.

6 Calderón, *El tesoro escondido*, auto sacramental.

7 Calderón, *Hado y divisa de Leonido, y de Marfisa*, Jornada 1.

8 Calderón, *El segundo blasón del Austria*, loa for auto sacramental.

9 Juan Bautista Diamante, *El defensor de el Peñón*, Jornada 2.

10 Juan Bautista Diamante, *Santa Juliana*, Jornada 1.

11 Juan Pérez de Montalbán, *Segunda parte del Séneca de España, Don Felipe Segundo*, Jornada 1.

12 "es modo de aborrecer amar por obligación" (Juan Pérez de Montalbán, *La toquera vizcaína*, Jornada 3).

13 Agustín Moreto, *El desdén con el desdén*, Jornada 3.

14 Calderón, *Mujer, llora, y vencerás*, Jornada 3.

15 E.g. "el agradecimiento parece de amor indicio" (Calderón, *Para vencer a amor, querer vencerle*, Jornada 2) or "un amor bachiller tiene indicios de apetito" (Francisco de Rojas Zorrilla, *Entre bobos anda el juego*, Jornada 1).

16 Francisco de Rojas Zorrilla, *Casarse por vengarse*, Jornada 2.

17 As in "Eso que dices hiciste, no fue amor, sino furor; que eso que llaman amor en su esperanza consiste" (Juan Pérez de Montalbán, *El sufrimiento premiado*, Jornada 3).

18 Juan Pérez de Montalbán, *La toquera vizcaína*, Jornada 1.

19 "no fue verdadero amor, sino mañoso artificio" (Juan Pérez de Montalbán, *El valiente nazareno*, Jornada 3).

20 Agustín Moreto, *El caballero del Sacramento*, Jornada 2.

21 Francisco de Rojas Zorrilla, *No hay amigo para amigo*, Jornada 3.

22 "¿qué mujer dejada se vio, que en odio no convirtió su amor, en ira su fe?" (Calderón, *El postrer duelo de España*, Jornada 2).

23 William Shakespeare, *Coriolanus*, in *The Complete Works of William Shakespeare* (New York: Gramercy, 1975), 773–812, I.9, p. 781.

24 Tirso de Molina, *Del enemigo el primer consejo*, Jornada 3.

25 Calderón, *Las armas de la hermosura*, Jornada 1.

26 Calderón, *Apolo y Climene*, Acto 1.

27 Juan Bautista Diamante, *Cuánto mienten los indicios, y el ganapán de desdichas*, Jornada 1.

28 Juan Bautista Diamante, *El jubileo de la Porciúncula*, Jornada 3.

29 For instance, "de enojo, a Amor no se pasa fácilmente" (Calderón, *Dicha y desdicha del nombre*, Jornada 3).

30 Calderón, *La viña del Señor*, auto sacramental.

31 Calderón, *Amado y aborrecido*, Acto 1. A similar example would be "pudiendo la voluntad reprimir, el cariño aprisionar" (Juan Bautista Diamante, *El sol de la sierra*, Jornada 3).

32 Kallendorf, *Ambiguous Antidotes*.

33 Vives, *The Passions of the Soul*, 8.

34 Carlos G. Noreña, "Foreword," in Vives, *The Passions of the Soul*, xiii.

35 Vives, *The Passions of the Soul*, 57.

36 Juan Pérez de Montalbán, *Como amante y como honrada*, Jornada 3.

37 See Kimberlé Crenshaw, *On Intersectionality* (New York: New Press, 2022).

38 Juan de Matos Fragoso, *El genízaro de Hungría*, Jornada 3.

39 On "virtue in the middle" see Kallendorf, "The Golden Mean," in *Ambiguous Antidotes*, 29–35.

40 Lope de Vega, *La buena guarda*, Acto 3.

41 Lope de Vega, *El caballero de Olmedo*, Acto 3.

42 Calderón, *No hay burlas con el amor*, Jornada 2.

43 Calderón, *El jardín de Falerina*, Acto 1.

44 Juan Bautista Diamante, *La Reina María Estuarda*, Jornada 3.

45 For scenes where a scale appears as an actual physical prop on stage, particularly in connection to Justice, see Kallendorf, *Ambiguous Antidotes*, 43; for the image of a scale in connection to Prudence, see Kallendorf, *Ambiguous Antidotes*, 139.

46 Calderón, *El Faetonte*, Acto 1.

47 Calderón, *La devoción de la Cruz*, Acto 1.

48 "En mí el amor con el valor se mide" (Calderón, *Nadie fíe su secreto*, Jornada 1).

49 Juan Pérez de Montalbán, *Amor, lealtad y amistad*, Jornada 1.

50 Agustín Moreto, *La fuerza de la ley*, Jornada 3.

51 Juan de la Cueva, *El viejo enamorado*, Acto 3.

52 Calderón, *Amor, honor, y poder*, Acto 1.

53 "probaré entre dos afectos tan poderosos, tan fuertes, como odio, y amor, cuál es el vencido, o el que vence" (Calderón, *Afectos de odio y amor*, Jornada 3).

54 Calderón, *Lo que va del hombre a Dios*, loa for auto sacramental.

55 Lope de Vega, *Los tres diamantes*, Jornada 1.

56 Calderón, *Las armas de la hermosura*, Jornada 2.

57 Juan Bautista Diamante, *El Hércules de Ocaña*, Jornada 3.

58 Kallendorf, "The Golden Mean," in *Ambiguous Antidotes*, 29–35.

59 Calderón, *Los misterios de la misa*, auto sacramental.

60 Francisco de Rojas Zorrilla, *El más impropio verdugo por la más justa venganza*, Jornada 3.

61 Tirso de Molina, *La peña de Francia*, Acto 3.

62 Lope de Vega, *El Amor enamorado*, Jornada 1.

63 Calderón, *A tu próximo como a ti*, auto sacramental.

64 Calderón, *A secreto agravio, secreta venganza*, Acto 1.

65 Calderón, *A secreto agravio, secreta venganza*, Jornada 2.

66 Calderón, *Argenis y Poliarco*, Jornada 2.

67 Yoandy Cabrera, "Ira y deseo: impulsos timóticos en la Grecia hispana," Ph.D. dissertation, Texas A&M University, 2019.

68 Calderón, *Las manos blancas no ofenden*, Jornada 2.

69 For example, witness the statement "[E]l 'soy quien soy' … [n]o se trata de afirmar un ser íntimo, ni una esencia individual, ni un yo interior" (José Antonio Maravall, *Teatro y literatura en la sociedad barroca* [Madrid: Seminarios y Ediciones, 1973], 103).

70 Calderón, *Los dos amantes del cielo*, Jornada 2.

71 "amor quita el miedo" (Lope de Vega, *La firmeza en la desdicha*, Acto 1).

72 "el respeto templará el deseo" (Antonio de Solís, *Eurídice y Orfeo*, Jornada 2).

73 "valor tu pecho encierra para empresas de importancia, que el miedo torpe destierra" (Tirso de Molina, *La peña de Francia*, Acto 1).

74 "¡que impida el golpe del odio el escudo del amor!" (Calderón, *En esta vida todo es verdad, y todo mentira*, Acto 1).

75 "Quítale el Amor la Espada al Furor" (Calderón, *La hidalga del valle*, auto sacramental).

76 Calderón, *Amado y aborrecido*, Jornada 3.

77 Calderón, *El encanto sin encanto*, Jornada 3.

78 Calderón, *En esta vida todo es verdad y todo mentira*, Acto 1.

79 Juan Pérez de Montalbán, *La deshonra honrosa*, Jornada 1.

80 Calderón, *Andrómeda y Perseo*, auto sacramental.

81 "¿Quién vio jamás dos afectos tan contrarios como severo el amor, y enternecido el agravio?" (Calderón, *Sueños hay, que verdad son*, auto sacramental).

82 Calderón, *Para vencer a Amor, querer vencerle*, Jornada 2.

83 "es amor muy honesto" (Juan Pérez de Montalbán, *La doncella de labor*, Jornada 2).

84 "mi amor decente" (Francisco de Rojas Zorrilla, *Casarse por vengarse*, Jornada 1).

85 "tú niegas afectos que debes a un noble amor" (Francisco de Rojas Zorrilla, *Los encantos de Medea*, Jornada 2).

86 "un inocente amor sin culpa alguna" (Juan Pérez de Montalbán, *La deshonra honrosa*, Jornada 1).

87 "No espera el perfecto amor ser de amor correspondido" (Agustín Moreto, *Industrias contra finezas*, Jornada 1).

88 "sustento / puro amor, contra un ciego / desvarío" (Juan de la Cueva, *El viejo enamorado*, Acto 3).

89 "con amor casto te di la mano de esposa" (Francisco de Rojas Zorrilla, *No hay ser padre siendo Rey*, Jornada 1).

90 "es ya feo amor vicioso" (Juan de la Cueva, *El tutor*, Acto 1).

91 "este amor es bastardo" (Juan Pérez de Montalbán, *Olimpa y Vireno*, Jornada 2).

92 "un amor vergonzante" (Francisco de Rojas Zorrilla, *Los áspides de Cleopatra*, Jornada 1).

93 "A ser el amor de Carlos indecente" (Juan Bautista Diamante, *Santa Teresa de Jesús*, Jornada 1).

94 "Crudo amor, templa tu ira" (Juan de la Cueva, *El tutor*, Acto 4).

95 "Sin duda es mi amor delito" (Juan Bautista Diamante, *Santa Teresa de Jesús*, Jornada 1).

96 "no hay amor tan honesto, que no llegue a descompuesto" (Juan Pérez de Montalbán, *El hijo del serafín, San Pedro de Alcántara*, Jornada 1).

97 "mudando de odio, y amor el noble afecto en el vil" (Calderón, *Las manos blancas no ofenden*, Jornada 2).

98 "mezclando de odio, y favor el noble afecto, y el vil" (Calderón, *La fiera, el rayo y la piedra*, Jornada 2). Observe the only very slight variation from the line by the same author – but appearing in a different play – quoted in the last note. Such instances are indicative of broader patterns of recycling material within a given author's total body of works.

99 Agustín Moreto, *Santa Rosa del Perú*, Jornada 2.

100 Juan Pérez de Montalbán, *Olimpa y Vireno*, Jornada 3.

101 Calderón, *El año santo de Roma*, auto sacramental.

102 Juan Pérez de Montalbán, *Segunda parte del Séneca de España, Don Felipe Segundo*, Jornada 1.

103 Juan Pérez de Montalbán, *El valiente nazareno*, Jornada 2.

104 Francisco de Rojas Zorrilla, *Entre bobos anda el juego*, Jornada 1.

105 Juan Pérez de Montalbán, *El valiente más dichoso, Don Pedro Guiral*, Jornada 2.

106 Juan Bautista Diamante, *Santa María del Monte, y convento de San Juan*, Jornada 3.

107 Francisco de Rojas Zorrilla, *No hay ser padre siendo Rey*, Jornada 2.

108 Calderón, *El verdadero Dios Pan*, auto sacramental.

109 The allegorical figure of Chastity instructs: "mi Precepto / es contra el Amor Lascivo" (Calderón, *El año santo de Roma*, auto sacramental).

110 Matthew 5:21–2, 27–8 (Douay-Rheims Bible, drbo.org).

111 For example, Erasmus of Rotterdam wrote a treatise titled *De libero arbitrio* (1524), and the notorious Molinist controversy began with the sixteenth-century Spanish Jesuit Luis de Molina. For more on these Renaissance debates, see the classic article by Charles Trinkaus, "The Problem of Free Will in the Renaissance and the Reformation," *Journal of the History of Ideas* (1949): 51–62. For a treatment that is more specific to Spain, including how these erudite debates intersected with popular culture, see Hilaire Kallendorf, "Lycanthropy and Free Will: The Female Werewolf in Cervantes' *Persiles*," *eHumanista* 42 (2019): 1–19.

112 Juan Pérez de Montalbán, *Cumplir con su obligación*, Jornada 1.

113 Calderón, *Auristela y Lisidante*, Jornada 2.

114 Juan Pérez de Montalbán, *Don Florisel de Niquea*, Jornada 1.

115 Guillén de Castro, *El desengaño dichoso*, Acto 3.

116 Agustín Moreto, *Primero es la honra*, Jornada 2.

117 Francisco de Rojas Zorrilla, *Casarse por vengarse*, Jornada 2.

118 María Tausiet and James S. Amelang (eds.), *Accidentes del alma. Las emociones en la Edad Moderna* (Madrid: Abada, 2009).

119 William F. MacLehose, "Fear, Fantasy and Sleep in Medieval Medicine," in *Emotions and Health, 1200–1700*, ed. Elena Carrera (Leiden: Brill, 2012), 67–94, at 90.

120 Juan Pérez de Montalbán, *El valiente más dichoso, Don Pedro Guiral*, Jornada 2.

121 Agustín Moreto, *El licenciado Vidriera*, Jornada 3.

122 Calderón, *Cuál es mayor perfección*, Jornada 3.

123 Calderón, *El valle de la zarzuela*, loa for auto sacramental.

124 Agustín Moreto, *Lo que puede la aprehensión*, Jornada 1.

125 Agustín Moreto, *El desdén con el desdén*, Jornada 1.

126 Calderón, *La banda y la flor*, Jornada 1.

127 As I wrote in the conclusion to *Sins of the Fathers*: "If I had to choose which side of this sliding scale to lean towards … I would choose the side of subjectivity and individual agency" (Kallendorf, *Sins of the Fathers*, 204).

128 Juan Bautista Diamante, *Santa Teresa de Jesús*, Jornada 1.

129 For a detailed study of free will in the *comedias*, see Hilaire Kallendorf, "Free Will a Fortress: The Self in Spanish Renaissance Drama," in *The Self in Premodern European Thought*, ed. José Luis Bermúdez and Catherine Conybeare (Cambridge: Cambridge University Press, forthcoming).

130 Agustín Moreto, *El mejor amigo, el rey*, Jornada 1.

131 Agustín Moreto, *El esclavo de su hijo*, Jornada 3.

132 On the conflicted or divided early modern Spanish subject, see George Mariscal, *Contradictory Subjects: Quevedo, Cervantes, and Seventeenth-Century Spanish Culture* (Ithaca: Cornell University Press, 1991).

133 Agustín Moreto, *El desdén con el desdén*, Jornada 1.

134 Guillén de Castro, *El conde Irlos*, Acto 3.

135 Juan Bautista Diamante, *Santa Maria Magdalena de Pazzi*, Jornada 2.

136 "Error que nace de amor … no merece tanta pena" (Juan Pérez de Montalbán, *El señor Don Juan de Austria*, Jornada 2) and "En habiendo amor no hay culpa" (Juan Pérez de Montalbán, *El señor Don Juan de Austria*, Jornada 3).

137 Juan de Matos Fragoso, *El amor hace valientes*, Jornada 3.

138 Juan de Matos Fragoso, *El hijo de la piedra*, Acto 1.

139 Francisco de Rojas Zorrilla, *Lo que son mujeres*, Jornada 3.

140 Guillén de Castro, *Don Quijote de la Mancha*, Jornada 2.

141 Cervantes, *El laberinto de amor*, Jornada 2.

142 Juan Pérez de Montalbán, *El sufrimiento premiado*, Jornada 2.

143 "voy forzado / de Amor paterno, / y del celeste Hado" (Juan de la Cueva, *La muerte de Ajax Telamón, sobre las armas de Aquiles*, Acto 1).

144 Juan Pérez de Montalbán, *Amor, lealtad y amistad*, Jornada 3.

145 "lo que el amor dispone es lo que quieren los Astros" (Juan Bautista Diamante, *Más encanto es la hermosura*, Jornada 2).

146 "el mismo Planeta, el mismo Astro que pudo inclinarme a su amor, le inclinó al mío" (Juan Pérez de Montalbán, *Olimpa y Vireno*, Jornada 2).

147 "donde hay fuerza de estrella siempre es más fuerte el amor" (Guillén de Castro, *Progne y Filomena*, Acto 1).

148 An example of a bad outcome would be, "pienso con su amor que me pega mala estrella" (Juan de Matos Fragoso, *El yerro del entendido*, Acto 1).

149 See Frederick de Armas, *La astrología en el teatro clásico europeo (siglos XVI–XVII)* (Madrid: Antígona, 2019).

150 Agustín Moreto, *Primero es la honra*, Jornada 2, in *Segunda parte de las Comedias de Don Agustín Moreto* (Valencia: Benito Macè, 1676), 125–64.

151 Calderón, *El hombre pobre todo es trazas*, Jornada 2.

152 Juan Luis Vives, *The Passions of the Soul: The Third Book of* De Anima et Vita, trans. Carlos G. Noreña (Lewiston: Mellen, 1990), 5.

153 Guillén de Castro, *La humildad soberbia*, Acto 1.

154 "como veo mi error, me desnudo del amor por estrenar el desdén" (Francisco de Rojas Zorrilla, *Lo que son mujeres*, Jornada 3). For a study of costume change

reflecting the 'putting on' or 'taking off' of Virtue and Vice, see Hilaire Kallendorf, "Dressed to the Sevens, or Sin in Style: Fashion Statements by the Deadly Vices in Spanish Baroque *Autos Sacramentales*," in *The Seven Deadly Sins: From Communities to Individuals*, ed. Richard Newhauser (Leiden: E.J. Brill, 2007), 145–82.

155 Francisco de Rojas Zorrilla, *Entre bobos anda el juego*, Jornada 2.

156 "Límite tiene el amor, término tiene su imperio" (Francisco de Rojas Zorrilla, *Los áspides de Cleopatra*, Jornada 3).

157 Lisa Perfetti, "Introduction," in *The Representation of Women's Emotions in Medieval and Early Modern Culture*, ed. Lisa Perfetti (Gainesville: University Press of Florida, 2005), 1–22, at 9. She quotes Daniel Lord Smail, *The Consumption of Justice: Emotions, Publicity, and Legal Culture in Marseille, 1264–1423* (Ithaca: Cornell University Press, 2003), 100–1.

158 Philippa Maddern et al., "Introduction: Performing Emotions in Medieval and Early Modern Worlds," in *Performing Emotions in Early Europe*, ed. Philippa Maddern et al. (Turnhout: Brepols, 2018), xiii–xxx, at xiv.

159 As summarized by Jonathan H. Turner, "The Sociology of Emotions: Basic Theoretical Arguments," *Emotion Review* 1.4 (2009): 340 54, at 346.

160 Peter Burke, "Is There a Cultural History of the Emotions?" in *Representing Emotions: New Connections in the Histories of Art, Music and Medicine*, ed. Penelope Gouk and Helen Hills (London: Ashgate, 2005), 35–47, at 43; quoting Anna Wierzbicka, *Emotions across Languages and Cultures: Diversity and Universals* (Cambridge: Cambridge University Press, 1999), 72–3; and Ronald de Sousa, *The Rationality of Emotion* (Boston: MIT Press, 1990), 182–4. Another scholar known for her work on emotion scripts is Agneta Fischer, who says "emotion knowledge is structured like a script" and "emotion scripts contain the following categories: antecedents, reactions (including physiological reactions) and regulation attempts" (Agneta H. Fischer, *Emotion Scripts: A Study of the Social and Cognitive Aspects of Emotion* [Leiden: DSWO Press, 1991], 12, 126).

161 See J.L. Austin, *How to Do Things with Words* (Oxford: Clarendon, 1975).

162 Barbara H. Rosenwein, "Emotional Space," in *Codierungen von Emotionen im Mittelalter / Emotions and Sensibilities in the Middle Ages*, ed. C. Stephen Jaeger and Ingrid Kasten (Berlin: De Gruyter, 2003), 287–303, at 300; paraphrasing William M. Reddy, *The Navigation of Feeling: A Framework for the History of Emotions* (Cambridge: Cambridge University Press, 2001).

163 Reddy, *The Navigation of Feeling*, 111. He further clarifies, "emotives … are like performatives in that they do something to the world" (111).

164 Jan Plamper, *The History of Emotions*, trans. Keith Tribe (Oxford: Oxford University Press, 2015), 257–8; citing Reddy, *The Navigation of Feeling*.

165 Walter Charleton, *Natural History of the Passions* (London: T.N. for J. Magnes, 1674), A4v; studied by Valentine Cunningham, "Readers Beside Themselves: Particular Pleasures and Generic Controls," in *Representations of Emotions*, ed. Jürgen Schlaeger and Gesa Stedman (Tübingen: Gunter Narr, 1998), 43–56, at 74.

166 On Renaissance theatres of memory in connection to Golden Age Spanish theatre, see John E. Varey, "Memory Theaters, Playhouses, and *Corrales de Comedias*," in *Parallel Lives: Spanish and English National Drama, 1580–1680*, ed. Kenneth Muir and Louise Fothergill-Payne (Lewisburg, PA: Bucknell University Press, 1991), 39–53.

167 Nova Myhill and Jennifer A. Low, "Introduction: Audience and Audiences," in *Imagining the Audience in Early Modern Drama, 1558–1642*, ed. Jennifer Low and Nova Myhill (Basingstoke: Palgrave, 2011), 1–17, at 4.

168 Steven Mullaney, *The Reformation of Emotions in the Age of Shakespeare* (Chicago: University of Chicago Press, 2015), 49.

169 Bridget Escolme, *Emotional Excess on the Shakespearean Stage: Passion's Slaves* (London: Bloomsbury, 2014), xvi.

170 Steven Mullaney, "Mourning and Misogyny: *Hamlet*, *The Revenger's Tragedy*, and the Final Progress of Elizabeth I, 1600–1607," *Shakespeare Quarterly* 45.2 (1994): 139–62, at 144.

171 Kristine Steenbergh, "Emotions and Gender: The Case of Anger in Early Modern English Revenge Tragedies," in *A History of Emotions, 1200–1800*, ed. Jonas Liliequist (London: Pickering & Chatto, 2012), 119–33, at 123.

172 Daniel M. Gross, *The Secret History of Emotion: From Aristotle's 'Rhetoric' to Modern Brain Science* (Chicago: University of Chicago Press, 2006), 111.

173 See Jean Howard, "The New Historicism in Renaissance Studies," *English Literary Renaissance* 16.1 (1986): 13–43.

174 Perfetti, "Introduction," 16. She cites Patrick Colm Hogan, *The Mind and Its Stories: Narrative Universals and Human Emotion* (Cambridge: Cambridge University Press, 2003).

175 Katherine Rowe, "Humoral Knowledge and Liberal Cognition in Davenant's *Macbeth*," in *Reading the Early Modern Passions: Essays in the Cultural History of Emotion*, ed. Gail Kern Paster, Katherine Rowe, and Mary Floyd-Wilson (Philadelphia: University of Pennsylvania Press, 2004), 169–91, at 184.

176 Vives, *The Passions of the Soul*, 48–9.

177 Irmgard Maassen, "Formal Ostentation, Maimed Rites, and Madness: The Theatrical Spectacle of Mourning in Shakespeare's *Hamlet*," in *Codierungen von Emotionen*, ed. Jaeger and Kasten, 271–86, at 272. For this term this scholar cites Michael Hattaway, *Elizabethan Popular Theatre: Plays in Performance* (London: Routledge, 1982), 54.

178 Hattaway, *Elizabethan Popular Theatre*, 54.

179 Thomas Rist, "Catharsis as 'Purgation' in Shakespearean Drama," in *Shakespearean Sensations: Experiencing Literature in Early Modern England*, ed. Katharine A. Craik and Tanya Pollard (Cambridge: Cambridge University Press, 2013), 138–53, at 141, citing OED definition 6d under "passion."

180 William Shakespeare, *Hamlet*, in *The Complete Works of William Shakespeare* (New York: Gramercy, 1975), 1071–1112, II.2.539–45, p. 1087.

181 Shakespeare, *Two Gentlemen of Verona*, in *The Complete Works*, 23–44, IV.4.163–6, p. 41.

182 Emma K. Rhatigan, "Audience, Actors, and 'Taking Part' in the Revels," in *Imagining the Audience in Early Modern Drama, 1558–1642*, ed. Jennifer Low and Nova Myhill (Basingstoke: Palgrave, 2011), 151–69, at 155, 157, 167n11.

183 Charles Whitney, *Early Responses to Renaissance Drama* (Cambridge: Cambridge University Press, 2006), 19, citing Andrew Gurr, *Playgoing in Shakespeare's London* (Cambridge: Cambridge University Press, 1996), 157, 166.

184 Daniel Goleman, *Emotional Intelligence: Why It Can Matter More than IQ* (London: Bloomsbury, 1996), 114.

185 S.J. Rachman, *Fear and Courage* (New York: W.H. Freeman, 1978), 103.

186   [D]escriba los amantes con afectos
         que muevan con extremo a quien escucha;
         los [soliloquios] pinte de manera
         que se transforme todo el recitante,
         y con mudarse a sí, mude al oyente.
                    (Lope de Vega, *Arte nuevo de hacer comedias en este tiempo* [1609], ed. Enrique
                           García Santo-Tomás [Madrid: Cátedra, 2006], vv. 272–6)

187 Keith Oatley and Mitra Gholamain, "Emotions and Identification: Connections between Readers and Fiction," in *Emotion and the Arts*, ed. Mette Hjort and Sue Laver (New York: Oxford University Press, 1997), 263–81, at 270–1.

188 Jonas Liliequist, "The Political Rhetoric of Tears in Early Modern Sweden," in *A History of Emotions, 1200–1800*, ed. Liliequist, 181–205, at 184.

189 Katherine A. Craik and Tanya Pollard, "Introduction: Imagining Audiences," in *Shakespearean Sensations*, ed. Craik and Pollard, 1–25, at 3.

190 Matthew Steggle, "Notes Towards an Analysis of Early Modern Applause," in *Shakespearean Sensations*, ed. Craik and Pollard, 118–37, at 121, in reference to J[ohn] B[ulwer], *Chirologia, or, The Naturall Language of the Hand* (London: Tho[mas] Harper, 1644), 30–1, 106–7.

191 Megan Cassidy-Welch, "Emotion, Place, and Memory at the Royal Abbey of St Denis," in *Performing Emotions in Early Europe*, ed. Maddern, 185–99, at 189.

192 Lachlan Turnbull, "Discursive Affect and Emotional Prescriptiveness: On the 'Man of Sorrows' in Fourteenth-Century Italian Painting," in *Performing Emotions in Early Europe*, ed. Maddern, 221–41, at 238.

193 Lucía Díaz Marroquín, *La retórica de los afectos* (Kassel: Reichenberger, 2008), 249. She refers to "la cuestión de si existierion manuales de técnica de interpretación [i.e., actors' manuals] en los siglos de oro" (249).

194 Díaz Marroquín, *La retórica de los afectos*, 258.

195 Martha Nussbaum, *Upheavals of Thought: The Intelligence of Emotions* (Cambridge: Cambridge University Press, 2001), 272.

196 William O. Beeman, "The Performance Hypothesis: Practicing Emotions in
Protected Frames," in *The Emotions: A Cultural Reader*, ed. Helena Wulff (Oxford:
Berg, 2007), 273–98, at 275.

197 Beeman, "The Performance Hypothesis," 288.

198   Por eso Tulio las llamaba espejo
        de las costumbres, y una viva imagen
        de la verdad.

                          (Lope de Vega, *Arte nuevo de hacer comedias*, ed. Enrique García
                          Santo-Tomás, 2nd ed. [Madrid: Cátedra, 2009], vv. 123–5, p. 138)

199 Richard Sorabji, *Emotion and Peace of Mind: From Stoic Agitation to Christian
Temptation* (Oxford: Oxford University Press, 2000), 154.

200 Penelope Geng, *Communal Justice in Shakespeare's England: Drama, Law, and
Emotion* (Toronto: University of Toronto Press, 2021), xii.

201 Geng, *Communal Justice*, 22.

202 Steven Mullaney, "Affective Technologies: Toward an Emotional Logic of the
Elizabethan Stage," in *Environment and Embodiment in Early Modern England*, ed.
Mary Floyd-Wilson and Garrett A. Sullivan, Jr. (Basingstoke: Palgrave Macmillan,
2007), 71–89.

203 Geng, *Communal Justice*, 129.

204 Martha C. Nussbaum, *Political Emotions: Why Love Matters for Justice* (Cambridge,
MA: Harvard University Press, 2013), 260.

205 "[P]laygoers are trained into proper subjectivity, in the Althusserian sense of the
word, by watching the behavior modeled for them" (Erika T. Lin, "'Lord of thy
presence': Bodies, Performance, and Audience Interpretation in Shakespeare's *King
John*," in *Imagining the Audience in Early Modern Drama, 1558–1642*, ed. Jennifer
Low and Nova Myhill [Basingstoke: Palgrave, 2011], 113–33, at 128). Meg Pearson
speculates about the precise nature of this interpellation, extending the notion of
"witness" beyond trauma studies to encompass early modern English theatrical
production: "Certain spectacular moments in plays recruit their audiences to
transform: Lavinia, her hands cut off, her tongue cut out, and ravish'd; Hermione,
'stone no more'; Richard II's improvised self-deposition. These instances – largely
visual but in cooperation with dialogue – encourage audiences to change from
spectators into witnesses … Onstage deaths, perhaps more than any other theatrical
moment, contain the potential to engage or alienate an audience" (Meg F. Pearson,
"Audience as Witness in *Edward II*," in *Imagining the Audience*, ed. Low and Myhill,
93–111, at 93).

206 Patrick Colm Hogan, *What Literature Teaches Us about Emotion* (Cambridge: Cambridge
University Press, 2011), 31.

207 Rowe, "Humoral Knowledge," 181.

208 Jean-François Marmontel (1723–99), quoted in Dominique Bertrand, "Contagious
Laughter and the Burlesque: From the Literal to the Metaphorical," in *Imaging*

Contagion in Early Modern Europe, ed. Claire L. Carlin (London: Palgrave, 2005), 177–94, at 191.

209 Vives, *The Passions of the Soul*, 48.

210 "The audience's affective reactions are often catalyzed – induced, felt, and experienced as emotions – most effectively when they are alienated from the emotions expressed or represented on stage" (Mullaney, *The Reformation of Emotions*, 49).

211 Mullaney, *The Reformation of Emotions*, 67.

212 Mullaney, *The Reformation of Emotions*, 70, 76, with reference to Kenneth Burke, *Permanence and Change: Anatomy of a Purpose* (Berkeley: University of California Press, 1954).

213 Shakespeare, *Hamlet*, II.2.562–6, p. 1087.

214 Irmgard Maassen, "Formal Ostentation, Maimed Rites, and Madness: The Theatrical Spectacle of Mourning in Shakespeare's *Hamlet*," in *Codierungen von Emotionen*, ed. Jaeger and Kasten, 271–86, at 272.

215 Stephen Laqué, "'Not Passion's Slave,'" 272, in reference to René Descartes, *Les Passions de l'Âme*, trans. Robert Stoothoff as *The Passions of the Soul*, in *The Philosophical Writings of Descartes*, ed. John Cottingham, Robert Stoothoff, and Dugald Murdoch, vol. 1 (Cambridge: Cambridge University Press, 1985), 325–404. Article 45 of Descartes's treatise reflects on the diverse array of emotions that books and plays stimulate in us.

216 I refer here to the concept of interpellation developed by Post-Structuralist and member of the Frankfurt School Louis Althusser. He defines *interpellation* as "hailing": "ideology hails or interpellates concrete individuals as concrete subjects … [I]deology … 'recruits' subjects among the individuals … or 'transforms' the individuals into subjects" (Louis Althusser, "Ideology and Ideological State Apparatuses," in *Mapping Ideology*, ed. Slavoj Žižek [London: Verso, 1994], 100–40, at 130).

217 Rowe, "Humoral Knowledge," 186.

218 Rowe, "Humoral Knowledge," 185.

219 Bruce R. Smith, "Afterword: Senses of an Ending," in *Shakespearean Sensations*, ed. Craik and Pollard, 208–17, at 212, citing Michael Schoenfeldt, "Shakespearean Pain," in *Shakespearean Sensations*, ed. Craik and Pollard, 191–207, and Allison P. Hobgood, "Feeling Fear in *Macbeth*," in *Shakespearean Sensations*, ed. Craik and Pollard, 29–46.

220 "Polybios objected to the way tragedy … acts as a dubious *psychagogia*" (Cunningham, "Readers beside Themselves," 47).

221 Plato, *Republic*, 605C–D; quoted in W.B. Stanford, *Greek Tragedy and the Emotions* (New York: Routledge, 2014), 3.

222 Sorabji, *Emotion and Peace of Mind*, 23.

223 Potkay, *The Story of Joy*, 167, citing Aristotle, *Politics* 1339a–1340a.

224 Victoria Kahn, "Happy Tears: Baroque Politics in Descartes's *Passions de l'ame*," in *Politics and the Passions, 1500–1850*, ed. Victoria Kahn et al. (Princeton: Princeton University Press, 2006), 93–110, at 107.

225 Richard Meek and Erin Sullivan, "Introduction," in *The Renaissance of Emotion: Understanding Affect in Shakespeare and His Contemporaries*, Richard Meek and Erin Sullivan (Manchester: Manchester University Press, 2015), 1–22, at 9.

226 Giambattista Guarini, *The Compendium of Tragicomic Poetry* (1599), trans. Albert H. Gilbert, in *Literary Criticism: Plato to Dryden*, ed. Albert H. Gilbert (New York: American Book Co., 1940), 504–33, at 511.

227 William Shakespeare, *The Taming of the Shrew*, ed. Ann Thompson, New Cambridge Shakespeare (Cambridge: Cambridge University Press, 2003), Induction, 2.126–31.

228 "Tragedies and Commedies stirre up affections" (Stephen Gosson, *Playes confuted in fiue actions* [London: Thomas Gosson, (1582)], F1r).

229   That Man giue mee; whose Brest fill'd by the *Muses*,
        With Raptures, Into a second, them infuses:
        Can giue an Actor, Sorrow, Rage, Ioy, Passion,
        Whilst hee againe (by selfe-same Agitation)
        Commands the *Hearers*, sometimes drawing out *Teares*,
        Then smiles, and fills them both with *Hopes & Feares*.
                            (Thomas Dekker, *If it be not good, the Diuel is in it* [1612], A4v;
                                    quoted in Matthew Steggle, *Laughing and Weeping in
                                    Early Modern Theatres* [Aldershot: Ashgate, 2007], 86)

230 Polimetes says to Roscio:

        By th'masse tis true, I have seen the knave paint griefe
        In such a liuely colour, that for false
        And acted passion he has drawne true teares
        From the spectators eyes, Ladyes in the boxes
        Kept time with sighes, and teares to his sad accents
        As he had truely bin the new man he seem'd.
                            (Thomas May, *The Heire* [1622], A4r; quoted in Steggle,
                                    Laughing and Weeping, 87)

231 "For not truth, but image, maketh passion: and a tragedy affecteth no less than a murder if well acted" (Thomas Hobbes, *The Elements of Law, Natural and Politic* [1640] [Oxford: Oxford University Press, 2008], I.13.2).

232 Francis Bacon, *De Augmentis Scientiarum*, in *Opera* (London: John Havilland, 1623), vol. 1, p. 109; translated and quoted in Steggle, *Laughing and Weeping*, 7.

233 Rowe, "Humoral Knowledge," 171.

234 Reddy, *The Navigation of Feeling*, 219, citing Philippe Pinel, *Traité médico-philosophique sur l'aliénation mentale ou la manie* [1801].

235 Nussbaum, *Political Emotions*, 179.

236 Hogan, *What Literature Teaches Us*, 68–9.

237 Shirley Prendergast and Simon Forrest, "'Shorties, Low-Lifers, Hardnuts and Kings': Boys, Emotions and Embodiment in School," in *Emotions in Social Life*, ed. Gillian

Bendelow and Simon J. Williams (London: Routledge, 1998), 155–72, at 157, citing T.R. Sarbin, *Narrative Psychology: The Storied Nature of Human Conduct* (New York: Praeger, 1986).

238 Martha Nussbaum, *Upheavals of Thought: The Intelligence of Emotions* (Cambridge: Cambridge University Press, 2001), 237.

239 Hogan, *What Literature Teaches Us*, 69, quoting Jerrold Levinson, "Emotion in Response to Art: A Survey of the Terrain," in *Emotion and the Arts*, ed. Mette Hjort and Sue Laver (New York: Oxford University Press, 1997), 23.

240 For an introduction to reader-response theory, see *Reader-Response Criticism: From Formalism to Post-Structuralism*, ed. Jane Tompkins (Baltimore: Johns Hopkins University Press, 1980).

241 Patrick Colm Hogan, *Cognitive Science, Literature and the Arts: A Guide for Humanists* (London: Routledge, 2003), 160.

242 Hogan, *Cognitive Science*, 183. In a subsequent book, Hogan offers a clearer definition of "emotional memories": "Emotional memories are 'implicit' memories, which is to say they do not, in and of themselves, bring representational content into working memory … [T]hey are not like 'memories' as we ordinarily think of them … [T]he activation of an emotional memory (roughly) leads one to re-experience the emotion. An emotional memory may be activated without a corresponding representational memory. In that case, we may experience the emotion but not understand why we are experiencing it. This is clear in cases of brain damage where the patient can form emotional memories but not episodic memories" (Hogan, *What Literature Teaches Us*, 51).

243 Jean-Michel Oughourlian, *The Genesis of Desire*, trans. Eugene Webb (East Lansing: Michigan State University Press, 2010), 90.

244 Giacomo Rizzolatti and Corrado Sinigaglia, *Mirrors in the Brain: How Our Minds Share Actions and Emotions*, trans. Frances Anderson (Oxford: Oxford University Press, 2008), 188; citing Antonio Damasio, *Looking for Spinoza: Joy, Sorrow and the Feeling Brain* (New York: Harcourt, 2003), 115–16.

245 Rizzolatti and Sinigaglia, *Mirrors in the Brain*, ix.

246 Jane Tylus, "'Par Accident': The Public Work of Early Modern Theater," in *Reading the Early Modern Passions*, ed. Paster et al., 253–71, at 257.

247 Rowe, "Humoral Knowledge," 186.

248 Gross, *The Secret History of Emotion*, 173.

249 Nussbaum, *Political Emotions*, 201–2, 258.

Bibliography

Abuelaish, Izzeldin, and Neil Arya. "Hatred – A Public Health Issue." *Medicine, Conflict and Survival* (2017). DOI: 10.1080/13623699.2017.1326215.

Adler, Cyrus, et al. "Beard." *Jewish Encyclopedia*. http://www.jewishencyclopedia.com.

Ahmed, Sara. "Affective Economies." *Social Text* 79 (2004): 117–39.

– "The Organisation of Hate." *Law and Critique* 12 (2001): 345–65.

Alberoni, Francesco. *Falling in Love*. Trans. Lawrence Venuti. New York: Random House, 1983.

Albertanus of Brescia. *Liber consolationis et consilii*. Ed. Thor Sundby. London: N. Trubner, 1873.

Alford, C. Fred. "Hatred Is the Imitation of Love." In *The Psychology of Hate*. Ed. J. Sternberg. Washington, DC: American Psychological Association, 2005. 235–54.

Alighieri, Dante. "Poem XX." In *The New Life (La Vita Nuova)*. Trans. Dante Gabriel Rossetti. Project Gutenberg. www.gutenberg.org.

Allen, Christopher. "Painting the Passions: The *Passions de l'Âme* as a Basis for Pictorial Expression." In *The Soft Underbelly of Reason: The Passions in the Seventeenth Century*. Ed. Stephen Gaukroger. London: Routledge, 1998. 79–111.

Althusser, Louis. "Ideology and Ideological State Apparatuses." In *Mapping Ideology*. Ed. Slavoj Žižek. London: Verso, 1994. 100–40.

Anderson, Ben. "Modulating the Excess of Affect: Morale in a State of 'Total War.'" In *The Affect Theory Reader*. Ed. Gregg and Seigworth. 161–85.

Ankowitsch, Christian. *Generation Emotion*. Berlin: BTV, 2002.

Aquinas, Thomas. *Summa theologiae*. Online edition. Corpus Thomisticum (Fundación Tomás de Aquino, 2013). "Prima secundae," quaestiones 22–48. http://www.corpusthomisticum .org/sth2022.html.

Arendt, Hannah. *Love and Saint Augustine*. Ed. and trans. J.V. Scott and J.C. Stark. Chicago: University of Chicago Press, 1996.

Aristotle. *Categories*. In *The Basic Works of Aristotle*. Oxford translation. Ed. R. McKeon. New York: Random House, 1941.

– *Rhetoric*. In *The Rhetoric and the Poetics of Aristotle*. Trans. W.R. Roberts. New York: Modern Library, 1954.

Augoustakis, Antony. "*Quaenam spes hominum*? Dashed Hopes in Statius' *Thebaid*." In *Hope in Ancient Literature*. Ed. Kazantzidis and Spatharas. 197–212.

Austin, J.L. *How to Do Things with Words*. Oxford: Clarendon, 1975.

Averill, James R., et al. *Rules of Hope*. New York: Springer, 1990.

Aviñón, Juan de. *Sevillana medicina* [1545]. Trans. Nicolás Monardes. Seville: Sociedad de Bibliófilos Andaluces, 1885.

Bachelor, Philip. *Sorrow and Solace: The Social World of the Cemetery*. Amityville: Baywood, 2004.

Bacon, Francis. *De Augmentis Scientiarum*. In *Opera*. London: John Havilland, 1623. Vol. 1.

Baier, Annette C. "The Ambiguous Limits of Desire." In *The Ways of Desire*. Ed. Joel Marks. Chicago: Precedent, 1986. 39–61.

Ballard, S.I., and H.G. Miller. "Psychiatric Casualties in a Women's Service." *British Medical Journal* (3 March 1945): 193–4.

Barasch, Moshe. "Despair in the Medieval Imagination." *Social Research* (1999): 565–76.

Bartra, Roger. *Melancolía y cultura. Las enfermedades del alma en la España del Siglo de Oro*. Barcelona: Anagrama, 2021.

Barzun, James Jacques. *A Stroll with William James*. Chicago: University of Chicago Press, 1983.

Bass, Laura. *The Drama of the Portrait: Theater and Visual Culture in Early Modern Spain*. University Park: Penn State University Press, 2008.

Bass, Laura, and Amanda Wunder. "Veiled Ladies of the Early Modern Spanish World: Seduction and Scandal in Seville, Madrid, and Lima." *The Hispanic Review* 77.1 (2009): 97–146.

Bataille, Georges. *L'erotisme*. Paris: Minuit, 2011.

Baumeister, Roy F., and Sara R. Wotman. *Breaking Hearts: The Two Sides of Unrequited Love*. New York: Guilford, 1992.

Beck, Brittney, et al. "On Navigating Despair: Reports from Psycho-therapists." *Journal of Religion and Health* 44.2 (2005): 187–205.

Beck, Ulrich, and Elisabeth Beck-Gernsheim. *The Normal Chaos of Love*. Cambridge: Polity, 1995.

Becker-Cantarino, Baerbel. "'Vana Rosa,' from Ausonius to Góngora and Gryphius." *Revista Hispánica Moderna* 37.1/2 (1972/73): 29–45.

Beeman, William O. "The Performance Hypothesis: Practicing Emotions in Protected Frames." In *The Emotions: A Cultural Reader*. Ed. Helena Wulff. Oxford: Berg, 2007. 273–98.

Behar, Ruth. "Sexual Witchcraft, Colonialism, and Women's Powers: Views from the Mexican Inquisition." In *Gender and Witchcraft*. Ed. Brian P. Levack. New York: Routledge, 2001. 218–44.

Belsey, Catherine. *Desire: Love Stories in Western Culture*. Oxford: Blackwell, 1994.

Bennassar, Bartolomé and Lucile. *Los cristianos de Alá: la fascinante aventura de los renegados*. Madrid: Nerea, 2001.

Bertrand, Dominique. "Contagious Laughter and the Burlesque: From the Literal to the Metaphorical." In *Imaging Contagion in Early Modern Europe*. Ed. Claire L. Carlin. London: Palgrave, 2005. 177–94.

Biagi, Laura. "Spider Dreams: Ritual and Performance in Apulian Tarantismo and Tarantella." PhD dissertation, New York University, 2004.

The Bible. Douay-Rheims Version. http://www.drbo.org.

– New International Version. https://biblehub.com/niv.

Blackhurst, Faith. "The Mediation of Love *por las rejas* in El *Quijote*." Paper presented at the XXVI Congreso Internacional de Literatura y Estudios Hispánicos (17–19 June 2020).

Blake, William. *Visions of the Daughters of Albion* (1793). The William Blake Archive. http://www.blakearchive.org/search/?search=joys%20grow.

Boase, Roger. "Ludic Dimensions of Courtly Love at the Court of Isabel *la Católica*." In *A Companion to Queen Isabel* la Católica. Ed. Hilaire Kallendorf. Leiden: Brill, 2023. 158–95.

– *The Secrets of Pinar's Game: Court Ladies and Courtly Verse in Fifteenth-Century Spain*. Leiden: Brill, 2017.

Bonanno, George. *The Other Side of Sadness: What the New Science of Bereavement Tells Us*. New York: Basic Books, 2009.

Bourke, Joanna. *Fear: A Cultural History*. London: Virago, 2005.

Braden, Gordon. "Senecan Tragedy and the Renaissance." *Illinois Classical Studies* 9.2 (1984): 277–92.

Brandes, Stanley. "Sugar, Colonialism, and Death: On the Origins of Mexico's Day of the Dead." *Comparative Studies in Society and History* 39.2 (1997): 270–99.

Brashear, William R. *The Gorgon's Head: A Study in Tragedy and Despair*. Atlanta: University of Georgia Press, 2008.

Braund, Susanna. "Haunted by Horror: The Ghost of Seneca in Renaissance Drama." In *A Companion to the Neronian Age*. Oxford: Wiley-Blackwell, 2013. 425–43.

Brehm, Sharon. "Passionate Love." In *The Psychology of Love*. Ed. Sternberg and Barnes. 232–63.

Brennan, Teresa. *The Transmission of Affect*. Ithaca: Cornell University Press, 2004.

Brigard, Felipe de. "Nostalgia and Mental Simulation." In *The Moral Psychology of Sadness*. Ed. Anna Gotlib. London: Rowman & Littlefield, 2017. 155–81.

Bringle, Mary Louise. *Despair: Sickness or Sin? Hopelessness and Healing in the Christian Life*. Nashville: Abingdon Press, 1990.

Brownlee, Marina. *The Severed Word: Ovid's* Heroides *and the* Novela Sentimental. Princeton: Princeton University Press, 1990.

B[ulwer], J[ohn]. *Chirologia, or, The Naturall Language of the Hand*. London: Tho[mas] Harper, 1644.

Bunyan, John. *Pilgrim's Progress* [1676]. Virginia Beach: CBN University Press, 1978.

Burke, Kenneth. *Permanence and Change: Anatomy of a Purpose*. Berkeley: University of California Press, 1954.

Burke, Peter. "Is There a Cultural History of the Emotions?" In *Representing Emotions: New Connections in the Histories of Art, Music and Medicine*. Ed. Penelope Gouk and Helen Hills. London: Ashgate, 2005. 35–47.

Burton, Robert. "Of the Moouing Faculty." In *Anatomy of Melancholy* [1621]. London: G. Bell and Sons, 1926.

Buss, David M. *The Evolution of Desire*. New York: Basic Books, 2016.

Byrne, Susan. *Ficino in Spain*. Toronto: University of Toronto Press, 2015.

Cabrera, Yoandy. "Ira y deseo: impulsos timóticos en la Grecia hispana." PhD dissertation, Texas A&M University, 2019.

Carrera, Elena. "Anger and the Mind-Body Connection in Medieval and Early Modern Medicine." In *Emotions and Health, 1200–1700*, ed. Carrera. 95–146.

– ed. *Emotions and Health, 1200–1700*. Leiden: Brill, 2012.

– "Introduction." In *Emotions and Health*. Ed. Carrera. 1–17.

Carter, Warren. "Cross-Gendered Romans and Mark's Jesus: Legion Enters the Pigs (Mark 5:1–20)." *Journal of Biblical Literature* 134.1 (2015): 139–55.

Carveth, Donald L. "Psychoanalytic Conceptions of the Passions." In *Freud and the Passions*. Ed. John O'Neill. University Park: Pennsylvania State University Press, 1996. 25–51.

Cassidy-Welch, Megan. "Emotion, Place, and Memory at the Royal Abbey of St Denis." In *Performing Emotions in Early Europe*, ed. Maddern. 185–99.

Catullus. *Odi et amo: The Complete Poetry of Catullus*. Trans. Roy Arthur Swanson. Stuttgart: Macmillan, 1959.

Cervantes, Miguel de. *Numancia*. Ed. Robert Marrast. Madrid: Cátedra, 1968.

– *Primera parte del ingenioso hidalgo don Quijote de la Mancha*. In *Obras completas*. Ed. Florencio Sevilla. Madrid: Castalia, 1999. 145–320.

– *Segunda parte del ingenioso hidalgo don Quijote de la Mancha*. In *Obras completas*. Ed. Florencio Sevilla. Madrid: Castalia, 1999. 321–508.

Charland, Louis C., and R.S. White. "Anatomy of a Passion: Shakespeare's *The Winter's Tale* as Case Study." In *Ordering Emotions*, ed. Broomhall. 197–224.

Chatterjee, Anjan. *The Aesthetic Brain: How We Evolved to Desire Beauty and Enjoy Art*. Oxford: Oxford University Press, 2014.

Childers, William. "Hispanic Casuistry Studies: Room to Grow." *Hispanic Review* 79.2 (2011): 317–26.

"Church to Remove Moor-Slayer Saint," *BBC News Online* (3 May 2004). http://news .bbc.co.uk/2/hi/europe/3680331.stm.

Cixous, Hélène. "The Laugh of the Medusa." Trans. Keith Cohen and Paula Cohen. *Signs* 1.4 (1976): 875–93.

Clark, Anna. *Desire: A History of European Sexuality*. New York: Routledge, 2008.

Clough, Patricia T. "The Affective Turn: Political Economy, Biomedia, and Bodies." In *The Affect Theory Reader*, ed. Gregg and Seigworth. 206–25.

Cole, Jennifer. "Love, Money, and Economies of Intimacy in Tamatave, Madagascar." In *Love in Africa*. Ed. Jennifer Cole and Lynn Thomas. Chicago: University of Chicago Press, 2009. 109–34.

Cole, Jennifer, and Lynn Thomas, eds. *Love in Africa*. Chicago: University of Chicago Press, 2009.

Collier, Jane Fishburne. *From Duty to Desire: Remaking Families in a Spanish Village*. Princeton: Princeton University Press, 1997.

Conde, Alfredo. *El griffón*. Madrid: Alfaguara, 1987.

Corbin, Alain. *Time, Desire and Horror: Towards a History of the Senses*. Trans. Jean Birrell. Cambridge: Polity, 1995.

Cormier, Sherry. *Sweet Sorrow: Finding Enduring Wholeness after Loss and Grief*. Lanham, MD: Rowman & Littlefield, 2018.

Covarrubias Orozco, Sebastián de. *Tesoro de la Lengua Castellana*. Madrid: Luis Sánchez, 1611.

Cowling, Erin Alice, et al., eds. *Social Justice in Spanish Golden Age Theatre*. Toronto: University of Toronto Press, 2021.

Craik, Katherine A., and Tanya Pollard. "Introduction: Imagining Audiences." In *Shakespearean Sensations*, ed. Craik and Pollard. 1–25.

"Creen haber hallado los restos óseos de Miguel de Cervantes y su esposa." Agencia EFE. https://www.youtube.com/watch?app=desktop&v=3ZpLT8VMkiE.

Crenshaw, Kimberlé. *On Intersectionality*. New York: The New Press, 2022.

Crisp, Justin E. "Introduction: A Bright Sorrow." In *Joy and Human Flourishing*, ed. Volf and Crisp. vii–xviii.

Cruz, Anne J. *Discourses of Poverty: Social Reform and the Picaresque Novel in Early Modern Spain*. Toronto: University of Toronto Press, 1999.

Cummings, Brian, and Freya Sierhuis. "Introduction." In *Passions and Subjectivity in Early Modern Culture*. Ed. Brian Cummings and Freya Sierhuis. Farnham: Ashgate, 2013.

Cunningham, Valentine. "Readers Beside Themselves: Particular Pleasures and Generic Controls." In *Representations of Emotions*. Ed. Jürgen Schlaeger and Gesa Stedman. Tübingen: Gunter Narr, 1998. 43–56.

Dalai Lama, Desmond Tutu, and Douglas Abrams. *The Book of Joy: Lasting Happiness in a Changing World*. New York: Avery, 2016.

Damasio, Antonio. *Looking for Spinoza: Joy, Sorrow, and the Feeling Brain*. New York: Harcourt, 2003.

D'Arcens, Louise. "Affective Memory across Time: The Emotive City of Christine de Pizan." In *Ordering Emotions in Europe, 1100–1800*. Ed. Susan Broomhall. Leiden: Brill, 2015. 85–104.

Darwin, Charles. *The Expression of the Emotions in Man and Animals*. London: John Murray, 1872.

De Sousa, Ronald. *The Rationality of Emotion*. Boston: MIT Press, 1990.

Descartes, René. *Les Passions de l'Âme*. Trans. Robert Stoothoff as *The Passions of the Soul*. In *The Philosophical Writings of Descartes*. Ed. John Cottingham, Robert Stoothoff, and Dugald Murdoch. Vol. 1. Cambridge: Cambridge University Press, 1985. 325–404.

Davies, Douglas. *Emotion, Identity, and Religion*. Oxford: Oxford University Press, 2011.

De Armas, Frederick. *La astrología en el teatro clásico europeo (siglos XVI–XVII)*. Madrid: Antígona, 2019.

DeYoung, Rebecca K. "The Roots of Despair." *Res Philosophica* 92.4 (2015): 829–54.

Del Río Parra, Elena. *Cartografías de la conciencia española en la Edad de Oro*. Mexico City: Fondo de Cultura Económica, 2008.

– *Una era de monstruos: representaciones de lo deforme en el Siglo de Oro español*. Madrid and Frankfurt: Iberoamericana / Vervuert, 2003.

– "*Suspensio Animi*, or the Interweaving of Mysticism and Artistic Creation." In *A New Handbook to Hispanic Mysticism*, ed. Kallendorf. 391–410.

– "La suspensión como acto estético en las letras áureas." *RILCE* 26.1 (2010): 157–67.

Devaney, Thomas. "Virtue, Virility, and History in Fifteenth-Century Castile." *Speculum* 88.3 (2013): 721–49.

Devlin, P. "Morals and the Criminal Law." In *Morality and the Law*. Ed. R. Wasserstrom. Belmont, CA: Wadsworth, 1971. 24–48.

Dholakia, Utpal M. "Three Senses of Desire in Consumer Research." In *The Psychology of Desire*, ed. Hofmann and Nordgren. 407–31.

Díaz Marroquín, Lucía. *La retórica de los afectos*. Kassel: Reichenberger, 2008. 160–1.

Dickinson, Emily. "'Hope' is the Thing with Feathers" (314). https://www.poetryfoundation.org/poems/42889/hope-is-the-thing-with-feathers-314.

– "I Cannot Live with You" (640). poets.org/poem/i-cannot-live-you-640.

Diez Roux, Ana V. "Despair as a Cause of Death: More Complex Than It First Appears." *American Journal of Public Health* 107 (2017): 1566–7.

Dion, Kenneth L., and Karen E. Dion. "Romantic Love: Individual and Cultural Perspectives." In *The Psychology of Love*, ed. Sternberg and Barnes. 264–89.

Dixon, Thomas. "'Emotion': The History of a Keyword in Crisis." *Emotion Review* 4 (2012): 338–44.

– *From Passions to Emotions: The Creation of a Secular Psychological Category*. Cambridge: Cambridge University Press, 2003.

Doebler, Bettie Anne. *Rooted Sorrow: Dying in Early Modern England*. London: Associated University Presses, 1994.

Dollimore, Jonathan. *Death, Desire and Loss in Western Culture*. New York: Routledge, 1998.

Domínguez, Freddy. "From Saint to Sinner: Sixteenth-Century Perceptions of 'La Monja de Lisboa.'" In *A New Companion to Hispanic Mysticism*, ed. Kallendorf. 297–322.

Donne, John. Elegy 19. https://www.poetryfoundation.org/poems/50340/to-his-mistress-going-to-bed.

Ducey, Ariel. "More Than a Job: Meaning, Affect, and Training Health Care Workers." In *The Affective Turn: Theorizing the Social*. Ed. Patricia Ticineto Clough and Jean O'Malley Halley. Durham: Duke University Press, 2007. 187–208.

Durkheim, Émile. *Suicide: A Study in Sociology*. Trans. John A. Spaulding and George Simpson. New York: Free Press, 1951.

Dylan, Bob. "Blowin' in the Wind." Song on album *Finjan Club* (1962). https://www.youtube.com/watch?v=MMFj8uDubsE.

Echevarría Arsuaga, Ana. "El azote del año mil: Almanzor, según las crónicas cristianas." In *Los protagonistas del año mil* (Actas del XIII Seminario sobre Historia del Monacato, 2–5 de Agosto de 1999). Madrid: Centro de Estudios del Románico, 2000. 91–116.

Ehlers, Benjamin. *Between Christians and Moriscos: Juan de Ribera and Religious Reform in Valencia, 1568–1614*. Baltimore: Johns Hopkins University Press, 2006.

Ekelund, Robert B., et al. "Rent Seeking and Property Rights' Assignments as a Process: The Mesta Cartel of Medieval-Mercantile Spain." *Journal of European Economic History* 26.1 (1997): 9–35.

Elliott, John. *The Count-Duke of Olivares: The Statesman in an Age of Decline*. New Haven: Yale University Press, 1989.

Elster, Jon. *Alchemies of the Mind: Rationality and the Emotions*. Cambridge: Cambridge University Press, 1999.

"Encuentran los restos de Miguel de Cervantes." https://www.youtube.com/watch?app =desktop&v=p9PJ_Wz6uGg.

Eppel, Alan. *Sweet Sorrow: Love, Loss and Attachment in Human Life*. London: Karnac, 2009.

Escolme, Bridget. *Emotional Excess on the Shakespearean Stage: Passion's Slaves*. London: Bloomsbury, 2014.

Ettinghausen, Henry. *Francisco de Quevedo and the Neostoic Movement*. Oxford: Oxford University Press, 1972.

Farnsworth, Kirk E. "Despair That Restores." *Psychotherapy: Theory, Research and Practice* 12.1 (1975): 44–7.

Fiadino, Elsa Graciela. "El juego festivo en *Santiago el Verde* de Lope de Vega." In *Actas del V Congreso de la Asociación Internacional Siglo de Oro* (Münster, 20–24 de julio de 1999). Ed. Christoph Strosetzki. Münster: Vervuert Verlagsgesellschaft, 2001. 575–82.

Figlio, Karl. "The Dread of Sameness: Social Hatred and Freud's 'Narcissism of Minor Differences.'" In *Psychoanalysis and Politics: Exclusion and the Politics of Representation*. Ed. Lene Auested. London: Karnac, 2012. 7–24.

Fischer, Agneta H. *Emotion Scripts: A Study of the Social and Cognitive Aspects of Emotion*. Leiden: DSWO Press, 1991.

Fisher, Nick. "Hope and Hopelessness in Euripides." In *Hope in Ancient Literature*, ed. Kazantzidis and Spatharas. 53–84.

Foucault, Michel. *Language, Madness, and Desire*. Ed. Philippe Artières et al. Trans. Robert Bononno. Minneapolis: University of Minnesota Press, 2015. 93–146.

Franks, David D., and E. Doyle McCarthy, eds. *The Sociology of Emotions: Original Essays and Research Papers*. Greenwich, CT: JAI, 1989.

Fuchs, Barbara. *Passing for Spain: Cervantes and the Fictions of Identity*. Champaign: University of Illinois Press, 2003.

Fulkerson, Laurel. "*Deos speravi* [*Miles* 1209]: Hope and the Gods in Roman Comedy." In *Hope in Ancient Literature*, ed. Kazantzidis and Spatharas. 153–69.

Gale, John. "Response to Part I: The Relics of Absence." In *Grief and Its Transcendence: Memory, Identity, Creativity*. Ed. Adele Tutter and Léon Wurmser. New York: Routledge, 2016. 51–63.

Galván, Luis. "'Valle de lágrimas' y lugares de la gloria: la *Celestina* y el Salmo 83/84." *Celestinesca* 28 (2004): 25–32.

Gamliel, Tova. *Aesthetics of Sorrow: The Wailing Culture of Yemenite Jewish Women*. Trans. Naftali Greenwood. Detroit: Wayne State University Press, 2014.

Garcés, María Antonia. *Cervantes in Algiers: A Captive's Tale*. Nashville: Vanderbilt University Press, 2005.

Garrod, Raphaële. "Conceptual Eclecticism and Ethical Prescription in Early Modern Jesuit Discourses about Affects: Suárez and Caussin on Maternal Love." In *Ordering Emotions in Europe, 1100–1800*. Ed. Susan Broomhall. Leiden: Brill, 2015. 180–96.

Gaukroger, Stephen, ed. *The Soft Underbelly of Reason: The Passions in the Seventeenth Century*. London: Routledge, 1998.

Gay, Peter. *The Cultivation of Hatred*. New York: W.W. Norton, 1993.

– *The Tender Passion*. New York: Oxford University Press, 1986.

Geng, Penelope. *Communal Justice in Shakespeare's England: Drama, Law, and Emotion*. Toronto: University of Toronto Press, 2021.

Gentilcore, David. "The Fear of Disease and the Disease of Fear." In *Fear in Early Modern Society*. Ed. William G. Naphy and Penny Roberts. Manchester: Manchester University Press, 1997. 184–208.

Ginzburg, Carlo, and Lucio Biasiori, eds. *A Historical Approach to Casuistry: Norms and Exceptions in Comparative Perspective*. London: Bloomsbury, 2018.

Godfrey, J.J. *A Philosophy of Human Hope*. Dordrecht: Martinus Nijhoff, 1987.

Golder, Harold. "Bunyan's Giant Despair." *Journal of English and Germanic Philology* 30.3 (1931): 361–78.

Goleman, Daniel. *Emotional Intelligence: Why It Can Matter More Than IQ*. London: Bloomsbury, 1996.

Gone with the Wind. Directed by Victor Fleming. Produced by David O. Selznick. Released 17 January 1940.

Goodheart, Eugene. *Desire and Its Discontents*. New York: Columbia University Press, 1991.

Gosson, Stephen. *Playes Confuted in Fiue Actions*. London: Thomas Gosson, 1582.

Gotlib, Anna. "Memory, Sadness, and Longing: Exile Nostalgias as Attunement to Loss." In *The Moral Psychology of Sadness*, ed. Gotlib. 183–205.

– ed. *The Moral Psychology of Sadness*. London: Rowman & Littlefield, 2017.

– "The Topographies of Sadness." In *The Moral Psychology of Sadness*, ed. Gotlib. 1–17.

Gouk, Penelope, and Helen Hills, eds. *Representing Emotions: New Connections in the Histories of Art, Music and Medicine*. London: Ashgate, 2005.

– "Toward Histories of Emotions." In *Representing Emotions: New Connections in the Histories of Art, Music and Medicine*. Ed. Penelope Gouk and Helen Hills. London: Ashgate, 2005. 15–34.

Greer, Margaret Rich. "Spanish Golden Age Tragedy: From Cervantes to Calderón." In *A Companion to Tragedy*. Ed. Rebecca Bushnell. London: Blackwell, 2005. 351–70.

Gregg, Melissa, and Gregory J. Seigworth, eds. *The Affect Theory Reader*. Durham: Duke University Press, 2010.

Groopman, Jerome. *The Anatomy of Hope*. New York: Random House, 2004.

Gross, Daniel M. *The Secret History of Emotion: From Aristotle's 'Rhetoric' to Modern Brain Science*. Chicago: University of Chicago Press, 2006.

Grossberg, Lawrence, et al. *Affect's Future: Rediscovering the Virtual in the Actual*. Durham: Duke University Press, 2010.

Guarini, Giambattista. *The Compendium of Tragicomic Poetry* (1599). Trans. Albert H. Gilbert. In *Literary Criticism: Plato to Dryden*. Ed. Albert H. Gilbert. New York: American Book Co., 1940. 504–33.

Guntrip, H. "Early Perceptions of the Schizoid Problem." In *Personal Relations Therapy: The Collected Papers of HJS Guntrip*. New York: Jason Aronson, 1994. 39–62.

Gurr, Andrew. *Playgoing in Shakespeare's London*. Cambridge: Cambridge University Press, 1996.

Harrison, Peter. "Reading the Passions: The Fall, the Passions, and Dominion over Nature." In *The Soft Underbelly of Reason*, ed. Gaukroger. 49–78.

Harvey, John H. *Give Sorrow Words: Perspectives on Loss and Trauma*. Philadelphia: Brunner / Mazel, 2000.

Hatfield, Elaine, and Richard Rapson. *Love, Sex, and Intimacy: Their Psychology, Biology, and History*. New York: HarperCollins, 1993.

Hattaway, Michael. *Elizabethan Popular Theatre: Plays in Performance*. London: Routledge, 1982.

Hawthorne, Nathaniel. *The Scarlet Letter*. New York: Barnes & Noble, 2003.

Heble, Ajay. "Trace." In *Encyclopedia of Contemporary Literary Theory*. Ed. Irena R. Makaryk. Toronto: University of Toronto Press, 1997. 646–67.

Hemfelt, Robert, et al. *Love Is a Choice: The Groundbreaking Book on Recovery for Codependent Relationships*. Nashville: Thomas Nelson, 1991.

Herzog, Dagmar, ed. *Brutality and Desire: War and Sexuality in Europe's Twentieth Century*. Basingstoke, Hampshire [UK]: Palgrave Macmillan, 2009.

Heuer, Keely Elizabeth. "The Face of Hope: Isolated Heads in South Italian Visual Culture." In *Hope in Ancient Literature*, ed. Kazantzidis and Spatharas. 297–327.

Hildner, David. *Reason and the Passions in the* Comedias *of Calderón*. Amsterdam: John Benjamins, 1982.

Hillbrand, Marc, and John L. Young. "Instilling Hope Into Forensic Treatment: The Antidote to Despair and Desperation." *Journal of the American Academy of Psychiatry and the Law* 36 (2008): 90–4.

Hirschman, Albert. *The Passions and Interests: Political Arguments for Capitalism before Its Triumph*. Princeton: Princeton University Press, 1997.

Hjort, Mette, and Sue Laver, eds. *Emotion and the Arts*. New York: Oxford University Press, 1997.

– "Introduction." In *Emotion and the Arts*, ed. Hjort and Laver. 3–19.

Hobbes, Thomas. *The Elements of Law, Natural and Politic* [1640]. Oxford: Oxford University Press, 2008.

– *Leviathan*. Ed. R. Tuck. Cambridge: Cambridge University Press, 1991.

Hobgood, Allison P. "Feeling Fear in *Macbeth*." In *Shakespearean Sensations*, ed. Craik and Pollard. 29–46.

Hofmann, Wilhelm, and Loran F. Nordgren, eds. *The Psychology of Desire*. New York: Guilford, 2015.

– "Introduction." In *The Psychology of Desire*, ed. Hofmann and Nordgren. 1–13.

Hofmann, Wilhelm, et al. "Desire and Desire Regulation." In *The Psychology of Desire*, ed. Hofmann and Nordgren. 61–81.

Hogan, Patrick Colm. *Affective Narratology: The Emotional Structure of Stories*. Lincoln: University of Nebraska Press, 2011.

– *Cognitive Science, Literature and the Arts: A Guide for Humanists*. London: Routledge, 2003.

– *The Mind and Its Stories: Narrative Universals and Human Emotion*. Cambridge: Cambridge University Press, 2003.

– *What Literature Teaches Us about Emotion*. Cambridge: Cambridge University Press, 2011.

Horwitz, Allan V., and Jerome C. Wakefield. *The Loss of Sadness*. Oxford: Oxford University Press, 2007.

Howard, Jean. "The New Historicism in Renaissance Studies." *English Literary Renaissance* 16.1 (1986): 13–43.

Irvine, William B. *On Desire: Why We Want What We Want*. Oxford: Oxford University Press, 2005.

Jaeger, C. Stephen, and Ingrid Kasten, eds. *Codierungen von Emotionen im Mittelalter / Emotions and Sensibilities in the Middle Ages*. Berlin: De Gruyter, 2003.

Jackson, Stanley W. "*Acedia* the Sin and Its Relationship to Sorrow and Melancholia in Medieval Times." *Bulletin of the History of Medicine* 55.2 (1981): 172–85.

Jankowiak, William. "Introduction." In *Romantic Passion: A Universal Experience?* ed. Jankowiak. 1–19.

– ed. *Romantic Passion: A Universal Experience?* New York: Columbia University Press, 1995.

Johnson, Paul. *Affective Geographies: Cervantes, Emotion, and the Literary Mediterranean*. Toronto: University of Toronto Press, 2021.

Johnston, Alexandre. "'Poet of Hope': *Elpis* in Pindar." In *Hope in Ancient Literature*, ed. Kazantzidis and Spatharas. 35–52.

Jonsen, Albert R., and Stephen Toulmin. *The Abuse of Casuistry: A History of Moral Reasoning*. Berkeley: University of California Press, 1990.

Kagan, Richard. *Lucrecia's Dreams: Politics and Prophecy in Sixteenth-Century Spain*. Berkeley: University of California Press, 1990.

Kahn, Victoria. "Happy Tears: Baroque Politics in Descartes's *Passions de l'ame*." In *Politics and the Passions, 1500–1850*, ed. Kahn et al. Princeton: Princeton University Press, 2006. 93–110.

Kahn, Victoria, et al., eds. *Politics and the Passions, 1500–1850*. Princeton: Princeton University Press, 2006.

Kallendorf, Hilaire. *Ambiguous Antidotes: Virtue as Vaccine for Vice in Early Modern Spain*. Toronto: University of Toronto Press, 2017.

– ed. *A Companion to Early Modern Hispanic Theater*. Leiden: Brill, 2014.

– ed. *A Companion to the Spanish Renaissance*. Leiden: Brill, 2019.

– *Conscience on Stage: The* Comedia *as Casuistry in Early Modern Spain*. Toronto: University of Toronto Press, 2007. 108–42.

– "Dressed to the Sevens, or Sin in Style: Fashion Statements by the Deadly Vices in Spanish Baroque *Autos Sacramentales*." In *The Seven Deadly Sins: From Communities to Individuals*. Ed. Richard Newhauser. Leiden: E.J. Brill, 2007. 145–82.

– *Exorcism and Its Texts: Subjectivity in Early Modern Literature of England and Spain*. Toronto: University of Toronto Press, 2003.

– "Free Will a Fortress: The Self in Spanish Renaissance Drama." In *The Self in Premodern European Thought*, ed. José Luis Bermúdez and Catherine Conybeare. Cambridge: Cambridge University Press, forthcoming.

– "Love Madness and Demonic Possession in Lope de Vega." *Romance Quarterly* 51.3 (2004): 162–82.

– "Lycanthropy and Free Will: The Female Werewolf in Cervantes' *Persiles*." *eHumanista: Journal of Medieval and Early Modern Iberian Studies* 42 (2019): 1–19.

– ed. *A New Companion to Hispanic Mysticism*. Leiden: Brill, 2010.

– *Sins of the Fathers: Moral Economies in Early Modern Spain*. Toronto: University of Toronto Press, 2013.

– "Splitting Hairs or Finding Threads: The Labyrinth as Metaphor for Moral Dilemma in the *Comedia*." In *DOCTA Y SABIA ATENEA. Studia in honorem Prof. Lía Schwartz*. Ed. Sagrario López Poza et al. A Coruña: Universidade da Coruña, 2019. 339–58.

– "Staging Penance: Scenes of Sacramental Confession in Early Modern Spanish Drama." In *Casuistry in Early Modern Hispanic Literature*. Ed. Marlen Bidwell-Steiner and Michael Scham. Leiden: Brill, 2022. 176–201.

– "La virtud como metáfora médica en el drama español de la Edad Moderna." *eHumanista: Journal of Medieval and Early Modern Iberian Studies* 39 (2018): 105–21.

Kallendorf, Hilaire, and Craig Kallendorf. "Catharsis as Exorcism: Aristotle, Tragedy, and Religio-Poetic Liminality." *Literary Imagination* 14.3 (2012): 296–311.

– "Conversations with the Dead: Quevedo and Statius, Annotation and Imitation." *Journal of the Warburg and Courtauld Institutes* 63 (2000): 131–68.

Kamen, Henry. *The Spanish Inquisition: A Historical Revision*. 4th ed. New Haven: Yale University Press, 2014. 232–3.

Kaster, Robert. *Emotion, Restraint, and Community in Ancient Rome*. Oxford: Oxford University Press, 2005.

Kazantzidis, George, and Dimos Spatharas, eds. *Hope in Ancient Literature, History, and Art*. Berlin: De Gruyter, 2018.

– "Introductory: 'Hope,' *Elpis, Spes*: Affective and Non-Affective Expectancy." In *Hope in Ancient Literature, History, and Art*, ed. Kazantzidis and Spatharas. 1–31.

Katzman, G.H. "Neurobiological and Psychological Mechanisms Explaining How Hatred Is Programmed into the Minds of Children." *Open Pediatric Medicine Journal* 3 (2009): 58–60.

Katritzky, M.A. "Literary Anthropologies and Pedro González, the 'Wild Man' of Tenerife." In *Medical Cultures of the Early Modern Spanish Empire*. Ed. John Slater et al. Burlington: Ashgate, 2014. 107–28.

Kemper, Theodore D. "Love and Like and Love and *Love*." In *The Sociology of Emotions: Original Essays and Research Papers*. Ed. David D. Franks and E. Doyle McCarthy. Greenwich, CT: JAI, 1989. 249–70.

Kesselring, Joseph. *Arsenic and Old Lace*. New York: Dramatists Play Service, 1969.

Kierkegaard, Søren. *Purity of Heart Is to Will One Thing*. Trans. Douglas Steere. New York: Harper and Brothers, 1938.

Kimble, Melvin A. "Human Despair and Comic Transcendence." *Journal of Religious Gerontology* 16.3–4 (2004): 1–11.

Kiwanuka, Musisi. "The Eternal Quest: Justice and Don Quixote in Sixteenth Century Spain." *Penn History Review* 16.2 (2009): 31–50.

Knecht, Ross. *The Grammar Rules of Affection: Passion and Pedagogy in Sidney, Shakespeare, and Jonson*. Toronto: University of Toronto Press, 2021.

Knight, Rachel. "Misrepresentation in Pop Culture" (16 December 2020). https://liberalarts .tamu.edu/blog/2020/12/16/misrepresentation-in-pop-culture/.

Knuuttila, Simo. "Medieval Theories of the Passions of the Soul." In *Emotions and Choice from Boethius to Descartes*, ed. Lagerlund and Yrjönsuuri. 49–83.

Koller, Kathrine. "Art, Rhetoric, and Holy Dying in the *Fairie Queene* with Special Reference to the Despair Canto." *Studies in Philology* 61.2 (1964): 128–39.

Kolnai, Aurel. *On Disgust*. Chicago: Open Court, 2004.

Konstan, David. "Hatred." In *The Emotions of the Ancient Greeks: Studies in Aristotle and Classical Literature*. Toronto: University of Toronto Press, 2006. 185–200.

Korsmeyer, Carolyn. *Savoring Disgust: The Foul and the Fair in Aesthetics*. Oxford: Oxford University Press, 2011.

Kräfft-Ebing, Richard. *Psychopathia Sexualis* [1886]. 12th ed. New York: G.P. Putnam's Sons, 1965.

Kristeva, Julia. *Powers of Horror: An Essay on Abjection*. Trans. Leon Samuel Roudiez. New York: Columbia University Press, 1982.

Kuchar, Gary. *The Poetry of Religious Sorrow in Early Modern England*. Cambridge: Cambridge University Press, 2008.

Kundera, Milan. *Immortality*. New York: Grove Weidenfeld, 1990.

Lagerlund, Henrik, and Mikko Yrjönsuuri, eds. *Emotions and Choice*. Dordrecht: Kluwer, 2002.

– "Introduction." In *Emotions and Choice*, ed. Lagerlund and Yrjönsuuri. 1–28.

Lampinen, Antti. "Against Hope? The Untimely *Elpis* of Northern Barbarians." In *Hope in Ancient Literature*, ed. Kazantzidis and Spatharas. 275–95.

Lange, Marjory E. *Telling Tears in the English Renaissance*. Leiden: E.J. Brill, 1996.

Lateiner, Donald. "*Elpis* as Emotion and Reason [Hope and Expectation] in Fifth-Century Greek Historians." In *Hope in Ancient Literature*, ed. Kazantzidis and Spatharas. 131–49.

Lauer, A. Robert. "Honor / Honra Revisited." In *A Companion to Early Modern Hispanic Theater*, ed. Kallendorf. 77–90.

– *Tyrannicide and Drama*. Wiesbaden: Franz Steiner, 1987.

Leclercq, Jean. *The Love of Learning and the Desire for God: A Study of Monastic Culture.* Trans. Catharine Misrahi. New York: Fordham University Press, 1982.

Lee, John Alan. "Love-Styles." In *The Psychology of Love*. Ed. Robert J. Sternberg and Michael L. Barnes. New Haven: Yale University Press, 1988. 38–67.

"'El lenguaje nunca es inocente,' según Juan Goytisolo." *El País* (1 December 1984). https://elpais.com/diario/1984/12/02/cultura/470790008_850215.html.

León, Luis de. "Vida retirada." In *Poesías*. Ed. Javier San José Lera. Alicante: Biblioteca Virtual Miguel de Cervantes, 2008.

Leslie, Ian. *Curious: The Desire to Know and Why Your Future Depends on It*. New York: Basic Books, 2014.

Levine, Stephen. *Unattended Sorrow*. Emmaus, PA: Rodale, 2005.

Levinson, Jerrold. "Emotion in Response to Art: A Survey of the Terrain." In *Emotion and the Arts*, ed. Hjort and Laver. 20–36.

Lewis, C.S. *The Allegory of Love*. Oxford: Oxford University Press, 1959.

– *Surprised by Joy*. New York: HarperOne, 2017.

Liliequist, Jonas, ed. *A History of Emotions, 1200–1800*. London: Routledge, 2016.

– "The Political Rhetoric of Tears in Early Modern Sweden." In *A History of Emotions, 1200–1800*, ed. Liliequist. 181–205.

Lin, Erika T. "'Lord of thy presence': Bodies, Performance, and Audience Interpretation in Shakespeare's *King John*." In *Imagining the Audience in Early Modern Drama, 1558–1642*. Ed. Jennifer Low and Nova Myhill. Basingstoke: Palgrave, 2011. 113–33.

Lombardi, Elena. *The Syntax of Desire: Language and Love in Augustine, the Modistae, Dante*. Toronto: University of Toronto Press, 2007.

Lombardo, Nicholas E. "Emotions and Psychological Health in Aquinas." In *Emotions and Health, 1200–1700*, ed. Carrera. 19–46.

López de Alvarado, García. *Breve compendio de confessión*. Venice: Juan Maria Bonelli, 1552.

López Pinciano, Alonso. *Philosophia antigua poética*. Ed. José Rico Verdú. Madrid: Fundación José Antonio de Castro, 1998. 54–6.

Low, Jennifer A., and Nova Myhill, eds. *Imagining the Audience in Early Modern Drama, 1558–1642*. Basingstoke: Palgrave, 2011. 1–17.

– "Introduction: Audience and Audiences." In *Imagining the Audience in Early Modern Drama, 1558–1642*, ed. Low and Myhill. 1–17.

Lowen, Alexander. *Joy: The Surrender to the Body and to Life*. New York: Arkana, 1995.

Loyola, Ignacio de. *Ejercicios espirituales*. In *Obras completas de San Ignacio de Loyola*. Ed. Ignacio Iparraguirre. Madrid: Biblioteca de Autores Cristianos, 1963.

Maassen, Irmgard. "Formal Ostentation, Maimed Rites, and Madness: The Theatrical Spectacle of Mourning in Shakespeare's *Hamlet*." In *Codierungen von Emotionen*, ed. Jaeger and Kasten. 271–86.

MacLehose, William F. "Fear, Fantasy and Sleep in Medieval Medicine." In *Emotions and Health, 1200–1700*, ed. Carrera. 67–94.

Maddern, Philippa, et al. "Introduction: Performing Emotions in Medieval and Early Modern Worlds." In *Performing Emotions in Early Europe*, ed. Maddern et al. xiii–xxx.

– eds. *Performing Emotions in Early Europe*. Turnhout: Brepols, 2018.

Magee, Brian. *The Philosophy of Schopenhauer*. Oxford: Clarendon, 1983.

Maravall, José Antonio. *Teatro y literatura en la sociedad barroca*. Madrid: Seminarios y Ediciones, 1973.

Mariscal, George. *Contradictory Subjects: Quevedo, Cervantes, and Seventeenth-Century Spanish Culture*. Ithaca: Cornell University Press, 1991.

Marks, I.M. *Fears, Phobias, and Rituals*. New York: Oxford University Press, 1987.

Marks, Joel, ed. *The Ways of Desire*. London: Routledge, 1986.

– "Introduction: On the Need for Theory of Desire." In *The Ways of Desire*, ed. Marks. 1–16.

Martínez Enamorado, Virgilio. "Héroe o villano. Guerrero o mecenas. Almanzor en la historiografía española moderna y contemporánea (siglos XVI–XXI)." *Boletín de la Real Academia de Córdoba de Ciencias, Bellas Letras y Nobles Artes* 81.143 (2002): 199–214.

Massumi, Brian. *Parables for the Virtual: Movement, Affect, Sensation*. Durham: Duke University Press, 2002.

Matsuda, Mari J. "Public Response to Racist Speech: Considering the Victim's Story." In *Words That Wound: Critical Race Theory, Assaultive Speech and the First Amendment*. Ed. Mari Matsuda et al. Boulder: Westview, 1993. 17–52.

McCloskey, John C. "The Theme of Despair in Marlowe's *Faustus*." *College English* 4.2 (1942): 110–13.

McClure, George W. *Sorrow and Consolation in Italian Humanism*. Princeton: Princeton University Press, 1990.

McGinn, Colin. *The Meaning of Disgust*. Oxford: Oxford University Press, 2011.

McKendrick, Melveena. "The 'mujer esquiva'. A Measure of the Feminist Sympathies of Seventeenth-Century Spanish Dramatists." *Hispanic Review* 40.2 (1972): 162–97.

– *Women and Society in the Spanish Drama of the Golden Age: A Study of the* Mujer Varonil. Cambridge: Cambridge University Press, 1974.

McMahon, Darrin M. *Happiness: A History*. New York: Atlantic Monthly Press, 2006.

Meek, Richard, and Erin Sullivan. "Introduction." In *The Renaissance of Emotion: Understanding Affect in Shakespeare and His Contemporaries*, ed. Meek and Sullivan. 1–22.

– eds. *The Renaissance of Emotion: Understanding Affect in Shakespeare and His Contemporaries*. Manchester: Manchester University Press, 2015.

Menache, Sophia. "Love of God or Hatred of Your Enemy? The Emotional Voices of the Crusades." *Mirabilia* 10 (2010): 1–20.

Merton, Thomas. *The Seven Storey Mountain*. San Diego: Harcourt Brace, 1948.

Merwick, Donna. *The Shame and the Sorrow: Dutch-Amerindian Encounters in New Netherland*. Philadelphia: University of Pennsylvania Press, 2006.

Michalopoulos, Andreas N. "Hope Dies Last at Tomis." In *Hope in Ancient Literature*, ed. Kazantzidis and Spatharas. 183–96.

Michel, Charles. "Les bons et les mauvais esprits dans les croyances populaires de l'ancienne Grèce." *Revue d'histoire et de littérature religeuses* new series 1 (1910): 193–215, 202–3.

Miller, Madeline. *Circe*. New York: Little, Brown, 2018.

Miller, Susan. *Disgust: The Gatekeeper Emotion*. New York: Routledge, 2013.

Miller, William Ian. *The Anatomy of Disgust*. Cambridge, MA: Harvard University Press, 1997.

Milton, John. *Paradise Lost*. London: Routledge, 1905.

Mitchell, Margaret. *Gone with the Wind*. Pan Books, 2014.

Mitchell, Timothy. *Passional Culture: Emotion, Religion, and Society in Southern Spain*. Philadelphia: University of Pennsylvania Press, 1984.

"El mito visto por Doré." Blog for *National Geographic*. https://historia.nationalgeographic .com.es/a/judio-errante-mito-eterna-culpabilidad_12248/6.

Moltmann, Jürgen. "Christianity: A Religion of Joy." In *Joy and Human Flourishing*, ed. Volf and Crisp. 1–16.

Monbiot, George. "Acceptable Hatred." *The Guardian* (4 November 2003).

Mooney, Gerry. "The 'Broken Society' Election: Class Hatred and the Politics of Poverty and Place in Glasgow East." *Social Policy and Society* 8.4 (2009): 427–50.

Moreto, Agustín. *Primero es la honra*. In *Segunda parte de las Comedias de Don Agustín Moreto*. Valencia: Benito Mace, 1676. 125–64.

Moretti, Franco. *Distant Reading*. London: Verso, 2013.

Morford, Mark. *Stoics and Neostoics: Rubens and the Circle of Lipsius*. Princeton: Princeton University Press, 1991.

Moschella, Mary Clark. "Calling and Compassion: Elements of Joy in Lived Practices of Care." In *Joy and Human Flourishing*, ed. Volf and Crisp. 97–126.

Muller, Marion. *"These Savage Beasts Become Domestick": The Discourse on the Passions in Early Modern Europe*. Trier: Wissenschaftlicher Verlag, 2004.

Mullaney, Steven. "Affective Technologies: Toward an Emotional Logic of the Elizabethan Stage." In *Environment and Embodiment in Early Modern England*. Ed. Mary Floyd-Wilson and Garrett A. Sullivan, Jr. Basingstoke: Palgrave Macmillan, 2007. 71–89.

– "Mourning and Misogyny: *Hamlet, The Revenger's Tragedy*, and the Final Progress of Elizabeth I, 1600–1607." *Shakespeare Quarterly* 45.2 (1994): 139–62.

– *The Reformation of Emotions in the Age of Shakespeare*. Chicago: University of Chicago Press, 2015.

Naphy, William G., and Penny Roberts, eds. *Fear in Early Modern Society*. Manchester: Manchester University Press, 1997.

Nelson, Jamie Lindemann. "Sadness, Sense, and Sensibility." In *The Moral Psychology of Sadness*, ed. Gotlib. 53–67.

Newton, Tim. "The Sociogenesis of Emotion: A Historical Sociology?" In *Emotions in Social Life*. Ed. Gillian Bendelow and Simon J. Williams. London: Routledge, 1998. 60–80.

Noreña, Carlos G. "Foreword." In Vives, *The Passions of the Soul*. i–xv.

– *Juan Luis Vives and the Emotions*. Carbondale: Southern Illinois University Press, 1989.

Notar, Beth E. *Displacing Desire: Travel and Popular Culture in China*. Honolulu: University of Hawai'i Press, 2006.

Nussbaum, Martha. *Hiding from Humanity: Disgust, Shame, and the Law*. Princeton: Princeton University Press, 2004.

– *Political Emotions: Why Love Matters for Justice*. Cambridge, MA: Harvard University Press, 2015.

– *Upheavals of Thought: The Intelligence of Emotions*. Cambridge: Cambridge University Press, 2001.

Oakes, Guy. "Eros and Modernity: Georg Simmel on Love." In *The Sociology of Emotions*, ed. Franks and McCarthy. 229–48.

Oatley, Keith, and Mitra Gholamain. "Emotions and Identification: Connections between Readers and Fiction." In *Emotion and the Arts*, ed. Hjort and Laver. New York: Oxford University Press, 1997. 263–81.

O'Hara, Denis J. "Psychotherapy and the Dialectics of Hope and Despair." *Counselling Psychology Quarterly* 24.4 (2011): 323–9.

O'Neill, John, ed. *Freud and the Passions*. University Park: Pennsylvania State University Press, 1996.

Oughourlian, Jean-Michel. *The Genesis of Desire*. Trans. Eugene Webb. East Lansing: Michigan State University Press, 2010.

Oxford English Dictionary. https://www.oed.com/.

Papaioannou, Sophia. "'A Historian Utterly Without Hope': Literary Artistry and Narratives of Decline in Tacitus' *Historiae* I." In *Hope in Ancient Literature*, ed. Kazantzidis and Spatharas. 213–32.

Papies, Esther K., and Lawrence W. Barsalou. "Grounding Desire and Motivated Behavior." In *The Psychology of Desire*, ed. Hofmann and Nordgren. 36–60.

"Parentesco en el Franquismo: mujer, sexismo y familia." https://www.youtube.com/watch?v=l7SPQHvalfQ.

Paschalis, Michael. "*uestras spes uritis*: Hope and Empire in Virgil's *Aeneid*." In *Hope in Ancient Literature*, ed. Kazantzidis and Spatharas. 171–82.

Paster, Gail Kern. *Humoring the Body: Emotions and the Shakespearean Stage*. Chicago: University of Chicago Press, 2014.

Paster, Gail Kern, Katherine Rowe, and Mary Floyd-Wilson, eds. *Reading the Early Modern Passions: Essays in the Cultural History of Emotion*. Philadelphia: University of Pennsylvania Press, 2004.

Patterson, Z. "Going On-Line: Consuming Pornography in the Digital Era." In *Porn Studies*. Ed. L. Williams. Durham, NC: Duke University Press, 2004. 104–23.

Payer, Pierre. *The Bridling of Desire: Views of Sex in the Later Middle Ages*. Toronto: University of Toronto Press, 2016. 52–3.

Pearson, Giles. "Species of Desire II: *Thumos* (Retaliatory Desire)." In *Aristotle on Desire*. Cambridge: Cambridge University Press, 2012. 111–39.

Pearson, Meg F. "Audience as Witness in *Edward II*." In *Imagining the Audience*, ed. Low and Myhill. 93–111.

Pedahzur, Ami, and Yael Yishai. "Hatred by Hated People: Xenophobia in Israel." *Studies in Conflict & Terrorism* 22 (1999): 101–17.

Perfetti, Lisa. "Introduction." In *The Representation of Women's Emotions in Medieval and Early Modern Culture*, ed. Perfetti.

– ed. *The Representation of Women's Emotions in Medieval and Early Modern Culture*. Gainesville: University Press of Florida, 2005.

Perry, Mary Elizabeth. "Deviant Insiders: Legalized Prostitutes and a Consciousness of Women in Early Modern Seville." *Comparative Studies in Society and History* 27.1 (1985): 138–58.

Pinsky, Robert. "Dante's Canto XIII: The Wood of the Suicides." *Boston Review*. https://bostonreview.net/archives/BR18.1/dante.html.

Plamper, Jan. *The History of Emotions: An Introduction*, trans. Keith Tribe. Oxford: Oxford University Press, 2015.

Planalp, Sally. *Communicating Emotion: Social, Moral and Cultural Processes*. Cambridge: Cambridge University Press, 1999.

Plata, Fernando. "On Love and Occasion: A Reading of the 'Tale of Inappropriate Curiosity.'" In *Cervantes and Don Quixote* (Proceedings of the Delhi Conference on Miguel de Cervantes). Ed. Vibha Maurya and Ignacio Arellano. Hyderabad: Emesco, 2008. 195–210.

Potkay, Adam. *The Story of Joy: From the Bible to Late Romanticism*. Cambridge: Cambridge University Press, 2007.

Prendergast, Shirley, and Simon Forrest. "'Shorties, Low-Lifers, Hardnuts and Kings': Boys, Emotions and Embodiment in School." In *Emotions in Social Life*. Ed. Gillian Bendelow and Simon J. Williams. London: Routledge, 1998. 155–72.

Quevedo, Francisco de. "*Farmaceutria* o medicamentos enamorados." In *Silvas*. Trans. Hilaire Kallendorf. Lima: Universidad Nacional Mayor de San Marcos, 2011. 115–21.

Rachman, S.J. *Fear and Courage*. New York: W.H. Freeman, 1978.

"Recuerdos TV: Anuncio coñac soberano (Machista)." https://www.youtube.com/watch?v=F49If5qxKC4.

Reddy, William M. *The Navigation of Feeling: A Framework for the History of Emotions*. Cambridge: Cambridge University Press, 2001.

Ree, Jonathan. "Mixed Emotions: Keeping Them In and Getting Them Out." *Los Angeles Times* book review section. 2 May 2000. 1ff.

Reid, Sally Frances, and Russell G. Smith. "Regulating Racial Hatred." *Trends & Issues in Crime and Criminal Justice* (Australian Institute of Criminology) (February 1998): 1–6.

Rhatigan, Emma K. "Audience, Actors, and 'Taking Part' in the Revels." In *Imagining the Audience in Early Modern Drama, 1558–1642*, ed. Low and Myhill. 151–69.

Richey, Cliff, and Hilaire Richey Kallendorf. *Acing Depression: A Tennis Champion's Toughest Match*. Washington, DC: New Chapter, 2010.

Rist, John M. *Stoic Philosophy*. Cambridge: Cambridge University Press, 1969. 25–6.

Rist, Thomas. "Catharsis as 'Purgation' in Shakespearean Drama." In *Shakespearean Sensations: Experiencing Literature in Early Modern England*, ed. Craik and Pollard. 138–53.

Rizzolatti, Giacomo, and Corrado Sinigaglia. *Mirrors in the Brain: How Our Minds Share Actions and Emotions*. Trans. Frances Anderson. Oxford: Oxford University Press, 2008.

Roos, Susan. *Chronic Sorrow: A Living Loss*. New York: Routledge, 2002.

Roosevelt, Franklin D. First inaugural address delivered on the steps of the U.S. Capitol building (4 March 1933). https://www.youtube.com/watch?v=rIKMbma6_dc.

Rosenblatt, Paul C. "Diversity in Human Grieving: Historical and Cross-Cultural Perspectives." In *Exploring Grief: Towards a Sociology of Sorrow*. Ed. Michael Hviid Jacobsen and Anders Petersen. London: Routledge, 2020. 37–51.

Rosenwein, Barbara H. "Emotional Space." In *Codierungen von Emotionen im Mittelalter / Emotions and Sensibilities in the Middle Ages*, ed. Jaeger and Kasten. 287–303.

– *Emotional Communities in the Early Middle Ages*. Ithaca: Cornell University Press, 2006.

Rowe, Katherine. "Humoral Knowledge and Liberal Cognition in Davenant's *Macbeth*." In *Reading the Early Modern Passions: Essays in the Cultural History of Emotion*. Ed. Gail Kern Paster, Katherine Rowe, and Mary Floyd-Wilson. Philadelphia: University of Pennsylvania Press, 2004. 169–91.

Ruiz Jaren, Eduardo. *Oliva Sabuco: filosofía y salud*. Madrid: Manuscritos, 2009.

Sachs, Arieh. "Religious Despair in Medieval Literature and Art." *Medieval Studies* 26 (1964): 231–56.

Sarbin, T.R. *Narrative Psychology: The Storied Nature of Human Conduct*. New York: Praeger, 1986.

Schiller, Friedrich. "An die Freude." English translation by the Schiller Institute. https://archive.schillerinstitute.com/transl/schiller_poem/ode_to_joy.pdf.

Schopenhauer, Arthur. *The World as Will and Representation* [1819/1844]. Trans. E.F.J. Payne. 2 vols. New York: Dover, 1966.

Scroggs, Nancy, et al. "'An Existential Place of Pain': The Essence of Despair in Women." *Issues in Mental Health Nursing* 31.7 (2010): 477–82.

Segal, Charles. *Euripides and the Poetics of Sorrow*. Durham: Duke University Press, 1993.

Shakespeare, William. *The Complete Works of William Shakespeare*. New York: Gramercy, 1975.

– Sonnet CXLIV. https://www.poetryfoundation.org/poems/50651/sonnet-144-two-loves-i-have-of-comfort-and-despair.

– *The Taming of the Shrew*. Ed. Ann Thompson. New Cambridge Shakespeare. Cambridge: Cambridge University Press, 2003.

Shanahan, Lilly, et al. "Does Despair Really Kill? A Roadmap for an Evidence-Based Answer." *American Journal of Public Health* 109.6 (2019): 854–8.

Shattuck, Robert. *Forbidden Knowledge: From Prometheus to Pornography*. New York: St. Martin's, 1996.

Sheffield, Frisbee C.C. *Plato's* Symposium*: The Ethics of Desire*. Oxford: Oxford University Press, 2006.

Slater, Niall W. "Up from Tragicomedy: The Growth of Hope in Greek Comedy." In *Hope in Ancient Literature, History, and Art*, ed. Kazantzidis and Spatharas. 85–110.

Smail, Daniel Lord. *The Consumption of Justice: Emotions, Publicity, and Legal Culture in Marseille, 1264–1423*. Ithaca: Cornell University Press, 2003.

– "Hatred as a Social Institution in Late-Medieval Society." *Speculum* 76 (2001): 90–126.

Smith, Bruce R. "Afterword: Senses of an Ending." In *Shakespearean Sensations*, ed. Craik and Pollard. 208–17.

Smith, Daniel Jordan. "Managing Men, Marriage, and Modern Love: Women's Perspectives on Intimacy and Male Infidelity in Southeastern Nigeria." In *Love in Africa*, ed. Cole and Thomas. 157–80.

Smith, Roger. "Self-Reflection and the Self." In *Rewriting the Self: Histories from the Renaissance to the Present*. Ed. Roy Porter. London: Routledge, 1997.

Snyder, C.R., ed. *Handbook of Hope*. San Diego: Academic Press, 2000.

– "Hypothesis: There Is Hope." In *Handbook of Hope*, ed. Snyder. 3–21.

Snyder, C.R., and B. David Feldman. "Hope for the Many: An Empowering Social Agenda." In *Handbook of Hope*, ed. Snyder. 389–412.

Snyder, Susan. "The Left Hand of God: Despair in Medieval and Renaissance Tradition." *Studies in the Renaissance* 12 (1965): 18–59.

Solomon, Richard L. "The Opponent-Process Theory of Acquired Motivation." *American Psychologist* 35 (1980): 691–712.

Sorabji, Richard. *Emotion and Peace of Mind: From Stoic Agitation to Christian Temptation*. Oxford: Oxford University Press, 2000.

Spinoza, Baruch. *Ethics* 3p18s2. In *Improvement of the Understanding: Ethics and Correspondence of Benedict de Spinoza*. Trans. Robert Harvey Monro Elwes. Washington, DC: M.W. Dunne, 1901.

Stallybrass, Peter, and Allon White. *The Politics and Poetics of Transgression*. Ithaca: Cornell University Press, 1986.

Stanford, W.B. *Greek Tragedy and the Emotions*. New York: Routledge, 2014.

Stearns, Peter N., and Carol Z. Stearns. "Emotionology: Clarifying the History of Emotions and Emotional Standards." *American Historical Review* 90.4 (1985): 813–36.

Stearns, Peter N., and Deborah C. Stearns. "Historical Issues in Emotions Research: Causation and Timing." In *Social Perspectives on Emotion*. Ed. William M. Wentworth and John Ryan. Vol. 2. Greenwich, CT: JAI, 1994. 239–66.

Steenbergh, Kristine. "Emotions and Gender: The Case of Anger in Early Modern English Revenge Tragedies." In *A History of Emotions, 1200–1800*, ed. Liliequist. 119–33.

Steggle, Matthew. *Laughing and Weeping in Early Modern Theatres*. Aldershot: Ashgate, 2007.

– "Notes Towards an Analysis of Early Modern Applause." In *Shakespearean Sensations*, ed. Craik and Pollard. 118–37.

Steinberg, Paul Ian, and John S. Ogrodniczuk. "Hatred and Fear: Projective Identification in Group Psychotherapy." *Psychodynamic Practice* 16.2 (2010): 201–5.

Steinbock, Anthony J. "The Phenomenology of Despair." *International Journal of Philosophical Studies* 15.3 (2007): 435–51.

Sullivan, Erin. "The Passions of Thomas Wright: Renaissance Emotion across Body and Soul." In *The Renaissance of Emotion*, ed. Meek and Sullivan. 25–44.

Swidler, Ann. *Talk of Love: How Culture Matters*. Chicago: University of Chicago Press, 2001.

Szende, Katalin. "Between Hatred and Affection: Towns and Sigismund in Hungary and in the Empire." In *Sigismund von Luxembourg. Ein Kaiser in Europa* (Tagungsband des internationalen historischen und kunsthistorischen Kongresses in Luxemburg 8.-10. Juni 2005). Mainz am Rhein: Verlag Philipp von Zabern, 2006. 199–210.

Swidler, Ann. *Talk of Love: How Culture Matters*. Chicago: University of Chicago Press, 2001.

Tausiet, María, and James S. Amelang, eds. *Accidentes del alma. Las emociones en la Edad Moderna*. Madrid: Abada, 2009.

Taylor, Bruce. "The Enemy Within and Without: An Anatomy of Fear on the Spanish Mediterranean Littoral." In *Fear in Early Modern Society*, ed. Naphy and Roberts. 78–99.

Taylor, C.C.W. "Emotions and Wants." In *The Ways of Desire*, ed. Marks. 217–31.

Teresa of Avila. *Let Nothing Disturb You*. Notre Dame, IN: Ave Maria Press, 2008.

Thomas, Lynn M., and Jennifer Cole. "Introduction: Thinking through Love in Africa." In *Love in Africa*, ed. Cole and Thomas. 1–30.

Thompson, Marianne Meye. "Reflections on Joy in the Bible." In *Joy and Human Flourishing*, ed. Volf and Crisp. 17–38.

Thurman, Howard. *Jesus and the Disinherited*. Boston: Beacon, 1996.

Tillich, Paul. *The Courage to Be*. New Haven: Yale University Press, 1952.

Tolman, Deborah L. *Dilemmas of Desire: Teenage Girls Talk about Sexuality*. Cambridge, MA: Harvard University Press, 2002.

Tompkins, Jane, ed. *Reader-Response Criticism: From Formalism to Post-Structuralism*. Baltimore: Johns Hopkins University Press, 1980.

"Tratado del aojamiento." *Estudios de Historia de la Ciencia y de la Técnica* 20 (2001): 177–211.

Trinkaus, Charles. "The Problem of Free Will in the Renaissance and the Reformation." *Journal of the History of Ideas* (1949): 51–62.

Trueblood, Alan S. *Experience and Artistic Expression in Lope de Vega*. Cambridge, MA: Harvard University Press, 1974.

Tsoumpra, Natalia. "The Politics of Hopelessness: Thucydides and Aristophanes' *Knights*." In *Hope in Ancient Literature*, ed. Kazantzidis and Spatharas. 111–29.

Turnbull, Lachlan. "Discursive Affect and Emotional Prescriptiveness: On the 'Man of Sorrows' in Fourteenth-Century Italian Painting." In *Performing Emotions in Early Europe*, ed. Maddern. 221–41.

Turner, Jonathan H. "The Sociology of Emotions: Basic Theoretical Arguments." *Emotion Review* 1.4 (2009): 340–54.

Tutter, Adele. "Prologue: Give Sorrow Words." In *Grief and Its Transcendence: Memory, Identity, Creativity*. Ed. Adele Tutter and Léon Wurmser. New York: Routledge, 2016.

Tylus, Jane. "'Par Accident': The Public Work of Early Modern Theater." In *Reading the Early Modern Passions*, ed. Paster et al. 253–71.

Van der Kolk, Bessel. *The Body Keeps the Score: Brain, Mind, and Body in the Healing of Trauma*. New York: Penguin, 2015.

Vangshardt, Rasmus. "The *Theatrum Mundi* of Celebration. Pedro Calderón de la Barca and the World Theatre as Aesthetic Theodicy." PhD dissertation, University of Southern Denmark, 2021.

Vann, Gerald. *The Pain of Christ and the Sorrow of God*. Oxford: Blackfriars, 1949.

Varey, John E. "Memory Theaters, Playhouses, and *Corrales de Comedias*." In *Parallel Lives: Spanish and English National Drama, 1580–1680*. Ed. Kenneth Muir and Louise Fothergill-Payne. Lewisburg, PA: Bucknell University Press, 1991. 39–53.

Vega, Lope de. *Arte nuevo de hacer comedias en este tiempo* [1609]. Ed. Enrique García Santo-Tomás. Madrid: Cátedra, 2006.

– *Fuenteovejuna*. In *Antología de autores españoles antiguos y modernos*. Vol. I: *Antiguos*. Ed. Antonio Sánchez-Romeralo and Fernando Ibarra. Hoboken, NJ: Prentice Hall, 1972. 296–346.

– *Rimas sacras*. In *Obras poéticas*. Ed. José Manuel Blecua. Barcelona: Planeta, 1989.

Velasco, Sherry. "Vision, Vulnerability, and the Provocative 'Higas' in Lope de Vega's *Santa Teresa de Jesús*." In *Women Warriors in Early Modern Spain* (A Tribute to Bárbara Mujica). Ed. Susan L. Fischer and Frederick A. de Armas. Newark: University of Delaware Press, 2019. 221–40.

Vignansky, Efrat, et al. "Despair Will Hold You Prisoner, Hope Will Set You Free: Hope and Meaning among Released Prisoners." *Prison Journal* 98.3 (2018): 334–58.

Vilches, Elvira. "Doing Things with Money in Early Modern Spain." in *A Companion to the Spanish Renaissance*, ed. Kallendorf. 508–30.

Villa-Flores, Javier, and Sonya Lipsett-Rivera. "Introduction." In *Emotions and Daily Life in Colonial Mexico*. Albuquerque: University of New Mexico Press, 2014. 1–14.

Vitz, Paul, and Philip Mango. "Kleinian Psychodynamics and Religious Aspects of Hatred as a Defense Mechanism." *Journal of Psychology and Theology* 25.1 (1997): 64–71.

Vives, Juan Luis. *The Passions of the Soul: The Third Book of* De Anima et Vita. Trans. Carlos G. Noreña. Lewiston: Mellen, 1990. 19–20.

Vlassopoulos, Kostas. "Hope and Slavery." In *Hope in Ancient Literature*, ed. Kazantzidis and Spatharas. 235–58.

Volf, Miroslav. "The Crown of the Good Life: A Hypothesis." In *Joy and Human Flourishing*, ed. Volf and Crisp. 127–35.

Volf, Miroslav, and Justin E. Crisp, eds. *Joy and Human Flourishing: Essays on Theology, Culture, and the Good Life*. Minneapolis: Fortress, 2015. 97–126.

Volpe, Edmond L. "Dry September: Metaphor for Despair." *College Literature* 16.1 (1989): 60–5.

Webster's New Collegiate Dictionary. Springfield, MA: G. & C. Merriam, 1976.

Weil, Simone. *Love in the Void: Where God Finds Us.* Ed. Laurie Gagne. Walden, NY: Plough, 2018.

Weller, Francis. *The Wild Edge of Sorrow: Rituals of Renewal and the Sacred Work of Grief.* Berkeley: North Atlantic, 2015.

Westlund, Andrea C. "Untold Sorrow." In *The Moral Psychology of Sadness*, ed. Gotlib. 21–41.

Whitney, Charles. *Early Responses to Renaissance Drama.* Cambridge: Cambridge University Press, 2006.

Wierzbicka, Anna. *Emotions across Languages and Cultures: Diversity and Universals.* Cambridge: Cambridge University Press, 1999.

Wilde, Oscar. "De profundis." Project Gutenberg. www.gutenberg.org.

Wilson, Robert Rawdon. *The Hydra's Tale: Imagining Disgust.* Alberta: University of Alberta, 2002.

Wittgenstein, Ludwig. *Remarks on the Philosophy of Psychology.* Vol. 2. Ed. G.H. von Wright and Heikki Nyman. Trans. C.G. Luckhardt and M.A.E. Aue. Oxford: Blackwell, 1980.

Wright, N.T. "Joy: Some New Testament Perspectives and Questions." In *Joy and Human Flourishing*, ed. Volf and Crisp. 39–61.

Wright, Thomas. *The Passions of the Minde in Generall.* London: Valentine Simmes, 1604.

Wunder, Amanda. "Women's Fashions and Politics in Seventeenth-Century Spain: The Rise and Fall of the *Guardainfante.*" *Renaissance Quarterly* 68.1 (2015): 133–86.

Wymer, Rowland. *Suicide and Despair in the Jacobean Drama.* New York: St. Martin's, 1986.

Zeki, Semir. *Splendors and Miseries of the Brain: Love, Creativity, and the Quest for Human Happiness.* Chichester: Wiley-Blackwell, 2009.

Index of *Comedias*

General Index

References to figures are in *italic*.

Abbas, Haly, 238
Abel, 79
Abencerrajes, 161
abject, 3
Abraham, 69
Abrams, Douglas, 142, 168
Abuelaish, Izzeldin, 84
acedia, 48, 119, 274n134
actors' manual, 247, 409n193
Adam, 9, 19, 141, 149
Aeneas, 395n326
affect (*afecto, affectus*), 7–10, 13
affection, 8–9
"affective turn," 4
afición (affinity), 90
Africa, African, 38, 156, 158, 169, 183,
    320n219, 326n311, 349n153; North, 181,
    367n267, 396n328
agape, 353n247
Age of Discovery, 176
Ahmed, Sara, 88
Alamo, 216
Albania, 41, 85
Albert the Great, 12
Albertanus of Brescia, 78
alborozo, 350n180
albricias, 150
Alcalá de Henares, 157
Alcázar (Seville), 108
Alcoholics Anonymous, 5
Alexander VI, Pope, 185
Alexander the Great, 316n165

Alfonso, King, 75
Alford, Fred C., 88
Algarve, 185
Algiers, 181, 182, 367n267
Alhambra, 125
All Souls' Night, 171
Allah, 45
Allen, Woody, 378n4
Almanzor, 45, 273n120
Althusser, Louis, 251, 410n205, 411n216
Amalfi, 73
America, American, 202, 363n199
amicitia, 307n33
Amnon, 76, 126, 190–1, 197
amor benevolentiae, 307n33
amor concupiscentiae, 307n33
amor sui, 327n336
amplificatio, 147
Andalucía, 182, 319n198, 332n41, 367n257
angel, 74, 169, 170, 360n134, 392n253
anger, *xii*, 3, 8, 10–13, 72, 76, 85, 169, 228,
    230, 238, 244, 248, 254, 262n81, 300n50,
    401n3
animales passiones, 12
anise, 356n42
Ankowitsch, Christian, 5
antisemitism, 107, 184
Antwerp Museum of Modem Art, 5
aojamiento, 184
apatheia (apathy), 8, 260n45
apetito (appetite), 9–10
apoplexy, 150, 172

Toronto Iberic